Design on the Land

Design on the Land

The Development of Landscape Architecture

Norman T. Newton

The Belknap Press of
Harvard University Press
Cambridge, Massachusetts, and London, England

TO THE MEMORY OF

MY MOTHER

JESSIE KING NEWTON

Contents

Foreword — xxi

I. Ancient Times — 1

II. The Middle Ages — 21

III. The World of Islam: Córdoba, Seville — 30

IV. The World of Islam: Granada, Iran, Mogul India — 40

V. The Renaissance in Tuscany — 55

VI. Rome and the Cinquecento — 67

VII. Roman Villas of Villeggiatura — 81

VIII. Villa Lante and the Villino Farnese — 99

IX. Later Italian Villas, 1610–1785 — 114

X. The Piazza in Italy — 132

XI. Beginnings in France — 153

XII. André le Nôtre: Vaux-le-Vicomte and Versailles — 165

XIII. England under the Tudors — 182

XIV. Seventeenth-Century England — 194

XV.	The English "Landscape Gardening School"	207
XVI.	Transition to Public Service	221
XVII.	Pückler-Muskau and Alphand	233
XVIII.	Early American Backgrounds	246
XIX.	Olmsted and Vaux: Central Park and Prospect Park	267
XX.	Olmsted's Work in Boston	290
XXI.	Two Pioneers: Weidenmann and Cleveland	307
XXII.	Charles Eliot and His Metropolitan Park System	318
XXIII.	Single-Track Eclecticism Takes Over	337
XXIV.	The World's Columbian Exposition of 1893	353
XXV.	The Influence of Charles A. Platt	372
XXVI.	Founding of the American Society of Landscape Architects	385
XXVII.	The American Academy in Rome	393
XXVIII.	The McMillan Commission's Plan of Washington	400
XXIX.	The City Beautiful Movement and City Planning	413
XXX.	The Country Place Era	427
XXXI.	English Town Planning and the "Garden City"	447

XXXII.	Town Planning in the United States: 1869–1915	464
XXXIII.	Town Planning in the United States: 1915–1929	479
XXXIV.	Town Planning in the United States 1929–1948	496
XXXV.	The National Park System: 1872–1929	517
XXXVI.	The National Park System: 1929–1964	538
XXXVII.	The State Park Movement: 1864–1933	555
XXXVIII.	State Parks and the Civilian Conservation Corps	576
XXXIX.	Parkways and Their Offspring	586
XL.	Urban Open-Space Systems	620
XLI.	Variations in Professional Practice	640
XLII.	Conservation of Natural Resources	659
	Select Bibliography	677
	Acknowledgments	691
	Illustration Credits	693
	Index	703

Illustrations

1. Temple of Queen Hatshepsut at Deir-el-Bahari   2
2. Reconstruction, Temple of Queen Hatshepsut   2
3. Mural showing house and garden of a high official at the court of Amenhotep III at Thebes   5
4. Reconstruction of house and garden from mural   5
5. Miletus, plan of city   7
6. Priene, map of city   7
7. Priene, bird's-eye reconstruction   8
8. Pompeii, scale model in Naples Museum   9
9. Pompeii, plan of typical house   9
10. Pompeii, House of the Vettii, plan   10
11. Pompeii, House of the Vettii, exterior reconstruction   11
12. Pompeii, House of the Vettii, peristyle   11
13. Rome, Forum Romanum, reconstruction   14
14. Rome, Fora of the Emperors, reconstruction   15
15. Rome, panorama from the Capitoline, reconstruction   16–17
16. Tivoli, Hadrian's Villa, plan of restoration   18
17. Horace's Sabine Villa, plan of restoration   19
18. Horace's Sabine Villa, restored section   19
19. Carcassonne, the Cité from below   22
20. Rome, cloister of St. John Lateran   24
21. Certosa di Pavia, Great Cloister   24
22. St. Gall, proposed plan of ninth century   25
23. Garden scene from *Roman de la Rose*   27
24. Córdoba, Court of Oranges from tower of Mosque   33
25. Seville, Alcazar gardens, plan   34
26. Seville, Alcazar gardens, Pavilion of Charles V   34
27. Seville, Alcazar gardens, fountain   36
28. Seville, Alcazar gardens, grilled window and seat   38
29. Seville, Alcazar gardens, newer fountain   39
30. Alhambra, the plateau complex   41
31. Alhambra, Arab Palace and Palace of Charles V   42

32. Alhambra, detailed plan of Arab Palace — 43
33. Alhambra, Court of Myrtles — 44
34. Alhambra, Court of the Lions — 45
35. Generalife, plan — 48
36. Generalife, Canal Garden — 48
37. Isfahan, Palace of Forty Columns — 52
38. Isfahan, Madrassa of Shah Hussein, pool — 53
39. Isfahan, Madrassa of Shah Hussein, sanctuary — 53
40. Agra, Taj Mahal — 54
41. Villa Careggi, engraving — 58
42. Villa Petraia, engraving — 58
43. Villa Palmieri, engraving — 58
44. Villa Medici, Fiesole, plan — 60
45. Villa Medici, Fiesole, elevation — 61
46. Villa Medici, Fiesole, from entrance drive — 62
47. Villa Medici, Fiesole, gateway from green garden — 63
48. Villa Medici, Fiesole, from lowest level — 64
49. Villa Medici, Fiesole, section — 65
50. Villa Medici, Fiesole, view down from wall of arrival terrace — 66
51. Vatican City, Belvedere, plan — 68
52. Vatican City, engraving of Belvedere by Brambilla — 70
53. Vatican City, Belvedere, Cortile della Pigna — 71
54. Vatican City, mural of Belvedere by Pierino del Vaga — 72
55. Villa Madama from below, about 1915 — 74
56. Villa Madama, plan as proposed, restoration — 75
57. Villa Medici, Rome, plan — 77
58. Villa Medici, Rome, engraving — 78
59. Villa Medici, Rome, view of palace from garden — 79
60. Frascati, Villa Mondragone, plan — 82
61. Frascati, Villa Aldobrandini, view from piazzetta — 83
62. Frascati, Villa Aldobrandini, plan — 85
63. Frascati, Villa Torlonia cascade, plan — 86
64. Frascati, Villa Torlonia cascade through bosco — 87
65. Frascati, Villa Torlonia cascade, detail of basins — 89
66. Tivoli, Villa d'Este, engraving — 90
67. Tivoli, Villa d'Este, plan — 91
68. Tivoli, Villa d'Este, Terrace of the Hundred Fountains — 92
69. Tivoli, Villa d'Este, Fountain of Arethusa — 94
70. Tivoli, Villa d'Este, Water Organ — 95
71. Tivoli, Villa d'Este, from lower end of viale — 97
72. Bagnaia, Villa Lante, plan — 100
73. Bagnaia and Villa Lante, map — 101
74. Bagnaia, Villa Lante, Lower Garden — 102
75. Bagnaia, Villa Lante, Fountain of Lights — 102
76. Bagnaia, Villa Lante, Water Table and Fountain of Giants — 104
77. Bagnaia, Villa Lante, Fountain of Dolphins — 105
78. Bagnaia, Villa Lante, Lower Garden from above — 106
79. Caprarola, Villino Farnese, plan — 108
80. Caprarola, Villino Farnese and palazzo, plan — 109
81. Caprarola, Villino Farnese, jet in vestibule — 110
82. Caprarola, Villino Farnese, caryatids in Box Garden — 111

83. Caprarola, Villino Farnese, scale model   112
84. Villa Gamberaia, plan   115
85. Villa Gamberaia, section   115
86. Villa Gamberaia, from Giuseppe Zocchi drawing   116
87. Villa Gamberaia, viale looking toward valley, 1924   116
88. Villa Gamberaia, viale looking toward hill, 1967   118
89. Villa Gamberaia, garden   119
90. Isola Bella, plan   120
91. Isola Bella, view from water   121
92. Rome, Villa Chigi, plan   123
93. Rome, Villa Chigi, pool and pines behind house   125
94. Rome, Villa Chigi, planting plan   127
95. Villa Balbianello, sketch plan   128
96. Villa Balbianello from water   129
97. Villa Balbianello, Bishop's Harbor   130
98. Florence, engraving of 1470   133
99. Florence, map of center, including Piazza della Signoria   134
100. Florence, Piazza della Signoria, view   136
101. Siena, Piazza del Campo, view   136
102. Siena, Piazza del Campo, plan   137
103. Venice, Piazza San Marco, plan   140
104. Venice, Piazza San Marco, aerial view   140
105. Venice, Piazza San Marco, looking toward San Marco   141
106. Venice, Piazza San Marco, from balcony of San Marco   142
107. Venice, Piazza San Marco, across Piazzetta toward water   143
108. Venice, Piazza San Marco, toward San Marco from
     Piazzetta   144
109. Rome, Piazza del Popolo, plan   148
110. Rome, Piazza del Popolo, engraving   149
111. Rome, Piazza del Popolo, from Pincio   150
112. Rome, Piazza di San Pietro, aerial view   151
113. Rome, Piazza di San Pietro   152
114. Amboise, engraving   154
115. Blois, engraving   155
116. Chenonceaux   157
117. Anet, plan   158
118. Charleval, plan   159
119. Paris, Tuileries, plan of 1652 by Gomboust   160
120. Paris, Tuileries, looking from Place de la Concorde, 1967   161
121. Paris, Tuileries, toward Place de la Concorde, 1967   161
122. Paris, Luxembourg gardens, aerial view   163
123. Paris, Luxembourg gardens, plan of 1652 by Gomboust   164
124. Vaux-le-Vicomte, plan   166
125. Vaux-le-Vicomte, parterres   169
126. Vaux-le-Vicomte from the Confessional   170
127. Vaux-le-Vicomte, aerial view   171
128. Versailles, early plan   174
129. Versailles, plan of 1746 by Delagrive   175
130. Versailles, aerial view toward gardens   176
131. Versailles, gardens at signing of Versailles Treaty   177
132. Versailles, Basin of Apollo and Tapis Vert   178

133. Versailles, allée in bosquets — 180
134. Warwick Castle — 183
135. Haddon Hall, plan — 186
136. Haddon Hall, lower courtyard — 186
137. St. Catherine's Court, plan — 188
138. St. Catherine's Court, the Jacobean porch — 189
139. St. Catherine's Court, view from hillside — 190
140. Montacute, plan — 191
141. Montacute, old arrival court — 192
142. Montacute, the "Italian garden" — 193
143. Hatfield House, plan — 195
144. Hatfield House, view east from house — 195
145. Melbourne Hall, plan — 198
146. Melbourne Hall, clipped allées — 199
147. Bramham Park, plan — 200
148. Bramham Park, pools at end of Broad Walk — 201
149. Bramham Park, T-canal — 201
150. Levens Hall, house and topiary — 202
151. Hampton Court, engraving — 203
152. Hampton Court, plan of Bushy Park — 204
153. Hampton Court, detailed plan about palace — 205
154. Stowe, across lake — 212
155. Blenheim, Vanbrugh-Wise plan — 213
156. Blenheim, Brown's revisions — 213
157. Blenheim, Brown's Lake — 214
158. Stourhead, composition — 215
159. Longleat, pools — 219
160. St. James's Park, from bridge — 222
161. The Green Park, open meadows — 222
162. Hyde Park, inner end of Serpentine — 223
163. Hyde Park, toward Marble Arch — 224
164. Regent's Park, Nash's plan — 226
165. Regent's Park, Weale's plan — 226
166. Victoria Park, Pennethorne's plan — 228
167. Birkenhead Park, the opening, contemporary print — 229
168. Birkenhead Park, plan — 230
169. Birkenhead Park, view across, contemporary print — 231
170. Birkenhead Park, the Temple, contemporary print — 231
171. Park at Muskau, plan — 234
172. Park at Muskau, Schloss Muskau — 236
173. Park at Muskau, looking south from castle — 238
174. Park at Muskau, meadow view — 238
175. Paris, Bois de Boulogne, "état ancien" — 242
176. Paris, Bois de Boulogne, "état actuel" — 243
177. Salem, Nichols garden — 248
178. Westover, Virginia, sketch plan — 251
179. Westover, Virginia, river facade — 252
180. Mount Vernon, aerial view — 254
181. Mount Vernon, plan of plantation — 256
182. Mount Vernon, detailed plan about house — 257
183. Downing's "English Flower-Garden" — 262

184. Downing's "Irregular Flower-Garden" — 262
185. "Suburban Villa" plan — 264
186. Blithewood — 265
187. Central Park, "Greensward" plan — 272
188. Central Park extended to 110th Street — 272
189. Central Park, aerial view — 278
190. Prospect Park, plan of 1866–1867 — 280
191. Prospect Park, plan of 1901 — 281
192. Central Park, transverse road — 282
193. Central Park, pedestrian underpass — 282
194. Central Park, carriage road and pedestrian paths — 283
195. Central Park, on the lake, 1912 — 284
196. Prospect Park, the Long Meadow — 285
197. Prospect Park, the proposed Nethermead Arches — 286
198. Prospect Park, the lake — 287
199. Central Park, the Mall — 288
200. Boston, Back Bay Fens, plan — 292
201. Boston, Franklin Park, plan — 296
202. Boston, Franklin Park, Ellicottdale, early days — 297
203. Boston, Franklin Park, Scarboro Pond — 297
204. Boston, Franklin Park, the Playstead — 298
205. Boston, "The Parkway" — 300
206. Boston, Ward's Pond in Olmsted Park — 301
207. Boston, Riverway, island construction, 1890s — 302
208. Boston, Riverway, later view of islands — 302
209. Boston, Riverway, Longwood Bridge, construction — 303
210. Boston, Riverway, later view of Longwood Bridge — 303
211. Boston, Riverway, grading, from Longwood Bridge — 305
212. Boston, Riverway, 1920 view from Longwood Bridge — 305
213. Minneapolis, proposed park system — 314
214. Charles Eliot — 325
215. Revere Beach before acquisition — 327
216. Charles River, Hemlock Gorge — 328
217. Middlesex Fells, Ravine Road — 329
218. Blue Hills Reservation — 329
219. Boston parks, 1890 and 1900 — 334
220. Boston Metropolitan Parks, 1912 — 335
221. Armsmear, residence of Samuel Colt — 338
222. Hudson River residence of Frederick E. Church — 340
223. Newport, Appleton "cottage" — 341
224. New York, the Villard house — 342
225. Boston Public Library — 343
226. Biltmore, detailed plan about house — 347
227. Biltmore, the Italian Garden — 348
228. Biltmore, plan of entire property — 349
229. Biltmore under construction — 350
230. Biltmore, completed — 350
231. Paris Exposition of 1889, sketch — 355
232. Paris Exposition of 1889, Galerie des Machines — 355
233. Chicago South Parks, Olmsted and Vaux plan of 1871 — 356
234. Chicago, Jackson Park, 1891 — 358

235. World's Columbian Exposition, Board of Architects 362
236. World's Columbian Exposition, plan 364
237. World's Columbian Exposition, Administration Building 365
238. World's Columbian Exposition, Court of Honor eastward 366
239. World's Columbian Exposition, Court of Honor westward 366
240. Chicago, Jackson Park, 1950s 367
241. World's Columbian Exposition, Transportation Building 369
242. Frederick Law Olmsted 371
243. Charles A. Platt's summer home at Cornish, plan 374
244. Terrace at Cornish 375
245. Faulkner Farm, plan 378
246. Faulkner Farm, flower garden 379
247. Garden of Weld 379
248. Timberline, plan 381
249. Timberline, sight-line to gardens 381
250. Timberline, main garden 382
251. Gwinn, plan 382
252. Gwinn, shore view 383
253. American Academy in Rome 396
254. L'Enfant plan of Washington, 1791 402
255. Ellicott plan of Washington 404
256. McMillan Commission plan of Washington, 1901 407
257. Scale model of Washington, existing state in 1901, westward 408
258. Scale model of Washington, proposed state, westward 408
259. Scale model of Washington, existing state in 1901, eastward 409
260. Scale model of Washington, proposed state, eastward 409
261. Bird's-eye sketch, McMillan Commission plan 410
262. Washington "kite plan" of 1928 411
263. San Francisco, Burnham plan 418
264. Manila, Burnham plan 419
265. Baguio, Burnham plan 420
266. Chicago, "Heart of the City" 422
267. Ormston, general plan 429
268. Ormston, aerial view 430
269. Ormston, Bowling Green 431
270. Killenworth, aerial view 432
271. Killenworth, entrance court 432
272. Killenworth, Green Garden 434
273. E. L. Ryerson residence, woods and lawn 436
274. E. L. Ryerson residence, woodland way 437
275. Landon K. Thorne country place, general plan 438
276. Landon K. Thorne country place, boat landing 439
277. Landon K. Thorne country place, birch allée 440
278. B. E. Taylor residence, terrace and garden house 442
279. B. E. Taylor residence, swimming pool 442
280. B. E. Taylor residence, entranceway 443
281. Edward F. Hutton residence, magnolia walk 444
282. Charles F. McCann residence, garden 445
283. "Victoria" 449
284. Port Sunlight, plan 450
285. Bournville, aerial view 452

286. Bournville, map — 452

287. Garden City diagram — 456

288. Letchworth, plan — 458

289. Letchworth, aerial view — 459

290. Welwyn, plan — 461

291. Welwyn, view on Handside Road — 462

292. Riverside, Illinois, 1869 plan — 466

293. Riverside, Illinois, riverside walk and road — 468

294. Roland Park, map — 469

295. Roland Park, street — 470

296. Kansas City Country Club District — 472

297. Forest Hills Gardens, plan — 475

298. Forest Hills Gardens, Station Square — 476

299. Forest Hills Gardens, sketch — 477

300. Longview, Washington, plan — 481

301. Mariemont, Ohio, plan — 485

302. Chicopee, Georgia, plan — 488

303. New York, Sunnyside Gardens, interior court — 490

304. Radburn, overall plan — 491

305. Radburn, plan of Section I — 492

306. Radburn, aerial view, 1930 — 493

307. Radburn, unit plan — 494

308. Chatham Village, plan — 498

309. Chatham Village, aerial view — 498

310. Chatham Village, interior mall, first unit — 499

311. Norris, Tennessee, plan — 501

312. Greenbelt, preliminary plan — 504

313. Greenbelt, plan of Community Center — 505

314. Greenbelt, along front of Community Center — 505

315. Baldwin Hills Village, plan — 508

316. Baldwin Hills Village, unit plan — 510

317. Baldwin Hills Village, garden court — 511

318. Baldwin Hills Village, aerial view — 512

319. Fresh Meadows, plan — 514

320. Fresh Meadows, interior court — 515

321. Yellowstone River canyon — 519

322. "Old Faithful" geyser — 520

323. Yosemite National Park, upper rim — 522

324. Mount Rainier National Park, Klapatche Lake — 523

325. Crater Lake National Park — 524

326. Devil's Tower National Monument — 525

327. Mesa Verde National Park, Cliff Palace — 526

328. Glacier National Park, St. Mary's Lake — 526

329. Rocky Mountain National Park, Nymph Lake — 528

330. Hawaii Volcanoes National Park, 1959 eruption — 531

331. Grand Canyon National Park — 533

332. Acadia National Park, Otter Cliffs — 534

333. Stephen T. Mather memorial tablet — 537

334. Morristown National Historical Park, Ford Mansion — 540

335. Salem Maritime National Historic Site, Custom House — 541

336. Statue of Liberty National Monument, existing conditions — 542

337. Statue of Liberty National Monument, general development
     plan after transfer from War Department   543
338. Great Smoky Mountains National Park   544
339. Olympic National Park, Olympic Mountains   545
340. Big Bend National Park, Santa Elena Canyon   547
341. Everglades National Park   548
342. Cape Hatteras National Seashore Recreational Area   553
343. Yosemite, valley floor   556
344. Adirondack Forest Preserve   559
345. Itasca State Park, Lake Itasca   560
346. Gorge of the Genesee River   561
347. Turkey Run State Park   563
348. Buttermilk Falls State Park   565
349. Jones Beach State Park, aerial view   566
350. Jones Beach State Park, East Bathhouse   567
351. Jones Beach State Park, Central Mall   568
352. Cook County Forest Preserve District, Schiller Woods, plan   570
353. Cook County Forest Preserve District, Schiller Woods,
     aerial view   571
354. Richardson Grove State Park   574
355. Civilian Conservation Corps park camps, 1935   579
356. Gilbert Lake State Park, cabin colony   581
357. Fairy Stone State Park, bathing beach   582
358. R. H. Treman State Park, swimming pool   582
359. Itasca State Park, horse trail   583
360. Palisades Interstate Park, Old Silver Mine Ski Center   583
361. Cook County Forest Preserve District, Skokie Lagoons   584
362. Parvin State Park, bathhouse complex   584
363. CCC enrollees, South Mountain Reservation   585
364. CCC enrollees, Parvin State Park   586
365. CCC enrollees, High Point State Park   587
366. Raccoon Creek Recreational Demonstration Area,
     Pennsylvania   590
367. Hickory Run RDA, Pennsylvania   590
368. French Creek RDA, Pennsylvania   591
369. Typical organized camp   593
370. Bronx River Parkway, before cleanup   598
371. Bronx River Parkway, after cleanup   599
372. Bronx River Parkway at Woodlawn, 1922   601
373. Bronx River Parkway approaching Scarsdale   602
374. Westchester County park system   603
375. Bronx River Parkway Extension   604
376. Saw Mill River Parkway, bridge at Pleasantville   605
377. Playland, Rye Beach, aerial view   606
378. Taconic State Parkway   609
379. Taconic State Parkway, overlook   610
380. Taconic State Parkway, divided ways   611
381. Blue Ridge Parkway, scenic easement   613
382. Mississippi River Parkway Survey, land controls   614
383. Palisades Parkway   615
384. Garden State Parkway   616

385. New York State Thruway near Suffern   618
386. Boston, Charlesbank, plan   622
387. Boston, Charlesbank, aerial photo about 1890   623
388. Chicago South Parks, Park No. 1   625
389. Chicago South Parks, Park No. 8   626
390. New York, Central Park Arsenal and Zoo   628
391. New York, Bryant Park   630
392. New York, City Hall Park, plan   632
393. New York, Williamsbridge Reservoir Playground   633
394. New York, Thomas Jefferson Park, East River Drive   633
395. New York, Orchard Beach   634
396. New York, Henry Hudson Parkway   635
397. Fresno, Fulton Mall   636
398. New York, Samuel Paley Park from above   637
399. New York, Samuel Paley Park   638
400. New York, Riis Houses, Plaza Playground   639
401. Excerpt, FHA *Land Planning Bulletin No. 1*   644
402. Williamsburg, Governor's Palace grounds   647
403. Weston, Massachusetts, the Country School   649
404. Los Altos, California, Foothill College   649
405. San Francisco, Ghirardelli Square   651
406. Pittsburgh, Mellon Square from above   652
407. Pittsburgh, Mellon Square   652
408. Hartford, Constitution Plaza   653
409. Boston, winning perspective for redesign of Copley Square   653
410. Chicago, Riveroaks Shopping Center   654
411. Kalamazoo, Upjohn Company   656
412. Timberline in the Olympics   662
413. Clear-cut slopes: resultant gullies   665
414. Gully erosion, California vineyards   665
415. Kentucky gully erosion   666
416. Dust storm approaching Springfield, Colorado, 1937   666
417. Olympic rain forest   667
418. Dying trees turn to humus   668
419. Contour furrows, Idaho   669
420. Gullies to heal in Georgia   670
421. Same gullies, healing   670
422. Smog over Denver   672
423. James River pollution   672
424. Canada geese, Yellowstone   674

Foreword

This book has arisen from a deep conviction that a sympathetic understanding of the development of landscape architecture—as an art and as a profession—can bring new richness to man's grasp of the world in which he lives. Landscape architecture: a profession only a little over a century old; an art as old as human existence. This book addresses itself to both. Moreover, it does not accept the lazy explanation that landscape architecture is simply what landscape architects do, for many of the finest examples of the art have been created by individuals who called themselves by other names.

What, then, should the term *landscape architecture* be taken to mean? It will be understood here to mean the art—or the science, if preferred—of arranging land, together with the spaces and objects upon it, for safe, efficient, healthful, pleasant human use. Whenever and wherever this art was practiced in the past, both the process and the product were, in present-day terms, landscape architecture. The ancient art became a new profession officially, when in 1863 the title Landscape Architect was first used by the state-appointed Board of Central Park Commissioners in New York City.[1] It had been employed unofficially by Frederick Law Olmsted and Calvert Vaux beginning in 1858, when they won the now famous competition for a design of the Central Park. They professed themselves "landscape architects," inventing the name to convey their intent to bear toward the total landscape the same relation that an architect bears toward a building, with essential emphasis on *design*.[2] This

1. Frederick Law Olmsted, *Forty Years of Landscape Architecture,* vol. II: *Central Park,* ed. F. L. Olmsted, Jr., and T. Kimball (New York, 1928), p. 74n. It is often incorrectly assumed that Humphry Repton and J. C. Loudon, in England, had earlier used the title "landscape architect"; both men styled themselves "landscape gardeners" (a title that Olmsted rejected), whereas by their infrequently used term "landscape architecture" they referred only to buildings in the landscape.

2. See also Olmsted's later comment, as recorded in *Forty Years of Landscape Architecture,* vol. I: *Early Years,* ed. F. L. Olmsted, Jr., and T. Kimball (New York, 1922), p. 127.

would customarily involve analyzing a problem, designing a solution, and supervising execution of the solution. What kind of problem? Any whatever, in a virtually limitless range, so long as its concern is with human use of outdoor space and the land.

Discussion of landscape architectural works, especially in a professional sense, necessarily includes the question of implementation. Even the most brilliantly designed solution to meet human problems is of little value except as it becomes an actuality through execution. Similar significance attaches to the consequent effect of a completed work in terms of public reaction and official support: what good did it do? As a profession, landscape architecture operates first as a social art, serving human values.

Naturally enough, the art and the profession have much history in common; how one approaches it will of course depend to some degree on his position as layman, practitioner, or student aspiring to practice. One need not have professional aims in landscape architecture to appreciate that the story of man's progress across the centuries can be interpreted as well through what he has built with and upon the land as through the battles he has fought and the wars he has won or lost. Consequently, the account of man's developing attitude toward the land, and of what he has done with it in different times and places to satisfy his varying needs, can be fascinating for every general reader; and as an aspect of socioeconomic history it is of intrinsic value quite apart from its applicability to the practice of landscape architecture in the twentieth century.

To a professional student or practitioner of landscape architecture, the past of this great land-planning art can bring, as it does to a general reader, the kind of deeper understanding of human history that is needed for fulfillment of one's role as an educated member of society. Beyond this, it can afford to the professional a clearer and more specific view of the part played by landscape architecture in the past and its potential for the future. And for him, in terms of direct aid to his own creative performance, it can be an ever-renewing source of technical assistance and inspiration—provided that he treats it always sensibly and does not make the mistake of trying to copy its forms. For both the general reader and the professionally oriented, hoping to benefit fully from studying landscape architectural works of the past, two simple suggestions on the question of time may be helpful: First: projecting oneself backward in time. To best understand a work of men in some past age, one must recapture as closely as possible the spirit of that age, sensing what someone of that time would have felt and thought about the example being studied. How did he evaluate it? What did he see in it, especially if he had never before seen anything like it? What were the contemporary affairs of men and how did they influence the character of the work?

Precisely how these *evaluational conditions* affected the actual form of the work—how it arose out of its cultural context—is not always easy to perceive. Usually far easier to see is the way the actual form of a historic work was affected by the *physical conditions* that surrounded it; and there is almost always evident a direct correlation, as in the use of shade and water to counteract the effects of a hot climate or the preponderance of vertical planes in a hilly terrain. Indeed, this is one of the most appealing characteristics in the best examples of the past, reflecting as it does the effortless way in which the result so often seems to have sprung quite naturally from the land.

Then there is the second suggestion in regard to time, obligatory for the professional but helpful to the general reader as well. From successful immersion in a bygone era, one needs to be brought back to confront the truth that one is living today, not long ago, that problems and circumstances now differ vastly from those of the past, and that accordingly it would make little sense merely to imitate in the present the physical form of the work under scrutiny. The professional can nevertheless gain much present-day value from the historic work if he but gives it his total attention, openmindedly, receptively. It is entirely possible that something intangible but fully applicable to present problems will be revealed: some relationship, bold or subtle, between causative factors and resultant form; some aspect of proportion or spatial structure, of color, scale, texture; or some one of the manifold invariant relations, of process or form or both, discoverable in many of the masterpieces of other times and places. In other words—the spirit of some interrelationship in the past can be of useful influence in the present.

In addition to the foregoing, a few comments should be made on landscape architectural design without reference to history. Despite the most earnest efforts of innumerable practitioners of the art, landscape architecture continues to be regarded by many laymen—and unfortunately by some individuals who call themselves landscape architects—as a horticultural field, an area in which plants and planting are the principal concern. This is a gross misconception. To be sure, because landscape architecture has to do with the total environment of man, and because plants are an important part of that environment, the landscape architect must know plant materials, not only biologically but also as a visual factor in design. But, in the strictest sense, plants are of importance to landscape architecture mainly in their capacity to aid in forming and modulating spaces. It is obvious that spaces are what humans do their living in; *space* must therefore be comprehended as the major medium of design.

The notion of the primary role of space seems for laymen and some professionals a very difficult one to grasp. It is thus appropriate to suggest here that one studying the history of landscape architecture, in the process of examining selected past examples, has an exceptional opportunity to further his understanding of what today's landscape architect means by the space that his profession is engaged in shaping and modifying upon the land; this can be done most effectively by looking carefully for certain spatial qualities in every work of the past encountered. To begin with, space must be appreciated as a material with which to work—as a vibrant, pliable fullness, not an emptiness. To speak of space as a void is to dismiss one of its chief potentials. Then, if it is to be truly effective and satisfying, a space must have a positive character; this means, simply, that the space must appear intended rather than accidental, the conscious product of a purpose rather than the mere by-product of other operations. Positive space never looks like something left over. One of the best sources of positive spatial character is clarity of overall form; this occurs most convincingly when one can readily perceive the boundaries or limits of the space, the vertical planes of masonry or vegetation implied or explicit that contain it. A space thus clearly bounded is felt to have integrity, to be something in and of itself; its form and size are un-ambiguous.

After determining that a space has positive character and form, its *structure* should be examined in search of whatever ordered relations one can see among its constituent parts. When these relations are easily comprehended and exhibit recognizable order, the normal human observer feels contentment, and the space is said to have strong, clear, positive structure. In studying the structure of a space, the arrangement of forms within it—or possibly the form of the space itself—impels the observer to look in some direction or sequence of directions. When one looks in a fixed direction even for an instant, the line along which he looks is called a *sight-line*. Especially in the case of manmade spaces, comprehension of the structure of the space, or of a series of spaces, depends in large part upon discernment of the relationships between or among the sight-lines. In a sense they become the skeleton on which the space is built. The same can also be said for the structure of a system of spaces.

These considerations can hardly be overemphasized. To repeat what often needs repeating, in design the role of space is primary. Whenever a design or configuration seems to be only an assembly of objects, with little or no attention to organization of the space between them, the space becomes visually a leftover, a negative quantity. An arrangement thus exhibiting misplaced emphasis earns for itself the annoyance that is normally felt, at least unconsciously, over the ambiguity of an aggregate of unrelated objects appearing to float vaguely in an amorphous field. Looking back through the centuries at what men have done, it is instructive to see that at times their efforts have for this very reason failed to achieve highest potential.

Attention to these basic factors in what the landscape architect means today by the design of outdoor space will be helpful as the reader traces the path from ancient times to the twentieth century. To be sure, this account makes no claim to encyclopedic treatment or comprehensive coverage. Typical high points, selected as the best existing illustrations of successive epochs, must suffice. But they should serve as a just outline of the story of landscape architecture, and of its development as an art and as a profession.

Design on the Land

I. Ancient Times

From a designer's point of view, which will be the prevailing one throughout this book, modern knowledge of the landscape architecture of man's earliest ages is necessarily for the most part conjectural; there is little remaining physical evidence from which to reconstruct the historic actuality in visible form. To be sure, there are many verbal references—as, for example, testimony to rich types of garden treatment around and upon the palaces and ziggurats of Mesopotamia, including, eventually, the "Hanging Gardens" of Babylon referred to by Herodotus. From still later times there are accounts of the Persian hunting parks or "paradises" that so fascinated the Greeks. There is documentary and site evidence of such earthwork operations as systems of channels for drainage and irrigation in early Egypt and Mesopotamia. These elementary networks, like the ones used in the same regions today, were presumably combinations of straight flowlines and thus were an ancient form of geometry on the land.

But, by their very nature, such outdoor works tend not to leave permanent vestiges as works of architecture do. And, for so visual a field as landscape architecture, physical remains are of the utmost importance to an acceptable grasp of past accomplishment; verbal descriptions are not enough. Moreover, for the purposes of this study, selective attention must be focused primarily on works whose actual form suggests their having influenced the landscape architecture of succeeding centuries—ultimately with relevance to the profession as it has been practiced in the modern era.

Accordingly, the first example to be discussed here is the mortuary temple of Queen Hatshepsut, at Deir-el-Bahari in Egypt, the remains of which make reconstruction clearly possible today (Figs. 1, 2). Built about 1500 B.C., it illustrates well the conditioning effects of the environmental factors referred

1. Remains of the mortuary temple of Queen Hatshepsut at Deir-el-Bahari.

2. Reconstruction of Queen Hatshepsut's temple, with the all-important processional line in the center.

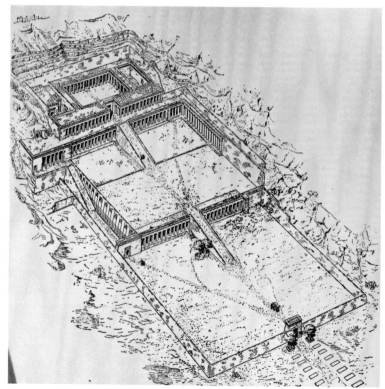

to in the Foreword. The physical ones, especially the topographic, are reflected in the temple's location well away from the periodically flooding Nile, with huge terraces stepping upward toward and literally carved into the high orange cliffs. Even the hot climate seems to have been recognized by the planting of trees in pits to shade the approach from the river.

The evaluational or cultural factors exhibit their influence here perhaps even more forcefully than the physical ones. Religion played a dominant role in Egyptian life; some authorities would go so far as to say religion *was* the life of Egypt. What has persisted of the ancient realms is almost entirely an architecture of temples and tombs. Seldom in history has a priesthood been more powerful—even the pharaoh, on whom national consciousness was largely centered, was supposed to have combined in him both god and king.

Against this background, it is not strange that the religious processional should have assumed a fundamental place in the scheme of things. Its effect is well demonstrated in the temple at Deir-el-Bahari, with its long, linear approach from a gated entry, straight onward and upward in ever more concentrated emphasis until the line of march and sight disappears into its mysterious terminal, the inner sanctum where only the god-king and the highest priests might enter.

Such a straight-ahead linear arrangement became almost a constant in the development of outdoor space in Egypt—and of indoor space, too, for that matter, as seen from the floor plans of most of the temples. Then the straight line of sight was normally accompanied by what must have seemed a logical corollary to Egyptian builders, who presumably sensed a condition clearly apparent to an observer today: when the eye looks at two points, it immediately "sees" a third one in virtually the exact center between them. The center seems to announce itself and to call out for attention. Thus, when so rigorous a line as that of the processional goes through an opening, it naturally wants to pass through the midpoint between the two sides. In the case of a doorway, the side points are of course the jambs; when the two points are free-standing verticals, they will in like manner be equidistant from the central line of march. This occurs typically in the gateway to a temple precinct, where the inevitable pair of pylons or giant seated figures flank the entry.

From this disposition it is but a short step to overall bilateral symmetry, a kind of mirror effect in the entire plan, with a right-hand part reflecting a left-hand part. Such an arrangement of elements—unimaginative, perhaps, but logical enough and easy—apparently became fairly common in the layout of grounds around Egyptian buildings public and private.

In the case of residential grounds, the picture is somewhat unclear. Excavations at Tel-el-Amarna have revealed an unusual amount of information about this one example of Egyptian town planning, including residential sections. But on the whole, because the homes of even the wealthy in Egypt seem to have been built of materials more perishable than the stone customary for temples, relatively little is known about the layout of the gardens and other grounds around residences, though there is helpful evidence in some of the mural paintings discovered in tombs.

One of the most remarkable of these paintings was found in the tomb of a high official at the Theban court of Amenhotep III; it is believed to depict his own house and garden. The layout (Fig. 3) is drawn in the strange Egyptian mixture of projections—partly in plan, partly in elevation, and even then with elements twisted around in place—requiring a bit of agility to read. The plan does, however, lend itself reasonably well to reconstruction (Fig. 4), showing a high-walled enclosure, the dominant central sight-line leading from an entrance gate at the front to the house at the far end, and fully bilateral symmetry in the distribution of the component parts. Here again the influence of environmental factors, especially climate, is evident. In an arid country of parching heat crossed by searing winds from the desert wastelands, vertical shelter against the winds, overhead shelter against the sun, and ample provision of water would naturally become usual in outdoor development. Hence the protective walls and the rows of trees, the vine-covered bower, the four rectangular pools with their waterfowl and the ever-present lotus plants.

To be realistic, one must suppose that exceptions to the method of bilateral symmetry undoubtedly occurred. But the straight-ahead linearity of a processional type remained a major characteristic through successive centuries of Egyptian constructions. Egypt did not offer much in its landscape architecture, so far as can now be deciphered; but what little it offered was unquestionably positive.

In contrast, the Greek phase of the present account is a perplexing challenge. Western civilization owes so much to Greece in architecture, sculpture, and letters that one would naturally like to record a rich Greek contribution to the story of landscape architecture in all its aspects. In some form not yet precisely known, the magnificent Minoan palaces of ancient Crete probably had surroundings of some richness. For a period of seven centuries, from the time of Homer's epics onward, Greek literature abounds with poetic allusions to trees and flowers, to sacred groves, to areas variously called parks and gardens. Plato's Academy, and the academies of other scholars through the years, are in effect described as gardens. Especially after the Persian wars there was much excitement about parks, inspired by experience of the Persian "paradises." As time passed, references to public gardens in the cities increased; it is known that the Athenian agora was furnished with trees. Men of importance appear to have acquired country villas and private gardens. Yet neither in the literature nor in the decorative painting on vases is there anything approaching clear, precise evidence as to the *design* of these open spaces, and there are virtually no physical remains to tell the story in visual terms.

4. Perspective interpretation of the mural shown in Fig. 3; all parts are organized on the central sight-line.

3. Wall painting from a tomb depicting house and grounds of an official at the court of Amenhotep III.

The Greeks obviously had a superlative capacity in one aspect of landscape architecture, the selection of sites and the fitting of individual buildings into them, as can be seen today in the ruins at Delphi or in the Greek theaters of Siracusa or Taormina in Sicily. But, so far as can be told from either descriptions or actual rémains, little is known about the arrangement or form of the surroundings of buildings beyond the mere statement that temples and other edifices were often set in extensive groves. Nor does much care seem to have been taken in organizing outdoor space in groups of buildings: the temples at Paestum, south of Naples, for example, or at Agrigentum or Selinus in Sicily, are quite unrelated to each other through any appreciable *spatial* structure, although each separate building is superbly joined to its own immediate site.

Beyond the siting of buildings, Greek interest in strong outdoor design seems to have been concentrated in what are recognized today as the beginnings of city planning. Even in this field, however, the performance remained oddly indifferent to the shape of the land and of outdoor space for a very long time. Hippodamos the Milesian, highly praised by Aristotle and generally regarded as the world's first city planner, strikes the modern eye as almost coldly theoretical in his development of the gridiron plan from the checkerboard layout of even more ancient times. In the rebuilding of Miletus, his home town in Asia Minor, he adopted a pattern that was practically superimposed upon the terrain, paying scant attention to the shoreline or to the slope of the land (Fig. 5). This gridiron method, called Hippodamian or Milesian, became for many generations the norm for building—or rebuilding after destruction—the many small cities established by the spread of the Greek world.

One of the best known of these cities, with well preserved remains, is Priene, newly built on a steep hillside above the River Meander, not far from the older Miletus. Here the streets of the rigid gridiron pattern lie with good reason along the land in one direction but slant steeply toward the valley in the other (Fig. 6). Somewhat more comfortably related to the terrain is the agora, the central public open space normally found in all Greek towns. With its longer dimension running parallel to the slope, the agora of Priene seems better fitted to the land than does the swarm of residential blocks (Fig. 7). Indeed, there is evidence that care—even devotion—was increasingly lavished upon the agora and other public elements of Greek towns, while the residential quarters were undistinguished until late in the history of Greece. In fairness, given the necessary brevity of this account, it should be pointed out that another development of later times was a relaxation in rigidity of the gridiron scheme and a closer fitting of plans to the land. This was especially true in the gradual improvement in conscious planning of the agora as a space framed by buildings.

Another Mediterranean town of early origin serves as a bridge to discussion of Roman landscape architecture: Pompeii, preserved in remarkably complete

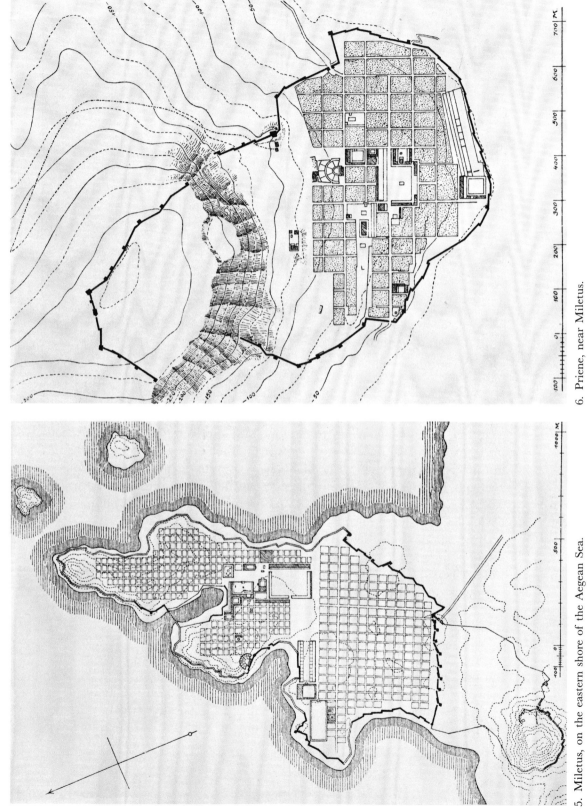

6. Priene, near Miletus.

5. Miletus, on the eastern shore of the Aegean Sea.

7. Priene: a reconstruction; many streets are too steep for use by wheeled vehicles.

condition because of volcanic inundation of it and Herculaneum by Vesuvius in 79 A.D. Originally an Oscan settlement and then influenced by the Etruscans in unrecorded times, it was strongly affected by the nearby Greek colony of Neapolis, later seized by the Samnites, and ultimately established as a thriving Roman town. Owing to the mixed nature of its long history, Pompeii can hardly be considered entirely typical of either Greece or Rome in any generalized sense; yet it does present a fascinating and rather comprehensive picture of life in a small Roman town from about 80 B.C. to 79 A.D. There were, of course, larger Greek cities in southern Italy and Sicily and still others developed by Rome in the north, often on Etruscan origins. But in no other case has there remained in place so much of the physical actuality as occurred through catastrophe in Pompeii.

As revealed today the street system of Pompeii, especially in the oldest sections (inherited, no doubt, from the settlement's earliest days), is rectilinear but only roughly so, looking from the air like a somewhat irregular checkerboard or honeycomb (Fig. 8). What may once have been the agora of the Greeks became in Roman times a forum, for generally similar purposes. Perhaps it had undergone reorganization; at any rate, whereas the very

8. Pompeii: scale model of the excavated remains.

earliest Greek agora had often had about it a haphazard, negative air, almost as if the space had been left over from something else, the Forum of Pompeii seems to assert itself as a conscious entity of space. It looks intended and purposefully positive.

The developed Pompeiian house, too, apparently presented a more organized aspect than the earliest Greek prototypes. In the process of becoming perceptibly more ordered it had developed an excellent interlocking of indoor and outdoor space. In the simplest case (Fig. 9) this was effected by a sequence of spaces threaded on a single line of sight—from the doorway on the street

9. Pompeii: a typical house is essentially simple in plan, with a visible sequence of spaces leading from the entry.

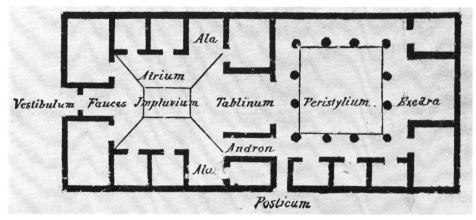

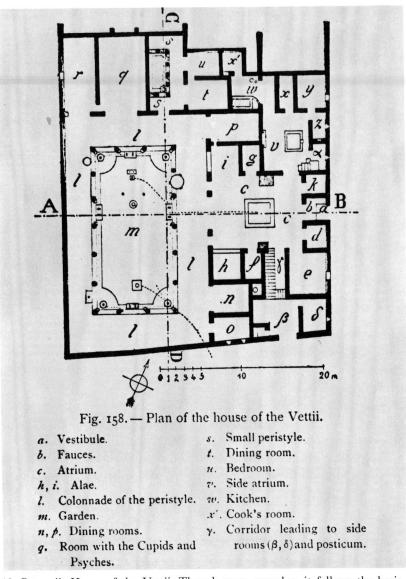

Fig. 158. — Plan of the house of the Vettii.

a. Vestibule.
b. Fauces.
c. Atrium.
h, i. Alae.
l. Colonnade of the peristyle.
m. Garden.
n, p. Dining rooms.
q. Room with the Cupids and
     Psyches.

s. Small peristyle.
t. Dining room.
u. Bedroom.
v. Side atrium.
w. Kitchen.
x'. Cook's room.
γ. Corridor leading to side
     rooms (β, δ) and posticum.

10. Pompeii: House of the Vettii. Though more complex, it follows the basic pattern of organization.

face of the house through the first room or atrium, then through a constricting doorway or passage to a larger, garden-like peristyle surrounded by a columned and covered walkway but otherwise open to the sky. The atrium, too, was partly open above and was covered by a roof that often sloped inward to a central rectangular opening directly over a pool of like dimensions in the floor. In a structure like the House of the Vettii, with the atrium light-flooded from above and the peristyle almost completely in the open air, the distinction between indoors and outdoors must have seemed minimal indeed (Figs. 10, 11, 12). The result, a merging of outdoor space with indoor space,

11. Exterior of the House of the Vettii; a reconstruction (note the inward orientation).

12. Peristyle of the House of the Vettii; indoors and outdoors are virtually one.

is well worth noting—especially in view of the importance given this phenomenon as a desirable characteristic in small-house design today.

There were other rooms in the Pompeiian house, of course, varying in number and complexity. Generally they were at the sides, opening only inward to the atrium or the peristyle, from which they obtained their light; there were few if any windows in the outside walls. To be sure, the outer face of the house might be occupied by shops opening solely to the street, but the residence itself was distinctly inward-oriented, practically turning away from the rest of the community. Repetition of this attitude in house after house throughout Pompeii naturally gave the town on overall visual texture of inwardness—a buttoned-up appearance oddly paradoxical in a community with individual houses more and more open to the outdoors.

This implied interest in life under the sky was not merely theoretical. From Pompeiian wall-paintings it is evident that gardens in the horticultural sense were held in high regard, and it is known that the peristyles of houses were customarily planted, though fortunately not in the raggedly ornate manner exhibited by many of them today. Some Pompeiian murals have been interpreted as depicting seaside villas, and these, considered along with physical remains uncovered in various locations, point to a growing trend toward country living. Evidence of this comes also from written accounts of Cicero and Horace, Vitruvius and Pliny, brimming with enthusiasm for the country even though they provide little basis for reconstructing the physical form of any particular *villa rustica*. It is heartening to know that as early as the second century B.C. Scipio enjoyed his country house; Cicero writes warmly of the family villa at Arpinum in the following century; Horace's odes leave no doubt as to his love of wild nature, and it has been possible to do a partly conjectural restoration of the little villa he had in the Sabine Hills near Rome. From Pliny the Younger come descriptions of his own several villas, all of which were treated with obvious affection. They appear to have been richly furnished, but the written record again does not provide enough information to establish plans of the villas with precision or detail. Nor can one determine to what degree there was genuine concern for design on visual levels. Such determinations will have to await considerable further excavation.

Such country villas of important or wealthy men, while surprisingly numerous, were relatively isolated. For greater abundance one must look to Rome itself. At the height of its opulence, the city was graced by a phenomenally large number of green open spaces of one kind or another, and on the Palatine a succession of emperors, from the early empire onward, built the sumptuous palaces and urban villas with which the hill was rather well covered. Each of these fabulous installations must have had its own gardens and promenades. From verbal accounts quite a bit is known about the plants employed, but there is little reliable evidence on the precise form or arrangement of these outdoor areas beyond the logical assumption that, as developments continued, the grounds echoed the increasingly regular geometry of the buildings.

For landscape architects it is in the valley north of the Palatine that the major theme of the Roman story unfolds. Here, nestled in the wide swale between its looming heights and the southward slopes of the Esquiline and the Viminal, with the towering eminence of the Capitoline at its western end, lies one of the world's most fascinating and important historic spaces, the great Forum Romanum (Fig. 13). Legendary in origin, this famous depression among the hills of Rome had long served many purposes—burial ground, marketplace, administrative and judicial center, place of public assembly and political gossip—before it ultimately became the symbolic hub of Rome and therefore of the world as it was known then. As early as the sixth century B.C., according to tradition, some of the first buildings were erected; in the fifth century the temples of Saturn and Castor, still partly standing today though much restored in ancient times, were built on the edges of the valley. Through the years the Forum Romanum held a bewildering mixture of nondescript minor public buildings, shops, and wooden market stalls, until its growing use for civic affairs pushed the markets out.

The second century B.C. saw the addition of two basilicas, great halls devoted to judicial, administrative, and at times commercial uses. The Basilica Aemilia, often restored but still in active service at the time, remained in place along the north edge of the Forum when in 46 B.C. Julius Caesar built the larger Basilica Julia on the southern side, roughly facing the Aemilia. The Capitoline hill had been architecturally faced off in 78 B.C. through construction of the Tabularium, or state archives, so that now a visually enclosed space began to take form, delineated by the two basilicas on the north and south and the Capitoline on the west. This development may have been fortuitous, but the chances are strong that it was influenced by Greek experience in forming civic centers through placement of public buildings in line along what thus became the sides of a space.

With the continuous colonnades of the two basilicas acting as boundary planes at the sides, especially looking down upon the scene from the Tabularium, it must have seemed that the space had acquired a sort of firm integrity, almost as though it were made of a transparent but material substance. The great vertical plane of the Palatine structures, reaching up behind the Basilica Julia, no doubt helped to confirm the sense of palpable spatial form. Sensations of this kind may well have stirred in Caesar himself when, just about simultaneously with the Basilica Julia, he had the Forum of Julius Caesar started just north of the main Forum Romanum—his own small version, with its Temple of Venus Genetrix at its western end. Here, as in the Pompeiian forum of the same period, one can feel an essentially systematic people striving somehow to achieve positive character in the spaces they create.

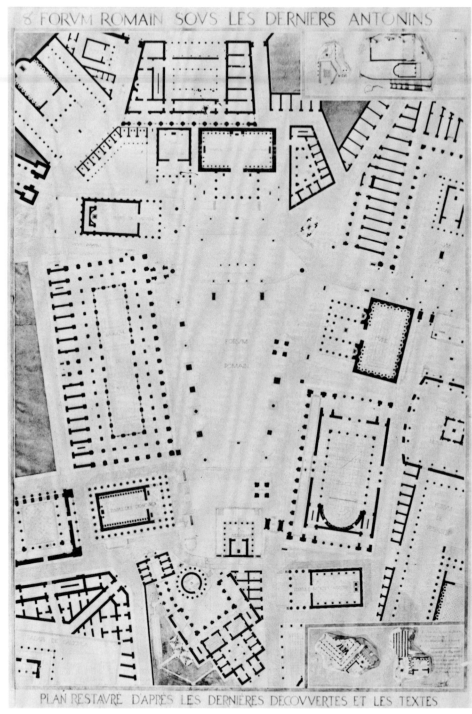

13. The Forum Romanum: a restoration.

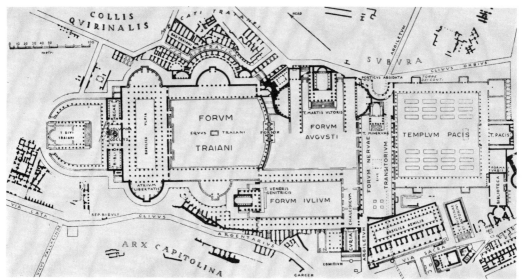

14. The Fora of the Emperors as restored.

After Julius Caesar's assassination, his nephew and successor Augustus, erecting in Caesar's memory the Temple of the Divine Julius, located it in the main Forum at the eastern end of the space between the two basilicas. However accidental this placement may have been on the part of Augustus and his architects in closing the far end of the space, it is improbable that the resultant effect can have been lost on them. For the new temple, at the end of an almost central line of sight through the space between the basilicas, attained a visual dominance that could hardly have gone unnoticed, and the now accented space of the Forum acquired a fully pronounced directional quality. It is much as though the viewers had suddenly had recalled to them mysteriously, out of a dim and unknown past, the overpowering impact of the terminal sanctum in the Temple of Queen Hatshepsut. At any rate, from that time forward, Roman handling of outdoor space reflected increasingly in its clearly ordered structure the major genius of the Roman empire: an undeniable capacity for organization.

Almost immediate evidence of this trend was provided by the great series of more elaborate and impressive spaces built during the next century and a half and known today as the Fora of the Emperors (Fig. 14). Just north of the Forum Romanum and the Forum of Julius Caesar, they were begun by Augustus. A few years after dedicating the Temple of the Divine Julius, he completed his uncle's unfinished little forum and, at right angles to it, began his own Forum of Augustus a bit to the north. To fulfill a vow made after repaying the assassins, he also erected at the north end of his new forum the Temple of Mars the Avenger. Balanced to right and left in the side boundary walls of the space, he built two large, semicircular recesses fronted by colonnades.

15a, b, c. Part of Bühlmann's famous panorama of restored Rome viewed from the Capitoline in the time of Constantine. Reading from left to right, in reverse chronological order: in 15a the top of Trajan's Column (which still stands today) appears to the left of the Basilica Ulpia; next is the main Forum of Trajan, reaching over into 15b, which also shows the Forum of Augustus (with its Temple of Mars the Avenger) and, in the foreground, the small Forum of Julius Caesar. In the foreground of 15c are: the corner of the Tabularium, the Temple of

During the next hundred years, two additions were made to the Fora of the Emperors: Vespasian's Forum of Peace, centered on a line of sight reaching eastward from the Forum of Augustus, at right angles to the main direction of that forum, and the Forum of Nerva (also called the Forum Transitorium), between those of Vespasian and Augustus. Then came the largest and most majestic of all, the huge Forum of Trajan, designed for the emperor by Apollodorus of Damascus and dedicated in 113 A.D. As a total complex, it consisted of a powerful sequence of spatial elements balanced on a single line of sight extending westward from the side of the Forum of Augustus— and, very possibly, on a continuation of the long sight-line from Vespasian's Forum of Peace.

This fantastic Trajan sight-line, on leaving the Forum of Augustus, passed first through a triumphal arch in the curving east side of the huge main Forum of Trajan, with its central statue of the emperor and twin hemicycles on the north and south sides. On the north side the hemicycle was cut into the slope of the Quirinal hill and supported several stories of markets. Across the west side of this broad space lay the vast Basilica Ulpia—covered, but with the sight-line continuing through the shadowy columned center, as through a kind of ancient breezeway, to the sculptured Column of Trajan just beyond, flanked by two libraries. Then, as a fitting climax at the far western end, came the Temple of Trajan, added after Trajan's death by Hadrian, his successor (Fig. 15).

Particularly notable in all the foregoing, from a designer's point of view,

Concord, and the Arch of Septimius Severus (still stands). Beyond is the space of the Forum Romanum, with the Curia and Basilica Aemilia on the left, the Basilica Julia and the Temple of Castor and Pollux on the right, backed by the heights of the Palatine, and in the center the eye-catching Temple of the Divine Julius. In the distance are the Basilica of Constantine (shown under construction), the Temple of Venus and Rome, and the massive Colosseum. On the horizon are the Alban Hills.

is the development in skillful handling of open space that appears to have occurred in the years between dedication of the Temple of the Divine Julius in 29 B.C. and completion of the Trajan complex over a century later. Whether the growth was accompanied by an awareness of increased understanding and facility or whether it was unconscious must be a matter for speculation in the absence of documentary evidence. But the physical remains discoverable on the site bear out the fact that growth occurred.

Vespasian's Forum of Peace and the Forum of Nerva, built during the hundred years after completion of the Forum of Augustus in 2 B.C., probably showed no great progress in the arrangement of outdoor space, but more excavation is needed to be sure. It is in the monumental complex of the Forum of Trajan and its supporting elements that Roman skill at spatial organization achieves its expert sophistication. Here are all the seemingly simple phenomena already suggested: the long sight-line connecting not merely two but an entire series of spaces; the clear delineation of each of these spaces not only as an entity in itself but also as an integral part of a whole; the terminal impact of the Column and Temple of Trajan. Beyond this, still another kind of relationship enters to breathe vibrancy into the total structure as an experience to be enjoyed by the visitor: the alternation of spatial size and quality along the sight-line—alternation of big and small space, sunlight and shadow, breadth and constriction, manmade ceiling and open sky—giving the whole sequence a sort of pulsation that addresses itself unforgettably to all the senses.

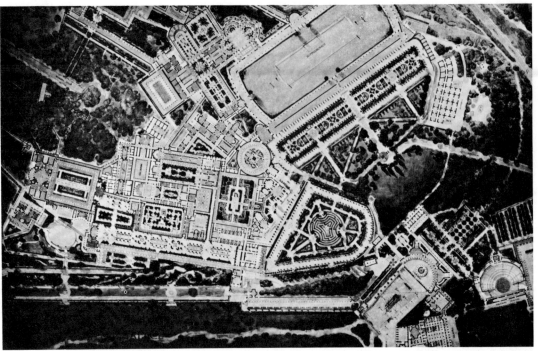

16. Hadrian's Villa, below Tivoli; restored plan of a monumental complex of interconnected buildings and outdoor spaces built in the second century A.D.

This is not to say that the Forum of Trajan was the ultimate in perfection; certainly much had yet to be learned about the behavior of open space under the hand of man. But, too, much that the Romans did was forgotten in subsequent centuries. That so high a degree of competence should have been attained under Trajan is entirely appropriate, for it was during his reign that the empire reached its widest scope. (And of course, one may be permitted the belief that skill in design was more to be admired than outward reach of empire.)

But it was under Hadrian, Trajan's cousin and successor, that perhaps the most fantastic single landscape architectural development occurred: Hadrian's extraordinary country villa, some fifteen miles east of Rome at the foot of the Sabine Hills below ancient Tibur, modern Tivoli (Fig. 16). There, on a tract of land several miles in circumference, he assembled a fabulous array of outdoor and indoor features recalling fondly remembered places in the length and breadth of the empire. Hadrian was a prodigious traveler and an avid collector of souvenirs, on a mammoth scale: as reminders of Greece he erected at his villa the great Hippodrome and Stoa Poikile, the Greek Theater, the Academy; to honor Alexandria, the Canopus and the so-called Temple of Serapis. There were great baths and lesser baths, libraries, a stadium, the Nymphaeum, a cryptoporticus, and of course the Imperial

17. Horace's Sabine Villa in the hills northeast of Rome; a restored plan.

18. Restored longitudinal section of Horace's Sabine Villa.

Palace. Today the whole is in ruins, but vast and stately ruins that conjure up without much difficulty the sheer opulence—and to modern eyes the remarkable extravagance—of the imperial establishment.

The most notable aspect of one's imagined reconstruction of Hadrian's Villa is the certainty with which, despite the all but bewildering number of buildings and outdoor areas, the strong visual tie can be sensed that must have existed among the components; for without it one could hardly have moved about in the conglomerate. Even today, with a bit of imagination, long sight-lines can be traced threading through these ruins in fascinating sequences of indoor and outdoor spaces, halls and courts, shadowy doorways and brilliant sunny pools, promenades and boschi and gardens—and always, at the far end of some sight-line, the receptive form of a great niche or other terminal. Over all of it now, as it must have been centuries ago, there is the aroma of sunwarmed cypress and box, laurel and olive and leather-leaved ilex.

A century and a half before Hadrian, Horace's joyous little country villa sheltered him only a few miles north of Tivoli in the Sabine Hills (Figs. 17, 18). The foundation walls, still visible, indicate a simple arrangement with house and enclosed garden intimately joined on a single sight-line. In early works like this and the Pompeiian house, which Horace's villa greatly resembled, one can see the germ of Roman genius for spatial organization that would bloom long afterward in such complexities as Hadrian's Villa. Essentially, the strength of those early places was in their basic simplicity, their unaffected acceptance of the facts of geometry. Roman works would ultimately become pointlessly involved, pretentious, and vulgarly ornate. But the underlying original basis, however brutally covered up, was always fundamentally simple—even in those later days when the majestic Roman empire, for one or more of many possible reasons, fell apart from inner splits and crumbled before the onslaught of vigorous "barbarians" who did not scare easily and were not impressed by the pomp.

II. The Middle Ages

With the final collapse of the Roman empire in 476, the Western world entered upon a period of several centuries called the Middle Ages—presumably because they lay between ancient times and the revival of classical learning. An age of profound religious dedication, of mysticism, of intuition and belief rather than of the rational methods of science, it had its own peculiar type of creative expression, spiritual and abstract rather than mundane and concrete. Of course there was affection for the immediate simple forms of nature; after all, the love of what men call beautiful is surely as old as man himself. But the major orientation in the Middle Ages was manifestly inward and introspective.

This was certainly as true in the area of what is now called landscape architecture as it was in other fields of effort. Circumstances of daily living in the Middle Ages were conducive neither to broad affection for the land nor to appreciative use of the wide outdoors. In this respect the period was retrogressive. During the best years of the Roman empire, man had at last come, if only in a limited way, to see himself as a part of the whole of nature. He had learned bit by bit to reach out into the open countryside and to use it with a sense of enjoyment. But during the Middle Ages this capacity virtually disappeared. Something akin to primitive man's fear of the wild seems to have taken hold of people, although in truth this was more from men's fear of each other than from any fear of the forces of nature in the raw. The countryside offered continual danger of attack—by highwaymen and robber barons on land, by pirates on the seas. To be sure, a clear amelioration of such fearfulness eventually accompanied the feudal system, with its fine code of interdependence of lord and vassal, but on the whole it is not too much to say that what passed for civilization was principally defensive.

In terms of outdoor space upon the land, this defensiveness was eloquently manifested in the castle and the walled community, as people huddled together like so many fear-ridden rabbits. Not that the wall was a medieval invention, by any means; as a device it had of course been known and used in earliest days. No one who has seen the foundations of Greek city walls or the cyclopean pre-Roman walls of Alatri is likely to forget their antiquity, and Roman emperors often followed the old custom. Wherever Rome had spread its colonial empire—even though by medieval times all evidence might have disintegrated except locations and vestigial ruins—protected towns appeared: Avila, Augsburg, Mainz, Trier, Strasbourg. The town completely surrounded by masonry walls is unquestionably representative of the Middle Ages. Even in the case of settlements too small for massive walls, safety of site was essential—witness today the numerous little hill towns, medieval or earlier, that still dot the landscape.

By general agreement, the oustanding example of the walled town, combining Roman origins, hilltop siting, and medieval masonry, is the Cité of Carcassonne, in southwestern France (Fig. 19). High on its plateau across the River Aude from the modern lower town, the Cité is double-walled, with fifty-three towers punctuating the inner and outer walls. There are a few remnants of the ruined old Roman fortifications, on which the Visigoths built in the fifth century, but the chief construction was done as a series of modifications in the twelfth and thirteenth centuries. A thorough repair of the walls and towers was executed under Viollet-le-Duc from 1855 to 1880, with commendable care taken to distinguish visibly between the authentic medieval work and the modern additions. Separating the outer and inner walls is a continuous strip of earth and paving of varying width. There are only

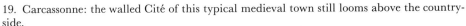

19. Carcassonne: the walled Cité of this typical medieval town still looms above the countryside.

two portals through the inner wall, within which are the fortress-like Château, the church of Saint-Nazaire, and a rather nondescript residential quarter much reduced from its original density. There are no indications of any significant medieval open spaces in the Cité other than the Place du Château.

When congestion became too great within the confines of some wall-encircled towns, houses sprang up beyond the defenses. But even then the tendency was to enclose the newly settled area with yet another wall.

Man's defensive attitude toward the outside world appears to have been characteristic of everyday medieval life in still another important sense. Figuratively turning his back on his physical surroundings, medieval man concentrated inwardly upon his own spiritual being, with perhaps more concern for the terrifying prospects of the hereafter than for what was going on around him. After all, Christianity was still suffering growing pains, and the Western world was in a theological ferment as it strove to throw off the older paganism. As a consequence, it is not surprising that on visual levels the greatest creative contributions of the Middle Ages were ecclesiastical. Whatever the shortcomings of the period in technology, it produced the wondrous Romanesque and Gothic cathedrals with their indescribably moving sculptures and stained glass.

It would be difficult to overestimate what the medieval growth of monasticism has meant to the continuance of civilization. In quiet retreats within monastery walls the literature and embryonic science of classical times were saved from disappearance. It is mainly in this sense that establishments like Monte Cassino served as bridges across the gulf between classical thought and the revival of learning when the Middle Ages had passed. And in the process of their copying and translating the monks produced the illuminated manuscripts and pictorial miniatures on which, in large part, modern understanding of the medieval visual environment is based.

The very nature of the monastic community, with its insistence on withdrawal from the secular world and on living under the Rule in prayer, silence, discipline, and manual work, gave rise not only to the isolated placement of the monastery itself but also to creation of the cloister, originally a grouping of the monks' separate cubicles with a covered walkway joining them around a central, common open space. The ambulatory, where the brothers could walk and meditate, was usually on all four sides; treatment of the open court varied greatly from place to place and with the passage of years, sometimes almost entirely paved, sometimes used as a garden for growing medicinal herbs. Nearly always there was a well in the center of the cloister; the stone wellhead has often survived, along with the ambulatory and its fanciful twisted and inlaid colonnettes. In time the cloister, as a form of square enclosed space, was found in close connection with urban churches; two outstanding examples in Rome are those in St. John Lateran and in St. Paul's-without-the-Walls (Fig. 20).

20. Cloister (chiostro) of Rome's cathedral church, St. John Lateran.

21. The Great Cloister of the Certosa di Pavia, its individual cells ranged along the outer wall.

After the founding of the Carthusian Order in 1086, an interesting variation in design of the cloister arose out of that Order's increased emphasis on work and study by the individual brothers. The great Certosa di Pavia, although almost too late to be classed as medieval (begun in 1396 and completed mainly in the fifteenth century), is an excellently preserved example of the

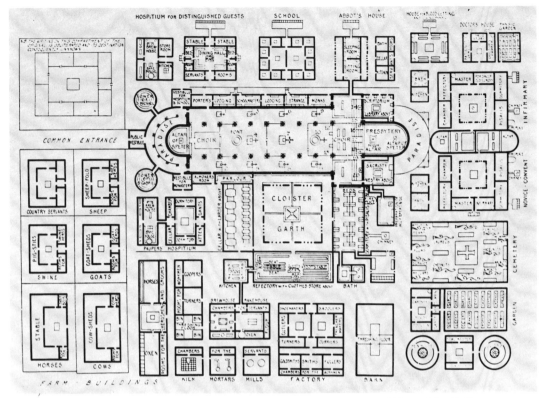

22. A redrawing of the monastery layout proposed about 830 A.D. to the Abbot of St. Gall (northeastern Switzerland). Note the completeness of the establishment, centering as always on church and cloister; the small cemetery at the right holds fruit trees, chestnuts, almonds, and hazelnuts.

typical Carthusian monastery. The monks' separate small houses, each with its own little garden, appear to march around in orderly precision outside the wall of the Great Cloister (Fig. 21). The latter, of unusual dimensions, has taken on today almost the character of a large tilled field.

The introspective attitude of the typical monastery is reflected in one of the most remarkable bits of evidence preserved through the centuries: the plan of an ideal monastery (Fig. 22), proposed in the ninth century to the Abbot of the Benedictine establishment at St. Gall in what is now northeastern Switzerland. It shows, though perhaps with exaggerated idealism, the astounding degree to which a monastery was expected to be self-supporting—to do its own farming, raise its own meat and wool and manufacture its own garments, perform its own day-to-day maintenance in every way, and ultimately to inter its deceased members in its own cemetery. The church, of course, is the heart of the whole complex, which includes the everpresent cloister.

Here again it is to be noted that the direction of major concern was consistently inward. The handling of indoor space in the Middle Ages, especially in the building of great churches, was highly skillful and progressive; the monasteries developed the cloister and the orderly grace of those serene inward-oriented spaces, open to the sky but nevertheless enclosed. For the truly outward reach of outdoor space there was apparently little if any appreciation and probably no feeling of necessity—except as the feudal system eventually devised clustered strips of ploughland about the manor houses. In the towns, the cramped streets left almost no space open and little of that unpaved. From illustrations in manuscripts, practically the only available evidence, the approach toward any cultivation of garden plots within the city would seem at best to have been a childish effort. Exactly how these little open spaces upon the land were used remains largely speculative: probably what started out as the practical use of precious bits of soil for growing vegetables and herbs was later expanded to include the cultivation of flowers. Vegetables were a major item in the staple diet of simple people, and from the very earliest days herbs were grown, especially by monks, for medicinal purposes. But eventually the monks needed flowers for altar decorations, and one can only imagine that the brothers preferred to grow them within their own walls.

Moreover, it is surely reasonable to suppose that, somewhat back in the long stretches of human history, man must have discovered his need for sustenance in a wider sense than merely of food for the stomach. To be truly effective, food for the *whole* man—or, as the Middle Ages might have put it, food for the spiritual self or soul—would also have to gratify hunger for the play of light on leaves and petals, for color and aroma, and above all for the ever-enthralling miracle of living growth. A study of the quaint miniature scenes in medieval manuscripts reveals their fascinating depiction of the gradual emergence of deep human craving for complete satisfaction of *all* the senses—or perhaps one should say the gradual re-emergence, for the chances are that successive ages have had to rediscover this homely truth again and again after times of turmoil or disruption.

At any rate, there is ample evidence that what began as an artless kind of cultivation of plants in checkerboard beds of soil became in time, at least in the secular world, provision of grass-carpeted and flower-bedecked pleasure gardens where gallants and their ladies whiled away the hours in merry persiflage (Fig. 23). One looks in vain for consciousness of spatial design; in its treatment of outdoor space the medieval period seems not to have progressed beyond an infantile simplicity that is none the less charming for its utter lack of sophistication.

To be sure, in the later phases of this austere age, various ways of forming patterns began to appear in gardens made less for human activity and more for show. Especially in England, where of course the climate was fully favorable to plant growth, patterns of the simplest kind, in beds and more often in clipped hedging, came to be used frequently: tight geometric configurations

23. Garden scene from the medieval manuscript *Roman de la Rose*.

called knots, or amusing devices like the maze or labyrinth, all of which grew more and more complex as gardeners became more facile. There were often simple pools and sometimes fountains where water was not too scarce. The clipping of trees into predetermined shapes, a revival of ancient Roman topiary work, came into favor as well, and in time even the simulated hilltop known as the mount was often included among the showpieces in this type of garden. But all of this was still only surface decoration, rather than the modeling of outdoor space.

One type of medieval outdoor space is much admired today: the town square. There is no evidence that the excellence of these urban spaces arose from any new awareness of spatial values or a suddenly acquired skill in design. In fact, it is most probable that medieval town squares appeal to the modern eye principally because they were obviously *not* preconceived as to form, but almost always seem to have evolved naturally out of the circumstances of location, need, and use—which comes close to echoing one of the most ardently held tenets of twentieth-century design.

To most observers these town squares, with very rare exceptions, have an atmosphere of unaffected simplicity—even awkwardness, on occasion—that is quietly but surely amusing. But it should also be noted that they possess qualities of great usefulness to present-day designers. For one thing, since they are seldom exactly square or even rectangular, they provide as a group a valuable laboratory in which to question the sanctity so widely but uncritically conferred on the right angle, and to study the effects of distortion on angles and on variants from prime geometric form.

Then, too, the invariably narrow streets entering the square very often do not continue through it. The space thus becomes a definite interruption or terminus to the entering sight-line, rather than a mere incident on a line that continues past the square. The stoppage is especially effective when the spatial corridor of the entering street comes in tangentially at the corner of the square, slides along one boundary plane of the space, and then stops against the far side. A complete case of the latter phenomenon, with a street sliding in at each corner of the square, produces what is known today as the "windmill" or the "whirling square," one of the most useful of basic forms, applicable in many areas of design.

Not every medieval city space has this blockage of sight-lines, but it is a major characteristic and occurs at least partially in most of them. Often, too, there is in these town squares an astonishing rightness of spatial volume stemming usually from happy proportions between horizontal and vertical dimensions. And beyond these considerations of overall form there is much to be learned from the casual use of paving materials—brick and stone in different shapes and sizes, laid random without the studied patterns introduced later, during the Renaissance.

The most charming, unpretentious, and therefore typical urban spaces are to be found in obscure little towns where medieval conditions have remained substantially unchanged. To be sure, there are among Italian town squares of the Middle Ages three famous ones in important cities: the Piazza San Marco in Venice, the Piazza della Signoria in Florence, and the Piazza del Campo in Siena, all of which will be discussed later. Of the three, only the second seems typically medieval; the Piazza San Marco, that greatest of all outdoor spaces, though medieval in fact has a magical aura of timelessness, and the Piazza del Campo, thoroughly medieval in its chronology and in the character of its architectural framework, nevertheless feels so consciously designed that it cannot be regarded fairly as an example of the medieval urban square.

By modern standards of judgment, characteristic medieval outdoor space was inward-oriented, consistently naive, obviously unpremeditated, and apparently not at all self-conscious. Thus it reflected, as the landscape architectural products of a people always tend to do, the spirit of the times. It is almost as though man's eyes were not yet wholly open to the wonders of the natural world, for he was busy contemplating his soul and its tortuous future. Daylight was too bright to bear; these were truly the Dark Ages, and openness to worldly experience would have to wait.

III. The World of Islam: Córdoba, Seville

While the Western world of Christianity groped along in the dark, a militant new religion sprang up in the Arabian desert in 622, spread within a century from Persia to the Pyrenees, and followed its conquests with a brilliant intellectual development of tremendous proportions: Islam, the world of the Muslims, followers of the prophet Mohammed. While Christian Europe was almost literally on all fours in mathematics, for example, the Muslims introduced Arabic numerals, positional notation, algebra, and new calculations in astronomy. Their curiosity was all-embracing: they experimented in the ancient pseudo-sciences of astrology and alchemy, made medical analyses of lasting value, and offered new techniques of poetry. What is known today of Aristotle rests in large part on discoveries and commentaries by Avicenna of Hamadan in Persia and Averroës of Córdoba in Spain. In the arts of design the contributions of Islam were distinctive, richly colorful, and highly imaginative. The whole was a cultural phenomenon in almost unbelievable contrast to the Dark Ages of the West.

By the year 700 the Arabs had swept across North Africa from Egypt to Morocco, converting or subduing the various tribes and races on the way; the amalgam of now Muslim peoples thereafter known generically as Moroccans or Moors stood poised at the ancient Pillars of Hercules, ready to invade Europe. In 711, Musa, the African viceroy of the Caliph of Damascus, dispatched a force across the narrow straits under command of a Berber chief named Tarik.

Moving swiftly inland, the Moors decisively defeated the last of the Visigoths, occupied Seville and Córdoba in 712, headed beyond the Pyrenees, took Narbonne in 720, and were stopped at last by Charles Martel in the epochal battle between Poitiers and Tours in 732. Despite this defeat, the Moors overran all of the Iberian peninsula except the very northern part and retained possession of it for centuries. The Catholic kings, keeping up intermittent pressure and aided by factional disagreements among the Muslims, slowly regained control, taking the stronghold of Toledo in 1085. Córdoba, the "Mecca of the West," an independent caliphate from 755 to 1031 and one of the greatest Islamic centers of culture, eventually suffered from sectarian strife, began to decline, and yielded to Ferdinand III in 1236. Twelve years later, with help from the Sultan of Granada, Ferdinand took Seville. For the next 250 years the successive kings of Granada, playing politics with the Christians and maneuvering adroitly among contending Muslim sects, maintained a wealthy and brilliant court. Then, torn again by internal dissension, Granada, the last Moorish possession in Spain, fell to Ferdinand and Isabella and was evacuated in 1492 after nearly eight centuries of Muslim rule.

The Islamic world, in striking contrast to Europe of the Middle Ages, showed profound appreciation for the outdoors. Owing to the climate that prevailed in most of the occupied regions and to a strong moral emphasis on family privacy, it was usual for even the simplest house to have at least one enclosed but unroofed court where a considerable part of the daily living took place. From east to west there was real affection for the land. The Muslims developed excellent forms of agriculture, with consequent high regard for water not only as a pleasant cooling agent but as the indispensible support of life in systematic irrigation.

Because religion and the state were inseparable, certain relatively uniform controls governed Muslim architecture and landscape architecture throughout the vast extent of Islam. There was some variation regionally in the rigor with which the requirements of the Koran were observed, as there was also in details of design, due to the Muslims' capacity for adapting themselves to local customs and conditions; but certain characteristics were consistent. Everywhere the mosques were vitally important centers of life, with their typical high minarets from which the muezzin called the faithful to prayer; and quotations from the Koran, reproduced in a wonderfully developed calligraphy, were used abundantly in decoration. That custom, together with the Muslim mathematical genius and the Koranic prohibition against physical representation of humans and animals, made virtually inevitable the distinctively fanciful geometric surface pattern now found throughout Islam. The Moorish version of Islamic landscape architecture was a lively one, expressing a patently happy acceptance of outdoor values. The influence of the Moors is evident even today in a large part of Spain, although centuries of Spanish modification have had their effect. Fortunately some noteworthy examples remain that have not been spoiled; all of these, as might be expected from the history of the Moors' gradual expulsion from the peninsula, are in the south, at Córdoba, Seville, and Granada.

In Córdoba, once the unquestioned focus of Islamic culture in the West, little is left standing of what was done in the great days of the Omayyad caliphs. There is written evidence that the city and its adjacent countryside abounded in luxurious palaces and gardens, but today only the gay atmosphere of the gardens and patios of a few private residences in the town reminds one of early culture and more scintillating days. In them the feeling, aside from occasional later Spanish architectural details, is strongly Moorish, and it is quite evident that this quality is carefully maintained.

Somewhat typical of what has happened frequently in Spain, the famous Mosque of Córdoba, one of the largest in all of Islam after numerous additions in Moorish times, was consecrated for Christian worship in 1238, immediately after the fall of the city, and has now been the Cathedral for centuries. It is a strange mixture of clearly Moorish forms with Spanish modifications, insertions, and overlays, the whole great pile dismally impressive in its bulky echo of majesty outside, but the interior with its forest of columns surprisingly light and spacious. It should be pointed out that the Spanish government and the church have long respected the original structure in systematic restoration and repair, and that the building is still known locally as La Mezquita (The Mosque).

Before entering the mosque proper, the faithful performed required ablutions; at Córdoba a large enclosed court served this purpose. It survives in almost pure Moorish character as the Patio de los Naranjos (Court of Oranges), with over one hundred glistening orange trees, each in a circular sunken well, arrayed in precise rows and the entire system connected by a network of brick-walled channels for irrigation (Fig. 24). At one side of the block of trees is a pool some thirty feet long with a high coping and, at each corner, a strangely detailed fountain, part Moorish, part Spanish-Renaissance, to which the people still come to fill their jars. There are four other minor pools in the courtyard; above the grove, tall palms wave their feather-duster heads.

The Court of Oranges is entered by a gate at the foot of the bell-tower, which was begun about 1600 on the foundations of the original Moorish minaret. On the three free-standing sides of the enclosure there apparently were at one time the covered walkways of a cloister, but the entrance side has been walled up to house administrative offices of the Cathedral. The great temple itself is on the fourth side of the court; originally there were some nineteen doors or gateways in this wall of the Mosque, allowing the multi-columned spaces of the interior to emerge into the grove of oranges—a remarkably perceptive example of providing for continuity of flow between indoor and outdoor space. There is a kind of hot, dusty serenity in the great court, which seems to serve also as a social gathering point, charming in the quiet animation of its groups of local citizens.

24. Córdoba: the Court of Oranges, originally a sort of open forecourt for the Mosque.

Seville today is a thriving, brilliantly colorful beehive of urban activity, whereas in Moorish times it was long subservient to Córdoba. While Córdoba withered, Seville flourished, reaching a peak of prosperity in the twelfth century, only to witness the end of Muslim control when the city fell to Ferdinand III in 1248. Much of the central part of the town still has the haphazard honeycomb street pattern of Muslim days, and here as in Córdoba, though more frequently, one sees the Moorish influence carried over rather faithfully in the treatment of gardens and patios of private houses.

Actually, much of the construction carried on by the Spanish in Seville during the opulent sixteenth century was entrusted to Moorish workmen. Such was the case in the gardens and patios of the Casa de Pilatos (also known as the Medinaceli Palace) and the Casa de las Dueñas (Palace of the Duke of Alba). The interior spaces of both are ample testimony to the wisdom of recognizing the good sense of Moorish practice in this bright, hot, arid climate and accepting it as naturally fitted to the circumstances. These are by no means flower gardens in the usual English manner; the growing of

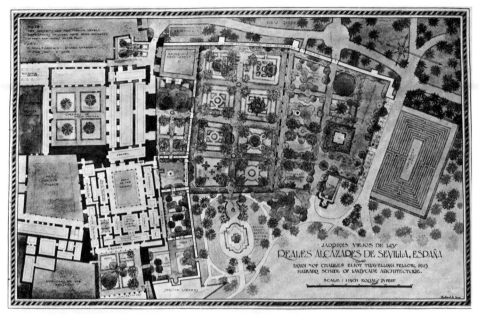

25. Seville: gardens of the Alcazar; the three distinct divisions are discernible in this measured plan.

26. The Alcazar gardens: Pavilion of Charles V.

turf would be practically impossible, and flower beds as such would not last under that kind of sun and water shortage. The predominant color of vegetation is the dark green of magnolias, oranges, and pepper trees, of box trimmed usually into hedging, and of cypress or juniper in tall hedges or trained into fanciful archways. A few evergreen flowering shrubs and vines supply brighter color, along with rows of potted plants set out according to season and the traditional polychrome tiles (*azulejos*) of Moorish origin. The patios are customarily paved throughout in tiles or in remarkable black and white pebble patterns; the garden paths, raised above the adjacent planting areas to ensure drainage into them from the paths, are either sand with tile edges or entirely paved in tiles. Emphasis is on the economical, but always audible, use of water, on concentrated richness of decoration and floral color against plain wall surfaces (normally white), and on the physiological and psychological cooling that accompanies all this when viewed from the shelter of deep shade.

The demonstrable excellence of such a combination of effects is to be seen in broader form in the patios and gardens of the Alcazar, the palace of the Moorish kings of Seville (Fig. 25). The massive, fortress-like establishment, as it stands today, derives from the even larger Moorish citadel built here in the twelfth century on ancient Roman foundations, with vast grounds extending to the banks of the Guadalquivir, far beyond the present gardens. The original Alcazar was completely destroyed, presumably during the siege of 1248; the palace was rebuilt by Peter the Cruel about a hundred years later, in a size somewhat reduced from the earlier one. His builders and artisans were Moors, faithful to their tradition, which accounts for the authentic character of the work despite its date. Subsequent additions and restorations, though possibly lacking in archeological accuracy, have generally adhered to the Moorish spirit, so that one senses here an eloquent evocation of past Muslim glory.

Within the Alcazar itself there are several handsome patios, but it is in the extensive compartmented gardens that the Moors' delight in open air is most clearly expressed. The chronology of the gardens is largely conjectural; it seems reasonable to suppose that a reconstruction of an earlier layout was done by the Moorish craftsmen hired by Peter the Cruel. It is known that Charles V made additions, and one of the most visible elements in the gardens is his pavilion, which to some degree acknowledges the Moorish tradition (Fig. 26). Still other work was done under Philip IV and Philip V; the several large, highly ornate gateways may be ascribable to them.

There is no overall scheme of design but, rather, three distinct divisions, each demarked by surrounding walls through which either simple gates or grilled windows connect the divisions. One enters the gardens at the northeastern corner, on an upper level containing a roughly rectangular reservoir. Extending along the area of the gardens, on the left, is a fortified wall built by Peter the Cruel; it is thick enough to house a long gallery, still at the upper level. The front of this simple stucco wall was later faced with an anachronistic mess of dark rococo blocks, the effect of which is visible from all parts of the gardens.

Immediately below the reservoir terrace and to the right, tucked against the wall of the Alcazar itself and reached from the reservoir by a double set of steps, is the charming little series of enclosures called the Gardens of Maria Padilla. Reaching outward from the palace between units of this area are two thick walls, pierced by simple grilled gateways at ground level and topped by ample promenades with rows of terracotta pots on the parapets. A similarly high thick wall, its elevated promenade at the level of the reservoir terrace and connecting with it, separates the Gardens of Maria Padilla from the second or middle division of the gardens. This is subdivided into eight hedged compartments, each treated in its own individual but rather non-descript fashion. The middle division has on its outer two free-standing sides an obviously later fence of ornamental piers and metal grilles (*rejas*), with two large, pretentious gateways. One of them leads to the third division of the gardens, that occupied by the Pavilion of Charles V and the baroque Pool of Joan the Mad.

The entire area of the gardens seems stuck together in the most naive way, almost like a patchwork quilt; yet it has undeniable charm. There is a certain luxuriant air about the place despite the known aridity of the climate—all the plots are surrounded by clipped hedges, vines trail over the white stuccoed

27. One of the many pools sunk into the patterned paving of unglazed tile in the Alcazar gardens.

walls, tall palms nod far above and cast their flickering shadows everywhere. But what is most memorable about the Alcazar gardens is neither the layout nor the vegetation: it is the details of tile and masonry and, above all, water. There is a surprising intimacy here, notwithstanding the sheer extent of the gardens, and the delicacy of scale in these details is certainly a major cause of the domestic character. It seems that wherever one looks a fountain meets the eye; yet these, with the single exception of the rather ambitious one at the center of the middle division of the gardens, are invariably modest (Fig. 27). All are sunk, usually without coping, into the paving of the path or patio, with water emerging in a small, quite unostentatious jet from a simple spout in the center of the pool or dripping from a shallow cup of marble or alabaster raised on a plain pedestal. In every detail—shape and lining of pool, form and material of water fixture—the fountains vary. But in every one the tinkling sound of gently falling water has a refreshing, soothing effect. The feeling of restfulness is further induced by the frequent benches and by such unexpected details as window seats built into the sides of a penetration in one of the thick old walls, with a metal grille through which one sees into the next division of the gardens (Fig. 28). Through the same thick walls the gateways for paths are straightforward, unadorned openings with the simplest kind of grilled gate and steps.

In all these details the chief performer is the azulejo, the polychrome tile for which Andalusia is justly renowned. The early, truly Moorish ones are extremely simple; as craftsmen became more skilled the patterns grew more complex, until in the sixteenth century the design and coloring had become somewhat elaborate. Both types are here; indeed, the style of the azulejos is one way of dating works in which they are used. The benches throughout all of the gardens' divisions are almost completely covered with azulejos; the risers in most steps are faced with one row of them; in the Pavilion of Charles V the inner wall of the surrounding arcade is solidly tiled; and in the recessed window seats referred to above the expanse of white wall over each seat has a large square of patterned azulejos embedded in it.

All paved surfaces in the gardens, as well as the treads of most of the steps, are of unglazed tiles, deep terracotta in color, mainly oblong and laid in either herringbone or basket-weave patterns. A variation is a basket weave with small glazed squares inset in windmill fashion; another is a combination of the small glazed squares with larger unglazed octagons. Virtually all of the fountains, except the large central one, employ azulejos in some way (Fig. 29). Some are wholly tile except for the water fixture; most have ingeniously continued patterns lining the sides and bottom of the pool, where the glazed color of the tiles enhances the water's glint.

There have been some relatively recent additions beyond the borders of the gardens here described, but such new developments are too clearly

28. A window seat in the thick wall, with a wall-facing of colorful tiles.

anomalous for inclusion in the present account. All in all, the Alcazar gardens, despite uncertainties of precise authenticity and patently off-key amendments, accomplish remarkably well the task of conveying the gay spirit of kingly Moorish gardens in urban surroundings.

29. A somewhat newer sunken fountain in the Alcazar gardens follows the flexible patterns of the Moorish workmen.

IV. The World of Islam:
Granada, Iran, Mogul India

Granada, in contrast to Seville, offers in the Alhambra and the Generalife supreme examples of what the Moors could do with outdoor space when relieved of the pressures of city life. This is not to deny that Granada is a city of significance; indeed, it was the last European stronghold of the Moors, where Muslim control continued for two and a half centuries after Córdoba and Seville had been lost. But the Alhambra and the Generalife, high above the teeming turmoil of the town, seem far removed and almost rural. The city lies in the dry valley of the Darro, at the foot of two long ridges some five hundred feet high—the Albaicin to the north of the Darro and the plateau of the Alhambra to its south. The Alhambra hill itself is separated by depressions from the slope bearing the Generalife on the east and from Monte Mauror on the south.

Soon after the conquest of 711 at the straits, the Moors built fortifications on the Albaicin, which they occupied; on Monte Mauror, where the Torres Bermejas (Vermilion Towers) still stand; and on the jutting western end of the Alhambra hill, where the walls and towers of today's Alcazaba are in large part original masonry. The Alhambra plateau (Fig. 30) was not used as a royal residence until Al-Ahmar, founder of the Nasride dynasty as Mohammed I, began his building there probably in about 1240. His successors added to the palace complex, with the major part of the work done under Yusuf I and Mohammed V between 1333 and 1391. Actually, today's Alhambra palace is what remains of a larger collection of buildings erected at various times; the name is an approximation of the Arabic for "red city," the term applied to the whole plateau by the Moors because of the color of the brick-like material used in the several buildings.

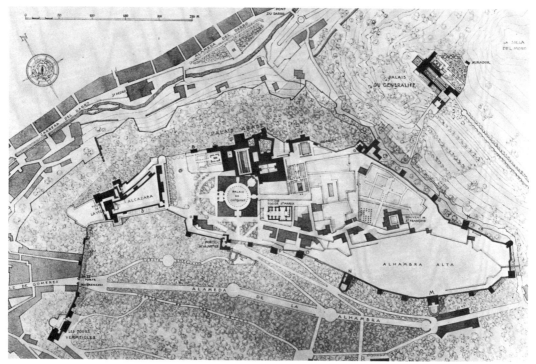

30. Granada: the Alhambra stands high above the town, the towers of the Alcazaba on the left end of the plateau, the Alhambra Alta on the right end, the Arab Palace in the middle; eastward and across a draw is the Generalife.

Ferdinand and Isabella, on Granada's surrender to them in 1492, respected the palace completely and had it restored and kept in good repair. But their grandson, the powerful Charles V, while professing admiration for the Alhambra, demolished some of it to make room for his own vast Italianate palace; begun in 1526 but never finished, although building continued intermittently for over a hundred years, it remains today—a large, intrusive pile of incongruity, utterly out of sympathy with its Moorish environment (Fig. 31). Fortunately, it is somehow possible visually to ignore it.

Surely few sights of man's handiwork are more compelling than the view approaching from the north of the great, orange-colored blocks of the towers of the Alcazaba and the Alhambra, framed in the green of trees on the almost vertical slopes of the rocky eminence over Granada, against a backdrop of white-capped Sierra Nevada. One's visit normally begins at a wide, rather formless plaza just inside the main gate to the high plateau. On the left are the towers of the Alcazaba; on the right, the outwardly unprepossessing Arab Palace and the monstrous Palace of Charles V. Straight ahead, from the northern edge of the plaza, the view is down into the valley of the Darro and across to the Albaicin. On the wall of the Arab Palace (Fig. 32), an inconspicuous door leads into a small, dark passageway at the other end of

31. Alhambra: aerial view of the Arab Palace and the unfinished Palace of Charles V.

which the visitor steps into a sudden flood of sunlight and the golden glow of one of the great spaces of the world, the Patio de los Arrayanes (Court of Myrtles).

This magical outdoor space is a lesson in silent contrasts. At the north end stands the formidable, fortress-like Torre de Comares—deep yellow or vermilion or reddish brown, depending on the season and on the hour, but massive always. Resting airily in front of it, at ground level, is a delicate arcade of seven arches on slender colonnettes of marble with fanciful capitals (Fig. 33). The entire surface above the arches, and even their soffits, are covered with a lacy, ivory-hued filigree of carved plaster, which catches every ray of light, especially that reflected upward from the smooth stone floor. The contrast between this concentrated enrichment and the plain wall behind it is as great as that between the seemingly frail arcade and the weighty tower. Centered behind the brightness of the arcade, the dark form of a pointed-arch doorway leads into the cavernous Hall of the Ambassadors, the sultan's official reception room.

In the center of the patio, flanked by two clipped myrtle hedges that give the court its name, is a long, rectangular pool, bordered by the paved walks that are the only coping and fed by a flat basin sunk into the paving at each

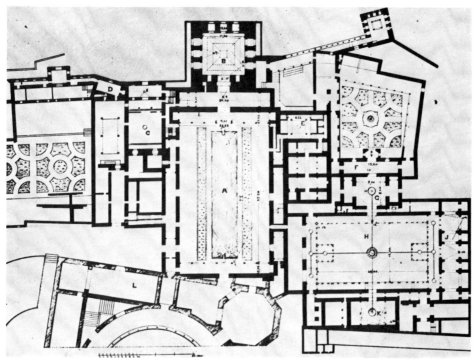

32. Alhambra: detailed plan of the Arab Palace; the Court of Myrtles is at A, the Hall of the Ambassadors within the Torre de Comares at B, the Court of the Lions at H.

end. The surface of the water is only slightly below the level of the surrounding walks; its complete stillness, reflecting to perfection the tower, the arcade, and the dark central doorway, projects their mirrored images as far below the level of the patio as they themselves rise above it, creating for the observer an eerie sensation of visual weightlessness—as though he and everything around him were floating in infinite space. There can be little doubt that this phenomenon is largely responsible for the feeling of pure serenity with which this wonderful space is blessed.

At the south end of the patio is an arcade like the one at the north, but in this case there is a windowed second story and above that another gracefully arched open gallery. Peering over the tiled roof of this uppermost story is the top of that invader, the Palace of Charles V. Behind the lower arcade, the central door (usually locked) leads to the remains of that palace. At the east and west sides of the patio, behind the myrtle hedges, are the clear boundary planes of the space, the simple walls of these wings of the Arab Palace, two stories high, roofed with the usual red tiles. Here again there is contrast—between the severe plainness of the walls and the snug areas of intricately carved plaster in geometric patterns around door and window openings.

33. The Torre de Comares, majestic above the still Court of Myrtles.

Near the southeast corner, a quite insignificant doorway across from the opening through which one has entered the court leads into a long, narrow room that, in turn, gives out upon the second of the Alhambra's most renowned outdoor spaces, the Court of the Lions or Patio de los Leones (Fig. 34). This fanciful open space is quite a change from the Court of Myrtles. The Court of the Lions is fairly jumping with visual activity and is even more jewel-like in the extraordinary richness of its decoration. Rectangular and somewhat longer in the east-west dimension than in the north-south, the court is completely surrounded by an arcade of tight, stilted arches on pipe-stem colonnettes, with additional square pavilions of similar construction at the east and west ends. Even more than in the Court of Myrtles, the surfaces of the arcade are elaborately carved in plaster, with geometric patterns and bands of cursive Arabic quotations; the soffits of the arches in the pavilions and in the rooms beyond the arcade bear the fantastic painted and gilded stalactite carving that so catches the reflected light as to be truly dazzling.

The central fountain of timeworn, darkened alabaster is of course the main act in this theatrical display. Twelve sturdy, stiff-legged, heraldic lions—looking rather like stuffed animals in stone—spit languid streams of water into a shallow surrounding channel while supporting an enormous flat basin. From the center of the basin a single wavering column of water rises lazily into the air, seems to give up, then topples back with a soft lapping sound. Overflowing from the basin, the water slides over an Arabic inscription

34. The Court of the Lions, with its intricately carved and colored colonnades and sturdily amusing Lion Fountain.

running around the lip and falls upon the apparently grateful lions. Indeed, the whole affair glistens and drips and looks exceedingly wet—no mean accomplishment with so little water, but this is a feat at which the Moors were masters. Its cooling effect on the quality of the space is remarkable, and most acceptable in the climate of Granada.

There are additional fountains; small bubblers in mere sinkages in the arcade paving at the ends of the court; and low basins in the side rooms opening to the patio, the Room of the Abencerrages (a noble Granadan family) on the south and the Room of the Two Sisters on the north. All of the basins are connected by shallow cut stone channels to the central one around the lion fountain. Aside from the channels, the open part of the patio is in reddish-brown gravel.

The relation of the two side rooms to the patio is technically worth noting because it illustrates a point of spatial design not yet encountered in this examination of Moorish handling of outdoor space. From either of these rooms a central sight-line goes directly to the lion fountain. In fact, if the fountain were not there, a sight-line from the Room of the Abencerrages would pass through the center of the court, at approximately right angles to the main east-west sight-line of the court itself, and on into the Room of the Two Sisters. The inter-relationships of the components thus tie the whole together in a readily apprehended spatial structure. Added strength of organization comes from the fact that the same sight-line continues through the Room of the Two Sisters to a mirador from which one looks directly down into the next open space, the Patio de Daraxa, at a lower level. In short, a visual connectedness has entered the spatial picture and positive structure becomes perceptible.

It will be recalled that in the Alcazar gardens there is no overall controlling scheme of design, and that up to this point the outdoor spaces of the Alhambra have not been tied together by sight-lines into any easily grasped relationship. From the outer plaza to the Court of Myrtles, and from this to the Court of the Lions, the connections seem entirely fortuitous. The observer, that is to say, can get from one space to the next, but nothing in the design *impels* him to do so or tells him visually where to go. In its internal organization of space the Court of Myrtles is of course clear and strong: the space is clearly defined, and the directional pull from south to north asserts itself beyond question. But, notwithstanding this internal geometric strength, there is no readily apprehensible visual tie to other spaces such as one feels, for example, on examining the Roman Fora of the Emperors.

With the Court of the Lions, built in 1377 (about a quarter-century later than the Court of Myrtles), the condition changes as indicated above, almost as though there had been a process of learning by experience. Whether the change occurred consciously or not, the results are there to be studied by today's designer as an object lesson in spatial organization. Technically, the

Court of the Lions is in several ways rather faulty. There is considerable confusion between directional and centralizing factors: the greater east-west length and the end pavilions say one thing; the central fountain contradicts this; a volume that is square in plan would seem to accommodate the forces better than the present oblong one. But these are perhaps minor objections, against the revealed strength of visual tie between the Court of the Lions and the Patio de Daraxa.

The Patio de Daraxa was not fully enclosed until the sixteenth century, but its spirit is generally Moorish. In its present detail, with a rather labored pattern of beds and hedges accented by tall cypresses, it is a relatively modern development. But the central fountain, while a hybrid assemblage of mixed parts, does show extremely well the characteristic use of light reflected up from water against the carved under-surface of the truly Moorish lifted basin. Another, even smaller open space, reached through a passageway from the Patio de Daraxa, is the Patio de la Reja, so named from the grilled window looking down upon it. It is seventeenth-century in origin but well worth attention because of its complete simplicity. It has a single quaint Moorish fountain, an excellent example of black and white pebblework paving, four slim cypresses, and unadorned white walls against which long shadows play.

There has been much difference of opinion as to whether the verdant Patio de Daraxa or the unplanted Court of the Lions, to cite the two extremes, conveys the more accurately the nature of Moorish outdoor space as the kings of Granada must have seen it. It would seem most probable that the truth lies somewhere in between: that the alleged dwarf oranges may indeed have existed in the Court of the Lions where all is now gravel; that the Court of the Myrtles did originally have an orange tree behind each myrtle hedge at each end of the patio, as was in fact the case early in the twentieth century; that in all likelihood the arcades did have many potted plants in colorful array along the sunny edges, for the Moors clearly loved color and had the horticultural skill to gratify almost any wish; but that no truly lush flower beds or massed plantings would have existed in the torrid climatic conditions. These details, however, would appear far less important than the form and arrangement of the spaces themselves, modulated as they are by the texture and color of the more permanent materials that now comprise their boundary planes. And one must not forget the intensity of the ever-present indigo blue sky. There can obviously have been plenty of color in older days, just as there is now, even without floral display. Color and calm and the marvelous use of a little water: the theme of the Alhambra.

The Generalife (Fig. 35), the gleaming white-walled summer retreat of the kings of Granada, stands on the westward slopes below the Silla del Moro, on the far side of a slight valley to the east of the Alhambra and nearly two hundred feet higher up. The present approach is by means of a long avenue of cypresses leading to an arrival court at the gate lodge. Beyond this building,

35. The Generalife, on the steep slope facing the Alhambra from the east.

36. The Canal Garden of the Generalife illustrates again the Moors' genius for economical yet remarkably effective use of water.

between it and the main house, lies the principal patio, the Canal Garden. With the gate lodge at one end and the higher house at the other, the patio is further enclosed on the west or downhill side by a long gallery joining the gate lodge and the house, and on the east by a service wing extending from the house and acting as a retaining wall for the series of garden terraces that step up the hill.

The main feature of this long garden is, as the name implies, the canal running from the house to the gate lodge along the central sight line. As though to make the wet pathway even more cooling—in sight and sound and actual temperature—thin streams of water spring into the air from both sides of the canal, arch toward each other, and fall with an audible whisper upon the surface of the canal. The effect is enchanting, especially viewed from the house end of the canal, looking against the sun into the backlit arches of sparkling white with the gate lodge in shadow behind them (Fig. 36).

The long planting areas on either side of the canal have been treated in various ways through the years. Most recently they have been framed with clipped hedges at the back, a few feet from the boundary walls, and with a row of moderately high cypresses along each side. The beds themselves are used for massed flowering plants. At the house end are two tall, spindle-legged evergreen trees of different sizes.

At each end of the patio, in the gate lodge as well as in the house, there is at ground level an open arcade with arches on the customary slender colonnettes, but with even richer surface decoration in carved plaster than on the arcade screens of the Alhambra. In the pavement of each arcade is a simple low marble basin, with a small bubbling jet and an overflow into the canal. The view of the Canal Garden from these arcades is the visitor's major experience at the Generalife.

On the uphill side of the service wing is another small patio, laid out as a water garden with rectilinear islands and spouting jets under towering old cypresses. Steps from this patio ascend to the first of four terraces that climb the steep hillside above the Canal Garden and parallel to it. The terraces are of decreasing size; each is treated in its own fashion with hedging of box and myrtle, modest but sprightly fountains, and patterned pebblework paving, mostly in black and white. At the top, reached by two long, converging pathways in brick and pebblework between stucco walls, is a high white mirador built in the nineteenth century but looking very much at home. The view from here, down over the Generalife gardens, to the Alhambra on its plateau, and further down to the sunbaked roofs of Granada, is a fitting climax to this experience of Muslim Andalusia.

Moorish landscape architectural accomplishments were of course not confined to Spain. Even today the character of the Moorish patio throughout north Africa remains fairly faithful to the early models; there are interesting examples in Marrakesh, Rabat, Fez, and to some extent in such gallicized cities as Casablanca and Algiers. But the outstanding cases are the ones discussed here.

Nor is the whole story of Islamic landscape architecture told, by any means, in Spain and North Africa. By the time Tarik and his forces had crossed the straits in 711, the Arabs pouring north and east from Mecca had overcome the Sassanid empire, had moved the Muslim capital from Medina to Damascus, and were preparing to move it further to Baghdad. As was usually their way, the conquering Arabs quickly adopted the Persian tradition in the design of outdoor space; and here in the eastern reaches of Islam there was, indeed, a tradition worthy of adoption.

It is to be noted that, whereas the Moorish conquerors of the Visigoths in Spain found only Roman ruins and the battlements of the Dark Ages awaiting them, the Arabs who swept into the Near East encountered an old and flourishing tradition of garden design stemming back to the earliest Persian parks and to the Hanging Gardens of Babylon. This is no mere figure of speech, but a matter of genuine antiquity. One might even say that the Persian garden antedates the Garden of Eden; actually, the word "paradise" is of ancient Persian origin. Greek records of the fourth century B.C. tell that troops invading the territory of the Medes and Persians came upon many examples of a kind of wooded oasis in the parched land—a pleasure grove about a supply of sparkling water—which the Persians called a paradise. *Paradeisos*, a Greek adaptation of the Persian word, came in time to mean not only the sublimity of a Persian garden but, indeed, any state of supreme bliss, including such a dream-place as the Garden of Eden or the celestial gardens promised the faithful by the Koran.

Thus it is entirely possible that the Moors in Spain were to some degree influenced by what had already been accomplished in Damascus, Mesopotamia, and Iran. This was especially true after Abd-er-Rahman, the only Ommayad prince to survive the onslaught of the Abbasides, fled to Córdoba and set up his own caliphate in 755, independent of Damascus. It can only be conjectured whether this older Eastern tradition affected the physical form of landscape architectural works in the Moorish West. There are no examples old enough to settle the point either way, though certain similarities of form undoubtedly arose out of the similarities of climate. But there is ample documentary evidence that the caliphs of the West sometimes imported Eastern plants, and there can be little doubt that, at least in Córdoba, well-remembered garden delights of Damascus were on occasion imitated in the early days.

Unfortunately, almost no instances can be found today of Persian gardens older than the sixteenth century; and there are few of even later date. The old tradition, however, appears to have persisted, for what does remain of the oldest gardens agrees remarkably with information available from literary sources and with patterns found in the earliest so-called garden-carpets. In its reputedly most authentic form the garden or enclosed space emphasized the water and shade demanded by a hot, dry climate: a pool in the center reached out by means of clearly delimited canals, at least in the longer dimension of the space but often crosswise as well. The total space was thus divided into the four quarters believed symbolic of the four corners of the world. The ancient correlation between food and pleasure was echoed by the presence of fish in the pool and canals and fruit trees in the sides and corners. For vitally necessary shade there were larger trees, particularly planes and cypresses. Thanks to highly skilled irrigation, beds of roses and other flowers were not only possible but rather frequent.

The modernization that has come to Iran with its naive copying of Western jukebox civilization has done much to destroy even the seventeenth-century versions of the older, traditional outdoor design of Muslim Persia. Perhaps the clearest remnants are in Isfahan, once the pride of Shah Abbas the Great, though little is left of the charm that must have graced the city when it had palaces and gardens galore, as many as six hundred thousand inhabitants, and no less than one hundred sixty-two mosques. If only the excellent land reforms of modern Iran had not been accompanied by Western chromium!

The largest remaining outdoor feature of Isfahan is the Maidan-i-Shah, an impressive though seemingly empty public open space. The Chehel Sutun, or Palace of Forty Columns (Fig. 37), shows the effectiveness of the long, mirror-still pool, reflecting the palace at one end and the great niche of a liwan at the other; the vegetation is only a mockery of what it must have been. Still pleasantly calm is the large enclosure of the Madrassa of Shah Hussein (Figs. 38, 39). The colorful tile facing of the buildings is still in place (notably the bulbous dome of exquisite blue over the sanctuary); in the great court the still water, veteran trees, and abundant flowers convey at least a reminder of ages past. But the famous Chahar Bagh, once a long promenade of cypresses and planes with channeled watercourses running the entire length and superb structures and gardens ranged along the sides, is today an asphalt traffic artery with few of the old buildings intact.

In Shiraz, to the south of Isfahan, the faint echo of old glories is still perceptible. In full accord with the older contemplative mood are the eighteenth-century Bagh-i-Dilgusha, Garden of the Heart's Ease, with its long canal and avenues of orange trees, and the relatively recent nineteenth-century Bagh-i-Gulshan, Garden of Roses, with pools, canals, and stately cypresses. More spectacular are the remains of the fantastic Bagh-i-Takht, or Garden of the Throne. This now broken pile of terraces, reflected in the huge, lake-like pool at the bottom, inevitably reminds one of what the Hanging Gardens of Babylon may have been.

Another early seventeenth-century garden based on the ancient tradition is the Bagh-i-Shah, or Garden of the Shah, at Ashraf, in the far north of Iran near the Caspian Sea. In common use the name applies to a whole group

37. Isfahan: pool of the Palace of Forty Columns, looking from the palace toward the great niche.

of gardens or, strictly speaking, to three groups of which two survive sufficiently for detailed reconstruction. The gardens of each group are a series of terraces strung together like so many jewels on a thread of continuous water channel, with a cascade splashing from each terrace to the next. These gardens at Ashraf were a favorite resort of Shah Abbas, who ordered their construction in 1612; since that time they have suffered greatly despite several spurts of restoration.

In terms of landscape architecture the eastern Islamic regions, though older historically, offer less present evidence of former greatness than do the western regions. Examples that can be studied in modern Iran were all built at least two hundred years later than the Alhambra. But, to see the Muslim art of the outdoors reach another peak of excellence—and to savor the lasting strength of its central dedication to landscape values—one can move on to the performance of the Mogul emperors of India. The Taj Mahal (Fig. 40), with its placid pools, has in its air of serene devotion and pure-white peacefulness something astonishingly like, yet entirely different from, the vermilion

38. Isfahan: Madrassa of Shah Hussein. Typical long pool in a photograph of about fifty years ago.

39. Madrassa of Shah Hussein, looking across toward the sanctuary at right angles to the preceding view. 1962 photograph; in a half-century the change is almost unnoticeable.

40. Agra: the Taj Mahal, built in 1630 by Shah Jahan.

silences of the Alhambra—built about three hundred years earlier and thousands of miles away.

The similarity between the two great Islamic monuments is not a matter of detailed form; it is not even an ostensible physical sameness. It is a unity of spirit. The two are superb expressions of a plain but powerful truth: that for over a thousand years, among peoples united in religious belief but as diverse in geography and racial origins as the Moors and the Moguls, against all the odds of time and circumstance, feast and famine, there persisted unbroken a deep-seated love of the outdoors and a delight in expressing it. In the long run this affection took many varied forms, but fundamentally it was always there—for over a thousand years. No passing fancy this, but an abiding sense of affinity based on understanding and acceptance of simple verities. To this end every Muslim was encouraged by the teachings of the Koran and by the customs of his religious observance. Of Islam's many remarkable accomplishments, this was by no means the least.

V. The Renaissance in Tuscany

It was probably inevitable that the Western world would sooner or later shake loose from the constrictions of the Middle Ages to experience the great awakening that is called the Renaissance. People must eventually have stirred somehow from their defensiveness and their introspective daydreaming about the hereafter to open their eyes, take a possibly surprised look around them, and discover that there was something indescribably marvelous about the sunlit world out beyond the walls and battlements.

To be sure, this aspect of the Renaissance was not its only significant characteristic; there were others, such as the revival of classical learning and the increased centering of attention on the physical human individual. But the rediscovery of the thrilling wholeness of the natural world—and of man's integral participation in it—would appear to have been the most clearly fundamental new characteristic, from which all the others emerge as almost self-evident consequences.

It has long been customary to regard the Renaissance as a movement beginning in about the year 1400. The new outward-oriented attitude, however, had already been voiced by a few exceptional men much earlier. None stands out in more startling contrast to his times than San Francesco (1182–1226), the gentle friar from the Umbrian hill-town of Assisi. Surely one of the greatest influences for good that the world has known, St. Francis was in a remarkably complete sense a herald of the Renaissance. As against the involved theology of his age, he preached an essentially simple religion based primarily on the golden rule and on an affectionate reverence for all living things. With happy eagerness he reached out to embrace the total earthly scene: one of his best known canticles, the "Cantico al Sole," is addressed to the sun; in his famous "Laudes Creaturarum," a hymn in praise of "all thy creatures," he speaks tenderly of his "brother sun," his "sister moon," and, even more revealingly, "our mother earth." His affection for the world of nature made a profound impression: in the historic series of frescoes of his life, painted by Giotto in the upper church of San Francesco in Assisi about 1295, one of the most significant episodes—and probably the best loved—is that known as St. Francis preaching to the birds.

It is most appropriate that Giotto should have been the creator of these frescoes of St. Francis: Giotto himself, though perhaps the inheritor of certain elementary advances made by Cavallini in Rome and Cimabue in Florence, was also a precursor of the Renaissance. Breaking away from strict enslavement to purely theological themes, he began depicting the events of sacred history in terms of daily life, with clearly communicated narrative, recognizable human expressions, and a background of familiar outdoor scenes. He introduced new visual depth, anticipating the later invention of perspective; on the whole he typified the new outlook, indeed the new way of seeing, that characterized the Renaissance. Small wonder that he is generally regarded as the father of modern painting—when he died in 1337 he had charted for the future an entirely new vision.

To this outward expansion of interest into the actual world there were important early contributors in the literary field, too. Dante, Giotto's contemporary, wrote the *Divina Commedia* and his exquisite sonnets in the *volgare,* rather than in the Latin used and understood by ecclesiastics alone. By giving new status and currency to the common tongue in written form, he vastly enlarged the opportunities for exchange of information and encouraged the ever-widening search for knowledge. A generation later, Boccaccio used the same Tuscan vernacular for his greatest prose work, the *Decamerone*—a milestone not only as the first novella, in itself a bright new form, but also as an instance of opening the literary field of interest to the day-to-day life of all kinds of men and women with all their trials and temptations. He was working steadily, though perhaps unconsciously, toward that humanism for which the Renaissance was noted—albeit his variety was an *umanesimo volgare,* a humanism of the people.

Petrarch, another prolific contributor to the pre-Renaissance drive, was revered as friend and master by the slightly younger Boccaccio. Fully dedicated to distant antiquity, and the actual discoverer of many writings of the past, Petrarch perhaps more than anyone else was responsible for giving the dawning Renaissance the stamp of classical revival. Perversely enough, though he professed to scorn whatever was not written in Latin, posterity remembers him best for the warmth and humanity of his poetry in the daily language of the people.

Other circumstances lent strength to this outward impetus. The development of siege artillery in the fourteenth century rendered old defenses obsolescent if not obsolete. With greater security on the highroads and seas, travel became more feasible. Meanwhile, the fantastic tales of Marco Polo about his years in remotest Asia had long been exciting interest in far-off places and things exotic; now the greater ease of travel released this latent curiosity in a compelling urge for exploration. Literally as well as figuratively, man's horizons were widening apace. As the conditions of travel improved, so did the dissemination of knowledge and the extension of trade and consequently the education and enrichment of families engaged in commerce.

The center of these developments was Florence, the glowing City of Flowers—Firenze in Italian, Florentia in ancient Roman days. Long a focus of the struggles between popes and emperors and later Guelfs and Ghibellines, Florence was a declared republic as early as 1115 and a commune even before that. A native devotion to creative industry had been apparent from well back into the Middle Ages, when Florence was widely known as a producer of wool, silk, and furs. An almost militant spirit of democracy led to the overthrow of the Teutonic nobles in 1266. In 1282 the powers of government were placed entirely in the hands of the Arti Maggiori, or Greater Guilds, the presidents (Priori) of which comprised the Signoria, the supreme governing body of the Florentine republic. The recognition thus accorded to creative production is well worth noting as fully symptomatic of the creative genius in the arts that characterized Florence throughout the Trecento and Quattrocento.

Into this context entered the new mercantile and financial aristocracy that arose with the phenomenal increase of trade in the closing years of the Middle Ages. As feudalism died out, the newly rich families replaced feudal lords and swept to enormous power, gaining, losing, and gaining again control of the guilds and the Signoria. Against this power from time to time the people, being passionately democratic, naturally revolted. After a century and a half of revolts and counter-revolts, during which Florence nevertheless gained recognition as a center of culture—and the arts had progressed amazingly despite whatever political squabbles were going on—control of the government was virtually seized in 1434 by the Medici, greatest of families in the mercantile aristocracy, under the benevolent despotism of Cosimo dei Medici, generally known as Pater Patriae (father of his country).

The Florence in which the Medici came to power, and over which they ruled almost monarchically for more than three hundred years, was limited to what is today the rugged heart of the city, with its narrow streets and irregular pattern of red-tiled roofs. Above this rippling, many-angled carpet rose the varicolored marble Campanile of Giotto and the castellated towers of the Bargello and the Palazzo Vecchio; Brunelleschi had erected his great mahogany-colored dome above the cathedral just before Cosimo seized control. The city lay on both sides of the Arno, with hills to the south and steeper ones to the north. Up and down that lovely Val d'Arno of countless poems the soft, blue-hazed scenery of Tuscany stretched away lazily—a countryside

41. The simple villa at Careggi built for Cosimo dei Medici by remodeling an older castle.

42. As in the Villa Careggi, medieval characteristics were reflected by the Villa Petraia with its fortress-like tower.

43. The Villa Palmieri.

of alluring gentleness, now that the Middle Ages had passed and men had rediscovered the sweetness and freedom of the open air.

Led by the Medici, the great families now began to go into this countryside for quiet comfort; thirteen centuries earlier Pliny the Younger had satisfied the same urge by building his Villa Tusci, but only his verbal descriptions of it remain. In 1417 Cosimo dei Medici had acquired a small property near the hamlet of Careggi, a few miles northwest of Florence. After his rise to power in 1434, he retained the architect Michelozzo to build what came to be known as the Villa Medicea di Careggi, or simply the Villa Careggi (Fig. 41). It should be noted that in Italy the term *villa* refers to the place as a whole—not to either house or grounds alone, but to the total complex seen as a unit.

Careggi, the first Medici villa, illustrates how transitional the early Renaissance country places were as they emerged from the Middle Ages. Little about the overall layout of the villa can safely be taken as authentic, but the house is still standing in what is presumably near its original state. It bears many of the defensive characteristics of the Middle Ages: the upper story corbels out over the lower one in typical fortress fashion, almost like an early American blockhouse, and a somewhat dour severity seems to cling to it. The villa has little to offer today's landscape architect save historical interest. Cosimo died here in 1464; here his grandson, Lorenzo the Magnificent, gathered about him on many occasions his favorite artists, writers, and neo-Platonic philosophers; and here he died in 1492. There is considerable evidence to show that the villa must have been a joyous place in Lorenzo's lifetime, which makes reasonable the discovery that Verrocchio's gay fountain of the winged boy struggling with a dolphin, now in the cortile of the Palazzo Vecchio in Florence, was originally in a Villa Careggi garden.

Farther out of town are three other villas eventually in Medici ownership: the Villa Petraia (Fig. 42) and the Villa di Castello, both near Careggi, and Lorenzo's massive country palace at Poggio a Caiano, some ten miles down the Val d'Arno. All, however, were built or remodeled so late as to be not at all representative of the early Quattrocento in Tuscany—aside from the extremely important fact that each is set right in the midst of its *podere,* or farm, usually in an olive grove. The typical early Tuscan villa lies close to the soil, literally as well as figuratively.

Nearer Florence, but still on the southward-facing slope of hills above the city, is the Villa Palmieri (Fig. 43), reputed to have been a favorite retreat of Boccaccio and believed by some to be the place where he wrote the *Decamerone.* The villa's exact age is uncertain, but it was already well known when Marco Palmieri bought it in 1457 and had it improved, possibly by Michelozzo; here again, the original plan is difficult to establish. The house has probably not undergone much change in external appearance since Palmieri's day. Its walls are decorated with a typical sgraffito pattern (cus-

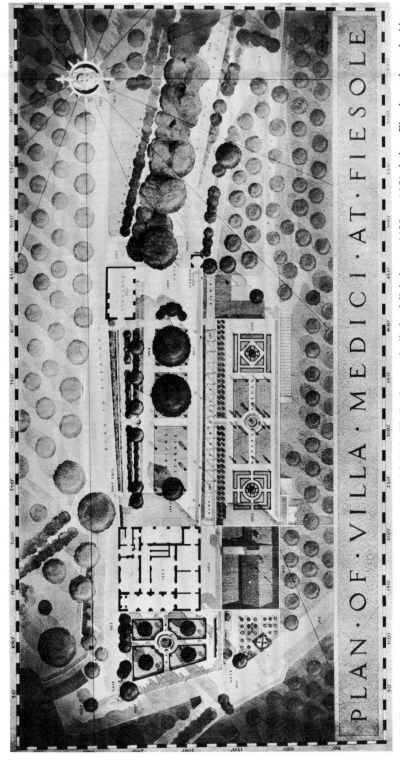

PLAN · OF · VILLA · MEDICI · AT · FIESOLE

44. For landscape architects, the most interesting Medici villa is the one built by Michelozzo, 1458 to 1461, below Fiesole and overlooking Florence and the valley of the Arno; this plan was measured and drawn in 1924.

45. This measured elevation shows the villa's most prominent feature, the great wall supporting the arrival terrace at the main-floor level of the house; farther down are the three other distinct levels of the villa.

tomarily in this region a light golden tan over chocolate brown). The upper-story loggia, from which one can look out over the rooftops of Florence, is an interesting example of this elementary but effective way of merging indoor and outdoor space.

Superior to any of these places, both as a work of landscape architecture and as a typical Tuscan villa of the Quattrocento, is the Villa Medici at Fiesole (Fig. 44)—a superb illustration of excellence in site selection and site development. Securely tucked into the steep slope just beneath the summit of the hill of Fiesole, it dominates Florence and the whole wide reach of the Val d'Arno. Through the wonderfully balanced emplacement of house and terraces on the hillside, the entire visible landscape, even to the farthest hazy hills on the horizon, is made an integral part of the villa itself. In this respect the Villa Medici is unquestionably a masterpiece; it is also one of the great examples of bold simplicity.

The villa was built by Michelozzo between 1458 and 1461 for Cosimo dei Medici's second son, Giovanni; Giovanni died soon after its completion and thenceforth it was associated with Lorenzo, Giovanni's more famous nephew. As one of Lorenzo's favorite spots, it became a literary center in the enormously productive period when Florentine arts and letters enjoyed the unstinted support of the Medici. At Fiesole as at Careggi, Lorenzo assembled for contemplation and discussion the members of his beloved neo-Platonic Academy—Marsilio Ficino, Poliziano, Pico della Mirandola, Landini—a notable manifestation of the revived interest in classical antiquity, so greatly stimulated by the arrival of Greek scholars fleeing westward after the fall of Constantinople to the Turks in 1453. The villa passed out of the hands of the Medici in the seventeenth century, but subsequent owners have maintained it well. Its high walls fit firmly on the cypress-clad hillside (Fig. 45)

46. The Villa Medici from the start of the long, curving entrance road.

just as they did when Giorgio Vasari, writing about Michelozzo a century after the villa was built, marveled that in all those years, "even though perched up on that height, it has never yet budged a hair."[1] (All the more remarkable, considering that Vasari wrote this four hundred years ago!)

One can enter the villa by a small foot-gate on the road leading down from Fiesole, but the normal carriage entrance is at some distance from the house (Fig. 46), so that from the long, curving drive one has occasional glimpses of the house and terraces through a screen of cypresses. Passing under the edge of a *bosco* of those magnificent dark Italian trees commonly called ilex but actually evergreen oaks (*Quercus ilex*), the road enters the arrival terrace, an area treated simply in gravel and grass with an orangery and a small oleander garden on the uphill side. Edging the gravel roadway are lemons and oranges in large red terra-cotta pots, a typical instance of the Italian villa's reliance on something other than flower beds for color. For many

1. Giorgio Vasari, *Vite degli Artisti*, ed. G. Milanesi (Florence, 1878), II, 443. Author's translation; English versions of the *Vite* do not normally include the chapter on Michelozzo.

years the terrace suffered the presence of two huge paulownia trees lined up right in the middle, which gave welcome shade but killed the feeling of space on the terrace itself; fortunately they did not affect the view outward. At the east end of the terrace are two ungainly garden houses, faced in somewhat rococo black and white marble chunks and presumably of a much later date than the main fabric of the villa. The whole terrace is supported by the high retaining wall that is the predominant visual feature of the villa seen from the valley.

47. A gateway from the evergreen garden at a lower floor level of the house.

48. Looking up from the lowest of the villa's four levels.

At the west end of the arrival terrace is the house, a simple, blocky structure with wide eaves overhanging cream-colored stucco walls. It is entered through a loggia, from which a hall leads through to another loggia facing the western sunsets. Below this, at the level of the lower floor, is a small green garden reached by stairs within the house. From the garden a gateway at the corner of the house (Fig. 47) leads to a small secluded terrace lying between the house on the left and the service building on the right at a lower level; the tile roof of the latter is neatly concealed by a parapet wall. Beyond, nestling along the foot of the great retaining wall of the arrival terrace, is an unpretentious arbor of grapes and roses that leads up at the

49. Cross-section reveals how effectively the villa's terraces were tucked back into the hillside, imparting visual and structural stability.

far end through yet another gateway to a sloping path and regains the entrance road.

A few feet below the level of the arbor is the lowest terrace, laid out in recent years as a simple garden, with varying degrees and forms of elaboration—sometimes, unfortunately, too ornate to be fully in character with the rest of the place. At each end of the garden is a service building. It is from this lowest area that one can best appreciate the straightforward boldness of the soaring walls and their sgraffito pattern: the three stories of the house and the forty-foot retaining wall of the arrival terrace (Fig. 48). These are the immense, light-colored surfaces that can so readily be seen from the tower of the Palazzo Vecchio in the heart of Florence.

At the outer edge of this bottom terrace the construction stops; just below it the olive trees begin, covering the hillsides with a profusion of silver-gray, in sharp contrast to the deep leathery green and bronze of the ilex and cypresses. As indicated earlier, this immersion of the villa into the immediate environment, done so naturally and seemingly without consciousness of intended effect, is one of the most welcome characteristics of Tuscan villas. So, too, is the complete balance with which such examples as the Villa Medici are fitted into the form of the land. An examination of a section across the terraces (Fig. 49) reveals how evenly the volumes of space have been carved into the slope—with just enough excess of cut, as against fill, to avoid the unstable feeling that so often haunts a protruding mass of fill. The spaces

50. Looking directly down from the edge of the arrival terrace to the lowest-level garden; comparison with the preceding cross-section demonstrates why the lowest level does not interfere with a view over the valley from a normal position on the arrival terrace.

of the terraces and house wrap around in a somewhat helical way, and the entire complex merges into the site with manifest firmness.

To be sure, the glory of the Villa Medici is its magnificent site; but without the skillful disposition of walls and spaces upon it the effect could well have been lost or at least irretrievably spoiled. As it is, the view of the villa from a distance—and, especially, the tremendous view outward from the arrival terrace—are what a visitor will most certainly remember. Technically as well the handling of the outward view is noteworthy: the foreground has been kept completely free of any competing elements, and the lower garden and service areas, placed by necessity where they might have proved quite distracting (Fig. 50), were kept so far below the normal cone of vision that they are hardly noticeable when one looks out to the far-distant hills across the valley. This distant view, the compelling object of attention, brings with it a sense of utter peace as the eye follows the silver ribbon of the Arno, gliding down from Pontassieve, hiding for a moment behind the golden towers of the city, then passing on into the blue haze on the way to Pisa. What could be more emblematic of the Renaissance than this: peace and a discovery of the joy in nature?

VI. Rome and the Cinquecento

After its elementary beginnings in the countryside around Florence in the 1400s, the Italian villa soon evolved into the rich, joyous, gloriously unified phenomenon that has excited the admiration of the civilized world in succeeding centuries. But this development began in Rome after 1500. While Florence during the fourteenth and fifteenth centuries achieved high status as a cultural capital, Rome was still a sleepy parochial town, almost completely medieval, its ancient monuments used as stone quarries for such buildings as were erected, its famous Forum Romanum half buried in the debris of centuries. Then a succession of vigorous popes, beginning with Nicholas V in 1447, struggled valiantly to make the city something more than the theoretical capital of Christendom. With such burgeoning activity, Rome became increasingly attractive to artists from the north, among whom the most distinguished was Donato Bramante, originally from Urbino.

It is generally agreed that development of the Cinquecento Roman villa had its start in a project designed by Bramante for Julius II shortly after the latter ascended the papal throne in 1503. Immediately upon his accession, the Pope decided to undertake three major projects: continuation of the rebuilding of St. Peter's church, begun about 1450 under Nicholas V but dormant ever since; additions to the Vatican, also built largely under Nicholas; and a connection between the Vatican palace and a sizable summerhouse called the Belvedere, which Innocent VIII had erected some sixteen years earlier on a low hill beyond the slight depression just north of the Vatican. All of these tasks Julius II committed to Bramante. The project connecting the Belvedere and the Vatican (Fig. 51) began the great evolutionary changes in the Italian villa.

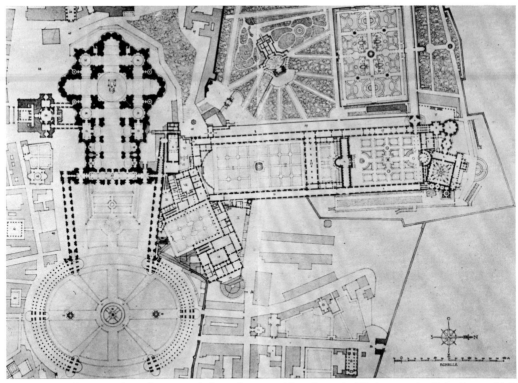

51. Bramante's project extended two long corridors from the Vatican to the Belvedere, which stood at an angle on a low hill to the north (far right). St. Peter's church and the Piazza di San Pietro are to the left in this plan, drawn by Gromort about 1900.

Bramante faced the problem in a spirit much influenced by his newly discovered interest in the actual forms of Roman antiquity, which he had been studying avidly since his arrival in Rome. A year before receiving the three commissions, he built the famous Tempietto, the little round temple in the cortile of San Pietro in Montorio, on the Janiculum. In this delicate structure he followed classical precedent but with typically personal inventiveness and imagination; as if to echo the still prevalent enthusiasm over things classical, the Tempietto was received with considerable acclaim.

In the Belvedere project Bramante designed two monumental three-story corridors, borne on series of Roman arches, reaching northward from the Vatican toward the Belvedere and enclosing a long rectangle of outdoor space. Then, across the front of the Belvedere itself, which stood at a marked angle to the new arcades, he constructed a false facade with a central hemicycle and exedra, bringing the Belvedere into visual conformity with the whole rectilinear scheme and providing the sort of terminal that had been so forceful in the days of the Roman empire. It has been determined that Bramante's main classical precedent was probably the Sanctuary of Fortuna Primigenia at Palestrina (ancient Praeneste).

The inequalities of terrain in the earth floor of the huge court, instead of being left in undulant softness, were resolved into horizontal planes at three levels by means of retaining walls and lordly stairways. The largest and lowest area, at the southern or Vatican end, was to have been a theater; a set of colossal steps across its northern end retained the intermediate level while providing seats for the theater audience. From the shallow intermediate level a double flight of ramps led to the uppermost level and its terminal exedra on the new facade of the Belvedere.

Work on the project suffered many interruptions and changes of command. Julius II died in 1513; Bramante died in 1514, after having completed most of the eastern corridor, the foundations of the western one, and a new court behind the Belvedere's facade. Julius was succeeded by another notable Pope, Leo X (Giovanni dei Medici, son of Lorenzo the Magnificent). As a Medici, Leo was understandably eager to see the work carried on, and he appointed as palace architect the young Raphael, Bramante's compatriot and heir. Work was continued on the eastern corridor in accordance with Bramante's plans, but then Raphael died in 1520 and Leo X in 1521.

Activity lapsed until the pontificate of Paul III, when the work planned by Bramante was vigorously resumed by his younger followers, Peruzzi in 1534 and Sangallo the Younger in 1541. The accession of Julius III in 1550 marked the beginning of changes from the Bramante scheme—which had possessed the clear strength to govern the work for nearly a half-century. Remodeling was started on the Bramante exedra at the north end of the Cortile; in 1551 Michelangelo did a new stairway to it. The enormous niche, the Nicchione, was built by Ligorio in the 1560s, modifying significantly the terminal aspect of Bramante's masterful design (Fig. 52).

The big changes in Bramante's Cortile del Belvedere were now well under way. Twenty years later, the great court as a spatial entity was chopped in two by the new Library, built across from one corridor to the other at the level of the intermediate terrace. In 1605 the huge pine cone was brought from St. Peter's and placed in the Nicchione. A second cross-court interruption (the so-called Braccio Nuovo) was added early in the nineteenth century, further modifying the original scheme by curtailing its uppermost level, which is now known as the Cortile della Pigna from the pine cone (Fig. 53).

The entire Belvedere project, especially during the period when Bramante's plans were adhered to, was tremendously influential in subsequent developments in villa design; indeed, it initiated a new era in the architecture of Renaissance Rome. The eminence of the Holy See and the professional reputation of Bramante were no doubt highly persuasive to potential imitators, but the great design itself had an impact the force of which did not diminish as construction proceeded. The project's epochal nature is reflected by the extent to which at the time other designers made sketches, drawings,

52. A sixteenth-century engraving, though less accurate than Gromort's in position of the Belvedere itself, shows the project before the new library was built, cutting the space in half.

and paintings of it; many of these have been preserved (Fig. 54). Both in plans and as the work progressed, the Belvedere court represented a totally new experience to its observers. Obviously, one cannot be sure that characteristics exhibited in the project were observed and then consciously emulated in other works; but in Italian landscape architecture from that time forward, certain of these qualities appear again and again with remarkable consistency. Presumably the sheer size of the great space and of all its constituent parts did not escape notice, being so different from medieval precedents and so

53. The Cortile della Pigna, so known since 1605, when the huge pine cone was placed in the Nicchione.

clearly an echo of ancient Rome: ever afterward, things Roman—and indeed Italian, in contrast, say, to French or English—were large, even huge, in scale.

The organized architectonic character so marked in the Belvedere project became virtually invariable in the Italian villa. To be sure, even the simplest Tuscan works had been architectonic, in the sense that the outdoors was obviously an extension of the house and needed to be treated accordingly. But in the Belvedere court, and in the subsequent typical Cinquecento villa, the space was not only architectonic in the general outline established by its boundary planes; it was internally structured as well. The sight-line leading

54. Mural by Pierino del Vaga, showing the projected use of the lowest level for naval pageantry, illustrates the widespread interest created by the Cortile del Belvedere.

from the Vatican to the hemicycle and exedra of the upper level was a spine on which the whole complex was organized, and this, too, would remain typical. To modern eyes, here is space treated positively as a material of design; it is in no sense whatever merely something left over from other operations.

This geometric organization appeared also in the crisp division of the whole court into the three clear-cut terraces, each an uncompromising horizontal plane echoing the architectonic vertical boundaries of the space. Horizontally, as well as vertically, there was a keen sense of spatial geometry and of clearly delimited planes—and this continued in the typical Italian villa. The same clarity was evident in the vertical planes supporting the terraces and especially in the firmly architectonic stairways, merged completely into the retaining walls as integral parts of the structure, rather than stuck on as mere additive accessories. This direct, skillful handling of walls and steps, devices inevitably necessary in a country as hilly as Italy, became one of the more frequent and delightful characteristics of the Cinquecento villa.

The relatively restricted urban situation of the original Belvedere project did not provide an opportunity for the wider overall schematic structure that was soon one of the most appealing merits of the typical villa of the open countryside, with sight-lines tying spaces together in an interlocking harmonious whole—often, but not necessarily, with bilateral symmetry. One need not go far from the Vatican, however, for an example of this development: only a short distance north, on the slopes of Monte Mario, Raphael began about 1516 (while still in charge of the Belvedere project) a country seat for Cardinal Giulio dei Medici. This elegant though unfinished villa, now almost engulfed by the swiftly growing city, has long been known as the Villa Madama.

A clear picture of the world in which such places as the Villa Madama came into being is hardly possible without some understanding of the crucial differences between the cultural or evaluational climate of the Roman Cinquecento and that prevalent today. The Holy See in those days was not only a center of religious authority but also a temporal power of considerable force, with papal states extending across the peninsula and from south of Rome to the River Po. One speaks of the reign of a pope, who was in fact a temporal monarch as well as a religious leader and in Rome the church *was* the state.

It was accepted as quite natural that great families should be ambitious to have their members achieve high status in the hierarchy of the church, including, of course, election to the papacy. Moreover, as a corollary to success the occupant of the papal throne was expected to appoint his relatives to office and to the cardinalate. Nor would it be realistic to look for a spirit of asceticism in the Holy See at that time, for it was not an ascetic era. The urge to joy and exuberant lightheartedness was perhaps one of the truest manifestations of this age of humanism, as it is so often termed. Leo X, a great and devout pope, expressed the prevailing attitude: "Let us enjoy the Papacy, since God has given it to us."[1] In the same spirit the cardinals, as princes of the church, were expected to glorify themselves and the establishment.

The Reformation undoubtedly had at least some bearing on the Cinquecento tendency toward what amounted to theatrical design, even in churches. After all, it was in 1517 (during the reign of Leo X) that Martin Luther put up his famous theses and in 1521 that he defended them in Worms. Fairly enough, inroads made upon the church by the Reformation quickly evoked a Counter-Reformation. If those responsible for the Church of Rome felt it good tactics to use dramatic, even awe-inspiring magnificence of color and form to attract and hold the faithful, they can scarcely be criticized for it. The same reasoning could not very well hold true in the case of a country seat—but there is little doubt that the Italian villa often shared in a prevailing spirit of visual grandiloquence.

The simple fact is that, in many respects, the moral climate of the early Cinquecento differed almost unbelievably from what is generally recognized as acceptable behavior today. The Puritan spirit, so soon to spring forth in

1. Edmund G. Gardner, *The Story of Florence,* 10th ed. (London, 1924), p. 141.

England, was certainly not present in Italy. Youthful elevation to high station in the church (at least on the part of influential families) does not appear to have been regarded with disapproval: Giovanni dei Medici became a cardinal at the age of 14; his cousin Giulio, the illegitimate son of Lorenzo's brother Giuliano, was also a young cardinal and in 1523, despite his acknowledged illegitimacy, was elected Pope Clement VII.

It was this Cardinal Giulio dei Medici for whom Raphael was commissioned to design what is now the Villa Madama (Fig. 55). The physical remains of this once fabulous project are not impressive; indeed, to appreciate its historical and technical significance the visitor requires prior knowledge of what can now only be imagined. In this respect a visit to the villa is an intellectual, rather than a primarily sensory experience.

Raphael's original scheme, if discovered sketches can be fully credited, was an elaborate series of inter-related outdoor spaces linked by sight-lines and fused geometrically to the indoor space of the house, which in turn was to have been handsomely enriched under his guiding hand with painting and sculpture. Not surprisingly, Cardinal Giulio had this display of opulence

55. The Villa Madama, on the northern outskirts of Rome, as seen from below about 1915; the surroundings are now built up.

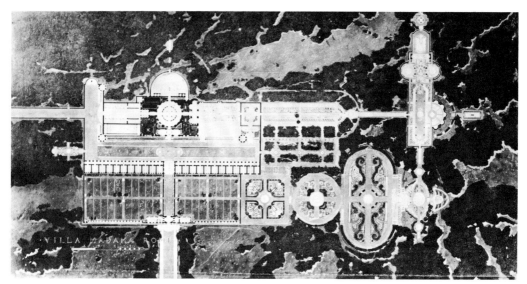

56. A reconstruction of the extensive Villa Madama layout as intended by Raphael.

begun during the pontificate of his cousin Leo X. As an essay in the visual grandiloquence already referred to, it may well have set the pace for all those who, in the good graces of the Holy See, found themselves moved to appropriate glorification of their status. Unfortunately, Raphael died in 1520, when little more than a start can have been made on his scheme. The work was continued by Antonio da Sangallo and Giulio Romano, who presumably were disposed toward Raphael's original intent.

In 1527 the villa, along with the city itself, suffered from intermittent warfare between the emperor, Charles V, and Francis I of France. Imperial troops, unpaid and mutinous, marched down the peninsula, took Rome, imprisoned Pope Clement VII in the Castel Sant'Angelo, and burned his pet villa. Some accounts have it that the Pope's political enemies in Rome did the burning; be that as it may, the unfinished villa was nearly destroyed and, though it was partly restored in later years, it never reached the full splendor envisioned for it by Raphael.

According to Raphael's plans and some later sketches, possibly by Sangallo, the villa was to have been organized on a basic north-south sight-line on which would lie, in sequence: the long, straight entrance road from the south, ending in an arrival court at the house; the house, with a series of indoor spaces threaded on the sight-line carrying it through the building; an outdoor terrace beyond the house; on the north side of the terrace, a wall and gate through which the sight line would continue to other outdoor spaces. From beyond the terrace a secondary sight-line, approximately perpendicular to the basic one, would run eastward down the slope through a clearly formed space, which in turn would serve as a fulcrum for yet another sight-line parallel to the main one. And so on—it is hard to tell just how many different areas were ultimately intended (Fig. 56).

Of this ambitious layout, only part was completed and only a fragment remains. The house was to have had a great circular space in the center (see Fig. 56), but because only the northern half of the building stands today, the present entrance facade is a huge unfinished semicircle. Passing through the house, one comes to a three-arched loggia at the north side, with an interior space reflecting each arch. These chapel-like bays are decorated with delightful stucco low reliefs reputedly by Giovanni da Udine. The three arches, now glassed in, open upon the one completed terrace, tucked back into the rising hill on the west, with niches for fountains set into the face of the retaining wall. On the north side of the terrace is the wall referred to earlier, its framed gateway flanked by two oversized statues. There is no development to the north beyond the gate. On the eastern or open side of the terrace is a parapet, across which some years ago one could survey open land leading down to the Tiber and beyond; this land is now built up. Below the high wall supporting the terrace is the only other remnant of the early work, a long rectangular pool fronting three deeply-set arches in the wall itself that were no doubt meant to be grottoes. At the northeast corner of the house, a set of steps leads rather casually from the terrace down to the level of the pool. And that is all.

From time to time, efforts have been made to cover the terrace with a pattern of box hedging; the interior of the house is kept in reasonable repair; somewhat fussy care is given to a motor turnaround at the bizarre semicircular entrance. On the whole, the place is but a sad ghost of things that might have been. But, given a modicum of imagination, one can rebuild Raphael's dream and see the Villa Madama as the historically significant example that it must have been.

The importance of the villa, historically and to a degree technically, rests upon the obvious fact that house and grounds were designed as an entity, upon the completeness of the visual tie that consequently exists between indoor and outdoor space and upon the emergence, in this relatively pioneer work, of a genuine attempt to create a system of positive spaces tied together into a unified overall structure carefully fitted to the site. All of these characteristics, except possibly the lavishness of the scheme, became normal in the Italian villa of the Cinquecento and afterward. If it could be seen today as it was originally projected, the Villa Madama would doubtless be one of the best examples in Italy of merger between indoors and outdoors in the organization of space for living and for show.

Within the city of Rome there are numerous villas of different ages, but only one of such character and fame as to warrant inclusion here: the Villa Medici (Fig. 57), home of the French Academy in Rome, on the Pincio. This

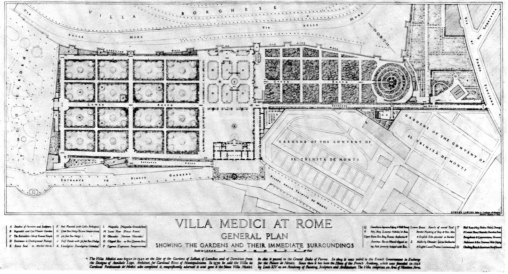

VILLA MEDICI AT ROME
GENERAL PLAN
SHOWING THE GARDENS AND THEIR IMMEDIATE SURROUNDINGS

57. Plan of the Villa Medici on the Pincio in Rome, as measured and drawn about 1919.

somewhat rigid, elaborate villa was begun by Annibale Lippi in about 1540 for Cardinal Ricci of Montepulciano, but a considerable part of the work was done after Cardinal Ferdinando dei Medici acquired the place some thirty years later, prior to becoming Grand Duke Ferdinando I of Tuscany. Specifically attributable to this Medici cousin is the unfortunate overloading of the villa, especially the garden facade of the palace, with assorted antique sculptures of differing sizes and scales, as well as the extension of the gardens by addition of the most northwesterly portion. The property was ceded to France in 1803 and has been the French Academy in Rome ever since.

The villa is built on a strip of high land between the edge of the Pincian hill (the ancient Roman "Hill of Gardens") and a stretch of old city wall. The great palace, bold on the forward margin of the hill, facing southwest, looms majestically over the roofs of Rome, its twin towers visible for miles. The usual approach today is by means of the viale leading from the Piazza della Trinità dei Monti, at the top of the Spanish Steps, to the large overlook in the Pincio gardens above the Piazza del Popolo. This road, well known for its fascinating panorama of Rome, passes the main lower door of the palace. A bit farther along toward the northwest, a ramp leads up from the road to a gate into the villa's gardens, which are at a level nearly one story above the lower entrance door. The palace thus acts effectively as a retaining wall supporting the main level of the grounds, and the added height of the lower story emphasizes the dominating posture of the palace as seen from the city far below.

The overall scheme of the villa is based on two sight-lines that cross at right angles some distance behind the palace. The shorter extends northeastward from the garden door of the palace and the graceful loggia before it, across a square open space or court, and through the main garden to a large allegorical sculpture at the far end, above the high old city wall. Unfortunately, the sight-line is blocked at its very beginning within the loggia by the well-known figure of Mercury by Giovanni da Bologna (a copy; the original was removed from here to the National Museum in Florence). Perpendicular to this line is the longer one running southeast to northwest: starting at a gate in the Via Pinciana, it follows a long, narrow road between walls, slides along the outer edge of the square court behind the palace, and plunges through a shady bosco to an architectural terminus at the northwest edge of the grounds.

The palace is L-shaped; a simple, two-story wing extends northeastward along the side of the square court behind the palace. Interrupted at this point by the long road from the Via Pinciana (Fig. 58), the vertical plane continues as a retaining wall about one story high and faced with niches to hold more of the overabundant statues. On the upper level supported by this wall is another bosco, with a rectilinear system of paths leading to a small earthen mount at the southeastern end—a feature associated with medieval English gardens but most unusual in Italy.

The main level of the gardens is of three distinct parts, all at the same level. Beyond the open square court, the main garden is a grid of gravel paths and six box-edged beds of grass containing a few palms and magnolias, with a random row of Italian stone pines (*Pinus pinea*) at the far edge. The entire open space directly back from the palace is almost equally divided between the square court and the garden; neither is dominant. There is not even a change of grade between the two to lend emphasis to one or the other. The

58. Contemporary engraving of the Villa Medici emphasizes the long straight access way to a gate on the Via Pinciana.

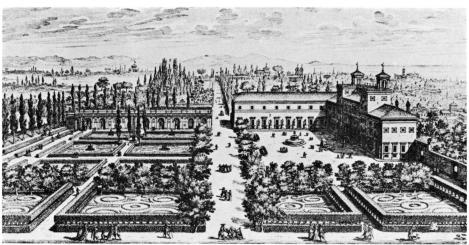

59. The ornate northeast facade of the twin-towered palace and the Villa Medici's main garden.

result is a regrettable lack of interest; the area is flat psychologically as well as physically, sunny but dull.

The third of the three parts comprising the main garden level is the shady bosco, about twice the size of the open space; it extends from that area to the villa's northwest boundary. Here again a rectilinear system of paths divides the bosco into four quarters, each of which is further quartered by paths. All sixteen compartments are outlined with high hedging, the monotony relieved only by the effect of the dark green canopy overhead and the flickering sunlight and shadow underneath.

The central section of the villa's grounds, the main garden level just described, seems disappointingly superficial—a fussy surface decoration, in contrast to the superb simplicity with which the villa's larger volumes of palace and outdoor space are fitted to each other and the site. What one remembers best about the Villa Medici is precisely this inter-relationship of the big forms, especially as the crisp definition established by their vertical planes is perceived. Three such vertical planes in particular are memorable: the garden facade of the palace (Fig. 59), despite its bewildering aggregation of embedded sculptures and bas-reliefs, clearly delimiting one edge of the outdoor space behind the palace; the long plane of the rearward wing and its extension marking the other edge of the space even while forming the level of the upper bosco; and, above all, the magnificent southwest facade of the palace, acting in effect as a vast retaining wall to support the entire villa. The whole plane of the facade glows with the warm golden patina that so often develops on Roman walls as the painted stucco mellows under sun and rain.

Just below this high plane, nestling under a clipped frame of small trees before the lower door of the palace, is the wide shallow basin and burbling jet of one of Rome's best known fountains. By its very placement it is made a part of the villa. Standing beside it at sunset, looking out over the city toward the great dome of St. Peter's in the distance as the bells in all the churches toll the Angelus—one has a sensation that is nowhere more vividly expressed than in the closing vesper music of Respighi's *Fountains of Rome*.

VII. Roman Villas of Villeggiatura

One of the major stimuli to the development of Cinquecento Roman villas was *villeggiatura*—an inheritance from ancient imperial times and still a practice in Rome today—the custom of going to the country for the punishingly hot days of summer. In fact, this was presumably the chief practical reason for the Villa Madama, quite apart from the promptings of self-glorification. The example having been set, the princes of the church sought out sites even farther from the oppressive heat of the city, going naturally to higher land in the hills within a few miles of the capital. In this way renown came to two small towns: Frascati, in the Alban Hills southeast of Rome, and Tivoli, in the Sabine Hills east of the city, just above the ruins of Hadrian's Villa.

The Alban Hills, some fifteen miles from Rome and clearly visible from any eminence in the city, are a volcanic group of which Monte Cavo, (ancient Mons Albanus) is the summit. On the northwest slope, facing Rome, lies Frascati. A mile or two farther away, and higher up the slope, are the remains of Tusculum, once the favorite summer residence of Cicero; the entire region was known in earliest times for its vineyards and villas. Faithful to its heritage, Frascati is famous today for its excellent but insidiously heady wine—the downfall of many a tourist—and for its many villas, of which no less than eight are listed as noteworthy in various guidebooks and treatises. Of these, three are well worth attention from a professional point of view: the Mondragone, the Aldobrandini, and the Torlonia, chronologically.

The Villa Mondragone (Fig. 60) was begun about 1567, in a modest way, by Martino Lunghi for Cardinal Marco Altempo; the present magisterial form of the villa is nearly all the result of work between 1605 and 1620 by many different architects in the service of Cardinal Scipione Borghese during the

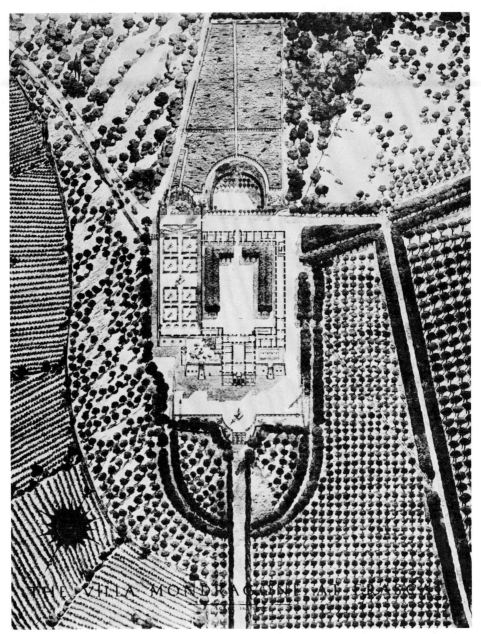

60. The Villa Mondragone at Frascati; plan measured and drawn in 1922.

reign of his uncle, Pope Paul V. It is a remarkably compact, highly architectural complex, set in the midst of extensive olive groves. The large palace rises grandly on the slope; behind it is a square open court with a low gallery along the west side and on the south an arcade leading to an amphitheater carved into the hillside. On the east side of the court, a wall separates this central space from what used to be a garden, with the remains of a once intricate water theater possibly by Giovanni Fontana at the south end, and a handsome monumental loggia at the north.

The most impressive feature of Mondragone is neither the palace nor the inner open spaces; it is the huge terrace on the north side of the palace, actually a roof over the underground kitchens, from which chimneys arise cunningly disguised as columns at the outer edges of the terrace. From the forward edge a semicircular projection juts out, at the center of which is a large fountain incorporating the Borghese winged dragons. It is worth observing that from the palace, or from the terrace close to the facade of the building, the fountain distracts one's attention from the wide prospect over the *campagna*. But as one moves far to the side of the vast terrace, or out upon the jutting forepart, thus removing the fountain from the cone of vision, the view is magnificent. Even so, the superb picture is split down the middle by the remains of a long, straight, cypress-lined viale reaching away toward the north. Tradition has it that this was once to have been a grand avenue all the way to Rome!

The Villa Aldobrandini, the most massive and noticeable of the Frascati villas, looms imperiously over the little piazzetta where one enters the town (Fig. 61). The palace's enormous facade is readily visible from the Janiculum hill in Rome, fifteen miles away; indeed, the villa is the usual means for

61. The vast bulk of Villa Aldobrandini's palace, visible from Rome across fifteen miles of campagna, towers over the piazzetta of Frascati.

locating Frascati from a distance. The place was built about 1598 by Giacomo della Porta for Cardinal Pietro Aldobrandini, a nephew of the reigning Pope Clement VIII.

A fanciful grille of stone and wrought iron hugs the edge of the piazzetta in Frascati. From a gate in the center of the grille a now disused road, covered by what remains of a long, dense tunnel of clipped ilex, leads straight up the hill to the base of the palace. The Aldobrandini tunnel seems utterly ridiculous, somewhat as the viale below the Villa Mondragone does but much more noticeably because of its location. The eye, instead of being led and funneled on a sight-line through the tunnel, finds it far easier and more comfortable to look uphill across the wide open fields on either side of the tunnel, which thus becomes only an annoying intrusion upon the very middle of the view whether up toward the palace or looking down from it.

Nevertheless, a powerful overall scheme is clearly organized upon this presumably effective central sight-line (Fig. 62). From the upper end of the ilex tunnel, two gigantic carriage ramps lead up, first to an intermediate terrace one story above the beginning, then another story to the main north doorway of the palace, already two whole floors above the downhill ground level. On the south or uphill side of the palace, at a level one story higher still, is a court that is used more often today for entrance than is the ilex tunnel. The court is cut boldly into the hill, with a highly ornate retaining wall and, in the center opposite the main south portal of the palace, a grandiose hemicycle cut even more deeply into the slope. In the central niche a figure of Atlas acts as the lower terminus of a long cascade that, emerging from a source far up the hill, passes between two high columns (down whose spiral grooves the water once actually ran), then plunges down the hill in a series of steps through a deep slot in the dense mass of ilex trees and ends in a splash over Atlas.

Of the villas discussed to this point, Aldobrandini is the first that demonstrates in characteristic degree the role of water in the typical Italian villa. Shade and water are so important under Italy's hot sun that the lack of either seems to render a villa alien to the native scene. In the Cortile del Belvedere and in each of the villas yet discussed, water was in fact used originally, but not in anything like its abundance at the Villa Aldobrandini.

The general plan of this villa is so well structured, so straightforward and bold even in its ostentatiousness, that one wishes its execution had been effected with more grace and better detail. Overelaboration tarnishes the plan even as compared with Mondragone, which in certain ways is larger but manages to have an air of restraint. Perhaps this is why one so often hears the Villa Aldobrandini referred to as being merely very big. The comment has considerable justice.

Of the delights awaiting a visitor to Frascati, none can have been greater than the cascade at the Villa Torlonia before its damage in World War II

62. Plan of the Villa Aldobrandini.

(Fig. 63). Frascati was the German headquarters at the time of the Allied landings at Anzio, and the occupied villas were often bombed. The Villa Torlonia suffered severely, but fortunately the worst damage befell the house, a building of little architectural merit. Even so, the cascade took some direct

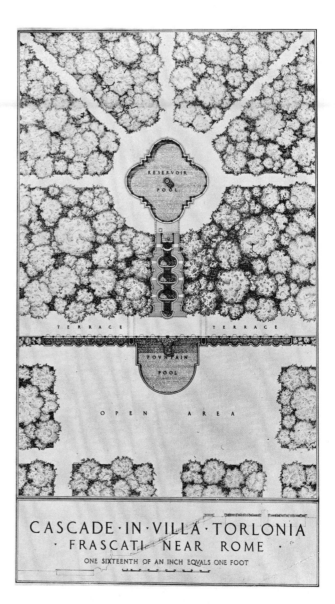

63. In the Villa Torlonia, only the cascade, its approach, and the pool at the top were noteworthy; now these suffer from inadequate repair of World War II bomb damage.

CASCADE · IN · VILLA · TORLONIA
· FRASCATI NEAR ROME ·
ONE SIXTEENTH OF AN INCH EQVALS ONE FOOT

hits in the upper basin, and the old bosco of ilex around the base was riddled by fragments. Repairs have been instituted, but it will be a long time before this superb piece of design regains its playful charm.

The Villa Torlonia is of uncertain age, and its peculiar fragmentary appearance suggests that, whenever it may have been begun, it was never completed as originally intended. It was most probably started by an unknown designer in about 1621, on the accession of Cardinal Alessandro Ludovisi as Pope Gregory XV (it was once known as the Villa Ludovisi). To be sure, the inscription on one of the fountains in the bosco refers to the

64. Approach to the Torlonia cascade through the ilex bosco, 1922.

time of Gregory XIII, which would place the villa as early as 1572 and support the claim that it is the work of Domenico Fontana, who died in 1607. But the general character of the details is closer to work of the later dates—and of course it is entirely possible that the inscribed fountain was brought from elsewhere.

The villa is readily accessible from the piazzetta of Frascati; it lies to the right looking uphill toward the Aldobrandini. Just within the modern entrance there is a set of implausibly grand stairways leading to a long, empty terrace that is only loosely related to the house at the far end. But behind the terrace and fronting the full length of it, on a shelf of land reaching back to the base of the hillside, there was for many years a dense, cool, ilex bosco. (In view of the wartime damage, it seems only fair to describe Torlonia in the past tense, as it was and, hopefully, as it will again be.) Because the growth overhead was so close as to make the bosco almost a solid block of foliage, only a little sunlight filtered through; the inky shade, especially on a sweltering summer afternoon, brought a welcome sense of cool relief. Slashed through the middle of the bosco, as if a giant had gouged into the mass of ilex, a corridor of open space led back to the splash of the great Torlonia cascade (Fig. 64). This contrast between the dark bosco and the diamond-like sparkle of sunshine on the falling water, often heightened by strong backlighting, created an unforgettable experience.

Emerging from the great swath, one came first upon a space extending right and left along an arcaded retaining wall at the base of the steep wooded hillside. In all the arches of the wall except the middle group on either side of a semicircular pool were shallow niches, each containing a small fountain. In the pool was a pile of moss-covered rocks. The arches adjoining the pool held stairs to the upper level. From atop the wall a fan-shaped spray shot outward and down to the pool from a markedly indifferent stone eagle. Above this point was the cascade, a handsomely modeled series of oval basins in stone with a rippled slanting plane between each, the whole flanked by stone stairways looping from level to level following the curves of the basins. At the top, the cascade was fed by a copious gush of water from the mouth of a large, grotesque mask. The fascination of the cascade lay not alone in the strong sculptural quality of its curving surfaces; from top to bottom it was covered with lichens, mosses, small ferns, and other plants to which the pitted travertine stone had offered hospitality (Fig. 65). The consequence was a subtle riot of pastel colors and an almost unbelievable intensity of wetness as water trickled and splashed down through the retentive tangle.

At the top of the hill, crowning all, was the reservoir basin, a balustraded pool of great visual strength with a high, foaming jet in the center. The numerous piers between ranges of balusters once had small jets in their tops, on the inner face of each a mask spouting water into the basin. The pool and a tight border of paving around it were centered in a space clearly carved out of the dense woods atop the hill. Here was water used as the wonderful vehicle it ultimately became in the Italian villa. It would be false to imply that even the most instructive of present-day visits could recapture the magical quality of the prewar experience; but even in damaged condition and glaring with new construction, the Torlonia cascade gives the serious designer valuable suggestions. In many ways it can remain the most rewarding of Frascati's offerings.

Cross-country, near the ruins of Hadrian's Villa and then up the hill, is

65. Detail of the Torlonia cascade in a dry midsummer of the 1920s; normally there was more water in the basins.

Tivoli, the other notable center of *villeggiatura;* here is the fabulous Villa d'Este, probably the best known—though by no means the best in design—of all Italian villas. As observed earlier, extension of life into the countryside by means of the *villa rustica* occurred with increasing frequency in the days of the Roman empire. Tivoli (known then as Tibur) was one of the chief centers of country life. One can still find the remains of several ancient villas about the town, in addition to what is left of Hadrian's; Tivoli is famous also for picturesque waterfalls in the River Aniene, overlooked by the vestiges of two Roman temples.

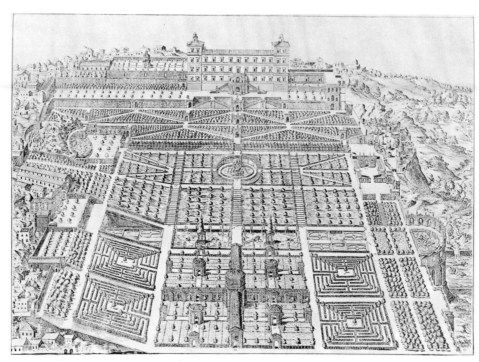

66. The Villa d'Este at Tivoli; judging by this contemporary engraving, it must have appeared garish and overelaborate when new.

Without much question, the chief attraction is the Villa d'Este. In the main it was probably the work of Pirro Ligorio, begun in 1549 for Cardinal Ippolito d'Este of Ferrara; evidence indicates that Giacomo della Porta was also involved somewhat later. The fantastic hydraulic effects for which the villa was justly renowned from the start were created by Orazio Olivieri. For this purpose a good part of the River Aniene was diverted and raised to the top of the villa, from which it still flows to produce by simple gravity the various water features for which the villa is most often remembered.

It must be pointed out that the enchanting effect of the Villa d'Este on today's visitors is surely in large part due to its overgrown condition. The whole area of the grounds, if the oldest engravings are reliable, was once visible at a glance, with far more subdivision into elaborate individual parts; the effect would thus have been, by modern standards of judgment, sadly overdone (Fig. 66). Today, however, a great massing of foliage, mainly ilex and cypress, prevents the eye from scattering its attention among a profusion of elements, most quite undistinguished in detail. As a consequence, the villa impresses virtually every visitor, whether layman or professional designer, with a sequence of stirring experiences and a sense of hidden mystery.

Topographically, the villa (Fig. 67) is most unusual in being cut into the slope of the land in two directions: predominantly to the south and somewhat

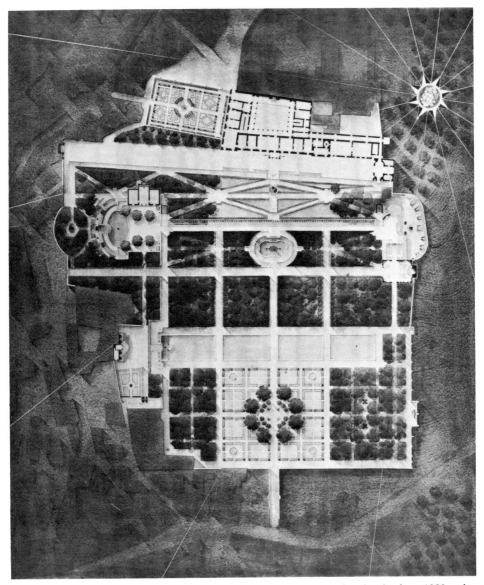

67. Plan of the Villa d'Este, measured and drawn as a restoration in the late 1920s; the happily overgrown condition is what one finds there today.

less to the east. The unfinished palace, a huge barracks-like affair of no great distinction externally, is on the height at the level of the town, facing roughly to the north. On this front of the palace is a tier of porches, one on each of three levels. A visitor usually enters the villa from a piazza in the town, going into the west end of the palace, then through it and out to the best vantage point, atop the porches.

68. Looking eastward on the long Terrace of the Hundred Fountains, with its sparkle and splash of more than three hundred streams.

From here one looks down the plunging main central sight-line of the villa, the spine upon which the entire layout is organized. This long line is not exactly perpendicular to the face of the palace, although to the unsuspecting eye it appears so. Following its entire length is a slot of space, seemingly carved out of the dense mass of ilex and cypress. Lying directly on this line at successive levels, though only partially visible from the upper end, are: a great beaker-like fountain, the Bicchierone; farther down the slope, the soaring jet of the Dragon Fountain; toward the lower end, the remains of a circular space with circumferential small jets, leading quickly to a large gate to the town at the very bottom of the slot-space. Although this long central corridor carries the major sight-line, some of the most exciting water features of the villa lie along or at the ends of the several east-west sight-lines that cross the main one.

Down the central line from the palace porches, one comes first to a long, narrow terrace along the base of the building. Immediately below, at the top of a sloping plane traversed by several diagonal walkways, is the Bicchierone, with languidly looping jets making irregular lapping sounds—an innocently deceptive quiet prelude to the noisy rush soon encountered below. Indeed, at the very next level comes the activity of the famous Terrace of the Hundred Fountains, the Cento Fontane (Fig. 68). This extraordinary cross-corridor of clearly formed space has a continuous double trough of stone running all the way across the face of the slope on the uphill side of the terrace—in effect a long, narrow basin with another immediately below and in front of it. The whole is much like a heroically long two-level sideboard of stone, topped along the back of the upper trough by a strange collection of alternating eagles, boats, trefoils, and other finials. These assorted objects are not in themselves at all distinguished, a lack in part atoned for by the playfulness and variety of their jets. From between the finials, streams arch down into the upper trough; from its front a second arching series falls to the lower trough. The narrow channel in the pavement picks up spillage.

From end to end the fountains are laden with lichens, mosses, and maidenhair fern, intensifying the sense of wetness. The whole is a riot of water in various forms: shooting vertically, then falling with a splash over pool and stone, in contrast to the two rows of arching streams. Quite apart from the measurable lowering of temperature, the sight and sound of the water have a psychological cooling effect that must seem impossible to anyone who has not experienced it. To appreciate this fully, one should feel it for the first time in the heat of an August afternoon, with the air full of the aroma of sun-baked ilex and box and cypress.

At the west end of the Cento Fontane, high above the campagna, is a somewhat childish miniature urban replica alleged to represent ancient Rome. At the east end of the terrace there is a walled enclosure containing the Fountain of Arethusa (Fig. 69), an ingenious semicircular waterfall from a basin whose lip is modeled to make the water come down in quivering, shimmering strands, supposedly recalling the hair of the legendary wood nymph. The oval pool into which the water spills has an arcaded, grotto-like rear wall. From the enclosure's gateway one has the reverse view back along the Cento Fontane to the far end.

Returning along the latter terrace to the center, there is a platform above a pair of stairways curving down to embrace the Dragon Fountain and its enormous vertical jet. There is something sublime about this tall column of water roaring to the sky from a moss-covered heraldic dragon, hesitating at its foaming pinnacle, struck dazzling white by sunshine, and crashing down into blue and purple shadows to bathe the dragon and its basin in a storm of spray. Numerous thin jets, arching and angling inward from several directions, supply an obbligato.

69. The Fountain of Arethusa at the eastern end of the Cento Fontane.

Continuing downward from the Dragon Fountain, still on the central sight-line, is a broad flight of ramped steps, their cheek walls a series of small bubblers and basins that emit a chuckling sound. At the sides, parallel to the central stairway, two runs of similarly treated steps descend straight from the Cento Fontane all the way through the bosco to the bottom of the slope—where, emerging from the shadows, one is at once in a broad sunlit area, the villa's largest single open space. Occupying most of it are four rectangular basins of mirror-still water, agitated now and then by ridiculously thin spurts arching from a few urns on the copings of the pools. Whether these placid basins appear dark or light, blue or green or silver, depends on season, day, and hour. To the west of the pools, behind some gnarled old ilex trees, the fill above a high retaining wall creates a platform from which one can usually see Rome, twenty-five miles across the campagna, the dome of St. Peter's appearing to float above the city like a great pearly bubble.

At the east end of the pool area, toward the town, is the elaborate Water Organ, with its astonishing symphony of fountains (Fig. 70). Surely landscape architecture can offer few, if any, more theatrical sights than this, seen alone and by reflection in the flat surfaces of the pools. Again, it is not the detailed sculptural form of the architectural components that overwhelms the viewer, for in truth these are little short of crude; it is, first, the ingenuity of the whole affair as a work of Cinquecento hydraulics, then the sheer splendor of the water display in its many simultaneous contrasting movements.

Although they can have little influence on today's visual effects, stories of the mechanical fantasy of the Water Organ in its heyday are still of genuine interest. When Montaigne saw the villa, about thirty years after it was begun,

70. At the bottom of the slope four quiet, rectangular pools provide foreground for the roaring riot of d'Este's Water Organ.

he marveled—as did John Evelyn some seventy years later—at the skill and imagination with which Olivieri and the Frenchman Claude Venier had contrived ways, using only the force of water and of air hydraulically propelled, to produce in the Water Organ such unusual sound effects as the booming of cannon, the song of birds, the bedlam of exploding fireworks, and tunes played on organ pipes. These sounds are now stilled, but in their place is the incessant roar of waters that perform their fabulous act in front of the high terrace, where an overelaborate dry organ house, built years later, surveys the noisy scene in silence.

The grandeur of the performance lies not alone in its magnitude, but in the variety of the water-play, to which a major contributor is the use of no less than six distinct levels with something happening at each. In the very center is a white band of solid-looking waterfall that emerges from just beneath the forward edge of the terrace and drops in two stages: first a long, straight fall to a pool about halfway down, then a more widely spread, veil-like sheet dropping forward and to the sides into a large basin at the bottom. The first drop, with the torrential appearance of a Niagara, is in fact a slide down a built channel that arches out from the face of the Water Organ terrace; indeed, one can walk from the side through a dripping archway into a gallery underneath the waterfall and from this level look out into the voluminous vertical sprays on both sides of the fall.

These high jets introduce four more levels of water-play. Immediately outside and below the viewing gallery just referred to, there is on each side of the central fall a deep shelf; six vertical jets from each of the shelves, a full dozen in all, shoot straight up, fill the air with spray, then drop back with a hiss upon the shelves, from which in turn a sheet of overflow falls into the first of two still lower basins. From this lower level, again on both sides of the central waterfall, the very largest pair of jets (actually a whole cluster of spouts in each basin) thrust their massive, foaming columns to a height above the upper terrace of the Water Organ. The great volume of water, reaching its apex and falling back with a resounding crash, falls mainly into the basins from which it rose but also into a larger flat basin in front of them and containing them. This basin also receives the final drop of the central waterfall; it is the largest of the basins thus far but not the lowest, for in front of it, surrounding it, receiving its flickering long band of quiet overflow is yet a larger and lower basin whose modeled edge gives one last fillip to the glistening water before releasing it into the reservoir at the base of the whole wild wonderment.

However strong the impressions of other instances of water-play in the villa—especially of the extraordinary variety in contrasting forms—one's sensations are almost certain to be magnified by the Water Organ in its flamboyant opulence. To most observers, the sheer volume of the water and its noisy turbulence are overpowering. Then there is the eye-catching sweep of the many streams—seemingly numberless verticals dashing swiftly upward, side by side with the equally uncompromising downward plunge of the waterfall and the slower, hesitant, delicate crystal sheets of the overflows. Every movement seems to have its opposite and to be emphasized by the comparison. Contrasting directions combine with contrasting speeds, while a myriad of flying droplets fill the air with diamonds in the sunshine.

From the theatrical Water Organ to the four plain reservoir pools before

71. Villa d'Este: from the far end of the central sight-line the deep slot-space of the viale leads back to the Dragon Fountain, the Bicchierone, and the palace at the top.

it—from tumultuous water to still, flat surfaces—is both transition and contrast. Then, as though to turn the corner from excitement to calm, there is the retreat to serenity in the circular space at the end of the great central sight-line. From there, looking back far up the hill toward the tier of porches at the palace where this visit began, the view, though obviously less commanding of prospect, is in some ways even more impressive than the initial view from the porches (Fig. 71). Here the sensation is of gazing upward to a distant sky from the bottom of a deep green canyon in the foliage. Here, surrounded by towering cypresses, with only gentle jets ascending from the remains of earlier fountains marking the circle, one can sit and reflect, perhaps better than at any other point, on the manifold variety within the total experience of this remarkable villa. Such wide variations are seldom found from the hand of man, and certainly no such abundance of water. It is a place unto itself, with few serious imitators anywhere.

The fortunate visitor can come to the villa at all seasons and all times of day, for no two moments ever seem quite alike: the villa is one thing at dawn, another at mid-day, another at sunset. If one is patient and outstays the hordes of tourists, perhaps, as evening shadows descend, the liquid warbling of a nightingale may be heard under the ilex trees.

VIII. Villa Lante and the Villino Farnese

Not all the notable Cinquecento villas are in the immediate vicinity of Rome. Indeed, two of those most widely admired are at some distance north of the city: the one regarded by most authorities as the finest of all, Villa Lante, is at Bagnaia, near Viterbo (about fifty miles from Rome on the road to Siena), and the somewhat later Villino Farnese is at Caprarola, about forty miles from Rome. In a strict chronological sense there is some question as to the accuracy of calling the Villino Farnese a Cinquecento villa, but it is usually so classified.

The exquisite Villa Lante (Fig. 72) was begun in its present form in about 1566. For nearly a century Bagnaia, a hamlet five miles east of Viterbo, had been associated with the bishopric of that busy medieval town as a summering place. Enclosure of woods above the village, creating a sort of park, had been started about 1475 by Cardinal Raffaello Riario, nephew of Pope Sixtus IV. As early as 1505 another Riario had built a hunting lodge in the park, and in 1532 an aqueduct had been brought in by Cardinal Niccolo Ridolfi, nephew of Pope Leo X. At last in 1566 Cardinal Gianfrancesco Gambara, bishop of Viterbo, began construction of the western of the villa's present pair of "little palaces"; it was completed in 1578, just in time to be admired and commented upon by Montaigne, who visited in 1581. On the death of Cardinal Gambara in 1587, Pope Sixtus V gave the villa to his nephew, Cardinal Alessandro Montalto, who built the second *casino* as a twin of the original and brought the entire villa to the state in which it has charmed so many succeeding generations. The place was church property, at the disposition of the Holy See, from the earliest days until 1875; in that year

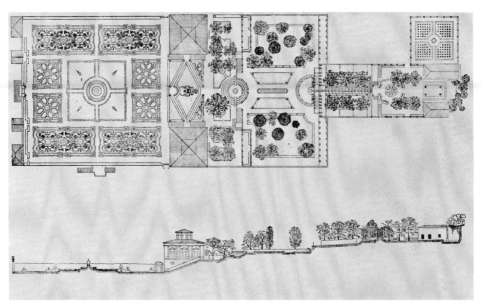

72. Plan and section of the Villa Lante at Bagnaia, generally regarded as the finest of Italy's villas.

it was given outright to the Lante family, to whom it had been allocated continuously since 1656. It appears to have been kept always in excellent condition. In 1953 it was acquired by the Società Villa Lante, which undertook a commendably complete restoration under the inspired leadership of Angelo Cantoni.

What is referred to today as the Villa Lante, in this account at least, is only the tightly knit central hillside complex, an architectonic, intimate composition of twin houses (*casini*) and their immediate grounds. The whole is enclosed by walls and situated within a larger wooded park, itself without strong design and tending toward the type of nondescript *parco inglese* that is never quite at home in Italy and merits relatively little attention from the visitor. The villa proper is essentially simple and unambiguous in design. The spaces comprising it are assembled with almost complete bilateral symmetry on a single center-line. Crisply delineated both vertically and horizontally, they step up the hillside in typical Italian fashion, with four specific levels separated twice by vertical walls and twice by clearly defined geometric slopes.

With regard to the bilateral symmetry, particular attention should be directed to the astute way in which this device is used in the Villa Lante. Although the single center-line forms a backbone on which virtually the entire layout is bilaterally constructed, almost without exception one cannot walk on the center-line. Consequently, the view is usually on a diagonal, which yields far less awareness of the bilateral symmetry than would be the case if, for example, a path were to go right up the middle of the spaces and split them visually in two.

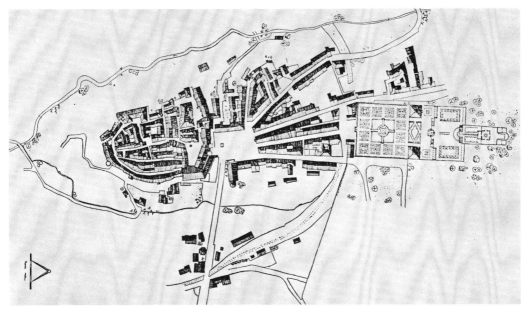

73. The Villa Lante is situated on the southern edge of Bagnaia, its lower gate opening on a street of the village.

The beginning of the long center-line is at a monumental gate leading from the narrow medieval streets of Bagnaia directly into the lowest level of the villa (Fig. 73). This entrance is no longer used regularly; one now reaches the same area (sometimes referred to as the Lower Garden) almost casually from the side, through a gate in the boundary wall at the southwest corner adjacent to the older of the twin casini, known as the Palazzina Gambara. Directly opposite, at the southeast corner and next to the later casino, the Palazzina Montalto, is another gate that is seldom used.

The Lower Garden is the one elaborate area of the villa. The dominant feature is a large, square pool, located of course on the basic center-line, surrounded by a low parapet with urn-like finials at corners and midpoints (Fig. 74). On this pool as a center the Lower Garden is developed in almost complete quadrilateral symmetry. The pool itself is divided into quarters by four balustraded bridges reaching from the outer edge to the circular central island. Upon this, in its own lifted basin, is a high fountain of four male figures traditionally called "Moors," holding aloft the heraldic Montalto beehive and star. Water, springing from the points of the star and from within the group, lends the four supporters a constant sheen before it falls into the central basin. Each of the four corner basins contains a small boat from which an amusingly modest squirt arches out to ripple the surface of the otherwise placid water. There are also languid small streams pouring from masks on the evenly spaced piers of the balustrades, but the overall spirit of the fountain and pool is one of mirror-like stillness.

The pool almost invariably takes on the indigo blue of the reflected sky,

74. The villa's Lower Garden and Palazzina Gambara.

75. The circular Fountain of Lights, joining two levels of the Villa Lante.

a vivid complement to the red and green of the garden's rather intricately patterned parterre-like beds. But the high coloration, true to the Italian norm, comes not from any permanent floral display, but rather from the bright red gravel and the evergreen box patterns and hedges of the beds. To be sure, small oranges and lemons and gay flowering plants—azaleas, geraniums, hydrangeas—are set out seasonally in simple terra-cotta pots. But the chromatic effect of the garden, especially as seen from above, arises chiefly from the blue of the pool and the red and green of the beds.

At the inner corners of the Lower Garden, nestled back into the base of the hillside, are the twin casini. Graceful structures of eminently satisfying proportions, they have three-arched loggias at ground level and square cupolas at the top. The interiors are profusely decorated with sixteenth-century frescoes, of which four in the loggia of the Palazzina Gambara are of special interest here: attributed to Raffaellino di Reggio, they are views of the Villa d'Este at Tivoli, the huge Palazzo Farnese at Caprarola, the Villa Lante itself, and the village of Bagnaia. From the garden a sloping plane of grass ascends between the twin casini to the second level of the grounds. The systematic avoidance of circulation on the center-line is immediately noticeable here: the middle of the slope is occupied by diagonal hedges and a coat of arms in box and the stairs are at the sides, one set of steps climbing the inward face of each casino.

The terrace reached by these stairs, at a level just below the main floor of the casini, has as its major element the ingenious circular water feature known as the Fountain of Lights (Fig. 75). Built in a series of concentric circles athwart the line of the retaining wall of the next higher terrace, the fountain has on the downhill side three stepped stone troughs curving outward. In the center is a circular halfway level with a flat, table-like fountain on a pedestal; above this, curving inward, another trio of stepped troughs climb against the retained upper terrace. The whole fountain is thus a circular form protruding over the lower level and cutting into the upper one, effecting a remarkable visual interlocking of the terraces. To make it all more delicate, the curving troughs have on their lips about seventy small candle-like jets, from which comes the fountain's name. Downward curving spouts fall from the vertical surfaces into the successive troughs, and the central table-like element is also a basin from which a jet rises gently. The simplest of steps are cut into the fountain's mass from each side to the middle level and from this to the upper one, but normally the transition from terrace to terrace is made by means of a pair of handsome stairways, one on each side at some distance from the fountain.

In the center of the third horizontal level is a fantastic piece of stone furniture in the regular form of a large banquet table but with a long basin for water cut into its top (Fig. 76). One can well picture this device, sometimes called the Cardinal's Table, serving as a cool buffet for outdoor refreshments

76. On the third level of the Villa Lante: the long stone Cardinal's Table, with the Fountain of the Giants beyond.

under the plane trees on a summer day. Behind the water table, still on the center-line, is the Fountain of the Giants. Presumably symbolizing the two great rivers Tiber and Arno, the giants are huge, recumbent figures, each propped on an elbow with a look of slightly annoyed boredom appropriate to having lain in a comfortless position for four centuries. In back of them are the stepped and gracefully carved cheek-walls of the two stairways to the next higher terrace; between them is a descending series of graduated bowls that receive the copious waters from above and spill them noisily into the large semicircular basin in front. The entire fountain—bowls, basin, figures from head to toe—is covered with lichens, mosses, and other small plants, suffusing the scene with wetness and bright color. The stairways and balustrades behind the giants, incorporating small jets and spouts of water at every imaginable point, are richly designed as an integral part of the immediate sculptural composition, which has about it an air of inevitability and rightness that is deeply satisfying.

Above the Fountain of the Giants, and supplying its torrent of water, is the long sloping cascade called the Water Chain. Gushing forth at the top from the mouth of a stone crayfish (*gambero,* a play on the name of the Cardinal Gambara), the water slides glistening down a channel between looping serpentine margins, flickering over minute, weir-like undulations in the bottom. At the lower end it spills out from between the claws of another crayfish to flood the top bowl of the Fountain of the Giants. For its entire length the cascade is on the villa's dominant center-line; here again—even

77. At Lante's topmost level, the foaming Fountain of Dolphins supplies the shimmering cascade of the Water Chain.

in this definitely directional space, emphasized as it is by the high flanking hedges of neatly clipped box—one walks not on the center-line, but on the ramped steps between cascade and hedges.

At the very top of the cascade, a final few steps lead to the villa's fourth horizontal level and the sumptuous octagonal Fountain of the Dolphins (Fig. 77). This crowning feature has nine vertical jets and about a hundred thin, linear spouts arching in five directions into a series of troughs that rise in tiers to a single circular basin on a pedestal at the apex. The fountain takes its name from the sixteen dolphins that do some of the spouting. At the rear corners of the shady space behind the fountain are two open-fronted pavilions installed by Cardinal Gambara, as attested by the inscriptions and the carved crayfish on the facades. Between the two shelters, at the rear of the area, is the so-called Fountain of the Deluge, a wild, naturalesque affair resembling a grotto and woodland cliff—as if one had fully penetrated the thick woods at the rear of the villa—with quantities of clear water pouring from its overgrown rocky face into a dark forest pool at the base. Here at the upper end of the great center-line is water in its most native state, in striking thematic contrast to the geometric, manmade intricacy of the architectonic pool and garden at the lower end.

Thus from a symbolically wild condition the water progresses down the slope through several transitional stages to reach its most sophisticated form in the Lower Garden. So too with the vegetation of the villa. The high southern end is virtually embedded in the woods of the hillside; the Fountain

78. Looking down to the Lower Garden of Villa Lante from just above the Fountain of Lights.

of the Dolphins is in an area relatively shaded by a mixed stand of native trees. From there on down the slope the cover thins until on the terrace of the Fountain of Lights, at the main-floor level of the casini, the sunlight filters down through the translucent leaves of the old plane trees to cast a pattern of dappled sun and shadow on the ground, the last hint of shade before the sunny expanse of the colorful Lower Garden (Fig. 78). Through all, from top to bottom in typical Italian fashion, the vegetative cover serves principally as a backdrop for the form and color of the more permanent materials—the red gravel, the blue and white water, the lichen-covered stone of walls and steps, balustrades and fountains—and for the brilliance of flowering plants put out seasonally in their red and orange terra-cotta pots.

For most observers, what makes the Villa Lante such a compelling experience is probably the handling of spaces in a wonderfully comfortable rhythmic sequence from level to level. But it is surely not this alone; in short, it is not just the plan of arrangement, fine as this is. Nor is it solely the imaginative treatment of water in its many forms and movements, including the mischievous "secret fountains" that the gardener can turn on here and there, squirting the visitor harmlessly to everyone's amusement. It is all of these and yet something more, something unforgettably intimate. Throughout the villa there is a detailed excellence, of scale, proportion, subtle relation between straight line and curve, and the same sort of impressively fundamental rightness that was noted in the Fountain of the Giants. The balustrades of the several terrace walls and their numerous vases and urns, whether fountains or dry finials, have a sinewy, muscular quality that makes them the epitome of the ancient virtues "firmness and delight." And all of these factors—all of the parts—play nobly together in happy symphony.

A belief has long persisted that the Villa Lante was designed by the famous architect Giacomo Barozzi, usually called Vignola. He was working on the vast palace for the Farnese family in nearby Caprarola when Cardinal Gambara began the Villa Lante, and it has been wishfully supposed that he would have been called in here as well. No document has yet been discovered that would either confirm or deny this assumption, however. Even if authorship of the Villa Lante is never finally determined, one fact is certain: whoever designed it was exceptionally skillful. For this, and for the villa's availability to modern eyes and ears, the world of the arts can afford to be grateful. Perhaps the finest praise for this villa is the fact that so many of the most fastidious designers, even among those wholly enamored of Italy, often speak of the Lante as the *only* Italian villa in which, after long reflection, they would still want to make *no changes at all*.

The visitor to the Villino Farnese retraces his steps about ten miles back to the south from Bagnaia and Viterbo to the hamlet of Caprarola. There, towering above the village, is the enormous bulk of the pentagonal Palazzo Farnese, begun in about 1547 for Cardinal Alessandro Farnese, nephew of the reigning pontiff, Paul III. In about 1559 Vignola was called in to design its final form over the earlier work of Sangallo the Younger and Peruzzi. Farther up the hillside and out of sight from the palace is the jewel-like Villino Farnese, sometimes called the Villa Caprarola. It would appear that the villino, though supposedly constructed from designs left by Vignola when he died in 1573, was not built until later (probably about 1620) for another member of the family, Cardinal Odoardo Farnese.

The villino is unusual in size, purpose, and fanciful character of detail (Fig. 79). To call it the Villa Farnese, as is sometimes done, overlooks its essentially summerhouse nature and implies a reasonable degree of development for daily living, whereas quite obviously the villino was intended primarily as a retreat from the more complex life of a princely establishment in the palace below. It is basically a joyous though quietly bemused plaything, neither so opulently riotous as the Villa d'Este nor so stiffly sedate as the Roman Villa Medici.

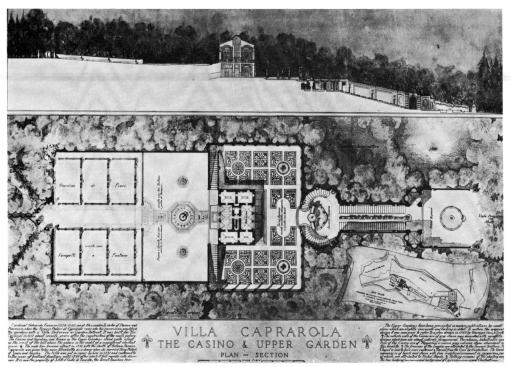

79. Plan of the Villino Farnese, also known as the Upper Garden of the Villa Farnese and as the Villa Caprarola.

The connection of the villino to the palace is rather tenuous (Fig. 80): one crosses a moat from the palace to what remains of a prosaic garden, then climbs gently by a footpath curving up through the chestnut woods to a sort of self-starting viale of fir trees. From the dark shadows at the sudden beginning of the viale a direct sight-line up the middle leads to the villino ahead, dazzling in the sunshine. The sight-line thus established continues as the central spine upon which the entire villino is assembled in virtually complete bilateral symmetry.

The viale of firs conducts one to the open side of a square vestibule at the bottom of a series of positive spaces comprising the villino (Fig. 81). The square is held in place by rather ornate walls on the right and left. In the center is a circular basin with one soaring jet that shoots noisily into the air, the sun often touching the white tip with silver, then falls to keep the stone coping continually shining wet. It is a powerful jet, pencil-thin but dramatic. Thanks no doubt to the shade of the fir trees and the steady spray, the viale and vestibule maintain even in hottest summer a surface of emerald green turf that is most unusual in Italy.

At the inner corners of the square vestibule are twin pavilions, each arched on the front and inward-facing side, with jauntily rusticated piers and an almost purely sculptural character. One senses already the playfulness that persists throughout the detail of the villino. Between the pair of pavilions is a steep slope carrying on its center-line a chain cascade reminiscent of that at the Villa Lante, though different in detail and less effectively connected to the whole scheme of water-play at top and bottom. As at Lante, there

80. Vignola's massive pentagonal Palazzo Farnese towers over Caprarola; it is connected rather thinly to the Villino Farnese on the hillside above.

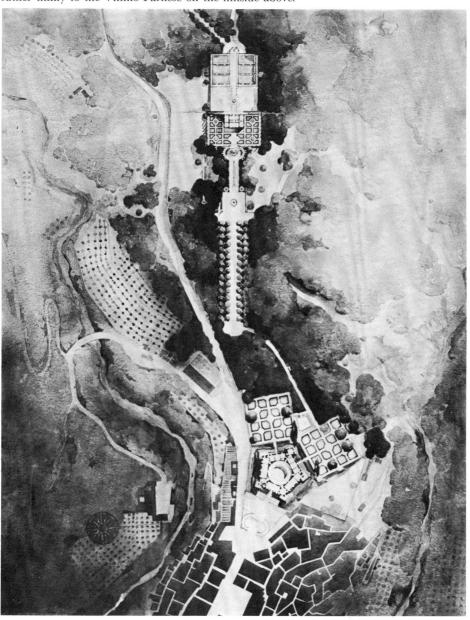

81. A single jet punctuates the square vestibule of space at the lower end of the Villino Farnese.

82. Fanciful caryatids en-
frame the box garden of the
Villino.

are ramped steps along the cascade on both sides, but here they are ampler
and bounded on the outer edges by paneled stone walls extending uphill from
the two pavilions. This rather deep protection maintains abundant grass
between the stone risers of the ramps.

   The slope levels off at the top of the cascade, and the walls sweep outward
and around to embrace an oval space containing a pair of curving stairs;
these culminate in two colossal river gods in stone, again much like the two
at Lante. But here the giants carry great cornucopias on their backs, from
which two ridiculously tiny squirts of water arch into a large beaker between
the gods, which in turn spills over into a semicircular pool at the base. The
curving stairs lead to the next level, a terraced rectangular box garden
delimited by walls with built-in seats, above which rise the ranks of high
caryatids that are among the most fanciful garden ornaments in all of Italy
(Fig. 82). The compartments of box hedging are further enlivened by two
sprightly little fountains, each a quartet of sea horses, echoing the pair of

83. Scale model of the Villino Farnese demonstrates its compact design.

like animals that mark the entry to this garden at the top of the curving stairways.

In effect the box garden serves as a patterned foreground to the exquisite two-story casino with its double loggia—its bright frescoes visible in the upper, major one—and its captivating air of quiet grace. To reach the level of the upper loggia there are stairs against the back retaining wall, entered at the right and left corners of the box garden and ascending toward the rear of the casino. The stepped cheek-walls of the stairways are topped by alternating dolphins and basins into which the dolphins spurt water untiringly. The level so attained is extremely simple. The casino itself, here but one story high, seems even more modest than from the lower level, although on this side, too, it has a well-proportioned loggia. The outdoor area on this level is in two nearly equal parts. The first, touching the casino, is a flat, grassy rectangle with a handsome central fountain surrounded by pebble-mosaic paving and two smaller basins at the sides. Higher up is a tilted area, divided into three successive terraced planes, with access steps at several points and a broad panel leading back on the center-line to an ornate triple gateway, semicircular in plan, opening into the surrounding chestnut forest. This upper triple-terraced area with its six distinct sections appears to have been intended for cultivation of flowers in crops; though it has a straightforward utilitarian feeling, it is enriched with stone basins, small finials, and some adroitly placed pebble-mosaic paving on the main lines of circulation.

The chief distinction of the Villino Farnese is of course its charming gaiety. But it deserves the serious attention of landscape architects as a lesson in completeness, as a compact example of the imaginative Italian villa in highly concentrated form (Fig. 83). Its plan is simple and direct; the spaces are clear and positive, the parts articulated smoothly in a single overall scheme. Its detail, though playfully extreme, is nevertheless consistent and controlled. As at the Torlonia cascade and at Villa Lante and Villa d'Este, the stone is everywhere covered with colorful lichens and the moist places welcome flourishing mosses and a host of other plants. The stone may be inanimate, but the whole place is vibrantly alive; and even those unbelievable caryatids look silently amused by the zany business. Water is not as abundant here as in some other villas, but the forceful accent of that single jet in the lower vestibule, especially viewed against the dark firs as one leaves the villino, is truly memorable.

IX. Later Italian Villas, 1610–1785

The vicinity of Rome was without doubt the area in which the Cinquecento villa achieved its most significant stature, but this is not to say that nothing happened elsewhere. There are at least a few villas of distinctive character though later date—reaching certainly into the 1600s and occasionally even the 1700s—that merit attention from those interested in landscape architecture. For example, taken chronologically, there are the Villa Gamberaia (1610) at Settignano near Florence; the spectacular Isola Bella (1632) in Lago Maggiore; the unique Villa Chigi (about 1760) on the outskirts of Rome, though remarkably Tuscan in appearance; and the gay little Villa Balbianello (1785) on the Alpine shore of Lago di Como.

It seems no more than simple justice to return to Tuscany and the Val d'Arno for the first of these villas; after all, this is where in a sense it had started long before. A few miles up the valley of the Arno from the heart of Florence is the sleepy village of Settignano—which produced more than its share of sculptors in the Quattrocento, incidentally. About a mile southeast, set on a slight rise amid olive groves, is the Villa Gamberaia (Figs. 84, 85), justly held in highest regard by all who love Italy and the Italian villa. Though built a century and a half later than the Villa Medici at Fiesole and without that kind of commanding view, Gamberaia seems completely Tuscan. It embodies many of the admirable qualities from which arises the Tuscan villa's characteristic serenity. It is simple, direct, uncomplicated.

Records in Florence refer to transfer of Gamberaia's site as a piece of farmland in 1398, but the earliest determinable date for the present villa is 1592, when Giovanni Gamberelli (of the family of the famous Rossellino brothers) acquired the property and began consequential improvements. On the house, an inscription dated 1610 provides the firmest indication evident of the probable age of the villa as it stands today.

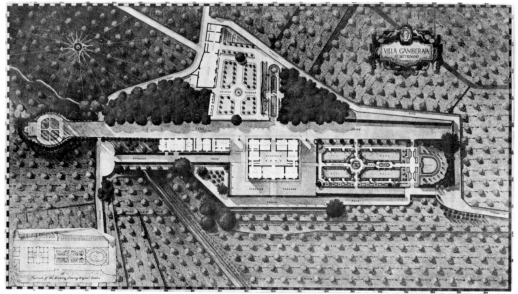

84. Plan of the Villa Gamberaia, near Settignano, measured and drawn about 1920.

85. Section of the Villa Gamberaia drawn to accompany the plan.

Approaching on the country road from Settignano (Fig. 86), just after glimpsing the house of Gamberaia across the fields the visitor sees ahead a tunnel through which the highway passes, with a line of cypresses across it at the upper level. It is perhaps an exaggeration to call this the first underpass in history, but an earlier one does not come to mind. Just short of the tunnel there is, on the right, a recessed gateway from which a short, straight, hedge-bordered entrance road leads directly toward the house and its wide surrounding terrace. There is no perceptible turnaround, and a service road angling off to the right hugs the terrace walls of the villa's developed area before reaching another highway beyond. Thus there are no curves in the road alignment, and the place has an almost pedestrian quality. It surely

86. Drawing by Giuseppe Zocchi shows the Villa Gamberaia in about 1750.

87. The turf viale of the Gamberaia, looking out toward the valley.

conveys no impression of accepting rapid traffic; indeed, this may be one of the sources of Gamberaia's undeniable quiet charm. Everything here seems unpretentious and unhurried.

The serenity of the villa undoubtedly rests also upon the calm simplicity of the house: its forthright plan, the restful proportions of its overall volume, the generous Tuscan overhang of its eaves, the gentle harmony between warm golden stucco walls and reddish-brown stone trim at openings and corners. The house is built around a central court, with a single sight-line that crosses the narrow dimension of the structure and emerges through doors on the east and west faces.

Outside the western door is a broad grassy terrace, open to sunsets. Across the low parapet, with its strangely raised finials and stone dogs, the towers of distant Florence rise out of the blue haze of the Val d'Arno. In the foreground the olive groves and vineyards, in true Tuscan fashion, come right up to the service road tucked beneath the terrace wall. The eastern door opens upon the villa's most unusual feature—a clearly exceptional sight in Italy— the long turf viale reaching from one end of the villa to the other (Fig. 87). At the south end is a balustrade, with a lonely stone figure unfortunately blocking the middle of the view down toward the Arno. At the north end the viale, framed in the rows of cypresses visible from the highway, digs into the hillside and terminates in a grotto-like niche deeply embedded in the dark green foliage.

The east face of the house is continued at both exterior corners by a sort of double arcade. That toward the north serves as a bridge from the second floor of the house to the small chapel and other outbuildings that lie between the viale and the short entrance road. The arcade toward the south, by means of an ingenious spiral stairway inside one of the piers, leads to the villa's lovely, and relatively recent, garden. The extended east face of the house, along with the opposite high terrace walls, rows of cypresses, and firm lines of hedge toward the southern end of the viale, thus plays an important part in giving this remarkable space its positive form. In its own different way this is as crisp an example of slot-space as the great central viale at the Villa d'Este (Fig. 88).

Directly opposite the eastern door, the sight-line across the house plunges into a fanciful alcove cut into the rising slope, tying outdoor to indoor space. Here Gamberaia shows a stage of development and sophistication not found in such Quattrocento Tuscan villas as the Medici at Fiesole—or elsewhere until after Bramante's work at the Belvedere. Even at Gamberaia it is the only case of such clear tying-in: neither the entrance road north of the house nor the garden on the south is visually tied to the indoor space.

The alcove feels almost like an extension of the indoor court. From viale level, stairways ascend the sides of the alcove to an upper level—on the south to a dense ilex bosco, on the north to a sunny garden of lemons and oleanders

88. Reverse of the preceding view, in later years, looking toward the hillside.

usually called the Lemon Garden, along the north side of which is a low
building for sheltering potted lemon trees in cold weather. In the alcove and
in this upper garden the detail of walls and steps is to some eyes rather crude,
with much of that strange surface decoration employing bits of broken marble,
usually black and white, that became so widely fashionable at one time and
that now tends to confirm ascription of a late date to some parts of the Villa
Gamberaia.

The main garden, south of the house (Fig. 89), is not much older than
this century. At one time the area held a garden much simpler than this,
though basically not dissimilar in plan. What distinguishes the garden today
is the division of its main rectangle into four pools of still water about a
smaller circular basin in the center. Another pool, apparently the far half
of an older oval form and backed by a high clipped arcade of hedging, is
at the end of the garden. Walks of pebble-mosaic paving separate the four
corner pools, and the divisions are further outlined by neatly clipped low
box hedges. The garden is accented by numerous pieces of fairly simple

topiary work. Some critics consider this "new" garden an anachronism, feeling that its use of too much unruffled water, too many flowers, and too many topiary pieces is not consistent with either the Italian ideal or the character of the villa. In a literal sense there is no doubt some merit in this argument, but the fact remains that most visitors, whatever their degree of professional skill or historical erudition, find this water garden an effective contributor to the pervading peacefulness of the villa.

In a similar vein, Gamberaia has been criticized for its abundance of turf, which certainly cannot be defended as normal to the typical Italian villa. To be sure, at points where concentrated wear is likely to occur—from the east and west doorways across the viale and the terrace, respectively, and at the house end of the entrance road—the turf is replaced by stone paving. Perhaps the best defense, and one that raises healthy doubts about such generalizing criticisms, is the fact that at Gamberaia, surely as the result of devoted care and watering, the turf of viale and terraces is almost always brilliant green. Only in hottest summer does it take on the glowing topaz hue that southern Californians recognize as the normal summer color of their own hills.

The shift north from Gamberaia to Isola Bella involves not only a leap in mileage and time, but also a more important one, in character (Fig. 90);

89. The famous water garden of the Villa Gamberaia, installed at the beginning of the present century.

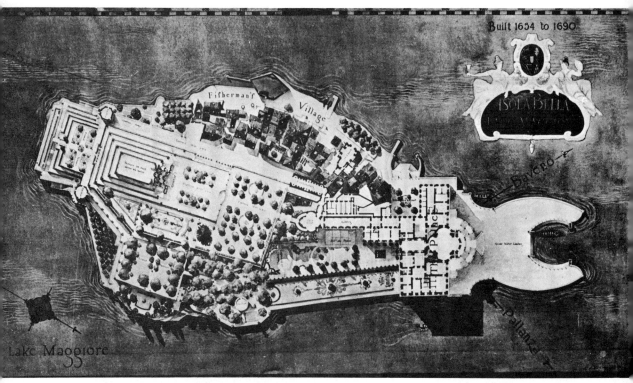

90. Isola Bella in Lago Maggiore.

from simplicity to elaboration, quiet modesty to outright showmanship. Offshore from Stresa in the languid waters of Lake Maggiore, Isola Bella represents the very extreme of man's capacity to remake the land: here an entire island, one of a group owned for centuries by the Borromei, a prominent family of Milano, has been made over and built upon. Work was begun by Count Carlo Borromeo in 1632 and continued under his son until 1671. Judging by the original model still exhibited at Isola Bella, the huge palace on the northern end of the island was not completed; but the gardens were, piling up to the south of it today tier upon tier like an enormous, extravagant but handsome wedding cake.

To best comprehend the technical skill employed in making Isola Bella what it is, as well as to savor the magical quality of this fantasy seemingly floating on the water, one should row out to it from Stresa (Fig. 91). Approaching from the south, the visitor sees the sturdy walls and arches built firmly as a base into the bare rock of the island; above this bottom level no less than ten rectilinear terraces pile up toward the sky, each treated luxuriantly but the fifth, sixth, seventh, and tenth specially developed. To comprehend the sequences and the sometimes intricately designed relations

91. The terraces of Isola Bella, tropically colorful seen from the lake against the snow-capped Alps.

the terraces should be followed attentively, either on the site or on the plan of the island.

Aside from various appurtenances that are not part of the major scheme, the terraces are in two rectangular groups, each in effect a truncated pyramid. The first, at the southern tip of the island, has its long dimension running east-west and thus presents its broad side to the water on the south. It consists of narrow strips and stairways, building up from the first or lowest level to the fifth, where a sizeable rectangular garden crowns the group of terraces. Just outside the back corners of the garden is a pair of octagonal pavilions, which open on the fifth level but reach down to foundations on rock at about the first. Both physically and visually the pavilions seem to anchor the entire composition. A broad walk at the rear of the fifth-level garden connects the two pavilions and continues on northward around the second group of terraces, for which the walk thus becomes a base. On the east side, the fifth-level walk expands to form another garden separate from either of the two main groups. On the west it moves straight along just above and behind the picturesque buildings of the Fisherman's Village.

The second rectangular group, unlike the lower set, has its long dimension running north-south. From the southern side, facing the water, this group seems to rise as pyramidally and regularly as those below it; but on the north, at the end toward the palace, variation appears in the sixth and seventh terrace levels. Ascent to the sixth level from the rear of the palace is by curving stairs famous for concealing a change of direction in the sight-line (the so-called "bent axis") by means of a very simple trick: the stairs are fitted against the outer circumference of a generally circular space just outside the palace. From below they *appear* to be symmetrical, but the steps themselves are screened by a high parapet wall on the inner circumference. Behind the screen the steps of the eastern arc have wider treads than those on the other side, so that the visitor arrives unsuspectingly on the upper platform at a point considerably west of the arc's center. From this platform, steps continue straight ahead on the *new* sight-line to the sixth level, and the new sight-line goes on to become the spine on which all ten terraces are organized.

The sixth-level terrace is not bilaterally symmetrical but swells out to the east and wraps around the remaining higher terraces. The seventh level is reached from the sixth by steps on the sight-line; it resumes a purely rectangular plan and is set forward snugly into the southern edge of the sixth-level terrace, thus picking up again the regular stepping effect. The north end of the seventh-level terrace is open for some distance; then come the top three terraces, tightly nested one above the other, completing the great truncated pyramid. The tenth or top terrace, practically enough after all this visual splendor, houses a cistern.

On walls and balustrades there is a profusion of obelisks, sculptures, and assorted finials—the entire villa has a carnival atmosphere. Since flowers in the equable climate of the Italian lakes are not so difficult a problem as in the hotter south, one looks down here on vividly colorful parterres, or outward to warm stone figures in sharp contrast against the indigo blue lake. All about the horizon the breath-taking mountains, now clear, now hazy, sometimes snow-capped in early summer are in marked opposition to the almost tropical abundance of verdure on all terraces and walls. Since the days of the Hanging Gardens of Babylon there can hardly have been anything quite so fabulous as Isola Bella.

The next chronological step in the list requires jumping forward about a century and moving back to the outskirts of Rome, or at any rate to what was the open countryside north of Rome only a few decades ago. The reasons for including the Villa Chigi (Fig. 92) may seem paradoxical, for it is quite definitely not typical of Italian villas. It is in the shadow of two hundred years of Roman villa development but is almost wholly Tuscan in feeling. It is far simpler than would naturally be expected in a creation of the florid Settecento. Though its plan has clear geometric strength, it is one of the few truly Italian villas whose spatial structure is formed primarily by vegetation. Nevertheless, the Villa Chigi with its unaffected charm illustrates well some technical points of which good examples are scarce.

PLAN OF VILLA CHIGI
BEYOND THE PORTA SALARIA · NORTH OF ROME
SCALE ONE INCH EQUALS THIRTY FEET

92. Until the Villa Chigi was measured and drawn in 1923 it had been considered a composition of perpendiculars and parallels, as shown in the panel at lower right. Actually the plan contains no right angles and no parallels.

The villa is thought to have been built for Cardinal Flavio Chigi in about 1760, a date so late in the development of Italian landscape architecture that the extreme simplicity of the plan is surprising. By the late 1700s much of Europe had succumbed to poor imitations of the so-called "English landscape gardening" school, but Villa Chigi resisted the onslaught. Indeed, the character of the villa—especially the house, with its widely overhanging eaves—seems to have clung loyally to a Tuscan prototype, fending off even the sophistication so typical of Rome. The Tuscan spirit may have reflected the origins of the family, whose Roman branch was established when the papal banker Agostino Chigi came down from Siena in the earliest years of the Cinquecento.

As in another notable instance, that of the Villa Torlonia at Frascati, it would seem sensible to visit Villa Chigi in terms of fifty or so years ago. To be sure, this villa suffered no damage during World War II; but even by that time the surroundings had changed so radically due to the frenetic expansion of Rome that the rural atmosphere, particularly with regard to the villa's offscapes, had all but vanished. Today, of course, Villa Chigi is almost completely engulfed by urbanization.

On an unimportant country road well beyond urban Rome traveling north on the Via Salaria, some two miles beyond the Porta Salaria and off a bit toward the east, there is a swelling of space accented by bordering high walls. On the right of this introduction on the open highway, two beehive-topped posts support an iron-grilled gate that opens directly into the Villa Chigi. From here, as one enters the grounds, there is a straight shot of over a thousand feet eastward down the slight slope to a distant shady terminus; this is the central sight-line on which the entire plan is structured.

The sight-line, impressively long in so small a property and yet not at all pompous, follows a fairly usual pattern of alternating sun and shadow. First inside the gateway is a sunny gravel area and across it the long, low, L-shaped house of faded orange stucco, pierced in deep shadow by an archway through which the sight-line passes to pick up a small raised pool in a second open graveled area on the other side of the house. Beyond this the sight-line tunnels its way, now in shadow again, between the high side walls of the villa's unusual long, narrow viale of laurel, ilex, and box. The viale consists of two parallel masses, much like two very thick hedgerows, of those species growing at random and densely mixed, then clipped high only on the inside faces. Halfway down the viale a sunny glade-like space interrupts briefly; then the tunnel-like effect continues to a terminal space in the shade of high unclipped ilex trees, beyond which a hidden stairway leads on down to the lower end of the viale.

Perhaps the most interesting single area is the open graveled space just east of the house, about the simple raised pool (Fig. 93). Beds of box hedging, cut in the pattern of the family's coat of arms, flank the pool; on either side

93. The great Italian stone pines and small raised pool behind the house of the Villa Chigi.

is a pair of fine Italian stone pines, bright green above the red-tiled roof. Pots of flowers add vivid color, as do the roses and wisteria that clamber up the walls of the house. Here can be observed one of Villa Chigi's technical excellences. The edge of this graveled area is demarked by a shoulder-high hedge of box through which small Grecian laurel trees are growing up. Beyond the hedge, to the right and left of the central viale, are pastures and cultivated fields; but the hedge is just high enough to screen them, while between the hedge and the luxuriant laurel tree tops a long open band of space, much like a ribbon-window, frames an undisturbed panorama of the Sabine Hills far to the east. A considerable portion of the villa's total area is devoted to agricultural use, but without the least intrusion of its activity upon the quiet view.

A secondary sight-line, crossing the graveled area close to the pool, extends north and south to two high baroque screens of modeled stucco in the deep shade of ilex boschi. The north and south boschi are further connected by another sight-line passing just west of the house and by a cool ilex tunnel along the boundary wall at the highway. Between the boschi and the house, scattered stone pines and ilex cast shifting shadows on eight box-hedged areas that were presumably once maintained as garden plots; for the most part these have been allowed to overgrow with a confusion of shrubbery. The pleasantness of this whole area around the house, and to the north and south of it, lies in the flickering pattern of sunlight and shadow from the overhead ilex and stone pine and the quiet transition from sunbathed house to purple shades of the boschi.

The angularity of the plan, with its long straight lines, might seem hard and unlovely were it not for the gentleness imparted by the soft, yielding outlines of box hedging, by the casual positions of the apparently random trees, and by the variation in angles formed by intersecting paths. Here again is an astonishing discovery: despite the highly geometric plan, there is nowhere in it a true right angle—even the house lacks right angles and presents on the entrance side a perceptibly concave facade. This departure from the uncompromising ninety-degree angle, whether intentional or accidental (as it probably was), is undoubtedly one of the elusive factors that give the villa its peculiar charm.

The land about the house is relatively flat, but the undulating fields to the east slope away from it, dropping about forty-five feet (and rendering them all the more invisible from the house). Surrounding the fields are long lanes bordered by unclipped ilex, laurel, and box in growth so dense that, passing along these shady walks, one is scarcely aware of the adjacent fields. The lanes thus further protect the opportunity to farm a large part of the villa without visual disturbance. Moreover, they contribute a remarkable sense of extent—making the villa seem much larger than it actually is.

The outer lanes provide another point of excellence of which examples are rare. By linking with the eastern end of the central viale, they allow alternate routes of return for a visitor who has accepted the invitation of the plan to walk the viale's length. All too often, even in plans of some magnitude and skill, the only way back from a distant point is a reversal of the way out, resulting in the monotony of mere repetition.

One other design factor of the widest applicability, in regard to planting, can be studied in the Chigi (Fig. 94). As noted earlier, the form of an Italian villa is seldom created by boundary planes of vegetation. But at Chigi the spaces are almost exclusively so formed: only behind the north and south boschi, along the highway, and in the house itself do masonry walls play any significant part in the spatial structuring. The villa, in short, is unusually

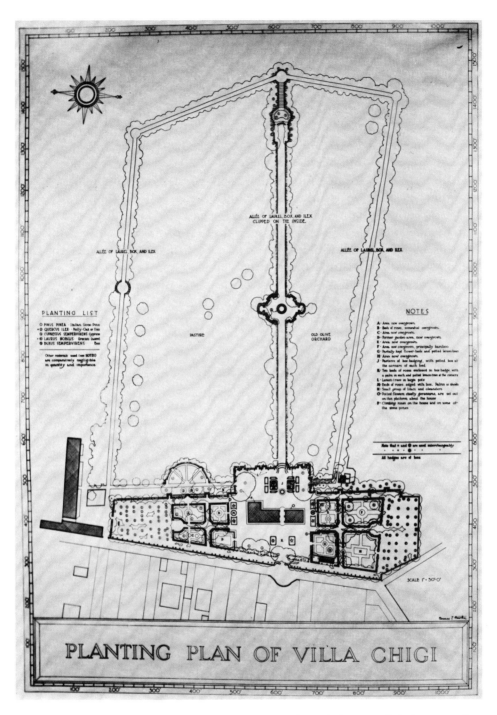

PLANTING PLAN OF VILLA CHIGI

94. Chigi, with its unusual feature of spatial structure formed almost entirely by vegetation, has a notably restrained plant list.

dependent upon plant materials, and one might rightly expect of it an extensive plant list with many species. All the more remarkable, then, the admirable restraint to be discovered instead. Though a quantity of non-descript shrubbery has been permitted to invade some portions of the grounds with the passage of years, the villa's character is actually, and most permanently, determined by the careful use of no more than five plant elements, all evergreen: ilex or holm oak (*Quercus ilex*), Grecian laurel or bay (*Laurus nobilis*), box (*Buxus sempervirens*), Italian stone pine (*Pinus pinea*), and cypress (*Cupressus sempervirens*). The other materials used are purely supplementary, contributing only incidentally to the total effect. For the simplicity of its planting scheme alone Villa Chigi would deserve enduring fame.

These are but some of the outstanding characteristics illustrated by this remarkable villa; what is most unusual about it is that so many useful hints are offered by so small a place. In its own particular way, so different from Villa Gamberaia and Isola Bella, Villa Chigi—assuming the imagination to visualize it today under the conditions of fifty years ago—embodies exceptional qualities of simplicity, restraint, and intimate grace that appeal directly and immediately to the well-trained eye and in large part to the untrained eye

95. The Villa Balbianello, on Lake Como, is one of the most playful of Italian villas.

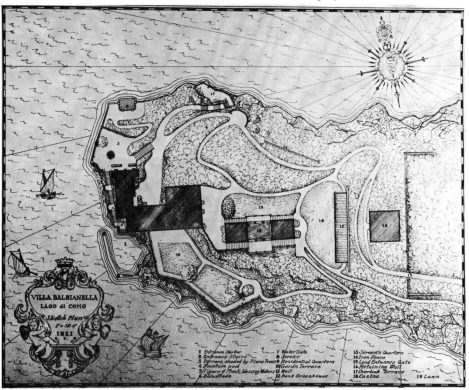

96. The normal approach
to Balbianello is by water.

as well. The place is wonderfully uncomplicated in form and apparent purposes.

The last of these relatively late villas takes one back again to the Italian
lakes—to the delightful Villa Balbianello, sitting snugly with its feet in the
waters of Lake Como, on the western or Alpine shore opposite Bellagio
(Fig. 95). The villa was built about 1785 for Cardinal Durini and served
for a considerable period as a summer residence for the Bishop of Como; later
it became a property of the Visconti-Arconati family. For many years it
has belonged to American owners who have maintained it with care and
sympathy.

As at Isola Bella, the most revealing way to approach Balbianello is by
water, preferably by rowboat across the lake from Bellagio (Fig. 96). The villa,
built on a peninsula that juts out into the lake, can be reached by road; but
the originally intended mode of access is clearly indicated by two distinct
water entrances. To the majority of visitors, the most memorable aspect of

97. The Bishop's Harbor at Balbianello.

Villa Balbianello is probably one or both of these entrances from the surface of the lake: approaching thus in leisurely fashion, one nears the golden-yellow walls, vine-clad and often flower-bedecked, rising from undulating reflections. The more ceremonious of the water gates, the Porta Nobile, is at the southeast corner of the point. It consists of an impressively broad flight of fifteen steps, leading from water level to a gate of intricately patterned wrought iron supported by gateposts with richly decorated vase-like finials.

The other water entrance, called the Bishop's Harbor (Fig. 97), is the more familiar. At the northeast corner of the point, tucked into the rocky shore below a corner of the house, it is a safe harbor for small boats, sheltered by a stone seawall on which stand two ecclesiastical figures in stone. From the Bishop's Harbor landing a long flight of steps, broken into three sets by two intermediate platforms, climbs the east face of the house to a terrace about thirty feet above water level. The parapet of stairway and terrace is one of the best known features of Balbianello: instead of the customary balusters there are panels with twin cherubs bearing stone swags between them. The piers, of unusual outline, support vases of bright flowers in season; colorful vines further soften the sinuous lines in their entire length. There is a gaiety about this balustrade—indeed, about the whole stairway and terrace—that is echoed felicitously in the low curved pool of the terrace and the dancing pattern of sunlight and shadow filtering through the canopy of plane trees.

South of this terrace is the landing platform of the Porta Nobile, some twenty feet below, reached by means of a winding path. On the north the terrace leads directly into the house and down the long stairway to the Bishop's Harbor. On the west a steep set of steps in the slope of the land leads to the level of a higher floor of the house; the east side of the terrace looks out across the water to the lush vegetation of the far shore below Bellagio.

Higher up on the ridge of the promontory are other structures: servants' quarters, a bank of greenhouses, and a splendidly sited arcaded casino from which the views up and down Lago di Como are justly famous. There are other outdoor terraces as well, farther back on the north and south fronts of the peninsula. All the outdoor and indoor areas are tied together by a system of paths that appears deceptively shapeless and disorganized in plan alone; but the topography would obviously not lend itself to incorporation of much rectilinear geometry, and in fact the paths are fitted so snugly and skillfully into the form of the rocky point that the whole scheme seems inevitable.

X. The Piazza in Italy

Italy's role in the design of outdoor space, as exemplified in the gradual development of the rural villa, is formidable indeed. But enthusiasm for the villa must not obscure that country's contribution to development of another landscape architectural form: the town square or piazza, in which the Italian genius for shaping outdoor space has again asserted itself effectively through the centuries.

From the early days of the Roman fora onward, Italy has served as an excellent ground upon which to study the development of town squares. On that ancient peninsula can be found examples of the entire gamut of evolving forms, from the simple Forum of Pompeii to the traffic-jammed madnesses of today. With the collapse of the Roman empire, the onset of the Middle Ages, and the all but complete burial of the Forum Romanum, there began emerging, apparently on its own terms and without reliance on Roman tradition, the unpremeditated, unaffected, seemingly accidental medieval town square or piazza. To be sure, there are cases in which open space within a city has preserved the form of a Roman precursor because it was built on those foundations, but the instances are rare. As a general rule, the urban spaces of medieval times evolved naturally out of their own specific circumstances of need, use, and location. To recall a suggestion made earlier: this organic self-development in the medieval town square may be what makes it a source of satisfaction to similarly oriented twentieth-century designers.

The most typical and unchanged medieval Italian piazze are usually in small towns: such examples as San Gimignano, Viterbo, and Orvieto come quickly to mind. But in larger cities there are piazze of outstanding importance and fame whose form is still essentially that of the Middle Ages. One is not likely to think of Florence (Fig. 98) without remembering the Piazza

98. Florence in 1470; a contemporary engraving.

della Signoria and the fortress-like Palazzo Vecchio. That is as it should be, for throughout the city's history, at least from the Trecento on, this rugged, stone-faced square has been the center of civic action. Here on a platform before their palace the Signoria met and addressed the people; here the Gonfaloniere received his standard of office; here in 1378 the riots of the Ciompi converged. Most memorably, perhaps, here Savonarola and his companions were burned at the stake in 1498.

A few years after membership on the Signoria was put completely into the hands of the Priori of the Greater Guilds, in about 1288, Arnolfo di Cambio was commissioned to build for the Priori a palace commensurate with their new status and dignity. Several houses were cleared away, a space was created for the building, and the Palazzo dei Priori, known shortly thereafter as the Palazzo della Signoria and today as the "old" palace or Palazzo Vecchio, was started. The great L-shaped space, wrapped around two sides of the palace, was thus partly an antecedent of the buildings and partly a consequence of the palace (Fig. 99). The handsome vaulted Loggia dei Priori (now called the Loggia dei Lanzi) was erected in about 1376 to accommodate some of the more ceremonial public functions of the Signoria. Precise data are not available on the timing of other buildings facing the piazza, but so far as has been determined these boundary planes (the actual building lines) have remained substantially as they were in the Quattrocento.

The piazza is thoroughly medieval in its complete lack of right angles, almost perfectly illustrating the characteristic form referred to earlier as the

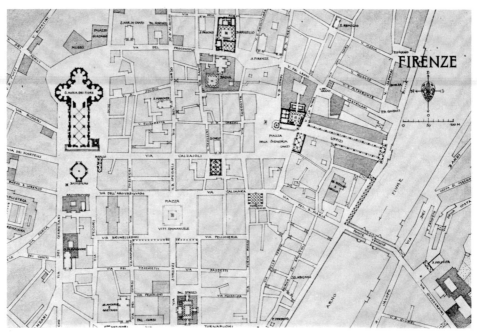

99. The heart of Florence, from the Ponte Vecchio to the Baptistry and the Duomo; the Piazza della Signoria is an integral part of this fabric. It is noteworthy that no street continues through the piazza.

"windmill" or "whirling square" arising from blockage of sight-lines. Coming in from the north, where it supplies the major connection with the Piazza del Duomo, the Via dei Calzaiuoli slides along the west side of the Piazza della Signoria and comes to a full stop against the south side. Also from the north, the Via dei Cerchi and the minor Via Magazzini end against the Palazzo Vecchio. Along the north face of the Palazzo, sliding in from the east, is the Via dei Gondi, which also stops in the piazza. From the south, the passageway between the two wings of the Uffizi Gallery (an addition by Vasari in 1560–1574) focuses its line of sight on the Palazzo Vecchio tower, going no farther. Only along the south side of the Piazza della Signoria does a line of sight appear even partially to pass through, from the Via Vacchereccia on the west past the Loggia dei Lanzi and into the Via della Ninna on the east. It is not a clear passage, however, and is scarcely noticeable, so that in visual effect the Piazza della Signoria is truly an example of the windmill, with no through sight-lines.

Though the piazza is convincingly positive in its total character, it does share with other L-shaped spaces, on visual levels, an inherent ambiguity, which in this case is resolved in a most interesting way. Usually an observer entering an L-shaped space finds himself in a quandary as to which of two basic alternatives he is experiencing. Does he feel himself to be in a single squarish volume, with a portion of its boundary planes hidden—but nevertheless implicit—within whatever intrudes at the corner? Or does the corner-occupying mass project so far that the spatial volume as a whole becomes visually two separate spaces trying hard but unsuccessfully to look like a single one? The dilemma causes many designers to regard the L-space as an invariably difficult form to handle.

Here in the Piazza della Signoria the problem is deftly solved, though probably in a self-suggesting or intuitive way rather than by deliberate plan—after all, its doing took some fifty or sixty years. A row of sculptures, reaching from the doorway of the Palazzo Vecchio northward toward the mouth of the Via dei Cerchi, acts in effect as a divider by prolonging visually the front plane of the Palazzo; two determinable spaces result with only a modicum of uncertainty.

The start came in 1504 when the *David* of Michelangelo was placed just north of the main door of the Palazzo Vecchio (it was replaced by a full-size copy when the original was moved to the Accademia). In 1534 Baccio Bandinelli's brutally ugly *Hercules and Cacus* was placed to the south of the doorway; at about the same time Donatello's *Judith and Holofernes,* already over seventy years old, was placed to the north of the *David,* and a row of verticals had clearly begun. Farther along, Donatello's *Marzocco,* the heraldic lion emblematic of Florence, still held its place on the steps of the platform, adding to the linear sense (it, too, was replaced by a copy when the original was taken to the Bargello). Then in 1557 the strange *Neptune Fountain* by Ammanati—a colossal marble Neptune disrespectfully known as the Big White Bully in the local vernacular, with an octet of sprightly bronze satyrs around the lower basin—was erected on a diagonal from the corner of the Palazzo Vecchio. A few years later, about 1560, the equestrian *Cosimo I* of Giovanni da Bologna took its place as the final element in the line.

To be sure, the line of sculptures is all postmedieval, the entrance cortile of the Palazzo Vecchio contains Verrocchio's fountain of the small winged boy struggling with a dolphin (the one originally made for the Villa Careggi), and the Loggia dei Lanzi houses some of the best-known examples of sculpture from classical times and the best Renaissance period. But the Piazza della Signoria itself is not a manifestation of Florentine softness or grace; there is something stern and hard-bitten about it (Fig. 100). Its paving is stone throughout; its vertical boundary planes are unyielding. The massive cubical form of the Palazzo Vecchio with its projecting battlements and soaring tower casts a forbidding air over the spaces around it. In short, not only in spatial relationships but in overall feeling the Piazza della Signoria is surely the most completely medieval, chronologically and in atmosphere, of all the famous urban spaces of Italy.

The Piazza del Campo in Siena, owing at least in part to design characteristics that are downright theatrical, is one of the most familiar medieval

100. The battlemented Palazzo Vecchio presides over the Piazza della Signoria.

101. Siena: the handsome brick and stone Palazzo Pubblico and its Torre del Mangia mark one side of the Piazza del Campo.

Italian city spaces (Fig. 101); but these characteristics are what make it seem less clearly a product of the Middle Ages. Thoroughly medieval in chronology, the piazza is not typical of that age: the city fathers manifestly had, from early days, a sharp appreciation of the space as a potential setting for important events such as the traditional horse race, the Palio, which even now is probably better known than the piazza itself. As early as 1262, legislation governed the height and character of houses facing the piazza; adherence to it has apparently remained a matter of public pride through the centuries, for today the uniformity of height and appearance in buildings across from the Palazzo Pubblico makes them an excellent background for the Palio.

The piazza is located at the upper end of a long swale, in a sort of half-bowl just below the juncture of the three ridges on which Siena is built. Thus from

102. Plan of the Piazza del Campo; radial ribs converge to an ample drain inlet with a shell-like hood.

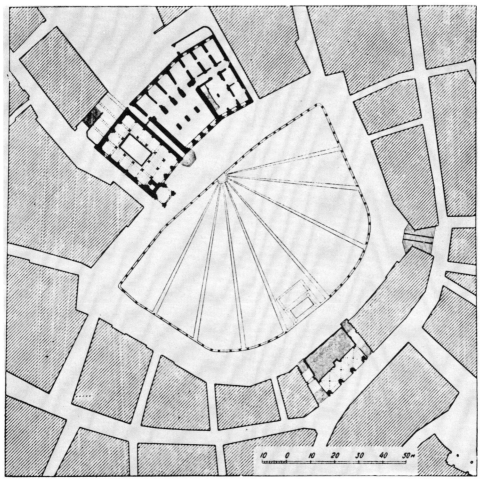

the very start the topography suggested a natural amphitheater, an effect heightened by the almost semicircular form of the space as it came to be delimited by buildings. Later the paving pattern of the whole was made clearly radial, with ribs of stone converging at the center of one side of the piazza and all the surfaces sloping down toward the fanciful drain inlet there. As a consequence of these factors, the Piazza del Campo looks and feels more consciously designed than one would expect in view of its authentically medieval history. Handsome as it is—electrical indeed if one sees it during the contagious excitement of the Palio—the piazza is not to be regarded as a true example of the medieval urban square. One medieval characteristic, however, it certainly has: blockage of sight-lines (Fig. 102). No less than eleven streets enter the piazza and end there; none goes through. But the roughly semicircular form is so dominant that most streets come in radially and not one slides in at a corner to create the windmill effect with which the space would seem more accidental and accordingly more medieval in spirit.

Aside from its amphitheatrical form, what renders the Piazza del Campo most distinctive is the contrast in colors of its materials: the deep red and warm gray or ivory of brick and stone, instead of the more usual dusty brown of medieval town squares in Italy. The combination is used in the impressive Palazzo Pubblico, built in a slightly concave curve on the southern edge of the piazza between 1288 and 1309. Two enlargements were made shortly thereafter, and then the graceful tower, the Torre del Mangia—named popularly, after the original bell-ringer—was erected between 1338 and 1349, the slim shaft in brick, the corbeled and battlemented top in stone. In 1352, as a votive offering after the great plague of 1348, the Cappella di Piazza, a small chapel in the form of a high stone loggia, was added at the base of the tower.

It is the same combination of materials that causes the radial pattern of the piazza's paving to stand out so noticeably: the near-white of the stone ribs in sharp contrast to the dark herringbone brick of the field. A wide stone border surrounds the whole, forming a relatively smooth promenade or track along the buildings on the curving north side and across the straighter front of the Palazzo Pubblico; there is a continuous row of stone posts or bollards on its inner edge. Just inside the promenade on the northern side is the reconstructed Fonte Gaia, a carved stone fountain, the original of which was erected here about 1410. At the edge of the strip in front of the Palazzo Pubblico, just below the row of bollards, is the central drain inlet referred to earlier. It is of carved stone in the form of a scallop shell, emphasizing the shell-like character that can be sensed in the entire piazza.

What this all amounts to is rather simple, except for the question of historical labeling, which is a matter of less than overwhelming importance to a designer. The Piazza del Campo, a space developed virtually as it is today by the end of the 1300s, is a medieval square that looks more like the deliberately designed creation of a later age. The appearance arises from at least a suggestion of the sort of ordered spatial structure that one tends to associate with the 1500s or after; and this very structure is undoubtedly a major source of the delight an observer feels in the piazza today. If the Piazza del Campo is historically a paradox, it is a most pleasant one.

The story is quite different at the Piazza San Marco in Venice, by general agreement one of the greatest outdoor spaces in the world (Fig. 103). Here a majority of the visibly constituent parts are definitely of the Cinquecento and even as late as 1810—despite which the piazza does not seem to have any of the conscious organization typical of work in these later centuries. The chief reason may well be the seemingly simple fact that the space itself, as a volume of plastic material, took form quite early. Its precise origins are of the hazy past; but it is known that the church of San Marco was begun in 830 as a chapel for the first Palazzo Ducale or Doge's Palace. There is ample evidence, too, that a parvis or open forecourt for the church existed as early as the year 1000 and that it was used also as a marketplace; the Campanile (bell-tower) had already been erected in timber in about 888. The church underwent a considerable alteration, beginning in 1063, to achieve its present form. The Palazzo Ducale was added to and modified through the years until about 1424, when its west face was built, fixing as it is now the eastern boundary of the Piazzetta, the smaller leg of the whole L-shaped space. The Campanile had been rebuilt in 1329 with brick and stone replacing the original timber. In short, though the piazza as a whole had been somewhat enlarged during the twelfth century, the great space had attained by the end of the Trecento or at latest by the first quarter of the Quattrocento essentially the form it exhibits today (Fig. 104).

Since then, that is, the boundary planes of the old L-shaped space have been almost completely maintained; new structures have been placed to front on essentially the same old building lines. The first of these was started in 1480, when the Procuratie Vecchie, a long row of administrative offices for the Venetian officials called Procurators, was begun on the north side of the main Piazza. The building was not finished until 1517, and in the meantime the Torre dell'Orologio (clock-tower) had been added in 1499 at the east end of the row to form an archway leading northward into the Merceria, the main land-based street of Venice.

The next boundary plane to be replaced was the western side of the Piazzetta, where Sansovino began his Libreria in 1536. It was not yet finished when Sansovino died in 1570, but in 1584 Scamozzi not only completed it but also undertook construction of the Procuratie Nuove, the new administrative offices on the south side of the main Piazza directly across from the old ones. In the process of this double operation, Sansovino and Scamozzi razed the structures along the south edge of the big Piazza and pulled back the building line on which to locate the north end of the Libreria and the

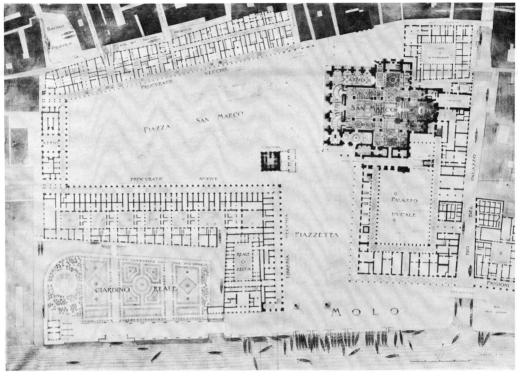

103. Venice: plan of the Piazza San Marco, surely one of the world's greatest outdoor spaces.

104. Aerial view of the San Marco complex, from a point above the lower right-hand corner of the preceding plan.

105. The Piazza San Marco, looking from the Fabbrica Nuova toward the church.

entire front of the Procuratie Nuove. Thus the Campanile was released from the buildings that had enveloped it on two sides and became a free-standing vertical (Fig. 105) to which Sansovino added the Loggetta, a sort of porch at the base of the tower. Two other sets of verticals are to be noted: the three handsome flagpoles in front of the church and the two columns standing at the open end of the Piazzetta. The flagpoles with their note of animation were done by Leopardi in 1505. The columns, one bearing the amusingly ferocious Lion of San Marco and the other a statue of St. Theodore, patron saint of Venice, were erected about 1189 and 1329 respectively.

Scamozzi did not live to finish the Procuratie Nuove; this was done by Longhena in 1640. There was no further change of major import until 1810, when the western end of the main Piazza was closed with the Fabbrica Nuova, built by Soli for Napoleon's Italian viceroy Beauharnais (Fig. 106). This structure, joining the Procuratie Vecchie and Nuove, allows passage through at ground level, with an excellent view of the church at the far end, but not on any central sight-line.

Oddly enough, though it is unquestionably L-shaped and should therefore be fraught with basic difficulties of design, the Piazza San Marco does not seem to suffer from this condition. There are no doubt many reasons for this, three of which merit attention here. First, the corner-occupying volume of buildings is so large in ground area, and relatively so low, that it conveys no sense of intrusion into a single rectilinear space. The Piazza and Piazzetta

106. Reverse of the preceding view, from the balcony of San Marco, near the four bronze horses.

107. The Piazzetta, with Sansovino's Libreria on the right; note the strength of the sight-line centered between the columns.

108. Looking from the Piazzetta toward the clock-tower.

seem more like broad ribbons of space with a remarkable feeling of continuity around the bend. The Campanile helps establish this flexible quality, acting as a kind of free-standing fulcrum on which the two spatial components turn; the relatively greater height of the tower, as compared with the Libreria and the Procuratie Nuove, undoubtedly enhances the space-turning role.

Second, the two legs of the L-space tend not to compete with each other; fortunately, the moving light of the sun seldom provides the Piazza and Piazzetta with equally exciting effects simultaneously. The two are different, yet each is distinctive: the Piazza with its canted north side and a quiet, architectonically closed west end, the Piazzetta parallel-sided and open at the south end to the high-keyed brightness of the waterscape (Fig. 107). The geometry of the two legs would seem to make the Piazza too overwhelmingly predominant: it is longer and larger and has the almost incredible fantasy of the great church as a terminal focus of attention, yet the sunlit view across the water from the Piazzetta to the island of San Giorgio, framed by the two free-standing columns, makes this smaller leg of the L-space so vibrant that it cannot feel like something left over or inconsequential. It generally yields primacy to the Piazza, but the Piazzetta is at all times a worthy accompaniment, fascinating but not competitive.

Third, a small space immediately in front of the church, implicitly rather than explicitly bounded, is shared by the Piazza and the Piazzetta and thus tends to unite the two legs of the L-space all the more firmly, supplementing the space-turning function of the bell-tower (Fig. 108). This little space is bounded on the east by the church, on the south by the implied plane from the corner of the church to the north side of the Loggetta and the corner of the Campanile, on the west by the implied plane from this corner of the Campanile through the line of Leopardi's flagpoles to the Torre dell'Orologio, and on the north by the clock-tower itself. One most clearly senses the integrity of this volume, naturally, when one is in it, especially upon entering it after traversing the length of either the Piazza or the Piazzetta. It is the inward terminal portion of space for both; standing in it, one is visually in both legs at once and thus in the great L-space as a whole, and the sense of a unifying force is so strong as to seem almost palpable.

Though these matters of spatial structure may seem too technical to have general effect, their subtle interplay probably forms the unconscious basis for the universal delight with which the Piazza San Marco is greeted and re-membered by all visitors, lay and professional. Obviously there must be other reasons, too. Now that both sides of the Piazza, and usually the front of the Libreria as well, are furnished with tables and chairs for outdoor refreshment, much animation and merriment add effect to the visual splendor of "the Pearl of the Adriatic." There is a sort of iridescence about the place—by day and even more by night—that makes one feel the very air is shimmering with gold-dust. The Byzantine sparkle of the church and its domes only heightens a sense of sheer wonder already hovering over the scene.

Awareness of the ageless quality of the piazza prepares one for its unspoken testimonial to the role of outdoor space as a sort of transparent cosmic cement. Where can one find a more positively compelling example of the power of an outdoor space to hold together and unify a group of highly disparate buildings? To landscape architects—indeed, to all designers—this is perhaps the most important contribution of the fabulous Piazza San Marco.

In sharp contrast to these three medieval spaces in Florence, Siena, and Venice, city spaces of Renaissance times reveal a quite different character. The early Cinquecento in Rome, under the leadership of Bramante, rediscovered the value of consciously ordered outdoor design; in city space also this came ultimately to be the accepted way of working. As in the villas, so in urban squares there was gradual development of skill, though the degree of sophistication lagged considerably behind that achieved in villas of the same period. Application of the newer tenets of design to the problem of the piazza naturally gave rise to the development of what may fairly be called Renaissance city space, in contrast to medieval space. The difference is one of spirit and attitude: the Renaissance type of urban space looks thoroughly conscious, the balanced carry-through of sight-lines is manifestly intentional and carefully planned, and spatial structure is clearly perceptible. There is virtually nothing of the casual, accidental, medieval quality in the typical Renaissance piazza.

Though much of the greatest development of Renaissance urban space occurred outside of Italy and somewhat later on—especially in France during the eighteenth century—it is clear that in this as in other areas of design the origins were Italian. Here again, Rome is the most appropriate site for examining the start and progress of the new notions, owing of course to the tremendous activities of a series of phenomenally energetic popes. The two outstanding Roman examples, illustrating not only the highest achievement of Renaissance urban space within the Eternal City but also the sketchy beginnings, are the Piazza di San Pietro, in front of the great church, and the Piazza del Popolo, at what was the usual northern entrance to Rome. Oddly enough, although the latter did not reach its present grandiose form until early in the nineteenth century, it was begun earlier than the Piazza di San Pietro.

From earliest Roman days the ancient Via Flaminia, coming down from the north, had passed through the city's walls at the Porta Flaminia, later called the Porta del Popolo. From the space naturally occurring just within the gate, the Via Lata, later called the Corso, continued straight to the heart of the city. There was early a rough suggestion of streets radiating from the gate, but in about 1520 the first Medici pope (Leo X) regularized what is now the Via di Ripetta (then the Via Leonina), fanning toward the right; between 1534 and 1549 the Farnese pope, Paul III, did the same with the Via del Babuino, fanning to the left. This was the situation at the Porta del Popolo when the great Sixtus V, elevated to the papal throne in 1585, began his monumental program of cutting new streets to connect the major churches and other significant points in the city.

Among the tasks committed by Sixtus V to Domenico Fontana, his favorite architect, was the unearthing of three huge Egyptian obelisks from the sites where they had been placed as trophies in ancient Rome and their erection in new locations related to the Pope's plans for the city. One of the selected new spots was in the then formless open space inside the Porta del Popolo, at the intersection of the sight-lines extending from the Via di Ripetta, the Via Lata, and the Via del Babuino. Here in 1589 Fontana raised the obelisk that Emperor Augustus, centuries earlier, had erected in the Circus Maximus.

Meanwhile, just inside the gate, the little church of Santa Maria del Popolo had been rebuilt under Sixtus IV about 1475. The gate itself had been improved by Vignola in 1562. In 1589, with the placement of the high obelisk at the focal point of the three radiating streets, a positive form of space was obviously suggested leading in through the Porta del Popolo and dispersing directly into the three streets. Actually, the Pope had intended to cut a long street from the obelisk straight to his favorite Santa Maria Maggiore on the Viminal hill and then on to Santa Croce in Gerusalemme on the far side of Rome, with obelisks marking the intermediate points. The grade up the Pincian hill at the start must have demonstrated the implausibility of completing the project—though the cut from atop the hill, in front of the Trinità dei Monti, was made to the southward and exists today, plunging over hill and dale all the way to Santa Croce, beginning with the familiar Via Sistina at the top of the Spanish Steps.

Even though the great three-mile swath of the Via Felice, as Sixtus V called it, could not be completed—nor indeed even started—at this northern end, the sides of the newly formed space about the obelisk were brought under some control; a large though somewhat lopsided trapezoidal form resulted, the new Piazza del Popolo of 1589. The next modification did not come until 1667, when the twin churches of Santa Maria in Monte Santo and Santa Maria dei Miracoli, designed by Rainaldi, were completed at the two points between the streets fanning toward the city. The directional force of the piazza, from the Porta del Popolo to the three radiating streets, was now clear and the rough trapezoidal space no doubt acted as intended. To be sure, this rather crude handling of space may seem a far cry from the suave skill exhibited in such contemporary rural works as the Villa Lante, but it was at least a start toward effective consciousness of the use of spatial structure.

Thus the Piazza del Popolo stood, from 1667 until 1820, when Giuseppe Valadier finished the monumental changes that took the space most of the way toward its present form. He had first proposed changes with a scheme published in 1794; the final plan, prepared in 1816, was fully executed in 1820. Basically, what Valadier did was to give larger and more obviously geometric form to the piazza, imposing upon the space a sumptuous grandeur it had not previously possessed. This he accomplished by remaking the simple east and west sides of the older trapezoidal space into great ornate hemicycles, incorporating curved carriage ramps and adding vegetation in a way that had not been usual in Italy (Figs. 109, 110). On the east side, against the slopes of the Pincio, the friars of the Augustinian monastery attached to Santa Maria del Popolo had grown their own vegetables in a garden adjacent to the church. This was replaced by a long, steep, winding carriage road up the slope and a huge terrace at the top overlooking the piazza and the northern part of the city. Behind the terrace was the public park of the Pincio (the Passeggiata del Monte), laid out only a few years earlier; still a popular promenade, it has contained for years a quasi-fashionable restaurant called Casino Valadier.

Opinions vary as to the merit of the Valadier enlargement of the Piazza del Popolo. There is some question whether so vast a space is justified at a point where large assemblies are unlikely. There is an even sharper question whether the north-south directional force of this entry to Rome was not vitiated by the strength of the countervailing east-west emphasis. (The latter question, be it said in Valadier's defense, became especially pointed long after his day when the westward sight-line from the Pincio terrace was grossly emphasized by the cutting through of a street directly on that line from the western hemicycle of the piazza, across the Tiber on the Ponte Margherita, and so on into the distance [Fig. 111].) The long east-west line has now become far too dominant for a piazza where entry to Rome was the clearly announced function; the result is the directional ambiguity generally felt in the Piazza del Popolo by designers today.

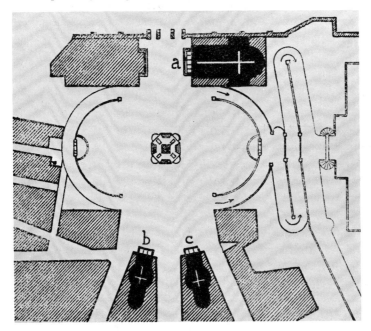

109. Rome: Piazza del Popolo as developed by Valadier but before the cut-through to the Tiber. Small a marks the church of Santa Maria del Popolo beside the city gate; at b is Santa Maria dei Miracoli and at c its twin, Santa Maria in Monte Santo.

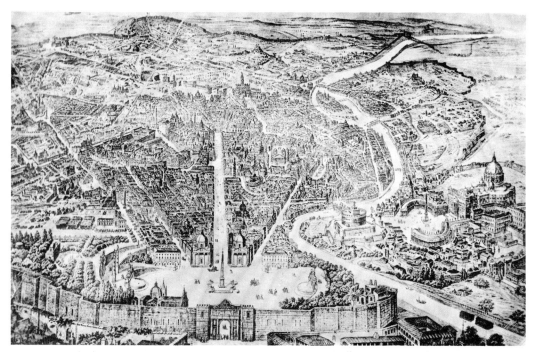

110. A much distorted engraving of Rome from north of the Porta del Popolo, showing the Valadier modification of the earlier trapezoidal piazza formed by the three streets fanning southward from the gate.

The Piazza di San Pietro also began with emplacement of one of the three ancient obelisks that Domenico Fontana raised in new locations for Pope Sixtus V. The one used here had stood close by, in Nero's Circus, on the spot later to be occupied by the sacristy of St. Peter's. In 1586 the great needle was placed—with enormous difficulty, according to the popular version—about three hundred fifty yards east of the center of the dome, on an extension of the center-line of the church. Although Pope Julius II had laid the foundation stone for the new St. Peter's in 1506, change had followed change in the plans and work was still going on when the obelisk was erected. Carlo Maderna would add the long nave, beginning in 1606, and complete the facade in 1614; just before this he would install the handsome fountain north of the obelisk.

But another half-century would pass before further steps were taken toward creation of the huge Piazza di San Pietro. It can only be presumed that during the interval the space about the obelisk and fountain remained amorphous, flanked on the north by the angular pile of the Vatican and on the south by nondescript smaller buildings. The isolated obelisk had been standing in its final place for seventy years when in 1656 Pope Alexander VII, a Chigi from Siena, commissioned Gian Lorenzo Bernini to work out an appropriate parvis for the church. Thus the famous piazza came into being as an integral work, all its component parts consciously designed by one man, clear in structure and purpose (Fig. 112).

As Bernini composed it, the space as a whole consisted of three portions, assembled in series on a single sight-line terminating uncompromisingly at the central doorway of the church and the famous papal balconied window above it. Each portion eventually acquired a specific designation. First, starting from the east, was the Piazza Rusticucci, strictly speaking not part of the main work, but simply an irregular space that existed between the Borgo Nuovo and Borgo Vecchio prior to Mussolini's fatuous decision to give St. Peter's a more pompous approach by cutting a swath to the Tiber. Second was the *piazza obliqua,* the elliptical space containing the obelisk at its center and bounded on the north and south by Bernini's superb colonnades. Third was the *piazza retta,* directly before the facade of the church.

The *piazza obliqua* is entered today from what was the Piazza Rusticucci through a wide opening between the outer ends of the north and south colonnades. The long dimension of the elliptical space is north-south, through the obelisk and the two huge fountains, of which the southern one was copied from Maderna's original when the piazza was being completed. The *piazza*

111. Piazza del Popolo looking down from the Pincio after the westward cut-through.

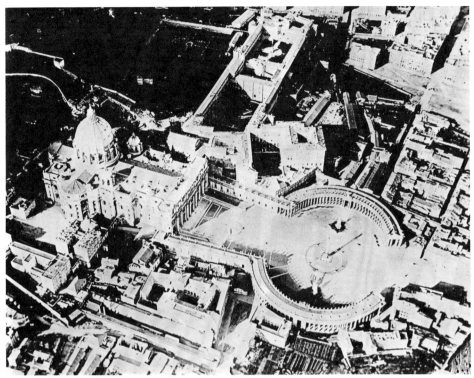

112. Rome: St. Peter's church, the Vatican (with the present form of the Cortile del Belvedere), and the Piazza di San Pietro.

obliqua is thus placed in opposition to the main directional pull, providing a pleasant intermediate pause in the swift rush of the chief sight-line toward the church. It should be noted, however, that the mistake of the Piazza del Popolo was not made here: the middle accents in the arcs of the colonnades are only mild ones, and sidewise attention tends not to stray beyond the two fountains. As a consequence, the north-south line does not compete with the main east-west one in the *piazza obliqua*. The cohesive tendency is then furthered by the slightly dished grade of the granite floor of the space and by the radial paving pattern.

Actually, focus is so insistently on the facade of the church that the notion of any competition with the main sight-line is almost ridiculous. The *piazza retta*, so called despite its having no right angles in plan, is bounded at the sides by closed corridors that diverge toward the church from the inner ends of the curved colonnades. The false perspective brings the facade somewhat forward, on visual levels, to an observer approaching from the east, and conversely increases the apparent distance to the obelisk and to the eastern opening in the colonnades as one looks in that direction from the church. In both instances the optical effect is minimized by the nearly square propor-

113. Piazza di San Pietro: the *piazza obliqua* and *piazza retta* from atop Bernini's colonnade.

tions of the *piazza retta* and by the consequent relative brevity of the slanting corridors; but the force of the false perspective, a favorite device of the late Seicento, is nevertheless discernible. The terminal power of the facade, especially the great central door and window, is heightened by the upward slope of the entire *piazza retta* toward the church and still more by the extraordinary lift of the pile of monumental steps, which reaches forward into the space as a majestic dais-like platform.

Important as all this is theoretically in a work of conscious design, the ultimate test of its excellence lies in the way the Piazza di San Pietro fulfills its two outstanding functions. It provides a wonderfully impressive and unequivocal approach to an important monument (Fig. 113); and on occasions when it seems that half the world has gathered to hear the white-clad figure on the historic balcony, the piazza becomes an outdoor assembly ground of stupendous capacity and character.

To a degree that is too often overlooked, a study of town squares, regardless of their age—and certainly regardless of the presence or absence of trees—offers an unequaled means for comprehending landscape architecture as an art of designing outdoor space for people. These crisp urban volumes, their boundaries almost always clearly perceptible, illustrate unequivocally the functioning of outdoor spatial geometry. The five piazze discussed here differ markedly in their effect on people within them, but they differ in effect because they differ in form.

XI. Beginnings in France

As the fifteenth was the century of Florentine awakening in landscape architecture and the sixteenth the century of the Roman villa, so the seventeenth
was France's great century. It was the era of Le Nôtre—of Versailles and
Louis XIV and French ascendency in Europe. Of course it did not burst
unheralded upon the scene; a century and a half of slow development went
before it as, toward the end of the fifteenth century, France emerged bit by
bit from the Hundred Years' War with England and the general turmoil of
the Middle Ages.

The continuation of warfare, both external and internal, over so long a
span—and until such a late date in comparison with progress of the Renaissance in Florence—left its mark on French developments for some time to
come. Medieval forms were retained in general use; the country house remained a battlemented castle with a moat around it; not until well into the
sixteenth century was there much extension of life into a placid landscape
beyond the defensive perimeter, and even then it developed hesitantly, almost
clumsily. Long after the influence of the Italian Renaissance had begun to
be felt, certain distinctively French characteristics persisted: the moat, no
doubt for reasons of appearance even when no longer needed for defense;
bastion-like corner towers, usually cylindrical, with pointed "candle-snuffer"
tops; steeply pitched roofs with high dormers. Then, strangely enough in an
atmosphere still tinged by medieval ruggedness, French ornamentation moved
toward delicacy of detail rather than toward the strong-muscled forms of
Italian prototypes.

The influence that the Italian Renaissance had on France came about
through a fact, or perhaps one should say quirk, of history. By 1477 Louis
XI, of the House of Valois, had at last achieved peace with England and

enough dominance over rival nobles to form a solid basis for an absolute French monarchy. His son Charles VIII, succeeding him in 1483, soon felt strong enough to press the family's dynastic claims to the Kingdom of Naples and in 1495 conducted a swift Italian campaign. By strict military interpretation, Charles won the war in Italy, but the more important fact is that Italy won his heart.

By his own admission Charles VIII fell headlong in love with Italy and felt that an entirely new world had been opened to him. On his return to France he brought a massive quantity of Italian works of art and more than a score of Italian artists and artisans. Among the latter was Pasello da Mercogliano, a Neapolitan priest who was also a skilled gardener. Especially enamored of the gardens he had visited in Italy, Charles brought Pasello to the family's favorite château, at Amboise on the south bank of the Loire, in the hope of improving the place so as to make it comparable with what he had seen on his southern expedition.

Amboise, however, a tightly walled medieval fortress on a rocky height above the river, offered little scope; and Pasello was no Bramante, though they were contemporaries. All that resulted at Amboise from these efforts in Charles's brief remaining lifetime was a small garden, probably of typical medieval pattern, close to the castle graveyard. Charles died unexpectedly in 1498 and was succeeded by a second cousin, the Duke of Orléans, who assumed the crown as Louis XII. The new monarch continued the efforts to improve Amboise, added a whole new wing, and somewhat elaborated the surroundings of the garden (Fig. 114), but his chief interest lay some twenty miles up the Loire in the château of Blois, his birthplace on the north bank of the Loire. The property—indeed, the entire county of Blois—was obtained by the House of Orléans late in the 1300s; it gained importance when Louis moved the French court from Amboise to Blois. To the older portions of the château he added the wing in brick and stone that now bears

114. Amboise, perched high above the River Loire, shows the timid early garden development begun by Pasello da Mercogliano for Charles VIII in the 1490s.

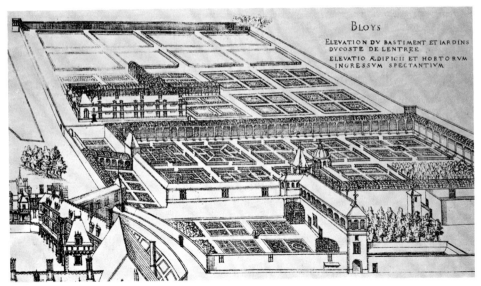

115. Blois: the layout of gardens begun here under Louis XII early in the sixteenth century was more elaborate but still almost medieval in its lack of organization.

his name and has a modern equestrian statue of him in a niche over the main portal.

Of more relevance here is the fact that he brought Pasello da Mercogliano from Amboise to Blois to begin ample but clumsy gardens. Though practically nothing remains of them today, one can at least glimpse what they may have been, thanks to the engravings published many years later (1579) by Androuet du Cerceau in his *Les Plus Excellents Bastiments de France* (Fig. 115). Looking at Du Cerceau's engravings—and he did views not only of Amboise and Blois but of most of the important works of the sixteenth century in France—one can readily see that here again, much like the case in Italy, a long and at times labored climb was being made from almost childlike medieval beginnings toward the skilfulness and sophistication of a well-developed understanding of design.

Because of its relatively late date, the Du Cerceau view of Blois naturally included additions made by Francis I, the cousin and son-in-law who succeeded Louis XII in 1515. There are the handsome Francis I wing and spiral staircase and the gardens toward which the wing faces: three separate levels, supported by high retaining walls and reached by a covered bridge from the château across a moat-like depression through which a street of the town runs today. The lower of these terraces were no doubt done by Pasello for Louis XII; the rest came with Francis I and later. The three garden levels are well organized, according to the engraving, in unimaginative checkerboard patterns of a medieval sort, with adjacent treillage and galleries; but the levels are not in any recognizable visual way related to each other, and the whole garden area is quite detached from the château.

The gardens at Blois, in short, appear to have given little promise of the strong spatial structure that would one day be regarded as typically French. Indeed, a similar obtuseness in outdoor design seems to have characterized the entire period of Francis I, despite his lively interest in the arts and the richness of the architectural developments during his thirty-two-year reign. Of course the precise detail of the many places created or begun by order of Francis I cannot be certain because none remains today in its original form; most were enlarged under Henri II, the son who succeeded him in 1547, or by later monarchs. But, on the whole, modifications of this kind do not tend to change the basic spirit of the early work as evidenced in Du Cerceau's views. Moreover, the question here is not of precise detail, but rather of overall spatial structure—or of its relative absence from French landscape architectural works of the first half of the sixteenth century.

The massive, moated château of Chambord, for example, started by Francis in about 1519 as a hunting lodge (incredible as this may seem for such an establishment) is widely known as a fabulous collection of towers, chimneys, pinnacles, and high dormers. But aside from its hunting preserve, a forested park many miles in extent, there is no evidence of outdoor development either by Francis I or by Henri II and those who followed. One encounters references to the cutting of long straight swaths through the forest in various directions, with great circular clearings, or *ronds-points,* at crossings from which groups of these *allées* radiated. The arrangement—which did become a custom at some time, if not actually at Chambord or as early as Francis I—was meant to provide a big open space where the ladies of the court could gather in comfort, with all the viands and trappings of the usual elaborate picnic, while their gallants hunted boar or stag in the forest. As riders pursuing their quarry crossed one or more of the radiating allées, the ladies could observe them and utter the expected exclamations of praise and wonder. Thus came into being, reputedly at least, what was one of the most unique devices of typical French landscape architecture.

The present château of Chenonceaux (Fig. 116), that most fanciful creation perched crosswise in the River Cher southeast of Amboise, was started on older foundations by the financier Thomas Bohier in about 1515, then came into the possession of Francis I in 1523. He continued the rebuilding, but most of the subsequent changes were made after 1547 by Diane de Poitiers, Henri II's mistress, or as late as 1559 by Catherine dei Medici, his widow. Here as at Blois there is in fact a garden, a sizeable rectangular plinth lifted on sturdy walls rising from the river on the near bank, wholly detached from the château. The garden has no doubt been treated in various geometric patterns from its earliest days, but it still has no strong connection to any overall scheme. Aside from this garden, a straight tree-lined avenue of ap-

116. Fanciful Chenonceaux, in the River Cher, eventually had gardens, but they were somewhat disjointed and detached from the château.

proach, and a square arrival terrace, Chenonceaux has no clearly developed outdoor areas.

Francis I also began, at Fontainebleau, the rather haphazard grouping of buildings that was enlarged and added to by his successors to reach the ultimate size and complexity of today's palace. From an engraving by Du Cerceau it is difficult to ascertain just which of the somewhat random gardens were done for Francis, but it is not at all difficult to see that throughout the sixteenth century the château's grounds developed little more schematic sense than a patchwork quilt.

In the closing years of the reign of Francis I, and during that of Henri II, the arts of France moved forward significantly. Francis called into service from Italy such known masters as Serlio and Primaticcio; from among the French a few able designers began to emerge, and more contact with Italian experience gradually brought a much stronger sense of design, including first of all the firm connection between indoors and outdoors that had been lacking

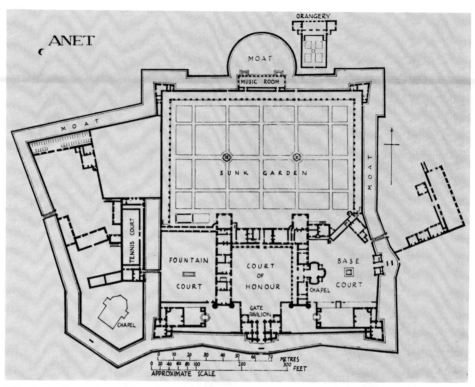

117. Anet, designed by Philibert de l'Orme, illustrates the first sense of spatial structure to creep into the persistent medieval tradition in France.

thus far in France. One French designer of prominence was Philibert de l'Orme, whose plan for Anet (Fig. 117), the place ordered by Henri II about 1550 for his favorite, Diane de Poitiers, reveals probably the earliest evidence in France of careful organization of outdoor spaces, with a strong tie by sight-line between a château and its grounds. At Anet, in the valley of the Eure some forty miles west of Paris, very little is left of what De l'Orme did; but Du Cerceau's engraving shows clearly the great contrast between the earlier medieval portions, angling around in several directions at the sides, and the almost too severe right-angled bilateral symmetry of the central portion. This new work, according to the engraving, is tightly organized on a single sight-line from a frontal drawbridge over the moat, through the Gate Pavilion and across the Court of Honor, then on through the main central wing of the château and along the center of a large rectangular garden, to terminate on the great Salle or Music Hall at the far end. The château and its appurtenances, basically U-shaped with wings, are developed with nearly complete bilateral symmetry around the Court of Honor and two slightly varying side courts. The large open garden, to be sure, is in the old medieval checkerboard pattern, with two fountains and no other internal relief; but for the first time in France one sees here a clearly defined outdoor space that is definitely anchored to the château by visual means. A moat still surrounds the whole complex.

After the early death of Henri II in 1559 his three weak sons, Francis II, Charles IX, and Henri III, each ruled in turn under the motherly but dominating hand of Dowager Queen Catherine dei Medici. In those thirty years France was too preoccupied with internal religious wars to produce much in the arts. About midway in the period, however, a remarkable project was initiated: Charleval, designed in 1572 for young Charles IX probably by Du Cerceau, whose plan for the great establishment is available today even though no physical evidence of Charleval itself remains (Fig. 118).

Charleval's exact location is uncertain; it lay somewhere near the Seine between Rouen and Paris. Du Cerceau's plan does not suggest the prior existence of any medieval foundations, though works of lesser magnitude in those days were seldom built entirely afresh. At any rate, if there were old walls to build on at Charleval they must have been demolished, for the Du Cerceau plan is such a sophisticated essay in rigorously bounded rectilinearity and bilateral symmetry as to seem academic almost to the point of theoretical formalism. Such extreme (some would say excessive) elaboration and refinement of Renaissance spatial design at a date relatively so early in France is all the more surprising when one considers that, even a generation or two later, many works of some renown had far less finesse.

In 1589, at Henri III's death, the House of Valois came to an end and was replaced on the throne by the House of Bourbon in the person of Henri IV, a distant cousin who had married Margaret of Valois, a sister of Henri

118. Charleval, designed by Du Cerceau for young Charles IX but never built.

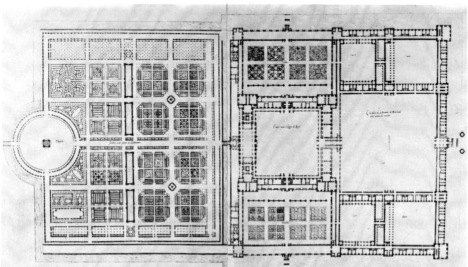

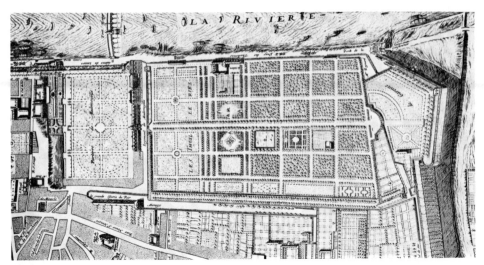

119. Paris: the gardens of the Tuileries as recorded by Jacques Gomboust in his famous map of Paris in 1652.

III. The religious wars over, active building was resumed and a period ensued that was of importance to the development of French landscape architecture, largely because of personal interest on the part of Henri IV. Credit is also due two of the king's loyal subjects: his chief gardener, Claude Mollet, whose influence was felt for generations and whose sons played a large part in transporting French ideas to England, and Jacques Boyceau, the ingenious developer of a major French contribution, the parterre.

To grasp the full significance of advances during the reign of Henri IV, it must be remembered that, once defensive siting such as that of Amboise or Blois was no longer needed, the great châteaux of France were usually located on wide extensions of flat terrain rather than on slopes as in hilly Italy. In the flatter topography of France this was only natural, and of course the broad treatment provided admirable background for the showy spectacles of a large court. In the change, however, the château garden had become a rather tedious flat expanse of checkerboard beds with nothing but typically child-like mechanical patterns of hedging, even though the French climate would have permitted a richness of floral growth that was all but impossible in the heat of Italy.

This was approximately the situation that felt the lively impact of Henri IV and Mollet and Boyceau. Their energy came to a focal point in the royal gardens of the Tuileries in Paris, where Catherine dei Medici a generation earlier (1564) had caused a very stiff layout to be done along with Philibert de l'Orme's designs for her grand new palace. Mollet proposed in the Tuileries a richer, more varied treatment (Fig. 119), less wearying than the habitual old checkerboard and more abundant in floral color. Boyceau occupied himself with devising for Mollet and the King ever more playful and intricate

120. The Tuileries today, toward the Louvre from the Place de la Concorde.

121. Reverse of the preceding view, looking toward the Place de la Concorde and the Arc de Triomphe.

patterns for use within the beds. A special goal was a single grand overall decorative pattern for the garden, with each bed or segment carrying its constituent part of the total design. In effect, Boyceau was working toward a reflection of the silken brocades and embroideries being used in fashionable dress—a species of floral embroidery on the ground or *broderie par terre,* from which came the habit of calling anything a parterre that had a pattern worked out in flowering plants.

Of all these improvements in the Tuileries little physical evidence remains today (Figs. 120, 121) because the place was redone again some fifty or sixty years later. From contemporary engravings, one would judge that in general arrangement the work of Mollet and Boyceau was not an overwhelming advance over what had preceded. But in its total effect there can be little doubt that the new spirit in the Tuileries prepared the way for much of the colorful splendor that was eventually considered the chief characteristic of French landscape architecture.

Passing attention should be paid to what Henri IV did at Fontainebleau, of which he was very proud. He made numerous additions to palace and grounds, but under Francis I the overall plan had so sadly got off on the wrong foot that these amendments could not bring order but only increased confusion. A truly notable place established under Henri IV was Saint Germain-en-Laye, down the left bank of the Seine about ten miles from Paris. Here the foundations of a thirteenth-century castle of Louis IX had been built upon by Francis I and added to by Henri II, but Henri IV ignored what had preceded and began anew. Although virtually nothing is left on the ground today except one so-called Pavilion of Henri IV, contemporary accounts and engravings do exist. They show clearly the Italian influence of the Queen, Maria dei Medici (whom Henri IV married in 1600 after divorcing Margaret of Valois). In simple fact the site plainly calls for hillside treatment and consequent vertical planes, rather than for the sweeping horizontality then typical of French châteaux. Under these circumstances, it must have seemed to Maria dei Medici an ideal solution to employ for Saint Germain-en-Laye the French architect Etienne du Pérac, who in 1582 had returned from Italy with unbridled enthusiasm for the Italian villa—and who had dedicated to the Queen a set of drawings of the Villa d'Este. The plans for the new place were done by Du Pérac and Claude Mollet with a Florentine, Tommaso Francini, called in to help with the waterworks.

What emerged, judging by contemporary accounts and engravings, must have been a monumentally impressive affair, as well as the center of court excitement as the favorite residence of Henri IV. There were no less than six large terraces, assembled with other intermediate levels on one central sight-line that plunged down the slope from the new palace at the top to the Seine at the bottom. Each level was treated in its own unique way; there were numerous fountains and grottoes; the transitions from terrace to terrace were made with compact stairways folded back against their retaining walls in the customary Italian manner. It is indeed regrettable that the great fabric has been allowed to disintegrate so completely, for it would be interesting to see how such an Italianate work would appear in France today under the beneficent mellowing influence of overgrown vegetation—as has occurred at the Villa d'Este, of which Du Pérac and Mollet must have been thinking while at work on Saint Germain-en-Laye.

Another royal project in Paris that was intended to seem Italian but never wholly succeeded was the Luxembourg (Fig. 122), ordered in 1615 by Maria dei Medici after the assassination of Henri IV (1610); the new young ruler, Henri's son Louis XIII, was born at Saint Germain-en-Laye in 1601 and was subject to the strong-willed regency of the Queen until 1617. She apparently took her Medicean heritage to heart and made herself thoroughly unpopular by attempting to rule with an iron hand; the story of her struggles with Cardinal Richelieu until both of their deaths in 1642 is well known. Her exaggeratedly firm will had an immediate effect upon the new residence on the left bank where, as Queen Mother, she planned to live during her widowhood.

It is quite generally accepted, unbelievable as it seems on a visit to the Luxembourg today, that Maria dei Medici ordered the place to be modeled on the Florentine Palazzo Pitti and its Boboli Gardens. Salomon de Brosse

122. Paris: the Luxembourg gardens of modern times.

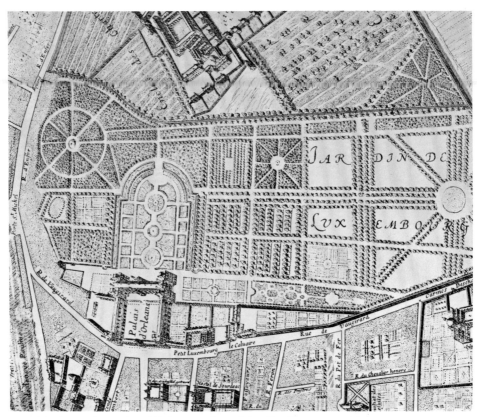

123. The Luxembourg in 1652 in a section of the Gomboust town plan.

designed the palace, and Boyceau is said to have created here some of his most famous parterres. But the flat terrain of Paris rendered imitation of Italy pointless if not impossible. The gardens of the Luxembourg have undergone so many changes that their original form can only be conjectured. Certainly the grounds were more extensive than they are now; but according to the Gomboust plan of Paris, dated 1652 (Fig. 123), the layout was rather clumsy geometrically. Today, of course, the gardens are among the most delightful of public parks, filled with lively but well-mannered Parisian children and their varicolored balloons.

In its historical context the Luxembourg serves principally as a milestone in the development of French landscape architecture from the crudities of Amboise and Blois to the high sophistication of the mid-seventeenth century. The Luxembourg ushers in the reign of Louis XIII, the king who built a momentous hunting lodge near the village of Versailles; thus it paves the way for his amazing son, the fabulous Louis XIV, and for the era of that greatest of French landscape architects, André le Nôtre, who was born during the reign of Louis XIII while the father, Jean, was a gardener at the Tuileries.

XII. André le Nôtre: Vaux-le-Vicomte and Versailles

In 1638 a son was born to Louis XIII and his queen, Anne of Austria, and a whole new epoch opened. The boy became king, Louis XIV, a mere five years later—starting a reign of stupendous influence on all of Europe, one that would make the seventeenth century of Western history undeniably the century of Louis XIV. For landscape architecture, too, it was an era of great dimensions: in the year of Louis XIV's birth the young André le Nôtre reached age twenty-five and his second year as successor to his father as head gardener of the Tuileries. The lives of the two, monarch and subject, in an unvarying atmosphere of mutual devotion and respect, would forever be associated through the subject's creation for his king: Versailles.

Before appraising this tremendous royal establishment it is wise to consider Vaux-le-Vicomte, a smaller and earlier work of Le Nôtre that is regarded by many authorities as technically superior to the larger project. At the Tuileries, André's father, Jean le Nôtre, worked under the supervision of Claude Mollet; the relationship must have been close, for Madame Mollet was André's godmother. There can be little doubt that the boy grew up in a creative climate, which became all the more significant for his future when his father sent him to the studio of Simon Vouët, one of the painters most in royal favor, for grounding in the arts. In the meantime, of course, son was learning the practicalities of horticulture from father, always under the reflected influence of Mollet, in the gardens of the Tuileries. When he was twenty-four (1637) André virtually inherited the appointment theretofore held

Légende

A _ le château
B _ la cour d'honneur
C _ le bassin des couronnes
D _ le confessionnal
E _ les cascades
H _ la grotte
I _ la gerbe
K _ la grille d'eau.

. ECHELLE o   50   100   200   300 METRES.

124. Vaux-le-Vicomte, near
Melun, plan.

by his father at the Tuileries. During the formative years that followed, some
independent projects appear to have held André's attention, such as work
for Cardinal Richelieu at Rueil and major responsibility for changes and
additions at Chantilly, the great château of the Condés. But the epochal

opportunity came when he was commissioned to do the grounds of Vaux-le-Vicomte for Nicolas Fouquet, finance minister to the king.

Fouquet, under the tutelage of the powerful Cardinal Mazarin, had himself become a figure of importance—and, incidentally, of great wealth—though in the process he had naturally developed political enemies. In 1656, having decided to build a country residence more magnificent than any previously done privately, he engaged Le Nôtre, along with the painter Le Brun and the architect Le Vau, to create the great place now known as Vaux-le-Vicomte near the village of Melun, between Paris and Fontainebleau. Work was begun in 1656 and finished in 1661, with the target a fête for Louis XIV, then twenty-three and already profoundly conscious of his exalted station.

The result was a triumph in every way except one. For the flamboyant court circles of the day, Vaux was an excellent theatrical backdrop; for succeeding generations of admirers it was an exquisite example of creative human handiwork; for Fouquet in a personal sense it was a disaster, as the King had already become suspicious of his handling of state finances, and the obviously lavish expenditures at Vaux brought these doubts to a climax. The headstrong young Louis XIV may well have taken a rather jaundiced view of such opulent display on the part of a mere subject, who thus appeared not to have carefully enough avoided outshining his monarch. Within a few days after seeing Vaux the King had Fouquet arrested. A long series of trials followed, in which the case against Fouquet was undoubtedly stacked by his enemies; he spent the rest of his life in prison and died there in 1680. Meanwhile, Louis XIV, deeply impressed by the successful work of the collaborative team, ordered the three to undertake at Versailles a development that would put Fouquet's place to shame.

The years have been kind to Vaux-le-Vicomte; it remains almost exactly as contemporary engravings depict it, and its owners for many years have guarded its original condition and given it superb maintenance. Its basic plan is very simple: there is one dominant sight-line central to the entire scheme, with several secondary sight-lines crossing the main one and visually perpendicular to it (Fig. 124). The primacy of the central line is immediately evident when one arrives before the gates, having traveled out the straight, poplar-lined highway from Melun. Suddenly a large semicircular clearing appears in the surrounding woods, south of which, beyond a long grille of wrought iron with high stone sculptured posts or terms, the château and its two generous forecourts lie backed into the sun. From the entrance gates, hung in the middle of the grille, everything that the eye can see is apparently balanced on the sight-line running from the gates to the main north portal of the château.

Immediately inside the gates is the open forecourt, a square space in four turf panels bordered and crossed by gravel roadways. Beyond it, still balanced on the central sight-line, is the arrival court, Le Cour d'Honneur, an integral part of the château and accordingly reached only by crossing the stone-walled moat that surrounds it. Across the middle of the forecourt a sight-line leads east and west to the two handsome brick and stone service groups, each wrapped around its own outdoor space, with a screen guarding the side toward the forecourt. The brick and stone of the two screens continues around into the ends of the long grille facing the highway and extends south toward the château, forming at the southern edge of the forecourt a pair of unusual arcades high above the corners of the moat.

Stepping through the arcade to east or to west and then turning at once toward the south, one descends a simple flight of steps, at the outer edge of the moat, to one of the two gay parterres, backed by heavy *bosquets,* at this slightly lower level to east and west of the château. The parterre on the east is about twice as wide as that on the west—the first noticeable instance of the plan's several departures from what seems at first glance a complete bilateral symmetry.

Observable also at this point is one of the technical devices for which Vaux is justly noted: the heightening of interest by accentuation of even the slightest difference in grade in a fundamentally flat countryside. Because the side parterres are at a lower level than the forecourt and the arrival court, the surface in the moat is nearer the observer here, the château seems actually to reach upward from the water, and the main indoor floor, about at the level of the arrival court, takes on an almost theatrical prominence above everything around it.

The elevated posture of the château becomes especially apparent on turning the corner of the moat to see the rather elaborately terraced bridge and steps from the main south portal across the moat and down to ground level. From the foot of these widening steps one has the full impact of the garden layout of Vaux (Fig. 125), spread to the south before the eye, held firmly at the sides by the dark green foliage of the heavy bosquets, their lower portion clipped or fronted by tall hedging. The whole magnificent prospect, though clearly an entity as one tremendous open space, may be regarded as comprising four integrated parts, all assembled on the dominant central sight-line: the upper level of highly ornate parterres, reaching as far as the crosswise pools called Le Petit Canal; the slightly lower level of the main garden, still rich but less intricate than the parterres nearer the château; the large canal lying across the central sight-line, with Les Cascades on the near side hidden from view and Les Grottes on the far side as a sort of terminal; above all, the long, grassy allée moving up over the hill and off into the unseen distance.

The first or upper level of parterres is itself composed of three divisions: a middle portion, holding two parterres in a brilliant pattern of red gravel, emerald turf, and darker green hedging; a western somewhat quieter portion, mainly in turf; and the eastern portion, wider than the others (and thus again departing from full bilateral symmetry), with turf panels and a fanciful gilt

125. View from the château over the expansive parterres of Vaux.

fountain known as La Couronne. The three divisions are actually at three distinctive levels, descending from west to east, but the differences of elevation are so slight and the transitions so subtle as to be noticeable only from the steps joining the levels. Fronting on all three divisions and above all three levels is the long gravel terrace at the foot of the bridge and steps across the moat. This terrace, narrow at the level of the side parterres east and west of the château, extends back into the bosquets a short distance—it is the first of the secondary sight-lines crossing the main central one, quite minor, with little emphasis at the ends. From this terrace, two successive sets of generously wide steps in the center lead down gently, by only six or seven risers each, into the middle portion of the upper parterres. At the far end of this level, directly on the central sight-line, is a low circular pool with a single high, elegantly thin jet. From it, extending east and west, is a wide gravel walk that reaches far back into the bosquets, a stronger secondary sight-line than the other one up near the château.

Immediately beyond the circular pool of the upper level, two sets of a few steps, again generous in proportion, descend to the lower level of the huge garden. The steps lie between the ends of the two long, quiet pools of the Petit Canal, whose east-west orientation reinforces the effect of the long gravel walk just described. The lower level of the garden, twice as long as the upper, has large turf panels, with two oval pools in the panels and a square one between them at the far end. Opposite the square pool, tucked into the eastern bosquet, is the somewhat surprising structure known as Le Confessionnal, a sort of overlook from which the diagonal view northwestward toward the

126. Vaux-le-Vicomte: diagonal view toward the château from the Confessional.

château provides a fairly comprehensive impression of the richness of the gardens (Fig. 126).

From here the wide-reaching horizontality of the whole is the outstanding characteristic: flat planes of land and somehow even flatter water, as still as a mirror. Even the subtle changes of grade, which lend so much interest and offset the vastness that might otherwise seem only monotonous, are scarcely perceptible when seen thus at an angle and from a distance. Over all is a sense of uncompromising vigor and firmness—of materials, form, color. There is nothing meager about the scene. Restless, perhaps, it seems to some observers, with too many statues and too many clipped global or conical evergreens, yet always positive, never unsure of itself. And color everywhere shimmers under the bright sun: warm pink in all the gravel walks and terraces, blue sky reflected in the quiet pools, red and emerald green parterres with deeper blue-green in the hedging; white or near-white in weatherbeaten marble statues—all of it gleaming surely against the dark masses of purple and green in the bosquets.

Another advantage of seeing the garden from the Confessional is that from there one questionable characteristic of the design, a flaw insistently troublesome in the view from the south portal of the château, can be avoided. The ample straight path all the way down the central sight-line tends to split the scene quite badly—recalling the happier effect at the Villa Lante and anticipating one in the Tapis Vert at Versailles.

Beyond the Confessional and the lower level of the garden, descent by ramps and steps leads to the only surprise, the row of fountains known, with their basin, as the Cascades. They are so concealed by the drop in grade as to be totally cut off from view until the observer is right upon them. They face the main crosswise Grand Canal, which lies athwart the main central sight-line and opens out at its nearby eastern end into a large circular stone-walled pool, where sham naval battles could be held and probably were in Vaux's heyday.

On the south side of the canal, across from the Cascades and facing the château, is the arcaded feature called Les Grottes. Its rough arches and basins are not themselves as interesting as the sophisticated series of low rectilinear terraces, in gravel with stone edging, around the square pool into which the Grand Canal is widened in front of the Grottos.

Above and beyond this, reached by ramps or steps, is the broad turf allée, lined by double rows of trees at the sides with dense bosquets behind them. In a fashion that so frequently renders a French allée different from a typical Italian viale, this long directional space appears to have no specific terminus but marches off over the hill to the infinitude of distant mystery. A gigantic gilded replica of the famous classical Hercules was placed in the allée years ago—surely not by Le Nôtre; ineffective and functioning not at all as a focal point, it would best be considered a well-meant recent mistake.

127. Vaux-le-Vicomte from the air.

As a whole, in its integrity as a single, strongly knit composition, Vaux-le-Vicomte is a superb example of French landscape architecture at its pinnacle (Fig. 127). This is not to say, of course, that it achieves the impossible by being perfect. Besides the few shortcomings already mentioned, some observers feel—and not entirely without justification—that the view of the garden from the château is too all-inclusive, that seeing so much of the total in one vast scene is oppressive, producing a condition of visual surfeit. Clearly, the original intent of this fabulous display was to impress and overwhelm rather than charm with subtle delicacies, and no doubt success attended these efforts for a glittering court. But somehow today, for all its richness of color and refinement of detail, one cannot help wishing that Vaux would hold more in reserve with which to greet the visitor in succeeding moments instead of bowling him over by showing him all, exposed and unframed, in a single first glance.

Vaux-le-Vicomte is nevertheless a truly great monument to the ability of Le Nôtre and perhaps his best creation. Versailles is better known, larger, and far more sumptuous, but in comparison Vaux is a little jewel, more delicate in detail, more intimate and even domestic in spirit. There is about it a kind of aristocratic restraint that is quite remarkable. The impression will be all the more certain and memorable if one contrives to see Versailles first.

It is the grandiose royal establishment at Versailles that most closely links the names of Le Nôtre and Louis XIV and that will remain always the most widely recognized physical symbol of the great Sun King, Le Roi Soleil, as he permitted himself to be called. Vaux-le-Vicomte was an accomplished fact when Versailles was nothing but the brick and stone hunting lodge on the edge of a wide, swampy tract built for Louis XIII by Salomon de Brosse in 1624, with a few parterres by Boyceau. The outlook at Versailles can hardly have been an enthralling sight to Le Nôtre, Le Vau, and Le Brun when Louis XIV, having pre-empted Fouquet's collaborative team, in effect ordered them to do at Versailles what they had done at Vaux but to do it bigger and better.

Work on the grounds began during winter 1661–62 and proceeded at a furious pace for many years. Cost was obviously never given serious consideration: millions were spent on materials, and labor could be had without limit. The army, of course, was available at all times and frequently used: the large Pièce des Suisses was so named because the Swiss Guards dug it! There is a long list of artists and artisans employed on the work, including over ninety sculptors. The king's personal interest in horticulture led to the importing of some three thousand orange trees from Italy, to be added to the twelve hundred "appropriated" from Vaux-le-Vicomte during the first winter of the operation. There were eventually twenty acres of kitchen gardens, with such exotic delicacies as pineapples and coffee trees, and asparagus at Christmas.

It did not take long for the king to center his full affection on Versailles and to cap this mood by moving the court bodily from the Louvre in Paris to this place that was more clearly his very own in a personal sense. In time the court numbered in the thousands: it is said that ultimately five thousand were accommodated in the enlarged palace and three times that number in the town that grew up around it.

Development of the grounds had gone on for some seven years before anything was done about the château. In 1668 Louis realized that more ample housing was required for his court and that the gardens had grown over-powering in relation to his father's little hunting lodge, of which he was inordinately fond. Accordingly, to meet the need but without damaging his childhood love, he directed Le Vau to provide additional room in the château while preserving intact the original building of brick and stone. By working around the old structure, Le Vau started the long process of adding more and more that eventually resulted in the enormous palace of the present. But it should be remembered that here, not as usual, the gardens came first and the palace was enlarged to fit them (Fig. 128).

The peculiar history of the palace, with its emphasis on the inviolability of the original hunting lodge, is important as a key to the design of Versailles as a whole. The very center of the "little pasteboard château" of Louis XIII was occupied by the king's bedroom, and Louis XIV—perhaps because of his affection for the older building, perhaps because he sensed the symbolic implications involved—saw to it that the dominant central position of the hunting lodge, and thus of the *chambre du roi* within it, was not modified or lost. At the court of France, a courtier's personal status was in large part measured by the frequency with which he was summoned by the king as one of a group to attend at his morning rising (*levée*), an event of remarkable ceremony that took place in the *chambre du roi*. Much as if it were literally the throne of France, it thus achieved a special and intimate distinction as the site for dispensing royal favor.

It is hardly conceivable that so astute a man as Louis XIV could have failed to appreciate the effect of his determination to retain the hunting lodge unchanged at the heart of the new developments. At any rate, as a conse-quence of the decision—reflecting an egocentric attitude apparently accepted as normal in the king by the society of his time—everything at Versailles was focused inescapably upon the all-important room in the center of the château, the one point of paramount significance as a symbol of the supremely exalted person of Le Roi Soleil.

If Versailles is to be truly appreciated, its background must be understood. The whole great scheme, for all its intricacy of parts, is built around an essentially simple skeleton consisting of two long sight-lines (Fig. 129). Of these the dominant one, naturally enough, extends from the center of the château to seeming infinity eastward and westward. The other, perpendicular

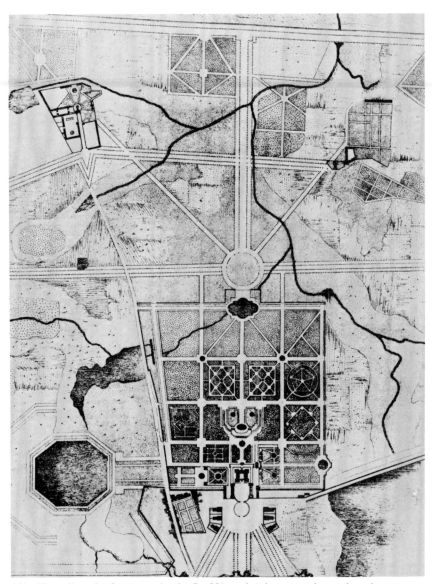

128. Versailles: the first stage in the Le Nôtre development shows the scheme growing outward from the hunting lodge of Louis XIII.

to the first, crosses it atop the very first terrace west of the château and extends to north and south, parallel to the face of the building. On this basic framework the main elements of the grandiose arrangement were in place by 1670; by 1685 all was about as it is today, including the huge Water Parterre, which had undergone three revisions. Additions and adjustments continued, of course, throughout the remaining years of the king's reign until his death in 1715, but none of the changes materially affected the total design.

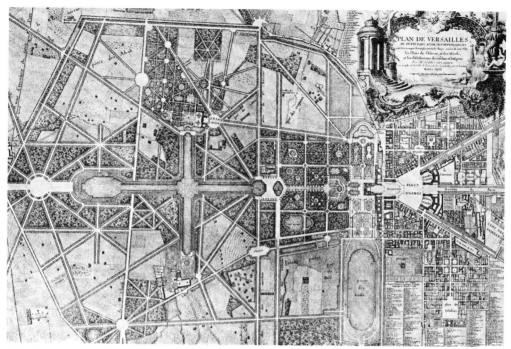

129. Versailles: the Delagrive engraving of 1746.

Approaching the east front of the château today from the town (Fig. 130), one is conscious primarily of an enormous expanse of unrelieved space—the Place d'Armes and a succession of smaller courts, demarked only by low stone balustrades and open wrought-iron fences, leading to the final intimate court below the windows of the king's bedroom in the old hunting lodge. The whole composition is obviously balanced on the great central sight-line, but the combined open spaces, along with the three avenues converging on the Place d'Armes from within the town, are so vast as to seem quite unintelligible unless one succeeds in imagining the scene thronged with people, carriages, horses, and other court trappings. After all, the two big stable groups facing the other side of the Place d'Armes could house, at their prime, some twenty-five hundred horses and a correspondingly large number of coaches.

There is a similar need for imagination on the part of an observer passing to the west or garden side of the palace; he must continually people the walks and terraces with crowds of courtiers and ladies in rustling silk finery. But no part of the grounds is so requisite of fancy as the area immediately to the west of the château (Fig. 131). Snug against the facade of the whole central block is the relatively narrow band of the first terrace, bordered only by the five wide treads of its own steps. On this terrace lies the long north-south sight-line of the plan. Directly in front of the terrace, and sweeping back around to right and left of the projecting central block of the palace itself,

130. Air view of Versailles from above the town.

is the immense Parterre d'Eau, the Water Parterre that was revised three times before, in 1684, it finally satisfied the king. Both here and on the terrace the question of scale is challenging; some impression of it may be gained from either of the single vases that stand at the two outer corners of the terrace. In plan, or from an aerial photograph, the vases appear modest enough; actually each is about twice as high as an average person. Similarly the vast Parterre d'Eau, with its two prodigious but low-coped basins of flat, normally still water, tends to dwarf the usual small groups of visitors but somehow becomes convincing if the observer envisions a mass of courtiers crowding around the wheeled sedan chair of the king.

The plateau covered by the Parterre d'Eau is apparently an earth fill put in place, and projecting much too far in the judgment of many critics, early in the building operation. From its outer edge, spread ahead to the west on the main sight-line, is one of the world's most famous and imposing views: across the Fountain and Parterre of Latona, down the Tapis Vert to the Basin of Apollo, and along to the Grand Canal reaching on and on toward the remote horizon—where during part of the year the brilliant setting sun becomes an exactly placed terminal feature, regarded by Louis XIV and his minions as a fitting counterfoil for the radiance of the great Sun King himself.

The Fountain of Latona, a four-tiered cake-like arrangement with a statue of the goddess on the top layer, is fitted with piping for an elaborate display

131. The Parterre du Midi, Parterre d'Eau, and Parterre du Nord in a historic moment at Versailles as delegates arrive to sign the peace treaty in 1919.

of gushing water. To be appreciated fully it should of course be seen with the waters operating to make it a marvelous confection in foaming white. This is true of the many fountains at Versailles, and the French government (owner of the property) provides the fantastic show of spuming water on certain preannounced days. On a day of *les grandes eaux,* the Latona is truly a sight to behold. Even dry it serves well its function as a sort of fulcrum between the Parterre d'Eau at the upper level and the Tapis Vert, at the top of which the Latona sits in its own florid Parterre; one of its chief merits to this end is the variety of ways one can descend to it from above, by wide central steps, narrower steps at the sides, or long circumferential ramps on the periphery.

The Tapis Vert, sloping gently down to the west from the Parterre of Latona, is an architectonic corridor in the best French tradition, tightly formed between the deep green bosquets. Down each side is a line of marble sculptures and behind these a row of trees, trimmed to a height of ten or fifteen feet, revealing a continuous line of high hedge or treillage behind the columnar trunks. The "green carpet" of the name refers to the broad central panel of turf; here again is an instance where placing the gravel walks at the sides, rather than in the middle, preserves the fine integrity of the space by avoiding the type of visual split encountered at Vaux-le-Vicomte.

132. The Bassin d'Apollon and the Tapis Vert, looking back toward the château early in this century.

At the foot of the Tapis Vert the edges of the bosquets retreat to form a sizeable open space; in the near end of this is the Basin of Apollo (Fig. 132), a sort of preliminary punctuation to the seemingly endless ribbon of the Grand Canal. In the center of the basin is the large bronze group of Apollo emerging from the water in his chariot, drawn by four galloping horses and preceded by three trumpeters astride leaping dolphins. On days of *les grandes eaux,* the whole is a mass of spouting white water with high and low jets shooting into the air in a welter of mist. To many designers this basin, when the waters play, serves as a more effective terminus to the central vista than the long canal, which appears to end in nothing unless it catches the setting sun.

Turning and retracing steps up the Tapis Vert, past the Latona to the high level of the Parterre d'Eau, one can follow the secondary sight-line to south and north while standing on the first narrow terrace. Southward, assembled on the sight-line, are three major units. First the broad expanse of the Parterre du Midi, large colorful panels and two very low circular pools, all against a field of wide pinkish gravel walks at a level only a few steps below the Parterre d'Eau. The floral patterns, changed from year to year and with the seasons, are rich in color but straightforward in design, without the feeling of fussy embroidery so often associated with French parterres. Beyond the Parterre du Midi, at a much lower level, is the garden of the Orangery, reached only by two ponderous flights of "hundred steps" at the sides. This large area is in front of the Orangery itself, which is under the Parterre du Midi; as a garden, it contains a large flat circular pool and trees set in their own tubs, sometimes oranges or lemons, sometimes palms. Still farther south is the placid surface of the big, rather formless pond called the Pièce des Suisses, with Bernini's equestrian statue of Louis XIV placed (with patriotic Francophile fervor?) at the far end, just barely visible against the dark background of bosquet.

The same secondary sight-line, as it runs north from the terrace of the château, is considerably more eventful than it is to the south. To be sure, the Parterre du Nord balances the Parterre du Midi in an overall way, but its pattern is changed to have a strong directional quality; the two circular pools are no longer central within their parterre panels but lie to the north, and a handsome fountain aptly known as the Pyramid is in the middle of the northern side of the whole space, right on the sight-line. Just beyond this, though partially blocked by the Pyramid, the sight-line slides almost too steeply down the slope of a nicely controlled slot of space carved through the bosquets. This is the Allée d'Eau, sometimes called the Allée des Marmousets, with a central walk and two long grass panels each with a widely spaced row of small fountains, formed by groups of children standing in round pools and supporting flat, saucer-like basins and small central jets.

At the bottom of the Allée is the Basin of the Dragon, a circular pool with a central half-submerged bronze dragon surrounded by dolphins and by swans ridden by arrow-shooting Cupids. When the waters are playing the dragon spouts a prodigious white stream high into the air; the other members of the group send smaller jets arching toward the edge of the pool. Then, as though this were not yet enough water, the sight-line finally reaches the Basin of Neptune, a broad pool with a lower water level than that of the Basin of the Dragon. Rather pretentiously shaped, it contains several complex bronze sculptural groups and has across its edge a row of many vases. When the "great waters" are working, jets rise from the vases in a wide white screen, to the accompaniment of arching, foaming sprays from the groups in the water and the higher and heavier jet from the Dragon.

The works thus assembled on the two principal sight-lines are impressive with the almost unbelievable grandeur and posturing of Versailles, but there is a different aspect to be considered (see Fig. 129). In the shadowy recesses of the thick bosquets lies a whimsical side of things, evidences of playfulness, of delight with the brightly ephemeral, that to modern eyes can make life at Versailles in the seventeenth century seem like one long glorious house-party weekend.

The wooded area as a whole extends from the large open spaces by the château outward on both sides of the Tapis Vert and the Grand Canal, but the portion usually referred to as the bosquets stops at the wide crosswise Allée of Apollo. These bosquets are divided into approximately square blocks by two pairs of internal allées, one east-west, the other north-south, with low circular basins at the four crossings (Fig. 133). Within the blocks a wide

133. A characteristic allée and crossing in the Versailles bosquets.

assortment of amusing features was installed, some intended to be permanent but most erected for immediate use and subsequent change. Accounts of the time mention elaborate temporary stage-settings for plays by Molière and Racine; music was written for specific occasions, often by Lully; there was gilt treillage in abundance and gaiety galore. At unexpected points throughout the bosquets, secret squirts of water played tricks on the unwary; apparently all was frivolity and a game to conquer boredom by inventing new trifles. Of particular interest today are the marble Colonnade, rich in fountains and sculpture, and the Salle du Bal, with its jets and cascade of fanciful work in *rocaille*. The Theatre d'Eau must have been charming, with its jet-framed stage, but little of it is left. In the block at the foot of each of the two ramps around the Fountain and Parterre of Latona, a carefully maintained quincunx fascinates visitors with its orchard-like five-way planting of trees. These quincunxes are of relatively recent growth, to be sure, but so are most of the trees of the bosquets. The entire wooded area has undergone devastation and regrowth several times, consequently only a few of the seventeenth-century creations can have remained. Indeed, the remarkable truth is that on the whole the place has succeeded well in conveying a sense of the spirit that must have prevailed, a fabulous mixture of serious and frivolous, pompous pose and impertinence.

XIII. England under the Tudors

As France had been understandably slower than Italy to show the impact of the Renaissance, so was England delayed and even more—as though distance from Florence were somehow a decisive factor in the absorption of the new enlightenment. The same slowly evolving pattern of time is discernible also in the achievement of national status in landscape architecture: the fifteenth century belonged to Florence, the sixteenth to Rome, the seventeenth to France. The eighteenth century brought England into position as the leader of fashion with its pervasive "landscape gardening school." The process of reaching that point, however, took just about two centuries after the first hint of Renaissance influence, even longer than it had taken France to reach pre-eminence under Le Nôtre.

Until well into the sixteenth century England was embroiled in intermittent warfare, first the Hundred Years' War with France and then the internal War of the Roses, which did not simmer down until rival claims of the Houses of Lancaster and York were merged in the bulky person of Henry VIII in 1509. That the succession should have fallen to this particular man is a matter of importance to the development of English landscape architecture.

It is not to be supposed that no significant building had occurred in England before Henry VIII and the dawn of the English Renaissance. The island had gone through the Middle Ages with much the same kind of richness as in other parts of the Western world, and here again the primary strength appears to have been ecclesiastical. From the days of Norman domination in the eleventh century, a succession of glorious cathedrals marked the passage of the years and remain today to excite one's admiration, from early Durham through Canterbury and Salisbury to Wells, York, and Gloucester; increasingly the monasteries, acquiring larger and larger holdings, enriched the land with

134. Warwick Castle; the defensive character of secular building in England echoes the Norman conquest.

abbeys and cloisters. There were secular developments, too, though less striking ones: the towns grew defensively on Roman remains; castles were frequent and as forbidding as elsewhere, with little or no attention to pleasant handling of the land. Such domestic examples as Warwick Castle (Fig. 134) and the early portions of Haddon Hall, in Derbyshire, continue to beguile today's observer with suggestions of the rudeness of country life in England from the eleventh century well through the fifteenth.

But in the reign of Henry VIII news at last trickled through about developments in Italy. Henry's great rivals, Francis I of France and Charles V of Spain, were by now thoroughly committed to the new forms and values of the Renaissance, and Henry naturally tried to follow suit within the limits of his comprehension. His tie with Rome was at first a firm one, his rejoinder to Martin Luther's doctrines having led Pope Leo X to designate him "Defender of the Faith"; and it was widely rumored that his favorite, Cardinal Wolsey, had hopes of election to the papacy himself. Then between 1527 and 1534 came the long quarrel with the Holy See over the King's divorce from Catharine of Aragon, ending in his complete break with Rome and excommunication.

It was the aftermath of the struggle between Henry and the Church of Rome that so strongly affected the course of life upon the land in England. In retaliation against Rome, the King in 1536 began suppressing the monasteries, dissolving them, and confiscating their properties. Between 1536 and 1539, it is estimated, about one-third of all the land in England changed ownership as Henry honored his favorites with grants of the newly "liberated" holdings. Some properties were occupied and enlarged by their new owners; other recipients of the royal favor sold their gifts to recently wealthy merchants or agriculturists. The redistribution of land ownership, together with the greater safety of rural conditions, quickly stimulated the growth of a kind of country living eventually regarded as a major characteristic of Britain. From the same sources arose also the typical English "country place"—a term designating as an entity the house and outbuildings, with sizable acreage, comprising a country residence, usually for the summer season but in many instances for all-year use.

From the first, of course, topography and climate exerted their expectable influence on development of the new country places. In England, where the forms of land vary a great deal—from abrupt hills to sweeping plains, with almost every other geological type between them—neither the verticality of the Italian villa nor the horizontality of the châteaux of France could become dominant. The English country house is seldom found at either the top or the bottom of a slope; usually it is halfway up. If it is on a flattish terrain it will be set on a slight rise for purposes of surface drainage, a matter of no slight importance in this damp climate.

Even more than the topography, however, the English climate was and is the controlling factor. The most thoroughly English characteristic of the island's landscape architecture arises from the abundance of moisture, and the relative sunlessness as contrasted with the other extreme in Italy. The English perennial border, that band of floral exuberance with which the country places of Britain are usually enriched, is a natural consequence of a climate perfectly adapted to plant growth. So, too, is the emerald turf of England's lawns and bowling greens. Throughout, whether in the extraordinary amount of glass in the walls of even the earliest houses, or in the scarcity of cooling fountains and shade-producing structures, the English country home reveals itself to be a heliotropic or sun-seeking affair and just the opposite, in this sense, of the Italian villa.

In England, to a degree perhaps more pronounced than elsewhere, works of landscape architecture were affected by the political or evaluational conditions of the times, as well as by the usual physical factors. The break between Henry VIII and Rome had another marked consequence: instead of bringing in large numbers of Italian artisans, as Francis I had done, Henry VIII and his new landed gentry called upon Flemish and German craftsmen or on local workers even less familiar with the classical details of the Renaissance. This may be the reason for the peculiar, but distinctively English, mixture of techniques in architectural detail and for the almost doll-like scale in even the most Italianate of forms. Especially noticeable in English houses is the woodworking character given to details, presumably by North European artisans, even when they were working in stone.

Stability and safety had blessed the English countryside as the brawling Middle Ages died away under the prosperity and the centralized regal strength of the Tudor regime. Thanks no doubt to the sense of security, the new country homes of England came to have a comfortable domesticity to which the somewhat diminutive scale quite naturally contributed. The homely atmosphere, in fact, has persisted through the years and has sometimes puzzled the archeologically minded. Owners have shown no hesitation about keeping up with the times and adding new elements to house and grounds simply as a matter of comfort. The result is that in many instances the place one visits today is a composite of many times and many influences; the "pure" specimen is hard to find among English country places.

This tendency toward mixture of types was further affected by another characteristic that developed among the English in the course of time, manifesting itself in design as well as in political matters: the national genius for cultural assimilation, noted in its governmental form as one aspect of the remarkable British capacity for colonial administration. In the applied arts it appears in the amiable ease with which the English adopted—and adapted, to be sure—modes of design developed in other lands. Thus, on top of the impact of the Italian Renaissance, felt in all European countries though somewhat less in Britain, the landscape architecture of England underwent in the two centuries following Henry VIII a French influence, a Dutch influence, and what was thought to be a Chinese influence.

These two centuries began with the year 1500 or, more precisely, after Henry VIII's accession in 1509. For the reasons discussed above, it is virtually impossible to find in England a purely pre-Tudor domestic work, unmodified by later additions. At Haddon Hall the earliest portions of the baronial mansion itself still show Norman and Gothic forms of the period from the twelfth century to the fifteenth (Fig. 135). But, aside from the adroit siting of the complex above the River Wye, there is little indication of any attempt to treat the land itself in pre-Tudor days (Fig. 136). The somewhat ungainly high retaining wall and terraces on the south front were added toward the end of the sixteenth century.

An excellent example of the small manor house and chapel of early Tudor times, with subsequent additions that do not seriously alter its character, is St. Catherine's Court, in the softly rolling hills northeast of Bath. Some small parts, especially the chapel, are almost certainly pre-Tudor; the chief work on the house is clearly Elizabethan; the handsome stone porch on the north face, at the main floor, is Jacobean; other additions are very recent. The spirit of the place is nevertheless remarkably harmonious in its charming, lived-in quality. The construction is of warm gray stone, tucked comfortably into the steep hillside with a series of terraces ranged above stone walls in what appears

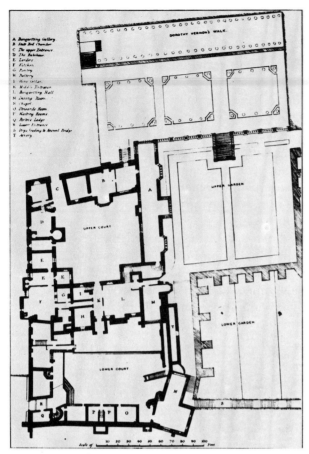

A Banqueting Gallery.
B State Bed Chamber.
C The upper Entrance.
D The Bakehouse.
E Larders.
F Kitchen.
G Pantry.
H Buttery.
I Wine Cellar.
K Middle Entrance.
L Banqueting Hall.
M Dancing Room.
O Chapel.
P Steward's Room.
P' Waiting Rooms.
Q Porter's Lodge.
R Lower Entrance.
S Steps leading to Ancient Bridge.
T Armory.

DOROTHY VERNON'S WALK.

UPPER GARDEN

UPPER COURT

LOWER GARDEN

LOWER COURT

Scale of 10 20 30 40 50 60 70 80 90 100 Feet

135. Plan of Haddon Hall.

136. The Lower Court of Haddon Hall illustrates the absence of outdoor development in this work.

to be an earnest effort to emulate the Italian villa (Fig. 137). The situation of the house is quite unusual, in that the main floor rests at the third of seven levels stepping westward up the hillside, with four levels above it and only two below. Presumably the house was set this low for easier access to the highroad at the bottom of the slope.

As is so often the case in relatively early landscape architectural works of any country, the organization of St. Catherine's Court on sight-lines is rather tentative and a bit clumsy. Directly before the Jacobean porch (Fig. 138) is a small sunken garden, built just after World War I to supplant an earlier misplaced roadway entrance. From the pool in the middle of the garden a sight-line descends to the east, centered on a path and steps leading to a pedestrian gate on the highroad. The present entrance court is at a lower floor, on the east or downhill face of the house, and forms the first of the seven levels. From a point just in front of the porch, an older sight-line leads up the hill westward between two enormous clipped yews. First a few steps rise to a garden with flower beds cut into the turf in patterns that have varied through the years; at its upper or western edge is a flight of steps jutting out into space from the terrace wall, instead of being folded back against the wall as in the Italian prototype. The Renaissance intent, however fumbling, is apparent in the carved stone balusters topping the entire length of the wall.

Above this wall is the famous turf terrace known as the Bowling Green. Along its upper edge, supported by a low wall, is a dark blue-green hedge of clipped yew, pierced by an archway and a short flight of steps right on the main sight-line. Uphill from the hedge is a slightly tilted strip of cutting-garden, then another low wall topped by a hedge, with another short flight of steps to the seventh or uppermost level. Along all of these areas and south of them, reaching from the top level to a lawn terrace south of the house, is a broad grass walk, with three sets of turf steps for which St. Catherine's is noted.

South of the house, reaching out across the open meadow, is a sight-line of relatively recent origin, with successive panels of lawn stepping downward first and then up again to a terminal at the far end. The series lies athwart the wider-open space of the meadow, with the result that spatial boundaries are somewhat ambiguous. This is the only component of the total scheme that does not seem entirely at home—simply because the other spaces are so firm and clear in structure. On the whole, St. Catherine's Court, in its quiet compactness, soft colors, and warmly domestic quality (Fig. 139), is a most appealing example of English country places.

By the time Elizabeth came to the throne in 1558, the Renaissance was more nearly in full swing in England—though with a strange kind of incomplete comprehension, a typical example of which is Montacute, built about 1580 near Yeovil, Somersetshire. Here is a beginning of conscious effort to

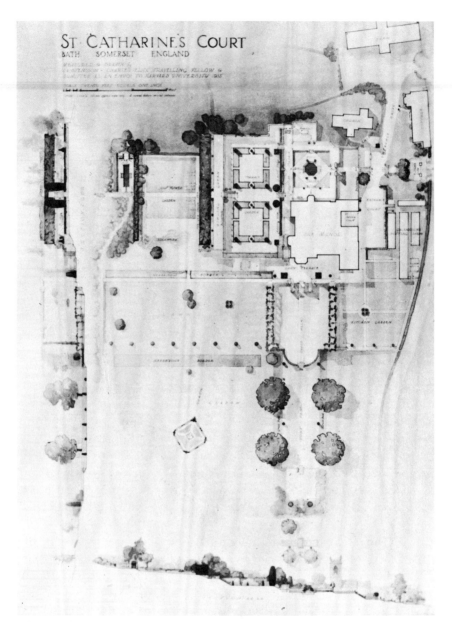

137. St. Catherine's Court, Somersetshire; the hillside situation is shown in the
section at the bottom of this measured drawing.

tie spaces together by means of sight-lines—seventy-five years after Bramante's
Belvedere, thirty years after De l'Orme's plan for Anet. The layout of Montacute is basically simple (Fig. 140): from the center of the H-formed house
a long sight-line extends in both directions, to the northwest across the arrival
court and along a straight entrance road, and to the southeast across a walled

court with two handsome pavilions and on out into the park. Crossing the latter court at right angles, near the southeast face of the house and cutting through gates in the court wall, is another sight-line that ties in, on the lower or northeast end, a square sunken area sometimes called the "Italian garden." On the southwest end this line connects with an area called the Upper Garden, of which little strong form remains.

The approach to Montacute today is the reverse of what it was at an earlier time, when the present walled court was the arrival and a long straight entrance drive came to it from the southeast through the park. Now this colorful square space is virtually a garden enclosure; its turf center is framed by a gravel walk, with deep borders of perennials on three sides against a carved stone, baluster-topped wall, lichen-covered and glowing with the same golden warmth as the house. The section of wall across the southeast side, between the two pavilions in the corners, is slightly lower than those on the other sides, reinforcing the directional effect of the old entrance gate and

138. The "new" sunken garden and the Jacobean porch, just after World War I.

139. St. Catherine's Court from the hillside in 1922; there have been some slight changes in the house since then.

enhancing the sense of outward view into the wide vista through the park, especially to one standing on the stone terrace that stretches from wing to wing of the house, facing the court.

The details of this court contribute greatly to its charm (Fig. 141). The twin pavilions or garden houses, with their curving roof-lines, bowed window bays, and diamond-leaded glass, though unique in their individuality, are typical of the amusing mixture of medieval and Italianate forms that characterized so much work of the Elizabethan period. Similarly revealing are the two fascinating objects midway in the side walls: each has a cylindrical base and a group of small classical columns under a circular entablature, above which three curving members—of stone, though strongly suggestive of strap-like wood carving—converge to support a finial that even more clearly looks like woodwork detailing. The finial, with its two interlocking, square-sectioned stone rings and the ultimate single spike, is exactly like those on the pinnacles of the garden houses and the piers of the entrance gate.

The visitor to the "Italian garden" passes through the gate in the northeast side of the walled court, crosses a wide gravel terrace, and continues on the sight-line into the sunken part of the big, sunny turf square (Fig. 142). The difference between the two levels is taken up by a trim grass bank, above which a gravel walk surrounds the garden. From this walk, in the middle of each side, an ornate but lonely set of steps carries a path to the center of the space and a balustraded pool, faithfully Italianate though small in scale. This green space perhaps typifies the frequent misplaced emphasis in what appear to have been sincere attempts at imitating in England what travelers of the time had seen in Italy. For despite the obviously geometric structuring of the plan—almost too bluntly obvious to be thoroughly Italian—and the meticulous detailing of the central pool, the overall atmosphere is almost anything other than Italian. The wide expanse of unwalled, unshaded space, its bright green turf, its sloping grass banks instead of vertical walls, and the general lack of continuous architectonic quality—all combine to say England rather than Italy. It is good that these matters have not been "corrected," for they are a valuable indication of the imperfect communications between Italy and England in the sixteenth century.

Much the same kind of partial understanding appears in the mansion of Montacute as well as in the grounds. On both facades an almost complete bilateral symmetry has crept in, to distribute bays and windows with amusing exactness, notwithstanding their casual pre-Tudor form and detail. It is almost embarrassing, yet it is unforgettably warm and colorful. There are valuable

140. Montacute, Somersetshire; plan measured and drawn in 1900. The square space at the left is sometimes referred to as the "Italian garden."

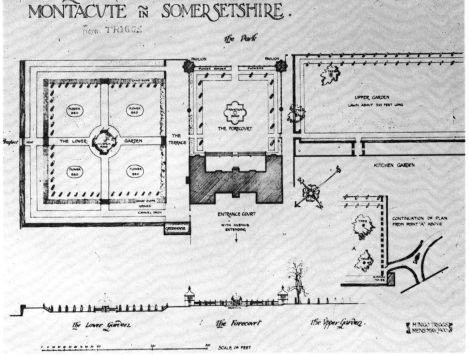

141. Details for which Montacute is famous: a strange mixture of medieval and classical forms as seen in the old arrival court.

142. Across Montacute's green "Italian garden."

lessons of both history and design at Montacute, but the place is so winning in its total charm that one tends to overlook the lessons while savoring the pleasure of visual experience. It is not surprising that authorities should so unanimously regard Montacute as the best existing example of fine Elizabethan country residences.

XIV. Seventeenth-Century England

In 1603 James VI of Scotland became James I of Great Britain, uniting England and Scotland under the Stuarts. Tudor days were over, but the distinctively English architectural combination—forms and details of medieval character mixed with a rather literal version of Renaissance order—continued into the Jacobean era. It persisted at least until about 1620, when the architect Inigo Jones brought back from Italian travels a new and more comprehending interpretation of the Renaissance.

Meanwhile, the Jacobean way of building was illustrated well by Hatfield House, in Hertfordshire, just north of London (Fig. 143). It was done in about 1611 for the Earl of Salisbury, reputedly by a French designer, Salomon de Caux. The great house, more brick than stone, is an amazing conglomerate of medieval elements with a few overlays of classical detail and a plan too stiffly symmetrical to seem fully at ease in the soft English landscape. From each face of the mansion a sight-line is projected, but not with equal success. To north and south the lines pass through open courts to long vistas through the park, set up by double rows of trees. Northward runs the approach road, quite simple and forceful as a long directional space; to the south the line is hurt at the outset by indecisive fragmentation of the large space by the house into part courtyard, part flower beds in turf, with the unhappy result that it is effectively neither one nor the other.

To the west of the house, though not strongly connected by sight-line, is a square garden that suffers from uncertainty as to which is dominant, turf or flower beds. Eastward from the mansion the sight-line starts off boldly enough, with a great stairway thrusting out from the house terrace into a garden of patterned beds, gravel paths, and clipped yews (Fig. 144); but the area seems to have no clear boundaries at the sides and feels like an object

194

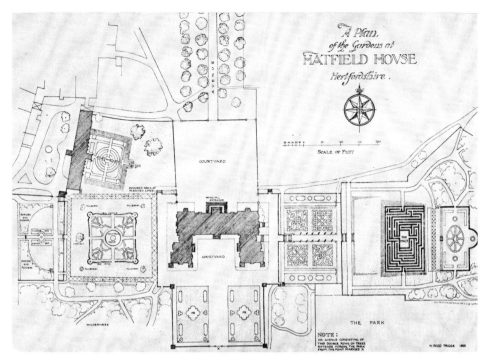

143. Plan of Hatfield House, Hertfordshire, done about 1611.

144. The stiff layout to the east of Hatfield House.

floating in a larger space. Then, unfortunately, the sight-line, carried by a central walk through this first garden, gets lost beyond it. To be sure, there is a genuine maze next on the east, with high hedges in an intricate labyrinthine pattern, and a small garden area follows, but neither is in any visible way spatially connected to the sight-line or into a determinable structure of the plan. Thus the general scheme of the grounds, rigid in its unimaginative adherence to geometric lines, demonstrates the inadequacy of merely laying down a rectilinear system of intended sight-lines and then assembling upon them some loosely related elements—things rather than spaces—like so many odd objects impaled on a pin. The *structural* sense of Renaissance planning was not yet understood at Hatfield, or indeed in England, to judge by other places of the period.

But even though Hatfield House turns out to be, from a landscape architectural point of view, primarily a famous Jacobean country place exhibiting fundamental weaknesses in layout on the land, it makes a notable contribution through the terra-cotta details of its unique balustrades. These are pierced panels, made up of flat-faced units, obviously preformed before baking and then assembled in patterns of astonishing diversity. The panels are held in a framework of molded terra-cotta piers, bases, and copings.

The first half-century of the Stuart era was noted more for the struggle between Parliament and the Crown than for any marked improvement of native trends in England's country places, which did tend to grow larger and more sumptuous as years passed. Then at last the internal quarrel exploded into civil war, Charles I was executed, and the austerity of the Commonwealth effectively put a stop to what was frowned upon by the Cromwellians as a royalist extravagance. The brief eleven-year period of the Commonwealth and the Protectorate, 1649 to 1660, saw country places destroyed rather than developed.

Meanwhile, two important influences had emerged. The first was that of Inigo Jones, whose Italian studies and grasp of the Renaissance had pushed England far ahead in architecture and led eventually to such high points of achievement as the career of Sir Christopher Wren. The second influence was that of the sons of Claude Mollet, especially André and Gabriel, whose talents were in some demand in England as well as on the Continent. Their chief effect was to introduce French directness, invention, and sense of structure into the handling of spatial geometry, and more specifically to perpetuate and enlarge upon the techniques developed by their father long before. André Mollet, who published his volume *Le Jardin de Plaisir* in 1651, was active in England as was his brother from the time of James I until their death in 1666; they may fairly be regarded as having paved the way for the royally induced fashionability of French design that held sway after the Restoration had brought Charles II to the throne in 1660 from lengthy French exile. Given the groundwork of the Mollets plus the King's understandable affection for things French, England was more than ready for the profound impact that the development of Versailles, in all its pomp and glory, had on the entire Western world by 1670.

It would be difficult to overstress the importance of the period of French influence in the story of English landscape architecture. Not only did the countryside, far less hilly than that of Italy, somehow lend itself more agreeably to the French way of projecting horizontality in space and vegetation than it did to the often unsure attempts at the walled verticality of the Italian villa. Beyond this is the implicit historical circumstance that it was chiefly French influence, albeit an exaggerated version, against which the great eighteenth-century revolution set in, leading to the controversial but purely English "landscape gardening school."

The expression *"chiefly* the French influence" is used here with full awareness of its implied indecisiveness. The remarkable English capacity for adopting and adapting the design of other peoples enters the story again at this point—first from the Dutch, later from the Chinese. As for the Dutch influence, it was again at least partly the vicissitudes of monarchy that affected the situation. In 1689, with the overthrow and flight of James II, Britain reached across to Holland and offered the throne jointly to Mary, daughter of James II, and her husband, Prince William of Orange. As William and Mary they occupied the British throne until her death in 1694, when William III ruled alone until 1702. Upon his death in that year Anne, the younger daughter of James II, succeeded him.

For some years prior to the accession of William and Mary, there had been a considerable trend in England toward the use of some of the techniques on which tightness of space had forced Dutch gardens to depend. With the arrival of William of Orange, the amiable imitation naturally acquired some of the unreasoning quality of fashion, and Dutch influence became even widespread. Among the Dutch techniques, one of the best known was trimming and training evergreens, usually box or yew, into fanciful shapes, presuming to create variety of interest on a small area of ground. This topiary work was by no means a Dutch invention; the term comes almost directly from the Latin *topiarius,* the Roman name for a gardener, and the technique was at least as ancient as Rome itself. At any rate, topiary became fashionable in England and was regarded as something Dutch, along with proliferation of tulips and the simplifying of ornate French parterre designs into tighter forms.

The infusion of these different influences from across the Channel had the effect, on the whole, of creating a thoroughly mixed period from about the middle of the seventeenth century until well into the reign of Queen Anne. On the one hand there was the impressive work of such architects as Inigo Jones and Christopher Wren, inspired by a fresh understanding of the Italian Renaissance. At the same time, French influence was strong in many of the larger country seats and continued to a much later date than one would expect. Of the places most affected, only a few examples remain intact, notably Melbourne Hall, Bramham Park, Wrest Park, and of course Hampton Court, the royal palace on the Thames that is a veritable museum of all the "styles" of English landscape architecture.

Dutch influence, meanwhile, with its compactness and topiary work, was more generally felt, since its merits were more applicable to small than large places. Remnants can still be found throughout England, but Levens Hall in Westmorland has long been considered the outstanding example. Such a barrage of foreign influences—Italian, French, Dutch, all on top of the medieval base that was essentially English and all subject to the eminently practical British acceptance of change at any time for comfort's sake—leaves little wonder that this was a mixed-up period.

Melbourne Hall, in Derbyshire, is not a large place; though thoroughly English in domestic quality and lush vegetation, it possesses in a peculiar way some elements of French design (Fig. 145). It is thought to have been developed, partly on older work, about 1704 and thereafter. The new form is usually attributed to the nurseryman Henry Wise; he and his partner, George London, were the first of England's flourishing commercial gardeners. The French feeling at Melbourne arises from various component parts rather

145. Melbourne Hall, Derbyshire, a somewhat scrambled case of French effects without French breadth.

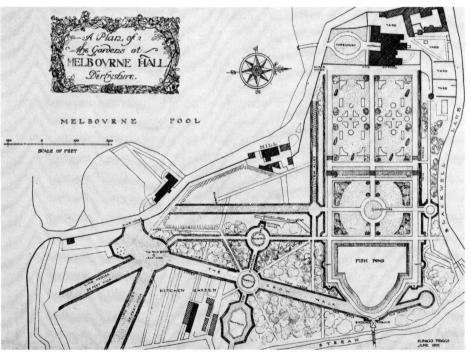

146. There is a reminder of France in Melbourne's allées, pools, and clipped hedges.

than from plan, although a sight-line extending from the house to the east carries a rectangle of three successive spaces, of which the third is a Fish Pond, sometimes called the Great Water. There is a gravel walk down the center of the spaces; others at the sides, in front of high yew hedges, lead around the Fish Pond to its far side. There an arbor of delicate wrought iron, widely known as the Bird Cage of Melbourne, serves as a terminal to the view from the house. The seemingly French character of the flat water and the tall evergreen hedges gains a modicum of support from the wide sets of steps in the paths, steps that would be appropriate at Vaux-le-Vicomte or Versailles but seem out of scale in this more domestic spot.

The rest of Melbourne, almost without plan, consists of a number of loosely related but somewhat radiating green-walled allées of turf between tall hedges of yew and linden, all cut through dense woods with simple pools at crossings (Fig. 146), a *clair voyée* (grille opening) to outward view, and the collection of lead garden figures for which Melbourne is especially noted. The network of allées is only partially tied to the open rectangle of spaces east of the house, though an ancient tunnel of gnarled yew trees parallels the south side and two of the minor allées stem at right-angles from the central sight-line.

Bramham Park, in Yorkshire, is more in the "grand manner" than Melbourne and for this reason appears more assuredly French in character (Fig. 147). Quite apart from size, it has a firm basis for such an impression in a carefully structured plan, with sheets of geometrically formed flat water and long allées through the woods—three essentials of typical French landscape architecture. Bramham was built about 1710, the house by an Italian archi-

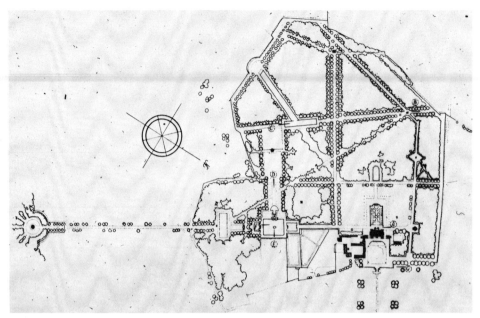

147. Plan of Bramham Park, Yorkshire.

tect, the grounds obviously by someone holding to an interpretation of the
current French idiom. The stone house and stables, almost self-conscious in
their columned Italianate propriety, embrace a clearly defined entrance court
into which a long road through the park arrives between elaborate gate piers.
On the other side of the house is a large, open grassy space, with a flower
garden uncomfortably in its midst opposite the curving stairway from the
main floor of the house. This garden, floating uncertainly in the larger open
area, is the only element in the plan of Bramham that seems not rigorously
controlled.

Parallel to the garden face of the house, a long sight-line carries from the
Chapel at the north end along a wide gravel pathway known as the Broad
Walk to a somewhat involved arrangement of pools at the south end. It
continues beyond these across a swale, up a distant slope, and off into the
blue haze in what has come to be accepted as the usual French manner. The
pools at the south end of the Broad Walk are crisply architectonic, with strict
copings and terraces about them (Fig. 148). They serve as a fulcrum for a
secondary sight-line to the west; on the line of this perpendicular is an inlet
called the Cascade, beyond which the sight-line leads to a Gothic revival
summerhouse and a broad green vista. Tied into this framework is a network
of allées through heavy beech woods. These walks feel entirely French, with
controlled edges of tree trunks, clipped hedging, and upper foliage, with
carved stone urns at several important crossings, and with a magnificently
simple body of water called the T-Canal from the form of its plan (Fig. 149).

148. Looking across Bramham's somewhat elaborate pools from above the Cascades.

149. One arm of Bramham's T-canal.

150. Levens Hall: the house and some of the fanciful topiary work.

Such canals, of which not many still exist, were one of the clearest manifestations of the French vogue in England; that at Bramham is surely one of the finest examples. Its arms are not perpendicular, but each lies in an allée; the slots of cool blue sky overhead, the green light filtering through the tightly bordering tall trees, the reflection of the whole in the dark mirror of the canal—all in the stillness of the woods—are for most observers the high moment of experience at Bramham Park.

Wrest Park, in Bedfordshire, has long been regarded as one of the best examples of French influence. It is included here solely because of its canals, for the present house and much of the grounds are actually nine-teenth-century. But the canals, magnificent yew hedges, and allées through the remarkable forest of mixed hardwoods are surely relics of the older time. Wrest is one of the few great places built on terrain level and extensive enough to accommodate the broad horizontality of French design, points clearly taken advantage of to the utmost in the several redesignings of Wrest. One strip of space and water, called the Long Canal, has at its far end a pavilion of ornate design, dated 1709. When maintenance of Wrest was at its height, this canal, bordered by straight grass margins, wide gravel walks, and clipped hedges backed by a forest growth of huge trees, was a superb example of French impact on England.

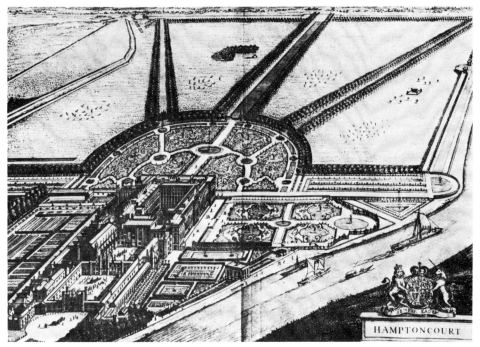

151. Kip's engraving of Hampton Court at the time of William III: an array of types, from the turreted west entry for Henry VIII to the broad French treatment facing Wren's additions on the east.

For Dutch influence in English gardens, Levens Hall in Westmorland—or, more particularly, its topiary garden, tucked into the angle between house and stables—is generally looked upon as the most nearly complete example. It is compact and neatly fitted into small compass, but its fame rests mainly upon an unequaled assembly of topiary sculptures (Fig. 150). The garden is thought to have been done by a French gardener named Beaumont in about 1700. Levens as a total property is of course much older than that.

No place illustrates the succession of foreign influences better than Hampton Court, on the Thames just above London. The palace covers the whole gamut of architectural development, from the medieval castellated western portal and courts started for Cardinal Wolsey about 1515 to the eastern end, added by Sir Christopher Wren in 1699 (Fig. 151). The grounds, while not so clearly tied to specific periods, retain much authentic work of later times and serve as an excellent summary of the development of landscape architecture in England prior to the great eighteenth-century revolution.

The visitor to Hampton Court normally enters at the west end and thus begins with the earliest work. Little is known of what was done on the grounds for Cardinal Wolsey; but after 1525, when he gave the place to Henry VIII, there is documentary evidence that the King established a much enlarged garden with the enclosures, banks, turf seats, knots, and arbors typical of

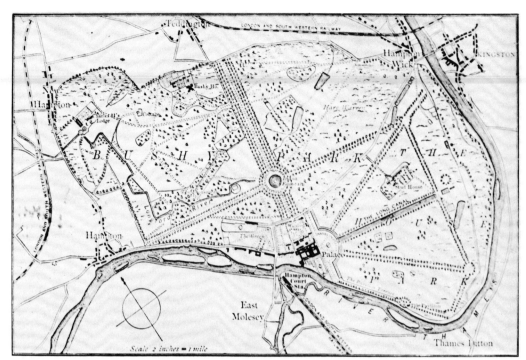

152. The larger domain of Bushy Park at Hampton Court today.

England's emergence from the Middle Ages. The fashion of the day also dictated the erection of numerous figures in painted wood or stone, including the "Kynge's Beastes" that are recalled today by the carved heraldic posts at the west portal. Henry added some two thousand acres of deer park around the palace complex, much of which remains as Bushy Park (Fig. 152).

Passing from the west end to the right around the palace, one reaches the neat, geometric, colorful Pond Garden, often called the Dutch Garden. This little rectangular space, with the Banqueting House of Henry VIII angled across one corner beyond, is such a favorite with visitors that one hesitates to quibble about its authenticity as an example of the Dutch influence. Suffice it to say that the Pond Garden in its rectilinear compactness and gay floral color is not inconsistent with the period of William and Mary—and it is well established that the two sovereigns were mainly responsible for the greater part of the Hampton Court grounds as they exist today.

Farther along the south side of the palace, one comes to the Privy Garden, a sizable area laid out in a geometric pattern of straight gravel paths, but so abundantly furnished with trees and shrubs that it has lost any sense of rigidity. There is a circular pool, and on each side a raised grass terrace recalls this characteristic of early Tudor gardens. Flanking the western terrace is a dark tunnel of arched old trees called Queen Mary's Bower. North toward

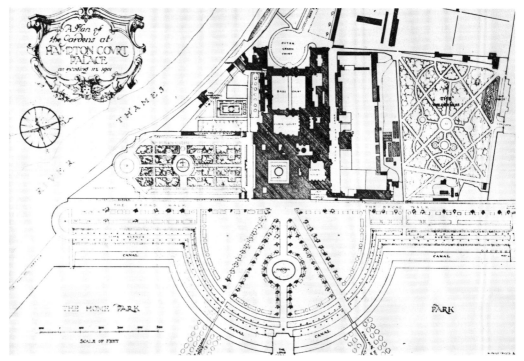

153. Detailed plan of the grounds around Hampton Court Palace.

the palace from the end of the bower, or from within the Privy Garden, it is clear where Wren's addition joins the older building.

But the full effect of the noble eastern portion of the palace is to be had only from beyond the Privy Garden. William and Mary, on accession in 1689, decided to rebuild the palace by adding what is now the entire eastern block; Sir Christopher Wren, then engaged in rebuilding St. Paul's Cathedral, was commissioned to do the work. At the same time Henry Wise, having been appointed superintendent of the gardens, undertook to rearrange the eastern end of the grounds to accommodate the alterations and additions to the palace.

The story of this whole eastern development, so obviously French in its spirit, actually reaches back at least thirty years earlier, beginning with the Mollet brothers, those busy practitioners of the French mode. Gardeners to Charles II in 1661 just after his return to the throne, it is only reasonable to suppose that they authored the first grand plans for development from the palace eastward—the only room available for the broad treatment desired by the King in his enthusiasm for emulating Louis XIV. The Mollets were probably responsible for laying the original basis for today's great *patte d'oie* (goosefoot) with its radiating avenues; they had already used this typically French device elsewhere.

When the Mollets died in 1666, they were succeeded by John Rose, an English gardener who had been sent to France to study, reputedly under the great Le Nôtre. One of Rose's pupils at Hampton Court was the George London who was later joined by Henry Wise in the ubiquitous commercial gardening firm, London and Wise. Clearly, in 1689, when Wise took charge of the new work for William and Mary, he was continuing a course of French influence well established by an unbroken line of Francophile designers. The result, though far less grandiose than Versailles, is another excellent example of the French influence in England (Fig. 153).

The Broad Walk, a long gravel promenade, straight and wide, bordered by beds of perennials, marches along the east front of the palace all the way from the Thames on the south to the Flower Pot Gates at the north end on the Kingston Road. Opposite the center of the great east facade, the three radiating avenues of the goosefoot spring out, the central one interrupted momentarily by an oval pool with vertical jets before continuing into the distance as the tree-lined Long Canal. The two other avenues reach out similarly into the park, tree-lined but without canals. Another canal, with fine old lindens hanging over both sides, parallels the ends of the Broad Walk but curves in a great semicircle at the center to embrace the geometry of the goosefoot and meet the inner end of the Long Canal.

North of the palace is a workyard and beyond that, through a gate in the Broad Walk wall, lies the Wilderness. This enclosed square is a strangely self-conscious combination of geometrically laid paths, straight and curved, running through a relatively wild growth of all sorts of plants, from the smallest ground covers and wild flowers to mature trees. Near the Lion Gate, where the north side of the Wilderness reaches the Kingston Road, is a true Maze of clipped hedging, probably the lineal descendent of the labyrinth known to have been developed for Henry VIII. These northern areas of Hampton Court have less to do with the present account than those on the south and east; but, thanks to their having been well maintained, they certainly provide a helpful package of illustrations for the rise and fall of fashion in English landscape architecture.

XV. The English "Landscape Gardening School"

It is impossible to single out any one factor and declare with truth that *this* was the cause of the great revolution of the eighteenth century in England, with its destruction of so much that had gone before, and with its substitution of "landscape gardens" in professed imitation of nature. It is equally pointless to attempt singling out an exact date to mark the advent of the revolution. Several contributory reasons and several plausible dates have been advanced by critics; all deserve consideration. One approach that involves perhaps an oversimplification, though a helpful one, is to regard the whole movement toward the "landscape garden" as but a natural manifestation of the wave of romanticism inundating the Western world. This was of course fundamentally a literary romanticism, a configuration primarily of the verbal world. One may fairly question whether trying to translate verbal involutions into visible, tangible forms—a reversal of the natural process of seeing an object before naming it—did not guarantee confusion.

It is not the intention to minimize the era's purely literary dimensions. The entire period, from Milton's occasional pleas for unmodified wild nature to Peacock's ridicule of Repton in *Headlong Hall,* was intensely productive in literature, whatever one may think of the landscape architecture of the time. Indeed, even those who heartily dislike the "landscape gardening school" can ill afford to dismiss the flourishing literary epoch that began in the days of Queen Anne, just after the start of the eighteenth century. For at no other time in history has there been such general interest in gardens and in the total physical landscape, so much writing and criticism and open debate, so much articulated concern. Landscape architects today would have good reason for rejoicing if there were to arise again such widespread public awareness of their professional accomplishments.

During these times a laudable interest in nature was growing steadily, but it was deeply affected in unfortunate ways by both the romanticism of the age and its literary expression. The consequence was the worship and virtual deification, largely sentimental, of a strangely limited something capitalized as "Nature," though it excluded humans and somehow managed to overlook the obvious, that man is as truly a biological organism as grass and flowers and trees and other denizens of the wild. The mistaken premise put "Man" and "Nature" verbally in opposition instead of treating humans as part of the totality of nature. One regrettable effect of this false premise was a downgrading of things produced by the human organism, a regarding of them in one verbal sweep as manmade-and-therefore-unnatural. Actually, of course, the pastoral and sylvan arrangements of vegetation comprising the landscape garden were themselves manmade, but by a convenient slip of logic the proponents of the "new style" contrived to ignore this contradiction—at least verbally.

The prevailing romantic and literary attitude toward Nature held also to certain misleading verbal abstractions about the natural world. These varied in intensity and detail from decade to decade as debate continued, but basically they found expression in such tenets as the dictum "Nature abhors a straight line," and even Hogarth's "line of beauty," the S-curve. To put it bluntly, the sophistry of the times asserted, in effect, that "nature wiggles," that natural forces are casually haphazard, that they generate only irregular forms, and that any kind of curved line is somehow more natural—and therefore better—than a straight one. All this despite the observable fact that nature is essentially orderly—and that "straight lines" often occur in the wild, as well as in creations of the human organism. It seems odd that so fallacious a doctrine of natural disorder could persist when one of the most revered writers, naturalists, and leaders of thought in mid-century, Jean Jacques Rousseau, said about nature: "Not contented only to establish order, she has taken effectual methods to prevent its being disturbed."[1] Instead, the interpretation of natural forces that prevailed during the landscape gardening epoch and that affected much of the work performed was seriously limited and distorted. It could readily have yielded to correction if a more rational attitude, based on actual investigation of the natural world, had been allowed to counteract the pretty romantic verbalizations.

One often hears the suggestion that the great changes in English gardens arose from retrospective fascination with the dramatic, imaginative landscape paintings of Poussin, Claude Lorrain, and Salvator Rosa. There is no doubt that these seventeenth-century masters were much admired in eighteenth-

---

1. Jean Jacques Rousseau, *Profession of Faith of a Savoyard Vicar,* Harvard Classics ed. (New York: P. F. Collier & Son, 1910), XXXIV, 260.

century England and that they influenced designers considerably, not only with their pictorial composition, but especially with their romantic ruined temples and the like. It may well be that the very term "landscape garden" came from a wish to have "a garden just like one of those landscapes." But there is no known evidence that a conscious effort was made by anybody to reproduce a specific painting in full actuality upon the land. Perhaps the inapplicability of such a method, so obvious to landscape architects in the twentieth century, was already sensed in the eighteenth: that a mere pictorial approach to design would imply a fixed station-point for the viewer, whereas a garden for living would have to be not just something to look at, but a volume in which the observer would move about.

Another occasional opinion is that interest in the Far East, particularly the celestial calm of Chinese gardens, was a major factor in the growth of the landscape gardening school. The accuracy of this view is highly doubtful. An Oriental influence was surely felt in some of the arts, such as ceramics, textiles, wallpapers, furniture, and interior furnishings in general, though even then it was evidently only a Western guess at something dimly understood. The actual effect upon English gardens appears to have been minimal, with the exception of Sir William Chambers' admitted fakery installed as "Chinese effects" at Kew. To render the entire matter even more ridiculous, designers on the Continent too often fell headlong for their own sort of *chinoiserie* added to an already grossly misinterpreted "English landscape garden," heaping a second error on the earlier one with the result a kind of *jardin anglais* or *giardino inglese* that is usually pathetically out of place in France or Italy.

However greatly opinions differ as to the influence of these various factors, there is virtually unanimous agreement that the essayists Joseph Addison, Richard Steele, and Alexander Pope did much to turn the public against the accepted mode of English garden design with its heavy French and Dutch overburden. At first the attack was principally against the current excesses in topiary. The generally regarded opening gun in the assault appeared as a mildly complaining essay by Addison in *The Spectator* for June 25, 1712: "our trees rise in cones, globes and pyramids. We see the mark of the scissors upon every plant and bush . . . I would rather look upon a tree in all its luxuriancy and diffusion of boughs and branches."[2] A year later *The Guardian* published a piece variously attributed to either Steele or Pope, bitterly attacking the topiary fad and appending the now famous catalogue of greens for sale, including "Adam and Eve in yew; Adam a little shattered by the fall of the tree of knowledge in the great storm. Eve and the serpent very flourishing. St. George in box; his arm scarse long enough, but will be in condition to stick the dragon by next April . . . A lavender pig, with sage growing in his belly."[3]

2. *Spectator, no. 414.*
3. *Guardian, no. 173.*

To be sure, the campaign of derision was aimed almost exclusively at topiary work for which the Dutch had perhaps unfairly been blamed. The fashionable public, however, in its enthusiastic acceptance of the Addison-Steele-Pope essays, soon began broadening the onslaught to cover garden layout as well, with strong support from the steadily rising tide of romanticism and its misconception of Nature.

The undeniable effectiveness of these essays naturally raises the question of what the conditions truly were and whether the complaints were justified. Could it be that in fact the protest was not so much against the older forms themselves, with their obvious geometry and manmade character, but against obviously maladroit ways in which those forms had come to be used? Such a possibility does not appear to have received the attention it deserves. In this area of inquiry may be found one of the clearest answers to the fundamental question of why so complete and cataclysmic a turnover in public taste can have come about.

Unfortunately, many older places were so modified in the course of the landscape gardening revolution as to be all but completely destroyed, and present-day judgments about the time are fragmentary at best. If, however, the protests of the essayists were fair (and it must be admitted that they sound alarmingly credible), then surely things had come to a pretty pass in the field of topiary. As for overall design, one has only to examine carefully the contemporary engravings of English country places toward the end of the seventeenth century—in such bird's-eyes as the famous Kip's views—to conclude that far too often the uncomprehending imitation of French and Italian design had led to elaborate exaggerations, awkward rigidities, and especially the indiscriminate thrusting of allées in all directions with little if any purpose. In short, and simply enough, in about the year 1700 there appears to have been in England a plethora of such examples of poor design, along with a few works of major merit. Revolt against such crudities would have been justifiable in any age; sadly, too many of the fine things were destroyed at the same time as the poorer ones.

From among all the possible contributing factors one may estimate the origins and allocate the blame or praise in various ways. The unalterable truth is that the gardening revolution of Britain's eighteenth century did in fact occur and that it influenced the whole of the Western world. Its first visible signs most probably came in the work of Sir John Vanbrugh, the self-trained architect best known for his monumental collaboration with Henry Wise at Blenheim for the Duke of Marlborough. Although long committed to strongly structured, geometric, balanced plans, Vanbrugh early in the century began toying with the romantic fashion, at times going so far as to suggest a compromise between the older way of working and the "new style."

Another busy designer of the day, Charles Bridgeman, who had been a pupil of London and Wise and sometimes collaborated with Vanbrugh, swung over from the older method into a strange amalgam of straight and wobbly lines. This queer combination is illustrated by plans of Stowe House, in Buckinghamshire, where Bridgeman and Vanbrugh are both known to have been working soon after 1714. It was Bridgeman who adapted a well-known military device, a line of sharpened pickets at the bottom of a ditch known as a *fosse*, and thus gained attention as the reputed "inventor"of the *ha-ha*. Across such a sunken fence an observer could look without seeing any physical barrier, which of course broke down any clear boundary definition of organized spaces. Whether Bridgeman realized it or not, he had struck upon something that fitted perfectly with the trend of the new fashion toward relative formlessness. (Quite apart from theoretical values, the *ha-ha* offered the practical usefulness, occasionally availed of even today on both sides of the Atlantic, of holding cattle at a distance from a house without requiring a visible fence.)

William Kent, the next key figure, had been a painter and scenic designer of sorts, was munificently supported by the Earl of Burlington, and had the literary allegiance of Alexander Pope. About 1727 they embarked upon a development at Chiswick House, in Middlesex, usually considered the first avowed example of the new landscape garden even though, according to plans in existence a decade later, the place was another mixture of the old regularities, rather crudely handled, and patches of what appear to be "wilderness" areas with paths wiggling and twisting through the woods. There is no clear evidence that Kent planted dead trees at Chiswick, although he did go to this extreme in the Kensington Gardens. At Chiswick there were imitation classical temples and bridges, a somewhat architectonic artificial waterfall, and other samples of romantic persuasion. In retrospect all this looks ridiculous; one is hard-pressed to believe it could have been done except with tongue in cheek. But to judge by Pope's florid verbalizations, it was meant in complete seriousness.

Hardly less peculiar was Kent's theory, illustrated by his published sketches, about planting trees always in clumps—like dumplings floating in a sea of sauce—to modern eyes an almost perfect model of "scatteration," having no sense whatever of spatial form or structure. Here would be a clear example of what might be termed "thingy" design, in which all the emphasis is on things in the aggregate and none on the useful spaces between them. Kent was also called upon to improve the gardens at Stowe, where his major effort went into destroying those portions of Bridgeman's work that had followed geometric lines. Whatever one's ultimate opinion may be about the landscape gardening school, it is reasonably clear that Kent made no great contribution toward its development—despite the glowing praise of Horace Walpole, who after all was not a designer.

Most critics would agree that the first to show genuine creative powers in this direction was a younger man, Lancelot Brown, who worked under Kent at Stowe until the latter died in 1749. Brown, then about thirty-three, quickly

154. A waterside scene of great conviction at Stowe, where Bridgeman, Kent, and Brown all worked.

began demonstrating at Stowe the skill that led to his being called in on a long series of places during the next three decades. Because of his propensity for talking about the "capabilities" that he always professed to see in the places he was asked to work on—master-salesman that he was—he came to be known as Capability Brown. While employed as head gardener at Stowe, he undertook several outside commissions, including a lake at Wakefield Lodge for the Duke of Grafton. This turned out to delight everyone, quickly spreading Brown's fame, and soon he was appointed royal gardener at Hampton Court. In short order he had become the darling of the fashionable world, with projects throughout England.

At Stowe, after Kent's death and again in later years, Brown worked to complete what Kent had begun toward virtual obliteration of the geometric portions of the Bridgeman-Vanbrugh layout. The work destroyed was hardly of the highest order, and the replacement is regarded by landscape garden enthusiasts as among the best examples of Brown's method (Fig. 154). One regrettable consequence of that method, however—all too usual in his projects—was the complete removal of rectilinearity from immediately about the great house, leaving it to sit without a base, somewhat unsteadily in a visual sense, in an oversoft surrounding of undulant meadow.

Blenheim, the joint effort by Vanbrugh and Wise (Fig. 155), underwent at Brown's hand a drastic overhauling in one of his most widely heralded "improvements" (Fig. 156). Immediately south of the great mansion he

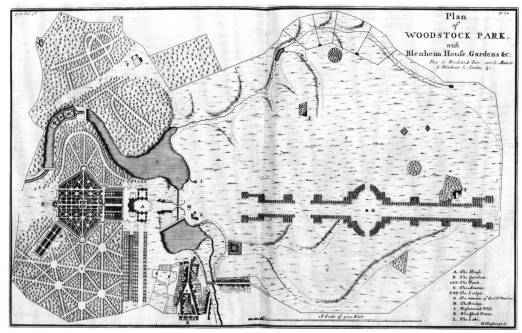

155. Blenheim: plan by Henry Wise and Sir John Vanbrugh.

156. Blenheim decades later, showing modification of the Wise-Vanbrugh work by "Capability" Brown. In a destructive sense, the polygonal garden was removed and pieces were lopped out of allées; constructively, the two water bodies were merged, making sense out of the previously ridiculous bridge siting, and more fluent ground forms were created.

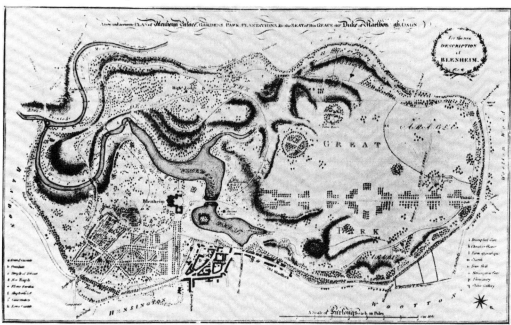

157. Blenheim today: Brown's Lake.

removed the overelaborate polygonal parterres, but instead of simplifying or regularizing them, which would doubtless have helped immeasurably, he introduced a sweep of lawn reaching to the walls of the house and leaving the latter with no architectonic support whatever on the ground. To the southeast and southwest of the house the rather pointless networks of allées were attacked, but only by removing whole sections here and there so that what was left must have had a motheaten appearance for some time. A similarly unimaginative fate befell the meaningless floating allées of trees marching through the open fields to the north. Offsetting these questionable amendments, Brown altered Wise's two bodies of water with excellent results, raising the surface level to create a continuous lake known as Brown's Lake (Fig. 157) and rearranging the shores east and west of the abutments to give Vanbrugh's bridge the appropriate setting it had lacked. Elsewhere at Blenheim, Brown appears to have unhesitatingly remodeled the surface of the land in other ways, producing striking pictorial compositions of pastoral scenery.

It is in this latter sense that Capability Brown made his contribution to progress in the art of landscape architecture, but it must not be forgotten that he was aided by nature's capacity to evolve wondrous effects if carefully placed trees and groups of trees are only left alone long enough. Brown had an unusual eye for the composition of individual pictures, which in large part accounts for the fine photographs possible today from selected points of view

158. Stourhead, another "landscape garden" faithfully preserved; similarity to a romantic landscape painting is unquestionable.

in many of his projects (Fig. 158). Of course this does not mean that these places are necessarily well composed in the larger multidimensional sense of spatial design. Indeed, there is little indication that Brown ever considered space a working material, that he was much concerned with the mechanical functioning of his creations, or that he was aware of what has come to be known as the *design* of outdoor *space* for human *use*. But in those instances where the passing of two centuries has brought beneficence of natural growth, without destructive changes, it is clear that in his day Brown assembled some exquisite bits and passages of large-scale landscape to be looked at with genuine pleasure.

The most heated arguments about Brown's efforts developed after his death in 1783, but even during his active lifetime he seems to have been controversial. A majority admired his work and referred to him as "the magician," but a few found fault with the soft sameness of the results and declared their opposition in polemical publications. In effect this controversy, to which Brown himself made no verbal contribution whatever, fed new life into the incessant literary output—books, pamphlets, essays, poems, letters to the editor—that had started with the Addison-Steele-Pope essays in *The Spectator* and *The Guardian*.

As early as 1718 Stephen Switzer, who had worked and studied under London and Wise, published his *Iconographia Rustica,* a book on practical gardening that boldly attempted to present the new style in written form.

Batty Langley in 1728 and Phillip Miller in 1731 produced volumes mainly on horticulture but offering some rather ludicrous instructions on layout. Alexander Pope continued for years his enthusiastic applause for Kent. In time Horace Walpole, too, lent the force of his literary reputation in praise of Kent, though mostly after the latter had passed from the scene. By 1750 the poet and amateur gardener William Shenstone, having begun building his own place at the Leasowes, started publishing his pet theories; these were principally literary and derived almost exclusively from landscape paintings. Thomas Whateley's *Observations on Modern Gardening,* published in 1771, though moderately critical of Kent, treated Brown's work with appreciation.

The opposition to Brown was headed by Sir Uvedale Price, advocate of "the picturesque" as an improvement on "the sublime" and "the beautiful." His picturesque, however, did not mean "like a picture"; it must be like a particular *kind* of picture—rough, rugged, savagely dramatic, and melancholy! In his *Essay on the Picturesque,* finally published in 1794, Price was downright abusive to the work and memories of both Kent and Brown, castigating them for producing scenes too soft and smooth, too sleek and feminine, to qualify truly as "Nature." It was all quite vituperative at times. Price was fervently seconded by his friend and neighbor Richard Payne Knight. Around the two a considerable school evolved, but it was an almost exclusively literary cult, given to verbal argument but not to much performance on the land. And it had its opponents, notably William Marshall, whose *Planting and Rural Ornament* (1796) neatly located the obvious flaws in the Price-Knight thesis.

The literary squabble became rather a brawl, quite inconclusive, as might have been expected in such a miasma of verbal metaphysics. In the midst of it—though without settling the argument, by any means—arose the major professional figure of the landscape gardening school, Humphry Repton. Repton's name appears at this point in the narrative because Price's diatribes of 1794 were aimed as much at him as at the shades of Kent and Brown. And for good reason: Kent and Brown were dead. Repton was very much alive and practicing as a Landscape Gardener, a term that Price acidly condemned as too pretentious. Repton's letter of July 1, 1794, replying to Price, firmly established him as an able polemicist in the sharp and sometimes bitter spirit of the day.[4] The letter also presaged the prolific writing and published theory upon which, together with executed work, Repton's professional reputation was founded.

Repton's entry into his chosen profession is one of the strangest on record. With no special training, though with some facility in drawing and an apparently innate bent for rearranging scenery, he suddenly reached a decision in the 1780s, when nearly forty years of age, and announced one fine morning by letters sent to all his friends and acquaintances that his services

4. For the letter and Repton's further comments see J. C. Loudon, *The Landscape Gardening and Landscape Architecture of the Late Humphry Repton, Esq.* (London, 1840), pp. 104–116.

as a Landscape Gardener would thenceforth be available. He appears to have been the first person to use the term as a professional title.[5]

Repton was inventive and remarkably articulate. For each of the many country places on which he was engaged he prepared a bound volume, setting forth his recommendations in great detail, injecting a bit of theoretical discussion, and incorporating sketches with an ingenious kind of hinged-flap overlay, showing the difference between what existed and what he proposed. Each volume was bound in red, and these "Red Books", with their fascinating before-and-after views, soon brought as much acclaim to their originator as did the actual developments he carried out upon the ground. He worked on a prodigious number of places; of the unknown total of his "Red Books", he quoted from over a hundred in his theoretical publications. In the long run, it is for the latter that his name has been most vividly remembered. By his own declaration this was how he wanted it to be: "It is rather upon my opinions in writing, than on the partial and imperfect manner in which my plans have sometimes been executed, that I wish my fame to be established."[6]

Through the years since Repton died in 1818, so much attention has been paid his writings that his actual work is relatively little known or studied. Certain it is that, in the course of some twenty-five years of active practice, he modified his views considerably, as suggested by his *Inquiry into the Changes of Taste in Landscape Gardening* (1806). At first he seems to have regarded himself as a disciple of Brown, whom he defended valiantly. Later he was not so sure, as he indicated in *Sketches and Hints on Landscape Gardening* (1794): "some modern improvers have mistaken crookedness for the line of beauty, and slovenly carelessness for natural ease; they call every species of regularity formal, and, with the hackneyed assertion that 'nature abhors a straight line,' they fatigue the eye with continual curvatures."[7] This was of course aimed mainly at the follies of Kent and the Burlingtonians a half-century earlier, but Repton soon came to see the illogic of the Brownian palace without visual support in a grassy field. For reasons of operational good sense rather than noticeable concern about form, he advocated return to some of the rectilinearity once regarded as a normal outward extension of the house: "I have discovered that *utility* must often take the lead of beauty, and *convenience* be preferred to picturesque effect, in the neighbourhood of man's habitation."[8]

The major strength of Repton, judged by twentieth-century standards, lay in his rejection of black or white extremes—and this in the midst of contemporary literary polemics. His way of putting it was: "I do not profess to follow either Le Nôtre or Brown, but, selecting beauties from the style of each, to

5. *Ibid.,* pp. 2, 15.
6. *Ibid.,* p. 127.
7. *Ibid.,* p. 86.
8. *Ibid.,* p. 99.

adopt so much of the grandeur of the former as may accord with a palace, and so much of the grace of the latter as may call forth the charms of natural landscape. Each has its proper situation; and good taste will make fashion subservient to good sense."[9]

Some critics have belittled Repton as a sort of grand compromiser who tried to be all things to all men. In this vein he has been called a promoter of eclecticism, to use the term in a somewhat different meaning from its usual one today. A more charitable view would be that Repton put some sense—though perhaps not enough—into the landscape gardening movement. He withstood the worst blandishments of the sentimental "wiggly Nature" school, yet stood his ground staunchly against the "wild improvers" of the Price-Knight cult. Unfortunately, he appears never to have succeeded in combining well the softness of park-like scenery with the strongly structured design of the more architectural portions of his projects; he simply was not skilled enough in design. But he made more sense than any other character to be found among the landscape gardeners of his time.

Repton, his profession's first credible theoretician, lived in an age so be-fuddled with a rigidly stratified society, so immersed in notions of social propriety, "polite refinement," and "correct taste," that in some ways his comments appear stuffy to modern eyes and ears—fit prelude to the Victorian era. But on the whole his observations are remarkably verifiable today, largely because his verbal assertions were usually tested in actual practice; and for his times he was refreshingly free of involvement in mere verbal metaphysics. His professional writings were assembled by J. C. Loudon and published in one volume in 1840. Loudon was the self-appointed spokesman for something he chose to call the "Gardenesque School of Landscape." This "school" was indicative of the lamentable state of affairs into which matters had slumped after Repton's passing, with emphasis now given exotic plants, single specimen trees, and other botanical and purely horticultural interests of the country's practical head gardeners. There had been a brief manifestation of theoretical concern in the writings of William Gilpin, whose *Practical Hints upon Landscape Gardening* (1832) strove earnestly to support the "picturesque" plea of the Price-Knight set. Gilpin's words flow sweetly, but the book's illustrations of "improvement" must be seen to be believed possible. By Loudon's time nobody seemed to care about design and layout anyway; the hodge-podge of the day was touchingly revealed by Loudon's own statement that "the Gardenesque School of Landscape has been more or less adopted in various country residences, from the anxious wish of gardeners and botanical amateurs to display their trees and plants to the best advantage."[10] The result, all too often, was a scattering of specimen plants and grotesquely

9. *Ibid.,* p. 234.
10. *Ibid.,* p. ix.

159. Longleat, worked on successively by Brown and Repton; the rigidly outlined sheets of water appear uncomfortable in the undulating landscape.

shaped flower beds willy-nilly throughout the turf of the so-called "dress ground," an almost perfect example of "thingy" formlessness.

In light of these developments, it is only fair to stipulate that the term "English landscape gardening school" be used only for Repton's work and what preceded it, back to Queen Anne's day. Overall evaluation of that period, culminating in Repton, will probably always be—as for many years it has been—controversial. Some years ago Henry Hubbard summed up one view in his usual pithy way: "The landscape gardening school did not supply a new kind of order, as professed, in place of an older one; they substituted *disorder.*"[11]

A majority of present-day landscape architects would probably agree that the eighteenth century brought, mainly, an unfortunate distortion of nature and a failure (at least until late in Repton's career) to distinguish between the native glories of open landscape and the architectonic requirements of areas closely associated with human habitation. Their complaint against the expression "landscape garden" is not against "landscape," as a noun, but solely against its use as an adjective to imply that the only admissible *kind* of garden is one composed of soft, bucolic scenery. Twentieth-century objection is hardly to the landscape, it is to what the eighteenth century wanted to do with it (Fig. 159).

11. Conversation, Hubbard and author, 1939.

It is in this wider area of the manmade landscape *outside* the garden that the landscape gardening school made its one unquestionable contribution to progress. For the first recorded time in the history of outdoor design, the landscape gardeners actually *built* landscapes in presumed conformity with wild nature. Whether they misconstrued nature is not now the point; they tried hard to make country scenery look as though man had not had a hand in it. In the process they gave England the basis for a gentle, universally admired countryside of ineffable charm. Further, they did something of even greater importance, in taking the first hesitant, blundering, and no doubt often accidental steps toward evolution of what would later be consciously developed as a new form of outdoor space. This is not to say that the landscape gardeners were space-conscious—there is every indication that they merely arranged objects in ways that seemed pictorially pleasing; but in so doing they automatically set up space relationships, of which the most effective would of course be enhanced and perfected in time by the normal processes of nature. Eventually these open spaces appealed to keen observers, like Prince Pückler-Muskau and Frederick Law Olmsted, as recognizable entities in their own right—examples of a new type of spatial form, with curving boundaries of untrimmed vegetation seldom parallel to the sight-line, floored by the undulant surface of the land, and subject to purposeful manipulation and modeling. Today this kind of plastic, gently formed, pastoral space is taken for granted as a normal component of the landscape architect's palette; one needs to be reminded that it did not exist as a medium of design until after the English eighteenth century.

There is another important consequence of this contribution by the school. At first glance it may appear only a quirk of nomenclature, but it is worthy of note. In almost every instance, major attention of the landscape gardener was centered upon the great expanse of land and woods that in the typical large country place was called simply the Park. This term followed the original usage, denoting "an enclosed piece of ground stocked with beasts of the chase." In its oldest and most usual form it was the Deer Park of the nobility and landed gentry. At Repton's death, however, the time was not far distant when forward-looking students of society, such as the Reformers of the 1820s and 1830s, would urge that the ordinary citizen, too, was entitled to his version of the Gentleman's Park. The new form, when it came—as in London and at Birkenhead—would no longer enclose deer but in appearance would resemble the works of the landscape gardening school, and would invariably be called a *public park*.

XVI. Transition to Public Service

Despite its unhappy deterioration under Loudon and his followers, the landscape gardening movement was included, some twenty years after Repton's death, in an epochal shift from private to public service. This event, of great significance to the then imminent *profession* of landscape architecture, came at a moment when two historic streams of progress were converging. One was the rapid growth of technology, the other a steady increase in concern for the living and working conditions of all men.

Of the many technological advances of the nineteenth century, surely none was more amazing in consequence than man's seemingly simple mastery over iron. With the development of sheet iron came steam engines; with the development of structural iron, iron columns and iron trusses to build factories with floors strong enough for heavy, engine-driven machines. The development of rolled iron brought metal rails and, with steam-engine locomotives, railroads. With the increased transportation potential, factories no longer had to be located at the source of raw materials. All of these factors in combination meant, inevitably, a prodigious growth in tightly packed industrial towns, with more and more workers drawn from agricultural pursuits to the factories. Then, to top it off, someone demonstrated the sanity of the preposterous notion that iron could be made to float!—steamships followed, and England's ports expanded at a fantastic rate; London and Liverpool were naturally among those most affected.

In 1819, the year after Repton died, the Factory Act protecting women and children to some extent against the mounting evils of mechanized manufacture became law. Through the succeeding decades, more and more concern for workers' health and safety occupied public attention. As early as 1825 Robert Owen was making his paternalistic proposals for industrial com-

160. St. James's Park, London, looking toward Buckingham Palace; here a long rectilinear canal of the seventeenth century was "landscaped" by John Nash.

161. The Green Park's meadow-like spaces are much used by Londoners sunning themselves in deckchairs on pleasant summer weekends.

162. Hyde Park: inner end of the Serpentine.

munities carefully planned to ensure contentment of the workers—and accordingly better production. In 1832 came the Reform Bill, broadly symbolic of the progress of liberal thought in England. By 1840 the so-called Reformers were having some effect on public opinion; and of course that decade brought the several European revolutions of 1848.

The two great progressive trends, the technical and the social, joined hands with what was left of the landscape gardening movement to bring into being two works of immense importance as marking the transition of landscape architecture from the service of wealthy private patrons to service of the public at large: Victoria Park in East London and Birkenhead Park across the Mersey from Liverpool. In origin the two differed somewhat. Victoria Park, created in a congested urban surrounding, was more clearly a response to the Reformers' drive. Birkenhead Park, provided as part of a virtually new town, resulted from technical advances as well as social ones.

Victoria Park, though of inferior quality by professional standards today and a disappointment even to its designer, was the earlier of the two in getting started. In the 1830s London had an unusual series of parks: St. James's Park, the Green Park, and Hyde Park and Kensington Gardens (Figs. 160–163); the new Regent's Park was on its way. All these were Crown properties even when open to the public, and all were in the fashionable West End. The

163. A more spacious expanse in Hyde Park, leading to Marble Arch and the Speakers' Corner.

crowded East End, meanwhile, was a murky maze of poverty with no outdoor breathing space whatever. It was a perfect target for the Reformers in their campaign to improve the overall social climate of London by reducing its destitution and consequent violence, crime, and epidemics. More humane conditions in the East End, they maintained, would certainly remove one of the worst sources of trouble; and one of the best ways to bring this about would be through establishment there of a park for public use.

To support their plea the Reformers needed only to point out the effect quite correctly noted in residential areas about the Royal Parks in the West End. Especially cited—with incontrovertible logic but also neat political acumen—was the section where in 1811 the Prince Regent, as a real-estate venture, had caused a portion of the ancient royal hunting park of Marylebone to be laid out by John Nash, with "terrace houses" around the open space thereafter known as Regent's Park (Figs. 164, 165). Nearing completion in the 1830s, its salutary effect on the entire vicinity was obvious. If this could be true for the affluent aristocrats of the West End, the Reformers asked, could not a similar device be beneficial to the poverty-ridden masses of the East End?

A petition to the Queen and pleas to Parliament were successful, at least initially, though governmental apathy later impeded progress. Bills for the creation of Victoria Park were passed in 1842 and a royal grant was allocated, which led to the park's being regarded for some years thereafter as a Royal Park. James Pennethorne, architect to the Commissioners of Woods and Forests, had already prepared a plan for the park in 1841 with an accompanying report to the Commissioners; indeed, it was his ardent support of the campaign that in large part persuaded the Commissioners to give it official approval. The 1841 plan by Pennethorne became the guide for the new park, though it was twice modified by 1846.

In view of the argument for an East End park to function like the royal ones in the West End, it seems too bad that Pennethorne did not follow the basic simplicity of the larger Royal Parks. These, aside from Nash's work, were chiefly the remaining areas (though much reduced) of once-huge native tracts of royal forests and fields, remarkably little the product of landscape gardening. But of course the acreage destined to be Victoria Park enjoyed no such hunting-preserve origins and was only a half-mile wide at best. Here one had to start from scratch; and for Pennethorne this apparently meant landscape gardening, then the only generally recognized method of "improvement."

He had worked on Regent's Park under John Nash but evidently did not have the same skill in landscape composition as Nash, who may have profited from earlier close collaboration with Humphry Repton on a few projects. And of course Loudon's influence and the "gardenesque school" were firmly in vogue by 1840. That Loudon could personally have affected the Victoria Park design is improbable, but a later version of Pennethorne's plan presents a spotty appearance, in the usual manner of the gardenesque school, and lacks any convincing sense of spatial organization. Unfortunately, the work was never wholly completed as Pennethorne had intended; but the park has continued to serve the people of East London. The paramount point is that Victoria Park was built at all; nevertheless, one could wish that such a milestone in landscape architectural history might have been a more worthy example of design (Fig. 166).

Birkenhead Park had somewhat greater success in birth and development; some critics feel this was because of its freedom from the tugging and hauling of London politics. The entire situation, of course, differed geographically, sociologically, and technically from that of Victoria Park. In 1820 nothing but thinly populated country lay along the west bank of the broad Mersey estuary directly opposite Liverpool. In that year a merchant of the city crossed over, bought land, and built a house, starting the growth of Birkenhead, slow at first and then accelerating as commercial opportunities multiplied. The first shipyard was installed in 1825, a street system laid out in 1826, and prospects of expansion soon became so obvious that an Act of 1833 vested power and

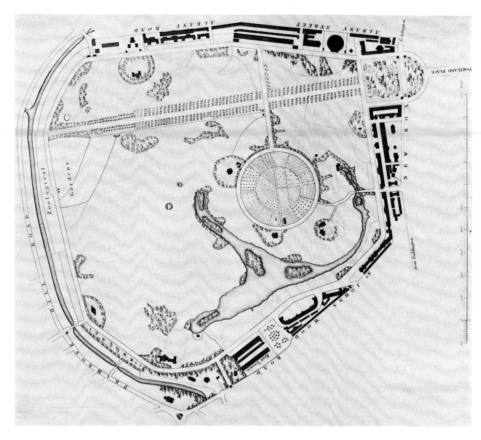

165. Map of Regent's Park as completed by 1841, drawn by the ironwork designer John Weale; note the changes from Nash's plan.

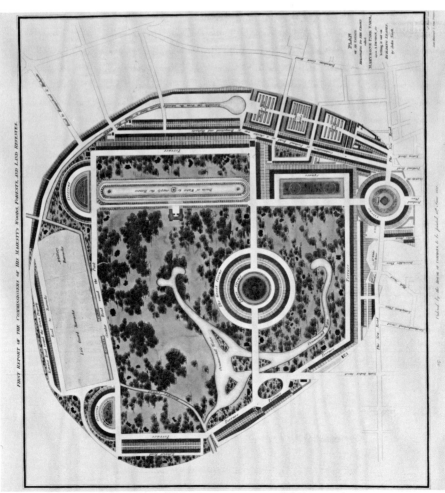

164. Original plan by John Nash for the Prince Regent's real-estate project of 1811, Marybone Park Farm, with "terrace houses" to be constructed around the periphery.

responsibility for development in a board of sixty Commissioners; since Birkenhead was clearly a product of Liverpool's rise in shipping and industry, it was no more than reasonable that about half the Commissioners should be Liverpool businessmen. Construction proceeded well, streets were paved, the simple utilities of the time were put in place, and Birkenhead thrived.

The Improvement Commissioners, however, were not satisfied with mere increase in size and business activity. Under heavy pressure from the burgeoning Reform movement—but, it must be admitted, with a canny weather eye for profit from land speculation on the part of a few—the Commissioners came to the inspired conclusion that a public park, such as did not then exist even in Liverpool, Manchester, Birmingham, or Leeds, would surely redound to Birkenhead's fame. To the credit of at least some of the Commissioners, in the spirit of the times they conscientiously felt it only right for working men, especially those so recently from farming occupations, to have *their* version of the landed Gentleman's Park; the congestion and drudgery of factories and docks would in some measure be offset by an open place reflecting country-type scenery. So was born in the brains of a few forward-looking men the phenomenon to be known within a few decades as the "country park." The park could have around its edges plots of land for sale as home-building sites to purchasers who would recognize the value of facing an open area. The income would accrue to municipal coffers, helping defray the costs of construction and maintenance. Good precedent existed for the economics of such a plan, though on a private rather than public basis, in the successful development of Regent's Park.

Convinced of their case, the Commissioners sought from Parliament in 1842 the power to use public funds for securing land and developing upon it a park to be used and owned by the people of Birkenhead. The Third Improvement Act was passed in April 1843, to become effective that September. Contracts for purchase of the land had been entered into by the Commissioners a year earlier in anticipation of their granted power. A total of 225 acres was bought, 125 of which were allocated to public recreational purposes in perpetuity and the remaining 100 for sale as house lots. In August 1843 the Commissioners engaged, as designer of the park, Joseph Paxton, who had a considerable reputation as a landscape gardener and who in 1842 had prepared a design for Prince's Park in Liverpool, a private real-estate venture known to the Commissioners. Paxton was also a figure of some national prominence as a practical botanist and as head gardener for the Duke of Devonshire at Chatsworth, Derbyshire. To help him on the ground the Commissioners also engaged his protégé, Edward Kemp, as superintendent.

Joseph Paxton was an amazing and versatile man. Born a Bedfordshire farmer's son in 1803, he early became an apprentice gardener. He was working in the gardens of the Horticultural Society when in 1826 the Duke of Devonshire offered him the post as head gardener at Chatsworth. His energy and

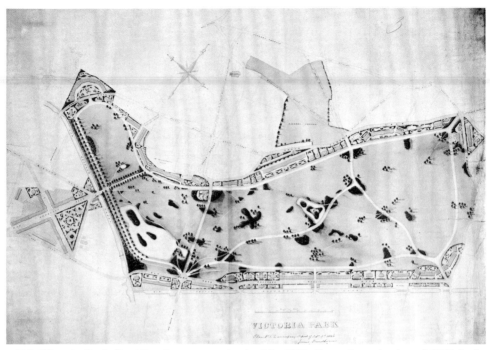

166. Victoria Park, East London, was authorized in 1842; Pennethorne's plan of 1841 had been modified several times before this one was inscribed, in his hand, "Plan No. 1 to accompany Report of Octr. 3d. 1846. James Pennethorne."

astuteness so impressed his employer that before long he was virtually manager of the Duke's affairs, a position that allowed him wide travel under the Duke's patronage. Experimental work in horticulture at Chatsworth had brought him into contact with J. C. Loudon, whom he succeeded in 1843, on the latter's death, as England's best-known gardener-botanist. Experiments led to ingenious hydraulic devices and continually improved glass houses, including the famous Great Conservatory at Chatsworth. This work led to Paxton's patent for construction of glass roofs and then to his greatest fame—and subsequent knighthood—in the design of the Crystal Palace of 1851, eight years after his engagement for Birkenhead Park. Even before the Crystal Palace, Paxton had achieved some recognition as an architect, a career second only to his "landscape gardening." Active also in business as an organizer, especially of railways, he was a Member of Parliament for some years prior to his death in 1865.

Rough work on the park began as soon as Paxton had sufficiently familiarized himself with the terrain to make general dispositions. Two lakes were dug and several of the "lodges" built during 1844, and by midsummer 1845 the rough work was finished in the main and much of the planting done. Continuing work of a detailed and finishing nature went on for another year

ENTRANCE TO THE PARK.

167. A pouring rain did not prevent the inaugural ceremony of April 7, 1847, for the new Birkenhead Docks and Park.

or so, and on April 7, 1847, the official opening was presided over by Lord Morpeth. Also completed in 1847 were the Egerton and Morpeth Docks, the town's first; the contemporary engraving of the park's inaugural ceremony (Fig. 167) is entitled "Opening of the Birkenhead Docks and Park"—a perfect reminder of the technological advances that so magnified Liverpool's industry and shipping as to bring about Birkenhead's birth.

Paxton's design for the park is fairly typical of its times, with the over-curvaceous quality bequeathed by the landscape gardening school (Fig. 168). But it is refreshing to see in his plan far less influence of Loudon and his gardenesque school, with its customary spottiness, than might have been expected in view of the close relationship of the two men. Even the car-riage-drive system, though restless in its abrupt reversals of curvature, is less writhing than it might have been. To be sure, the clumsy joining of the park road to the two northern entrances is regrettable, as is the pinched effect impressed upon the park spaces in the middle, where it would seem an effort was made, though unsuccessfully, to ease the harmful effect of the road that cuts directly across the heart of the park. But on the whole the carriage road no doubt has done the job assigned to it—an ambiguous one at best because of the decision to have a belt of house lots for "villas" around the periphery,

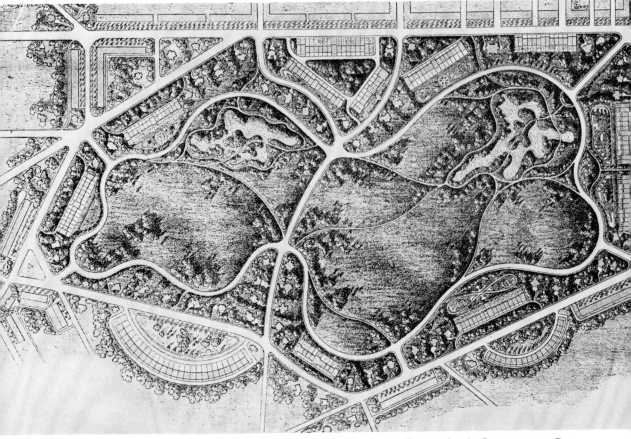

168. Plan of Birkenhead Park: started in 1843 by Joseph Paxton for the Improvement Commissioners of the Borough.

between the road and the straight boundary streets. As a consequence, one is left with an uncertain feeling as to where the park's limits actually lie; it is almost as though the town and its housing were ruthlessly invading it. The internal spaces of the park (Fig. 169), while individually positive and reasonably clear of gardenesque scatterings of trees, are difficult to assess as a total structure because of the road system, both in Paxton's plan and from the air today. The two sizable lakes contribute to the overall spatial effect but are so narrowed and twisted to almost river-like proportions that they lose something in outdoor scale.

The strange eclecticism of the era is reflected in many details, such as the incredibly ponderous Ionic archway at the main or northeast entrance to the park. The monument was designed not by Paxton but reportedly by Gillespie Graham, the same Scottish architect who had made Birkenhead's first street plan. Paxton apparently had his heart set on nine small gate lodges; the four

169. Contemporary engraving, "Scene in Birkenhead Park," looking across the park to the grandiose entrance and the masts clustered at the new docks beyond.

170. Two of Birkenhead's bridges, in keeping with the fashion of the day: the Temple on the right and the more distant Swiss Bridge.

actually built were quaintly named the Gothic, Italian, Castellated, and Norman Lodges! The bridges, too, were faithful to the requisite early-Victorian modishness; the Swiss Bridge, the Rustic Bridge, and the Temple (Fig. 170) were among the most curious bits.

When all is said and done, the technical quality of the design is obviously of far less importance than the simple fact of the park's having come into being. Almost as noteworthy, in a historical sense, was the effect of the park on a young American traveler, Frederick Law Olmsted, who little anticipated becoming within a few years the designer of the first new "country park" in the New World and the founder of the profession of landscape architecture in the United States. In 1850, at the age of twenty-eight, Olmsted spent several months in England. Having landed by packet in Liverpool, he and his companion set out by crossing the Mersey to Birkenhead; there they stopped at a bakery, and Olmsted, as was his custom, fell into conversation with the baker. Among other information freely given, the baker "begged of us not to leave Birkenhead without seeing their *new park.*" They went to it at once, and Olmsted was profoundly impressed. In his fascinating book, *Walks and Talks of an American Farmer in England,* published in London in 1852, he voiced his enthusiasm in glowing terms. After all, he had never seen anything like this anywhere in completely *public* ownership: "I was ready to admit that in democratic America there was nothing to be thought of as comparable with this People's Garden . . . And all this magnificent pleasure-ground is entirely, unreservedly, and for ever the people's own. The poorest British peasant is as free to enjoy it in all its parts as the British queen. More than that, the baker of Birkenhead has the pride of an OWNER in it . . . Is it not a grand good thing?"[1]

1. Frederick Law Olmsted, *Walks and Talks of an American Farmer in England* (London, 1852), pp. 74–83.

XVII. Pückler-Muskau
and Alphand

Arising from the better aspects of the English landscape gardening school were two continental phenomena of great importance. The first, which made a valuable contribution to the improvement of "landscape gardening," was a single man and his personal endeavor, Prince Pückler-Muskau and the park he created on ancestral lands in Germany. The second, significant historically rather than technically, was the team headed by Adolphe Alphand that worked some years later under the fabulous Baron Haussmann in Paris.

Hermann Ludwig Heinrich, Fürst von Pückler-Muskau, was born in 1785, the son of a count, a privy councilor of the King of Saxony. The title of Fürst (prince) was received later from the King of Prussia. Pückler's domain, including the *schloss* where he was born, the adjacent village of Muskau, and many square miles of territory, lay on both sides of the River Neisse, in old Silesia, about a hundred miles southeast of Berlin (Fig. 171). The River Neisse became after World War II the unrecognized boundary between East Germany and the Soviet version of Poland, so that, tragically, the park of Muskau is cut in two. The portion remaining unquestionably in East Germany contains the castle and the finest part of the park, as well as the village and the mineral baths through which the locality is now shown on maps as Bad Muskau. Although the schloss was completely gutted by fire during the war, the place is reported to have suffered no other harm. The East German portion is well maintained and obviously held in high esteem by the government, even to the extent that the village is advertised as *Parkstadt Bad Muskau* and foreign tourists are encouraged to visit it.

Pückler was on all counts an active individual. Having started to prepare for the law at Leipzig, he dropped that for the sweep of a military career.

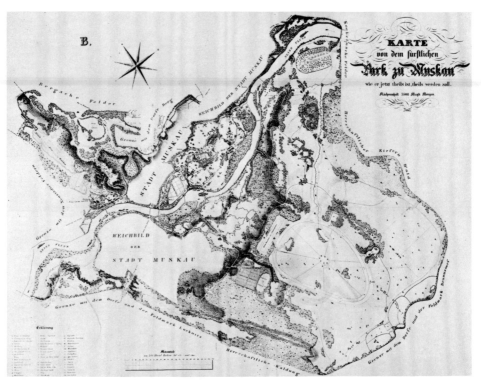

171. "Map of the princely Park at Muskau, as in part it now is, in part will be," from Prince Pückler's book. The portion to the left of the River Neisse is now East Germany; that to the right, never completed, is Poland.

The last decade of the Napoleonic wars found him dashing about incessantly, an able officer, a skilled swordsman and rider, always enthusiastic, always ambitious, always dreaming of wider horizons and limitless wealth. Through his life he was a gay blade—a ladies' man and a model of fashion. An inveterate traveler, he visited England at least twice in his younger days, then wandered almost continuously over Europe and North Africa for some years after Waterloo had brought a measure of quiet to his world. During these years he courted and married a wealthy widow, the Countess Pappenheim, and plunged all the more deeply into the social and diplomatic frivolities of the times.

Before long the frothy life began to pall, and Pückler's innate creative bent asserted itself. The family properties centering on Muskau had meanwhile come to him on his father's death and, harking back to boyhood dreams of improving these beloved lands, he recalled the encouragement his plans had once received from Goethe, in Weimar. Without fully realizing what the project would eventually cost, he dedicated himself to the task with the abiding conviction that, as he put it, "it does not become a man, who has succeeded to estates owned by his forefathers for centuries, to turn his back on them."[1]

"I desired," he later wrote, "to lay out as a park . . . the whole river domain with its bordering plateaus and hill chains . . . and to surround the town itself in such a way that it would become merely a part of the park . . . the main idea . . . was nothing less than to present a sensible picture of the life of our family, or of the aristocracy of our country . . . For this purpose it was only necessary to utilize what was already there, to elevate and enrich in the same spirit, but not to violate its locality and history" (*Hints,* pp. 130–131).

Having determined his course of action, Pückler naturally turned to his knowledge of what the English landscape gardening school had done. In visits to England as a young man, he had seriously studied many country places, particularly the works of Brown and Repton, and had come to the "firm conviction that England must for a long time remain an unattainable model in the art of worthy . . . enjoyment of life, especially with regard to country life" (p. 4). It should not be supposed, however, that he was an indiscriminate admirer of everything English. He criticized with refreshing candor, generally preferring Repton's work to that of Brown, which he found "often crude, angular, and uncouth" (29). He condemned especially the mistaken German imitation of the "*so-called* English style," in which "straight roads are then turned into corkscrew forms which are just as mechanical, serpentining in the most tedious manner . . ." (6).

The comments and criticisms quoted here and later in this account were the result, either direct or indirect, of another trip to England and Ireland in 1828. During this visit Pückler sent back a series of letters, later published in Germany as *Briefe eines Verstorbenen* and in England as *Letters of a German Prince.* Perhaps emboldened by the genuine success of the letters, and their praise by the aged Goethe himself, Pückler published in 1834 the now famous *Andeutungen,* or *Hints on Landscape Gardening,* with which he included a chapter on the park at Muskau. In this chapter one is continually reminded by Pückler, the incurable optimist, that the whole place is necessarily described as completed even though some features may still be only projected. The unhappy fact is that he never did finish the development as planned, but exhausted his resources by 1845 and in that year had to sell the entire property to Prince Frederick of the Netherlands. He thereupon retired to his smaller holding at Branitz, which he continued to play with until his death in 1871.

What Pückler did at Muskau was not spectacular; indeed, its charm for over a century has lain in its quiet simplicity and straightforwardness. When he began, the domain already included not only the moated castle, with its

---

1. H. L. H. Pückler-Muskau, *Hints on Landscape Gardening,* trans. Bernhardt Sickert, ed. Samuel Parsons for ASLA (Boston, 1917), pp. 118–119.

172. Schloss Muskau across the artificial lake about 1910; the castle is now a burned-out ruin, but the rest remains.

orangery, stables, and "theater," but the town of Muskau, the alum mines and refining works, the mineral baths, a mill, a brewery, a wax bleachery, numerous cultivated fields, pastures, and farmhouses, and, on the edges of the property, the tiny villages of Berg, Lucknitz, Kraunsdorf, and Köbeln. It is particularly to be noted that Pückler retained all of these, repairing and rehabilitating where necessary; all were, he felt, an integral part of the "locality and history" of the place. Even before beginning work, he felt required to buy some two thousand acres more; meanwhile, he was clearing out and cleaning up the unkempt fields and other signs of what he considered the careless, insensitive treatment of the land by his ancestors.

The greatest single stroke was undoubtedly Pückler's diverting a small part of the flow of the Neisse, leading a new stream toward the town from above the old mill and converting the existing moat into a lake partly enveloping the castle (Fig. 172). To do this, he first had to buy and remove an entire street of the town, then blast out the thick foundations of old fortifications as well as the walls of the moat itself. Beyond this point the new stream still meanders gently northeastward, forms another small lake, then rejoins the Neisse. The artistry of the stream-work, especially where shrubs on the margins dip softly into the water as though they and the stream and lake had always been there, is amazingly skillful.

The whole scheme was tied together with a flowing system of roads, paths, and bridges that provided routes of great variety and ingenuity as described by Pückler in the "three carriage drives" on which he conducts the reader of his book. The crowning glory of the park, however, is the firm integrity of its magnificent pastoral spaces (Figs. 173, 174). Here Pückler seems to have revealed most clearly the innate understanding of spatial structure—the awareness of spaces as components of design—sought in vain among the usual English landscape gardening works. It cannot with any certainty be stated that Pückler was conscious of this; obviously he did not write of space as a working material of design. Yet in this masterful creation of his one sees again and again the handling of spatial sequences on clearly enunciated sight-lines—first a large sunny space, then a shadowy constricted space, next a still larger sunny one again—with a kind of pulsation that imparts a vibrant, living quality to the entire great composition.

Selecting from what the Prince actually did on the land and from what he offers in his writings, the modern student of landscape architecture can find a surprising number of visible examples or verbal precepts that are as helpfully applicable today as they were in Pückler's time. It is appropriate here to touch briefly on some of these discoverable "hints," one by one.

1. *Unity.* "The indispensable foundation for the building of a park," wrote Pückler, "is a controlling scheme. It should be begun and carried out with entire consistency." This quality of oneness or wholeness, he urged, is "the same principle which . . . makes of the true work of art a microcosm, a perfect self-contained world in little" (*Hints,* 14).

2. *Inwardness.* Another aspect of unity, this quality is noticeably manifested in the park at Muskau because the whole is a hollow or valley, with the skyline generally under visual control. Such a condition, in effect a large concavity or bowl composition, tends to direct the interest inward and confer a sense of cohesion. It stresses also the extreme importance of recognizing topographic units and treating them homogeneously.

3. *Outwardness.* Pückler was keenly aware of the almost universal human craving for elbowroom, for the outward reach of space that gratifies the eye quite apart from any actual measurement. "Laid out with equal intelligence I should always prefer the more extensive to the smaller park, even if the latter should be more favored by Nature" (p. 21). Later he wrote: "it is obvious that every interesting feature of the distant landscape should be included in the park . . . Distant views . . . lying away beyond the actual grounds, give an appearance of measureless extent" (30).

173. Looking southward from the carriage entrance of the castle at Muskau, the integrity of spaces as components of the design can be sensed.

174. The outward reach and pulsation of spaces across the meadows of Muskau.

4. *Simplicity.* While acknowledging frankly the difficulties that confronted him in the effort to bring order and loveliness to the basically dreary valley of the Neisse, Pückler never wanted the result to *look* difficult. "When all is finished, the greater, nay, the greatest part of the real merit of the work will remain unnoticed by the casual stranger, and the more this is true, the better it is" (117). When a visiting "lady of intelligence and understanding" remarked that the place gave "the general impression of quietness and simplicity," Pückler declared that no comment could have pleased him more deeply (16). He sought effortlessness and ease of appearance, not show.

5. *Man as nature.* The Prince felt that English country places, by too often excluding humans from the landscape scene while insisting on the presence of sheep and cattle, had grossly misrepresented the position of man in the totality of nature. In word as well as deed he strongly favored including in the scene those evidences of man's activity that reflected a human contribution toward making the environment what it was. "Even in painted landscape, we demand something which reminds us of human effort—as we say, to *animate* it . . . If one can bring within the park a manor house with its fields adjoining, a mill or a factory, this will give it only the more life and variety, which is much to be recommended" (pp. 4, 40). This is precisely what he did in the park at Muskau.

6. *House-garden unified.* Again accepting manmade forms as a legitimate part of the scene, Pückler resolved the problem that had so confused the early landscape gardeners. "Near the house one should seek for the charm of a garden of modest proportions, which, whenever possible, would contrast with Nature around . . . an extension of the art of architecture from the house to the garden . . . as the park is Nature idealized within a small compass, so the garden is an extended dwelling" (pp. 22, 42). At Muskau he put this tenet into practice by creating beside the schloss a number of shaded sitting places that were veritable outdoor living rooms, anticipating what would be called, over a century later, the interpenetration of indoor and outdoor space.

7. *Ecology for humans.* Further demonstrating his profound grasp of a total ecology that included the human organism, Pückler wrote: "In the park I avail myself, as a rule, of native or thoroughly acclimated trees and shrubs, and avoid all foreign ornamental plants, for idealized Nature must still be true to the character of the country and the climate to which it belongs . . . Such grounds should represent Nature, it is true, but Nature arranged for the use and comfort of man" (65).

8. *Variety.* It is doubtful that the Prince ever thought in such a twentieth-century term as that of space-time. Yet he seemed to sense intuitively the dynamic quality of the time dimension, whether in recognizing the variation of light at different times of the day or in calling for changes of viewpoint as one progresses along a given travelway. He even hints at the wise suggestion that in any circuit it is preferable to have, for variety's sake, a return route

different from the route out. "Drives should be laid out so that chief points of interest and the most noteworthy objects in the entire park may be visited one after another without passing the same object twice—at least not in the same direction—on the round trip" (83–84). He was apparently fully conscious of the value of perceptible sequences, whether of spaces or of things. The drives he laid out in his own park illustrate this eloquently.

9. *Educational values.* Pückler's Muskau was barely emerging from medieval despotism. The lands he inherited were "a free lordship, endowed with subordinate sovereign rights and including the dependent vassal property covering an area of ten to eleven miles square" (119). It is therefore all the more remarkable that he held very advanced views about the use of his park as a training ground for educating the public away from vandalism. He was quite specific about it: "I allowed everyone, without consideration of persons, access to my grounds, although many landowners assured me that . . . people would cut down all the young trees and pluck all the flowers. It is true that some excesses occurred at first. They were sharply punished when the culprits could be identified, and when not, the damage was quickly and patiently repaired, and the gates remained as before, open to everyone. Very soon people were impressed by this steady perseverance; when often hundreds take their pleasure in the spacious park, I must admit, for the credit of the public, that any serious mischief is quite exceptional" (123–124). Little did Pückler realize that he was using a technique depended upon by landscape architects today in the design of state parks, to help a day-use tenderfoot become a skilled long-term camper who knows how to conduct himself in the presence of wild nature.

In the opinion of most present-day critics, there was one glaring exception to the rule of excellence in Pückler's performance—one that is difficult to reconcile with his unquestionable talents and the wisdom of his "hints." This was his adoption of what can most charitably be regarded as a fashion, foisted on a gullible public by the times (or maybe by the gardenesque school of J. C. Loudon): the screamingly bright, usually odd-shaped, floating flowerbeds invading the green of turf without evident reason. The strangest part is that the Prince actually seems to have been proud of them, appearing to have lost sight of their disruptive effect in design while waxing enthusiastic over the mere horticultural accomplishment. It is sometimes even claimed, as if this were a virtue, that Pückler *invented* carpet-bedding.

"To the flower beds themselves," he wrote, "I give a distinct, defined shape and surround them preferably by basket-work . . . On the ground plan, no doubt, there may be a singular appearance in the fan-shape; the 'H' set in a star; the square shaped like the breastplate of a Jewish high priest; the cornucopia; the colossal flower made up of various plants; an 'S' of roses and forget-me-nots; the peacocks' feathers, etc. As a matter of fact, the effect is rather rich and original, and not more heterogeneous than the bazaar effect is usually in the room of an elegant lady" (pp. 73, 143). The Prince clearly entertained a few doubts about the matter himself!

When all is considered, perhaps this isolated errant foible can be excused—except for a single especially harmful instance, on the south front of the castle, where a few broad steps descend toward Muskau's most compelling meadow vista. In the grass, athwart the bottom of the steps in the foreground of the prospect—as Pückler shows it in one of his illustrations—he placed a row of four square flower beds of the glaring sort here described, virtually challenging the eye to get across without trouble.

Aside from this one peculiarity, however, it must be obvious that the contribution of Prince Pückler-Muskau was astounding, not only in high creative quality but also in originality and inventiveness far ahead of his time. All the more remarkable, surely, when it is recalled that he had no training in this field. His understanding and foresight must inevitably be attributed to intuition and to a profound sense of dedication to the loftiest practical ideals.

Even after he retired to Branitz in 1845, the benefit of Pückler's judgment and experience was sought by others facing problems similar to his upon the land. Among the most important of these projects, at least historically, was the Bois de Boulogne, in Paris. This former royal hunting forest was undergoing changes as one part of the monumental series of works carried out between 1853 and 1870 by Louis Napoleon and his energetic prefect, Baron Georges Eugène Haussmann. Louis, the nephew of Napoleon I, having been proclaimed President of France by popular vote in 1848, became Emperor Napoleon III in 1852 when a second plebiscite ratified restoration of the empire. Along with his countrymen in general, he had long been infatuated with the English landscape garden or *jardin anglais,* as the French misinterpretation was usually labeled. The Emperor had especially envied London its Hyde Park and Serpentine and had resolved to modify the Bois de Boulogne accordingly.

The Bois, some 1100 acres of woods on the western outskirts of Paris, had been established at least as early as the seventeenth century, with characteristically French allées radiating from *ronds points* in the dense forest (Fig. 175). Now Louis Napoleon wanted the sinuous water and sweeping curves that he associated with the new fashion. On visits to London he had studied Hyde Park earnestly, assuming it to be typical of "landscape gardening." He had firm ideas about the changes he wanted in the Bois, positive individual that he was; but he did seek the advice of the eminent Prince Pückler-Muskau, whose work on his family estates had achieved such fame and whose helpful writings had appeared in both English and French.

Then Louis Napoleon made his worst mistake, assigning the task of redeveloping the Bois to his father's head gardener, one M. Varé, who quickly demonstrated that for his abilities the job was too big and too difficult. In attempting to create a single long body of water like the Hyde Park Serpentine, Varé overlooked so essential a matter as checking the actual grades of the land and found himself in an impossible fix with an excavation that would be either too steep to hold the intended water or too unreasonably deep at the upper end.

At this point the Emperor's new Prefect of the Seine fortunately appeared on the scene. Georges Eugène Haussmann, after some twenty years of service in the Prefectoral Corps, had been appointed Prefect of Bordeaux in 1851. His record there, as administrator and executive, had been so outstanding that in June 1853 the Emperor summoned him to Paris, appointed him to this top prefectoral post, and confided in him the imperial hopes for grand alterations in the capital city. Between 1853 and 1870 the projects completed under Haussmann's administration were little short of fantastic. To a large degree the Paris that captivates visitors today is the result of Haussmann's efforts: the many *rues percées* and such major ways as the Boulevard Saint Germain and the Boulevard Saint Michel, as well as the much revised Bois de Boulogne and Bois de Vincennes, to say nothing of several small local parks and the city's charming aura of sunny, tree-lined openness as exemplified by spaces like the Etoile, the Place de l'Opéra, and the Place de la République.

175. Paris: the earlier state of the Bois de Boulogne, with allées and ronds points normal to the French tradition.

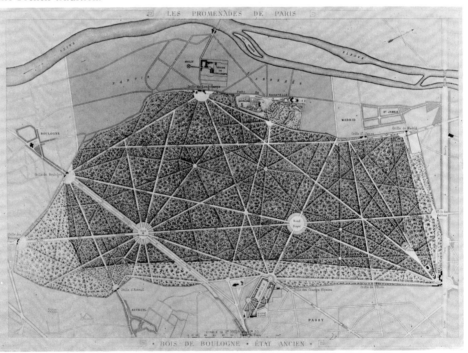

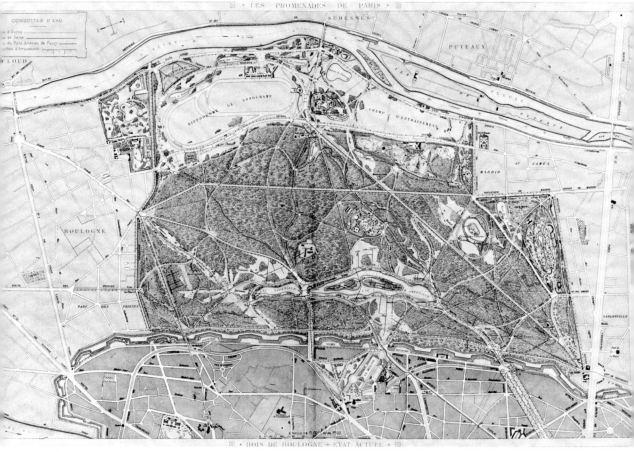

176. Paris: the Bois de Boulogne as "improved in the English fashion" for the Emperor by Haussmann and Alphand.

Of all this, the work on the Bois de Boulogne is of chief interest here. When Haussmann first saw it, almost immediately after his arrival in Paris, he swiftly comprehended not only the dimensions of the task as a whole but especially the mistake that Varé had made. With the Emperor's permission he sent to Bordeaux for his right-hand man, Jean Charles Adolphe Alphand, to come to Paris for a job that was hardly habitual in the Corps of Bridge and Highway Engineers. Alphand was officially classed as an engineer, but his outlook and skills would qualify him today as a landscape architect. He had been a mainstay for Haussmann in Bordeaux and was even more valuable to him in Paris.

In the Bois, Alphand promptly rectified the bungled excavation of Varé by shortening the proposed long body of water into two lakes, upper and lower, with a carriage crossing and waterfall between them. He did what he could to modify most of the long straight allées into winding roads and paths, as the Emperor wished (Fig. 176). Though these changes have aroused much technical controversy in the century since they were made, it is only fair to say that among Haussmann's many projects the Bois was in public acceptance one of the most successful. By obtaining permission to sell some peripheral portions for residential purposes, particularly in the fast-growing and fashionable section of Neuilly, Haussmann was able to acquire other land toward the Seine on the west and to develop there the great race course of Longchamps, while gaining surplus income with which to cover a large part of construction costs and thereby ease the burden of taxation—then as now a highly commendable move in Parisian eyes.

Alphand was a figure of genuine importance, not only for the work he did in his twenty years of association with Haussmann, but beyond this for the two large volumes he later produced entitled *Les Promenades de Paris,* published between 1868 and 1873. The exquisitely drawn plates became the standard reference on Parisian parks and boulevards. They included, too, many examples of the peculiar talent of a younger man, Barillet-Deschamps, a horticulturist summoned from Bordeaux as a member of the original Haussmann team of 1853. Barillet-Deschamps had somehow developed a remarkable flair for the twists and curlicues of the *jardin anglais;* in time he achieved the rank of Chief Gardener of the City of Paris, while his immediate superior, Alphand, became the city's Director of Works and Inspector General of Bridges and Highways. The name of Alphand was known also to later generations because of the popular book *L'Art des Jardins,* first published in 1868 by Baron Alfred Auguste Ernouf "avec le concours de A. Alphand." This volume, containing a mixture of history, theory, and working instructions on a variety of "parks, gardens, and promenades," was illustrated profusely with engravings, many taken from Alphand's more highly regarded *Promenades.* The book does not begin to compare with Pückler-Muskau's writings in total value, but it is nevertheless an interesting reflection of attitudes of the era.

In a quite specific sense, Alphand and the Bois de Boulogne have historical significance in the prelude of what was about to happen in the United States. Prince Pückler-Muskau had perhaps less immediate effect, but only because his place, after all, was private rather than public. But, as had been the case with Birkenhead Park, so now the Bois de Boulogne a few years later helped guide public opinion in America and the thinking of Frederick Law Olmsted as the time approached for him to join Calvert Vaux in creating Central Park in New York. In fact, according to the subsequent testimony of Olmsted himself, the Board of Commissioners, before instituting the famous competition of 1857, had seriously considered trying to get either Paxton or Alphand to design Central Park.[2] Certain it is that Olmsted, traveling abroad in 1859

2. Frederick Law Olmsted, *Forty Years of Landscape Architecture,* vol. II: *Central Park,* ed. F. L. Olmsted, Jr., and T. Kimball (New York, 1928), p. 311. Cited hereafter as *Olmsted Papers, Central Park.*

after starting work on the park, visited Birkenhead again, and then in Paris not only conferred with Alphand, but went with him on eight visits to the Bois de Boulogne.[3] How helpful these visits were in a professional sense is doubtful, for Central Park is by general agreement a far greater work of art than the Bois. But the Bois, even in its newly modified form, did come first and in this respect must be accorded historical precedence.

3. *Ibid.,* p. 56.

XVIII. Early American Backgrounds

Developments in the New World had proceeded as might have been expected in a series of overseas offshoots from Europe. In the first century after Columbus there was only sporadic exploration of North America and virtually no settlement; Spain and to some degree Portugal were engaged in conquering South America. From about 1600 onward, when settlements were at last made by the Spanish, French, English, Dutch, Swedish, and Finnish, for many years the primary concern regarding the land was plain: clearing the forest and preparing arable soil. Staying alive was the persistent central problem as each group of hopeful colonists tried to meet the needs and fulfill the purposes of its own particular adventure.

European settlers found no tradition of land planning established by the natives. Peaks of culture and creative achievement had certainly been reached among the American Indians, but there was little or no arrangement of terrain in a landscape architectural sense. So, too, with the earliest colonists, the Spanish, whose feverish activity in the south and west seldom paused long enough to embrace orderly treatment of land areas, aside perhaps from eventual small gardens in the missions of California. The founders of New France, vigorous in building a fur trade and converting Indians, were on the whole far too busy to indulge any capacity for outdoor design, even if the climate had encouraged such niceties. There may well have been a few tiny gardens in Quebec or Montreal, but there was little scope in Canada for this kind of thing, even in the age of Le Nôtre and Versailles.

New Sweden, the little colony of Swedes and Finns on the Delaware River, lasted only seventeen years before being annexed by New Netherland. The

Dutch are known to have had a few small gardens in New Amsterdam, and their enormous patroonships along the Hudson were forerunners of the later manors and country places that would front on that river in the nineteenth century. But actual developments of any extent upon the land, so far as design was concerned, were minimal in Dutch times—and then in 1664 New Netherland was relinquished to the English. Thus it happens, almost by default, that landscape architectural accomplishment in colonial North America seems restricted to English settlements. Even here the story progresses slowly, for in this Western wilderness the moment of relaxation needed for developing gardens did not arrive until well into the eighteenth century. When, in time, an effort could be afforded in this direction the patterns normally followed were the well-remembered ones of England, though with the time-lag of a generation or two so common in colonial societies.

In attempting to reconstruct colonial examples, a major difficulty lies in the nature of the available evidence. With a few lucky exceptions, chiefly in the south, most early work on the land was done with relatively impermanent materials of which practically nothing is left, so that verbal accounts must be relied on. There is an ample supply of these in letters, descriptions, and early nursery catalogs, but of course this evidence, though better than none, is usually about plant materials only and provides little firm basis for determining specific plans. From a designer's point of view, knowing *what* materials were used is necessary but not enough; he needs also to know *how* and precisely *where* they were used.

In their landscape architecture, the degree of difference among the colonies was remarkable—especially considering that in the most basic elements of design the regions differed very little. The internal structure of gardens, wherever they existed, was apparently a simple geometric arrangement of beds, usually rectilinear but on occasion circular, rather uniformly in all the colonies up and down the Atlantic seaboard. But differentiation among them must be clear, particularly as they were affected by climate, economics, and social organization.

The region most distinctive in comparison with the others was New England, where the long, rigorous winters and the generally stony soil militated against the large, widely spread layouts possible in the warmer south. Moreover, in New England the stern demands of an austere morality tended to emphasize plain practicality and reject whatever could too readily be interpreted as display. New England farms were normally small, operationally compact, and close to each other or to settlements. They were situated near highways to reduce the risk of isolation by heavy snows, even in those later cases when merchants and mill-owners, having attained wealth, built "mansions" away from the towns. Throughout New England distinguished houses of the eighteenth century are extant, but in most instances their original outdoor surroundings can only be imagined.

177. Salem, Massachusetts: the Nichols garden with its faithful mulberry tree.

It is mainly in the towns that a fortunate habit of not bothering to change the old has sometimes lent a degree of credibility to small gardens accompanying houses of unquestioned authenticity. Examples are the Nichols garden in Salem and other smaller ones there and in Marblehead, Governor Hutchinson's garden in Milton, and somewhat later gardens in Newburyport—all in Massachusetts. The Nichols garden retained until recently what appeared to be its original plan, centered on a long, straight path heading downhill from an archway in a carriage barn behind the fine old house (Fig. 177). The side areas were no doubt subdivided in different ways through the years, but an old mulberry tree stood as a symbol of constancy beside the central path, midway down the hill. Even up to a few years ago, when the lower end of the garden had been chewed away by a concrete highway, the mulberry tree stood its ground.

So far as can be established, the usual pattern in New England gardens was the expectable one: a tight rectilinear layout of paths and square beds, with some sort of edging. Thanks to numerous nursery catalogs of the time, preserved by the Massachusetts Horticultural Society, there is rather full evidence of the commonly used trees, shrubs, and herbaceous perennials, many of which were imports from England. In contrast to the dearth of reliable information about the form of private gardens, examples of typical New England public open spaces can still be seen in such village greens as those of Ipswich and Lexington and in Commons like those of Boston and Cambridge. Of course these public green spaces offered no signs of design intent, nor could they accurately be called parks. They were originally intended as common cow-pastures (hence the name) and for drilling the local militia, but they provided a strong background of tradition when the time came for fostering the new notion of "country parks."

The New York part of the colonial story brings in a new dimension. Under New Netherland's rule, patroonships were granted in 1629 to members of the Dutch India Company who brought fifty or more settlers and received in return vast acreages along the Hudson—sixteen miles on one side or eight on both sides of the river, as deep inland as conditions permitted. When the English took over in 1664 under the Duke of York the patroonships were confirmed, along with other huge tracts granted as manors under English law. There were at least sixteen manors, the most influential being those of Van Rensselaer, Van Cortlandt, Livingston, and Philipse, plus the Sylvester Manor on Shelter Island. These five retained their manor houses or other pre-Revolutionary buildings of like age and character; the Philipse Manor Hall in Yonkers and the two Van Cortlandt houses, one at Croton-on-Hudson, the other in New York's Van Cortlandt Park, are probably the most widely known today. But, aside from an 1847 survey of grounds at Philipse Manor Hall and an existing box garden on possibly old lines at Sylvester Manor, these early holdings offer no remnants of landscape architectural treatment. There are of course contemporary references in writings about small gardens connected with New York's town houses and to country places of a few wealthy merchants on upper Manhattan Island, but no authentic physical remains are known.

In the vicinity of Philadelphia the available evidence becomes more positive and less dependent on verbal accounts alone. In Germantown, such fine early stone houses as Wyck and Wister's Big House have simple gardens of box-bordered squares and walks that may well descend with little modification from the originals. High on the banks of the Schuylkill, the ultimate preservation of what is now Fairmount Park meant also the saving of several excellent eighteenth-century houses, among them Mount Pleasant, built in brick and stucco after 1761 with part of its grounds restored some years ago in conformity with an earlier survey showing a series of terraces, with earth banks, stepping down toward the river from the house.

As attention moves south, evidence of early landscape architectural effort improves considerably, for a combination of reasons: gentler climate, frequent use of such permanent materials as brick, greater number and wider distribution of country places and their relative freedom from the pressures of subsequent urbanization. The case of Virginia is particularly illustrative. From the earliest days of the Jamestown landing, dispersal rather than settlement in towns was the rule because of Virginia's growing dependence on tobacco culture and on the head-rights method of acquiring land in sizable parcels. Land speculations and successful tobacco ventures resulted in an entirely new class of surprisingly wealthy landowners. Large tracts of land, leading eventually to typical southern plantations, became a usual pattern especially toward the end of the seventeenth century, when slave labor began to be a vital element in the economy. Moreover, the mild climate and the multiplicity of servants, both white and black, nourished in Virginia a culture much like that of the landed gentry in England. Out of these factors arose the characteristic plantation life of the south, on agricultural-residential properties considerably larger and more widely dispersed than individual private places in the north even on the vast manors of New York.

In certain ways Virginia did not differ greatly from her northern counterparts. In the detailed layout of gardens, the same basically simple geometric patterns prevailed. Apparently the small town-gardens of Alexandria and Williamsburg did not differ essentially from those in northern cities, except that a low hedging of imported English box became more common in the south. Similarity between north and south was further emphasized by the design of houses, which followed throughout the colonies a version of what in England was known as Georgian architecture and in America was inventively modified just enough to give rise to the term Georgian Colonial. Residential construction was predominantly of wood in New England and brick in Virginia, but in grace of detail and nicety of proportion the two were fundamentally alike.

In the landscape architecture of the plantations, a difference between regions was early reflected. On the larger place, where several distinct elements comprised the whole, some sort of overall organization of parts was naturally required. It is in these layouts that Virginia and the other southern colonies exhibited the tendency of colonial societies to cling to the oldest forms brought out from England and to lag far behind in any shift in the vogue. In the layout of the typical plantation, even to the end of the eighteenth century and into the nineteenth, the organizing force was usually the strong geometric influence of the English Renaissance rather than the landscape gardening trend that had long since become the fashion in England. As a rule, then, the southern plantation had a readily discernible spatial structure that was not always skillful and in fact was rather often childishly bungling, but that nevertheless clearly evidenced an effort at creating an overall scheme of organization, with perceptible sight-lines tying the spaces together.

For ease of water-borne communication in the early days, many of Virginia's oldest plantations were located on river fronts. Within a few decades after the first landing at Jamestown in 1607, several large tracts were acquired both above and below it on the James River. On some of these, notably such properties as Shirley, Westover, and Brandon, brick houses of remarkable distinction had been erected by the mid-eighteenth century. Similarly, other brick houses had been built farther north, such as Chatham on the Rappahannock and Gunston on the Potomac; handsome Mount Airy in stone had arisen on the Northern Neck, between the Rappahannock and the Potomac; the first frame buildings of Mount Vernon had appeared, a few miles up the Potomac from Gunston. Available information as to the layout of the surrounding outdoor areas on these plantations is in most cases neither precise nor complete, but the general lines of some can be reasonably surmised, either on the ground or from descriptions.

Of the James River places, Westover retains enough of its original plan to warrant being cited as a typical and fairly authentic example. Some forty miles from Richmond, on the north bank of the river, it was built by William Byrd II in the 1730s. The handsome brick house, of two stories with a steep-roofed, dormered attic, is quite generally considered one of the finest existing specimens of American colonial residential architecture. It faces almost exactly south, with lower wings to east and west, about 200 feet from the river

178. Westover, on the James River in Virginia: a paced survey made just before World War I.

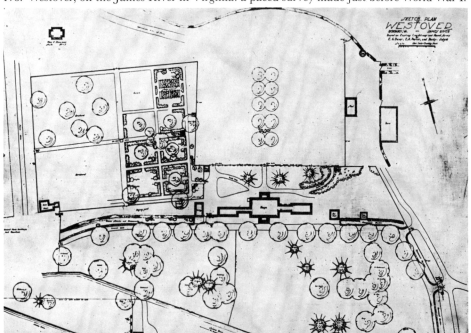

179. The south front of Westover, facing the James.

bank and at a slight angle to it (Fig. 178). A strong north-south sight-line passes across the center of the house, through two large doorways on the north and south faces, each with exquisite carved wood trim painted white. The first floor is lifted a few feet off the ground, and a pile of carved stone steps ties each doorway to a walk at its foot. Though impeccably simple, the house has an undeniable air of elegance.

The central sight-line extends from the south door across an open lawn to the river and over it to the far southern shore. From the north door it indicates clearly, by means of a pair of delicately wrought gates with brick gateposts topped by stone falcons, where a straight approach road once lay, bordered by trees and entering the house area through a wrought-iron fence punctuated by brick piers with cut-stone finials. The area between the fence and the north face of the house has obviously lost its original arrangement, no doubt as a consequence of abandoning the old approach road. The more usual present entrance is on the river front of the house, coming from the east, parallel to the south facade and flanked by a row of magnificent old trees (Fig. 179). The flower garden, lying west of the house, is bordered as usual by heavy box hedges. It appears to have been in a checkerboard pattern; what remains is neatly compact in its old-fashioned charm, but the garden is not clearly tied to the central organization of the house and the spaces north and south of it. Whether it was ever so tied is very hard to tell.

Shirley and Brandon are also distinguished James River houses, but the evidence of their original layout is even less complete than that of Westover. At imposing Mount Airy, north of the Rappahannock, there is a strong organization of turfed earth terraces and planting beds, but it can only be guessed that this was the original plan.

Gunston on the Potomac was developed by George Mason, author of Virginia's Bill of Rights and first Constitution and friend of General Washington, in the 1750s. Though a man of means, he chose to build a tiny house on his extensive lands. Perfect in proportion and detail, Gunston Hall sits well back from the Potomac, with gardens lying between the house and the river. Both house and grounds have recently been restored with meticulous care, the house by removal of extraneous additions and the grounds on the basis of existing material, chiefly very old box hedges.

The general plan of the place is completely straightforward. A long sight-line cuts through front and rear doorways of the little house, carrying a tree-bordered approach road on the entrance side and, on the side toward the river, a central gravel path between two magnificent hedges of box so high and full as to seem an evergreen tunnel lined up on the rear doorway. Garden areas lie to right and left of the central path and its high old box. They are open, sunny, and quite unaffected in their detailed treatment, consisting mainly of turf with box hedging and some individual specimens of box and magnolia. Beyond the garden is a pavilion, then the land slopes abruptly toward the river.

Gunston Hall is a striking illustration of the timeworn adage that truly impressive works are as a rule basically simple. Here is an instance of something almost doll-like in size that was nevertheless the home of a man who could have had a palace if he wished. There is a tradition that Mason, though a public figure in great demand, was so fond of Gunston that he begrudged every day spent away from it. This depth of affection is somehow clearly conveyed by the place even today.

A few miles up the Potomac from Gunston Hall is Mount Vernon (Fig. 180), known as the home of George Washington. The first buildings were erected in 1743 by Lawrence Washington, half-brother and guardian of young George, then only eleven years of age. George, who later inherited the place,

knew no other home from his fifteenth year. Throughout his life he was
devoted to Mount Vernon, continually making additions and adjustments,
even to the extent of sending precise written instructions to his local manager
in his enforced absences during the Revolution. Again and again in the eight
years of the war the General revealed in his writings how deeply he missed
"dear Mount Vernon." When at last the battles were over and he could
return, he made a few final changes; by 1785 the place had achieved its
present form. Washington returned permanently in 1797 after his two terms
as President, and in 1799 he died there. His tomb, between the house and
the river, is one of the cardinal points in a pilgrimage to Mount Vernon.
The entire place has been preserved as a national shrine through the devoted
efforts of the Mount Vernon Ladies' Association of the Union, established
in 1853 to rescue it. In the early 1930s it was made the terminus of the Mount
Vernon Memorial Highway when this was constructed southward from
Washington, and a thorough restoration of the entire property was effected
during the years immediately following.

The white frame house, set on a rise above the Potomac, faces southeast
at an angle to the river. The steep lawn goes right up to the two-story
columned porch, with only a grassy bank seeming to supply a base for the
structure. This uneasy formlessness—and the lovely soft view up the Potomac
over the trees bordering the river—are Mount Vernon's only suggestions of
the landscape gardening school fashionable in England for at least a generation by the time this place was completed. With the sole exception of the
treatment on the river front of the house, Mount Vernon is strongly organized

180. Mount Vernon on the Potomac: aerial view of the river front. Visible beyond the roof
are the Bowling Green and the vista into the far woods.

in what can now be described as the fairly usual Virginia version of the English Renaissance. A main sight-line runs from the center doorway of the house inland toward the northwest (Fig. 181) and a minor sight-line crosses it at right angles through a carriage turnaround just before the house. In sequence on the main sight-line, going inland from the house, are the gravel turnaround itself; an area of lawn called the Bowling Green; at the far end of this, a low wooden gate opening to a circumferential drive; beyond the gate, a meadow-like field leading in the distance to a long, straight vista that cuts into the surrounding woods.

The Bowling Green has symmetrically wavy sides that give it a gently sophisticated air. The edges are marked by gravel pathways that were originally carriage roads leading from the gate at the far end to the turnaround at the house and are now used only by pedestrians. Their unusual curvature is not at all the type of wiggly line associated with the landscape gardening school; the paths are definite in alignment, with a thoroughly clear geometry. To right and left of the Bowling Green, hidden and fitted in behind the bordering trees, are two gardens known as the Box Garden on the right, looking from the house, and the Kitchen Garden on the left (Fig. 182). The two, crisply delimited, each with a graceful small garden house at the far end of the shield-like plan, are again almost exactly symmetrical on the main central sight-line.

On the secondary sight-line, straight roads head out to left and right from the carriage turnaround, pass various little service buildings, then curve to become the aforementioned circumferential drive. The straight road to the left descends past a small paddock and the stables to a boat landing at the water's edge. The corresponding road to the right leads to greenhouses and workyards for the garden, then takes present-day visitors to the parking space at the terminus of the Mount Vernon Memorial Highway.

Aside from its historical significance, Mount Vernon deserves attention as an example of the Virginia plantation at its unpretentious best. It is not especially remarkable for any perfection of detail, but rather for its coherence as a total scheme. The house, with its wings and the curved arcades linking them, is not exceptional; indeed, there are certain endearing awkwardnesses about it. But the plan of the whole is extremely satisfying, particularly when one recalls that no professional designer is known to have helped General Washington with it. In fact, it is almost too competent in overall landscape architecture to be classified as *typical* of Virginia plantations of the post-Revolutionary period. Of course the entire place profits greatly from careful maintenance today.

More highly regarded architecturally than the house at Mount Vernon are two superb creations of that amazing Renaissance Man of America's eighteenth century, Thomas Jefferson: his beloved home, Monticello, and the quadrangle he designed and built for the University of Virginia at Charlottes-

181. The stately reaches of Mount Vernon as measured and drawn in 1931.

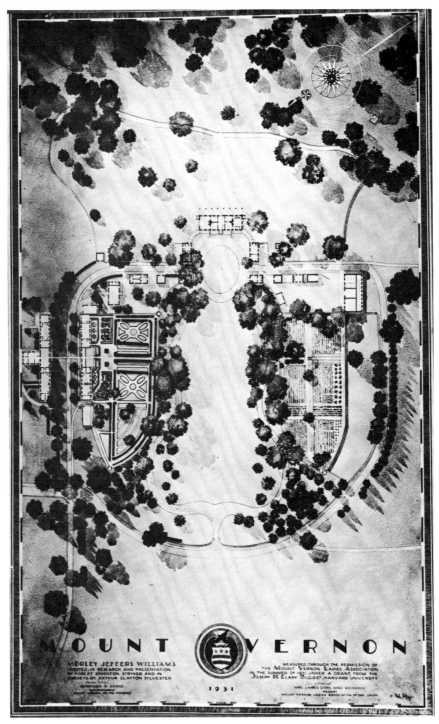

182. The immediate surroundings of the house at Mount Vernon: the Bowling Green in the center, the Box Garden on the left, the Kitchen Garden on the right.

ville. Interested in design from college days at William and Mary, Jefferson read and studied avidly, including especially the published works of Palladio. As a confirmed classicist he was drawn to Palladio's exposition of Roman architecture, of which he became a lifelong devotee. In the process he acquired remarkable skill as a draftsman (using simple graph paper) at a time when America did not yet offer any professional training for architects.

Monticello, the house on Jefferson's "little mountain," was four miles from Charlottesville and near Shadwell, where he was born in 1743 and lived as a boy. This gem of American architecture, begun in 1771 and remodeled extensively between 1796 and 1809, is regarded by many critics as a precursor of the classical revival. Though Jefferson wrote and sketched many instructions about the terracing, walks, flower beds, orchard spacing, and the like, the treatment of Monticello's grounds appears to have been quite casual and, surprisingly enough, without architectonic design. This aspect of his genius[1] is revealed in other ways: in his careful selection and handling of offscapes from the approach road up the hill and from the house itself; in the ingenious treatment of connection with service outbuildings by means of a subterranean tunnel; and in the fascinating contents of his famous *Garden Book,* in which he made almost daily entries from 1766 to 1824 about his wide-ranging interests, including an enormous amount of information on plants and planting. It emerges rather clearly from the *Garden Book* that at Monticello he was more concerned with general agriculture and his farming than with what he called "pleasure gardening."

The great campus quadrangle of the University of Virginia was the pinnacle of Jefferson's achievement as architect—and as landscape architect as well, in fitting the complex to the site. Though based of course on classical precedent, the plan was otherwise original with Jefferson; it involved two long buildings, called East and West Lawns, each consisting of five two-story Pavilions for faculty lodging and classrooms, joined by continuous arcaded dormitories for students. The two Lawns face each other across a terraced grassy panel, with the library Rotunda lifted high above steps at the upper end. Behind each of the two Lawns, as finally determined, is a double series of gardens (with the famous serpentine brick walls) and beyond these an additional row of arcaded dormitories, facing outward, called the East and West Ranges. Jefferson not only designed the whole, but meticulously supervised its construction from the laying of the first cornerstone in 1817. The work was substantially completed before his death in 1826.

In addition to these two masterpieces Jefferson made many other architectural contributions, among them designs for numerous country houses in Virginia for personal friends, participation with the French architect Clérisseau in designing the new capitol in Richmond, and his own competitive

1. An interesting study is the chapter by Warren H. Manning (a founder of the ASLA) in W. L. Lambeth and W. H. Manning, *Thomas Jefferson as an Architect and a Designer of Landscapes* (Boston, 1913).

design for the White House in 1792. He had an abiding interest in landscape architectural matters. During his years as American Minister to France he went often to Versailles and saw many of the more important châteaux. In 1786, following descriptions in his copy of Whateley's *Observations*, he visited some of the English country places, including Hampton Court, Stowe, Leasowes, and Blenheim, and commented on them.[2] As Washington's first secretary of state, from 1790 to 1793, he participated actively in the preparation and adoption of Major Pierre L'Enfant's plan for the new federal city.

As indicated earlier, the geometric design of seventeenth-century England tended to remain dominant in the American south. But even Jefferson the inveterate classicist was so favorably impressed by English places seen on his visits that, upon return to Monticello, he obviously began leaning toward "landscape gardening" observed in England. By 1801, when he became president, he appeared to be thinking mainly in landscape garden terms. The sketches he did in 1807 for the "winding or Roundabout Walk" at Monticello[3] seem beyond understanding in a disciple of Vitruvius and Palladio.

Meanwhile, in the north of America views of the English landscape gardening school had found a sympathetic home. To a degree this may be attributable to the appearance of newly rich merchants and manufacturers in the booming northern cities following the course of fashion-worship, in which sudden acquisition of wealth is often accompanied by eager but uncritical acceptance of "the latest thing." But this would account for only a portion of the growing number of country places, some of which had of course been in family possession for generations. A more probable underlying factor was the lack of any real need in the north for extensive layouts—compared to those of the southern plantations—and the early tendency to leave handsome sites alone as unimpeded natural scenery. Thus, when the time came for instituting "improvement," the background was well adapted to landscape gardening treatment without the kind of wholesale destruction of existing forms that occurred at the time of change in England. At any rate, what emerged eventually was a clear dominance of the "landscape garden" and its pastoral character in the north.

Of the country homes around Boston a good example is Gore Place, in Waltham, the residence of Governor Christopher Gore on land he had begun acquiring in 1786. By 1796 he had achieved sufficient legal eminence to head the United States Commission for settling claims under the Jay Treaty with England; in 1799, while he was living in London, his original wooden house in Waltham burned and he at once began plans for rebuilding. He returned to America in 1804, and a year later construction was started on the present brick house—a handsome building with admirable refinement of detail. The Gores had the advice of a French architect, one M. Legrand, but it is not

2. Edwin M. Betts, ed., *Thomas Jefferson's Garden Book* (Philadelphia, 1944), pp. 111–114.
3. *Ibid.*, pl. 24–25, p. 349.

known by whom the plans were actually drawn. The grounds were treated in the landscape gardening idiom, no doubt influenced by the Gores' residence in England at the height of Humphry Repton's fame. The "mansion" is on a rise of land, unsupported by any architectonic base other than the landing platform on the north face. Evidently the only garden lay somewhere to the northwest of the house and completely detached from it. Surrounding the house, and reaching to its very walls in true landscape gardening fashion, are extensive undulant lawns that originally reached all the way to the Charles River. There are many fine trees, some of obviously ancient vintage, and the whole scene retains a quiet, rural atmosphere despite its reduction by suburban encirclement to what in older days was only the "homestead" portion. In the vicinity of Boston the few other country places at about the turn of the nineteenth century are exemplified by the summer home of Theodore Lyman, also in Waltham, with its house by McIntire and its almost completely natural grounds, or the more ostentatious Cushing-Payson place in Belmont.[4]

Another region that showed signs of interest in careful outdoor development was the Hudson River valley. Through patroonships and manors properties of considerable size had become rather usual in lower New York by the time of the Revolution; many of the vast family holdings were parceled off in time, but even then a tradition of almost baronial places remained, especially along the banks of the Hudson. During the first half of the nineteenth century, as economic growth brought more and more concentrated wealth, the owners of some of these properties seem to have begun giving thought to their development as summer homes or, increasingly, as country homes for year-round use.

The first man to engage in providing the desired improvements along the Hudson was André Parmentier, a nurseryman from either Belgium or France who appeared on Long Island in 1824 and established a nursery there; he busied himself on the Hudson River places, but he died in 1830. There is no authoritative list of his work; but Hyde Park was mentioned specifically as Parmentier's by his admiring successor in landscape gardening activities along the Hudson.[5] That successor was a young resident of Newburgh, Andrew Jackson Downing, the first American writer on landscape architectural topics. Born at Newburgh in 1815, the youngest son of a wheelwright and nurseryman who died when the boy was only seven, Downing received from an elder brother thorough schooling in the propagation and use of plants. He was an eager student and, while still a young man, achieved a well-merited reputation as an authority on horticulture.

4. For an interesting evaluation of these three "Bostonian country-seats" in 1889, see Charles William Eliot, *Charles Eliot, Landscape Architect* (Boston, 1902), pp. 240–250.

5. A. J. Downing, *A Treatise on the Theory and Practice of Landscape Gardening Adapted to North America* (New York, 1841), p. 22. See also Eliot, *Charles Eliot*, pp. 250–260, for descriptions of Clermont, Montgomery Place, and Hyde Park (all on the Hudson).

Downing's deepest urgings went beyond botanical considerations and led him to a laudable concern for visual quality—for the appearance of country places as well as their operational efficiency. In effect, he asked that the places be judged as works of art. He had had no training in the arts; it is actually sometimes to be wondered whether he had a clear vision of what the term stood for to himself. But Downing loved scenery, as might be expected of a boy growing up in the glorious highlands of the Hudson; he had seen something of what he regarded as "elegant" living in some of the great houses; and he obviously had an innate bent for persuasive writing. As a consequence, he eventually became a figure of enormous popularity, not so much through occasional work on country places as through his book, *A Treatise on the Theory and Practice of Landscape Gardening Adapted to North America,* published in 1841 when he was only twenty-six. The first American book on "rural art" that was not just another volume on practical gardening, it sold actively both at home and abroad, brought its young author nearly instant fame, and went through no less than six editions. Through it Downing stimulated interest in the improvement of home properties and ultimately had an extraordinary influence on the American countryside. Because the *Treatise* was so widely read and had such far-reaching effects at a time when the arts of America were groping forward eagerly for expression and guidance, it must be examined in some detail.

One of the most remarkable characteristics of this unusual self-made man was his firmly held conviction—perhaps ill-expressed, yet far ahead of his time—that human behavior is greatly affected by environment. For his anticipation of what became an accepted precept of designers nearly a century later, Downing deserves applause. How he went about applying his conviction, however, is another matter. Unfortunately he was a child of his age, steeped in romanticism and resounding, sentimental, high-order abstraction. With seemingly uncritical enthusiasm he plunged into the metaphysical jargon of the English landscape gardening writers whom he admired and at times even outdid in elaborate vagueness. To make matters worse, he was heavily influenced by the gardenesque school of J. C. Loudon, to whom he refers in the *Treatise* as "my valued correspondent . . . the most distinguished gardening authority of the Age."[6] It will be recalled that Loudon published his edition of Repton in 1840, the year before Downing's book appeared; also that he was mainly responsible for the sorry closing chapter to the story of English landscape gardening. Was it perhaps Loudon's influence that caused Downing to point with approval at "the necessity of introducing largely exotic ornamental trees, shrubs and plants, instead of those of indigenous growth"?[7] Surely any doubt should be dispelled by the truly Loudonesque spottiness

6. Downing, *Treatise,* p. iv.
7. *Ibid.,* p. 35.

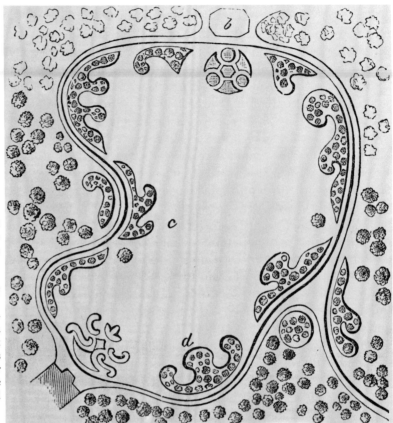

183. An engraving of the "English Flower-Garden" in Andrew Jackson Downing's *Treatise*.

184. Another engraving from Downing's *Treatise*, "The Irregular Flower-Garden," offered as "a suitable accompaniment to the house and grounds of an enthusiastic lover of the picturesque, whose residence is in the Rural Gothic style."

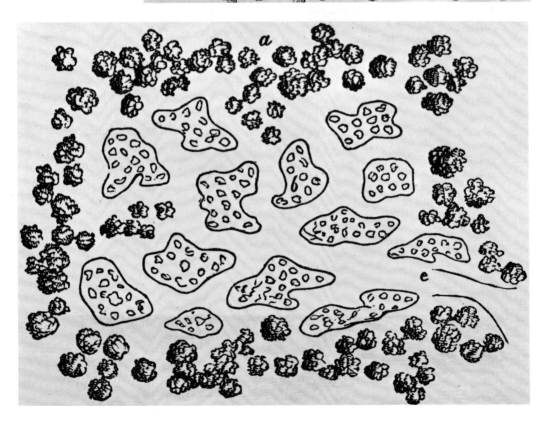

of two engravings in Downing's book (Figs. 183, 184), one illustrating the "English Flower-Garden," the other, more unbelievably, "The Irregular Flower-Garden."

Eager and enthusiastic as it was, Downing's writing was astonishingly obscure as can be readily attested by dipping into the *Treatise* at almost any page. One can hardly escape wondering not only what Downing meant, but also whether *he* clearly understood what he was writing about. Here and there are flashes of light, but on the whole fog prevails. Downing showed a most human failing by complicating the simple and oversimplifying the complex. Blandly ignoring all the historic modulations (or, possibly, unaware of them), he divided this "tasteful and refined art," as he called it, into "two distinct modes . . . One is the Ancient, formal or Geometric Style: the other the Modern, Natural, or Irregular Style."[8] He thereupon dismissed the "Geometric Style" as something too easy to do; "the ends in view were to be attained in a merely mechanical manner, with but little study or theory upon the subject" (p. 29). This was perhaps typical of Downing's judgment, for again and again he appears to evaluate things by whether they were difficult of accomplishment, or costly, or had enough "polish and elegance" to be impressive. What a contrast between this and the simple, uncomplicated attitude of Prince Pückler-Muskau voiced only a few years earlier!

Downing set forth with firm finality what he termed the "grand principles" (apparently there were only four) essential to the "successful practice of this elegant art." They included, fairly enough, *unity* ("The Production of a Whole") and *variety* ("The Production of Variety"), explained in statements that can be sensibly interpreted today. But the "principles" included also the following: "The Recognition of Art, founded on the immutability of the true as well as the beautiful;" and "The Imitation of the Beauty of Expression, derived from a refined perception of the sentiment of nature" (42–43).

For many present-day readers, the most disappointing aspect of Downing's book is the patronizing way in which he appears to have preyed upon an assumed status-consciousness among those who sought guidance from his book. In effect one was continually urged, though often by subtle implication only, to show that one belonged, so to speak, on the right side of the tracks— that one was of the "imaginative and cultivated few" who were capable of "refined enjoyment" because they had "cultivated and refined minds." Maybe this should not seem surprising, in view of the earlier supercilious reference to "a larger class of independent landowners, who, in many respects, are intelligent and well educated" (19).

As a matter of design approach, perhaps the most regrettable element in Downing's brand of snob appeal was the persistent and heavy leaning on what he called "correct taste in art," rather than on dependable and meas-

8. *Ibid.*, p. 10.

urable characteristics. Things, he indicated, would be done "in a tasteful manner" by those who had "cultivated susceptibility and taste." A "man of taste" naturally had a "tasteful and enlightened mind" with which to comprehend a "tasteful and refined art," with its "expression of tasteful design, or an air of correct elegance" (26). He made it quite clear, of course, that not everybody was of the elite; among the "mass of uncultivated minds" (54) one would expect to find "false taste," if only because "in an infant state of society, in regard to the fine arts, much will be done in violation of good taste" (27). The quotations here are gathered from various parts of the book but with full care to avoid unfair juxtapositions. The point is that Downing's era had not yet learned what miserable creations can result in *any* age, and all too usually do, from reliance on "Taste" alone.

So far as actual work is concerned—the layout, that is, of specific areas of land—Downing offered no particular system or method, nor do the examples shown in illustrations of what he did or admired appear materially

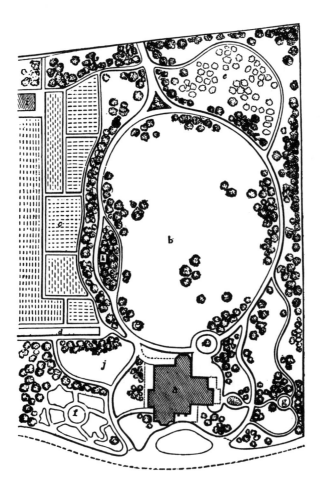

185. To illustrate "suburban villa residences," the *Treatise* offers a plan of "this admirable villa at Burlington, New-Jersey"— not Downing's own work but used with his unquestioning approval.

186. The frontispiece of the 1841 edition of Downing's *Treatise,* "View in the Grounds at Blithewood, Dutchess Co. N.Y." Both the majestic background of the Hudson and the spottiness of elements in the grounds are fairly represented in this engraving.

different from what was then being done by the gardenesque school in England (Fig. 185). By modern standards, the illustrations look as if no design had been involved at all. Much the same can be said of the work Downing is believed to have executed on some of the Hudson River places (Fig. 186). There he did, indeed, assemble fine collections of trees that in the course of time naturally became stately, though there was little or no sense of spatial structure in their arrangement. To be sure, Downing always had the requisite respect for site, and, working as he usually did with the superb scenery of the Hudson valley as a backdrop, the result was almost bound to look tremendously impressive.

If, then, Downing's book and his fieldwork leave so much to be desired, how can it truthfully be said that he had an important impact on the American scene? In all candor, it seems clear that he has probably received more adulation than merited either by the quality of his executed landscape architectural work or by the theoretical value of the *Treatise.* He was hardly to be blamed for whatever exaggeration occurred; after all, because his *Treatise* was the first book of its kind published in America, and because it was written by an American, both he and the book naturally became objects of patriotic acclaim. This in itself would account for much of his popularity.

In justice to Downing it should be noted also that he became widely known for his books on architecture and that he is credited with—some would say blamed for—considerably influencing architectural fashions at mid-century. No assessment of this aspect of Downing is ventured here, other than a comment that he and many of his present-day admirers appear to deal almost exclusively with "styles." As pointed out repeatedly, this account assumes a *designer's* point of view; and a designer "realizes that a historical 'style' is but a verbal label attached to a work of design after it is done, and then usually by someone other than the designer. He sees a 'style' as a label of the historian, not as a tool of the designer."[9]

But the fact remains that beyond all this Downing had a beneficial effect that merits full recognition. No matter what the reason for his popular appeal, it is true and vastly important that he awakened Americans to the desirability of improving the wholeness of their residential properties. It is not so much *what* he wrote in his book or did in the field; it is, rather, the simple fact that he wrote or acted at all, and that in this way he encouraged people to *do* something about their environment.

Downing's place in the history of landscape architecture rests also upon two other significant acts of service. It was he who in 1850 found and brought to America the young English architect Calvert Vaux. Seven years later, Vaux asked Frederick Law Olmsted to join him in the competition for a plan for Central Park and the two won. Even more worthy of note—and in the opinion of many his greatest contribution—was Downing's journalistic campaign, along with William Cullen Bryant, for a public park in New York. Though Downing was drowned in 1852, in a tragic boating accident on his beloved Hudson, the writing he had already done in the press from the mid-forties onward was in large part responsible for the 1851 passage of the first Park Act in New York—the legislation that, as amended in 1853, brought into being the first new "country park" in the Western world.

9. N. T. Newton, *An Approach to Design* (Cambridge, 1951), pp. 71–72.

XIX. Olmsted and Vaux: Central Park and Prospect Park

When in 1851 the Legislature of the State of New York passed what has come to be known as the First Park Act, a historic milestone was reached in the provision of public land to be developed as a park for the people's enjoyment and recreation. Urban open spaces, such as the town square or piazza and the English common, had of course existed for centuries. There had been parks of a sort in ancient times, to be sure, but in every known instance ownership had rested in the hands of the ruler; the parks of Rome, for example, were pleasure gardens owned by the emperor, who granted admittance to the people but usually only on special occasions, as a gesture of imperial favor. Versailles had become the property of the people of France, but only after bloody revolution had wrenched the great gardens from the royal ownership under which they had been built and developed. The Royal Parks of London, in existence since the days of Henry VIII, had long been open to public use, but they remained the property of the Crown.

In short, public open spaces were not in themselves an innovation, but those that did exist were not intended for recreation. Parks were not unknown, nor was public access to them; what is important is the public's complete lack of any *right* of access. A combination of these hitherto unknown dimensions characterized the public park as it emerged from the reform-conscious 1830s and 1840s. To summarize an earlier chapter, prior to the creation of Victoria and Birkenhead Parks there is no recorded instance of outdoor recreational space on land acquired and owned by the people themselves, developed with public funds and open indiscriminately to all. Now, only a few years after the completion of Birkenhead Park, the Western hemisphere, too, was to have its first public park—to be carried out, like Birkenhead but with far greater skill, as a "country park" evoking the visitor's memory of rural scenes and his instinctive attraction to them.

For many decades there had been open spaces in New York, as elsewhere in the American colonies—notably the squares of Savannah and Philadelphia and the generous provision of green crossing-spaces in Major L'Enfant's 1791 plan for Washington—but on the whole they were only pleasant accents fortuitously arrived at wherever street patterns developed natural areas of openness. The Battery and Bowling Green at the lower tip of Manhattan Island, and the so-called park at City Hall a little way north, were no doubt happy interludes in the expanding town. But they had neither the extent nor the character to encourage any considerable amount of recreational activity.

It should not be overlooked that a completely American invention, the "rural cemetery," may possibly have influenced public interest in park-like scenery. The first of these, Mt. Auburn Cemetery, had been established in Cambridge, Massachusetts, in 1831 through the efforts of Dr. Jacob Bigelow, a Boston physician and botanist who was convinced that the traditional churchyard burying ground was a menace to public health. After some years of campaigning on this issue he joined forces with the newly organized Massachusetts Horticultural Society, which wanted to found an "experimental garden" but lacked the necessary funds. Thus, oddly enough, it was the Horticultural Society that received from the State Legislature the authority to dedicate real estate for a "rural cemetery." Apparently Mt. Auburn soon became very popular as a quiet place in which to escape the bustle and clangor of the city—for strolling, for solitude, and even for family picnics. Following its success, other cemeteries of the same type began springing up, among them the Greenwood Cemetery in the City of Brooklyn. Andrew Jackson Downing recorded in 1849 his impression of Greenwood as "grand, dignified, and park-like."[1]

But in the 1840s the notion of acquiring land in the public interest, then developing it solely for recreation in a pastoral or sylvan way, was for New Yorkers quite without precedent. A few of the better educated or more widely traveled citizens no doubt knew of the efforts being made by reformers in England, and some may even have followed the halting steps toward realization of their hopes in Victoria Park and at Birkenhead. But the time was ripe for persuasion of the many by two gifted and intensely dedicated writers: Downing and William Cullen Bryant, poet and also very effective editor of the New York *Evening Post*. Bryant in the press and Downing there and in the *Horticulturist* began pleading in the early 1840s for recognition of society's responsibility to the burgeoning population of working people. Both on visits to England wrote enthusiastic pieces about the popular use of the Royal Parks

---

1. Quoted in *Olmsted Papers, Central Park,* p. 21.

and urged setting aside land in New York before it was too late. Bryant specifically expressed regret that nothing had been done years earlier to anticipate "the corrupt atmosphere generated in hot and crowded streets" by preparing for "a range of parks and public gardens along the central part of the island or elsewhere."[2]

With the 1848 eruption of revolutions in Europe, and such catastrophic blows as the Irish potato famine, immigrants began arriving in New York in larger masses than ever, lending greater weight to the arguments advanced by Bryant and Downing. The years of striving bore fruit at last. In April 1851 Mayor Kingsland, newly elected with the support of the *Evening Post*, sent to the Common Council a message officially recommending that the State Legislature be petitioned for authority to acquire land for a public park. The petition went promptly to Albany, and on July 11, 1851, the Legislature passed the First Park Act, authorizing the City of New York to purchase a tract of land bounded by Third Avenue and the East River, 64th and 75th Streets. The area, known as Jones's Wood, was the one Bryant had first proposed for park use as early as 1844.

But now Bryant realized that he should have advocated a larger area. Jones's Wood had seemed in 1844 a high goal to shoot for; it was now obvious that for the growing city this acreage would not suffice. Bryant, Downing, and others awakened to forceful action by their enthusiasm, encouraged by success, started a campaign for another, much larger park, more centrally located. Bryant and his *Evening Post* came out vigorously for acquisition of *two* areas: Jones's Wood on the East River and a tract based on the Croton Reservoir in the middle of the island; the latter was being urged by Downing in the *Horticulturist*. The upshot of all the clamor was the passage in Albany, on July 21, 1853, of legislation known today as the Amended Park Act, granting the City of New York authority to take an area bounded by Fifth Avenue, Eighth Avenue (now Central Park West), 59th Street, and for the moment 106th Street—northward extension to 110th Street was approved in 1859. Unfortunately, not enough pressure was exerted in favor of retaining the East River tract, already authorized under the Jones's Wood Act, and that legislation was repealed in 1854; there was much uninformed opposition to having even one park, let alone two.

The years 1853–1856 were spent in taking the land now comprising Central Park as far north as 106th Street; the additional 65 acres up to 110th Street were not acquired until 1863. It is noteworthy to municipal administrators as well as landscape architects that the postponed addition cost $18,147 per acre, as against the price of $6,838 per acre paid for the site of the New Reservoir in 1856, only seven years earlier (and of only $2,316 per acre for the Old Reservoir site, bought in 1838). Such is the effect of park development

---

2. *Ibid.*, p. 23.

on the market value of land, included and adjacent; such also is the cost of piecemeal acquisition of land for parks.

From the outset, partisan politics proved the major enemy of the park. Through 1856, in the absence of appropriate legislation from Albany, affairs were in the hands of the Mayor, the Street Commissioner, and, in effect, the Common Council. For the most part these worthies—when the land had been secured and a chief engineer appointed—used the park for handing out jobs to politically faithful workers; no real progress was made in its development. At last in April 1857 the State Legislature, by compromise among political factions, passed an act setting up the theoretically nonpartisan Board of Commissioners and vesting control of the park in them rather than the city government. One of the Board's first actions was appointment of a super-intendent to supervise the labor force under the general direction of the chief engineer. At the urging of one of the Commissioners, the post was applied for by Frederick Law Olmsted. Born in Hartford, Connecticut, on April 26, 1822, Olmsted lived on Staten Island. He had systematically trained himself for work on the land. A skillful traveling observer, he wrote easily and by 1857 was widely known for articles on agriculture and a series of brilliant reports on social conditions in the South, *A Journey in the Seaboard Slave States* (published in 1856) and *A Journey in Texas* (1857). He was finishing the manuscript for a third volume, *A Journey in the Back Country,* when sought out for the superintendency.

Olmsted was immediately attracted to the prospect of being closely associ-ated with the new park. Fascinated with natural scenery from boyhood, he had long been interested in parks, as indicated in his comments of seven years earlier on Birkenhead and other English parks. As he put it, "while others gravitated to pictures, architecture, Alps, libraries, high life and low life when traveling, I had gravitated to parks."[3] He applied for the superintendency, and with the active support of such men as Washington Irving, Peter Cooper, Horace Greeley, William Cullen Bryant, Whitelaw Reid, and Asa Gray he was elected by the Board of Commissioners and appointed to the office of superintendent on September 11, 1857.

His first contact with his new duties was not a happy one. On reporting to the chief engineer, he was told brusquely that the real need had been for a "practical man." To be sure, Olmsted's reputation was primarily as a literary figure; but after all the years he had spent on precisely the type of work to be carried on in the park, he felt the slur deeply. Indeed, when twenty-five years later he wrote his famous paper "The Spoils of the Park," in justification of his work, he subtitled the piece "with a few leaves from the deep-laden notebooks of 'a wholly unpractical man'."[4]

On October 13 appeared the public announcement that is for landscape architects one of the truly historic milestones of the profession: "The Board

3. *Ibid.,* p. 320n.
4. *Ibid.,* p. 117.

of Commissioners of the Central Park offer the following premiums for the four designs for laying out the Park, which may be selected: For the first, $2,000; for the second, $1,000; for the third, $750; for the fourth, $500. The plans to become the property of the Board."[5] This eminently wise provision for overall planning, surprising because so contrary to the insensitive "practical" atmosphere that surrounded the nascent park, not only gave rise to the great plan by Olmsted and Vaux, but laid a basis for Olmsted's insistent plea, reiterated through the years, that the park always be treated *as a whole*. Oddly enough, the strongest plea for such careful master-planning had come from a firm of "landscape gardeners" who later entered the competition, though unsuccessfully: Copeland & Cleveland, of Boston, publishers in 1856 of a noteworthy little pamphlet entitled *A Few Words on the Central Park,* an excellent argument for the virtues of comprehensive planning. More will be said subsequently about the remarkable Horace W. S. Cleveland.

As for the competition itself, Olmsted had no intention of entering at first. Even when asked by Calvert Vaux, the English architect brought over by Downing, to join in preparing a design for submittal, he demurred out of consideration for the chief engineer, who was technically his superior and was himself entering the competition. But when the engineer's reaction to the courtesy was an expression of contemptuous indifference to Olmsted's participation, that settled it. Olmsted thereupon joined Vaux in an enthusiastic effort to devise during the winter months the best solution they could for the manifold problems of the park. Meanwhile, of course, Olmsted continued his daily supervision of preparatory ground work in the swamps and rocky outcroppings of the Central Park acreage.

The competition was judged the following spring. On April 28, 1858, having examined at length the thirty-three drawings submitted, the Board voted first prize to Plan No. 33, presented under the name "Greensward" (Fig. 187). On opening the sealed envelopes containing the competitors' names, the "Greensward" plan was found to be the work of Olmsted and Vaux. At once, as so often happens with such groups of laymen, various Commissioners put forward suggestions for the plan's amendment. Fortunately, good sense prevailed, a small subcommittee was appointed to confer with the designers, a few minor changes were agreed upon, and in all major respects the "Greensward" plan was accepted officially as the basis for execution on the ground. The only early recommendation worth specific mention here was the one (Fig. 188) "that the Superintendent be requested to prepare the sketch of a plan for an extension of the Park to One Hundred and Tenth Street."[6]

On May 17, 1858, the Board of Commissioners abolished the posts of superintendent and chief engineer, assigned the duties of both to a newly created "Chief executive officer who shall be styled the Architect in Chief

5. *Ibid.,* pp. 40–42.
6. *Ibid.,* p. 234.

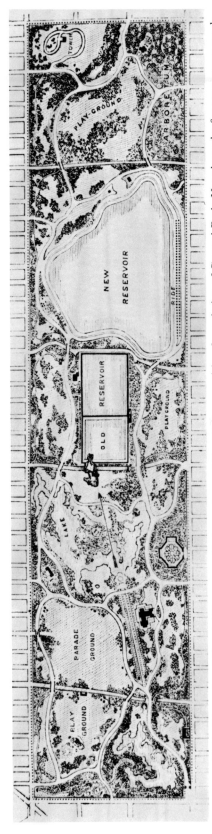

187. New York: Olmsted and *Vaux's* "Greensward" plan, winner of the 1857 competition for a design of Central Park. Note how the four transverse roads (a stated requirement in the competition program) were depressed so as to pass beneath the north-south park roads. Note also the Tower on Bogardus Hill at the northwest corner, where the park reached only to 106th Street.

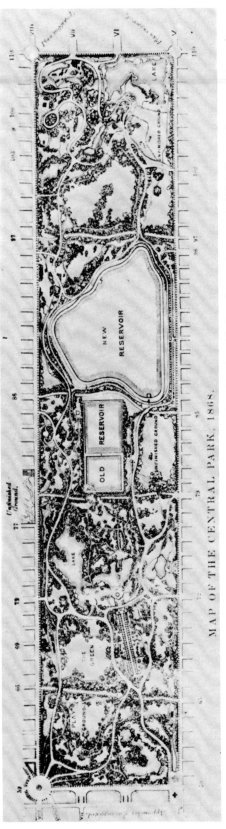

MAP OF THE CENTRAL PARK, 1868.

188. Central Park: the winning plan was modified almost at once to use the four blocks added at the north to reach 110th Street, the present boundary; the loop road planned for Bogardus Hill thus came well within the park and the lake in the northeast corner could be built. The illustration is from the 1868 reprinting of the "Greensward" report, hence the date.

of the Central Park," and appointed Olmsted to the new office.[7] As architect-in-chief he was also authorized to call in the services of Vaux and six field assistants. By autumn 1858 over 2,500 men were at work, a prodigious amount of construction and planting had been done, and in December enough water could be let into the partly built lake to permit a start of the public skating for which the park soon became famous. By late summer 1859 the work force had grown to over 3,600, the lake was nearly completed, and Olmsted felt he could safely undertake a brief trip to visit European parks as requested by the Commissioners. It was on this trip that he met Alphand, studied the Bois de Boulogne, and revisited the park at Birkenhead.[8]

After the outbreak of the Civil War in April 1861, work on the park continued as a buttress to public morale but the pace was modified. In June Olmsted was granted leave of absence for appointment in Washington as secretary of the commission supervising medical care of the Union forces—later known as the U.S. Sanitary Commission, and the predecessor of the American Red Cross. To this demanding work Olmsted gave himself unstintingly, striving nevertheless to visit New York and the park as often as possible. Meanwhile, relations of Olmsted and Vaux with the Board of Commissioners, deteriorating steadily since 1859 when a Comptroller had been appointed over them, finally came to the breaking point. On May 12, 1863, the two resigned, stating "that it will be impracticable for either of us to give a continual personal attention to the Park operations during the ensuing summer." They signed the letter of resignation "Olmsted and Vaux, Landscape Architects." The Board, accepting the resignation at a meeting on May 14, also used the designation "Messrs. Olmsted and Vaux, Landscape Architects," and placed on record the Board's "unabated confidence in their high artistic taste and in their superior professional abilities."[9]

This exchange in May 1863 marks the first *official* use of the title Landscape Architect. To be sure, the plan of the park used in the annual report of January in that year had also been signed "Olmsted and Vaux, Landscape Architects," and the two men had probably used the term privately before then. But the official use in a government document of May 1863 serves to establish that date perhaps better than any other as the birthday of the *profession* of landscape architecture.

At first, it would appear, Vaux was more enthusiastic than his partner about the designation; but Olmsted overcame any early objections, adopted the term for himself and his successive professional firms, and continued to use it throughout his life. He came to regard the title as truly expressive of his professional role: to bear toward a landscape the same relation that an architect bears toward a building.

7. *Ibid.,* p. 49.
8. *Ibid.,* pp. 55–56.
9. *Ibid.,* p. 74 and n.

This was but the first in a long series of resignations, and threats to resign, that marked the story of Central Park and the incessant political interference with which Olmsted and Vaux had to contend. Reappointed the Landscape Architects of Central Park in 1865, they resigned again in 1870 as a protest against the rascality of the infamous Tweed ring. Just a year later, in November 1871, after the electorate had revolted against Tweed, they were appointed again under a total reorganization, this time as Landscape Architects to the New York Department of Public Parks. In 1872 the two decided, for mutual convenience and quite amicably, to dissolve their partnership; Olmsted continued to serve as Landscape Architect to the Department, Vaux as Consultant. The next year, increasingly dissatisfied with the Commissioners' administration, Olmsted resigned his post—consenting, however, "to resume service . . . upon a modified arrangement, vindicating my professional standing."[10] Under these terms the devoted services continued, though seldom happily, until 1878, when the Tweed ring had so fully regained control of the city's government that Olmsted was finally forced out entirely—after twenty arduous years of battling for ideals against political harassment, often of the most virulent and calloused kind.

At the time of the first of these many resignations, that of 1863, Olmsted's health suffered under pressure of the heavy load of organizational work for the Sanitary Commission, so that by midsummer he felt compelled to resign from the latter also. At this juncture there came an unexpected call from a quite different quarter, resulting in a two-year period of great importance historically though geographically far removed from Central Park. Knowledge of Olmsted's skill as an expert in the management of land had spread so widely that the Mariposa Mining Company of California now offered him the superintendency of their extensive gold-mining properties. Worn out physically, exhausted mentally, Olmsted accepted the proposal and left for California in September 1863. California was then a far distant land: one sailed to the Isthmus of Panama, crossed this usually on muleback, and then sailed up the Mexican coast to San Francisco, landing there after nearly a month of travel. Olmsted, arriving in October 1863, went at once to the Bear Valley headquarters of the Mariposa Estates.

Providential it was, for the sake of America's future attitude toward state and national parks, that a man of Olmsted's insight and stature should be in California at this particular moment in history. In the following June, by Congressional action with the approval of President Lincoln, Yosemite Valley and the adjoining Mariposa Grove of Big Trees were withdrawn from the public domain and ceded to California, becoming the first state park and indeed the first scenic area in the United States reserved explicitly for public enjoyment in perpetuity. As manager of the Mariposa Estates, Olmsted was known to be enthusiastically familiar with the magnificent Yosemite terrain

10. *Ibid.,* pp. 132, 305.

and overwhelmed by its grandeur. Moreover, his reputation had preceded him: it was therefore entirely natural that Governor Low should appoint him to the Yosemite Commission when this was created in September 1864 to manage the newly ceded lands for the state. The writing of a preliminary report on behalf of the Commission logically fell to Olmsted, and in this remarkable paper, presented in 1865, he spelled out for the first time a clear and sensible pattern of sound thinking about the fundamental purposes, social values, and appropriate development of such great scenic areas, then unprecedented as a type of public reservation. His counsel had lasting influence; and the report, though some portions disappeared from sight until recovered in 1952, remains one of the great basic documents in the story of American state and national parks.

Olmsted found the western climate invigorating, and in 1864-1865 he also produced plans for "a village and grounds for the College of California,"[11] now the University at Berkeley, plans for a new cemetery at Oakland, and preliminary plans for Golden Gate Park in San Francisco (not carried out). Though he kept in touch with the progress of operations on Central Park, he felt that there was little hope of ever achieving a workable arrangement with New York's political authorities and accordingly thought seriously of remaining in San Francisco and founding a newspaper. Meanwhile, Vaux was writing frequently pleading that he return to New York, not only for the sake of Central Park but also because Vaux had been consulted by Brooklyn officials about a possible new park there.

Then, in July 1865, Vaux wrote that the partners had been reappointed "Landscape Architects to the Board" for Central Park, and in September that they had actually been asked to design the big new park in Brooklyn. The attraction was too great to be resisted; in November Olmsted landed in New York again with his family, settling on Staten Island for convenience in ferrying to Brooklyn for the new project. What many consider the greatest single work of Olmsted and Vaux, Prospect Park in Brooklyn, was in the making.

Brooklyn in those days was an autonomous municipality, separate from New York City, and the popularity of Central Park had not failed to arouse understandable envy. The city's Common Council as early as 1859 had obtained from the State Legislature an act setting up a commission "to locate parks and a parade ground . . . and to report such selection to the Common Council."[12] On the basis of the commission's report a second act was passed at Albany in 1860, authorizing acquisition of land for a parade ground in the New Lots section of Brooklyn but providing for only about half the

11. Frederick Law Olmsted, *Forty Years of Landscape Architecture,* vol. I: *Early Years,* ed. F. L. Olmsted, Jr., and T. Kimball (New York, 1922), p. 11. Cited hereafter as *Olmsted Papers, Early Years.*
12. Brooklyn Park Commissioners, *Annual Report, 1861,* pp. 5–6.

acreage comprising today's Prospect Park. It took three successive acts of the Legislature, in 1861, 1866, and 1868, to complete the taking of all the land now included. A separate act of 1868 relocated the proposed parade ground, placing it south of the park, where it lies now.

It had been late in 1864, while the question of boundaries was under discussion by the duly appointed Board of Commissioners of Prospect Park, that Vaux was called in for advice. His report, dated February 1865, made a good start toward achievement of the present boundaries: he recommended doubling the holding south and west, selling off the quite unmanageable portion to the northeast of Flatbush Avenue, and providing an oval space at the northern tip of the park for a main entrance. When Olmsted arrived late in 1865, he concurred fully in the recommendations that Vaux had made, and these were incorporated in the preliminary report and plan presented by Olmsted, Vaux & Co., Landscape Architects, dated January 24, 1866. In May they were formally appointed "Landscape Architects and Superintendents to the Board of Commissioners of Prospect Park."[13] Field work was begun in July 1866, but it was not until 1868 that the State Legislature finally enacted extension of the boundaries to their present state through addition of a crucial belt of twelve blocks of land along the Ninth Avenue side. Inclusion of this area—vitally important because it controlled a significant stretch of the proposed Circuit Drive as well as the western edge of the park's major open space, the Long Meadow—had been advocated by Vaux in his preliminary study, assumed by him and Olmsted in their original plan for the park, and repeatedly recommended in their annual reports.

On the whole, the fieldwork proceeded happily; but operations in the northern part of the park were necessarily stop-and-go for a period of over two years, pending acquisition of the Ninth Avenue piece. As the landscape architects reported in January 1868, "at many points the works . . . have been suspended in consequence of the uncertainty in regard to boundary lines."[14] In fact, once the boundary question was settled and the needed land became available in 1869, work in the northern portion went forward quickly, so that by the end of the year it was "finished, with the exception of a little planting."[15]

The difficulty with definition of boundaries may seem unduly emphasized here, but it points up a major difference between what Olmsted and Vaux experienced in Prospect Park and what they suffered over Central Park. In Brooklyn they had troubles, to be sure, but these were problems on the site rather than political interference. Reading the successive annual reports of the Commissioners and of the landscape architects, one cannot fail to be

13. *Ibid., 1867*, p. 138.
14. *Ibid., 1868*, p. 173.
15. *Ibid., 1870*, p. 354.

impressed by the sympathetic understanding consistently given Olmsted and Vaux. Even in the matter of boundaries it was not the Commissioners, but rather the Common Council and even more the State Legislature, that slowed matters. So far as can be determined from the public record, the landscape architects were invariably supported by the Commissioners.

By January 1871 Olmsted and Vaux could report to the Commissioners: "The primary construction of the park is now essentially complete in all of the territory which was at first placed under your control." And, in the portion not so fully finished because of the delayed land acquisition, "the design is so thoroughly fixed upon the ground that the character of the scenery, and of the public accommodations aimed at, can hardly be questioned."[16]

When, at the close of 1873, funds regularly appropriated for Prospect Park came to an end, Olmsted and Vaux had every reason to feel contented with what had been accomplished "during the eight years in which we have had the honor to serve your Commission."[17] Only a few permanent but relatively expensive stone structures, replacing sturdy wooden ones of an admittedly temporary nature, remained to be built whenever extraordinary funds should become available. The landscape architects voiced a special plea for the ultimate completion of the main entrance on the Plaza. "The Park gateway," they wrote in January 1874, "should be a handsome architectural structure, with an arcade extending over the walk . . . and the pavement necessary to carry out this feature has been designed and laid."[18]

It was nearly a quarter-century before this last suggestion was acted upon. As late as 1895 the construction of exterior walls and gates was still going on, and at the Plaza the huge Soldiers' and Sailors' Arch had been erected to commemorate the Union forces of the Civil War. The great oval space designed by Olmsted and Vaux, thenceforth called the Grand Army Plaza, clearly required a degree of modification to accommodate the Arch. Fortunately, Brooklyn authorities had the good sense in 1896 to consult Olmsted and his firm (known then as Olmsted, Olmsted and Eliot) for redesign of the Plaza itself. The present monumental entranceway, designed by McKim, Mead and White, was erected at the same time.

To those who are familiar with both Central Park and Prospect Park—or the Brooklyn Park, as Olmsted and Vaux invariably called it—comparison is inevitable. Both are masterpieces as "country parks," yet they differ. Along with Franklin Park in Boston, they constitute the great triad of Olmsted's works. There can be little question that Central Park, as the first of its kind in the Western hemisphere and as the vehicle through which Olmsted founded the profession of landscape architecture, is historically pre-eminent. But,

16. *Ibid., 1871*, p. 422.
17. *Ibid., 1873*, p. 23.
18. *Ibid., 1874*, p. 28.

189. Aerial view of Central Park from the south.

measuring the two parks in simple terms of human preference—or, indeed, regarding them quite without preciosity as works of art—Prospect Park would appear to win out in the judgment of a good majority.

In this light it is perhaps not surprising to read, in the report of Olmsted and Vaux in January 1870: "If, as is now frequently stated in the public prints, the Brooklyn Park is in some respects more attractive than the Central Park in New York, it is because we have, from the outset, been sustained by your board in our effort to improve a considerable portion of the ground with special reference to the development of this element of pastoral effect."[19] Apparently there was already something about Prospect Park, unfinished as it was in 1870, that people found unusually appealing. Or does the passage perhaps reveal that the designers themselves felt a stronger affection for this park than for their other work across the river?

In fairness it should be pointed out that in certain respects such as boundaries, relation to street plan and external traffic, accommodation of predetermined reservoirs, and rocky terrain the task confronting Olmsted and Vaux in Central Park was clearly more difficult than the later one in Prospect Park. The matter of boundaries alone had several consequences. The legislation

19. *Ibid., 1870,* p. 357.

authorizing Central Park set the boundaries rigidly into a single adamant grid-system of streets, with the result that the park is a rectangular strip five times as long as it is wide (Fig. 189). This may seem logical on the ribbon-like island of Manhattan, but it provided the designers with an extremely trying area to handle. Moreover, since the grid-system of streets was laid out with no attention to topography, the boundaries were likewise unrelated to the conformation of the land. Prospect Park, in contrast, had its boundaries adjusted on the advice of the landscape architects, who naturally were guided by topographic considerations. Even then the boundaries were fitted to streets, not in a single grid-system, but in several systems. These factors combined to make the park a well-rounded chunk of land rather than a strip and therefore a less arduous design problem (Figs. 190, 191).

The position and length of Central Park on its narrow island were sure to render it, sooner or later, an obvious impediment to crosstown traffic. Hence the entirely sensible requirement, written into the program for the 1857 competition, of four transverse roads. Though truly necessary, the transverse roads would have seriously interrupted any continuing sense of south-north unity if Olmsted had not *sunk* them in deep-walled trenches—surely the most brilliant single stroke of the Greensward plan—thereby allowing the park to flow visually across them (Fig. 192). In Prospect Park there was no problem of cross traffic.

As a further challenge to its cramping side boundaries and its narrowness, Central Park contained two municipal reservoirs that had to be kept: the old one a walled rectangle built about 1838, the newer one, of about the same age as the park itself, a large, amorphous blob reaching in an unbroken sheet almost all the way across the park and from 86th to 96th Streets. The "old" reservoir was removed about 1930, leaving only the stone Belvedere tower at its southwest corner and a small pond of water; the "new" one, though still the largest single open space in the park, is wholly unused for park purposes, while in effect it tends to separate the upper and lower parts of the park. No such obstruction occurred in Prospect Park.

As if all of this were not enough to try the souls of the designers, there was in Central Park one other condition: the area was extremely rocky. This in itself could be handled, and was, by sensitive exposure of rock outcroppings. But it meant also that much of the park had only a thin layer of soil, which made planting far more difficult to do and to maintain than in Prospect Park, where the soil was deeper and the tillable areas more widespread.

In many respects, of course, the two parks are much alike in problems to be solved and technical excellence of the solutions. The vertical separation of traffic types, with arched underpasses (Fig. 193) leading pedestrian walks under the carriage (now motor) drives—one of the best examples of Olmsted's capacity for being ahead of his times—is executed with great similarity in the two. Both have suffered in some measure from becoming arteries for

190. Prospect Park, Brooklyn: the original Olmsted-Vaux plan of 1866-1867.

191. Prospect Park plan as modified by the designers and Park Commissioners before 1875. This plan of 1901, when Brooklyn had become a borough of New York City, is close to the present condition.

192. Central Park: one of the four sunken transverse roads as depicted in an early report of the Commissioners; although the traffic has changed in type and increased in volume, the roads still function admirably.

193. An old but valid photograph of one of Central Park's many pedestrian underpasses; Prospect Park has similar ones. The facing is typical of Vaux's brownstone detail.

194. Central Park about 1912: pedestrian crossing of a carriage road was only occasionally placed at grade; today, heavy north-south traffic has made these roads one-way, and grade-crossings are now governed by lights.

lengthwise motor traffic (Fig. 194), though Central Park for obvious reasons of placement and population has the larger volume. Both have excellent bodies of water: in each a large, picturesque, heavily used lake (Fig. 195) is supplemented by several smaller ones. Both have the well-defined green spaces with undulant floors of turf that provide the "pastoral effect" so much desired by Olmsted and Vaux.

It is on examining these green outdoor spaces that one is most likely to hit upon a noticeable difference between the two parks. The open spaces of Central Park, such as the Green and the Playground in the lower part, (to use the place names Olmsted was so fond of conferring on spaces and features in his parks) are indeed well-formed, positive, placid but firm on readily perceptible individual sight-lines. They exemplify what was referred to in an earlier chapter as an unconscious product of the English landscape gardening school that would one day become a conscious medium of design in the hands of such men as Pückler-Muskau and Olmsted. The same can be said, of course, for the outdoor spaces of Prospect Park. But, whereas those of Central Park are perforce limited by the squeeze of the side boundaries, the Long Meadow of Prospect Park (Fig. 196) has ample room to swing away to south and west in a sweeping curve—as calmly overwhelming a space as one could reasonably hope to experience anywhere. Coming as it does at the very beginning of the visitor's walk into the park, as he emerges from the shadowy underpass beneath the Circuit Drive to be suddenly confronted by sunny openness, the Long Meadow somehow establishes for the whole park an impressive generosity of scale and atmosphere of peacefulness. Small wonder that so many critics regard it as one of the truly great outdoor spaces of the world.

The Long Meadow illustrates with compelling force the psychological effect of curving space. As one enters from the north, first eyes and then feet are pulled irresistibly toward the hazy distance of the south where the meadow curves to the right and out of sight. Moving along under the impulse, one feels the pull continue and senses the start of an outstanding characteristic of Prospect Park that is hard to find in the older sister across the river: sequence. This is where the narrowness of Central Park and its crosswise interruptions, skillfully handled as they were by Olmsted, deprived the older park of the ready opportunity for a continuing sequence of spaces ranged on a structure of serially connected sight-lines. And in landscape architectural design a perceptible spatial sequence is so basically important as to be almost a necessity.

As a matter of fact, there are many spatial sequences in Prospect Park. The most pronounced pulls the visitor down the left side of the curving Long Meadow toward a small pond tucked into the margin of the space. Crossing the outlet from the pond, one is drawn left into a shady wood and continues along the stream, now a gurgling rivulet sliding down in the dappled light between banks of glacial boulders, with a footpath on the near side and a bridle path on the other. Following the path, all three of these lines are seen to go under the ingenious triple Nethermead Arches (Fig. 197), which carry

195. Central Park: the lake about fifty years ago; skating has been popular in both parks since earliest days.

196. Prospect Park: the Long Meadow.

overhead a midpark section of the Circuit Drive. Coming out into the open from the woods and the arches, on the right is the sunny greensward of a glade known as the Nethermead and on the left the stream continues into the small natural basin, now somewhat overgrown, that Olmsted named the Binnenwater.

The path leads across the stream again and so around the eastern side of an appropriately quiet pool called the Lullwater. Here stands a sadly decrepit boathouse of ornate dirty-white tile, mercifully overlooked entirely. The Lullwater itself turns and goes westward in a narrow, winding stretch with a closely clinging path. One follows this beyond the low Lullwater Bridge and along the grassy margin until the water and a path on each side pass beneath the arch of the Terrace Bridge, the highest in the park, carrying a section of the Circuit Drive from Breeze Hill on the east to Lookout Hill on the west; south of it the Lullwater widens out to form the relatively small northern arm (Fig. 198) of the Lake. Drawn along the shore past the terraced Rose Garden and the Concert Grove, one finally reaches the main body of the Lake, which occupies nearly the whole width of the southern end of the park.

This route is but one of several effective sequences from north to south in the park. There are others from any side entrance to another, across the park or skirting its wooded perimeter—much of which has an extended high berm of earth along the boundary, thickly planted with trees and shrubs to exclude the sights and sounds of the nearby street. And then, whatever sequence one may have followed in length or breadth of the park, it is of equal importance in design that in returning the selfsame route need not be retraced. Prospect Park has in remarkable degree what may be called *around-ness,* for want of a better term.

No discussion of Central and Prospect Parks would be complete without reference to the battles that had to be fought, in Olmsted's time and for many years after, to keep them from being interfered with in one way or another. This has been especially true of Central Park; Prospect, because of its different location, has fortunately been freer from meddling. The chief source of trouble through the years has been the misguided and often completely senseless desire to put into the park some structure or other facility utterly unrelated to its park purposes. As long ago as the 1920s, it was pointed out that Central Park would be entirely filled, and spilling over at the edges, if all the irrelevant structures proposed for inclusion had been built. It was in the course of resisting repeatedly this kind of instrusion that Olmsted made one of his most often quoted statements: "The only solid ground of resistance to dangers of this class will be found to rest in the conviction that the Park throughout is a single work of art, and as such, subject to the primary law of every work

197. Prospect Park: the Nethermead Arches, as proposed in the Commissioners' *Report* of 1869—footpath left, stream middle, bridle path right, carriage road overhead.

198. Prospect Park: northern arm of the lake, fed from the Lullwater; the broader expanse of the main body of water is around and beyond the point at the right.

of art, namely, that it shall be framed upon a single, noble motive, to which the design of all its parts, in some more or less subtle way, shall be confluent and helpful."[20]

A second type of interference, though far less frequent, is nevertheless serious because it involves the question of design. Of late it does not appear to happen so often, but only recently it seemed that some well-meaning soul or other was forever popping up with the proposal that all or part of Central Park—and Prospect Park, too, on a few occasions—be redesigned in "the more truly urban" form of, say, the Luxembourg in Paris. No condemnation of the latter is to be inferred through pointing out that in such a suggestion the original intent of Olmsted and Vaux is wholly overlooked. Their primary aim was avowedly the provision of a tract of rural scenery as a relief for workers hemmed in by the city. Indeed, the very opposite of urban forms and conditions was consciously sought.

20. *Olmsted Papers, Central Park*, p. 45.

199. Central Park: the Mall, looking toward the Music Hall, Terrace, Esplanade, and Bethesda Fountain—the only strongly architectonic area within either of the two great parks.

To this general rule there was one sensible exception: there was to be in the park one carefully delimited area where masses of people so characteristic of the city would be encouraged to congregate: the Mall (Fig. 199), the Music Hall, the Terrace, and the Esplanade with its quaint Bethesda Fountain. This tightly-knit complex of urbanity was accordingly designed in thoroughly architectonic fashion and paved against the pounding of feet. It was and still is a strong design, no matter what one may feel today about Vaux's amusingly Victorian details. As shown by the arrow drawn on the Greensward plan, the central sight-line of the series of spaces was firmly anchored on a distant stone tower proposed for the corner of the old Reservoir (today called the Belvedere and used as a weather station). At the southern end, regrettably, the sight-line was less well fixed; it is reached almost fortuitously by the system of roads and paths from the main entrance at 59th Street and Fifth Avenue. As a consequence, a clear connection with the geometric urbanity of the city is lost, and the Mall tends to float loosely in the total design, despite the inner strength of this architectonic set of spaces. At Prospect Park this problem does not arise: the connection between urban rectilinearity and the softer forms of the park occurs within the embrace of the street system itself, in the strong oval design of the Plaza.

These two bits of architectonic design, introduced with fine judgment where large crowds of visitors would challenge—or very possibly destroy—a pastoral treatment, do not contradict the basic human purpose for which the two parks were built, best voiced by Olmsted: "It is one great purpose of the [Central] Park to supply to the hundreds of thousands of tired workers, who have no opportunity to spend their summers in the country, a specimen of God's handiwork that shall be to them, inexpensively, what a month or two in the White Mountains or the Adirondacks is, at great cost, to those in easier circumstances."[21]

To say that Central Park and Prospect Park were successes would merely recite the obvious. Through the enthusiastic public reception accorded these two pioneering parks, even before they were near completion, the fame of Olmsted and Vaux—as partners until 1872, as individuals thereafter—was firmly established. They set a standard for park work that has not been materially improved or altered in subsequent years. Even while still working on Central and Prospect Parks, they were engaged by an ever larger number of municipalities: Buffalo and Albany, Newark, Providence, Fall River, Hartford, and New Britain. Perhaps most important of all was Chicago, where they prepared the remarkable subdivision layout of 1869 for Riverside, Illinois, and the 1871 report for the Chicago South Park Commission, including plans for Washington and Jackson Parks, both of which gained national prominence twenty years later. Even after dissolving their formal partnership, the two friends collaborated on matters in New York—notably Riverside Park—until Vaux retired; he died in 1895.

Meanwhile, Olmsted's growing practice took him over a wide range of territory with a multitude of projects. He was called in to improve the grounds of the capitol in Washington and the state capitols in Albany and Hartford. There were college campuses to do, grounds for summer resorts, land subdivisions, and some private places. In addition to continuing occupation with cities where park systems had already been started by the firm or by Olmsted himself (Buffalo, Hartford, Louisville, Baltimore, for example), he undertook Belle Isle Park in Detroit and Mount Royal Park in Montreal. He was fascinated by conferences with Sargent and Gray on a proposed arboretum in Boston. Always at heart a conservationist, he was extremely active in campaigns to save Niagara Falls and the New York Adirondack Mountain region. At last, in 1883, thoroughly wearied of New York City and increasingly busy on landscape architectural matters in the Boston area, he closed his New York office and moved to Brookline, where he bought the house at 99 Warren Street that was his home and office for the rest of his life.

21. *Ibid.*, p. 46.

XX. Olmsted's Work in Boston

Surviving today in deplorable condition after many decades of neglect and misuse, Olmsted's public work in Boston was at least as important, technically and historically, as that in New York. It was somewhat slow in getting started; actual work did not begin until twenty-five years after the birth of Central Park. Despite the widely heralded early success of Central and Prospect Parks, it was not until 1869 that public interest was sufficient in Boston to cause circulation of a citizens' petition to the City Council urging the creation of such a park.

Early in 1870 the Mayor, on behalf of the Council, managed to get a park bill through the General Court, the State Legislature. But as amended, the bill provided that in order to become effective the measure would require a two-thirds favorable vote of the people. Unfortunately, not enough preparatory work had been done, and in the municipal elections that fall the support was not forthcoming. Indeed, it was five more years before the Park Commission Act of 1875 was passed by the Legislature and accepted by popular vote. Even then, although Park Commissioners were duly appointed, the act gave the City Council the responsibility for providing funds. When that body was backward about voting the Commissioners any appropriations for land acquisition, action was blocked again, and nothing much happened until the City Council's hand was forced in 1877.

In the meantime, Olmsted had been on the Boston scene at frequent intervals since 1867, when he was first called in for professional advice by Professor Charles Eliot Norton, of Harvard. In 1872 he had prepared a study and report for Massachusetts General Hospital on possible sites for what is now the McLean Hospital, and in 1875 he laid out this establishment on the site he had recommended in Waverly. Late in 1875 the Park Commissioners sought his counsel on areas tentatively selected as possible park sites. In a letter of April 8, 1876, reporting on his field inspections, Olmsted recommended approval of four specific units, along the Charles River, in the marshy Back Bay, around Jamaica Pond, and in West Roxbury. Because of lack of funds, no development was feasible. In 1877, however, it became clear to the City Council that the public's patience was exhausted, especially with respect to the much-discussed further filling in and use of the Back Bay marshlands. Pressures were brought, too, by owners of property in the Back Bay area who knew what park development could do for the market value of adjacent land. Under the compulsion of this somewhat inglorious marriage of interests, the City Council finally borrowed and authorized the acquisition of land and the laying out of a park in the unimproved portion of the Back Bay.

The Park Commissioners thereupon announced a competition, but Olmsted chose not to enter and also declined the invitation to judge the submissions. When asked to comment professionally on the winning plan he agreed, and he immediately sought a conference with the city engineer. From him Olmsted learned that the competitors had obviously failed to recognize and solve the severe drainage problem that existed in the area, where on virtually flat land the rise and fall of the tidal Charles River had to meet the steady outflow of two streams, Stony Brook and Muddy River, both of which tended to flood badly when high tides backed up on the Charles. The problem, Olmsted saw at once, would have to be solved before any scenic development was attempted. The city engineer, who naturally concurred, had proposed a large rectangular storage basin with a tide-gate arrangement to control the water level. Olmsted persuaded him to modify the rectangular form so as to give the banks more nearly the alignment of a natural backwater, retaining otherwise the engineering solution.

This eminently sensible combining of practicality and creative imagination so pleased the Park Commissioners that they forthwith engaged Olmsted as landscape architect for the entire project. The scheme was further studied, revised, and brought to acceptable form in 1878. This meant that filling in and regrading, in accordance with Olmsted's plan, could be started at once, for land acquisition had already begun in 1877. In December 1878 articles of agreement were signed by Olmsted and the Park Commissioners, who published the preliminary plan for the Back Bay Park, or the Fens, as Olmsted preferred to call the area, in their annual report of 1879.

The Back Bay Fens (Fig. 200) comprise an area of land and water about a quarter-mile wide at its maximum, extending in an irregular arc for just over a mile from the tide-gate on the Charles River at the northeastern end to the Fens Bridge, near the present buildings of Simmons College, at the western end. The area is bounded by park roads that have become city streets. As originally designed, the park and its waterway were crossed by bridges

200. Boston: Olmsted plan for the Back Bay Fens as shown in the Park Commissioners' *Report* for 1879.

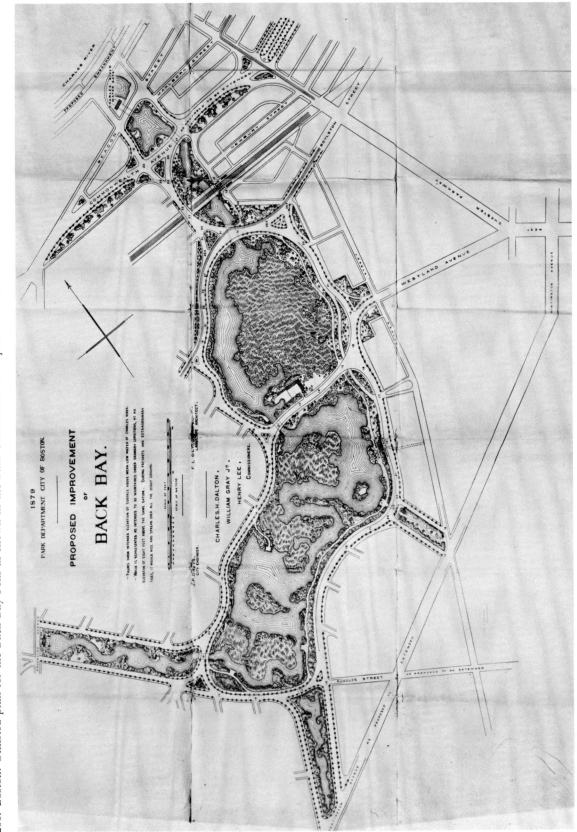

1879

PARK DEPARTMENT CITY OF BOSTON.

PROPOSED IMPROVEMENT
OF
BACK BAY.

— Figures show intended elevation of surface, above mean low water of Charles river.
— Water is represented as intended to be maintained under ordinary conditions, at an elevation of eight feet above the same datum. During freshets and extraordinary tides, it would rise and spread over all the beach ground.

F. L. OLMSTED,
LANDSCAPE ARCHITECT.

J. P. DAVIS,
CITY ENGINEER.

CHARLES.H.DALTON,
WILLIAM GRAY Jr.,
HENRY LEE,
COMMISSIONERS.

carrying Beacon Street, Commonwealth Avenue, the Boston & Albany Rail-road, and Agassiz Road. There were six entrances: the arm called the Charlesgate linked to the river; the Boylston and Westland entrances from the east; the Huntington entrance from the southeast; the Parker Hill or Tremont entrance from the southwest; and the Longwood entrance at the western end beyond the Fens Bridge. All simply entered the park and ended there except the Boylston entrance, from which the visitor was led across the area, high above the waterway, on the arch of the massive bridge designed by Olmsted's good friend and frequent collaborator, architect H. H. Richardson.

From the various entrances there were pleasant paths for strolling; there was also the start of what was intended as an extensive bridle path system that Olmsted named the Ride. As the channels of the waterway would be relatively narrow and winding, it was decided to limit boating to canoes. One of the most attractive aquatic features, occurring naturally even while dredg-ing was being done and continuing to the present, was the adoption of the Fens by native waterfowl in surprising numbers. As the excavation and filling progressed, the forming of artificial salt meadow and other appropriate planting kept pace, on the fast land as well as along the wet margins, with a view to creating a scene described by Olmsted as "the waving fenny verdure, the meandering water, the blooming islets, and the border of trees and underwood following the varied slope of the rim of the basin, like the hanging woods of a river bank."[1]

Because of inadequate annual appropriations, the Back Bay Fens took a long time to finish. In the process there were a few revisions, but they were minor compared to what has happened since. The damming of the Charles, resulting in a controlled basin instead of the former tides, has of course greatly modified the basic drainage problem. The old Stony Brook channel has been put underground at the Huntington entrance, and the Museum of Fine Arts has been erected facing the Fens to the west of this point. Offsetting these improvements, however, one sees in the area today the sad results of decade upon decade of indifference, both official and public, compounded with an all but complete failure to grasp the inherent values of the park as envisioned by Olmsted.

In the western part of the Fens, from Aggasiz Road to the end, at least half of the original water area has been filled in. The "blooming islets" that Olmsted planned are gone. What were once quiet marsh-meadows are now occupied by an athletic field of indifferent quality, a geometric rose garden, and a war memorial. East of Aggasiz Road the former marsh-meadow has been given over for many years to "victory gardens," flower and vegetable plots planted and maintained by individual citizens on application and

1. Boston Park Commissioners, *Annual Report, 1879,* pp. 11–12.

permit. All of these varied elements are of course laudable in themselves, but they hardly represent appropriate uses for the Fens, if only because they are wholly disruptive of what would otherwise be a placid scene. Moreover, for their own good these activities deserve locations better adapted to their several purposes.

At the inner end of the Westland Entrance an undistinguished yet pretentious fire station blocks the view into the Fens. The old line of the Boston & Albany Railroad, now used by the Penn Central, is paralleled across the park by the new Massachusetts Turnpike, and the entire Charlesgate arm of the Fens is effectively smothered under a welter of concrete roads and ramps to accommodate not only the turnpike but also Storrow Drive along the Charles.

In hot weather a foul smell often arises in the whole length of the Fens; but in fairness to present authorities it may be noted that the problem has apparently existed off and on through the years. Severe droughts of recent years have undoubtedly contributed to the stagnation. On the other hand, however, it can legitimately be wished that the authorities would do a better and more frequent job of cleaning the water surfaces of filth and giving a reasonable degree of maintenance to the vegetation.

While studying the Back Bay Fens in 1879–1880, Olmsted quickly saw the possibility and value of continuing a strip of parkland up the valley of Muddy River to Jamaica Pond, one of the park sites he had recommended in 1876. The potential must have appealed also to the Park Commissioners, for their next annual report contained a preliminary plan by Olmsted and his report, dated December 1880 and entitled: "Suggestion for the Improvement of Muddy River and for completion of a Continuous Promenade from the Common to Jamaica Pond." This was the start of the epochal "green fingers" project of the Riverway, but construction did not begin until ten years later.

West Roxbury Park was another tentative park site recommended by Olmsted in 1876. At last, on November 7, 1881, the City Council authorized the Park Commissioners to start acquiring land for the park. The site was in a region of suburban and rural residences, with much of the artificial appurtenance of such development. The process of securing the property was lengthy; the City Council found it necessary to amend its legislation several times during the next two years, and as late as December 1883 the Park Commissioners were voted additional authority to purchase certain holdings to improve the boundaries of the park.

Meanwhile, although Olmsted was studying the area and working on preliminary plans, these were for him extremely busy years. His office remained in New York, but he spent much of the winters of 1881–1883 with friends in Brookline and Cambridge. From 1881 on he leaned more and more on his nephew (and stepson) John Charles Olmsted, who had become his apprentice in 1875 on graduation from Yale and was himself a remarkably competent landscape architect.[2] Then, as noted earlier, in 1883 Olmsted closed his New York office and moved everything permanently to Brookline. That year he accepted in tne office, as an apprentice, Charles Eliot, son of the president of Harvard. In 1884 John Charles Olmsted was taken into full partnership under the firm name of F. L. and J. C. Olmsted.

Appropriately enough, the first big project to emerge from the new firm after the move to Brookline was a preliminary report on West Roxbury Park dated December 22, 1884, and referring to plans being prepared in the new office. The preliminary was published by the Park Commissioners in their annual report for the year 1884. The final General Plan and accompanying report came shortly thereafter and were printed as supplements to the Commissioners' report for 1885. This plan was the first to use the name Franklin Park. It had become known that the Franklin Fund, set up in 1791 by the will of Benjamin Franklin, would make available to "the Town of Boston" in 1891 (after a century's accumulation, as provided by Franklin) a sum sufficient to extinguish the debt incurred for the purchase of the West Roxbury Park. The Park Commissioners, in gratitude and as a memorial to one of Boston's most noted sons, voted on November 10, 1885, to name the area Franklin Park. Prior to approval of the General Plan in 1885, work on the park had necessarily been limited to clearing the ground, removing the most insistent evidences of residential occupancy, building walls with the stone lifted from the fields, and so on. Serious construction of the park as such, in accordance with the approved plan, did not get under way until 1886.

Franklin Park (Fig. 201) is generally known as the third in Olmsted's great triad of parks; the first two, of course, are Central and Prospect Parks. On a technical basis, Franklin Park in its heyday was a close rival of Prospect for top rank among the three as a work of landscape architecture. Indeed, in a paper presented in 1905, John Charles Olmsted, who had himself played a strong role in the park's creation, wrote: "As an illustration of park designing . . . Franklin Park is probably the best piece of work . . . done by its designer, Frederick Law Olmsted. The topography and ledges and trees lent themselves not only to many picturesque bits of landscape designing, but afforded, with moderate grading, excellent fields for such sports as are permissible in a landscape park."[3]

Franklin Park has about the same overall size as Prospect Park, with chunkier dimensions. Its core is a large central space from which a relatively level meadow, called the Playstead, once led off to the north; a curving space called Ellicottdate (Fig. 202) still pulls one to the northwest. Between the

2. In 1859 Frederick Law Olmsted married the widow of his brother, John Hull Olmsted, thus becoming the stepfather of her children, John Charles, Charlotte, and Owen. In 1870 another son, Frederick Law Olmsted, Jr., was born.

3. *Transactions of the ASLA,* I (1899–1908), p. 52.

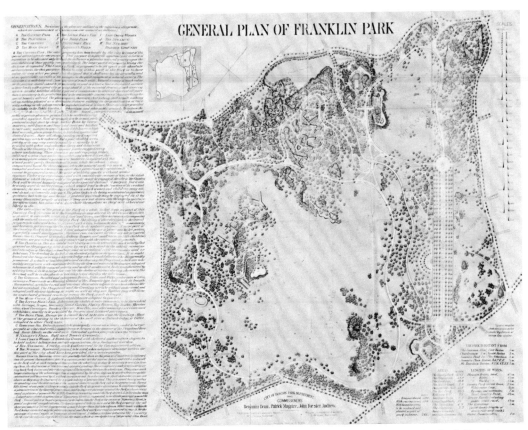

201. Franklin Park: the General Plan with copious "Notes" printed by the Park Department in 1886.

two Schoolmaster Hill thrusts forward, with Hagborne Hill and the rocky woods of the Wilderness behind it. On the west side of the central space is Scarboro Hill; Ellicottdale curves around beyond it; south of it lies charming Scarboro Pond (Fig. 203). On the east side of the park, surrounded by woods, is an architectonically formed mall originally called the Greeting that now leads in from the strong semicircular entrance on Blue Hill Avenue. This awkwardly monumental yet effective gateway, near Refectory Hill, is a modification of the Olmsted plan; the entire Greeting was held in abeyance for years. Today the Boston zoo lies alongside it, where Olmsted had intended a children's play area named the Little Folks Fair. There is a Circuit Drive around the park, just inside the belt of woods of varying width that screens out the exterior urban vistas. Here, as in Prospect Park, there was no serious transverse traffic problem.

Franklin Park today would not be likely to elicit from John Charles Olmsted a repetition of the words of praise he voiced in 1905, save as they reflected his justifiable admiration for the sensitivity and skill with which

202. Ellicottdale in Franklin Park at the turn of the century, with tennis courts of the pat-ball variety marked out on the grass.

203. Scarboro Pond, Franklin Park.

204. The Playstead before its pre-emption for a stadium of little distinction.

his elder had realized the fine potential of the area. In 1905 the younger man questioned "the introduction of golf playing,"[4] which had already occurred; now almost the whole open space in the park is a municipal golf course, heavily played. The entire northern meadow, formerly the Playstead (Fig. 204) with its quiet Overlook, has been pre-empted by a stadium and parking lots; the area is lost completely in terms of park value, nor has the new work any of the distinction that such a municipal installation deserves, even when built in the wrong place. The main open spaces of the park are used as a cross-country course by the local colleges—and an excellent course it is, according to the runners, provided one is adept at dodging well-hit golf balls.

Maintenance—or lack of it—has long been an annoying problem in Franklin Park; it has varied greatly, markedly worse in some years than others. Emphasis, clearly enough, is on maintaining not a park but a golf course. The so-called Club House on the slopes of Refectory Hill is well treated, whereas buildings elsewhere in the park have been neglected. Fire has damaged some of the oldest shelters, which have then been allowed to stand half-charred for years. The former Refectory, near the Blue Hill Avenue gateway, has long been in scandalous—even dangerous—condition. Admittedly the fault is largely one of public apathy, illustrated with shocking clarity when just a short while ago there was only minimal outcry against a proposal

4. *Ibid.*, p. 53.

to destroy the rough, wooded Wilderness area in the north and invade it with a high school for which the virtually unbuildable site was not at all well suited. The incredible part is that the blunder was avoided by only the thinnest margin in a highly political School Committee that is elected by popular vote.

Notwithstanding John Olmsted's opinion of over a half-century ago, many landscape architects today find that Franklin Park, quite apart from questions of upkeep, somehow impresses less positively than Prospect Park. Judgments vary as to the reason; some point to the extent and mystery of the main Lake in Prospect Park as against the compactness of Scarboro Pond. Others fail to find in Franklin Park clear spatial sequences equal to those of Prospect. There is another important reason that may not strike one immediately on a first visit. Although basically the two parks have much in common, both being masterpieces of their kind, there is a distinct difference between their respective central open spaces; as has been observed, this is what sets the scale, the tone, the overall impression in a park of the "country" type. To a discerning eye, a major flaw in Franklin Park is the high hill that rises in the very heart of the great central space, detracting noticeably from the needed sense of containment and giving the space a feeble, scattered effect as compared to the magnificent Long Meadow of Prospect Park. After all, experience has demonstrated that one of the surest ways of killing or negating a space is to put something high in the middle.

Perhaps the most poignant aspect of Franklin Park is the fact that, despite its tragic neglect and mishandling, the greatness of Olmsted's creative power manages to shine through, as though to justify the customary listing of this work in the great triad of his parks. In so evaluating it one is of course thinking primarily of its excellence well into the present century rather than of its present state. But even today, with all its shortcomings, Franklin Park remains a source of pleasure and healthy exercise for a multitude of people. It can almost be said that as a quiet park it no longer exists. Yet it is unquestionably a legitimate member of the famous triad.

While Franklin Park was being built, only spasmodic activity occurred on Olmsted's "Continuous Promenade from the Common to Jamaica Pond." One of the earliest attempts to let the atmosphere of surrounding country penetrate the urban complex with park-like corridors, the "green fingers" project became widely known and admired in the United States and abroad. To the Park Commissioners, this offshoot of the Back Bay Fens was known as the Muddy River Improvement and also briefly as Riverdale. In December 1881 the City Council authorized the Commissioners to purchase land for the project whenever the Town of Brookline concurred. Concurrence of Brookline was essential because the boundary between the two municipalities ran for the most part along the middle of the stream. The Commissioners' annual report for that year contained a General Plan for Muddy River

205. "The Parkway" (Olmsted's "promenade") from Boston Common to Franklin Park, as shown in the Park Commissioners' *Report* for 1886.

Improvement, drawn by "J. C. O." For one reason or another no substantial action followed, other than minor acquisitions of property, until 1887. In that year the Longwood entrance to the Back Bay Fens was widened to accommodate connection with the anticipated Muddy River Improvement. Hope for eventual accomplishment was indicated also in 1887 (Fig. 205), when the Commissioners voted "that the intended public promenade . . . be named as a whole The Parkway" and that its lower sections be named successively Charlesgate, Fenway, and Riverway.[5]

The entire Parkway, or Promenade, as Olmsted conceived it originally, was to start with Boston Common and the Public Garden. From there, Commonwealth Avenue, a handsome tree-lined street, would lead directly to the Back Bay Fens. From the Fens the route would follow the course of Muddy River upstream, first northwest in the Longwood entrance of the Fens to beyond Brookline Avenue, where the stream made a ninety degree turn, southwest to cross upper Brookline Avenue again, and on across Huntington Avenue. South of this crossing a large cat-tail swamp would be converted into Leverett Pond. Then the route would lie in a belt of woods filling the valley around two small pools, Willow Pond and Ward's Pond (Fig. 206), before reaching Jamaica Pond, a source for Muddy River. The portion from the Fens to upper Huntington Avenue is what the Commissioners' 1887 vote named the Riverway; the section from Leverett Pond to Jamaica Pond came to be called the Jamaicaway. By the time the whole run was completed a park strip called the Arborway was added, joining Jamaica Pond with the Arnold Arboretum and an entrance to Franklin Park.

5. Boston Park Commissioners, *Annual Report, 1887*, p. 22.

At last the Park Commissioners, in their annual report for 1889, published an authoritative Revised Plan for the Muddy River Improvement, and in 1890, just ten years after Olmsted's first "Suggestion," grading of the banks was begun. In the meantime a good start had been made, through the purchase of adjacent parcels of land, toward elimination of scores of squalid shacks and a dump that had come to border the stream and endanger public health. The slopes were minutely plotted, staked, and graveled against slumping, and footpaths were laid out on both sides of the stream and a carriage road on the Boston side. The Newton branch of the Boston & Albany Railroad, which ran beside the lower part of Muddy River on the Brookline side, was blocked out visually by means of a continuous mound with heavy planting, and several sinuous islands were built in the stream at this point as an additional screening measure (Figs. 207, 208). Bridges, designed by Richardson's successors from sketches by the Olmsteds, were thrown across at several points; Longwood Bridge, of seam-faced granite, is the most noteworthy (Figs. 209, 210). The planting that followed was done with typical Olmstedian care, using almost exclusively native materials.

According to the 1895 annual report of the Commissioners, work on the Muddy River section was substantially finished, as was Leverett Park, and the final steps for Jamaica Park were in sight. This was the year when the elder Olmsted, now feeble after forty arduous years of professional practice, felt compelled to retire. In tribute to him, as the work neared realization,

206. Ward's Pond, in the wooded area later renamed Olmsted Park by the Commissioners.

207. The Riverway: spotted old negative shows lower end of the Muddy River, near Brookline Avenue, under construction in the 1890s.

208. The Riverway at the same site after several years of growth on the islands.

209. The Riverway: construction, looking downstream toward the temporary Longwood Bridge, in the 1890s.

210. The Riverway at the same site after completion of Longwood Bridge; Brookline left, Boston right.

the Board of Park Commissioners voted on December 24, 1900: "That those parts of the parks heretofore known as Leverett Park and Jamaica Park be called *Olmsted Park* in honor of Frederick Law Olmsted."[6]

In its present condition, over a half-century later, Olmsted's Promenade—or the Riverway, as the entire Muddy River stretch now seems to be called—is a sad tribute to his genius. Surely it is a far cry from the delight it must have been during the first two decades of this century. An official attitude of disrespect seems almost to have been deliberately established at the very start of the Riverway proper, at the lower Brookline Avenue crossing: the former flow of visual continuity from Fens to Riverway has been thoroughly obliterated by the introduction of a massive concrete parking lot for the benefit of a nearby department store. The leisurely carriage drive of other years has yielded to the times and become a heavily traveled motor road, a major traffic artery consisting of Arborway, Jamaicaway, Riverway, Fenway, and what is left of Charlesgate. To call it a "parkway" is by now a complete misnomer, for in most of its length it is lined with private residences and has far too many side-access roads to qualify as a parkway in modern terms.

To be sure, there are still pedestrian paths along the stream on both sides, the Brookline side usually well maintained, the Boston side relatively ignored. The same comparison must be made, though the difference in this regard is not so sharp between the two sides, as to care of vegetation along the margins of the stream, where water-loving species have naturally tended toward overgrowth. The islands at the lower end of the Riverway are so overgrown as to be nearly indistinguishable, and the entire waterway is badly blocked, not only with silt, which is understandable, but with refuse, which is not. One of the mid-century sights not soon to be forgotten is the iridescent plumage of a duck sitting incongruously on one of the discarded automobile tires that too often ornament the water.

One of the most widely reproduced views of the Riverway was taken in 1920, looking upstream from atop Longwood Bridge (Fig. 212; compare Fig. 211). The canoeists are paddling along a shadowy stream bordered by dogwood and other verdure; today the stream is clogged and impassable, its banks much eroded, and the water sluggish and brown, streaked with oil and floating trash. But the overhanging green is still there, the high old trees are more mature, and in spring the dogwood flowers; one can walk here in peace and comfort, at least on the Brookline side. As with other Olmstedian masterpieces, the original bright spirit, the grace and loveliness—the greatness of the fundamentally simple and right—seem to flicker down through the overstory in disregard of man's capacity for destruction.

The Back Bay Fens, Franklin Park, the Muddy River Improvement—and the Arnold Arboretum, too, that world-renowned combination of the scientific

6. *Ibid., 1901,* pp. 4–5.

211. The Riverway: looking upstream in the 1890s from the temporary Longwood Bridge. Tracks of the Boston & Albany branch line are on the right (now the Riverside rapid transit line); a footpath is being built along the regraded stream banks.

212. The Riverway from atop the permanent Longwood Bridge in 1920.

and the recreational worked out by Olmsted and Sargent for Harvard University and the City of Boston: these were rich years in the productive life of Frederick Law Olmsted and a strong foundation for the firm that continued his professional ideals for so many decades from the office in Brookline. With John Charles Olmsted as his partner from 1884, he next admitted the gifted Henry Sargent Codman in 1889. Codman died four short years later in the midst of work on the World's Columbian Exposition. In that year (1893), Charles Eliot returned to the man under whom he had been an apprentice from 1883 to 1885 and the firm became Olmsted, Olmsted, and Eliot. The new partner had traveled and studied further after apprenticeship, had opened his own office in Boston, and had already earned a solid name for himself.

XXI. Two Pioneers: Weidenmann and Cleveland

Despite Olmsted's resounding success, the profession of landscape architecture had very few practitioners in its early years. During the period when Olmsted had his headquarters in New York he worked in close association with two men at different times: until they dissolved their partnership amicably in 1872, he and Calvert Vaux practiced together for some fifteen years, and the association continued less formally on various occasions afterward; from 1874 for at least a few years before the 1883 move to Brookline Olmsted had an office arrangement, though not a partnership, with Jacob Weidenmann.

In 1888, when a park commissioner in Rochester, New York, sought advice regarding available landscape architects, Olmsted wrote pungently about the state of his new profession:

> With reference to your undertaking there is less room for choice than may be supposed among the landscape gardeners or landscape architects of the country . . . Of those who have given themselves the title of landscape gardeners not one of many more than a hundred have the smallest right to it . . . in all Europe and America, among all the men who with no dishonest intention take the name of landscape gardeners (or architects) there are very few who have shown or are likely to possess any respectable power of dealing with problems of the class that properly come before the Park Commissioners of a large and growing city . . . Of those among them likely to be available to you the man of highest proved ability is my old partner Calvert Vaux of New York . . . There

are in the country but two other (properly speaking) landscape designers who have had any experience that would specially qualify them to advise you.[1]

One of these two was Olmsted's former associate Jacob Weidenmann, "the author of a book . . . on landscape gardening; a Swiss by birth. He laid out and superintended for years, the public park at Hartford, Conn."[2] Weidenmann was born in Winterthur, Switzerland, on August 22, 1829. After a brief apprenticeship with an architect in Geneva, he went to Munich for further architectural training. After working as an engineer and architect in Panama and South America he returned to New York (which he had visited earlier), and in 1861 he became superintendent of parks in Hartford. During his seven years there he worked closely with the Reverend Horace Bushnell on Bushnell Park and designed and promoted the Cedar Hill Cemetery.

In 1870, soon after moving to New York City, he published *Beautifying Country Homes: A Handbook of Landscape Gardening*. In 1874 he entered into a working agreement with Olmsted. Their announcement read: "Mr. Olmsted and Mr. Weidenmann can at all times be commanded for any business of their common profession."[3] With Olmsted, Weidenmann was engaged on a number of works including the Schuylkill Reservoir in Philadelphia and Congress Spring Park, Saratoga. He was also employed upon the Hot Springs Reservation in Arkansas, on the grounds of the state capitol at Des Moines, and on other public and private works, sometimes alone and sometimes in collaboration with Olmsted.

A pioneer in the movement for cemeteries in which enclosures would be eliminated, monuments restricted, and the whole maintained in park-like form, Weidenmann in 1881 wrote several articles pleading for the "modern" cemetery and in 1888 published *Modern Cemeteries*. It was his intention to compile and publish illustrations of his designs in a volume for which he prepared many plates; the work was never finished, but some plates are on file in the New York Public Library. At the time of his death, on February 6, 1893, he was laying out the Pope Park in Hartford. In his memory, the Jacob Weidenmann Prize was endowed at Harvard for annual award to a student of landscape architecture.

The other man referred to by Olmsted in his letter was Horace William Shaler Cleveland. "He is a cultivated Boston born and bred man, has been employed in responsible positions on the public parks of Brooklyn, Chicago and Minneapolis. He is the oldest landscape gardener in the country."[4] It is unforgivable that so little attention has been accorded by the profession

1. *Olmsted Papers, Early Years*, pp. 127–130.
2. *Ibid.*, p. 130.
3. *Ibid.*, p. 18.
4. *Ibid.*, p. 130.

to Cleveland, a completely dedicated early practitioner, and indeed that so little is known about him. Born in Lancaster, Massachusetts, on December 16, 1814, he died in Hinsdale, Illinois, on December 5, 1900; between those dates he packed a lifetime of hard work, high idealism, professional practice, and writing.

Almost nothing is certain about Cleveland's early years and training except that he worked for a while in his teens, during five years spent in Cuba while his father was vice-consul at Havana. After his return to the States he continued an active interest in agriculture with a partial admixture, apparently, of practical civil engineering and land surveying. In the early 1840s he acquired a farm near Burlington, New Jersey, and there in 1842 he brought his bride, Maryann Dwinell. A son Henry was born in 1846, and a second son Ralph in 1851; the latter eventually became his father's partner.

Shortly after Ralph's birth Cleveland moved again, back to New England this time. He settled first at his grandfather's home in Salem, Massachusetts, and then for ten years in nearby Danvers. About 1855, while still in Salem, he formed a partnership with Robert Morris Copeland, of Lexington; the two set up an office in Boston for the practice of what they termed "landscape and ornamental gardening." The services offered by the new firm of Copeland & Cleveland reveal, albeit somewhat quaintly, how a new profession was emerging—or at least trying to emerge—from the botanical atmosphere of horticulture. The firm, as advertised in a one-sheet flyer now in the Library of the Harvard Graduate School of Design, "will furnish plans for the laying out and improvement of Cemeteries, Public Squares, Pleasure Grounds, Farms and Gardens, as well as for the construction of every species of Building connected with Agriculture, Horticulture, and general rural improvement."

In 1856, when land for New York's Central Park had been acquired and the rough fieldwork of clearing begun, Copeland & Cleveland came forward with the first public pronouncement of the new profession hovering on the threshold: a small (seven-page) pamphlet, probably written by Cleveland, entitled *A Few Words on the Central Park*. To be sure, the piece bore the imprint of its times: there is a certain flowery grandiloquence about it, some of the unctuous emphasis on "moral influence" that characterized many writers of the 1840s and 1850s and none more noticeably than Andrew Jackson Downing, who seems to have been held in awe as a sort of patron saint in the years just after his tragic death. There is in the Copeland & Cleveland paper, as in Downing, an American version of the English verbal involvement with "the sublime, the picturesque, and the beautiful," and an echo of Loudon's "gardenesque school of landscape." Nevertheless, the treatise was a remarkably persuasive plea for the virtues of planning, and in particular for early preparation of what would be called today a general or master plan for the entire park. The following excerpts are especially significant:

It is foolish to say that we should plan only what we can immediately execute. The design should embrace all possible, or at least all probable wants, and adapt itself to them from the beginning . . . We have heard it objected that it is not safe or wise to plan too largely at first; that people are appalled at the thought of so vast an outlay, and that the result will be, that we shall accomplish nothing. To this we reply, that in this, as in every public or private enterprise, the truest economy lies in considering beforehand every possible necessity, and beginning the work knowingly, making the needful appropriation not only of money but of time for its accomplishment; and in such a work as this, embracing such variety and amount of labor and expenditure, we cannot be too careful in arranging for their judicious apportionment.[5]

The Copeland & Cleveland argument for foresight and planning may well have influenced the decision of the Central Park Commissioners to hold the 1857 competition; it is of course impossible to be sure, yet the paper was unquestionably remarkable and timely. Copeland & Cleveland, naturally enough, entered the competition, but their plan was not among the premiated four.

The Civil War made obvious inroads on the firm's professional practice, and apparently the formal partnership was dissolved during the war years. In fact, little is known of Cleveland in the decade that followed except that he was busy in Tarrytown, New York, in 1867 and that for some part of 1869 he was with Olmsted & Vaux on Prospect Park in Brooklyn. Although he was eight years older than Olmsted, Cleveland recognized Olmsted's genius and enjoyed working with him. A warm friendship sprang up between them, resulting in extensive correspondence throughout their lives though they did not often meet in later years.

In 1869, having learned that Chicago, following the example of New York and Brooklyn, had acquired public lands for future development, Cleveland moved there and opened an office. Precise information about his early years in Chicago is scanty because all his papers, notes, and books—except two documents that had already been published—were destroyed in the great Chicago fire. The first of the publications, *Public Grounds in Chicago: how to give them Character and Expression,* came out in 1869; a twenty-page pamphlet, it discussed mainly the problem of infusing a degree of interest into the flat and unvarying topography of Chicago. Especially intriguing today, in view of Cleveland's later vigorous campaigns against the rigidity of grid-system town plans, is a passage about the proposed "grand avenue, or 'boulevard,' three hundred feet in width and fourteen miles long," connecting the parks of Chicago. Here Cleveland shows his flexibility and willingness to let the circumstances and good sense, rather than dogma, govern:

5. R. M. Copeland and H. W. S. Cleveland, *A Few Words on the Central Park* (Boston, 1856), pp. 2, 5.

The drive way, extending throughout its whole length, should not be less than sixty feet wide. To carry it straight from end to end would be fearfully formal and dreary, yet to make a turn in a road, without any obvious necessity or object, is a violation not only of the rules of landscape gardening, but of common sense. When Mr. "Capability" Brown . . . created in the last century a revolution in the old geometric manner of arranging grounds, in England, by the introduction of what was termed the "natural style," he was for a time, regarded as the arbiter of taste, and every one was so delighted with the change from angles to curved lines, that it was not at first perceived that in his zeal to hit upon the line of beauty, which he fancied to consist in a series of graceful curves, he had fallen into an equally formal system as the one he condemned; so that one of his critics remarked of his serpentine paths, canals, etc., that you might walk from one end to the other, stepping first upon zig, and then upon zag, for the whole length. And this kind of formality is the danger which is most to be apprehended in the construction of such a drive as the one we are considering, for, whenever, by the introduction of water, or plantations, or whatever object may be devised, a reason is furnished for a variation from a straight course, the necessity immediately stares us in the face of providing something on the other side, to turn it back again, before it reaches the boundary within which it must be retained, and the continuation of such variations, with a repetition of scenes of woodland, lawn and water, which, however tastefully arranged, must consist essentially of the same elements of attractive interest, would result eventually in a *monotony of variety,* scarcely less fatiguing than that of the straight road.[6]

The other document, published early in 1871, was a pamphlet announcing the availability of Cleveland's professional services, in association with two engineers of known competence. In it he referred to "Twenty years' experience in landscape gardening, during the last two of which I have been actively engaged in designing the arrangement of grounds for a great variety of purposes, in Illinois, Indiana, Michigan, Wisconsin, Iowa and Kansas."[7] A number of commissions were cited specifically, including institutional and cemetery designs in locations as widely dispersed as Rhode Island, Massachusetts, Iowa, and Kansas.

In 1870 the firm of Olmsted & Vaux had signed an agreement with the Chicago South Park Commission, for whom a report and plans were printed in 1871. In late summer 1872 Cleveland was appointed "Landscape Architect of the South Park and connecting Boulevards," with the understanding that

---

6. *Landscape Architecture,* 20 (January 1930), pp. 96–98.
7. H. W. S. Cleveland, *A Few Hints on Landscape Gardening in the West* (Chicago, 1871), p. 2.

execution would be guided by the Olmsted & Vaux plans.[8] His relations with the South Park Commissioners, however, were not wholly agreeable and ultimately ended in litigation.

The Chicago years, though not exactly happy, were on the whole productive once Cleveland had recovered from the wreckage of the fire. Throughout the midwest his projects, the details of which are unfortunately now lost, increased. But the outstanding event of his Chicago period was the publication in 1873 of his remarkable little book, *Landscape Architecture as Applied to the Wants of the West*. So far as available evidence shows, this essay was the first *book* to use the term "landscape architecture" in the professional sense. Olmsted had of course adopted the title at least ten years earlier; but, though he wrote much—and more clearly than Cleveland—he does not appear ever to have published anything on landscape architecture with the implied permanence of book form.

It is obviously not to be expected that professionals today will find in Cleveland's book anything startling technically. The remarkable fact is that in so early a treatise the aims and techniques of a new profession could be in such large part analyzed and clearly enunciated. There is a distinctly contemporary flavor in Cleveland's terse complaints about "the inadequate conception of the scope of the art" and "the idea . . . that landscape gardening is solely a decorative art."[9] Here he is, nearly a century ago, voicing today's plea that the landscape architect be called in *early enough,* and stating firmly "the conviction . . . that it is the original design of arrangement which confers upon any place its intrinsic expression or character . . . the want of which cannot be atoned for by any amount of subsequent dressing or decoration" (p. 17).

To a modern reader, the zeal of a pioneering spirit still illumines the book. Cleveland was genuinely brimming with concern over the probable visual fate of the "vast regions yet lying undisturbed between the Mississippi and the Pacific" (29). He used only about one-fifth of the volume for "illustration of the meaning of landscape architecture" (18) by discussing his approach to a private residential project, devoting the remaining four-fifths to an intense dissertation on "landscape architecture applied to the arrangement of towns" (28). Indeed, in terms of the present Cleveland emphasized almost exclusively the broad land-planning aspects of the profession, rather than those detailed considerations of specific form more closely associated with the design aspects.

As in the case of the earlier *Few Words on the Central Park,* so in the 1873 volume a twentieth-century reader finds Cleveland's exposition suffering somewhat from the Victorian, status-conscious, right-side-of-the-tracks terminology of the times—or perhaps of Downing, whom he admired and emu-

8. Chicago South Park Commissioners, *Annual Report, 1872–73*, p. 12.
9. H. W. S. Cleveland, *Landscape Architecture as Applied to the Wants of the West* (Chicago, 1873), pp. 13–14.

lated. But notwithstanding this burden of "picturesque romanticism," the eloquent sincerity comes through to the present with a persuasive appeal for decent common sense and a vigorous attack on the stupidity of gridiron town plans unrelated to topography. A few excerpts illustrate:

> Before the introduction of railroads the settlement of the West was by a gradual process of accretion, a vanguard of hardy pioneers keeping ever in advance . . . nothing approaching to scientific or artistic designs of arrangement of extended areas, based upon wise forethought of future necessities, was attempted. The government system of surveys of public lands formed the only basis of division, the only guide in laying out county roads, or the streets of proposed towns; and if the towns grew into cities it was simply by the indefinite extension of the straight streets, running north, south, east or west, without regard to topographical features, or facilities of grading or drainage, and still less of any considerations of taste or convenience, which would have suggested a different arrangement . . . yet the custom is so universal and offers such advantages in simplifying and facilitating descriptions and transfers of real estate, that any attempt at the introduction of a different system encounters at once a strong feeling of popular prejudice . . . Every one who is familiar with the river towns of the West will recall innumerable instances of enormously expensive works in cutting down hillsides and building up embankments; of the almost total destruction of valuable building sites; in one place by their being left in an inaccessible position on the top of a precipice; in another by being exposed to all the drainage of a street which is far above them, while all the naturally beautiful or picturesque features of the place have been destroyed or rendered hideous in the effort to make them conform to a rectangular system, as if the human intellect were as powerless to adapt itself to changing circumstances as the instinct of insects, whose cells are constructed on an unvarying pattern. (Pages 30–33)

> Whatever may be thought of such an arrangement . . . for a perfectly level site, it is hardly conceivable that any sane man will attempt seriously to defend the rectangular system when applied to a tract comprising much inequality of surface. Wherever it has been applied it has proved enormously costly, inconvenient and destructive of natural beauty. And yet the selfish greed of real estate proprietors prevents a departure from the practice, and renders them callous to the sufferings they inflict upon the future inhabitants, provided only that they can secure the largest immediate returns from the sale of lots, with the least possible outlay in preparing them for the market. (52–53)

One can hardly help wondering how appalled Cleveland would be if he were to see with what tenacity developers today cling all too often to the very ways

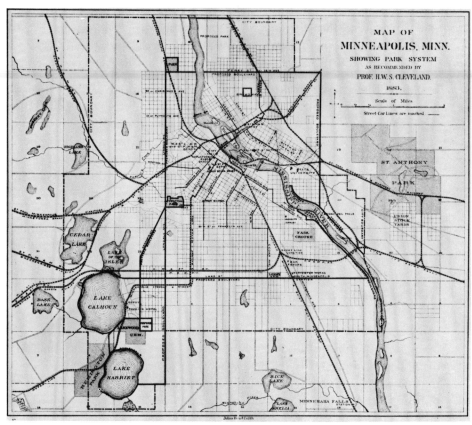

213. Horace W. S. Cleveland's proposal of 1883 for a park system in Minneapolis, the basis for the city's excellent present network of parks.

he excoriated nearly a hundred years ago—and how little our mid-twentieth-century society does to combat them.

In the course of travels east and west on professional tasks during the Chicago years, Cleveland found Minneapolis and St. Paul exceptionally attractive. As early as 1872 he had begun urging authorities of the two cities to be more aware of the area's unusually fine natural potentials for a system of public parks. Contacts continued intermittently for over a decade; then in 1883 a Board of Park Commissioners for the City of Minneapolis was created by the State Legislature and popular vote, despite bitter opposition by some elements of the population. The new Board forthwith engaged Cleveland to prepare a general plan for a city park system. His report, entitled "Suggestions for a System of Parks and Parkways for the City of Minneapolis," was presented at a meeting of the Board on June 2, 1883. It made a profound impression on the Commissioners, who published it in pamphlet form with its accompanying plan for a network of parks and boulevards (Fig. 213), and distributed it widely.

With characteristic directness Cleveland's report launched at once into assurances for those whose fears of heavy costs had led them to oppose the park legislation (he was aware that the Park Act had been approved by 5,327 to 3,922 votes in the popular election):

> The subject of public improvements in the form of parks and parkways is sure in its first inception to meet with opposition, owing to a natural misconception in the minds of inexperienced persons who imagine that such improvements must necessarily involve the immediate outlay of very large sums of money . . . the repeated experiences of other cities, in this country as well as Europe . . . have invariably demonstrated that . . . a judicious expenditure for such objects is always a wise and safe investment.
>
> In the ten years succeeding the commencement of work on Central Park in New York, the increased valuation of taxable property in the wards immediately surrounding it was no less than $54,000,000, affording a surplus . . . sufficient, if used as a sinking fund, to pay the entire cost of the park in less time than was required for its construction . . . The expenditures which but yesterday were so bitterly denounced have proved the best investment that could possibly have been made. The popular idea, however, that the purchase of lands for parks and parkways involves the necessity of immediate large outlay for their improvement is not only erroneous, in fact, but in many cases would be inconsistent with a wise economy.[10]

The important point, he urged, was to anticipate future needs with a view to "securing the areas that are needed before they become so occupied or acquire such value as to place them beyond reach (p. 4) . . . Look forward for a century, to the time when the city has a population of a million, and think what will be their wants. They will have wealth enough to purchase all that money can buy, but all their wealth cannot purchase a lost opportunity" (6).

The development of individual components of such a park system, he suggested, could await the corresponding growth of the city, but in the meantime adoption of an overall scheme was fundamental. Here as in the case of the *Few Words on the Central Park*, Cleveland earnestly advocated a master plan for the entire park system: "The plans for the general arrangement of the parks should, however, be prepared as soon as may be, so that the amount and character of each year's work may be predetermined and kept in progress, with the certainty that every step is towards the ultimate object, and the unity of design preserved throughout" (4–5). It must not be

10. H. W. S. Cleveland, *Suggestions for a System of Parks and Parkways for the City of Minneapolis* (Minneapolis, 1883), pp. 3–4.

overlooked that in this report, as in all his communications, Cleveland emphasized the metropolitan picture: "The growth of Minneapolis and St. Paul into one great metropolis is as certain as the existence of the vast wealth now lying latent in the regions beyond" (5).

Although Cleveland's comprehensive scheme for Minneapolis was enthusiastically received by the Board of Park Commissioners, progress in its realization was understandably slow. He was retained in 1884 and 1885 to design specific units of the system; in March 1885 he wrote his friend Olmsted that prospects in the area were becoming quite lively, and that "I have every reason to believe that the work of design will be placed in my hands." [11]

Three months later, at the invitation of the Common Council and Chamber of Commerce in St. Paul, Cleveland proposed a regional park system in an address entitled "Public Parks, Radial Avenues, and Boulevards: Outline Plan of a Park System for the City of St. Paul." Again he indulged in a bit of prophecy: "It seems so evident that St. Paul and Minneapolis eventually, and at no distant day, will become virtually one city, and the interests and future welfare of each must be so intimately connected with that of the other, that it is very desirable that they should unite in the designing and arranging of improvements of the area which now separates them, by which they are to be mutually benefitted." [12]

Even though the park systems of the two cities were not being developed as fast as he had hoped, Cleveland's professional engagements, public and private, in the area increased steadily; in 1886 he moved his office from Chicago to Minneapolis, where to his delight Olmsted visited him shortly thereafter. In 1887 he delivered another address in St. Paul, on the "Park Systems of St. Paul & Minneapolis." In 1888 he again sounded the metropolitan plea before the Minneapolis Society of Fine Arts: "The Aesthetic Development of the United Cities of St. Paul and Minneapolis." The published version, in pamphlet form, contained a plan of Cleveland's dream, a regional park system.

It was still too early in the growth of the American park movement to expect immediate public acceptance of so far-reaching a scheme as the one Cleveland envisioned for the Twin Cities. Indeed, it was many years before even his plans for Minneapolis approached full realization; numerous other dedicated public servants and private citizens eventually took part in building the park system that is today the city's proud possession, but Cleveland is quite generally regarded as its father. For many years the annual reports of the Board of Park Commissioners continued to carry as a foreword the quotation, "I would have the City itself a work of art. —H.W.S.C." The annual report of the Board for 1898, fifteen years after publication of Cleveland's overall plan, includes the following tribute: "It was the great good

11. *Landscape Architecture,* 20 (January 1930), p. 104.
12. *Ibid.,* p. 107.

fortune of Minneapolis to secure the services of one of the masters of American park designing, Mr. H. W. S. Cleveland, and to enjoy the advantages of his experience, taste and skill, until his powers were exhausted by age and disease." [13]

The morbid tone at the end of the testimonial was not without some justification; after all, when he moved to Minneapolis Cleveland was seventy-two. There is evidence that he enjoyed excellent health and remained active for several more years, until about 1890, traveling hither and yon on projects of many kinds. In 1891 he took his son Ralph into partnership under the firm name of H. W. S. Cleveland & Son; a plan under that name for Powderhorn Park in Minneapolis was dated 1892. But the next known record of the two is in Chicago, where the son was a photographer in the mid-1890s and the father was visited in 1898 by his friend Charles M. Loring, long the president of the Minneapolis Board of Park Commissioners. At the latter's instigation, Cleveland wrote his last published paper in that same year, "The Influence of Parks on the Character of Children." On December 5, 1900, nearing his eighty-sixth birthday, he died in Hinsdale, Illinois; appropriately, he was buried in Minneapolis.

13. Minneapolis Park Commissioners, *Annual Report, 1898*, pp. 26–27.

XXII. Charles Eliot and His Metropolitan Park System

Of Frederick Law Olmsted's young apprentices in Brookline, none made a name for himself more swiftly—or more remarkably, considering the short span of his life—than Charles Eliot. Born in Cambridge on November 1, 1859, when his father was assistant professor at Harvard, Eliot spent much of his youth in the outdoors, camping, sailing, and hiking cross-country. He was an avid student of the natural sciences and a keen observer of scenery, but even when he took his A.B. degree in June 1882 he had no firm conviction as to a future career.

Although landscape architecture was then almost unknown and no university offered instruction in it, Eliot had heard something of the profession through his uncle, Boston architect Robert S. Peabody, who knew Olmsted and had on occasion collaborated with him. What Eliot heard of the new field, especially its emphasis on outdoor activity, appealed to him so strongly that he resolved to prepare himself as well as he could for entry into the profession. In September he enrolled in the Bussey Institution, at that time the only Harvard department dealing with agricultural and horticultural matters.

The practicality and relevance of courses at the Bussey captured Eliot's interest, but an unexpected turn of events prevented his finishing the school year there. President Eliot had come to know Olmsted after his move to Brookline and had sought advice from him on the course of training Charles ought to pursue. The upshot was that in April 1883 the young man was introduced to Olmsted in Brookline by Robert Peabody and a week later entered the office as an apprentice, suspending his studies at the Bussey.

During the next two years Eliot gained experience of incalculable value, accompanying the elder Olmsted on many trips in the field, working closely in the office with John Charles Olmsted. Though only a few years older than Eliot, the younger Olmsted had developed unusual skill and became a partner in the firm during Eliot's apprenticeship. Both afield and on the board there was a wide variety of work, for those were extremely busy years. There was field experience immediately at hand in the building of the Back Bay Fens; in the office, among other projects Eliot worked on plans for the West Roxbury (Franklin) Park, for the ill-fated City Point design, for the Boston & Albany Railroad development, and for revision of the plantings in the Arnold Arboretum.

In April 1885, after two highly instructive years with the Olmsteds, Eliot resumed his studies at the Bussey Institution and completed his year's courses. That summer and fall he traveled extensively in the east, going as far south as Charleston, continually observing and making notes, with focus always on topography and flora. In November he sailed to England to begin the foreign travel and study he had been planning since the moment, three years earlier, he had made up his mind to head for the profession of landscape architecture. The year abroad was a mixture of learning and frustration. Armed with innumerable letters of introduction—perhaps too many, he sometimes felt— and warmly received in the homes of his father's friends, he was still too much a novice in a little-known, infant profession to be sure exactly what it was he wanted to know or to see, or even what others could best do to help him. As President Eliot later characterized the problem, which to his educator's mind seemed a particularly annoying one, "in short, he experienced to the full the difficulty of studying a profession in preparation for which there is no recognized school or course of study."[1]

The distribution of Eliot's time during the year may seem strange to twentieth-century students of landscape architecture, but it no doubt reflected fairly the influences and assumptions prevalent in the mid-1880s. He spent half the year in England: three months of the winter in London; over two months of the early summer traveling about from Devonshire to Edinburgh; a final two weeks in London and Liverpool before sailing home. To France he gave more than three months: February and May in Paris, often in conference with André, Alphand's professional successor; and some forty days in southern France, mainly on the Riviera. From there he went to Italy, where he limited himself to three weeks and went no farther south than Florence. A period of about two months he devoted partly to a trip through Scandinavia into Russia, partly to Germany and Holland. Of this portion the park at Muskau was the high point; indeed, today's best available description of Prince Pückler's place is the one Eliot wrote after his visit in 1886.

1. Charles William Eliot, *Charles Eliot, Landscape Architect* (Boston, 1902), p. 132 (cited hereafter as Eliot, *Charles Eliot*).

Eliot's itinerary, supplemented by his notes, is most revealing; it suggests how strongly Britain and things British continued to be the major background of New England culture in the 1880s. In professional terms, though only a few traces of the "landscape school" were to be found in the Olmstedian techniques that Eliot admired so much, Repton still remained for him the master—in print if not on the ground. Even Pückler-Muskau's brilliant German masterpiece, which Eliot held in justifiably high regard, he saw as a reflection of Repton! What satisfied Eliot more profoundly than any other type of design was "quiet, peaceful, soul-refreshing scenery," which usually reminded him of England. He respected the "formalities and eccentricities of the great gardens" at Versailles, but obviously preferred the *parc anglais* effects of the Petit Trianon.[2] The 1880s were simply not much interested in the great examples of Renaissance design, whether in Italy or France or England; the typical Italian villa and its compact wholeness would not be "rediscovered" until some years after this trip of Eliot's.

By the end of October 1886 he was home again in Cambridge, and in December he set himself up in practice at 9 Park Street, Boston. In this office and at two successive State Street addresses, Eliot saw his professional engagements grow slowly and selectively during the next six years. Of greater long-range importance to the profession, however, was the writing he did in this period. He had been encouraged by Olmsted, who valued Eliot's capacity with the pen: "You will not think it flattery if I say that you can give the public what the public most needs better than any other man now writing . . . You ought to make it a part of your scheme to write for the public, a little at a time if you please, but methodically, systematically. It is a part of your professional duty to do so."[3]

Although in those early office years Eliot's writing naturally had to include the usual reports in connection with his practice, he performed a lasting service to the profession with communications to the press, bringing landscape architecture repeatedly and favorably to public attention. Especially notable were his letters to the editor of *Garden and Forest* and the many articles he wrote at the request of that magazine. Running consistently throughout all of these were two themes: an eloquent plea for heightened public awareness of visual quality in the environment and for appropriate standards of value; a simple, straightforward exposition of how the services of landscape architects could help toward achieving the desired goal.

The letters to *Garden and Forest* led to one of Eliot's happiest accomplishments: creation of the Trustees of Public Reservations. In February 1890 he wrote to the editor of the magazine a letter entitled "The Waverley Oaks: a Plan for their Preservation for the People." In it he offered not only a plan

2. *Ibid.*, p. 123.
3. *Ibid.*, p. 207 (see also *Landscape Architecture,* 11 (July 1921), pp. 189–190, for entire letter, Olmsted to Eliot).

to save the famous oaks, but in yet wider scope "an imperfect outline of a scheme by which . . . the finest bits of natural scenery near Boston might perhaps be saved to delight many future generations." These little areas or "bits of scenery," he suggested, might best be entrusted to "an incorporated association, composed of citizens of all the Boston towns, and empowered by the State to hold small and well-distributed parcels of land free of taxes, just as the Public Library holds books and the Art Museum pictures—for the use and enjoyment of the public."[4]

On March 5, the very day his letter was published in *Garden and Forest*, Eliot wrote to Professor Charles S. Sargent, director of the Arnold Arboretum, and to George C. Mann, president of the Appalachian Mountain Club of which he was an active member, seeking their support for the plan of trusteeship. They were in hearty agreement. Eliot, with characteristic speed, drew up a statement of reasons for his proposal and presented it on March 10 at a meeting of the Council of the Appalachian Mountain Club. The Council forthwith authorized Eliot and Mann "to draw up an invitation to societies and individuals to meet and consider a plan for preserving natural scenery."[5]

The next day Eliot prepared a circular letter, which he sent out to various influential people throughout Massachusetts with an inquiry regarding their interest in the problem. The replies were so encouraging that, when Eliot and Mann reported to the Appalachian Club Council at a meeting on April 2, presenting also a "Preservation Scheme" drafted by Eliot for the occasion, the Council voted unanimously to call the proposed "meeting of persons interested in the preservation of natural scenery and historical sites in Massachusetts."[6] With such heartening progress in only a few short weeks, Eliot now felt justified in devoting large amounts of time—during the busiest season of the year for his office practice—to the necessary preliminaries for the projected meeting: gathering names and addresses of possible participants from all parts of Massachusetts; assembling an outline of the proposed scheme, to be issued with the invitations; preparing actual papers to serve as positive bases for discussion.

The conference took place on May 24, 1890, at the Massachusetts Institute of Technology, then on Boylston Street in Boston. It was a huge success, thanks largely to Eliot's careful groundwork and to the persuasiveness of his oral presentation. About one hundred people were there from all sections of the state, and some four hundred cordial letters had been received from other individuals unable to be present but wishing to express sympathy with the proposed organization and its purposes. The meeting voted formally to authorize appointment of a committee "to promote in such ways as may seem to it advisable the establishment of a Board of Trustees to be made capable

4. *Ibid.*, p. 318.
5. *Ibid.*, p. 321.
6. *Ibid.*, p. 324.

of acquiring and holding, for the benefit of the public, beautiful and historical places in Massachusetts."[7]

The committee as finally constituted had twenty-nine members, drawn from towns throughout the state, with Eliot as secretary. Subcommittees were charged with the specific tasks of formulating a scheme of organization for the proposed board of trustees and of drafting a bill for introduction in the General Court (Massachusetts legislature). Studies continued through July, and in August two circulars, written in the main by Eliot, were widely distributed in Massachusetts to inform the public of the proposed legislation and solicit support. As the 1891 session of the General Court drew near, work was finished on an act of incorporation and an appropriate form of legislative petition. One of Eliot's typically astute moves was to have the petition signed by at least one citizen from each county.

A public hearing before its Judiciary Committee was scheduled by the Senate for March 10. Eliot immediately sent invitations to all those who had manifested firm interest; the value of these tireless advance efforts was evident when hundreds of people attended the hearing and many spoke in favor of passage. Four days afterward Eliot, still leaving as little as possible to chance, wrote all the members of the original twenty-nine-member committee, as well as all the incorporators, urging them to send individual letters to members of the legislature.

Without difficulty the bill was passed by both houses of the General Court and, on May 21, 1891, Governor Russell signed into law the act creating the Trustees of Public Reservations; it had taken just fifteen months from the day Eliot's letter to *Garden and Forest* was published. As President Eliot later commented justly: "The qualities which brought this quick success were capacity for rapid and yet accurate work, persuasiveness, and good judgment about both men and measures."[8] But even this evaluation omitted two central characteristics: Eliot's apparently inexhaustible, driving energy and his complete attention to even the smallest detail relevant to the project in hand.

The Trustees of Public Reservations, as incorporated, were a remarkable group of twelve distinguished citizens of the state. Having elected Eliot as secretary and established by-laws and rules of procedure (summer 1891), they turned to the ways in which they could best serve Massachusetts. Eliot had been pondering the entire problem for so many months that he was immediately ready when asked for suggestions. He indicated that there was pressing need, first for a gathering of the facts on existing open spaces in the state and on existing legislation, then for concentrated work on the most crucial question of all, the possibility of a metropolitan system of parks around Boston.

This matter had long been in the forefront of Eliot's thinking; indeed, he had written a letter to Governor Russell several months earlier, in December

7. *Ibid.*, p. 329.
8. *Ibid.*, p. 335.

1890, recommending inclusion of remarks on metropolitan parks in the governor's forthcoming address to the 1891 session of the General Court. In the suggested paragraphs Eliot had emphasized the narrow-mindedness that impeded metropolitan action—and that, unknown to him, would still do so three-quarters of a century later:

> What provision is being made within this metropolitan district for securing those public open spaces which the experience of all great cities has proved to be essential to the welfare of crowded populations? It is obvious that no adequate provision of this sort is either thought of or attempted. The City of Boston is creating a limited system of public pleasure drives and parks, but the other municipalities within the metropolitan district are allowing their few remaining open estates to be divided and built upon one by one and year by year. The excellent public park Act of 1882 remains for these cities and towns a dead letter: and why? Largely because of local jealousies. One city refuses to seize its opportunity to obtain for all time a charming natural park which the loving care of an old family has preserved, because it fears that the people of the adjoining city will enjoy what it has paid for. The towns are influenced by similar selfish fears, and the very wards within the cities are similarly jealous of each other.
>
> There seems to be no remedy for this state of things except the establishment of some central and impartial body capable of disregarding municipal boundaries and all local considerations, and empowered to create a system of public reservations for the benefit of the metropolitan district as a whole.[9]

Recognizing the sensibility of Eliot's suggestions, the Trustees of Public Reservations accordingly decided to act in four specific directions: to publish a survey of existing public open spaces in Massachusetts, to collect and publish the laws of the State regarding public open spaces, to call together the park authorities from the separate communities of the district around Boston in the hope of fostering joint action, and to ask the legislature of 1892 to investigate the park situation.

As a result of the first two decisions, the Trustees were able to add, as appendixes to their first annual report, a useful study of "The Public Holdings of the Shore Towns of Massachusetts," a thorough analysis of "The Province Lands at Provincetown," and a compilation of all the statutes of Massachusetts pertinent to the problem of public open spaces. But the third and fourth decisions had the most far-reaching effect, for they led to the creation of the Metropolitan Park Commission and the first *metropolitan system* of parks in America. In the opinion of many landscape architects and students of

9. *Ibid.*, pp. 356–357.

urban government, this was Charles Eliot's greatest contribution toward fulfillment of what he regarded as his social responsibility.

Having resolved to bring together the park authorities of the Boston area, the Trustees of Public Reservations called them to a meeting on December 16, 1891, at the office of the Boston Park Commission. When asked to make the opening statement on behalf of the Trustees, Eliot did not repeat the language of his letter of a year earlier to Governor Russell, valid as those comments still were. He wisely chose to describe the picture graphically, instead of flatly accusing the assembled representatives of politically inspired stupidity. Following an adopted custom, he had written out beforehand a brief of what he wanted to say. An extract from this outline illustrates the persuasiveness of his logic:

> Here is a rapidly growing metropolis planted by the sea, and yet possessed of no portion of the sea-front except what Boston has provided at City Point. Here is a city interwoven with tidal marshes and controlling none of them; so that the way is open for the construction upon them of cheap buildings for the housing of the lowest poor and the nastiest trades. Here is a district possessed of a charming river already much resorted to for pleasure, the banks of which are continually in danger of spoliation at the hands of their private owners.
>
> Here is a community which must have pure drinking water, which yet up to this time has failed to secure even one water basin from danger of pollution. Lynn has come nearest to it. In the Fells they are working towards it, but the ridiculous town boundary difficulty there prevents concerted action.
>
> Here is a community, said to be the richest and most enlightened in America, which yet allows its finest scenes of natural beauty to be destroyed one by one, regardless of the fact that the great city of the future which is to fill this land would certainly prize every such scene exceedingly, and would gladly help to pay the cost of preserving them today.
>
> Compare the two maps—one showing the opportunity, the other the miserable present result. Do not the facts speak for themselves? Is it not evident that present methods are too slow and inefficient? Can this community afford to go so slowly? Is not some form of joint or concerted action advisable at once? [10]

Other speakers, representing most of the cities and towns of the metropolitan area, followed Eliot, all in favor of joint action. So uniform was the sentiment of the group that they set up a committee, comprising representatives of Brookline, Everett, Lynn, Milton, and Waltham with General

10. *Ibid.*, pp. 351–352.

214. Charles Eliot: founder of the first metropolitan system of parks.

Walker of Boston in the chair and Eliot as secretary, and charged it to prepare a petition to the 1892 session of the General Court, urging a legislative study of the park situation.

The Trustees of Public Reservations, in addition to having called this important meeting, also sent a petition on their own asking that an inquiry be instituted by the General Court. To reinforce this petition and the one submitted by the associated park commissions, Eliot sought signatures from other interested people in all the cities and towns around Boston. In this he again had the loyal aid of Sylvester Baxter, a journalist from Malden whose excellent contacts with newspapers throughout the state had been so helpful in the 1890 campaign for establishment of the Trustees of Public Reservations. Baxter was interested not only in the preservation of open spaces but also, and perhaps even more profoundly, in the political and administrative aspects of a metropolitan solution to urban problems. In 1891 he had published a remarkable pamphlet entitled *Greater Boston*, the earliest recorded plea for the kind of sensible metropolitan thinking that unfortunately still meets local resistance in the Boston area. In his pamphlet Baxter proposed what he termed a "federated metropolis" that would involve merging many governmental functions and services under centralized metropolitan departments instead of leaving them scattered among a dozen cities and towns. One of the many interlocking parts of his plan would in effect have created a system of parks encircling Boston, a result so much like what Eliot had been advocating that he naturally greeted with enthusiasm at least this part of Baxter's forward-looking proposals. So, in 1892, the two joined hands for the common cause. Thanks largely to their efforts, several thousand additional signatures were obtained to support the petitions to the General Court.

A public hearing before a Joint Committee of the legislature on March 11 was heavily attended; a Metropolitan Parks bill was promptly passed by both houses in response to the popular demand; on June 2, 1892, Governor Russell approved the bill, thus authorizing appointment of a temporary commission to study the problem and report on it to the next session of the General Court. Some brief difficulty ensued in getting three qualified citizens to serve, but on July 9 the temporary Metropolitan Park Commission of 1892 was appointed: Charles Francis Adams of Quincy, Philip A. Chase of Lynn, and William B. de las Casas of Malden. The Commission thereupon engaged Eliot as landscape architect and Baxter as secretary.

The task facing the temporary Commission, that of giving the project appropriate study and coming up with a sound report and recommendations for the 1893 session of the General Court, was by no means a small one. In fact, if Eliot (Fig. 214) had not already spent so many months and years familiarizing himself with the region's topography, the Commission's work could hardly have been finished in time for presentation. In response to questions from chairman Adams, Eliot offered from time to time his thoughts on organization of the Commission's work, on the ultimate structure of a permanent Commission, and on the overall character of the park system as he had envisioned it. He suggested that "for a district such as ours" the system as a whole ought to include five types of area: spaces on the ocean front, shores and islands of the inner bay, the courses of the larger tidal estuaries, two or three large areas of wild forest on the outer rim, and small squares, playgrounds, and parks in the densely populated sections, to be provided by the local communities.[11] During the fall of 1892 the Commissioners, guided and accompanied by Eliot and Baxter, visited all the potential sites within ten miles of Boston, continually reviewing on the ground Eliot's comments on each area. Following the field trips, Eliot addressed to the Commissioners

11. *Ibid.,* p. 381.

215. Revere Beach, Boston, before acquisition and clean up; in the project to establish a public bathing beach, Eliot had no precedent whatever to guide him.

on January 2, 1893, a full professional report in three parts: a summary of the physical and historical geography of the metropolitan district; an analysis of the way in which this geography should govern the selection of park sites; a review of available opportunities for setting aside new open spaces along the lines discussed.[12] The report in its entirety is a document that anyone seriously interested in landscape architecture would profit from studying.

For each type of area he had earlier suggested for inclusion in the system, Eliot made in the report a specific recommendation. On the ocean front, even though there was no precedent for so taking land for public recreational use, Revere Beach—an excellent stretch of sand northeast of Boston (Fig. 215)—should be acquired and developed if only to save it from continuance of its use for a highway and railway line; "the present condition of this fine beach," he wrote, "is a disgrace." [13] For the shores and islands of the inner bay he recommended no general development for public recreation, but simply preservation through judicious planting. As for the estuaries, all possible land should be secured, at least above the line of commercial useful- ness, on both sides of Boston's three large tidal rivers, the Mystic, the Charles, and the Neponset, including specifically the Mystic Lakes, the Hemlock Gorge

12. Commonwealth of Massachusetts, *House No. 150: Report of the Board of Metropolitan Park Commissioners* (Boston, 1893), pp. 82–110.
13. *Ibid.,* p. 108.

216. Hemlock Gorge on the Charles, one of the three streams and estuaries in Eliot's scheme.

on the Charles (Fig. 216), and the Neponset marshes. The need for peripheral areas of wild forest would be met by the Middlesex Fells (Fig. 217) on the north and the Blue Hills (Fig. 218) on the south, with two smaller supplements, Beaver Brook (with the Waverley Oaks) in Belmont and Waltham, and Muddy Pond Woods (later Stony Brook Reservation) on the Hyde Park line. The intown squares, playgrounds, and parks were already provided in

217. Ravine Road, Middlesex Fells: the northern of Eliot's "areas of wild forest on the outer rim."

218. Typical rock outcrop in the Blue Hills Reservation, the southern peripheral area on Eliot's list.

fair degree by the several communities whose responsibility this should be, according to Eliot.

The final report of the temporary Commission, presented at the end of January 1893, contained first a brief statement and recommendations of the three Commissioners, with a draft of a proposed act to create a permanent Metropolitan Parks Commission. Next came what the Commissioners termed an "elaborate report prepared by the secretary,"[14] in which Baxter availed himself of the opportunity to expose the "peculiar political geography" (p. 3) of the Boston district, with its "community disintegration" (5) and "local jealousies" (10), and to point to the clear administrative advantages of metropolitan planning. Eliot's landscape architectural report to the Commissioners, already referred to above, followed; the Commissioners called it "Mr. Eliot's scheme of park development" (x) and included it in full. As printed, *House No. 150* also contained in appendixes several proposals made by Baxter personally, though not by the Commissioners, and a reprint of a study made by the elder Olmsted in 1887 for the Boston Park Department on the regrowth of trees on the shores and islands of Boston Harbor.

The recommendations of the temporary Commission were well received by the General Court, and a Park Act creating the permanent Commission was passed and signed by the Governor on June 3, 1893. Following closely the form proposed by the temporary Commission, it provided for five members to serve without salary, granted the appropriate powers including the right of eminent domain, set up a Metropolitan Parks Trust Fund of one million dollars, and specified the twelve cities and twenty-four towns comprising the Metropolitan Park District. The three members of the temporary Commission were included among the five appointed to the permanent one, which ensured continuity of policy, and the new Metropolitan Park Commission was fully organized by August 1893.

In the meantime, changes had occurred in Eliot's professional life. On January 13, 1893, Henry Codman, the gifted young junior partner of the Olmsteds, had died unexpectedly in Chicago, where he had been in charge of the firm's work on the World's Columbian Exposition. This left the Olmsteds with a heavier burden than they felt they could handle, and almost at once they asked Eliot to join them as a partner. On March 1 he did. Thus in the fall of 1893 it was the Olmsted office—or Olmsted, Olmsted & Eliot, to use the firm's new name—that was officially appointed Landscape Architects to the permanent Metropolitan Park Commission, although Eliot continued his unbroken personal attention, acting as the firm's representative.

The epochal historic fact was that the Metropolitan Park Commission, with its legally delineated Park District, came into being. It was the first of its kind, a source of inspiration and encouragement to other metropolitan com-

14. *Ibid.*, p. x.

munities everywhere. But for its landscape architects inception did not mark the end of work. The next several years meant for Eliot an unending succession of studies and recommendations. In the first six months of 1894 his "metropolitan work" required attendance at six legislative hearings and twenty-five meetings of the Commission, and more than fifty appointments in the field.

The problems of the Commission were further complicated by the legislature's hasty passing of the so-called "Boulevard Act" of 1894 to relieve unemployment, saddling the Commission with the construction of "boulevards" connected with the several reservations. This function went beyond the purposes for which the Commission had been created, wholly overlooked the need for preparatory groundwork, and failed to recognize the amount of time and study required to prepare sound plans for such projects. At first Eliot and the Commissioners objected strongly to being assigned the task; but he soon saw, and convinced the Commissioners, that the provision of such access ways might serve to tie the parts of the system together and would certainly be a boon to the public.

By the end of 1894 land had been acquired by the Commission for the Middlesex Fells, Blue Hills, Stony Brook, and Beaver Brook Reservations. During 1895 Revere Beach, the Hemlock Gorge on the Charles, and other portions of the Charles River and Mystic River Reservations were secured, and the boundaries of the Middlesex Fells and the Blue Hills were modified positively. The year 1896 found Eliot still devoting much time to the work of the Commission, primarily on details of the development of Revere Beach, on securing more parcels of land along the Mystic, the Charles, and the Neponset, and in a campaign (which did not succeed until several years later) to create a nontidal basin on the Charles River through damming.

From the very beginning of the Commission's work on developing the reservations, once the areas had been acquired, Eliot experienced the difficulty that so often confronts landscape architects when their clients, whether individuals or public bodies, fail to comprehend the basic good sense and economy of planning—and especially of the general plan. Having repeatedly and patiently explained, orally and in writing, the meaning and value of general plans, Eliot was at last, by midyear 1896, constrained to write to the Commission on behalf of his firm: "We asked that we might be definitely and publicly freed from all responsibility for work done in the new reservations, or else that we might be definitely engaged to draw up for the consideration of the Commission those comprehensive schemes or programmes of work which are commonly called 'general plans.' You will readily understand that we cannot professionally afford to have our names associated with work done regardless of comprehensive studies." [15]

15. Eliot, *Charles Eliot*, p. 658.

Even beyond such obvious requirements as general and working plans for the layout and construction of roads, if these were to make sense, Eliot was distressed by the Commissioners' seeming inability to comprehend the need for overall advance planning of what he classed as "landscape forestry": silvicultural operations, especially in the larger areas, done for the sake of preserving and enhancing the inherent scenic merits for which, in the main, the tracts had been acquired. He wrote highly perceptive papers on the topic. Professionally worthy of study even today are such writings as Eliot's famous letter of January 8, 1896,[16] on the importance of cutting out trees under certain conditions (the letter often referred to as "the use of the axe"), and his "summary report" of a year later, February 1897, on "Vegetation and Scenery in the Metropolitan Reservations" (pp. 715–732), covering the extensive field survey conducted during 1896. Both papers emphasized the value of general plans as a safeguard against wasted effort; both recommended systematic forest operations carried out in close accordance with such adopted plans and under landscape architectural guidance. As it turned out, these were to be the last in Eliot's many though unavailing attempts to prevent the Commissioners from wasting funds and scenic resources on "planless or non-comprehensive work" (659).

Unfortunately for Eliot's health, the mounting sense of frustration in the development phase of the Metropolitan Parks came at a time when he had expected pressure from this direction to become easier. Throughout the period of his service to the permanent Commission as the representative of Olmsted, Olmsted & Eliot he had carried his fair share of the firm's other work. With the park system successfully past its formative stages, he had counted on more time for other obligations and had therefore undertaken a larger portion of the office load. Now he drove himself ceaselessly, not only in the effort to keep the Park Commission on the right track, but in a multitude of other projects. There were parks, playgrounds, and parkways to study in field and office for communities from Brooklyn to Portland, college campuses, botanical gardens, hospital grounds, and of course the usual private places. There were magazine articles to write and public meetings to attend. To all of these Eliot gave himself unstintingly.

Thus it was that a wet, snowy day in March found him tramping out a new road-line in the woods of Keney Park in Hartford. The next day, back home in Brookline, he stayed in the house with what seemed a heavy cold. But it was not a cold; it was meningitis, for which there was then no known treatment. Only a few days later, on March 25, 1897, he died—at thirty-seven.

In its commemorative resolution the Metropolitan Park Commission referred to Eliot as the "father of the Metropolitan Park System, which will be a memorial of his short but eminently fruitful professional life."[17] In its

16. *Ibid.,* pp. 709–713.
17. Metropolitan Park Commissioners, *Annual Report, 1898,* p. 31.

1898 annual report, the next after his death, the Commission reproduced the whole of the report he had written in 1893 for the temporary Commission;[18] for this report of Eliot's was rightly regarded by all as "the basis of the great undertaking" (p. 55).

If Charles Eliot were to see the condition of his Metropolitan Park system today it is doubtful that he would think it much of a memorial. Surely this is one of the supreme ironies—that something so far ahead of its times when he conceived and brought it into being (Figs. 219, 220) should be so far behind today, measured against the progress made elsewhere in state, county, and regional parks. Yet if he were to see it now, maybe he would not be so surprised after all; he might recall the thankless task of trying to get the Commissioners to adopt general plans for the reservations and his despair over their "irresponsible, hap-hazard, and planless methods."[19] To a modern observer it would appear that much the same uncomprehending attitude must have persisted through the years. For it seems that little can have been done to develop these areas thoughtfully for human use, whether in overall master planning, in provision of well-designed facilities except in a few rare instances, or in prosecution of carefully considered practices of forest management.

All too often the reservations have been gouged out for the sake of highways, but this is only one manifestation of a still larger fault: utter obeisance to the automobile in administration of what was born as a park system. The focus is no longer on the parks themselves, but primarily on a series of highways—to call them parkways is in most cases fallacious—and on a sizable uniformed police force to regulate the consequent motor traffic in addition to policing the parks. The Commission also maintains a scattered group of local playgrounds and swimming pools, all undoubtedly useful but not closely related to Eliot's basic system of parks.

This state of affairs is by no means new. When in 1920 the direction of the metropolitan parks was merged with functions of water supply and sewerage under a new body, the Metropolitan District Commission, it was perhaps inevitable that the parks would suffer. At any rate, as long ago as 1923 Eliot's friend and coworker Sylvester Baxter, in an article for the *Boston Evening Transcript* (September 29) wrote:

> The parkways and boulevards . . . intended to be strictly subordinate . . . to make the reservations pleasantly and easily accessible . . . have become the primary factor in the scheme of the park system . . . The service of motor-traffic, recreational in only a minor degree so far as the park system is concerned, has become the main consideration for the park administration. Hence the chief stress is laid upon the development, maintenance and policing of the boulevards and parkways; the personal

18. *Ibid.*, pp. 119–149.
19. Eliot, *Charles Eliot*, p. 666.

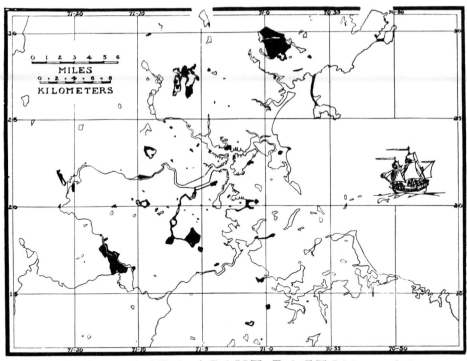

OPEN SPACES ABOUT BOSTON 1893

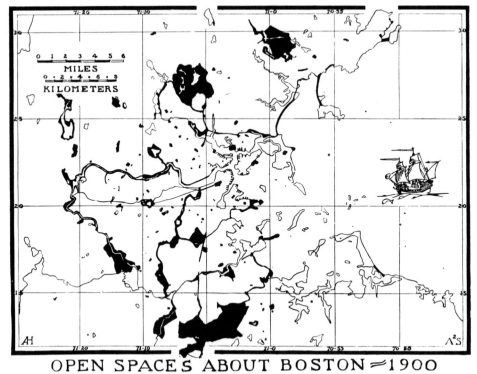

OPEN SPACES ABOUT BOSTON 1900

219. Charts showing the actual growth of a metropolitan park system in seven years.

LOCAL OPEN SPACES   METROPOLITAN OPEN SPACES

220. Map of the parks around Boston in 1912; Middlesex Fells on the north and Blue Hills on the south are easily seen.

> organization of the several divisions of the system is with almost exclusive reference to policing. Policing is of vast importance . . . Yet it is fundamentally wrong that policing should be the dominant factor.

What Baxter wrote in 1923 is no less true today, when the mad rush of civilization has rendered greater, not less, the need for relaxation, for contemplation, for the slower pace of walking, for the occasional calm solitude of such open spaces as are still retained.

Fortunately, a memorial exists of a quite different nature. President Eliot, who had been so distressed by the lack of a "recognized school or course of study" to guide his son's preparing for the profession, had an unexpected opportunity to see the situation corrected shortly after the son's death. In

1899 a generous donor, Nelson Robinson of New York, came to Eliot in Cambridge to offer a gift in memory of his own son. As the wish of Nelson Robinson, Jr., to become an architect had been denied by his death while still at Harvard College, President Eliot suggested that endowing the recently inaugurated courses in architecture at Harvard would be a most appropriate memorial. The suggestion was warmly received; then, when in conversation he learned that Eliot, too, had suffered a similar bereavement, the donor asked that his gift be used also for a curriculum in landscape architecture as a memorial to President Eliot's son.

Thus it was that Harvard in 1900 established the first university course of professional training in landscape architecture in memory of Charles Eliot, with a professorship and, a few years later, a traveling fellowship endowed in his name. And, to the extent that it has been built upon this beginning, the entire scheme of university education for the profession—in which America is unique—may justly be regarded as a memorial to Eliot.

At least one other memorial deserves reference here: the poignantly commemorative volume *Charles Eliot, Landscape Architect*, published in 1902 by his father, without question one of the classics in the literature of the profession. The authorship is not given as such, but the simple dedication reveals it quietly: "For the dear son who died in his bright prime, from the father." To the generations of landscape architects who have inherited Charles Eliot's fine sense of social mission, no characterization of the man could seem fairer than the one used by the father as the subtitle in this book: "A lover of nature and of his kind, who trained himself for a new profession, practised it happily, and through it wrought much good."

XXIII. Single-Track Eclecticism Takes Over

In the course of about three-quarters of the nineteenth century, architecture in America underwent a gamut of changes that were not closely paralleled by landscape architecture. Though the design of buildings endured successive eclectic "revivals" and then went on to the romantic, picturesque eclecticism of multiple choices from predetermined "historic styles," the landscape architectural environments of the buildings remained in the soft, naturalesque, relative amorphousness of Reptonian neutrality or the later spottiness of the Loudon or Downing manner. In fact, the shifting modes of architecture had little or no impact on treatment of the landscape until roughly the late 1880s, when a marked new direction manifested itself and affected landscape architecture noticeably.

By the late 1850s the romantic fashions of architecture had already moved through classical and medieval revivalism into a full-fledged addiction to the so-called picturesque, borrowing freely from different foreign types and "styles." But around the buildings—especially in the case of country houses—manmade "landscape garden" continued as the basic norm, even though Pückler-Muskau and Olmsted had by then made notable advances in the more truly natural handling of outdoor space. Feverish industrial development in the years after the Civil War, with an ever larger number of newly rich owners craving symbols of culture and social status, pushed the picturesque romanticism to often ridiculous extremes, if only in envious imitation of similar eccentricities popping up in the country homes of old-line families.

Some of these results can be seen in a volume entitled *The Homes of America,* by Mrs. Martha J. Lamb, published in 1879. The opening paragraph of Mrs.

221. Armsmear, near Hartford, "carries out no decided principles of architecture."

Lamb's chapter on the "Modern Period" reveals the prevailing mood: "Within the present half century domestic architecture has been running a race with the general development and prosperity of America. Countless styles from all climes, with modifications and abbreviations, have been made subservient to the convenience and tastes of a mixed population. Cottages and villas . . . dot the length and breadth of our land. Many of these are in themselves the expression of sentiment, self-respect, and artistic culture."[1] The illustrations, from engravings of excellent black and white quality, are supplemented by a voluble text. Unfortunately, the author's commentary is cute and cloying in the approved feminine manner of her day, with an almost audible gasp of admiration for costliness and size. This is annoying, of course, but it does in its peculiar way convey something of the scale of values that marked the times. And the visual evidence tells the story even better than the words.

Among the twoscore country places included in the section on the "Modern Period," one of the most astonishing is Armsmear, near Hartford, the "villa" of Samuel Colt, inventor of the revolver (Fig. 221). Mrs. Lamb describes the house in part as follows:

1. Martha J. Lamb, *The Homes of America* (New York, 1879), p. 148.

The mansion itself, unique and costly as it is, carries out no decided principles of architecture: like the mind of its originator and builder, it is bold and unusual in its combinations. It is spoken of as an Italian villa . . . But the lofty, solid tower, and substantial, home-like aspect are distinctively English, and the capacious dome in the rear, quaint pinnacles, minaret effects, profusion of balconies, and light, lavish ornamentation everywhere, indicate a severe touch of the Oriental. It is constructed of stone, and, however contradictory in its architectural features, is massive, majestic, and refined. (Pages 177–178)

Another example, "in the Persian style, so far as our climate and requirements permit," was built by the eminent painter Frederick E. Church on the Hudson across from Catskill (Fig. 222). Mrs. Lamb is impressed by the "pleasing variety of colors"; the strange tower has "red, yellow, and black bricks, arranged in characteristic patterns." There are "mosaic tiles" around the main doorway, and "the cornices, which are very bold, are richly painted in colors and gold." To top it off, "the roofs are covered with green, red, and black slates, relieved by a few gilt slates." This place, later known as Olana, was recently saved from demolition by a group interested in preserving historic monuments. As a museum piece it obviously has its points; in Mrs. Lamb's words: "The building is certainly very unique, and is wholly an individual structure, departing distinctly from precedents in America" (176–177).

One of the most amusing examples, "the picturesque brick-and-wood cottage of Thomas G. Appleton" at Newport, Rhode Island (Fig. 223), "is a bewildering mass of outcropping fancies, Swiss roofs, overhanging balconies, and novel conceits" (205–206). It appears to have been chosen by Mrs. Lamb as something simple in contrast to the "more stately homes" in the community! Of the town itself she says:

> Newport is a city of architectural surprises . . . gradually blossoming into cottages that are palaces until its costly dwellings in endless succession line the avenues . . . Every known and unknown order of domestic architecture is represented here. The seeker after the picturesque has not infrequently adopted the grotesque, but the styles of old Germany and of modern France, of Switzerland, of Spain, of Italy, of England, and of the isles of the sea, are faithfully reproduced. (204)

If this is the state of eclectic confusion in which American architecture found itself by the 1870s, it is not surprising that an eager welcome was extended, during the decade after 1875, to the visual stability and cohesiveness of some rather literal new works from three distinct sources: Richard Morris Hunt, the first American to return from the French Ecole Nationale des Beaux

222. Residence of Frederick E. Church near Hudson, New York.

Arts; Henry Hobson Richardson, eleven years Hunt's junior but a far greater designer; and, later, the firm of McKim, Mead and White.

Hunt, then regarded by other architects as dean of the profession, was a dedicated Francophile who made a name for himself with unbelievably magnificent mansions for wealthy industrialists. A house by Hunt might be virtually a copy of some French château, but at least it was all of a piece instead of a mere jumble of unrelated parts. Richardson, surely one of the foremost of all American architects, made a quite different contribution.

223. The Appleton "cottage" at Newport.

Basing his designs on Romanesque precedents, he developed with masterly freedom and originality a personal idiom of massive strength. Trinity Church in Boston, built between 1872 and 1877, was his first work of distinction. In general, unfortunately, his fine potential influence was vitiated by imitators who too often copied him stupidly, without the innate sense of design that enabled him to move on brilliantly in his own way from the Romanesque basis.

Stanford White had been in Richardson's office before he joined Charles Follen McKim and William Rutherford Mead in the firm of McKim, Mead and White. In 1877 the three young men made a trip through New England to sketch and study examples of American Colonial architecture. Deeply impressed, according to Mead they tended thereafter toward "the classic

MADISON AVENUE FACADE

ENTRANCE GATEWAY

224. New York: the Villard house, Madison Avenue, about 1915. Now used chiefly for archdiocesan offices.

225. The Boston Public Library, about 1908.

form" in their practice.[2] Pursuing that theme further, they reached back for prototypes to the Italian Renaissance; a notable example is their Villard house, on Madison Avenue in New York (Fig. 224). Completed in 1885, this enormous building has the stolid appearance of an Italian palace of the late Quattrocento. With today's hindsight, one may well question what an Italian Renaissance *palazzo* was doing in midtown New York at the end of the nineteenth century. Be that as it may, this building and others of equally consistent and cohesive quality—such as McKim's handsome Boston Public Library (Fig. 225)—made a profound impression in their time.

Each of these new sources, to be sure, still looked backward historically for "inspiration." But eclecticism, after all, had been the rule one way or another for some seventy-five years. More important at the moment was the undeniable fact that the three designers' respective products, by being held in such close conformity to their historic prototypes, achieved thereby a recognizable homogeneity that must have brought to perceptive observers a sense of blessed relief from the current multidirectional giddiness. The headed-for-all-points eclecticism, in short, was supplanted by another eclecticism: a resolute, single-track sort. The reception accorded the new trend, especially the work of McKim, Mead and White, was at least enthusiastic

2. Charles Moore, *The Life and Times of Charles Follen McKim* (New York, 1929), pp. 41–42 (cited hereafter as Moore, *McKim*).

enough to mark the beginning of over a half-century of what Sigfried Giedion later termed "mercantile classicism."[3]

Now landscape design, too, was encouraged to imitate "historic styles" on occasions when it was closely tied to single-track eclectic architecture. This perforce involved breaking away at last from strict and exclusive adherence to the "landscape gardening" effects dominant since the eighteenth century despite the shifts in architectural climate. How this came about is best seen from a brief review.

Even though the pastoral "landscape gardening" character remained essentially unmodified through the years, the changes in architectural temper were of course reflected in whatever buildings happened to be included in the overall landscape architectural scheme. Among the earliest designs for projected structures in the park at Muskau were those of Pückler's much admired friend Friedrich Schinkel, Germany's chief protagonist of the classical revival. Birkenhead Park had not only its pretentious pseudo-classical Grand Entrance and the arcaded Temple, but also the Swiss Bridge and the series of Lodges called Norman, Italian, and Gothic. In America such early nineteenth-century examples as Gore Place and the Hudson River properties, with either Georgian Colonial or neoclassic houses, had grounds done in emulation of the English fashion in landscape gardening. Later, Downing's "tasteful" landscapes embraced buildings of a wide romantic range—as were also his apparently influential illustrations of cottages in his treatises on "rural architecture." His own house at Newburgh was actually of a turreted pseudo-Gothic persuasion, but the grounds, like most of his layouts elsewhere, were done in the staccato manner with emphasis on specimen trees that seems to have constituted his interpretation of the "landscape garden."

Central Park in its way continued the softer tradition of Repton's earlier days. Yet in at least two important respects the park was *not* the same. Whereas the landscape garden was, by self-profession, a matter of fashion for residential purposes, the task before Olmsted and Vaux was a markedly different one: creation of a tract of genuine country scenery to give urban workers a means of relaxation and relief from the oppressive confines of the city. Moreover, in this park Olmsted achieved, as to some degree Pückler-Muskau had twenty years earlier—and no doubt just as unconsciously—a new realization of outdoor space that gave firm structure to the composition as against the old scattered, accidental effect of the landscape gardening school. At one particular location the park broke away from old practices noticeably. In the only place where significant numbers of people were expected to congregate, the sequence of spaces from the Mall to the Bethesda Fountain, the pastoral character was logically dropped entirely in favor of a thoroughly architectonic plan. The spatial structure here was and still is commendably strong, with

3. Sigfried Giedion, *Space, Time and Architecture,* 5th ed. (Cambridge, 1967), p. 395.

a sight-line from the beginning of the Mall through the outdoor concert area to the Terrace, then down to the Esplanade around the Bethesda Fountain at the south edge of the lake. Originally, as indicated by the arrow on the Greensward plan, the sight-line went all the way to the Belvedere tower at the southwest corner of the Old Reservoir; but the growth of trees in the Ramble blocked out this longer view years ago.

It should be noted that this geometric arrangement of paved spaces, though it clearly abandoned the pastoral theme, did not imitate any "historic style" either in overall form or in details. In fact, one is hard pressed to determine how Vaux could conceivably have arrived at some of his strange designs of piers and parapets, a "style" that succeeding generations of young designers have irreverently classified as "late Pullman" or "early U.S. Grant." In truth, what was seen in these details, as well as in the stone-faced underpasses, was most probably a reflection of the prevalent romantic Gothicism with a laudable admixture of sheer personal invention on Vaux's part.

Perversely enough, though its purposes were definitely *non*residential, Central Park's nationwide appeal undoubtedly did much to encourage the perpetuation of the landscape gardening fashion in residential landscape architectural design. At any rate, during the 1860s and 1870s, as long as American homes continued to be relatively formless in their indecisive lines of hybrid ancestry, equally formless "landscape gardening"—a potpourri of rolling lawns and shrubs and specimen trees—remained virtually the only customary treatment of the grounds around them. Not all the houses of this fantastic period, of course, were as bizarre as some of those described by Mrs. Lamb, though she had obviously chosen what she believed "the best." Then, with the 1880s, came the big change, already referred to as the probable beginning of "mercantile classicism" in architecture and of a generally similar eclecticism in landscape architecture.

The better to understand the impact of this revolution on landscape architecture, it is helpful to remember one of the earliest unhappy actions of the English landscape gardening school in the eighteenth century: outright destruction of the geometric spatial forms immediately surrounding such great mansions as Blenheim. By making the undulant green lawns come right up to the houses, the "landscape gardeners" deprived these buildings of the firm bases they clearly needed to retain visual stability. Conversely, so long as the landscape gardening vogue remained consciously in force, it was thought unfashionable to have any sort of architectonic lines close to the house. The soft envelopment readily became habitual; what seems like doing nothing is of course an easy habit to acquire. Then, as the years went on and the houses grew more and more indefinitely formless, the absence of an architectonic outdoor framework mattered less and less. In fact, it would have been increasingly difficult to provide one for houses so nondescript in form.

But then came the "new" architecture, marked by an avowed one-track eclecticism, such as the imitation French of Hunt or the revival of "classic Renaissance" by McKim, Mead and White. Their great houses, no longer vague in form but positively architectonic in line and volume, forcefully projected their geometry outward in spirit, seeking an outdoor design that would enable them visually to grasp the earth and achieve stability on the site. In short, these houses demanded that the immediate environs be as architectonic as the house itself; and common sense appeared to require that they be architectonic in the *same way*. As the house became eclectic, so did the landscape architecture, and the inadequacy of the old landscape gardening treatment for the purpose at hand resulted in its being discarded—or at least relegated to the farthest reaches, away from the house. The latter is precisely what did happen, giving rise eventually to a distinct American contribution to the techniques of landscape design.

As if still further to guarantee this peculiar turning point in the history of the arts, American industrialists and financial operators of the breed later referred to as "Robber Barons" now wanted bigger and bigger country places, more and more surely seeming to symbolize culture. Nothing could better prove their status, they confidently believed, than apparent familiarity with things European. The combination of wealth, desire, and a kind of infantilism that had bedeviled American attitudes for decades, causing the insecure to look ever backward to Europe for assurances of worth, created a climate completely conducive to the now concentrated eclecticism of both architecture and landscape architecture.

Such were the forces that brought about what has been called the Country Place Era of landscape architecture, a period of steadily increasing and strongly eclectic activity that lasted through the 1920s. One of the earliest and most famous of these magnificent places, a collaborative endeavor involving Hunt and the elder Olmsted, was Biltmore, the property of George W. Vanderbilt, near Asheville in the mountains of western North Carolina. Begun in 1888, it illustrates well several aspects of the new eclecticism. Biltmore shows to what ludicrous extremes the architecture of the time could go: Hunt, a Francophile to the core, built here a house that echoed Francis I, in the overall and in every detail, even to a spiral staircase reminiscent of the one at Blois. The great white pile is unquestionably imposing, provided one can manage to overlook how Francis I might have felt in the wilds of North Carolina.

Biltmore (Fig. 226) shows also how natural it was for Olmsted to develop the immediate grounds as an extension of the architectonic lines of the house; indeed, it is readily seen how inept a landscape garden setting would have been. The house faces approximately east and west. On the west side it looms high above a steep, wooded slope that reaches down to the distant French Broad River. On the east side a broad Esplanade extends from the house to a double set of stone-cheeked ramps leading up to the foot of a vista much

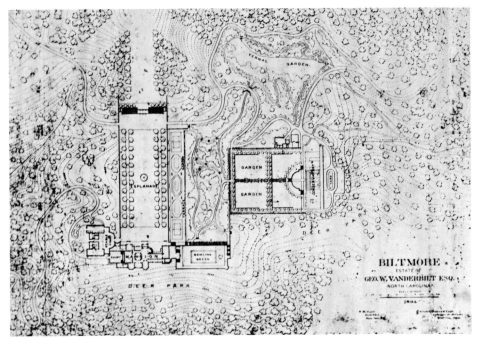

226. Biltmore, North Carolina: a collaborative effort by Frederick Law Olmsted and Richard Morris Hunt.

like the great allée at Vaux-le-Vicomte. Just below the ramps, Biltmore's main approach road enters a rectangular graveled area at the east end of the Esplanade, which thus becomes the chief arrival space before the mansion. A similar rectangular area is at the end next to the house, and two straight roadways join the ends. It is obvious from the sharp corners that the use of automobiles was not anticipated in the Esplanade. Double rows of trees border the sides; in the central turf panel is a pool.

To the north of the house and at a lower level are stables and two service courts, reached by a branch of the long uphill approach road. Below the south side of the Esplanade and parallel to it is a long strip overloaded with three pools; for some strange reason this is called the Italian Garden (Fig. 227). Immediately south from the end of the house a rectangular mass juts somewhat awkwardly into space; it was originally labeled a Bowling Green, but in later years a swimming pool occupied it. Down to the south of the entire house-complex, and effectively detached from it, is an elaborate pair of flower gardens known today as the Walled Garden and the Rose Garden, with a large Conservatory. Beyond these, already far enough from the house to have a feeling of wild nature, is what Olmsted named the Vernal Garden; it is now maintained as an experimental ground for azaleas.

To be sure, the detailed area right around the house is not convincingly "French," nor is it one of Olmsted's best designs. Perhaps the notion of historical imitation bothered him. It is known that for him the most absorbing side of the work at Biltmore lay in the thousands of acres of farmlands and forests that the owner was buying—and in the projects of road construction, tree planting, and general silviculture to be carried on within them. Out in that larger domain (Fig. 228), removed from the house and free from both the architectonic necessity and the seeming obligation to "look French," Biltmore still shows how completely the imitative spirit of eclecticism can vanish from landscape design when eclectic architecture is not an integral part of a joint composition. Throughout the vast expanses of field and forest, landscape architectural problems could be solved in their own terms, and forms could thus arise without affectation directly from the circumstances of topography and functions to be served. For example, the long approach road, as it wound up the hill from Biltmore Village to the mansion, had only to meet with care the requirements of land and purpose; it accomplished the task with becoming simplicity.

Even in these wild wooded acres, however, one sees illustrated the way in which architecture, thrusting outward the influence of its form, calls for an architectonic order in its immediate vicinity. Accordingly, for a short distance on either side of the "French" gate lodge near the village, and again when coming close to the architectonic area around the mansion, the same approach road perforce took on a rectilinear alignment, reflecting to this extent the geometry of the buildings. To go beyond Biltmore for a moment, it should be noted that this phenomenon—the insistent occurrence of strong geometric form—proved widely applicable and by no means limited to the surroundings of architecture (the instance in Central Park will be recalled).

227. The Italian Garden at Biltmore.

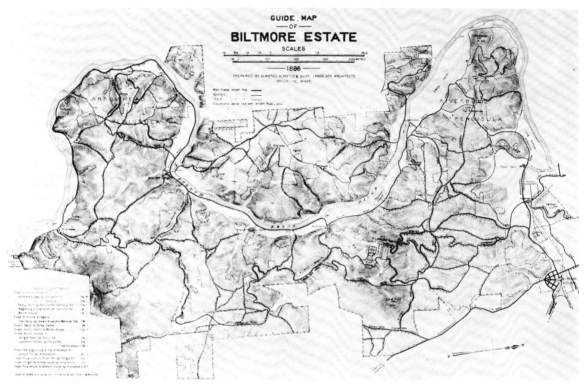

228. Biltmore: general development plan of the whole extensive property.

Indeed, designers working later on large-scale parks discovered that, even in the midst of wild nature, any organized group activity of people seems almost invariably to demand a visually perceptible architectonic order in design.

Thus Biltmore, through its great extent, the variety of its natural conditions, and the specific requirements of the owner, almost automatically became a background against which certain precepts of landscape design asserted themselves, with particular reference to the new type of eclecticism of the 1880s. In another, quite different, respect—not a design precept but an operational policy—it set an example well worth following, too. However false and unjustified the French appearance, the house and grounds were built simultaneously (Figs. 229, 230), ensuring at least their integrity as a single composition. In subsequent years far too many country places suffered through their owners' failure to have architect and landscape architect work together from inception. At Biltmore the first field activity in 1888, well ahead of work on the house and grounds, was the topographic survey of the whole property carried out under Olmsted's direction as lands were acquired. Thereafter he stayed in close contact with every aspect of the development until his retirement in 1895, which happened to be the year when Biltmore House was formally opened.

229. The "mansion" and outdoor areas under construction simultaneously, seen from above the end of the Italian Garden.

230. Biltmore: the house and immediate grounds completed together.

Olmsted had regarded Biltmore all along as clearly semipublic in potential; accordingly, in the closing years of his active practice, he said that for this reason he would continue to give the job his personal attention even though he had decided he must otherwise drop private commissions. His prediction was well borne out, for Biltmore became a major center for the rise and perfecting of American forestry.

The Biltmore School of Forestry, established in 1898, served for some twenty years as a crucially needed training ground for professional foresters. In 1914, on the death of the owner, a considerable portion of the Biltmore acres was turned over to the United States to form the nucleus of a national forest. Subsequently another portion was made a municipal forest for the town of Biltmore, and a sizable strip was sold to be included in the Blue Ridge Parkway. In recent years the property has consisted of some 12,000 acres, only about one-tenth of its original size but still in large part a demonstration area for modern dairy farming and sustained yield forestry. In 1930 the house and grounds were opened to the public, and they are maintained today as a museum.

So, with houses like Biltmore—yet in many ways unlike it, for its copybook imitativeness, vast size, and splendid pomp can hardly be considered entirely typical—the shifting architectural moods of over three-quarters of a century came to be replaced by a purer, more "correct," more concentrated eclecticism. Some critics would one day regard this new type as archeological in its classical outlook; certainly the half-century of its dominance would be marked by a sounder derivative scholarship than were earlier decades, a careful "going by the book," perhaps to offset its lack of inventiveness. The "mercantile classicism" would rule in public and commercial buildings. In residential design the takeover would be slower and less uniformly "classical."

To landscape architecture this new kind of eclecticism brought an even sharper change. For almost the first time since the eighteenth century, something other than the soft monotonies of the "landscape gardening school" gained recognition. The new way was slow in development, mainly because there were few professional landscape architects. But in due course a stronger sense of conscious design was restored to the scene: a spatially well-structured order, usually architectonic as a consequence of its close relationship to the clearer, more firmly designed buildings. Although this approach to landscape design—actually the rebirth of a former excellence—came in on a tide of concentrated architectural eclecticism, it is interesting to note that the results would not themselves always be eclectic. Happily, the power of simple geometry is independent of "historic styles." As the level of landscape design improved, a significant number of practitioners achieved a commendable vigor without being historically imitative.

The forty years of the Country Place Era were a period of heartening advance in design quality, but they also had one regrettable effect on public opinion. Despite Olmsted's having founded the profession on a park for all the people, followed by other public works from coast to coast, residential practice increased rapidly in response to growing demand as individual accumulations of wealth multiplied. To be sure, some landscape architects kept on doing primarily public work throughout the Country Place Era. But at the height of the period's activity, in the second decade of the twentieth century, many practitioners devoted so much professional time and energy to the design of large residential properties that, as an entirely natural but unfortunate consequence, landscape architecture was regarded generally as a profession serving only the wealthy. This was of course truly a misconception, but not a surprising one. In fact it persisted, with more than a little justification, until America's economic circumstances were radically modified, first by the 1929 collapse and then by the new legislation of 1933.

XXIV. The World's Columbian Exposition of 1893

Aside from its customary position as a historic event in the growth of the arts in America, the World's Columbian Exposition of 1893, or the Chicago World's Fair as it is frequently called, has a special reason for treatment here. In a manner all its own it bridged a gap across several generations of students in the arts of design, serving as the vehicle for expressing a diametric change of attitude within the span of a relatively few years. From the 1890s until as late as the end of the 1920s or even the early thirties the Exposition was usually held forth as marking the pinnacle of achievement in the arts of America. But by the late 1930s, or at any rate very soon after World War II, exactly the opposite evaluation prevailed: "everybody knew" that the Columbian Exposition represented the very bottom of a thoroughly muddy barrel.

As is the case with black and white judgments generally, both extremes were untrue. A more valid view would see the Exposition as having had two distinctly positive points and a single offsetting negative one. The two pluses were an extraordinary stimulus to interprofessional collaboration and an unprecedented awakening of public interest in civic design. The large minus was a lamentable dedication to a "classical ideal." Before analyzing these three points, a brief look at earlier large expositions of the nineteenth century is helpful. The important ones were connected with men already mentioned. Prince Albert, expanding on Roman and French precedents of the seventeenth century, organized at London in 1851 a huge international exhibition to advertise the manufactures of Britain. It was for this Exposition of 1851 that Sir Joseph Paxton invented and built the Crystal Palace. In Paris, Baron Haussmann, profiting by the British success, installed in 1855, in a building erected for the purpose on the Champs Elysées, the first of the great French Expositions Universelles. In 1867 he held another and larger one, in the Champ de Mars on the left bank of the Seine, with grounds by Alphand and Barillet-Deschamps in the tortuous manner of the French *jardin anglais.* Though Haussman fell from office in 1870, the value of his expositions held convincingly enough to bring about another in 1878, on the Champ de Mars and with the added attraction of the Trocadéro built to face it from across the river.

The Exposition Universelle of 1889 (Fig. 231) was the most epochal of the series. It occupied the Champ de Mars again, and showed phenomenal progress in the use of structural steel, resulting in new forms arising freely without precedent. Gustave Eiffel erected his soaring tower where it stands today as a major landmark of Paris. And out behind it, away from the river, was the Palais de l'Industrie with its marvelous Galerie des Machines, which used a series of hinged steel arches (Fig. 232) to span a vast indoor space— unlike anything that had gone before. Then as now forward-looking designers greeted with enthusiasm any evidence of technological progress in the use of new materials to devise new solutions for human needs. The Tour Eiffel and the Galerie des Machines were eye-openers that acquired even more significance when it became known that within three years the United States would have an exposition to celebrate the four-hundredth anniversary of the discovery of America. In the bright New World, the hopeful were sure, these new methods and skills with steel would have unlimited opportunity to move forward. It was a moment of excited anticipation. Little did the hopeful realize what would happen to their dreams!

Rumors about an American exhibition to be held in 1892 were correct. As early as summer 1889 four cities, New York, Washington, St. Louis, and Chicago, began competing with each other for Congressional favor. In April 1890 the Act of Congress was passed authorizing the Fair, naming it the World's Columbian Exposition, and awarding it to Chicago; it was to be opened to the public May 1, 1893, since there was insufficient time to prepare for opening in 1892 as originally intended. A national World's Columbian Commission was appointed by the President, and to organize the work locally in Chicago the State of Illinois licensed a corporation of distinguished citizens.

Almost immediately a controversy arose regarding the site. To resolve the dispute, after four months had been wasted in debate by the corporation, the elder Olmsted was called in to examine possible locations and report on them. He and his talented young partner Henry Sargent Codman arrived in Chicago on August 10, 1890, and were shown seven sites, three on the shore of Lake Michigan and four inland. It was quickly apparent that the three lakeside sites had far more to offer than the inland ones, thanks not only to the view of the lake but also to the animation of shipping activity. Of the three the northernmost appeared best, but Olmsted learned from the

231. Paris: bird's-eye sketch of the Exposition of 1889; the Galerie des Machines is at the left of the Eiffel Tower.

232. Paris Exposition of 1889: interior of the Galerie des Machines.

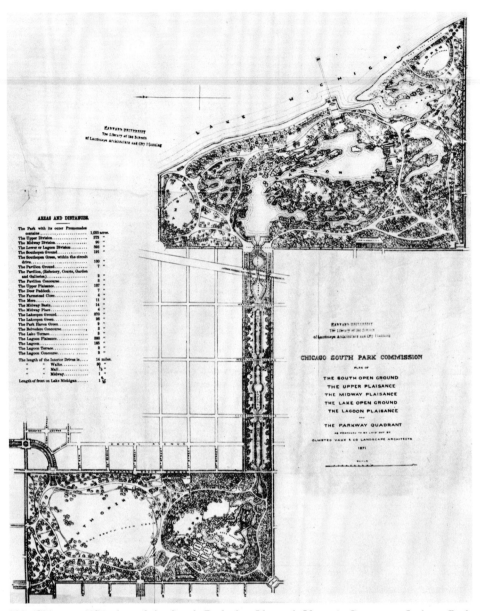

AREAS AND DISTANCES.

The Park with its outer Promenades
  contains . . . . 1,055 acres.
The Upper Division . . . . 272 "
The Midway Division . . . . 90 "
The Lower or Lagoon Division . . . . . . 593 "
The Southopen Ground . . . . 191 "
The Southopen Green, within the circuit
  drive . . . . 100 "
The Pavilion Ground . . . . 7 "
The Pavilion, (Refectory, Courts, Garden
  and Galleries) . . . . 2 "
The Pavilion Concourse . . . . 3 "
The Upper Plaisance . . . . 187 "
The Deer Paddock . . . . 7 "
The Farmstead Close . . . . 4 "
The Mere . . . . 11 "
The Midway Basin . . . . 14 "
The Midway Place . . . . 4 "
The Lakeopen Ground . . . . 270 "
The Lakeopen Green . . . . 26 "
The Lake Haven Green . . . . 9 "
The Belvedere Concourse . . . . 2 "
The Lake Terrace . . . . 8 "
The Lagoon Plaisance . . . . 260 "
The Lagoon . . . . 105 "
The Lagoon Terrace . . . . 2 "
The Lagoon Concourse . . . . 3 "

The length of the Interior Drives is . . . . 14 miles.
  "   "   Walks . . . . 20 "
  "   "   Mall . . . . ⅝ "
  "   "   Midway . . . . 1 "
Length of front on Lake Michigan . . . . . 1⅖ "

CHICAGO SOUTH PARK COMMISSION

PLAN OF

THE SOUTH OPEN GROUND
THE UPPER PLAISANCE
THE MIDWAY PLAISANCE
THE LAKE OPEN GROUND
THE LAGOON PLAISANCE

AND

THE PARKWAY QUADRANT

AS PROPOSED TO BE LAID OUT BY

OLMSTED VAUX & CO LANDSCAPE ARCHITECTS

1871

233. Chicago: 1871 plan of the South Parks by Olmsted, Vaux & Company; Jackson Park at the top, Washington Park at the bottom, the Midway between them.

corporation that the railway companies were unwilling to meet the cost of providing the needed extension of transportation facilities. The middle site was too cramped against the business center of the city. The choice went to the southernmost of the three, an area of about six hundred acres known as Jackson Park.

Olmsted knew the tract well from former years. In 1870, when with Calvert Vaux he made studies for the Chicago South Park Commission, this land had already been reserved by the city for park use. The plan of 1871 by Olmsted, Vaux & Company (Fig. 233) shows in some detail the proposed landscape treatment of the lakeside area, a nearby inland block, and a strip connecting them. By 1890 plans for the inland section, now known as Washington Park, had been partly carried out—though not at all as Olmsted would have wished. Very little had been done toward creating the proposed lagoons in the lakeside section (Jackson Park), which had been left a flat, uninteresting piece of sandy soil with some scrubby trees. But at least in 1890 it presented a clean slate, so to speak, on which to work. Here, it seemed to Olmsted, the method contemplated in 1870, when he had called the area Lagoon Park, could still be used to advantage, dredging channels inward from the lake and depositing the material on the fast land to give it greater height and variety. Codman agreed but suggested that, because the Fair would undoubtedly have numerous buildings in a group, terrace-like bases for them could readily be provided by making the edges of the channels vertical and then filling in behind these walls with the excavated material. The resultant effect would be not unlike that of the canals of Venice.

With these thoughts in mind, the two men conferred with the Chicago architectural firm of Burnham & Root—Daniel Hudson Burnham, upon whose advice the corporation had depended because of his reputation as an efficient manager of major building projects, and his younger partner, the brilliant designer John Wellborn Root. The two had been in active practice for nearly twenty years and had done much of the work that would one day be the start of the so-called Chicago school. On August 20, F. L. Olmsted & Company were appointed consulting landscape architects to the Fair, and immediately thereafter Burnham & Root were appointed consulting architects. Fortunately the four men found that they saw eye to eye about the Fair, and from the start a whole-heartedly collaborative spirit prevailed.

Both Burnham and Root were immediately impressed by the good sense of the Olmsted-Codman proposals for the selection of Jackson Park and its treatment. Indeed, even before the Fair was awarded to Chicago, Root had envisioned and sketched out a somewhat similar possibility, with lagoons supplied from the lake, for a waterfront site farther north, opposite the center of Chicago. But, when the four consultants' unanimous recommendation for Jackson Park reached the Fair corporation, the report met dogged resistance. Opposition was based on a preference for Washington Park, presumably because to untrained eyes it seemed somewhat finished, whereas the Jackson Park area was clearly forbidding (Fig. 234). Consequently, the four were required at a very late hour to submit a second report, in which they pointed out that Jackson Park "offers original soil to be modeled at will . . . leaving Washington Park for the pleasure and overflow ground for which it is fitted."

234. Twenty years later: Jackson Park, Chicago, 1891.

Jackson Park's advantages were cited, with an eloquence matching the sincere conviction of the consultants, as "those which are most characteristic of the region: its proximity to Lake Michigan and its free use, not only of the rare beauty of this great sheet of water, but of such festive and Venicelike lagoons as may be supplied from Lake Michigan, imparting to the whole Fair grouped about them double enchantment . . . the Fair on Jackson Park will be directly associated with the existing grandeur, beauty, and interest of the one distinguishing natural, historic, and poetic feature of this part of the American Continent—its great inland seas." [1]

Happily, that did it: the Jackson Park site was approved. Olmsted said of this, in a later address: "In the end the Commission accepted our advice, not, I think, because a majority of its members understood the grounds of it, but because they could not be led to believe that we should have given this advice without having, as experts, sound reasons for so doing. The result was due to respect for professional judgment. Comparing this experience with some of my earlier professional life, I can but think it manifests an advance in civilization." [2]

Olmsted could now see committed more precisely to paper the general disposition he had outlined, first to Codman, then to Burnham and Root, when discussing the possibility of using in Jackson Park the dredging methods advocated in 1871. The National Commission for the Fair had insisted that a plan be submitted for their approval. The four consultants went to work. The basic scheme was Olmsted's, started by picking up from the 1871 plan a sight-line approximately perpendicular to the lakefront. Balanced on this line would be a strong architectonic space, with a basin in the center and buildings facing upon it from a firm boundary line. From the central sight-line, extending north at right angles, another narrower space and canal would lead to a naturalesque lake and wooded island. On this framework a preliminary arrangement of terraces, bridges, landings and the like was roughed out. Following generally a schedule furnished them by the corporation, the four men determined the number and sizes of buildings. A large-scale sketch plan was drawn up in pencil on brown paper by Root and Codman; this was submitted to the National Commission and the Illinois corporation and on December 1, 1890, adopted officially as the controlling plan for the Exposition. Only minor changes occurred in it thereafter.

Meanwhile, in order to simplify the organization of the work, Burnham & Root had resigned as consulting architects; Root alone had been reappointed consulting architect and Burnham designated Chief of Construction—or Director of Works, as he would often be called in the ensuing months—with the sole responsibility to the corporation for guiding the whole project. This complete centralization of management had been insisted on by the railway president in charge of work for the corporation as chairman of its Grounds and Buildings Committee. In going along with the arrangement, Burnham had in view also the fact that, because of their privileged involvement in all the planning of the Fair to date, Burnham & Root as a firm could not in his judgment accept a commission for the work or for

1. *Report to Joint Committee on Site* (Chicago, 1890), pp. 10–12.
2. American Institute of Architects, *Proceedings, 27th Annual Convention* (Chicago, 1893), p. 163.

any part of it. Moreover, the Fair would be too vast a project, given the stringent limitations of time, to be sensibly undertaken by any single firm. It would have to be a group effort with one individual coordinating.

Burnham prepared a memorial of these thoughts, to be addressed to the Grounds and Buildings Committee if the other consultants concurred. To his relief, Olmsted, Codman, and Root agreed wholeheartedly, as did A. Gottlieb, who had been appointed consulting engineer to the Fair. All thereupon signed the communication, dated December 9, 1890, and authorized Burnham to present it. The memorial explained that planning had reached a point where methods for obtaining designs for individual buildings would have to be determined. It discussed several possible procedures and recommended one: "This is to select a certain number of architects, choosing each man for such work as would be most nearly parallel with his best achievements. These architects to meet in conference, become masters of all the elements to be solved, and agree upon some general scheme of procedure. The preliminary studies resulting from this to be compared and freshly discussed in a subsequent conference and, with the assistance of such suggestions as your advisors may make, be brought into a harmonious whole." [3]

After some sharp debate, the Grounds and Buildings Committee adopted the recommendations and on December 11 approved the five architectural firms selected by Burnham at the Committee's request: Richard M. Hunt of New York; McKim, Mead & White of New York; George B. Post of New York; Peabody & Stearns of Boston; Van Brunt & Howe of Kansas City. The next day Burnham wrote to each of the five explaining the situation and inviting participation. The eastern architects met at once at the office of McKim, Mead & White; on December 22 Burnham met Hunt, Post, Mead, and Peabody at dinner in New York. Van Brunt had wired his firm's acceptance. What Burnham learned in New York was that the eastern group had unanimously elected to "use the classic motive." This was a fateful decision, but there is no evidence that Burnham protested. As Charles Moore records it: "The choice of the classical motive . . . was absolutely new to Chicago, no architect in that city having used it up to the time of the Fair." [4]

It is fascinating, though academic, to speculate about what the Columbian Exposition might have been if Burnham had not called in the eastern group, and if Burnham & Root had been able to do the buildings in a pre-Exposition Chicago vein on Olmsted's brilliant plan. But the facts might as well be faced: the new eclecticism of the 1880s was securely in the saddle, at least on the eastern seaboard. After the Fair, of course, Burnham—who appears to have been won over completely—became one of the staunchest protagonists of the "classical motive."

3. Charles Moore, *Daniel Hudson Burnham, Architect, Planner of Cities* (New York, 1921), I, 39 (cited hereafter as Moore, *Burnham*).
4. *Ibid.*, p. 42.

On his return to Chicago from the New York meeting, Burnham was given approval by the Committee to extend additional invitations to five Chicago firms: Burling & Whitehouse; Jenney & Mundie; Henry Ives Cobb; S. S. Beman; Adler & Sullivan. The first meeting of all selected architects was held January 10, 1891, at the offices of Burnham & Root. Hunt presided; Louis Sullivan acted as secretary. In the afternoon the group visited Jackson Park, and that night the Grounds and Buildings Committee gave them a dinner. Enthusiasm reigned, and the great endeavor was off to a vigorous beginning. Almost at once, however, came the tragic death of Root, the gifted designer on whom Burnham had so long depended. Felled by pneumonia, he was the first of two irreparable losses; before the Fair could open in 1893, Codman too was taken.

For a week after the first meeting discussions continued in Chicago, then the following assignments were agreed upon:

F. L. Olmsted & Company	Landscape Architecture
R. M. Hunt	Administration Building
Peabody & Stearns	Machinery Hall
McKim, Mead & White	Agricultural Building
G. B. Post	Manufactures and Liberal Arts
Van Brunt & Howe	Electricity
S. S. Beman	Mines and Mining
Adler & Sullivan	Transportation
H. I. Cobb	Fisheries
Burling & Whitehouse	Venetian Village
Jenney & Mundie	Horticultural Building

To fill the void left by Root's death, Charles B. Atwood was brought on from New York. Eventually he designed many of the buildings, including the Art Gallery at the northern end of the Fair and the Peristyle at the eastern end of Olmsted's great central space.

The next big Chicago meeting was a month later, on February 24. Olmsted and Codman came with a more exactly detailed general plan worked out by Codman at the Brookline office. Each architect brought his preliminary sketches and presented them in a frankly critical all-day session (Fig. 235). The spirit of teamwork was remarkable as each member generously sought to contribute to the harmony of the composition as a whole rather than to glorify himself through his building. On this occasion Augustus Saint-Gaudens, the leading sculptor of the time, was added to the group. It was typical of the prevailing atmosphere that he offered to help by advising on all sculptural matters and enlisting the services of such other sculptors as Daniel Chester French and Frederick MacMonnies, declining the opportunity to seize the spotlight with a work of his own.

235. World's Columbian Exposition: the Committee of Architects in session. Olmsted at corner of table, leaning on elbow; McKim at right, presenting plan of a building.

By the end of February 1891 both the Illinois corporation and the National Commission had approved all aspects of the work, and final execution could proceed. At the site, dredging of the waterways and filling of the central terraces began under Codman's supervision. Burnham erected a temporary wooden structure, known as the Shack, with rough living quarters and a drafting room where Atwood, as senior designer, saw to the final preparation of such working drawings as were needed beyond what the participating architects brought with them on their periodic visits to the grounds. For over two years the work went on at a strenuous pace, driven continually by Burnham. Soon after the start, on the recommendation of Post and McKim, he engaged Francis D. Millet as Director of Color, to coordinate the work of painters as Saint-Gaudens was doing for the sculpture. Several of the most highly acclaimed mural painters, such as Edwin Blashfield, Kenyon Cox, and Gari Melchers, took part; but it was early decided that the exteriors of all the buildings of the central group would be uniformly white. Millet soon "organized the white-wash gang,"[5] as Burnham put it, using a new method for spraying on the paint.

This treatment accorded perfectly with a certain superficiality characteristic of the Fair. Because the whole enterprise was by definition temporary, the

5. *Ibid.*, p. 50.

buildings were to be constructed of staff, a mixture of plaster and fibrous binding material, on metal skeletons or armatures. A far cry indeed from the hopes for advances in steel engendered by the Galerie des Machines and the Tour Eiffel in 1889! In justice, the use of these plaster-cast fronts can hardly be objected to in view of the temporary factor. But is there not a note of irony in the obeisance to a "classical ideal," with its necessary imitation of the forms of an ancient stone architecture, in a situation requiring the use of plaster instead of stone? Under these conditions it is all the more astonishing that the Fair should have been so influential, perpetuating as it did for the next half-century of American architecture the new eclecticism of the 1880s.

The Exposition opened its gates to the public, as advertised, on May 1, 1893. A version of the official map (Fig. 236) is available today on which to approximate the visitor's experience. Emerging from the Fair's railway station on the west edge of the area, he found immediately in front of him Hunt's tall Administration Building, given this dominant position out of deference to his seniority among the architects (Fig. 237). Wide passageways led around either on the right, past the lengthy Machinery Hall of Peabody & Stearns, or on the left, past Beman's Mines and Mining and the Electricity Building of Van Brunt & Howe.

Either passage took him to the front or east side of the Administration Building, from which the tremendously impressive central space, named the Court of Honor (Figs. 238, 239), lay grandly ahead, the ruffled surface of its basin glinting in the sunlight. Directly in front, at the near end of the basin, was MacMonnies' lively fountain group. Across the farthest end of the space, only partly screening the waters of Lake Michigan, was Atwood's multicolumned Peristyle, with French's heroic single figure of the Republic standing in the basin before it. Along the right side of the space, fronting on the terrace and its walkways, stood McKim's rather delicate Agriculture Building. Opposite this, fronting on the left-hand terrace, was Post's bulky exhibition hall for Manufactures and Liberal Arts.

Just beyond the MacMonnies fountain and to the west of McKim's and Post's buildings, narrow crosswise canals led to minor buildings on the south and to the large naturalesque lake and its wooded island on the north. Ranged around this northern area, without much apparent order, were more minor buildings. On the east was the long side of Post's enormous exhibition hall; north of it, the Federal Government Building; then Fisheries, by Cobb; at the far end Atwood's Art Gallery; next the Illinois State Building, the Women's Building, the Horticultural Building by Jenney; and, at the southwest corner, partly tucked in behind Mines and Mining, the fanciful Transportation Building of Adler & Sullivan.

Through October 1893 the Fair continued to receive its awestruck thousands. Then it closed; the buildings were torn down and the site in due time

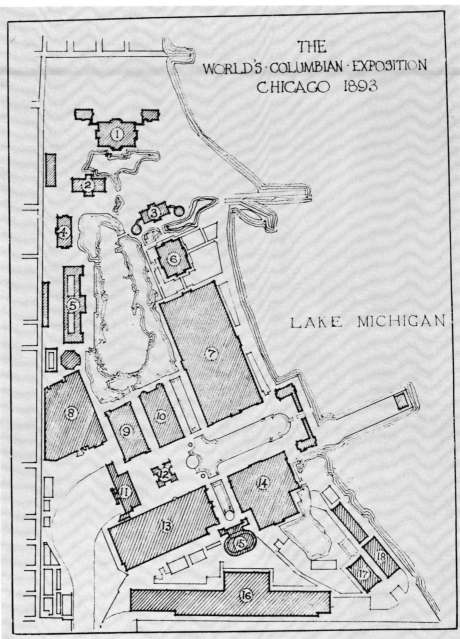

THE WORLD'S · COLUMBIAN · EXPOSITION CHICAGO 1893

LAKE MICHIGAN

1 Art Galleries; 2 Illinois Building; 3 Fisheries; 4 Women's Building;
5 Horticulture; 6 U.S. Government; 7 Manufactures and Liberal Arts;
8 Transportation; 9 Mines; 10 Electricity; 11 Station; 12 Administration;
13 Annex Machinery; 14 Agriculture; 15 Stock Pavilion;
16 Stock Exhibit; 17 Anthropology; 18 Forestry

236. Plan of the Fair.

237. World's Columbian Exposition: Hunt's Administration Building.

became Jackson Park again, vastly improved (Fig. 240) over its appearance in 1891. Aside from its primary function of exhibiting the products of men's handiwork and mechanical skill, what did the Exposition accomplish? What of the two positive and the single negative points suggested at the outset of this chapter?

It is doubtful that any other single event in the history of the arts in America served as notably as the Fair in stimulating the practice of inter-professional collaboration. Certainly the opportunity was unusual. Saint-Gaudens appears to have sensed the possibilities when, at the end of the group session of February 1891, he asked Burnham: "Do you realize that this is the greatest meeting of artists since the fifteenth century?"[6] The teamwork involving architects, landscape architects, sculptors, and painters, all striving—not separately, but together—toward an agreed goal, proved its own value in the visual harmony and wholeness of the Fair itself. But it did more: the lesson of the Fair encouraged perpetuation of this entirely sensible collaborative method of practice. Fortunately, through their own experience the participants learned the lesson well: that, to be successful, collaboration means

6. *Ibid.*, p. 47.

238. World's Columbian Exposition, Court of Honor: the core of the Olmsted-Codman plan, looking east from the Administration Building; at the right, McKim's Agriculture; at the left, Post's Manufactures and Liberal Arts.

239. Court of Honor, looking westward from Atwood's colonnade.

240. Jackson Park, 1950s. Olmsted's Wooded Isle remains essentially unchanged.

more than the mere amiable willingness of practitioner A to have practitioner B, from another field, execute his work on the project independently at the same time. It means joint involvement from the beginning in an open-eyed and open-minded acceptance of mutual help and interdependence. Collaboration, then, may be marked up as the first of the two positive points of the Columbian Exposition. It is not too much to say that at least two manifestations of belief in the collaborative process would be directly brought about by the experience of the Fair: establishment of the American Academy in Rome in 1894 and the McMillan Commission's plan of 1901 for Washington.

The second positive point about the Columbian Exposition, and the best known, was the unprecedented awakening of public interest in civic design. In fact, the degree of excitement about the Great White City, as it was often called, far exceeded anything its creators had hoped for. The use of electric lights, then still a novelty, to outline some of the buildings at night surely contributed to the general sense of enchantment. After all, the country had never seen anything like it before, and to most visitors the Fair was like a dream of unimaginable opulence. Far and wide a vibrant new interest was aroused in what design could do for America's towns and cities.

In part, the impressiveness no doubt arose from the use of a uniform sixty-foot order in all the buildings around the Court of Honor and from the seeming homogeneity of white surfaces everywhere, even on buildings actually disparate in character and in some cases rather badly misguided "classical" imitations. There can be no doubt, however, as to the tremendous impact made by the Court of Honor itself—the spatial core that demonstrated, as nothing else had done for a century or more, what a wonderfully unifying force is exerted by well-structured outdoor space. To present-day eyes it would seem this contribution of Olmsted, Codman, and Root must surely have been the dominant factor in the Fair's awakening of public interest. That Olmsted's influence was appreciated by his colleagues, too, is clear in the following excerpt from remarks made by Burnham at the testimonial dinner of some two hundred persons tendered him in New York just as the Fair was about to open:

> Each of you knows the name and genius of him who stands first in the heart and confidence of American artists, the creator of your own parks and many other city parks. He it is who has been our best adviser and our common mentor. In the highest sense he is the planner of the Exposition—Frederick Law Olmsted. No word of his has fallen to the ground among us since first he joined us some thirty months ago. An artist, he paints with lakes and wooded slopes; with lawns and banks and forest-covered hills; with mountain-sides and ocean views. He should stand where I do tonight, not for his deeds of later years alone, but for what his brain has wrought and his pen has taught for half a century.[7]

At the same dinner Charles Eliot Norton, responding for "Architecture, Sculpture, and Painting," included some comments of particular interest here:

> The general design of the grounds and of the arrangement of the buildings was in every respect noble, original and satisfactory, a work of a fine art not generally included in the list of poetic arts, but one of the most important of them all to America—that of the landscape architect. Of all American artists, Frederick Law Olmsted, who gave the design for the laying out of the grounds of the World's Fair, stands first in the production of great works which answer the needs and give expression to the life of our immense and miscellaneous democracy.[8]

It is now well known that the two positive points of the Fair were strongly affected in their ultimate results by the one negative point, dedication to a so-called classical ideal. But the first two points were nevertheless commendable in themselves, quite apart from the "classicism" that clouded their

7. *Ibid.*, p. 74.
8. *Ibid.*, pp. 78–79.

application. Interprofessional collaboration remains today an extremely valuable mode of working, and a lively concern about design on the part of the total citizenry is a necessary characteristic of any sound society. It is simply too bad that for so long after 1893 both the collaborative process and public interest should have been marred by uncritical acceptance of the Fair's "classicism" as though this were its essential merit.

As a continuation of the new eclecticism of the 1880s, dedication to the classic motive may have been entirely natural for eastern architects: their sincerity is not questioned. But use of the "classical ideal" in Chicago, of all cities, was neither natural nor necessary—nor was it agreed upon unanimously. One cannot help wondering what might have been the outcome had Root remained alive. He, after all, not Burnham, was the designer of the firm; he had already given thought to the approaching Fair, and this thought, as far as it had gone into details, was a continuation of what he had been doing in Chicago—fresh, free, colorful, and certainly not whitewashed "classic." He might have resisted the blandishments of McKim and Post and Hunt as Burnham did not. But this is pure speculation, and must always be just that.

One member of the architectural group who had agreed with Root's hopes for a forward-looking, gaily-colored Fair, and who mourned all the more

241. Sullivan's Transportation Building with its famous Golden Door, the focus of controversy at the Exposition.

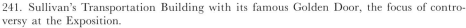

deeply the loss of his friend, was Louis Sullivan. He too had participated in the resurgence of building in Chicago; as a member of the firm of Adler & Sullivan, he had done the Auditorium, and the surprisingly different Wainwright Building in St. Louis was under construction. Evidently, without making an open issue he disagreed flatly with the Fair's "classical ideal," and his Transportation Building (Fig. 241), with its great Golden Door, was in its own idiom—and in its own place, *outside* the Court of Honor. In its peculiar way eclectically imitative to a degree, and not notably inventive structurally, the Transportation Building was by no means up to Sullivan's best. Yet modern generations, seeing it perhaps as a symbol of their own antipathy to the classical ideal and its aftermath, tend to regard it as the only noteworthy work of architecture in the entire Columbian Exposition. A similar view, in fact, was expressed at the Fair by numerous foreign visitors, especially those who had come hoping and expecting to see some outstanding architectural progress, stimulated by innovations of the Paris Exposition.

Some years later, no doubt further embittered by the decline in his private practice and the dominance of the type of classical architecture he despised, Sullivan made the withering pronouncement about American architecture that has been so often quoted: "The damage wrought by the World's Fair will last for half a century from its date, if not longer."[9] To be sure, it would be a mistake to accept this dictum of Sullivan's too literally.[10] The prediction was nevertheless in a sense amazingly accurate, appearing to have missed the target by a few months at most. Anyone who has followed the course of American schools of architecture in recent decades will recall that the question whether to "go modern" was still heavily argued in many schools in the years just before World War II. After the war one heard virtually no debate about the question. The twentieth century had at last been discovered in American architecture; the Battle of the Modern had finally been won—in just about 1943, or fifty years after the Fair.

To landscape architects, and to the history of their profession, the Columbian Exposition brought additional significance—thanks to Olmsted (Fig. 242), even beyond the sentiments expressed so fairly by Burnham and Norton. At the Fair Olmsted and Codman not only created an overall scheme of marked excellence as a work of landscape architecture. In its most important component, the Court of Honor, they gave clear proof of the remarkable integrative capacity inherent in the landscape architect's major material, outdoor space. This cohesive effect of the Court of Honor was exercised quite independently of the "classical ideal" of the buildings. Indeed, the spatial form would have retained its basic strength, and would have required no essential modification even if Root or Sullivan or both had been in charge of all the architecture.

9. Louis Sullivan, *The Autobiography of an Idea* (New York, 1924), p. 325.
10. See the early part of this chapter; also Lewis Mumford, *Roots of Contemporary American Architecture* (New York, 1952), p. 14.

242. Frederick Law Olmsted about 1890.

What Olmsted accomplished at the Fair was thus an object lesson of exceptional value to the profession—or *could* have been, especially at a time when the Country Place Era was getting under way. Landscape architects were becoming increasingly involved in collaborative work on country residences, in which the houses tended to follow the current eclectic fashion all the more earnestly after the Exposition. Olmsted's work there should have encouraged younger landscape architects to concentrate on the basic importance of clear spatial geometry and structure, instead of bowing to the imitative eclectic mode of the architecture. For this was the potential lesson offered by the Court of Honor: architectonic vigor requires no obeisance to eclecticism. Unfortunately, few of Olmsted's colleagues learned the lesson well enough; so landscape architecture, too, fell into the predicted half-century of slumber, awaiting the dawn when rational design would come into its own.

XXV. The Influence of Charles A. Platt

Almost immediately after the Columbian Exposition, though not in any way connected with it, a man appeared quietly upon the scene who would have a profound effect on design in landscape architecture: Charles Adams Platt. At this moment the still young and thinly manned profession needed all the help it could get as it headed into its Country Place Era. Platt's impact was a double one. Through publishing in 1894 a small volume about the Italian villa entitled *Italian Gardens* and through the example set by his own early work, he influenced the basic trend of landscape design, enriching its directions and infusing it with a new spirit at a critical point in its history. Second, in four decades of active professional practice he demonstrated in works of superlative quality his fine understanding of order in the arrangement of outdoor space upon the land.

To grasp the importance of Platt's contribution, the state of landscape design when he published his illustrated book on the little-known Italian villa must be considered carefully. With the advent of the clarified architectural eclecticism of the 1880s, a stronger type of landscape architecture had seemed a logical necessity. Now, however, though Olmsted had shown the way in such places as Biltmore and the World's Fair Court of Honor, the force of the old "landscape gardening" fashion was hard to break down, and the new spirit was correspondingly slow to advance. The relatively few attempts at a more architectonic design were at best tentative. What they most often lacked was a sense of overall organization or structure—exactly what characterized both Platt's own work and the typical Italian villa as he revealed it in his book.

Platt was by no means a newcomer in the world of the arts. He had been working for a decade in painting and etching, had spent five years studying in Paris, and was exhibiting successfully in New York, when as though by divinely inspired accident a turn of events markedly affected his further career, to the great good fortune of American architecture and landscape architecture. A younger brother, William Platt, had been briefly engaged in the Olmsted office in Brookline, with some thought of becoming a landscape architect. As an artist, Charles was naturally interested in scenery and in gardens and during his Paris years had given considerable attention to architecture. It required no great amount of persuasion to get him to join his brother for an extended trip to Italy. There the two made voluminous notes, sketched avidly, and became wholly enamored of the strength and integrity of the Italian villa as a work of art.

In 1892, shortly after the brothers' return to America, William died suddenly; Charles carried out their joint determination, publishing in *Harper's Magazine* a series of articles on Italian villas, about which nothing was then available beyond the early volumes of Percier and Fontaine and a later study in German by Tuckermann. These Platt articles became in 1894, along with reproductions of his paintings and sketches, the epochal book. Today, when so much more is known about Italian villas than was the case then, it is heartwarming to see in Platt's text such unmistakable evidence of complete rapport with his subject. It is hardly too much to say that he and the Italian villa were made for each other. The book did not profess to be a technical treatise; there is no minutely detailed analysis, nor are there plans or sections of the villas. The visual strength of the volume lies in reproductions of photographs and of the author's paintings. What it does—and what it must have done for many readers when it appeared, for it became quite popular—is to convey through its text a simple, direct, unromanticized yet quietly enthusiastic appreciation of the typical Italian villa as the distinctive phenomenon that, on the whole, it was and is: a marvelously integrated combination of indoor and outdoor space, of architecture and landscape architecture, fitted with consummate felicity to its site and its role in the life of the time.

One of the most heartening aspects of the book's approach is Platt's completely honest critical evaluation. He does not go head over heels for every villa just because it is Italian, as some unbridled enthusiasts do. His deep admiration for excellence is all the more forceful in contrast to this basic reserve. The reader can see repeatedly in these youthful essays the same gently balanced feeling for appropriateness and proportion, the same exquisite but fully virile sense of discrimination, that marked Platt's own work.

It is interesting that the book apparently made quite an impression on Charles Eliot, who wrote an excellent review. Eliot, having rather slighted Italy in his early professional travels, preferred the soft Reptonian method. Now he agreed with Platt in "rightly thinking that these villas of Italy may

243. Charles A. Platt's summer home at Cornish, New Hampshire.

teach lessons of value to the America of today." He may even have revealed something of the prejudices still common among conservative folk in the 1890s when he commented: "The gardens of the Renaissance in Italy, France, and England have been thoughtlessly ridiculed in modern days because of their

244. The entrance pathway and terrace at Cornish.

unlikeness to wild nature. As well revile a palace for its unlikeness to a wigwam."[1]

But the impact of the villas meant far more to Platt than mere material for a book. It takes no clairvoyance to see that he had been drawn to them because what he found in them accorded with his own instinctive way of designing; they must have seemed a reinforcement of what he felt intuitively. The essentially simple layout of his own summer home at Cornish, New Hampshire (Fig. 243), even in those early days, had the clarity and strength of spatial organization that became an ever-present design characteristic of the many country places he did in ensuing years.

The layout (Fig. 244) was certainly not "Italian." But from earlier chapters of this account it will be remembered that organized structure of space was an unfailing factor in the Italian villa at its best. Obviously Platt and that villa spoke the same clear language of geometric form. There is no great mystery about it; both in Platt's work and in the typical Italian villa, organizational strength came from a pair of quite simple fundamentals, as true today as in the past. The first is the observable fact that a line of sight connecting one space with another, or several spaces in a series, ties them together visually and imparts to the beholder an appreciable and satisfying

1. Eliot, *Charles Eliot,* pp. 547–549.

psychological sense of clear inter-relationship, of structure, of strength. The second, an antecedent to the first, is the equally observable fact that, when the spaces thus tied together are unequivocally formed, having their boundaries perceptibly defined or implied by vertical planes so that each individual space is easily grasped as an entity, then the sense of structural strength is even greater and more satisfying.

To achieve such unequivocal form, the individual spaces—both in Platt's design and in the Italian villa—were as a rule crisply geometric, usually rectilinear, always firmly under control. They fitted well into that readily comprehensible surety of overall order for which humans always appear to be seeking, and to which they respond with such an abiding sense of contentment when they find it. For further strength and continuity, house and grounds were invariably treated as a single, fully integral composition. In the villa Platt saw this at once; indeed, he specified in the introduction to his book "that the word 'villa' is used in the Italian sense" to refer not merely to the house or palace, but to "the design as a whole, including gardens, terraces, groves, and their necessary surroundings and embellishments, it being clear that no one of these component parts was ever considered independently."[2]

These are the characteristics that gave to the Italian villa, and to Platt's own work from first to last, a vigorous architectonic quality. This quality was apparent not only in the easy transition from house to grounds as the geometry of indoor space extended itself into the equally definite geometry of outdoor spaces, but also in the transition from space to space under the sky, especially in the close attachment of outdoor spaces to the earth itself in clear-cut planiform areas, with distinct recognition of the vertical dimension through walls and steps. Contrary to a widely held belief, bilateral symmetry—the mirrored balancing of a right-hand with a left-hand part on a center-line between the two—was by no means an essential of this architectonic structure in the plan of Italian villas. It occurred in them, as it had occurred again and again since ancient days, but it was not essential. What *was* essential was the sight-line itself, tying spaces together.

Given the framework of such an architectonic complex, it is obvious that an overall scheme could not well contain any of the undulating surfaces and soft pastoral spaces of the park-like "landscape style" until one got out beyond the influence of the perceptibly geometric. That the park-like forms of space could exist in those outer reaches, connected to the architectonic area by means of an entirely different kind of strong transition, was often demonstrated not only in Platt's work but in that of numerous other landscape architects in the years that followed. In fact, as pointed out earlier, gradation from the architectonic into the park-like became, in the opinion of many

2. Charles A. Platt, *Italian Gardens* (New York, 1894), p. 6.

critics, one of the specific contributions of American landscape architecture.

This development in America, incidentally, was in healthy contrast to the lengthy debate that split opinion in England during the latter half of the nineteenth century. William Robinson, a self-appointed defender of the old "landscape school," wrote voluminously, especially in horticultural journals; in *The English Flower Garden* he castigated any departure from the soft, wavy lines of the "natural" landscape. His most effective opponent, architect Reginald Blomfield, with fully equal vehemence in *The Formal Garden in England* insisted on architectonic design not only around the house but everywhere, and attacked the "landscape gardeners" for their indecisive wobbling. The ridiculous extremes to which the two went, each demanding that everything be done *only* in *his* way, is another illustration of the senselessness of black-and-white, either-or, two-valued arguments. American landscape design found a way to use both types, assigning to each the role for which it was uniquely fitted. It is worth noting that Charles Eliot voiced this American view, revealing the growth of his own thinking, as early as 1892, in a review of the Blomfield book.

It may be objected at this point that Platt and his influence came during the period when the eclecticism of the 1880s had been further reinforced by the unhappy effects of the "classicism" of the World's Fair. This is true. But precisely the sort of development that was seen as possible, even in the Country Place Era, was in Platt's work—a case of architectonic design not imitatively eclectic. For in fairness to Platt it must be made clear that he never consciously imitated any Italian villa. He never copied one, or wanted to; no designer who truly loves Italy would think of doing so. Moreover, though it is probably true that his way of working was more widely accepted, even when misunderstood, because of the prevailing eclecticism, it is certainly true that everything he did had an intangible personal quality quite unlike anything done by others before or since. The major point is that neither the strength of Platt's personal style nor that of the Italian villa was in any way affected by the existence of an American eclectic period, for they were wholly independent of it.

The historically noteworthy fact is that, at a moment when landscape design was greatly in need of help, Platt came along with his little book and such work as his place at Cornish. The combination had quick impact on the profession and on client after client in constantly growing numbers. The appeal of what he did and wrote manifested itself soon in the increasingly coherent, organized, architectonic type of design that began to appear on the drafting boards of landscape architects. This is not to say that strong landscape design had not existed before. There had indeed been a few gardens with perceptibly geometric form, but they were scarce; and the connection between house and grounds was often disappointingly loose and the amount of well-knit integrity in the total composition small. At about the turn of

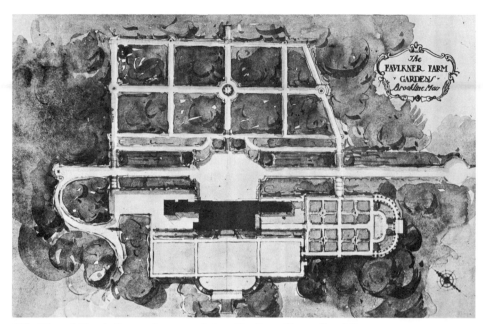

245. Plan of Platt's first major commission, Faulkner Farm, Brookline.

the century, landscape design took an upswing in overall strength and vitality, especially in residential projects. Platt's genuine modesty and reserve being what they were, it would have been inconceivable in him to claim he had been in any measure responsible for this rebirth. But there can be no doubt of his fundamental role.

The first outstanding opportunity to try his hand professionally as a landscape architect was in Brookline, at Faulkner Farm, where in 1897 work was started on execution of what Platt entitled a "plan of grounds surrounding his house" for Charles F. Sprague (Fig. 245). This early work, later known as the Brandegee Estate and now the home of the American Academy of Arts and Sciences, was substantially completed by 1898. In its overall structure the plan of Faulkner Farm was simple, direct, and strong. Unfortunately, widespread attention has been focused on the flower garden (Fig. 246), actually too fussily elaborate to be typical of Platt's work. To be sure, it contained several elements associated in popular conception with Italy— pergola, pool, terminal pavilion—but it had not yet achieved the sureness of detail that Platt developed in works of only a few years later. Already much more in his natural vein was another Brookline project of a similar nature, the Garden of Weld, done about 1901 for the Larz Andersons (Fig. 247). In overall plan it, too, had clear structural strength; but the forms were considerably simplified, and the central open space, with its turf panel, gave the garden a more placid aspect than the one at Faulkner Farm.

246. The flower garden at Faulkner Farm.

247. The Garden of Weld, Brookline; its center is more spacious than that at Faulkner Farm.

Even though they were not completely representative of Platt's mature ability, these two early commissions illustrate well an unusual factor in his professional development. In these instances Platt's task was the creation of gardens only—and this is precisely the way his career in architecture and landscape architecture began. According to the report of an interview with Platt a decade later, in 1912, "he gained opportunities for designing gardens in this country, work which he found congenial but in which he was hampered by the architects' lack of skill in designing the house to fit the grounds, so that he was never able to do such a garden as he wished. It was easy for him to take the next step and to design both house and garden. He is said to have entered architecture through the garden gate."[3]

It did not take long for potential clients to discover the advantage of asking Platt to do both house and grounds, and with this greater latitude he came into his own as a superlative designer of country places. Year after year, a long and remarkable list of commissions followed. Among the most widely acclaimed were Timberline, at Bryn Mawr, Pennsylvania (Figs. 248–250); Woodston, at Mt. Kisco, New York; Maxwell Court, at Rockville, Connecticut; Gwinn, at Cleveland (Figs. 251, 252); the McCormick "villa" at Lake Forest; Villasera at Warren, Rhode Island; and Girdle Ridge at Katonah, New York. In the houses themselves Platt's design sometimes had its only hint of eclecticism. That is, with differences in materials it was on occasion possible and not unjust to attribute terms of "historic styles" to the houses, but only in the sense that a stucco-faced house "looked Italian," or a brick and limestone one "looked Georgian." Even so, the house always bore Platt's personal style more noticeably than it did anything historically imitative. And in each case the overall plan of the place—that is, its landscape architecture—remained untouched by eclecticism.

All of Platt's work was distinguished, not only for the reasons already noted, but also for the painstaking care with which each commission was studied and carried out, from big general conception to smallest detail; it was this unremitting perfectionism, as well as the overall strength of layout, the restraint, the eye for proportion, and the impeccable use of materials, that gained Platt the frank admiration of his colleagues and made him virtually the idol of the younger generation of designers through the 1920s.

Of all the distinctions that graced Platt's designs for country places one of the most fascinating, and surprising, was the successful resolution of a seeming paradox. Although without exception each of the plans had its faithfully rigorous system of sight-lines tying positive spaces firmly together either in series or in opposition—so that, as the saying went, "you can always tell a Platt plan"—there was actually among the different schemes an almost incredible variety and individuality. This was all the more remarkable in

3. *Landscape Architecture,* 2 (January 1912), p. 127.

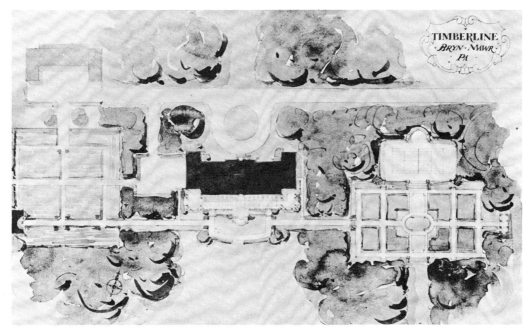

248. Plan of Timberline, Bryn Mawr; here Platt had Olmsted Brothers as associated landscape architects.

249. Terrace steps and the long sight-line to gardens at Timberline.

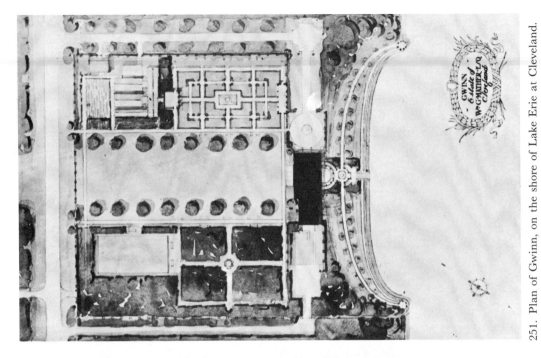

251. Plan of Gwinn, on the shore of Lake Erie at Cleveland.

250. In the main garden at Timberline.

252. View along the curving shoreline of Gwinn.

view of the number of projects executed. Within the first twenty years after publication of his little book on the Italian villa, Platt had done such a quantity of superb work that a monograph on it appeared in 1913, with a warmly appreciative introduction by his good friend, the critic Royal Cortissoz. Examination of the plans and photographs in this visual summary of Platt's work tells more than the present words can hope to.

During the remaining twenty years of his lifetime after 1913, Platt created many more buildings and, by himself or in collaboration, some outstanding works of landscape architecture to add to those already done. Quite a few were institutional projects, among them plans for the University of Illinois and Phillips Andover Academy. The work published in the 1913 monograph, however, is thoroughly representative and remains the authoritative source for an understanding of the Platt genius.

In that year, 1913, Platt was elected to corresponding membership by the American Society of Landscape Architects in recognition of the tremendous good he had done for the profession. By that time, of course, he had completed many noteworthy buildings and was known as an architect, rather than as a painter, an etcher, or a landscape architect—all of which he had been, successively and successfully. To practitioners in each of these arts he always seemed one of their own. To landscape architects he will always be a landscape architect and one of the greatest the profession has known. To those privileged to work with him, Platt will be remembered not only for his sure touch and seemingly effortless ability, but for the depth of his modesty and for his unfailing kindness to younger designers.

XXVI. Founding of the American Society of Landscape Architects

In the 1890s, as the new century approached, the profession of landscape architecture drew near its fortieth birthday. But it was not yet organized; there was no systematic method of training, other than the time-worn one of apprenticeship, and the number of practitioners was small. Nevertheless, some of these few began to feel the urgent need for uniting in some form of organization. By 1898, when efforts in this direction became serious, the profession had suffered losses it could ill afford. Two potential leaders had died, Codman in 1893, Eliot in 1897. In the west, Cleveland was no longer active. The elder Olmsted had retired from practice in 1895 and shortly thereafter lapsed into a child-like state, completely worn out by the years of strenuous uphill work for the profession he had created; he continued in this helpless condition until his death in 1903.

As early as the winter of 1896–97, one of Olmsted's early apprentices, Warren H. Manning, who had just opened his own office in Boston after eight years with the Olmsted firm, sought to arouse interest in establishing a professional association of landscape architects. Naturally he wrote to Eliot, who had returned to the Olmsted office as a partner while Manning was working there. Eliot replied from the field, in an admittedly hurried note: "I can tell you frankly that I do not believe a league of professional men . . . is worth attempting while the number of professional men concerned is only four or five, and while the profession is so generally unrecognized by the public." Eliot advocated instead "organizing, not a professional, but a general association, to be made up of all who desire the advancement of landscape art . . . in our country. In such a general association, amateurs, . . . foresters, gardeners, and anybody interested might become members."[1] Eliot's suggestion for a general association was in fact adopted in summer 1897, when the American Park and Outdoor Art Association was organized in Louisville, Kentucky. By that time, Eliot had passed away. The Association engaged the interest of numerous landscape architects, including Manning, but it did not satisfy what he felt the profession needed, nor did it last for many years.

Meeting so little enthusiasm for a professional association in the Boston area, Manning did not for the time being persist. Meanwhile, the spirit for organization was stirring more actively in New York, where initiative was taken by Samuel Parsons, Jr., who had been a partner of Calvert Vaux and was now landscape architect to the recently enlarged City of New York. On February 24, 1898, Parsons sent out a letter that started a series of small meetings looking toward formation of a professional society. At first he thought only of including practitioners of his acquaintance in New York, but he was soon persuaded to broaden the effort to include Boston people known to him.

Parsons found at first, as Manning had earlier, that there was no great interest in Boston for a national organization. In July 1898 John Olmsted replied to Parsons to the effect that the few landscape architects of Boston thought it "entirely unlikely that any such comprehensive and elaborately organized professional association as you seem to have in mind will be successful until there are more experienced and well recognized practitioners willing to join it." Olmsted did say that the Boston group had agreed to start a purely informal local club, the Repton Club, to meet occasionally for dinner and discussion of each other's plans and sketches. He added: "It seems to us reasonable to suppose that similar societies may be organized from time to time in different parts of the country, and that when there are a sufficient number of recognized practitioners, they can get together in a National Society."[2]

Manning, on the other hand, was enthusiastic over the New York efforts and clearly eager to cooperate with Parsons. By December 1898 the two had met in New York, and Manning had agreed to communicate again with "two or three" of the Boston landscape architects, inviting participation. This time circumstances were more persuasive, and John Olmsted said he would come to a meeting in New York, as did his younger half-brother, Frederick Law Olmsted, Jr., now in his late twenties and a new member of the firm.

1. Eliot, *Charles Eliot*, p. 703.
2. *Landscape Architecture*, 40 (January 1950), p. 59.

Accordingly, on January 4, 1899, in the office of Parsons & Pentecost in the St. James Building at Broadway and 26th Street, New York, eleven charter members ("original Fellows," as they designated themselves) met and organized the American Society of Landscape Architects: Nathan F. Barrett, Miss Beatrix Jones (later Mrs. Max Farrand), Daniel W. Langton, Charles N. Lowrie, Warren H. Manning, John Charles Olmsted, Frederick Law Olmsted, Jr., Samuel Parsons, Jr., George F. Pentecost, Jr., Ossian C. Simonds (of Chicago), and Downing Vaux. Officers were elected: president, John Olmsted; vice-president, Parsons; treasurer, Lowrie; secretary, Langton. A committee was appointed to draw up a constitution and by-laws, which were duly adopted at the next meeting, held on March 6, 1899.

Considering the historical importance of their action in establishing the profession's first organized body, the eleven founders were a strangely uneven group—in age, training, skills, and apparently personal dedication. Parsons, at fifty-five, was the eldest, Pentecost at twenty-four the youngest. Thirty years later only five were still professionally active, Mrs. Farrand, Lowrie, Manning, F. L. Olmsted, and Simonds. Of course none of the eleven had received university training for landscape architecture. The Olmsteds and Vaux had been brought up in landscape architects' families; Barrett, Manning, and Parsons had started in family nurseries. Lowrie and Simonds were graduate civil engineers; Miss Jones had enjoyed early training under Sargent. Langton and Pentecost appear to have been drawn to the field simply by personal predilection. As might be expected, available information about all eleven varies greatly.

Nathan Franklin Barrett was born on Staten Island in 1845. After three years in the Union forces during the Civil War he spent another three in his brother's nursery, studying plants with a view to a professional career as a "landscape gardener." His first commission came in 1869 for the Central Railroad of New Jersey. From this he branched out into town planning and park work; in 1872 he planned the experimental town of Pullman, Illinois. More town planning followed, along with considerable residential work in which he was one of the early proponents of geometric or "formal" design. In 1895 he was appointed landscape architect of the newly formed Essex County Park Commission in New Jersey; from 1900 to 1915 he was a member of the Palisades Interstate Park Commission. It is of particular interest that he should have served professionally with both the first county park system and the first interstate park body in the United States. He was president of the ASLA in 1903 but not very active in the Society after 1907. He died in Pelham, New York, October 17, 1919.

Beatrix Cadwalader Jones was born in New York City in 1872. From earliest childhood she was fascinated by the outdoor environment, and at the age of eleven she participated in laying out the family place, "Reef Point," at Bar Harbor, Maine. As a young woman she lived in Brookline with the Sargents while studying under Professor Sargent at the Arnold Arboretum. From the large office that she later maintained for some years in New York, she carried on an extensive and demanding practice, mainly on private residential projects but also as a consultant landscape gardener—a title on which she always insisted—to Princeton, Yale, the University of Chicago, Oberlin, and other institutions. In 1913 she married Max Farrand, a professor at Princeton; when he was appointed director of the Huntington Library in Pasadena they moved to the west coast. From 1922 on, she was in full charge of all outdoor efforts at Dumbarton Oaks; these gardens and the great quadrangles of Princeton and Yale are generally regarded as her most outstanding professional work. Yale made her an honorary Master of Arts in 1926 and Smith College a Doctor of Humane Letters in 1935. She was an honorary member of the American Institute of Architects. After her husband's death Mrs. Farrand lived in Bar Harbor, and there she died February 27, 1959, the last surviving charter member of the ASLA. Throughout the sixty years of her membership she maintained loyal, unflagging enthusiasm for the Society.

Daniel W. Langton, a southerner, was the Society's first secretary; but failing eyesight compelled him to relinquish that post and, ultimately, his practice as well. Some of his gardens had achieved public notice in the middle 1890s, and the memorial minute adopted by the ASLA after his sudden death on June 20, 1909, referred to "his active career as a public official and designer of parks, country estates, and playgrounds."[3] In certain municipal park work he was associated with Lowrie.

Charles Nassau Lowrie was born at Warrior's Mark, Pennsylvania, in 1869 and was graduated as Civil Engineer from the Sheffield Scientific School of Yale in 1891. Establishing his private office in New York in 1896, he built a wide practice, especially in parks and institutional grounds. Some of his earliest studies were for state parks, but he became known primarily as an authority on municipal parks and recreational areas. For thirty years he was landscape architect of the Hudson County Park Commission in New Jersey. He was on the Fine Arts Commission of the State of New York for some six years and in 1938 became by appointment the first landscape architect on the Art Commission of New York City. One of the most energetic organizers of the ASLA, he was its president in 1910–11 and remained active in the Society throughout his life. He took a primary part in arranging the Society's 1939 annual meeting at the New York World's Fair only a few weeks before his death on September 18, 1939.

Warren Henry Manning was born in Reading, Massachusetts, in 1860. His father was a prominent nurseryman; with his three brothers, he immersed himself early in the study of plants, with emphasis on native species. In 1888 he entered the Olmsted office, serving first as a horticulturist and later as

3. Board of Trustees, American Society of Landscape Architects, Resolution of June 28, 1909.

an assistant in design; in 1896 he opened his own office in Boston. Later he worked for many years from the Manning Manse in Billerica; there the office became large but remained always highly personal, so that all the work bore indelibly the Manning stamp. He was deeply interested in the development of young "landscape designers," as he called them; the Billerica office was a training ground remembered affectionately in later years by young men of whom many became prominent in the profession. Manning's practice, covering just a half-century in time, was remarkably varied: general city planning, parks, and institutional grounds, as well as many country places. Among his best-known works were the park and parkway system along the Susquehanna River at Harrisburg, Pennsylvania; the Hampton Institute in Virginia; the Jamestown Exposition of 1907; municipal park systems in several states. He was incessantly active, always a vigorous participant in ASLA affairs. He was president of the Society in 1914. In his last years his office was in Cambridge, Massachusetts; he died February 5, 1938.

John Charles Olmsted was born in Geneva, Switzerland, in 1852, the son of John Hull Olmsted. After his father's death he became, at the age of seven, the step-son of his uncle, Frederick Law Olmsted. A graduate of Yale in 1875, he entered his uncle's office in New York, was allowed a share of the enterprise in 1878, and rose to partnership in 1884 after the office had been moved to Brookline. At the time of the founding of the ASLA he was unquestionably the most widely experienced in the group and probably the ablest. Prior to his uncle's retirement in 1895, the projects most clearly associated with John Olmsted were such Boston ones as Franklin Park, the Arnold Arboretum, and the Riverway; for in those days he managed the Brookline office and traveled much less than in later years. After 1895 he was the senior partner in the firm (Olmsted Brothers from 1898 on), and can thus be credited with a high degree of responsibility for its manifold operations during the rest of his life. He was a prolific designer, genuinely admired by his colleagues as leader of the profession after his uncle's retirement. He was the first president of the ASLA, serving from 1899 through 1901 and again in 1904–05. He died in Brookline on February 25, 1920.

Frederick Law Olmsted, Jr., was born on Staten Island in 1870. He took his A.B. magna cum laude from Harvard in 1894. After working diligently in the field on projects of the Olmsted office until 1898, he joined his elder half-brother John in partnership and the firm name became Olmsted Brothers. In 1900 he was selected by President Eliot to organize and head at Harvard the first university curriculum of professional training in landscape architecture. In 1901, when he was only thirty-one, he was chosen as a member of the famous McMillan Commission to revive the L'Enfant plan of Washington; the great Mall is primarily his creation. Later he was a member of the National Commission of Fine Arts from its inception in 1910 until 1918. During World War I he led the collaborative teams of architects, landscape architects, and engineers that planned the government's war housing and military cantonments. The notable State Park Study of 1929 for California was another of his major accomplishments. Throughout a phenomenally busy life he was always somehow able to find time to guide and counsel students and younger landscape architects. There can be little question of his place as the outstanding practitioner of his times, with a store of energy and a capacity for application that wore out many a younger man. One of his last undertakings was a survey of the Colorado River Basin, carried on in field and office when he was in his seventies. He was at all times a devoted servant of the profession and of the ASLA, of which he was president in 1908–1909 and 1919–1923. He spent his last years in retirement in California, where he died at Malibu on December 25, 1957.

Samuel Parsons, Jr., was born in New Bedford, Massachusetts, in 1844, the third of his name in an old Quaker family of horticulturists. Taking his B.S. degree from Yale in 1862, he served during the remaining years of the Civil War with the U.S. Sanitary Commission, of which the elder Olmsted had been the organizer. He then returned for several years to his father's nursery, farmed for a while in southern New Jersey, and began to offer his services in laying out private residential properties. In 1880 he became a partner of Calvert Vaux, with whom he practiced until the latter's death in 1895. Meanwhile, Parsons had been appointed superintendent of planting in Central Park in 1882 and superintendent of parks in 1885. Eventually he went on to be landscape architect to the City of New York and commissioner of parks. Even after leaving the Park Department in 1911, he continued to lead an unrelenting campaign against any threatened maltreatment of Central Park. Primarily as defender of the parks, he was for years a well known and highly respected public figure in New York. In private practice he did residential projects in some thirteen states, as well as parks throughout the country. A prime mover in establishing the ASLA, he was its president in 1902 and 1906–07. He died in New York City, February 3, 1923.

George F. Pentecost, Jr., was born in 1875, started his practice in New York in 1896, and was Parsons' partner at the time of the ASLA's founding in their office. Shortly thereafter they were engaged in Washington on work between the White House and the Washington Monument that antedated the McMillan Commission studies. Pentecost did numerous residential projects, land subdivisions, parks, and golf courses. He was intermittently active in affairs of the Society; the last meeting at which his attendance is recorded was the twentieth annual meeting in New York in 1919, and he resigned from the Society in 1921.

Ossian Cole Simonds was born in Grand Rapids, Michigan, in 1855. He took his degree as Civil Engineer from the University of Michigan in 1878 and for a time was a member of the architectural firm of Holabird, Simonds & Roche in Chicago. He then became superintendent and landscape architect of Chicago's Graceland Cemetery, which he developed into one of the most remarkable park-like cemeteries of the Western world. After 1888 he branched out into an extensive private practice, starting with the layout of Fort Sheridan, Illinois; but Graceland continues to be regarded as his masterpiece. The ASLA elected him president in 1913, the first sign of a move away from the Atlantic seaboard. In 1929 the University of Michigan conferred upon him the honorary degree Master of Arts, citing his creative work in landscape architecture. In his latter years his firm was known as Simonds, West & Blair. He died in Chicago, November 20, 1931.

Downing Vaux was the son of Calvert Vaux and worked with his father from the middle 1880s onward. After the father's death in 1895, the son practiced alone on a wide variety of projects including parks, institutional grounds, and the usual residential properties. Elected secretary of the ASLA at the first annual meeting in 1900, he served in that capacity with complete devotion through the Society's difficult first decade. Poor health finally compelled him to retire; after an extended illness he died in Kingston, New York, May 15, 1926.

Anyone familiar with the ever-widening practice of landscape architecture is fully aware that this is not likely to be an overpopulated profession. There is good reason for its relatively small size, as professions go. An unusual combination of concerns and capacities has proved essential in a well-rounded landscape architect. He must have a compelling interest in, and sensitivity to, the environment as a whole. This requires of him a *total* view of ecology: a deep and abiding grasp of the natural world as an ongoing process of which humans are an integral part. He needs innate responsiveness to people, to their problems, and to the quality of life surrounding them. With it all he must be a visualist: fundamental to his approach is a sense of design, an intimate concern for specific form at every scale, and a keen appreciation of visual relationships as these affect human behavior. His mission insists on a creative urge and a dedicated search for excellence. It asks of him the ability to see, feel, and think—all with clarity—and to communicate visually as well as verbally.

Then, above all, he must possess the capacity, both as a lone practitioner and in collaboration as an equal with other professionals, to blend his outlook, knowledge, and varied skills into effective action for the service of society at all levels. Ideally, this demands of every landscape architect a combination of faculties not to be found in many individuals, even in the embryonic form of early interests and aptitudes. Landscape architecture accordingly is not and in the opinion of some probably never can be a massive profession. The public need—which becomes greater every day in the face of society's destruction of the environment—will inevitably exceed the supply of competent landscape architects. Nevertheless, that little group of founders assembled in

1899 could hardly have envisioned their organization with a membership approaching fifteen hundred just seven decades later.

Such at least was the conclusion one had to reach from conversations, during their latter years, with the last four survivors of the original eleven: Manning, Lowrie, F. L. Olmsted, and Mrs. Farrand. Symbols of a conviction well served through years of effort, yet invariably warm and human and compassionate toward their young successors, they were a joy to know. One could long remember Manning's piercing gaze and vigorously jutting white beard, Lowrie's calm energy, quiet good humor, and quick encouraging smile, Olmsted's wise and twinkly eyes over the half-spectacles, and the gracious bearing of that great lady Mrs. Farrand, who always referred to herself in unfailing telegrams to annual meetings of the Society as "ancient charter member."

XXVII. The American Academy in Rome

Before moving too far in time from the Columbian Exposition, it would be well to consider three phenomena that resulted more or less directly from the Fair and from associations formed during its design and execution: the American Academy in Rome, established in 1894; the plan of Washington by the McMillan Commission of 1901; the so-called City Beautiful movement, stimulated by publications of Charles Mulford Robinson in 1901 and 1903 and culminating in Burnham's Chicago Plan of 1909.

The American Academy in Rome was the creation of McKim, who had fully enjoyed the happy collaborative spirit that had encouraged unity at the Fair. Completely convinced that in the arts paramount merit stemmed from Rome, he even felt strongly that for those like himself who had been trained at the Ecole in Paris a final period of observation and study in Rome was a necessity. It was no more than natural for him to seek means whereby to establish in the Eternal City an American institution to foster the collaborative process and perpetuate the "classical ideal," which he obviously and sincerely believed to have been in the main responsible for the success of the Columbian Exposition.

For what he wanted to do McKim saw as precedent the French Academy, founded in Rome by order of Louis XIV in the seventeenth century and since 1801 housed in the Villa Medici on the Pincio. McKim's aim was to develop, along much the same lines, what he referred to as "a School of Contact and Research (not of original design), National in character, endowed and maintained through the public spirit of individuals."[1] He had talked of his hopes

1. Moore, *McKim*, p. 138.

in conversations with Burnham in the Shack, and Burnham remained a staunch ally through the years. Though his goal was the eventual founding of a fully collaborative American academy in the allied arts, McKim approached the problem by seeking first to establish what seemed immediately possible: a Roman atelier, as he called it temporarily, for postgraduate study in architecture. After the Fair had closed, he went to New York to work on the deans of the existing schools of architecture, hoping that he could persuade them to send the annual winners of the schools' traveling scholarships to such a Roman atelier, making at least a start for the ultimate.

McKim met with enthusiastic response from the heads of the schools and from leading members of the architectural profession. Agreement was reached in autumn 1894, and the American School of Architecture in Rome was formally established. Pending endowment for independent "Roman Prizes," the first students were to be the three holders of traveling scholarships from Columbia, Pennsylvania, and the Rotch Committee in Boston. Temporary quarters were obtained on an upper floor of the Palazzo Torlonia, and frankly primitive equipment was installed. Running expenses for at least the year ahead had been raised (mainly from the pockets of McKim and Burnham), and a campaign was begun to raise money for the permanent establishment.

In the spring of 1895 the American School of Architecture was incorporated in New York State, with Burnham as president and McKim as vice-president; in Rome it moved into the Villa dell'Aurora, formerly part of the Villa Ludovisi, near the French Academy. These visible signs of progress for architecture quickly encouraged similar activity in other fields. Within a short time steps were taken to set up "departments" of archeology, sculpture, and painting, with lively cooperation from leaders in each area. All concerned agreed upon the desirability of forming an American academy to embrace the three arts, as originally contemplated by McKim. The archeologists, representing the Classical Schools at Rome and Athens, felt that unfortunately they had not the power to join with the others.

The American Academy in Rome was at last formally organized at a meeting held on June 8, 1897, at the Century Club in New York. A constitution was adopted, assumption of the rights and obligations of the American School of Architecture in Rome was agreed upon, articles of incorporation in the state of New York were approved, and the nine professional members of the first Board of Trustees were elected. They were Blashfield, John La Farge, and Frederick Crowninshield, painters; Saint-Gaudens, French, and J. Q. A. Ward, sculptors; Burnham, McKim, and F. W. Chandler, architects. Among them, four of McKim's friendly colleagues on the World's Fair collaborative team—Burnham, Blashfield, Saint-Gaudens, and French—had been actively helpful from the start. A few weeks later the nine professional board members, as provided in the articles of agreement, added to their number by electing five lay members to represent the community at large. In September the whole Board met and elected McKim as president of the Academy.

Meanwhile, things continued to run smoothly in Rome, so far as one could tell, year after year. The Academy was still in the Villa dell'Aurora when in 1904 private generosity made possible the start of negotiations to purchase the larger Villa Mirafiore, on the Via Nomentana out beyond the Porta Pia. In a financial sense, these first ten years had been far from easy; the Academy was kept going solely by McKim's energy in raising funds among public-spirited citizens, with frequent and generous additions from himself and Burnham. The high point had come in 1901, when Henry Walters of Baltimore and J. Pierpont Morgan of New York agreed to lend their names to an endowment campaign, which they later topped off with their own large contributions.

The year 1905 was a momentous one. A firm foundation for the Academy's endowment was laid by the munificent Walters-Morgan gifts and those of a few other donors, all of whom were thereupon designated Founders of the American Academy in Rome by the Board of Trustees. Then on March 3, 1905, President Roosevelt signed into law an Act of Congress incorporating the Academy and granting it a national charter. This had been one of McKim's major hopes and was realized mainly through his persistence. In 1907 the endowment fund had reached a point where the Trustees could award the first regular Fellowships in Architecture, Painting, and Sculpture on the Rome Prize, each for a term of three years. In the same year the Academy was moved into the Villa Mirafiore, the purchase of which had been effected the year before.

Continued periods of illness compelled McKim in 1908 to leave the office of McKim, Mead & White for what was intended as a long vacation. But his health did not improve, and on September 14, 1909, he died at St. James, Long Island. In the main, of course, his dream for an American Academy in Rome had been realized. Ironically, a final momentous step that led to the Academy's present superb location overlooking the entire city came immediately after McKim's death. Only a month later the Trustees learned that Mrs. Clara Jessup Heyland, an American who had lived in Rome, had bequeathed to the Academy the historic Villa Aurelia, her property on the Janiculum. Here at the Porta San Pancrazio and along the roads outside it, Garibaldi and his faithful followers had fought in 1849 one of the fiercest of his battles, defending the walls of the new Roman republic. The Villa Aurelia (or Savorelli, as it was then known), though badly shattered, had served as Garibaldi's headquarters during the tragic month-long siege.

The trustees accepted the Villa Aurelia in 1910 and shortly thereafter received the gift of enough additional adjacent land to accommodate a whole new establishment. In 1912, the Congressional charter having been appropriately amended, the Academy was joined by the American School of Classical Studies (founded in Rome in 1895), and a new building was started in which to house the enlarged American Academy in Rome. Occupied in the autumn of 1914, it became and still is the home of the Academy (Fig.

253. The American Academy in Rome occupied this new building by McKim, Mead and White on the Janiculum, overlooking the city, in 1914.

253), with its two components, the School of Fine Arts and the School of Classical Studies.

Despite the deceptive terminology, the Academy was not intended as a school in the usual sense: it offered no instruction or fixed courses. Winners of the Rome Prize, chosen competitively (normally one a year in each of the arts and two or three in the classics), were expected to have reached a high level of competence in their respective fields and to be capable of using effectively the terms of their Fellowships for further advancement by individual effort. Major reliance was placed on the value of collaboration—on the Fellows' acquiring understanding of the aims and ways of each other's arts from living, working, and traveling together. In effect the Academy, the sort of place so aptly described by McKim in 1894 as "a School of Contact and Research," was for postgraduate study. These governing conditions of the Academy continue.

In 1915, thanks primarily to the efforts of Ferruccio Vitale and Frederick Law Olmsted, landscape architecture took its rightful place at the Academy as one of the allied arts, and a three-year Fellowship in Landscape Architecture was established. This was followed in 1921 by the founding of Fellowships in Musical Composition. By the end of the 1920s the Academy had a full complement of Fellowships: three each in Architecture, Painting, Sculpture, Landscape Architecture, Musical Composition, and Classical Studies.

It was also at about this time, as the Academy approached its fifth decade, that the first signs of revolt against the policy of *perpetuating* the "classical ideal" appeared among the Fellows. To creatively intelligent young people a deep-seated conviction had been growing steadily for some years, especially after the first world war, that there was something basically unsound about following the forms of a distant past to meet the different needs and problems of an immediate present. The rational spirit of the twentieth century was asserting itself, despite the persistent effects of America's long eclectic hibernation. The writings of Le Corbusier were eagerly read and exerted considerable influence. The revolt, of course, was not against the historic monuments themselves. There was little if any disposition to question the greatness of these things, in their own time and place: the majesty of the Pantheon, the delicate strength of the Cancelleria, the fitness of the Roman villas to their sites, the sheer brilliance of the sculptors and painters of the Florentine Quattrocento. But the more profoundly one knew and admired these works, the more clearly one saw them as great in their own context of space-time, not to be transported bodily to other times and places for other purposes.

These problems were naturally of no special moment to the Fellows in Classical Studies, but to those in the arts they were increasingly insistent. To some of the Trustees, on the other hand, the Fellows' questioning attitude was distressing indeed; it seemed like the stumbling of a wayward child. Unfortunately, the Trustees tried to combat the tide by adopting an official "Credo," a statement of belief in eternal supremacy of the "classical ideal" and a promise to support the traditional policy that was to be signed as a condition of receiving the Rome Prize.

This thoroughly ill-advised measure did not last, and it accomplished little except to intensify the spirit of rebellion and magnify falsely the Academy's image as a stronghold of traditionalism and resistance to change. Meanwhile, the arts in America were clearly swinging away from the jaded habits of eclecticism toward a brighter day. It was a period of much confusion and only partial understanding. With the exaggerated zeal that seems to flourish at such times, too many young Americans took to denying the existence of anything older than yesterday afternoon and to looking askance at all foreign travel and study. The term of the Rome Prize Fellowship, in response to the mood of applicants, was reduced in 1931 from three years to two. Although the number of applications remained high, throughout the 1930s the Academy suffered from the reputation that had been unjustly fastened to it for addiction to worship of the past. Actually, eclecticism had been rejected by the Fellows themselves, and the valuable collaborative experience remained the major asset. But the actuality was not enough; what was needed was official recognition of the new spirit. And this rejuvenation of the Academy was not fully accomplished until after World War II.

During the war, the Academy's physical properties were placed under protection of the Swiss legation and came through unharmed. The Fellowships were actively resumed in the fall of 1947 but with several changes. Official dedication to the "classical ideal" was at last abandoned and creative freedom was guaranteed. The term of the Fellowship was further reduced from two years to one, with the possibility of renewal for another year. Married applicants were declared eligible, the age limit was lifted, and the lengthy prewar competitions were eliminated, awards thereafter to be made on the basis of submittals of work already done. The Fellowships in Fine Arts were opened to women (those in the Classics had been open to them all along). A Fellowship in Art History was added in the School of Classical Studies, and the archeological frame of reference was broadened so as to include postclassical periods.

Since the reopening in 1947 there have been a few other changes, leading mainly toward even more diversification. In 1951 a Fellowship in Literature was established for creative writing; most recently, Fellowships in Musicology have been awarded. In cooperation with the Fulbright Commission, a large number of American holders of Fulbright Fellowships have been accepted at the Academy, and hospitality has been extended to Italian scholars whose Fulbright Research Grants allow them to work there instead of in the United States. The expanding roster and the wider range of the Academy's officially recognized interests, coupled with changing times and rising costs of operation, may eventually alter the essential character of the Academy or modify its mission. Some observers regard these changes as inevitable; only time will tell.

Regardless of whether changes are still to occur, the profession of landscape architecture, in the half-century or more since its Fellowships were established at the Academy, has already gained much through its representatives—perhaps more than the other arts. Certain it is that, in the days of revolt against perpetuation of the "classical ideal," the Fellows in Landscape Architecture were envied at the Academy because they, like the Fellows in Musical Composition, were allowed almost complete freedom from official "classical" restraints. Neither group had any difficulty obtaining approval for travel to England and other territory to the north; whereas, incredible though it may seem today, the architects, painters, sculptors, and classicists were generally restricted to travel in what were known as "classical lands." To the landscape architects and composers virtually the whole of Europe was then open, as it is now to all Fellows of the Academy. And Italy itself, not to mention travel elsewhere, has long offered a remarkable array of superlative works of landscape architecture: country villas, urban piazze, hill-hugging medieval towns, boldly ordered later city plans—instances in wide variety demonstrating techniques old and new for successfully arranging outdoor space upon the land. Such experience is all the more valuable today, as against what it was in the eclectic era, in that no designer is now expected to reproduce these works or imitate their detailed forms in another context.

To all the arts and to scholarship it is obvious that the Academy has made an outstanding contribution. It has given highly skilled young people the opportunity to experience the best accomplishments of other epochs and to increase their own skills with depth of understanding. Within the limitations imposed by the values, customs, and tastes of a period, the Fellows in the arts have represented consistently the highest level of technical and creative achievement. As outlooks have shifted with the times, the Fellows have themselves participated in the new directions—or, indeed, have on occasion anticipated them.

Though present-day judgment may find McKim sadly mistaken in his desire to perpetuate the "classical ideal" of the Columbian Exposition, tribute must be paid him on other counts. In creating the American Academy in Rome he gave selected young men and women, free for a time from financial pressures, a firm operating base from which to enlarge their comprehension through travel and firsthand observation. Above all, he earned the lasting gratitude of succeeding generations for having sensed the importance and fostered the development of what is still the Academy's main strength, the collaborative spirit.

XXVIII. The McMillan Commission's Plan of Washington

Another direct consequence of the World's Columbian Exposition took form eight years after the Fair: the work of the Senate Park Commission of 1901, usually called the McMillan Commission, in revival and preservation of Pierre L'Enfant's original plan for the Federal City of Washington in the District of Columbia. The members of the Commission—the younger Olmsted, Burnham, McKim, and Saint-Gaudens—owed their selection primarily to the resounding collaborative success of the Columbian Exposition. The services they performed, as well as the events preceding them as far back as the founding of the nation, are of cardinal importance not only to designers but indeed to all Americans; for Washington is every citizen's national capital. Generally considered one of the handsomest capitals in the world, it cannot stay that way without the attention of a devoted citizenry. In the context of this account the city has added significance as an outstanding example, not only of landscape architecture, but of collaboration in the finest sense of the term. Here four professionals, each of top rank, worked hand in hand, merging their efforts unselfishly toward achievement of a common goal. Their opportunity to do so was due to the devotion and initiative of Senator James McMillan of Michigan.

The District of Columbia was created in July 1790 by Congress, then sitting in Philadelphia. This federal area was to be approximately ten miles square, on land straddling the Potomac River and ceded to the United States by Maryland and Virginia. The task of locating the District precisely and creating a capital city within it was given to President Washington, who placed it just below the falls of the Potomac at the head of navigation and sent Major Andrew Ellicott to survey and mark the boundaries. Washington then called in a young French military engineer, Major Pierre Charles L'Enfant, to lay out a federal city in the District in consultation with the President himself.

L'Enfant, having studied the ground carefully—often by himself and later in the President's company—first selected locations for the Congress House (now the Capitol), on a rise known as Jenkin's Heights, and for the President's House (now the White House). Then, true to French tradition as he had known it all his life, he projected from the two locations a pair of sight-lines perpendicular to each other, one westward from the site of Congress House, the other southward from the site of the President's House. On each sight-line he provided a wide swath of space, and where the two crossed, at a point then close to the Potomac, he indicated an "equestrian figure of George Washington." Upon this basic skeleton L'Enfant set up next a rather elaborate system of radiating avenues, focusing on Congress House and the President's House and including a straight vista between them. In the best Versailles tradition, crossings of the radiating avenues were to be marked by open spaces. Unfortunately, the diagonal avenues occasionally made awkward angular intersections with the rectilinear grid of north-south and east-west streets that the three Commissioners of the District and Secretary of State Thomas Jefferson had already specified to be named "alphabetically one way and numerically the other, from the Capitol."[1] Otherwise, however, it was a distinguished and impressive plan. On December 13, 1791, President Washington transmitted the L'Enfant Plan to the Congress with a favorable recommendation (Fig. 254).

The plan was quickly approved, but L'Enfant himself became so intractable—flatly refusing to accept orders from the three Commissioners legally responsible for management of the District of Columbia—that his services had to be terminated in March 1792. He refused the compensation recommended by the President, demanded a fee some twenty times as large, and spent the rest of his life, a pathetically haughty figure, petitioning Congress for what he insisted was due him. He died in 1825; his tomb, marked by a raised stone tablet, is in front of Arlington mansion in a spot from which today one can survey the sweep of the entire Federal City. On L'Enfant's dismissal, work on the city plan was turned over to Ellicott. The Ellicott plan (Fig. 255) followed that of L'Enfant closely but was much more carefully and exactly drawn. Though it clarified in a few instances the pattern of diagonal avenues, it was essentially an excellent delineation of the original L'Enfant plan.

The seat of government was officially moved from Philadelphia to Washington on December 12, 1800; the Capitol and the President's House were

1. Commission of Fine Arts, *Thirteenth Report* (Washington, 1939), p. 11.

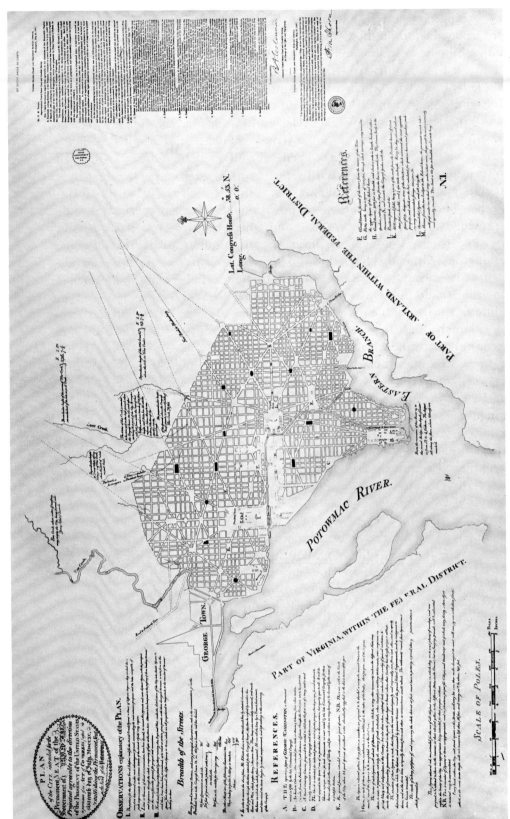

254. The plan of 1791 by Major Pierre Charles L'Enfant for the Federal City, traced from the original by the Coast and Geodetic Survey in 1887.

in place and nearly four hundred dwelling houses had been built, but much of the projected city was still a tract of swampy land. The L'Enfant plan continued to be followed, on the whole, as long as Jefferson lived. From 1830 through the nineteenth century, however, the city grew in haphazard fashion, with little or no attention to what had been the L'Enfant plan. Several serious blunders were made through ignorance and lack of foresight. In 1837 President Jackson caused the Treasury Building to be erected athwart the sight-line of Pennsylvania Avenue, blocking the vista that L'Enfant had intended from the Capitol to the White House (as the President's House was called when painted after the British had burned it in the War of 1812). The Smithsonian Building, begun in 1846, was so placed that it jutted into the space L'Enfant had planned as a wide allée from the Capitol westward. In the same year the Virginia portion of the District was foolishly ceded back to the state. Perhaps the most vexing departure from the L'Enfant plan was treatment of the railroad problem, for which L'Enfant had of course been unprepared. Tracks were introduced in about 1835 across the main sight-line westward from the Capitol, and then in 1872 Congress permitted construction of a railroad station in the middle of what is now the Mall.

L'Enfant's proposal for a monument to General Washington was carried out, but not precisely as to either form or location. Fortunately, the indicated "equestrian figure" was not erected; it is obvious today that an equestrian statue at this position in the great plan would have been either too small to fulfill its design function or too massive to make sense as a horse and rider. In 1836 a competition was held, and a relatively unknown young architect, Robert Mills, emerged as winner with an admirable obelisk design. But when the cornerstone was laid in 1848 the engineers, seeking firm subsoil for foundation, ignored L'Enfant's intent and located the base about four hundred feet to the southeast of the crossing of sight-lines from the Capitol and the White House. Moreover, the monument was allowed to stand unfinished, a truncated stub, from 1854 until 1884, when at last it was completed in its soaring white eye-compelling simplicity.

By the close of the nineteenth century, Washington was thus but a faint suggestion of the imposing national capital that L'Enfant had envisioned. To be sure, the land area had been extended through reclamation of swampy acres from the river southwest of the Washington Monument, but nothing had been done to use this extension. On December 12, 1900, the centennial of the transfer of government from Philadelphia to Washington was celebrated with appropriate fanfare. One of the many events was a gathering at the White House, by invitation of President McKinley, to see a new set of plans for enlargement of that building—plans that were quickly opposed by the American Institute of Architects, convening in Washington for the centennial, by Senator McMillan, chairman of the Senate Committee on the District of Columbia, and apparently by almost everybody else. The Senator was

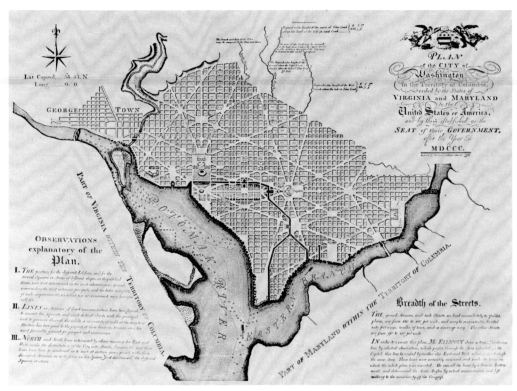

255. Plan drawn by the American surveyor Andrew Ellicott, essentially a clarification of L'Enfant's plan.

particularly irked because, convinced that the shabby, unfinished appearance of Washington could be corrected, he had urged an appropriation to cover a study of the District's parks. Use of the appropriated funds to pay for the unacceptable White House plans he regarded as an especially inexcusable diversion. He thereupon introduced a resolution, adopted by the Senate on March 8, 1901, authorizing his Committee to study and report on the entire park system of the District and for this purpose "to secure the services of such experts as may be necessary for proper consideration of the subject." [2] The term "such experts" shortly came to mean the four members of the famous McMillan Commission, chosen carefully by the Senator.

Keenly aware of the landscape architectural nature of the Washington problem, Senator McMillan wished he could call in the elder Olmsted, whom he had been instrumental in commissioning to create Belle Isle Park in Detroit over twenty years earlier. He had also been much impressed by Olmsted's brilliant contribution to the Columbian Exposition, and he admired the man profoundly. But he knew that Olmsted had retired from practice and was

2. Moore, *Burnham*, I, 137.

unavailable. So, assuming the likelihood that the father's great ability had been passed on to the son, the Senator settled on Frederick Law Olmsted, Jr., then only thirty-one but already widely experienced in association with his father. To join Olmsted the Senator selected Burnham, not only because of his reputation as a successful architect of large projects, but especially because the Senator had great respect for his job as director of works at the Columbian Exposition, where he had acted as coordinator of a first-rate collaborative team. Burnham and Olmsted, asked to choose an additional architect, agreed immediately on McKim; he accepted after some persuasion, and a few weeks later, at his suggestion, Saint-Gaudens was invited to join the group—the Senate Park Commission of 1901. As the eldest, Burnham was designated chairman. To aid the Commission Senator McMillan assigned his political secretary of the past eleven years, Charles Moore, whose familiarity with administrative matters in the Senate and in the District proved extremely helpful.

At one of the earliest meetings of the Commission, Burnham suggested that together they should take a brief European trip to study the major examples of landscape architecture done on the grand scale that would aid them in the Washington task. Senator McMillan concurred in the proposal and volunteered to advance funds personally for expenses, trusting to the Senate to reimburse him later. Such an expedition at government expense was then almost unheard of; it must be remembered, however, that the Commission served through many months of arduous work without salary. Plans were made to sail in June. In April, Burnham, Olmsted, and McKim did a quick circuit of Virginia places, including Williamsburg, Upper and Lower Brandon, Westover, and Shirley, to refresh their understanding of the kinds of surroundings enjoyed by Washington and Jefferson in their day.

On June 13 the three members and Moore sailed for Cherbourg; unfortunately, slow recovery from recent illness prevented Saint-Gaudens from joining them. Before landing again in New York on August 1, the travelers had visited Paris, Rome, Venice, Vienna, Budapest, and London. Together they had studied and discussed the Bois de Boulogne, the Tuileries and the Luxembourg, Villa d'Este, Hadrian's Villa, the Piazza di San Pietro and the Piazza San Marco, Fontainebleau, Versailles, Vaux-le-Vicomte, Hyde Park, Hatfield, and Hampton Court, as well as numerous other places. Olmsted had drawn up the itinerary and brought along a tin cylinder of District of Columbia maps, which were customarily taken out for each evening's discussion of the day's experiences and their relevance to the Commission's complex project. Only Olmsted had given much concentrated professional thought to the Washington problem before appointment of the Commission: his father, after all, had been engaged on layout of the Capitol grounds nearly a half-century earlier, and the son had been exposed to talk about the capital from boyhood. At the AIA Convention of 1900 in Washington, a paper by "young

Rick Olmsted" on the city's problem had been a major contribution. Accordingly, despite his relative youth, his service on the McMillan Commission was of exceptional value and enabled him to crystallize thoughts about Washington that had long occupied his professional attention.

Before the travelers returned to America, one of their most bothersome problems was unexpectedly solved. Even before the Commission was appointed, Burnham had been retained by President Cassatt of the Pennsylvania Railroad to design a new Washington station for the company. Burnham had done his utmost to persuade Cassatt to build on a new site, one that would not continue to block development of the L'Enfant plan westward from the Capitol. In July, when the group reached London on the homeward leg of their trip, Burnham was called to a conference with Cassatt at the latter's hotel; he returned to his colleagues with momentous news. The Pennsylvania Railroad had recently acquired control of the Baltimore and Ohio, and Cassatt was willing to give up the Mall location in favor of a union station on the B&O site north of the Capitol, provided that Senator McMillan could get the government to appropriate $1,500,000 toward the cost of a railroad tunnel under Capitol Hill for lines running south. Burnham was fully confident that Congress would complete this bargain, and events within a few short months proved him right.

The travelers returned on August 1; on August 20 they reported to Senator McMillan at his summer home north of Boston and laid plans for preparing and presenting the Commission's recommendations publicly. The chief components of the proposed plans had been sketched out and agreed upon in the course of many discussions during the trip. To prepare the whole for submission to the Senate Committee on the District, two workrooms were made available. In April, immediately upon appointment, the Commission had secured drafting space in the Senate Press Gallery. Here a small staff under a job-captain from his own office had been charged by Olmsted with gathering material on the entire District of Columbia, preparatory to a study for a completely integrated park system for the District. In August a second workroom was set up in McKim's New York office, where he and Olmsted, with Saint-Gaudens as frequent consultant, worked with a sizable staff on drawings embodying the Commission's proposals for the great central composition of the Washington plan (Fig. 256). Burnham, in his Chicago office, worked on plans for the new Union Station, a plaza in front of it, and approaches to the Capitol from this railroad gateway. Meanwhile, the Commission's report to the Senate Committee on the District was being prepared in Washington by Olmsted and Moore.

Two highly important visual aids were incorporated in the presentation. Before going abroad, Burnham had obtained Senator McMillan's approval for construction of a pair of scale models to show existing and proposed conditions; built by George C. Curtis of Boston under Commission guidance, the models were strikingly effective in impressing President Roosevelt, Con-

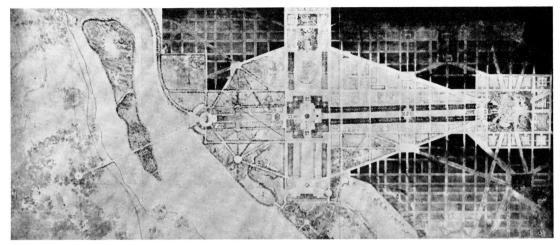

256. The McMillan Commission's plan of 1901, proposing virtual reinstatement of the L'Enfant plan.

gress, and the public (Figs. 257–260). For much the same anticipated result, McKim was authorized to enlist the nation's foremost illustrators to render the proposals in color; among them was the exquisite series by Jules Guerin that became famous as models of rendering for several successive generations of architectural and landscape architectural students. The wealth of material assembled—plans, perspectives, bird's-eye views (Fig. 261), models, renderings, and telling enlargements of some of Olmsted's European photographs—made a smashing display in rooms provided at the Corcoran Gallery of Art. The grand opening was on the evening of January 15, 1902. On that morning the Senate Committee on the District of Columbia had approved unanimously its report conveying the final report of the Park Commission and recommending adoption of the Commission's plans. The Committee Report, later printed as *Senate Report No. 166, 57th Congress,* was formally presented by Senator McMillan when the Senate met that noon.

In effect, the Senate Park Commission Plan of 1901, as it came to be known, was an exact revival of the L'Enfant plan of 1791. The new plan differed from L'Enfant's only in steps taken to correct some of the worst nineteenth-century blunders. The off-center placing of the Washington Monument was accommodated by establishing an entirely new sight-line from the Capitol dome *through* the monument in its actual position, then extending the line westward across reclaimed swamp land on a long reflecting basin to a proposed monument to President Lincoln near the new edge of the river. From a *rond-point* surrounding this monument a memorial bridge would span the Potomac to the Virginia shore and Arlington Cemetery.

The old north-south sight-line from the White House was unchanged but was to be strengthened by locating a large circular basin and fountain at the crossing west of the Washington Monument; the line was prolonged

257. The McMillan Commission's scale model of Washington as it existed in 1901; looking westward from above the Capitol.

258. Similar view, companion to the preceding model: Washington as proposed for the future by the McMillan Commission.

southward to a subsidiary group where the Jefferson Memorial stands today. Around the Monument itself an elaborate setting was proposed, with broad terraces and stairways instead of the grassy mound that existed. The extended sight-lines were made the definite center-lines of a spatial structure even stronger than that of the L'Enfant plan. The problem of disparate buildings bordering the Mall or jutting into it was solved by the use, at Olmsted's suggestion, of two double rows of elms on the sides. As a result, the long central allée would be clearly formed by verdure, rather than uncomfortably by variegated buildings, and the buildings themselves would be effectively screened.

The Commission's proposals were not limited to treatment of the central composition of what has come to be known as the "kite plan." The 1901 study also incorporated a new Potomac Park along the river and a proposed parkway to the northwest. The Anacostia Flats, southeast of the center, were to be regained for recreational use, and park roads were projected to Mount Vernon on the south, to the Great Falls of the Potomac upstream, and to quiet islands in the river. Throughout the city, the open spaces suggested by L'Enfant were retained with appropriate emphasis.

The exhibits in the Corcoran Gallery—nearly two hundred of them—were enthusiastically received and widely publicized, both in America and abroad. All in all, the 1901 plan offered not only a rededication to the ideal of the great national capital envisioned by L'Enfant over a century earlier; it also rectified ways in which that early dream had been violated and went on to

259. Model showing existing conditions in 1901, looking eastward toward the Capitol.

260. Similar view, companion model: the Commission's proposal.

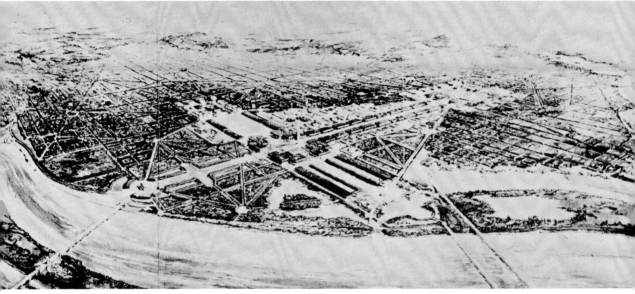

261. Bird's-eye sketch of the McMillan Commission's plan.

project an even larger magnificence. On the whole, development of the Federal City since 1901 has been in conformity with the McMillan Commission's plan (Fig. 262). The only noticeable omission is that of the proposed base of extensive terraces for the Washington Monument. Unstable subsoil, the very condition that prompted the shift in 1848, is still a serious problem. Many studies have been made to provide a suitable architectonic platform for the monument, but it must be remembered that this area was once almost surrounded by water, and the possibility of affecting the subsoil water table or of otherwise undermining the obelisk itself has counseled against major excavation for walls in the vicinity.

Another impediment to full realization of the potentials has been the apparent need in times of national crisis for makeshift "temporary" buildings, mainly in the Mall, with a stubborn resistance to removal even after the generating emergency has passed; continual expansion of federal activity renders their displacement ever more difficult in a city where demands for space tend always to exceed supply. Some solutions to the space problem have been found by moving whole agencies to other cities, but that is another story. So too is the extent to which the impressive grandeur of the great showpiece has been allowed to develop cheek by jowl with lamentably impoverished slum areas behind the scenes. This is, fortunately, being corrected, but all too slowly.

Adherence to the 1901 plan has not been accomplished without some struggle. Senator McMillan's death in August 1902 removed the most in-

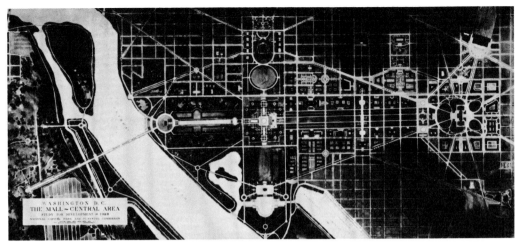

262. Official "kite plan" of the city, prepared in 1928 by the National Capital Park and Planning Commission.

fluential supporter of the plan. Almost immediately it became necessary to fight against intrusions upon the Mall; at various times in this campaign all four Commission members took active part. Although the Commission itself had expired with the submission of its report, President Theodore Roosevelt asked the members to continue advising him unofficially. Later he added others to form in 1905 a large Council on the Arts. Congress, however, apparently feeling insufficiently consulted, killed the Council by withholding funds.

The need for some duly constituted advisory body in Washington was nevertheless completely obvious, and in 1910 President Taft, sidestepping the difficulty encountered by his predecessor, persuaded Congress itself to establish the national Commission of Fine Arts. This seven-man group, its members appointed by the President for four-year terms, has customarily consisted of three architects, a landscape architect, a painter, a sculptor, and an art historian or critic. President Taft appointed Burnham chairman and Olmsted and Moore members of the first Commission. The landscape architect members have been, after Olmsted, James L. Greenleaf, Ferruccio Vitale, Gilmore D. Clarke, Elbert Peets, Michael Rapuano, and Hideo Sasaki. Though by law purely advisory, the Commission has been called upon freely by Congress and the executive departments. Mistakes of planning even more disastrous than the infamous ones of the nineteenth century have on several occasions been prevented by patient advice of the Commission.

In recent years the Commission of Fine Arts has often been criticized as reactionary in its outlook, an accusation that is far from just. By the very nature of its establishment for a protective purpose over a half-century ago, the Commission has had to be conservative rather than experimentally progressive or avant-garde. To be sure, much of Washington's public architecture smacks of the overopulent, overcolumned "classical ideal," but reasonable criticism recalls that America's inane form of eclecticism persisted as a sort of national idiom far into the 1930s; surely the Commission cannot be blamed for it. As for the Commission's conservatism—far more to the point is the understanding and protection accorded to the McMillan Commission's Plan of 1901 and thus, in turn, to the inspired vision of Pierre L'Enfant.

XXIX. The City Beautiful Movement and City Planning

A third consequence of the Columbian Exposition was the direct product of the Fair's stimulus to public interest in civic design. It is hardly probable that many visitors were conscious of such matters as design implications in any technical sense—or even knew clearly what it was they liked about the Fair beyond the sheer size, the fantasy, the whiteness, the sculpture, and surely the magical electric lights. But, whatever the reason, people were tremendously impressed. And when they returned to their homes in cities all over America they carried with them a certain starry-eyed excitement over the possibility of emulating in hometowns some of the impressiveness sensed at the Fair.

Heightened public awareness brought about tangible results in varied ways both large and small. Among the most active participants in the process of educating the public—for that is what it amounted to—were a relatively unknown young journalist from Rochester, New York, named Charles Mulford Robinson and the Fair's now famous director of works, Daniel Hudson Burnham. Their backgrounds and approaches were naturally quite different. Robinson, who had taken his A. B. degree at the University of Rochester in 1891, was an editor on the *Post-Express* of that city at the time of the Fair. He was fascinated by the splendor of the Exposition and also by its appreciable effect on public opinion. In fact, one of his earliest independent writings, based on his own reactions, was "The Fair as Spectacle," a description and history of the Columbian Exposition issued by its Board of Directors in

Chicago. Experience of the Fair added impetus to Robinson's intuitive preoccupation with the form and functioning of cities at a time when little attention had been given city planning as a distinct area of professional activity.

To be sure, William Penn had laid out Philadelphia with predetermined open spaces, Oglethorpe had given Savannah its early squares, and L'Enfant's plan for Washington had recently been rediscovered. The elder Olmsted had been engaged in planning portions of New York and of Boston's Back Bay, all as a normal part of his landscape architectural practice. Cleveland had been an active missionary in the midwest, but his work was little known elsewhere. Eliot had included some town planning in his practice, along with his great regional work on metropolitan parks. But these were comparatively isolated instances; it would be another decade at least before any considerable number of landscape architects would make city planning a major part of professional operation. Moreover, no study or writing had been done about cities in general; so Robinson was truly a pioneer in his articles and editorials about the planning of cities, or more especially about their improvement, with constant emphasis on their *appearance*. "Civic aesthetics" became for him a rallying-cry, the driving force behind an exceptionally productive though tragically brief lifetime of writing, lecturing, counseling, and more writing. Coming as it did at a moment when popular interest was unusually keen as a consequence of the World's Fair, Robinson's activity had even greater cogency.

The upshot of the shorter pieces was his series for the *Atlantic Monthly* in 1899 entitled "Improvement in City Life." There were three parts in successive monthly issues, "Philanthropic Progress," "Educational Progress," and "Aesthetic Progress." The series aroused a heartening response and led to Robinson's being offered an opportunity to go abroad by *Harper's Magazine*, to observe municipal improvements in Europe and to prepare another series embodying the results. The articles for *Harper's* appeared in 1901 and 1902, but in the meantime Robinson had amassed so much additional material that he brought out his first book, *The Improvement of Towns and Cities, or the Practical Basis of Civic Aesthetics,* in 1901. As an indication of how untraveled was the literary ground he entered, let it be noted that for this book, which was to go through no less than eleven printings in fifteen years, Robinson could find nobody willing to take the original risk of publication—so he brought it out himself. It was almost immediately a best seller.

This little volume did not pretend to be one of the "how to do it" species. Essentially it was a summary or compilation, in narrative form, of what had been done successfully in many towns and cities in America and Europe. It listed over a hundred individual "societies which have done some definite thing to improve a community's appearance."[1] The writing was filled with

1. C. M. Robinson, *The Improvement of Towns and Cities* (New York, 1901), p. ix.

deep conviction and a sublime confidence in "the world-wide civic battle between Ugliness and Beauty" (p. 294). Robinson's remark that "something very like religious fervor can be put into the zeal for city beauty, sustaining it through long patience and slow work" (288), may well have been self-revealing.

The book had a most enthusiastic reception and was reprinted within a few months and then again within a year. It extended hopeful encouragement to hundreds of communities, not only by the sheer multiplicity of examples of actual accomplishments but also by the grass-roots emphasis: "civic art is not an outgrowth only of fashion and large gifts. They can do much to make beautiful a village, but in a populous community the roots should reach down to the common people, to the people who individually have little money but who by the force of their numbers stamp the public taste and opinion, to those to whom the city's care is ultimately committed. There can be no exclusiveness in civic art" (287).

The success of the first book impelled Robinson to enlarge upon it in a second and larger volume, *Modern Civic Art, or the City Made Beautiful.* This came out in 1903, with a second edition in 1904 and a third in 1909. Nowhere is Robinson's profound sense of dedicated mission more firmly and clearly expressed than in the preface to the second edition:

> That there has been a call for a new edition of this volume may be understood as meaning much more than the success of a book. It stands for the progress of the Cause for the furtherance of which the book came into existence. Nothing, indeed, has been more remarkable than the growth of the "civic improvement" movement during the last few years . . . upwards of twelve hundred local "improvement" societies in the United States alone are now recorded . . . The best phase of the movement is not, however, its extent, nor even its vigour and growing efficiency, but the dependence it puts on the ideal. By selecting here and selecting there, the dreamed "City Beautiful" becomes a reality, is made a tangible goal.[2]

"City Beautiful!" That would be the watchword, echoing in one form or another through all of Robinson's general writing. His short pieces entitled "The City Beautiful" appeared in newspapers in 1903 and 1904. Perhaps unfairly, this would be the name bestowed upon all the activity that followed his pleading, the "City Beautiful" movement.

Robinson became phenomenally busy as a city planning consultant, doing no less than twenty-five reports for as many municipalities from New York to Honolulu. This brought him into frequent contact with the increasing number of landscape architects who had meanwhile begun to include the urban scene in the scope of their practice, though usually with concentration

---

2. C. M. Robinson, *Modern Civic Art, or the City Made Beautiful,* 2nd ed. (New York, 1904), pp. iii–iv.

on topography and the utilitarian needs of people rather than on the architectural impressiveness emphasized by Robinson. Of the ASLA founders, Manning, Lowrie, and the younger Olmsted were by now often engaged in city planning projects. In 1903 John Nolen began in Cambridge, Massachusetts, what would soon become his nationwide city planning practice; soon thereafter came Arthur A. Shurtleff (later Shurcliff) and Henry Vincent Hubbard in Boston, and Sid J. Hare with his son, S. Herbert Hare, in Kansas City. In 1909 the National Conference on City Planning was organized, with Olmsted as its first president.

In the same year the first university courses in city planning were offered by Professor James Sturgis Pray at the Harvard School of Landscape Architecture. Robinson, eager for a few months' respite from practice, went to the school the following spring as a guest for research and study. In 1911 he published *The Width and Arrangement of Streets,* in part an outcome of his work at Harvard. Then in 1913, tying himself more formally to the educational field, he accepted appointment to a newly established chair in civic design at the Department of Landscape Architecture (or Landscape Gardening, as it was still called in the midwest) at the University of Illinois. In the midst of his other work he visited the University for several weeks each term. The American Society of Landscape Architects in 1915 elected him to associate membership. In 1916 he completely revised and enlarged his earlier book on streets, publishing it as *City Planning: With Special Reference to the Planning of Streets and Lots.* Then, suddenly and unexpectedly, at the age of forty-nine, he died in 1917 at Albany, New York.

In contrast, whereas Robinson's contribution to the rise of city planning was largely general and theoretical, Burnham's was almost wholly specific and physically actual. In his case, the impact of the Columbian Exposition on civic affairs was immediate. In 1894 James W. Ellsworth, a leading citizen of Chicago and one of those most closely associated with the Fair from the day of its inception, urged Burnham to make a study of Chicago's lakefront, uniting the Jackson Park area more definitely with the city center. Burnham's plan, presented in 1896 at a dinner given by Ellsworth, was received with much enthusiasm and offers of financial support, but for reasons never entirely clear it was shelved without further action until just ten years later. Meanwhile, Burnham had become deeply involved in the Washington efforts of the McMillan Commission and on Union Station with its approaches to the Capitol—work that brought on other calls for his services. In 1902 he was appointed to a three-man commission to advise the city of Cleveland about a civic center. The Group Plan Commission, on which Burnham served as occasion required for some ten years, produced a rather unimaginative plan for a pompous rectangular space tightly bordered by uniformly "classical" buildings.

Also in 1902, Burnham visited San Francisco to confer with members of the Merchants Exchange about a plan for the city. He returned there again that autumn; but nothing developed until 1904, when he was called in by a newly organized Association for the Improvement and Adornment of San Francisco ("Adornment" a revealing title in light of today's hindsight) "to direct and execute a practical and comprehensive plan." As the Association recorded it in a preface to the eventually completed report, "Mr. Burnham accepted the task, giving his services gratuitously, the association paying the expenses incidental to the work and the salaries of his subordinates. At his request a bungalow was built on a spur of Twin Peaks, Willis Polk being the architect. At this point of vantage, selected to command a panorama of the city and to permit uninterrupted study, the work was begun on October 20, 1904."[3]

With Edward H. Bennett in charge of the project locally, Burnham had the plan and report substantially completed by September 1905. They were accepted with formal ceremony by the Mayor and the Board of Supervisors, who thereupon ordered them printed as a municipal publication. The task of preparing a profusely illustrated book containing not only the Report on the Plan but also reproductions of the base maps and all the plans, was finished and bound volumes ready for distribution on April 17, 1906 (Fig. 263). Delivery of the books, however, did not occur, for on the very next day San Francisco suffered the earthquake and fire that left much of the city in ashes. Senator Phelan of California later reported those harrowing days: the people naturally "dropped the ideal plan in order to house themselves and rehabilitate their affairs. It was the worst time to talk of beautification."[4] The Burnham Plan for San Francisco never adequately reached the public and was virtually forgotten. Perhaps this was just as well, for sooner or later the plan would surely have been found too grandiose, with its elaborately monumental plazas superimposed upon the face of the city, connected by diagonal streets and boulevards carved across the already awkward existing gridiron system of streets.

Early in 1904, even before the study of San Francisco had got under way, Burnham was asked by Secretary of War William Howard Taft to visit the Philippines and make plans for Manila and the proposed summer capital at Baguio. Leaving San Francisco in October, Burnham spent about four months in the Orient including six weeks in the Philippines studying conditions and working on plans with his future partner, Peirce Anderson. They submitted the Manila Plan and Report to Secretary Taft in June 1905 and those for Baguio in October. In the Manila plan (Fig. 264), Burnham made the principal visual focus not the old walled town, but an entirely new "Government or National Group" arranged as "a single formal mass" so as to create "a hollow square opening out westward to the sea."[5] From the group

3. D. H. Burnham, *Report of D. H. Burnham on the Improvement and Adornment of San Francisco* (San Francisco, 1905), p. 8.
4. Moore, *Burnham*, II, 3.
5. *Ibid.*, p. 188.

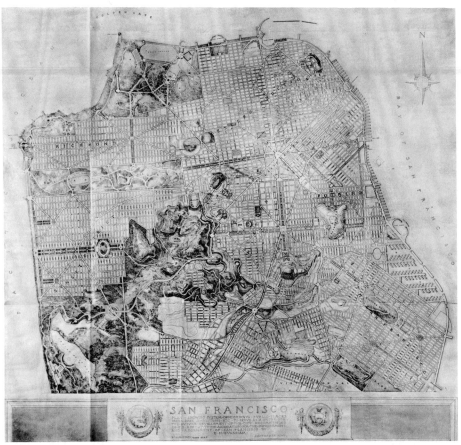

263. The Burnham plan "for the improvement and adornment of San Francisco," presented the day before the earthquake of 1906. Note the number of superimposed monumental nuclei among the plan's proposals.

and its plaza, radials would reach out to the proposed new railway station and other centers. On this framework Burnham laid out an overall street system the aim of which was: "to leave the old city streets untouched except for the creation of a few indispensable new arteries . . . The old walls, left undisturbed except for the street openings through the angle bastions . . . In the outer part of the town, a rectangular street system . . . provides especially ample streets in the line of heaviest traffic toward the town centre, and by means of radial and diagonal arteries makes every section of town readily accessible from every other."[6] Emphasis on accessibility through radials and diagonals gave the Manila plan a distinctive overall fan-shaped pattern, with the town divided by radials into five sections, each with its own internal orientation of rectangular blocks, reducing appreciably the number

6. *Ibid.*, p. 187.

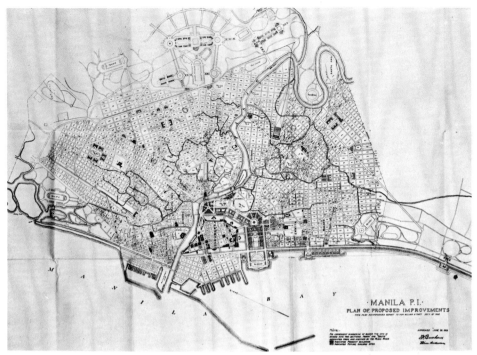

264. The 1906 Burnham-Anderson plan for Manila, requested by Secretary of War William Howard Taft.

of clumsy intersections. This was possible only because in the outer districts there were at that time neither approved streets nor improved properties to stand in the way.

In the Baguio problem Burnham at last encountered land that was apparently too rough for him to handle. After all, he was not a landscape architect; as an architect of the imperial eclectic era he was more at home in urban, table-top surroundings. The plan for Baguio was far from successful and had a clearly willful character in the arrangement of its two major centers. In the final report he attempted to excuse the shortcomings: "the aim of the plan has been to lay down a geometrical scheme which will adapt itself as closely as possible to the ungeometrical contours of the Baguio Valley. This street system may seem at first sight somewhat arbitrary, failing as it sometimes does to conform strictly to the lay of the ground. Such partial failure is, however, inevitable in any orderly arrangement."[7]

Inevitable indeed! Had it not occurred to him that ground-consuming bilateral symmetry, and unduly extensive level areas, would prove unmanageable in this intricately rugged mountainous terrain—and that neither was at all necessary? A "geometrical scheme" and an "orderly arrangement" could

7. *Ibid.*, p. 198.

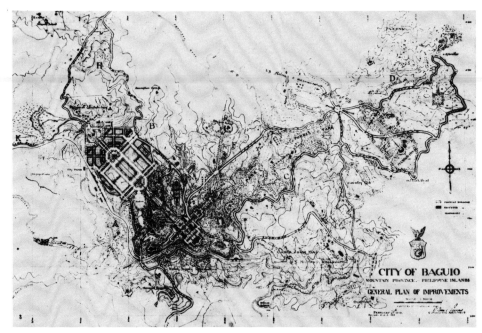

265. The astonishing general plan for Baguio, in the Philippine mountains; table-top design on rough topography.

certainly have been worked out, but not with the bilateral balance and the regal scale that Burnham apparently believed normal. To present-day eyes his Baguio plan seems downright brutal in the way it ignores the topography to jam down upon the land the "Government Center" and the "Municipal Center," as the two pretentious groups are called (Fig. 265). The crudeness of the centers is made all the more noticeable by the simple and unaffected treatment of the subsidiary portions of the layout, on roads that respect the "ungeometrical contours of the Baguio Valley."

Because the Burnham plan for Chicago has been so lavishly praised as his major monument, all the work elsewhere—Washington with McKim and Olmsted, Cleveland, San Francisco, Manila and Baguio—is perhaps to be regarded as mere rehearsal for Burnham's return in 1906 to what had been interrupted ten years earlier. Even then he begged off for a year longer because the approach was from a group other than the one before which he had presented his lakeshore plan in 1896. But a new proposal in 1907 by the Commercial Club, supported by a promise to raise the needed funds, set the gears in motion. Burnham gave the project almost undivided attention personally through the early months of 1907; then work by a staff under Bennett continued even when Burnham was away from Chicago attending to a multitude of other jobs. The plan covered not just the lakeshore but a great metropolitan area around Chicago.

The finished Chicago Plan and Report were published by the Commercial Club on July 4, 1909, in a large, handsome volume edited by Burnham's friend from McMillan Commission days, Charles Moore, with abundant illustrations. The report was exhaustive in its coverage: the history of city planning, of Chicago, and of the Chicago plan; analyses and proposals regarding parks, transportation, streets and boulevards; a comprehensive and fully detailed treatment, with exquisite rendered plans and elevations, of the "Heart of the City," including a monumental yacht basin and museum group for Grant Park in the long lakeshore park system, and an inland civic center of gigantic proportions and overwhelming magnificence. The volume closed with a lengthy legal opinion by counsel, presented with the concurrence of an impressive list of public, semipublic, and private attorneys. Among its many illustrations were three unusually eye-compelling types of display, inserted in some instances as doubly or triply folded sheets: colored charts of proposed park, street, and boulevard systems; color reproductions of the extraordinary paintings of Jules Guerin (illustrator for the McMillan Commission); and spectacular renderings, in plans and elevations, of the "Heart of the City" and the "Grand Axis," done in thorough Ecole des Beaux Arts manner by Jules Janin, brought from Paris for the purpose.

Within four months after official presentation of the plan, the Mayor and the Common Council, at request of the Commercial Club, appointed the Chicago City Plan Commission, under the chairmanship of Charles H. Wacker; the purpose of this body was to campaign through the years for funds to carry out the provisions of the Chicago plan. This they did—and in fantastic amounts. An observer today cannot escape the conviction that the fame of the Burnham Plan of Chicago, especially after Burnham's death in 1912, rests in large measure on promotional activities of the City Plan Commission. Important among these was *Wacker's Manual of the Plan of Chicago*, published in 1920 by Walter D. Moody, managing director of the Commission, as a means of indoctrinating the school children of Chicago toward final realization of the plan.

The Chicago Plan of 1909, like Burnham's other city planning efforts, was a strange mixture. In part it was clearly based on a study of existing physical conditions and opportunities (though not so clearly on any analysis of social facts). Whenever the proposals arose organically from actual circumstances and needs, they made sense and were a sound contribution to the slowly growing art and science of city-building. On the other hand, there were proposals that must have come almost wholly from Burnham's passion for bigness and boldness in the grand manner, as in the "Heart of the City" and its incredibly vast Civic Center, and that seemed to be thrust bodily into the fabric of the city by sheer will-power, as if by imperial decree (Fig. 266). These inspired awe for a time, to be sure, but eventually they were seen as making little sense in twentieth-century human terms.

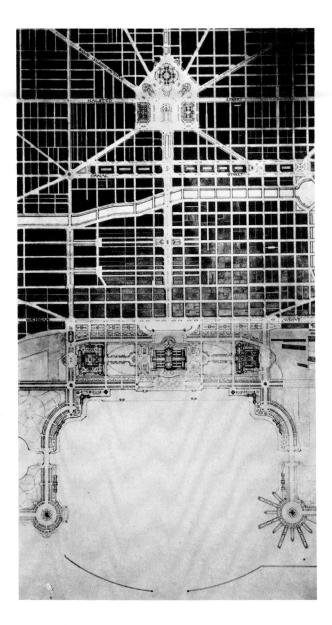

266. The implausibly monumental "Heart of the City" proposal of the Burnham Chicago Plan of 1909.

It was this aspect of the Chicago plan—as of those for Cleveland, San Francisco, Manila, and Baguio—that soon led observers to class Burnham's work as part of the City Beautiful movement associated with Robinson. This was an almost ludicrous juxtaposition of personalities: the gentle, eager young dreamer-journalist and the brusque, burly, experienced protagonist of majestic architecture and large affairs. Yet it was reasonable, for in large part both were concerned primarily with *appearance*, Robinson by repeated profession throughout his writings, Burnham because visual stylistic conformity was for him essential to the eclectic "classical" architecture through which he sought impressiveness.

In fairness to Robinson it must be noted that he protested in his first book: "If the crusade is to amount to anything, it must begin with demands for comfort and well-being that will appeal to all as reasonable. The wish for a beautiful street will remain always visionary until the want is felt of a good street and a clean one."[8] He was undeniably sensitive to human lives and problems. But in actuality "beautification" was to be the means and the "City Beautiful" the goal. Nor was Burnham concerned solely with the looks of things; he attended duly to physical conditions, especially circulation, and to economic questions—or at least to the wants of the industrial and financial world. But his friend and disciple Willis Polk quoted him as saying of the art of architecture: "It is, after all, the art of creating an agreeable form"[9]—appearance, that is, came first among the virtues.

Certainly neither of the two could be blamed, least of all by designers then or now, for caring about appearance in a world that paid all too little heed to it. They could hardly be criticized for observing the power of well-formed space to unify discordant elements in a city plan. The question that arose in time was rather one of priorities, of sequence, of method in design. When basic conditions—social, economic, physical—were tackled first, and the solution of these human problems brought about pleasant spaces and forms, then all seemed logical and right. But when the forms of spaces or objects were preconceived as "beautiful" and then superimposed upon the city without clear relation to any generating human needs or forces, most especially if the overlaid scheme was pompous, then it all tended to seem somehow false and lacking even in genuine "beauty."

For Robinson and Burnham the situation was further snarled by two unfortunate tendencies of the time. First, firm dominance of the "new" eclecticism and, at least in Burnham's case, an implicit belief in the infallibility of the "classical ideal." Second, the persistent fallacy of treating "beauty" as though it were a substance, a kind of heaven-sent elixir of which something could be "full," a magic material that could somehow be added with curative effect to an otherwise "ugly" thing. Hence the repeated reference to "beautification" as a means of improvement; hence the eagerness for "adornment," reminiscent of hanging shiny ornaments on a Christmas tree.

In view of the spurious thinking reflected by these common usages, the unhappy term adopted by Robinson, City Beautiful, virtually invited trouble in application. But his own complete sincerity was never in doubt, nor was his dedication to the improvements he worked for. His valiant service to the cause of city planning was admired and appreciated by the landscape archi-

8. Robinson, *Improvement of Towns,* p. 286.
9. Moore, *Burnham,* II, 167.

tects with whom he worked closely; and one effect of his crusade had been to heighten the city planning activity in their offices. To the roster of older practitioners already mentioned, younger landscape architects were now being added: such men as Arthur C. Comey and Justin R. Hartzog in Cambridge, the latter an associate of Nolen for years; Lawrence V. Sheridan in Indianapolis; Russell V. Black in Pennsylvania; Earle S. Draper in the south. City and regional planning, as well as whole small communities of varied types, occupied these offices increasingly as the years went by.

Also with the passage of time, less and less was heard of the City Beautiful movement as such. At first, for a period of moderate duration, the prevailing attitude toward the movement was one of sensible discrimination— differentiating between the sound, socially oriented, organically derived elements on the one hand and the capricious, preconceived, often ridiculously pretentious superimposed ones on the other. But eventually, following the regrettable human habit of seeing things as all-black or all-white, it became fashionable, roughly in the decade after World War I, to deride everything about the City Beautiful movement indiscriminately. It is a fair conjecture that the patently shallow new attitude was at least partially influenced by two undercurrents: the dimly heralded approach of a fresh, twentieth-century view of design, the so-called modern movement, with its roots in rationality; and the development of a new direction among city planners, away from design and toward political science.

In 1923 the Harvard School of Landscape Architecture offered a city planning option toward its Master's degree; then in 1929 a separate Harvard School of City Planning was set up under the chairmanship of Professor Henry Vincent Hubbard, a landscape architect and partner in the firm of Olmsted Brothers. In this and other newly organized schools of city planning the changing trend manifested itself in students who were usually the very opposite of what the City Beautiful type was supposed to be. With obvious good sense they were actively concerned with the basic human problems, the socioeconomic maladies and functional disorders of the city. This, rather than a romantically preconceived form of "beauty," they wisely recognized as a valid starting point in the struggle for urban excellence. Unhappily, however, they were too often totally unconcerned about appearance and cared little if at all about physical form. On the whole, they tended to be verbally rather than visually oriented and accordingly concentrated their attention on statistical analysis, formulation of broad programs of action, legislation, administration, and political science in general rather than on design. The regrettable consequence was a steady drift in the direction of splitting off the crucial socioeconomic and programing phase from the wholeness of city planning.

This development had minimal effect on individual landscape architects whose practice included city and regional planning. They simply kept on doing as they had done before, concerning themselves not only with analysis of underlying social and economic factors, but also with physical planning that made visible, tangible results available for the use of human consumers. To a landscape architect, a fully healthful end product in physical form was a necessity; all the statistical analysis, the program writing, the legislative and administrative action seemed academic if it did not lead to a useful physical result.

The new trend in city planning did have a temporary effect on the profession of landscape architecture in an organizational sense. This became especially noticeable as the American Institute of Planners built its size and stature through a policy of including in its membership the many professional fields concerned with city and regional planning as a political science: economists, geographers, sociologists, lawyers, statisticians, psychologists, housing specialists, and others who were politically minded or otherwise interested in various levels of governmental administration. The rapid growth of the AIP, the skyrocketing public demand for city planners, the expanding activity of government agencies—and no doubt to some degree the glamor of seeming to deal responsibly with vast affairs—drew some younger landscape architects to the offshoot body, away from the ASLA. Their mistaken impression was that only thus could they meet what they knew to be the social responsibility of landscape architecture. Saying they just wanted to "practice planning," as they termed it, they overlooked the obvious fact that "planning," like thinking, is something done by *all* intelligent people in *any* field of endeavor, not only by one particular group in one particular field. They soon discovered that for genuine landscape architects this isolation could not last. Before long the "planning only" mode of operation, without necessary physical result, became too dryly partial for those who were visualists and designers at heart; they returned to the ASLA and again busily engaged themselves in the city and regional planning sectors of landscape architecture. Some quite properly retained their AIP connection; indeed, because most landscape architects consider "site planning" and "land planning" appropriate synonyms for landscape architecture, many ASLA members are affiliated with the AIP.

On the modern scene the question now arises whether the new sort of city planning, or generalized "planning" without specific reference—having emerged from landscape architecture originally—has not intentionally withdrawn from membership in the family of design in the visual arts. The process known as design may be regarded as comprising three interlocking or continuous phases: the analytical or programing phase, the physically creative phase, and the construction phase. Architects and landscape architects, with regard to indoor and outdoor space respectively, have by custom professed the intent and ability to perform all three phases, without which the task of solving people's problems cannot validly be thought complete.

It has been argued by some city and regional planners of the new breed that the mid-twentieth-century world is so complex that no one profession can sensibly propose doing all three phases of the design process. Therefore, they maintain, assignment of the first or programing phase, to be properly done, must be delegated to the specialists in this, the "planners," who do not then profess to concern themselves with the second and third phases. Assuming that such a disposition of effort is satisfying to the "planners," there may well be some sense in this proposal. But with equal validity it leads to another and wider consideration: that city and regional planning are best understood not as the field of any one profession, but as a *collaborative* area to which many professions can offer specialized contributions. Such a policy was advocated by the landscape architect Gilmore D. Clarke when in 1935 he was called in by Cornell University and appointed Professor of City and Regional Planning.

According to such a view there is surely ample room, in any problem of planning regions or cities, for enlisting the entire array—sociologists, economists, geographers, psychologists, and other social scientists, lawyers (legal planners), landscape architects (land planners), architects (building planners), and engineers (construction planners)—each concentrated upon that sector of the total problem to which he can presumably make a better contribution than anybody else. Of course the precise makeup of such a collaborative group, regarding not only individuals but also professions, would vary according to the task in hand. Or, to cite what is already a trend, an alternative could be the organizing of firms whose corporate structure would include the major contributory professions, with other experts to be called in as occasion demands. Several firms of this kind are now in operation, with results that are more than satisfactory to all the participants and the clients.

It is interesting to note the possibility—indeed, the probability—that the City Beautiful movement, having started out as a consequence of one effect of the Columbian Exposition, may now in its final and most workable form appear as a consequence of quite another effect of the Fair: the stimulus to collaboration. Perhaps the City Beautiful movement will ultimately prove to have fulfilled its brightest and best hopes by indirection, long after the movement itself and its authors had been forgotten.

XXX. The Country Place Era

In the latter years of the nineteenth century, landscape architecture entered a period of increasing activity in the design of large residential properties in the country. Not truly "country estates," however; the actual inheriting of an *estate* is not involved in these discussions of American country places. Regrettably, however, such misuse of terminology did gain currency, serving to magnify a problem already caused by the three or four decades of the Country Place Era: the mistaken but persistent popular view of landscape architecture as a profession geared solely to magnificence for the opulent few. This was, of course, a gross distortion of the profession's basic value to the whole of society as evidenced, even during the Country Place Era, by landscape architects working as the elder Olmsted had done almost exclusively on a variety of public projects. It is nevertheless true that in this period the time of many practitioners was occupied mostly by sizable residential commissions.

But it need not be assumed that these years were a total loss merely because of the narrowing effect on the profession's public image. As though to counteract such a cramping influence, the Country Place Era succeeded in becoming also a period of remarkable progress in quality of landscape architectural design. In retrospect it can now be seen that, in all probability, the intensive preoccupation with large residential problems more sharply emphasized the necessity of strong design, and did more to improve its character, than any less personally exacting or more physically limited type of problem would have done. It is unfortunate that these years of improvement coincided with the period of concentrated eclecticism in architecture. Historical imitativeness sometimes occurred in landscape architecture, too, but not by any means invariably. And if in a given instance the work now appears to have been eclectic, careful analysis discloses that where excellence graced the design it was *despite* historical imitation, never because of it; the power of simple geometry, as pointed out earlier, is independent of "historic styles."

To be sure, in its totality as a design for living even the simplest of plans for a manorial residence, sitting alone on a sweeping tract of the landscape, is not likely to offer a workable answer to the needs of present-day society. But in terms of sheer quality in design, a wealth of learning can be had by today's designer from studying outstanding works of the Country Place Era. In them are characteristics of excellence fully applicable to his current problems in design. Of what did this excellence consist? It would be fruitless to attempt specifying *all* that was best about the best examples, which naturally differed one from another. But certain characteristics were usually present: meticulous care for detail, for proportion and scale—especially outdoor scale, which can be so deceptive to architects and other designers accustomed to indoor scale; simple clarity of spatial structure, with space treated as a plastic material—always positive and primary, not just left over; clarity of circulation that was basic—equal clarity of correspondence between horizontal and vertical so that, for example, what was crisply geometric in plan did not slump into waviness in section; rightness of relation between form and material in the best cases—as true for plant materials as for masonry or metal or paving; usually short and generally restrained plant lists, with materials tending perhaps more often toward firmness than airy looseness and with reliance on evergreen compactness to convey a sense of the architectonic where needed to emphasize geometric form; understatement and reserve rather than exaggeration—bearing out the maxim that the truly great designs, whether in the Country Place Era or today, never appear to strut.

The part played by Charles Adams Platt's creative skill in affecting the growing strength of design was large. To some degree, it can now be discerned, his influence was evident in the work of others soon after publication in 1894 of his book on Italian villas; but major impact came in the first two decades of the twentieth century, as examples of his own work in the field increased in number and became more widely known. Platt was of course not the only leader of the period in the evolution of strong design. In fact, one of the most interesting phenomena in the closing decades of the nineteenth century was the growth of architectonic direction in the residential designs of the Olmsted firm following their work on areas about the mansion at Biltmore. As observed earlier, when Platt's book appeared Eliot wrote an appreciative review of it, indicating substantial agreement with the "lessons of value" to be had from Italian villas. Gardens done by the firm between Eliot's entry in 1893 and his death in 1897, though rather pretentious and rigidly mechanical by the firm's later standards, were already more deft in the geometry of their spatial structure than the work at Biltmore. The improvement continued in the new century as the office's residential projects multiplied, and soon the performance of Olmsted Brothers in the design of country places reached the level of distinction that came to be taken for granted as characteristic of that office. Contributing to this development were not only John Olmsted and Frederick Olmsted, Jr., but also such younger men as Percival Gallagher and Edward Clark Whiting, two of the profession's most skillful designers.

Gallagher, after study at Harvard's Bussey Institution, entered the Olmsted office as an apprentice in 1894, already an artist to the core. After ten years and a brief interlude in another partnership, he returned to Olmsted Brothers as an associate in 1906; later he became a full partner. His creative skills were great, his modesty even greater. He was a mainstay of the firm's operations until his untimely death in 1934. Whiting, seven years his junior, took his A.B. degree from Harvard College in 1903, did graduate work for two years in Harvard's new curriculum in landscape architecture, and went to the "OB Office" in 1905. Working closely with Gallagher, he sharpened an already keen sense of design. He, too, later became a full partner in the firm of Olmsted Brothers and for fifty-seven years was a dedicated servant of the profession, an inspiration to younger men not only for his unselfish ability but also for his vigorously youthful spirit. He died in 1962 in his eighty-first year.

Of the scores of country places by Olmsted Brothers from coast to coast, one regarded as a favorite throughout the profession was Ormston, the residence of J. E. Aldred near Glen Cove, New York (Fig. 267). It was built just

267. General development plan for Ormston, near Glen Cove, Long Island.

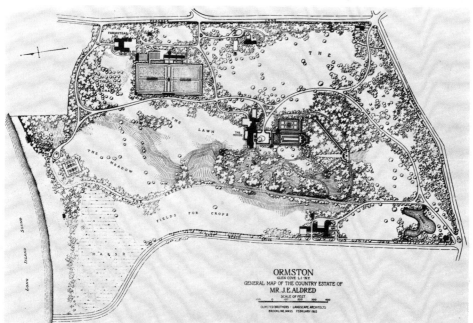

ORMSTON
GLEN COVE L.I. N.Y.
GENERAL MAP OF THE COUNTRY ESTATE OF
MR. J.E. ALDRED
SCALE OF FEET
OLMSTED BROTHERS · LANDSCAPE ARCHITECTS
BROOKLINE, MASS. FEBRUARY 1922

before World War I, on the north shore of Long Island in the area jokingly called "The Dukeries" by younger landscape architects in New York. The house, a large grey stone mansion by Bertram Grosvenor Goodhue, was faithfully imitative of Elizabethan England in accordance with the express wishes of the owner. For Olmsted Brothers, Gallagher and Whiting were the landscape architects in charge (Fig. 268).

With two branches from separate gates on Lattingtown Road, a long drive curved through the grounds to enter a stone-walled court on the south side of the house. Through a door in the south wall of this arrival court, directly opposite the main entry to the house, the visitor passed first into a small Blue Garden and then to a turf panel called the Bowling Green (Fig. 269) with a fountain at the far end. A single sight-line tied these areas together visually. In the Blue Garden, at the end of a stone and timber wisteria-covered pergola, stood a fascinating lead-roofed summer house of grey stone like that of the house and walls. East of the Bowling Green, screened from it by planting and a wall, was an area called the Rose Garden but used principally as a cut-flower garden. On the north side of the house a simple paved terrace at grade, a floor higher than the arrival court, looked out over a broad lawn and meadows sloping off toward Long Island Sound. At the beach were tennis courts and a bathing pavilion. On the eastern edge of the property, opening on Peacock Lane, was a farmstead with associated greenhouses and kitchen gardens, and on the western edge were the stables and garage. An ample system of roads and paths connected the several portions of the place, and to the southwest of the Bowling Green a pair of straight allées through the

268. Ormston: air view of the house and immediate grounds.

269. The Bowling Green at Ormston.

woods provided another variety of interesting walks. As a total composition Ormston had all the customary merits of an excellently organized country place, but by general agreement among contemporary landscape architects it was most noteworthy for its exemplary compactness of design.

One of the most highly respected creators of country places was James Leal Greenleaf. A graduate civil engineer from the old Columbia School of Mines in 1880, he taught engineering at Columbia until 1895, then opened an office in New York for the practice of landscape architecture. He was a gentle, gracious person, regarded with admiration by his colleagues and affection by the younger generation, to whom he was unfailingly helpful. Greenleaf succeeded Olmsted on the National Commission of Fine Arts, from 1918 to 1927, and was President of the ASLA from 1923 to 1927. Retired from practice in 1926, he died in 1933. His best-known works were in the New York metropolitan area, mostly in northern New Jersey and on Long Island. Especially notable was the group of country places for the Pratt family near Glen Cove, not far from the Aldred property. Of the four separate Pratt places, Killenworth, the residence of George D. Pratt, was the favorite among students of landscape architecture (Fig. 270). It gained a different kind of fame in later years when it was bought by the Soviet Union for the use of

270. Air view of Killenworth, also near Glen Cove.

their delegates to the United Nations. This is where Chairman Khrushchev held his studiously folksy news conferences, hatless, coatless, and on foot at the main entrance gates, during much-publicized visits to America.

The house at Killenworth, in grey stone somewhat like the Aldred one, was by Trowbridge & Ackerman. Roughly a T in plan, it had an open-ended arrival court at the crossbar of the T (Fig. 271). On the left side of the vertical shaft of the T was a long, narrow terrace, parallel to the house and reaching out to a simple garden house at the far end. At a lower level, down steps

271. Killenworth: the arrival court.

from the side of the long terrace, a deep pool was surrounded by evergreens. Somewhat to the left lay the famous grass-floored Green Garden (Fig. 272), a remarkable example of the use of box, yew, and other evergreens with turf steps to bring an appealingly soft quality to what might appear on paper a rigidly square plan around a central pool. Here as in many other spatial compositions, Greenleaf employed carefully placed trees with seemingly random spacing to remove all signs of harshness from an essentially rectilinear plan. In the opinion of most of his contemporaries, the Green Garden was Greenleaf's finest single achievement.

On the other side of the house, a paved sitting place at grade was connected with a simple grass panel at the foot of the T and faced out over a meadow-like lawn. Here the transition from geometric areas immediately about the house to undulant spaces and ground form in the distance illustrated well what has earlier been referred to as a clearly American contribution to the techniques of landscape design. Demonstrated here, too, were Greenleaf's flexibility and his capacity for breaking away from "the rules." In the years before World War I, when the Pratt place was being done, the use of Colorado blue spruce was generally frowned upon because of its attention-grabbing color. But Greenleaf used the tree in two ways: in the Green Garden architectonically in pairs, much like sculpture, and in the naturalesque areas of the meadow sprinkled casually along the edges of the woods, where it seemed oddly subdued and entirely at home. This was just one way in which Greenleaf often provided charming fillip by treatment that was a little "off" from theoretical perfection.

Three years younger than Greenleaf was the remarkable Jens Jensen, born in Denmark in 1860, an immigrant to the United States in 1884, and in his time one of the most controversial of leading American landscape architects. After two years in Florida and Iowa, in 1886 he settled in Chicago, his home throughout fifty years of activity. In 1935 he closed his Chicago office and withdrew to his summer home, "The Clearing," in Ellison Bay, Wisconsin, to do some writing and conduct an informal school. There, at the end of ninety-one unusually vigorous years, he died in 1951. Jensen, a "late bloomer," did not begin professional practice until he was in his forties. From his first Chicago job in 1886 as a gardener in the West Parks, he had risen to the superintendency of Humboldt Park only to be dismissed in 1900 for reasons of which he could well be proud: he had fought too hard against graft and political knavery. From 1900 on, he developed a growing private practice. In 1906, when the political picture had been cleaned up, he was appointed landscape architect and superintendent for the entire West Park system. But by 1920 the political scene had again deteriorated and Jensen cut his connection with the West Park Commission, disgusted with "politicians." He was a man of indomitable integrity and deeply-held convictions, personal, political, and professional.

272. The Green Garden at Killenworth.

It was the last of the three that tended to make him a controversial figure among landscape architects. An ardent student of nature from childhood, Jensen was a superb plantsman with a happily profound commitment to the use of native species. In time his brilliant work with indigenous trees, shrubs, and wildflowers—in compositions of quiet spaciousness emphasizing horizontality and stratification of the sort found in hawthorns, flowering dogwood, and native crabapples—came to be known and advertised as the "Prairie Style." There was of course nothing new about the idea of handling native materials in a natural way, but Jensen did it supremely. In a sense it is regrettable that he and his devotees made so much of the Prairie Style as a somehow "different" way of working, for this only tended to fasten upon it a parochial label of purely regional applicability—a fate that no sound program of planting design deserves. This probably contributed to Jensen's comparative isolation within the profession, especially when combined with his insistence that his naturalesque method constituted the *whole* of landscape architecture and was its only valid content! But the chances are strong that isolation, if that is the right word for it, was brought on willfully by Jensen himself, through his continued excoriation of any and all practitioners who indulged in geometric design or in any other way disagreed with him. He chose to attack "eastern landscape architects" in particular and resigned from the ASLA after a brief membership.

Many members of the profession looked upon Jensen—not without justice—as a "partial" landscape architect because he confined himself to planting, thus producing limited solutions. Planting, they pointed out, is a necessary component but by no means the invariable total of landscape architecture. The magnificent results achieved by Jensen where his methods were best adapted, in large parks such as Columbus Park in Chicago and the parks of Racine, Wisconsin, were rightly admired throughout the profession. But when he insisted on applying to residential properties, which comprised the bulk of his practice, the same exclusively wild-nature technique as in the parks, ignoring the architecture and scorning any organized visual tie between house and grounds, few of his colleagues could honestly applaud. Such a difference in views, exacerbated by Jensen's verbal fulminat' ns, led inevitably to his acquiring on a national scale, perhaps unjustly but none the less definitely, a reputation as an egocentric maverick best allowed to go his sublimely confident way undisturbed—and unmentioned.

On the other hand, in his thirty-five years of active practice Jensen built up a small but devoted popular following in the midwest, mainly among those who still thought in terms of "landscape gardening." In their eyes, it would appear, he could do no wrong. Professionally, there can be little serious doubt that he was excessively idolized by the few; but it is equally certain that in time he and his work became far too little known outside this worshipful circle. Few of Jensen's large private commissions have survived the march of land subdivisions. Among the older and more representative, the place he created in 1912 for E. L. Ryerson at Lake Forest, Illinois, has been preserved as the seat of a religious seminary. The house is by Howard Van Doren Shaw; spread before it is the expanse of a broad meadow, typical of Jensen's facility in the handling of large tree-bounded spaces. Much of the property is wooded, thoroughly native, and pleasantly traversed by winding, shadowy trails (Figs. 273, 274).

Whatever Jensen chose to do he did in full measure, not only in his intensely personal type of professional practice but also in public service. He worked on many committees, so long as he felt sure the current political complexion was clear. He played a significant part in the genesis of what later became the Cook County Forest Preserve District. Until after his retirement he published relatively little; but his 1939 book, *Siftings,* with its incandescent sincerity, amply rewards the reader who shares his clear and perceptive affection for wild nature and the land.

Surely one of the most active offices in New York was that of Vitale & Geiffert. Ferruccio Vitale, a Florentine by birth and a military engineer by training, came to the United States in 1898 as a military attaché of the Italian

273. Woods and open lawn, E. L. Ryerson residence at Lake Forest, Illinois.

embassy in Washington. On his return from the Philippines as an observer with American forces, he was introduced to landscape architecture in New York by George Pentecost, one of the founders of the ASLA. Vitale took to the profession with enthusiasm, began practice in 1904, and kept at it energetically until his premature death in 1933. His major professional interest, aside from his practice, was the cause of landscape architecture at the American Academy in Rome; to this he was completely dedicated. The first Fellowship in Landscape Architecture was established largely through his efforts, and he continued to take a lively interest in the work of the Fellows. He was the landscape architect member of the National Commission of Fine Arts from 1927 to 1931.

Alfred Geiffert, Jr., came to Vitale as an apprentice while still in his teens—he always insisted he had come as the office boy—and early showed himself a remarkably intuitive designer. This made him the best possible complement to Vitale, fundamentally a gifted critic with a naturally keen sense of discrimination, rather than a facile designer. Indeed, the steady improvement of work by this office during the Country Place Era can be attributed in large part to the development of Geiffert's innate ability under Vitale's

274. Woodland way, E. L. Ryerson residence.

watchful eye. Geiffert eventually became a partner and, after Vitale's death, continued the practice alone for another quarter-century until he died in 1957.

The commissions of Vitale & Geiffert, though extensive and varied, included many country places. One of the most unusual, done in the early 1920s, was the summer residence of Landon K. Thorne near Bay Shore, Long Island (Fig. 275). Here a flat, almost treeless tract, much of it salt marsh, was transformed into a delightful landscape with woods and sunny grasslands, several water bodies, and an abandoned ship canal stretching its considerable length inland from Great South Bay. The brick house, a rather literal adaptation of English precedent by William F. Dominick, was sited near a sizable lake at the inner end of the canal. The Thorne place was an instance of the kind referred to earlier in this account: despite the eclecticism of the architecture, the landscape design was carried out forcefully with simple geometry and common sense but without historical imitation.

Entering from the public highway that bordered the property on the north, a sweeping drive swung across a short bridge, from which it offered a view southward the length of the canal, then curved on to reach a graveled arrival area at the house. On the far side of the house was a paved sitting place

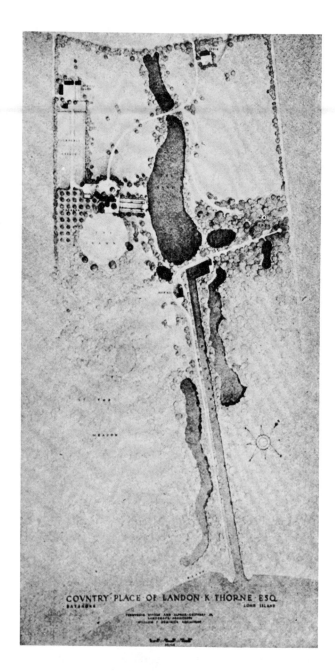

275. General plan, country place of Landon K. Thorne at Bayshore, Long Island.

at grade, and beyond this lay a circular lawn from whose edges the plantings of wild native growth extended all the way to the shore. Eastward from the house was a flower garden specifically requested by the owner; but in order not to interfere with the fine lake view, the flower compartments were placed at the sides and raised on low brick walls. Down the gently sloping turf panel

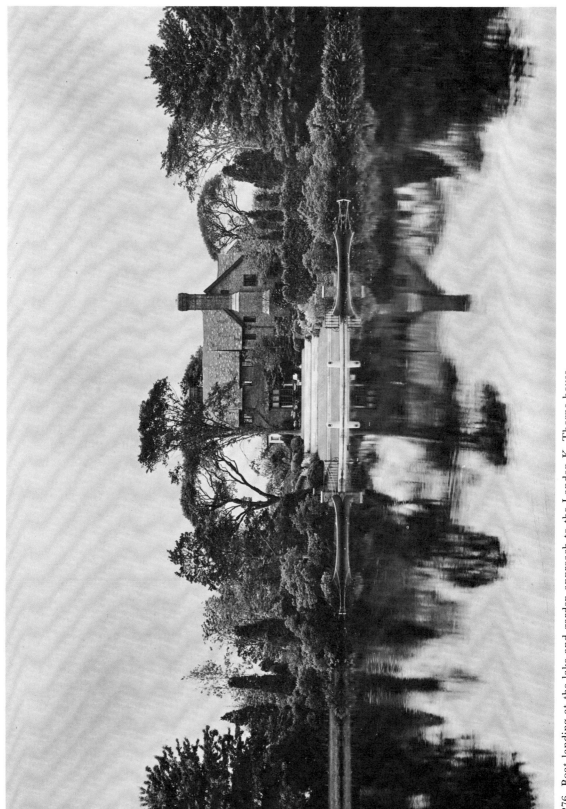

276. Boat landing at the lake and garden approach to the Landon K. Thorne house.

277. The birch allée at the Thorne place.

thus provided through the center of the garden, one descended to a fully operational boat landing at the water's edge (Fig. 276). The usual other components of a country place were also present (Fig. 277): service buildings and vegetable garden, tennis courts, bathing facilities, and an orchard west of the house. But in the judgment of the day, the chief merit of the Thorne job rested in the handling of the area between the house and the lake, and in the almost totally manmade environment of natural wildness.

These early practitioners of the Country Place Era could not, generally, have had formalized university training in landscape architecture. The apprentice method was the only means available until inauguration of the course at Harvard in 1900. A compromise between office and school was managed by a few. One was Bryant Fleming, who worked out his own selection of courses leading to a B.S. degree at Cornell in 1901, before a department of landscape architecture had been organized there, and followed this with three years under the eagle eye of Warren Manning. Fleming's professional career was notable for excellence and also unusual mobility. Forming a partnership in 1904, he started practice in Buffalo. The firm of Townsend & Fleming was soon busily engaged on country places over a wide territory: Louisville, Chicago, New York, Toronto, and in between. But the outbreak of World

War I abruptly suspended all the active projects, and, thanks to a kind benefactress, the office equipment was stored for the duration in the unoccupied old Middlebury Academy building in the village of Wyoming, western New York. Here Fleming picked up again after the war, in practice alone and with jobs extending even more widely afield than before. The working facilities were little more than primitive, and in 1924 the office was moved to Ithaca, where Fleming continued in the old Corson House until his retirement from practice in the late 1930s. Always a teacher at heart, he had helped, years earlier, to establish a course in landscape architecture at Cornell, taught there as a visiting critic, and was intensely loyal to the University. After retiring, he spent his last years in Wyoming, in the house he had built for himself; he died in nearby Warsaw in 1946.

Fleming's work was extremely individual and unorthodox, at times challenging all rationality, often guilty of the most whimsical exaggeration, yet somehow invariably delightful. During the 1920s, after registering as an architect in New York State, he often did both house and grounds. The large country place, with no holds barred and no costs open to question, continued to be his favorite type of project. But he also took pleasure in executing more compact commissions in the immediate outskirts of cities. One of these, the residence of B. E. Taylor in Grosse Pointe, just outside Detroit, illustrated his flair for the unexpected. The house had already been built when Fleming was called in. He added a terrace across the front (Fig. 278) that faced a wide lawn and Lake St. Clair. To the left, the terrace extended on a flat-arched bridge across a swale to reach a high-domed octagonal brick garden house; in its lower ground floor were dressing rooms to accompany a swimming pool beside the swale (Fig. 279).

Below the right-hand end of the terrace there was a small entryway, partly enclosed by brick walls into which projecting layers of rough stone had been laid like ledge rock. On closer examination, however, the layers were seen to be not stone but broken slabs of old cement sidewalk, bedded upside down, with crude lumps of jagged cinders still adhering. Over all ran a trickle of water, and moss had been encouraged to grow on all the rough surfaces by rubbing them with raw potato so that the moss spores would be caught and held. To everyone's amusement the trick had worked, to produce a result amazingly like the sopping, lichen-covered stone sculpture of fountains in Italian villas (Fig. 280). There was literally never any telling what Fleming would do next.

No summary of the Country Place Era would be truly representative without reference to the work of two women who were certainly among the most able designers of the profession: Miss Marian Coffin and Mrs. Annette Hoyt Flanders. Both were awarded the Gold Medal of the Architectural League of New York, Miss Coffin in 1930, Mrs. Flanders in 1932. Miss Coffin, after private tutoring, studied at Massachusetts Institute of Technology as

278. Terrace and garden house, B. E. Taylor residence, Grosse Pointe, Michigan.

279. Swimming pool and garden house, B. E. Taylor residence.

280. Entry walkway from the lakeside, B. E. Taylor residence.

the only woman in the Class of 1904. Unable to get a job in a New York office—indicative of prejudice against women landscape architects in those unenlightened days—she forthwith opened her own and operated it busily until 1927, when a serious illness felled her temporarily. She moved the office from New York to New Haven and made a courageous comeback. The same spirit of strength seemed manifest in her work. One of the most characteristic of her many projects was that for Edward F. Hutton at Wheatley Hills, Long Island (Fig. 281). Miss Coffin died in 1957, in her eighty-first year. Mrs. Flanders, a 1910 graduate of Smith College, later studied landscape architecture at Illinois and engineering at Marquette. She began practice privately in 1914, worked later with Vitale for some years, and opened her own New York office in 1922. In an extensive practice she was most noted for gardens of exceptionally vigorous quality. A widely admired example was her garden for Charles F. McCann at Oyster Bay, Long Island (Fig. 282). She moved her office in 1943 to her native Milwaukee; there she died in 1946.

The work of the few individuals and offices discussed here was of course not the whole story of the Country Place Era, although it gives a reasonable picture of the best aspects of the period. Many others were involved in producing country places with varying degrees of excellence; and, it must be kept clearly in view that some did no domestic work at all during these

281. Edward F. Hutton residence, Wheatley Hills, Long Island: the magnolia walk.

decades. But the design of large and necessarily costly residential projects remained the major preoccupation of many landscape architects, forming an overweighted component in the public image of the profession, until the Wall Street debacle of 1929 followed by the economic revolution of 1933 brought a revision of tax policies long needed in America's technologically advancing industrial society. As a result of the new taxation, the size and number of large domestic establishments in town and country soon waned. This changed the outlook completely for such landscape architectural offices as had subsisted mainly on large-scale residential work. In effect, the Country Place Era was over.

As the "great places" diminished in size and frequency, a vast number of moderately sized upper-middle-income domestic properties came into being. Given prevalent conditions, no one could have objected to such a sign of increasing health in the national economy. But the situation presented a difficulty for landscape architecture as a profession. It might at first glance appear completely possible to set up a successful practice—one that would lose neither high quality nor the landscape architect's shirt—on volume production of small residential jobs. Unfortunately, though, the small place is by its very limitations a relatively difficult problem in design, requiring a disproportionate amount of office time as against the actual cost of execution on the ground, which is normally very small. Practice of this kind, though dependent on a sufficient quantity of commissions, has in fact been carried

282. Garden of Charles F. McCann residence, Oyster Bay, Long Island.

on with success in some instances, particularly by women. But comparatively
few offices have found it generally workable. The nearest approach has been
that of some landscape architects who have found they could afford to include
an occasional small residential job or garden in practices consisting chiefly
of public or quasi-public projects. This has been done with marked success,
especially in California, by such inventive designers as Thomas Church,
Garrett Eckbo, Robert Royston, and Lawrence Halprin. The bulk of small
domestic work in a large part of the country has drifted into the hands of
"landscape nurserymen" who absorb the cost of designing, if any design is
exercised at all, in profits to be made from sale of materials and labor—which
is of course contrary to the accepted practices of professional landscape
architects.

In short, the Country Place Era, both during its years of existence and
in its sudden ending, exerted a marked effect on landscape architecture and
evoked strong differences of opinion within the profession. During the period's
three or four decades, landscape architecture acquired a public image that
was by no means universally applauded and that haunted it for a long time.
At the end of the era, the national economic changes that brought about
its demise were a source of dismay to some and delighted relief to others,
depending on their respective social and political beliefs. With the close of
the period the complexion of landscape architectural practice underwent a
tremendous change. It was naturally painful to those old-timers who hated

to see the big residential jobs disappear in such numbers; but it was just as naturally gratifying to youngsters eager to see their profession make a significant move back again toward more positive public service.

One consequence was clear beyond question or debate: the Country Place Era, whatever its faults and weaknesses, resulted in higher and stronger standards of design, especially among the scores of draftsmen and young designers working in the various offices. This was an advance that proved its value again and again in the years ahead. Just how this happened can be seen in residential arrangements for many families rather than just one—in the design of communities large and small, total and partial.

XXXI. English Town Planning and the "Garden City"

The sector of landscape architecture involving the design of total or partial communities, generically but rather loosely known as town planning, is best comprehended as a process that emerged in an effort to counteract the worst environmental effects of the industrial revolution. This immediately suggests looking to Great Britain, where the great mechanized upheaval first made large impact on human lives. In discussing the genesis of Victoria Park in London and Birkenhead Park across from Liverpool, it was shown how technological advances in metallurgy had given rise to congested industrial towns where employees usually suffered appalling conditions of living and working. One of the few industrialists deeply concerned over these unsavory circumstances in the early days was Manchester textile manufacturer Robert Owen, who during the first quarter of the nineteenth century, initially in his Manchester plant and later in the mills of New Lanark, Scotland, introduced many forward-looking policies to make the working situation more nearly bearable.

Of paramount interest here is Owen's conviction that environment affects character, that improved surroundings have a salutary effect upon workers, and that this in turn benefits industry itself. Although Owen is customarily regarded as the founder of modern socialism—a term he introduced in the 1830s—and was hailed by the workers as their champion, his early efforts were clearly paternalistic; that is, impetus for correction came directly from him, not from the workers. But, held down by partners who scoffed at his theories and wanted instead to pursue the old ways of sacrificing everything but profits, Owen in 1813 formed his own limited-dividend company to have greater flexibility in carrying out his advanced ideas. In addition to unprecedented modifications in management, he recommended setting up working communities of fixed size in both population and acreage, anticipating the "garden city" movement by nearly a century. He even went so far as to suggest precisely how the buildings should be arranged in a "model village": the dwelling units in a great square of continuous row-houses, with open space and gardens around them and community facilities grouped in a central space inside the square.

Owen was too far ahead of his times, however, found little sympathy among fellow industrialists, and in 1825 shifted activity to America. He bought outright from a Rappite religious group in Indiana an entire town, renaming it New Harmony. His attempt to establish a genuinely utopian existence, actually supporting it financially at the outset, was a failure because rapacious opportunists imposed upon his generosity and idealistic motives. Having sunk most of his fortune in New Harmony, he gave up in 1828 and returned to Britain; by then his partners had bought out his interest in the New Lanark experiment. He spent the rest of his days preaching his social and religious theories and died in 1858.

By mid-century, agitation against slum housing and the general squalor of industrial towns was more widespread. In 1849 James Silk Buckingham, a controversial figure for most of his life, published his *National Evils and Practical Remedies,* in which the frontispiece (Fig. 283) was an illustration of a proposed model town called "Victoria." Somewhat like Owen's quadrilateral "model village" of thirty years earlier, it had a more complex system of concentric squares of row-housing, with luxurious embellishment in the form of towers, colonnades, parks, and spouting fountains. But "Victoria" was theoretical and nothing more.

In 1853 Sir Titus Salt established on the banks of the River Aire, in Yorkshire, the new village of Saltaire, planned to accommodate workers from the Salt cloth mills. In its modest way this was probably the first example of a model community actually built and operated in conjunction with a large industry; it was also an early indication that some industrialists were becoming aware of the wisdom in moving works away from the pressure of crowded cities.

Next on the scene was a man whose experiments made a lasting contribution to the building of sane industrial towns: George Cadbury, of Birmingham. As early as 1859 he began working with the illiterate poor as a volunteer teacher. In 1861 he and his elder brother Richard succeeded their father in management of the family chocolate industry. The business had reached a low point, and the succeeding years required unremitting efforts to rejuvenate it. But the brothers somehow contrived to continue working on behalf of the poor, campaigning for improvement of the deplorable housing and for better education. Their energies were centered on conditions in Birmingham itself

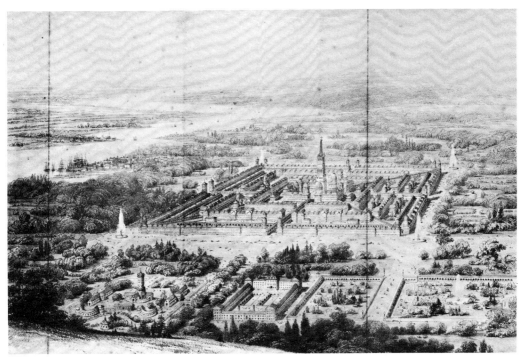

283. "Victoria," the model city of James Silk Buckingham, 1849.

until 1879. Then came the important step, when the firm of Cadbury Brothers built a new factory in the country to replace its plant in the heart of the city. The location was rural, more than four miles from the center of Birmingham, on the railway and on a small stream that gave the name Bournville to the development. Beside the factory, some twenty cottages were built for employees needed on the ground at once. It was a superb site, with rolling, wooded land, ample room for expansion, and excellent transportation facilities by road, railway, and canal. But because management of the rapidly growing industry made such demands on the brothers, for the next fifteen years, until 1894, Bournville was simply operated with dedication and studied as a pilot project.

Meanwhile, in 1887, the soap-manufacturing firm of Lever Brothers had started Port Sunlight, a one-industry development five miles up the Mersey from Birkenhead and seven from the center of Liverpool. The first purchase of land was an area of about 56 acres, of which 24 were intended for a newly built factory and offices and 32 for a village to house (only) employees of the firm. The land had numerous gullies or ravines, up which the water would flow at high tide; an early move was to fill the bottoms of the ravines above tidewater and develop the deepest as a park for the community. Later the ravines, except for the park, were filled in. But in the meantime the road

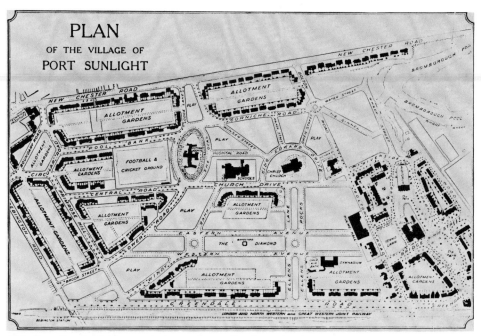

284. Port Sunlight, the one-industry Lever Brothers development near Liverpool begun in 1887.

system had been in great degree dictated by the curving lines of these long depressions, which bore little relation to the pair of rather grandiose mall-like spaces superimposed to cross each other in the midst of things. As a result, the plan of the village (Fig. 284) suffered from a certain stiff clumsiness; it was committed early and apparently lacked flexibility even when the conformation of the land became less rugged.

Port Sunlight's merit lies in its early use of what came to be known as the "superblock," in its park and individual buildings. From earliest years the houses were of excellent quality, in pleasant variety, based on older English prototypes; so too were the community buildings, on which a generous founder lavished extraordinary treatment. Within fifteen years after establishment the acreage had been increased to 230, of which 140 were in the village. Lever Brothers met the entire cost of installation—land, houses, schools, shops, institutions, clubs, parks, allotment gardens, recreational areas, and roads—without expectation of financial return other than the improved production of a contented work-force. The rents were calculated merely to take care of taxes, repairs, and maintenance. The founder, W. H. Lever (later Lord Leverhulme), was a truly benevolent industrialist, a great believer in "prosperity-sharing," as he called it, as a matter of "the truest and highest form of enlightened self-interest" on the part of capital and management.[1]

1. W. H. Lever, *The Buildings Erected at Port Sunlight and Thornton Hough* (London, 1902), p. 48.

There is no evidence of professional planning services early at Port Sunlight, although after 1905 the pioneer British landscape architect Thomas Mawson was a close advisor to Lord Leverhulme. Nor is the visual quality of Port Sunlight distinctive as an example of design. It did not even represent an attack on Britain's *general* housing problem; its aim was restricted and local. But sociologically and psychologically it was a big step forward, the practical realization of an industrialist's genuine concern for the health and happiness of his workers.

While Port Sunlight marched ahead, the Bournville experiment of the Cadbury Brothers marked time. But in 1893, when George Cadbury felt sufficiently free from the problems of running the factory, he bought an additional 120 acres of land. On this he began building in 1894, and by 1900 Bournville had grown to 330 acres, with 313 houses. Unlike the Port Sunlight development, Bournville was not restricted to workers in the factory; indeed, none of the houses built in this period was reserved for employees, and the Bournville Estate was fully independent of the firm of Cadbury Brothers. Port Sunlight and Bournville differed also in that the former grouped open space into large allotment gardens; dwelling units in the latter, through Cadbury's insistence, all had individual gardens (Fig. 285), and there was also a generous distribution of public open space. From the first, therefore, Bournville had a lightness of density that must have seemed incredible at the end of the nineteenth century, especially in housing for the working class.

In December 1900 George Cadbury founded the Bournville Village Trust, turned the whole development over to twelve Trustees, and renounced all financial interest in the property on behalf of himself and his family. In the half-century and more since then, several methods, usually the organization of cooperative housing societies, have been employed to develop portions of the total holdings on land leased from the Village Trust. By World War I, Bournville had its own shops, schools, Ruskin Hall for arts and crafts, churches, park, recreation fields, children's playgrounds, some allotments in addition to individual gardens, a garden nursery, and a working men's college. There was an attractive village green surrounded by shops and public buildings and a Village Council to foster social activities. In short, Bournville was no longer just an interesting housing experiment, but had the amenities, facilities, size, and character of a flourishing garden village (Fig. 286). In fact, it had been included within Birmingham when the city limits were extended in 1911.

Development was of course suspended during the two world wars, but activity in the years of peace resulted in a great variety of housing types—detached houses, row-houses, flats, bungalows, all in ownerships and rentals with specific accommodations for retired professional people, single women, the elderly and the infirm—laid out in village-like residential groupings of limited size tied together by an admirable system of open spaces and park

285. The Cadbury Brothers' Bournville, outside Birmingham; from the beginning there was emphasis on individual gardens.

286. Map of Bournville after expansion and incorporation within Birmingham in 1911.

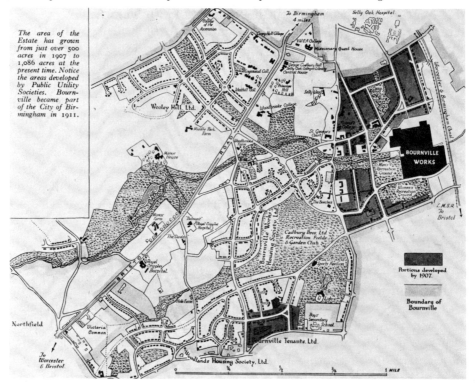

The area of the Estate has grown from just over 500 acres in 1907 to 1,086 acres at the present time. Notice the areas developed by Public Utility Societies. Bournville became part of the City of Birmingham in 1911.

strips. In keeping with the original premise of the founder, every residential unit was amply furnished with its own garden or an equivalent. There were, and still are, excellent facilities for recreation and for the education of old and young. George Cadbury, in addition to his concern for workers' housing, maintained active interest in the Adult School Movement for over sixty years, from his volunteer teaching in 1859 to his death in 1922.

Because ownership of the land has remained vested in the Village Trust, land speculation has been eliminated and the founder's original intent, decent economically feasible housing for low and moderate incomes, has been successfully observed. In 1955, when the Village Trust published a summary report following its jubilee celebration, Bournville had nearly 3,500 dwellings of diverse types and sizes on over 1,000 acres occupied by a population of about 10,500; it is of course still larger now. Because it has grown intermittently, with acquisitions developed bit by bit and from time to time, there has never been any single controlling master plan, and the whole now has an almost accidental character. Yet it has a definitely organic quality and the charm often found in accidental conformations, possibly in this case because Bournville is so clearly a heartening testimonial to the enduring strength of a selfless ideal like that of George Cadbury.

Even as Bournville and Port Sunlight were being brought to life as experiments in better housing for workers, a young Londoner named Ebenezer Howard put an inventive and inquiring mind to the complex problem of organizing better communities on the land. He was twenty-nine when the Bournville factory was built, thirty-seven when Port Sunlight began. On a brief stay in the United States he had seen how much harm can be wrought by land speculation; and he had been much impressed by Henry George, the American single tax exponent, during George's visit to London in the early 1880s. Though by occupation a court reporter, Howard became an enthusiastic land reformer, a student of the efforts of Cadbury and Lever, and in time the author of his own theory for a radically different kind of town, which he called a Garden City. After rewriting his thesis many times, he finally published it in 1898 as *Tomorrow: A Peaceful Path to Real Reform;* the second edition, in 1902, was retitled *Garden Cities of Tomorrow.* This modest little volume, accorded at first a mixed reception ranging from enthusiastic acceptance to outright rejection, is now recognized as an unquestionable classic of town planning history.

Howard's program rested on the belief, which he held to be "well-nigh universally agreed by men of all parties," that somehow people must be stopped from streaming "into the already over-crowded cities."[2] The flow he likened rather quaintly to electromagnetic attraction: "Each city may be regarded as a magnet, each person as a needle; and, so viewed, it is at once

2. Ebenezer Howard, *Tomorrow: a Peaceful Path to Real Reform* (London, 1898), pp. 10–11.

seen that nothing short of the discovery of a method for constructing magnets of yet greater power than our cities possess can be effective for re-distributing the population in a spontaneous and healthy manner" (p. 14). He illustrated the situation with a diagram, "The Three Magnets." It appeared that the "Town magnet" and the "Country magnet" offered, each in its own way, advantages that were quickly offset by parallel disadvantages. To this dilemma there was but one answer: "But neither the Town magnet nor the Country magnet represents the full plan and purpose of nature. Human society and the beauty of nature are meant to be enjoyed together. The two magnets must be made one . . . Town and country *must be married,* and out of this joyous union will spring a new hope, a new life, a new civilisation. It is the purpose of this work to show how a first step can be taken in this direction by the construction of a Town-country magnet" (17–18). Howard went on to describe "The Town-Country Magnet," as he titled the first chapter of the book. The magnet, of course, was his Garden City.

With what seems to have been habitual modesty, Howard made no claim of complete originality for his proposal. Indeed, he called it "a unique combination of proposals" and said it combined "three distinct projects" (101) advanced by others but never before united in a single effort. This was overgenerous to others and considerably oversimplified the case. Actually, a detailed examination of Howard's Garden City program reveals that it was in an even more ample sense "a unique combination of proposals"; for it was made up of a number of simultaneous parts or proposals, each essential to a full realization of the total intent. To what degree the parts were derived from the work of others—and to what degree modified by Howard's inventive genius—is immaterial. The main point is the efficacy of the parts *as a combination.* Howard did not enumerate or list the components, but they can be abstracted as follows.

1. *Town-country.* Developing the notion of the town-country magnet would be provision of the advantages of both town and country: a populated center limited and surrounded by a larger agricultural zone, bringing ready markets of the town to the farmer and delights of the country within quick reach of the town-dweller. Not a town *in* the country, and certainly not a garden suburb, but an entity of town-country in permanent combination.

2. *Transportation.* The tract must of course have reasonably available railway facilities.

3. *Limited size.* A total "area of 6,000 acres, which is at present purely agricultural, and has been obtained by purchase in the open market" (20) was to be divided into a central 1,000 acres for a town of 30,000 people and an outlying 5,000 acres of country with 2,000 people. The agricultural zone would act as a buffer against uncontrolled growth of the populated center.

4. *Land held in trust.* In order to prevent land speculation and to retain for the community the unearned increment in land value, the entire area of 6,000

acres "is legally vested in the names of four gentlemen of responsible position and of undoubted probity and honour, who hold it in trust" (21). Land would be leased only, not sold, to occupants.

5. *Control of planning.* Under trust ownership of all land there would be fully controlled planning prior to construction, including establishment of densities and general form but, again under municipal control, allowance for desirable individuality.

6. *Wards.* As preplanned, the central town would be divided into "six equal parts or wards," each with a population of about 5,000 and a public school, and "should be in some sense a complete town by itself" (22, 45). This anticipated the later neighborhood principle in town planning (though not so termed by Howard).

7. *Spaciousness.* In "this fortunately-placed community" there would be for all, not just a select affluent few, "ample sites for homes . . . ample space for roads . . . so wide and spacious that sunlight and air may freely circulate, and in which trees, shrubs, and grass give the town a semi-rural appearance . . . ample sites for town-hall, public library, museum and picture gallery, theatre, concert-hall, hospital, schools, churches, swimming baths, public markets, etc." (39). In the center of the town would be "a public park, containing 145 acres, which includes ample recreation grounds within very easy access of all the people" (22). Howard very nearly made this delightful aspect of his program seem too good to be true.

8. *Industrial employment.* One of Howard's basic aims was the outward migration of industry and workers from the overcrowded metropolis of London. "On the outer ring of the town are factories, warehouses, dairies, markets, coal yards, timber yards, etc. . . . The smoke fiend is kept within bounds . . . for all machinery is driven by electric energy" (25). Industries might be conducted either by the municipality, with experimentation strongly encouraged, or by private enterprise with great individual freedom of operation.

9. *Dispersal of towns.* As a corollary to the principle of fixed sizes, whenever the town reaches its planned population of 32,000 it "will grow by establishing . . . another city some little distance beyond its own zone of 'country,' so that the new town may have a zone of country of its own." Such leapfrogging would mean that "in the course of time, we should have a cluster of cities . . . grouped around a Central City" (129–130). Here Howard's "Social Cities" anticipated satellite towns.

A step-by-step examination of the intent of at least these nine components of his program will show beyond question how interdependent they were in combination, how essentially each contributed to Howard's dream of "a new civilisation" (18). To illustrate graphically what he described verbally, Howard included in his book a diagram of the whole Garden City (Fig. 287) and another, in greater detail, of a single ward within the town. At first glance

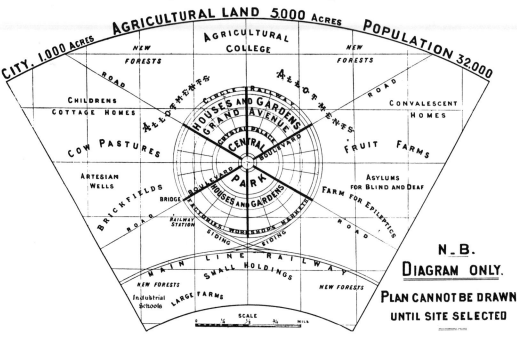

287. Ebenezer Howard's Garden City diagram, 1898.

the diagrams have the appearance of plans so rigidly mechanical as to seem ridiculous—which is the risk with diagrams meant to show only general relations but actually having so much positive geometric form that they look deceptively like intended plans. In fairness, Howard's precautionary note should be heeded: "N.B. Diagram only. Plan cannot be drawn until site selected" (at p. 22). Surely no landscape architect could object to this insistence on a topographic map as a first step.

In 1899, the year after *Tomorrow* was published, an interested group formed the Garden City Association. Discussion of Howard's program ensued, with a rising tempo of propaganda, until in 1902 the Garden City Pioneer Company Limited, made up principally of businessmen and including W. H. Lever and George Cadbury, was organized and set out to find a site for their experimental town. Four possible tracts were studied—with appropriate secrecy to prevent sudden boosting of prices—and one was selected: about 4,000 acres of rural land in Hertfordshire, thirty-five miles north of London on a branch of the Great Northern Railway, the so-called Letchworth Estate. Purchase contracts were signed with fifteen local landowners in July 1903, and on the following September 1 the First Garden City Limited was registered as a joint stock company authorized to sell shares for raising the needed capital. This meant that no formal trust was established; it was fully understood that eventually the company would transfer its land holdings to the community, but nobody could tell when this would occur. Meanwhile, this departure from Howard's "unique combination of proposals" was, and continued to be in one way or another for years, a major cause of trouble for Letchworth. The area available for the new garden city was only two-thirds of the desirable 6,000 acres, but in every other respect the site was excellent. It was well drained, with an abundant supply of water, and was occupied by only three small villages, Norton, Letchworth, and Willian. Within a year the land had been surveyed, work started on drainage and water supply, and a town plan prepared by Barry Parker and Raymond Unwin. This marked the start of a career in which Unwin became one of the most scintillating figures in the field of town planning.

The Parker-Unwin plan was a simple one (Fig. 288), carefully adapted to the land. It recognized the unfortunate fact that the railway bisected the community, instead of encircling it as suggested in the Garden City diagram, and that to some degree this would always be an impediment to full unity. A town square was located south of the railway; from the square a long, straight street—Broadway—was extended south to residential blocks and north past public buildings and shops to the railway station. Three existing roads across the tract, roughly parallel to the railway between Hitchin and Baldock, were retained and a partial set of radial streets from the town square added. On this framework a road system was developed, with much use of the cul-de-sac.

Industrial sites were indicated on the railway east of the town center; later another smaller industrial section would be added west of the center. North of the railway station, the existing Norton Common was to be kept as open space for recreation. The undisturbed villages of Norton and Willian would lie just beyond the northern and southern edges, respectively, of the agricultural belt (Fig. 289). The village of Letchworth, though nearer the town center, would be modified only slightly. Letchworth Hall, on the very edge of the agricultural belt, would be retained for use as a hotel in conjunction with the adjoining Golf Course.

The company ran into financial difficulty right from the start. This creation of a whole new town at once, not from some lordly munificence but as a public venture, must have seemed in 1904 a piece of unprecedented madness. Moreover, the spread of suburbs outward from London, in virulent competition with the "garden city idea," was fully fostered by the rapid growth of rail transportation. As authorized, the company issued shares to raise capital; but, because the company was committed to future transfer of its holdings to the community, a share of stock represented no ownership, even ultimately, of anything tangible. As the shares thus carried no equity interest, and at

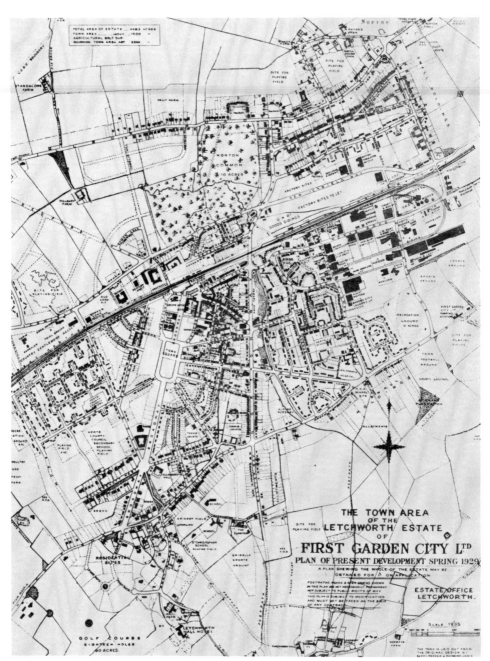

288. Letchworth, the first Garden City, as it had grown by 1929, twenty-six years after its founding.

a restricted dividend of 5 percent were clearly not intended as a business investment, they sold only sluggishly. At the end of the first year less than half the needed capital had been obtained, and much of this had been provided by the directors of the company.

289. Air view of Letchworth row-housing and the agricultural belt.

Various devices were tried in the hope of arousing public interest, but to little avail. In the summer of 1905 a Cheap Cottages Exhibition was organized, with some success in publicity, attracting visitors, and getting 121 permanent cottages built. A society for building cottages was started, and the first two industries appeared. Soon it appeared clear that Letchworth

Garden City was at last something more than a mere dream. But progress was slow, and pressure mounted to sell building sites instead of leasing them, particularly for industry; a majority of the directors felt committed to the original intent, however, and the leasehold system was not abandoned. Inevitably this meant comparatively slower growth, but it also meant that the basic ideal remained alive. After ten years, in 1913, a first dividend of 1 percent was paid to the shareholders; the originally intended 5 percent was not paid until 1923, twenty years after the town's foundation.

The first world war stopped all activity, but by that time Letchworth was well enough established to feel sure of survival. By 1919 the population had reached 10,000; from then on a sort of slow, plodding increase continued. But in 1919, out of eagerness to prove his theories, Howard handed Letchworth the further problem of nearby competition by starting a second garden city, Welwyn, only twelve miles away. He had found another tract of open land offered at public auction; it was only twenty-one miles from London, on the main line of the Great Northern Railway, at the junction of two branch lines a few miles north of Hatfield in Hertfordshire. It amounted to less than 3,000 acres, about half his recommended size for a total garden city, but he could not resist, and with financial help he bought the land. In April 1920, Welwyn Garden City Limited was registered as a joint stock company.

The development of a plan for Welwyn was a complex procedure as compared with the simple but fortunate hiring of Parker and Unwin at Letchworth. In twenty years the number of "qualified experts" had greatly increased, and a considerable team of them held many conferences before the plan of Welwyn evolved (Fig. 290). Then, too, whereas the planning of Letchworth had been done virtually from scratch with no precedent other than Port Sunlight and Bournville to help or hinder, the planners of Welwyn had nearly twenty years of Letchworth's experience to weigh before reaching conclusions. Preparation of the official plan was in the hands of Louis de Soissons.

In the Welwyn plan the total community, as at Letchworth, was divided by the main line of the railway; the two branch lines curving to east and west interfered somewhat less. A long, straight spine of space occupied by parkway and town square, west of the railway and parallel to it, formed the core of the plan. From the railway station a crosswise mall, called Howard's Gate, led to the town square. This became the civic and business focus, strong in design but sometimes criticized as too large in scale and a bit pompous for a garden city of modest proportions. The industrial section was planned to go along the railway, east of the main line and south of the branch to Hertford.

The residential layout was admirably fitted to the land; the road system, making use of some existing country lanes, was softer than that of Letchworth in terms of alignment and outdid the older city in its use of the cul-de-sac and the close or court. Neither town, of course, was designed to accommodate

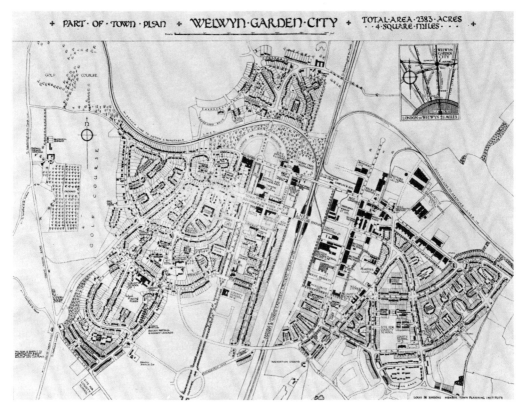

290. Welwyn, the second Garden City, started in 1920.

the motorcar in mid-century numbers; any attempt to provide for such a motorized society in 1920 and earlier would probably have been regarded as utterly insane. One of the happiest characteristics of Welwyn was the care with which many of the existing natural features were preserved (Fig. 291); also, there were ample spaces for recreation, chiefly on the periphery of the central town, along the edges of the agricultural belt.

In development and growth Welwyn struggled with much the same difficulties as Letchworth. At the outset shares were hard to market and the raising of capital was desperately slow. The garden city idea had become widely misunderstood, despite the relative success of Letchworth, and was commonly confused with the "garden suburbs" sprawling out cancerously from London— the very phenomenon Howard had sought to eliminate with his proposals. Ironically, the directors of the Welwyn enterprise actually thought of dropping the term "garden city" from the title of their company, feeling it might be a drawback; happily, they did not yield to this passing fear. The building of houses was begun in early 1920; the first recorded population was 400. Within a year it had nearly doubled, and in 1930 the ten-year-old Welwyn held about 8,000 people in over 2,500 dwelling units.

291. Welwyn: existing natural amenities rigorously preserved and incorporated in the town plan.

During World War II Letchworth and Welwyn acquired swollen populations through transferred war workers and evacuees from London. Development stopped, of course, while the nation concentrated on its war performance. With the end of hostilities the two garden cities took up again their slow but steady advance, but they faced an entirely new era when in 1946 the New Towns Act was passed. For many years prior to the war there had been mounting concern in Britain, influenced in no small part by the demonstrated merits of the garden city idea at Letchworth and Welwyn, over the frequently unwise use of land and the irrational spread of urbanization. The onset of aerial bombing naturally aroused thoughts of eventual reconstruction, and these in turn suggested the necessity of applying sound policies to the process of rebuilding after the war.

Then, in 1940, publication of the Barlow Report—the results of a three-year study by a royal commission appointed before the war—started the chain of legislative events leading to Britain's astonishing postwar development of progressive thought and action in town planning. The main thrust of the report urged dispersal of industry away from congested areas, under the direction of strong central authority. Other influential reports followed, notably those of the Uthwatt and Scott committees in 1942, supporting the Barlow proposal and making further recommendations: legislation to vest in the state virtually all private rights to develop land; universal application of planning controls; increased local authority for compulsory sale and purchase of land.

Publication of the reports led to the Town and Country Planning Act of 1944, empowering local authorities to acquire land for development by themselves or by letting it to private enterprise. With the end of the war, Britain was well prepared to implement the years of concern, study, and hardship with forward-looking legislation. One of the first manifestations was the New Towns Act of 1946, which enabled the Minister of Town and Country Planning (a new ministry had been established in 1943) to designate the site of a new town and create a development corporation as a public authority to plan, acquire, and build the town. In their response to the new legislation, Letchworth and Welwyn differed markedly.

At Welwyn, designated in 1948 as one of the New Towns under the Act, the new policies were accepted with only brief resistance from the company. In 1949 the Welwyn Garden City Development Corporation, appointed in accordance with the Act, bought outright the holdings of Welwyn Garden City Limited, and the company went into voluntary liquidation. Thus the community now owned its land, as originally intended by Ebenezer Howard. At Letchworth, however, the picture was complicated by dissension within the company and even more by fundamental disagreement between it and the Urban District Council as to the company's legal and moral responsibility. A period of stalemate and stagnation set in, further complicated by speculation in the company's stock and outside attempts to gain control of its management. The whole miserable dilemma was brought to a head in 1961, when the Urban District Council filed a private bill in Parliament "for the purpose of establishing a Corporation which in return for appropriate compensation will acquire the undertaking of the First Garden City Limited." The outcome was that the bill, though bitterly opposed by some elements in the company, became law in July 1962; on January 1, 1963, the holdings of the company passed over to the Letchworth Garden City Development Corporation. The people at long last owned the land on which their town was built. Howard's dream for Letchworth was now realized—but sixty long years after he had brought the town into being.

Thus for the purposes of this account ends the story of Port Sunlight and Bournville, of Howard's "garden city" program, of Letchworth and Welwyn. To be sure, a dozen or so New Towns were designated under the Act of 1946, including among the best known Harlow, Stevenage, Hemel Hempstead, East Kilbride, Cumbernauld, and Crawley. But results have been too varied, and the question of total success is still too controversial, to warrant any attempt to generalize about this bold step in civilization. Whether controversial or not, however, the progress Britain has made toward fully intelligent handling of the surface of the earth, and the spaces and objects upon it, should be studied by everyone interested in the town planning aspect of landscape architecture.

XXXII. Town Planning in the United States: 1869–1915

Given the obvious geographical difference in the nineteenth century between the settled compactness of Great Britain and the undeveloped continental spread of the United States, it is not strange that there were also differences between the beginnings of the town planning story in the two countries. One important variation, however, was not merely of size or geography; it involved the initiative role of industry. Can it be that the forces of industry in Britain achieved enlightenment much earlier than their counterparts in America? It would seem so. Of course Robert Owen, in the midst of failure, came nearest to success at New Harmony in America, and Ebenezer Howard received at least part of his impetus from the evils of land speculation as he saw it practiced here. But, whereas in Britain the early voices heralding town planning were those of industrialists—Owen, Cadbury, Lever—industrial concern for the workers in America did not early rise above the drab level of New England's mill villages or the infamous company towns around the coal mines and steel works of Pennsylvania and West Virginia.

In America the early voices of town planning were not those of industrialists but, instead, those of the first practitioners of the new profession landscape architecture. Moreover, involvement was not with industrial situations directly, but rather with the residential and more general aspects of community life. The early protagonists—Olmsted, Vaux, Cleveland—though ever concerned with human lives and values, were impelled by the problems at hand in their early works to place more emphasis on physical design than on the socioeconomic plight of factory workers. Aside from its historic importance, the major contribution of the 1869 plan of Olmsted and Vaux for Riverside, Illinois, was the inventive design of its road system. Cleveland, despite his never having much of a chance to prove his case in physical fact, published in 1873 one of the most compellingly forceful arguments ever heard against the inanity of the typical checkerboard or gridiron plan on land that could not happily accommodate it. To the credit of America, it is perhaps worth noting that both efforts antedated by several years erection of the factory at Bournville and the start of Port Sunlight.

Olmsted and Vaux were already widely known for their work on Central Park and Prospect Park, although neither was completed, when in 1868 they were called in by Emery E. Childs, of Chicago, to advise his newly organized Riverside Improvement Company. The project was a real-estate venture to establish a "suburban village" on 1,600 acres of land along the Des Plaines River, nine miles from the center of Chicago.[1] Today it is of more than passing interest to find Olmsted, Vaux & Company, in their preliminary report of a hundred years ago, reassuring Childs that, although the dominant characteristic of the time had been the flocking of people into ever larger cities, there was already "clearly perceptible" a reverse trend toward the formation of suburbs, "especially affecting the more intelligent and more fortunate classes."[2] The Riverside gamble was accordingly, they thought, a reasonably sound one.

Though there was by then at Riverside the first out-of-town railway station on the main line of the Burlington, the landscape architects considered this "a very inadequate and unsatisfactory means of communication between a rural habitation and a town";[3] they recommended construction of a wide, well-treed approach road or "park way" reaching to Chicago. The task of creating here a village-like suburb with a sylvan domestic atmosphere was challenging. A few spots in the tract were slightly higher than the surrounding flatness; some, as well as the riverbanks, were occupied by trees. But all around Riverside was "the low, flat, miry, and forlorn character of the greater part of the country immediately about Chicago" (p. 259).

The preliminary report is a fascinating document in several respects, illustrating as it does what was commonly known and understood by laymen—and what was not—a century ago about landscape architectural practices. Those who assume that well-laid roads and underground drainage systems have "always" existed, in suburbs as well as cities, will profit from Olmsted's patient explanation of the reasons for constructing such roads and such "underground channels, secured against the accumulation of drift-stuff

1. See "Riverside, Illinois," *Landscape Architecture,* 21 (July 1931), pp. 257–291.
2. *Ibid.,* p. 260.
3. *Ibid.,* p. 263.

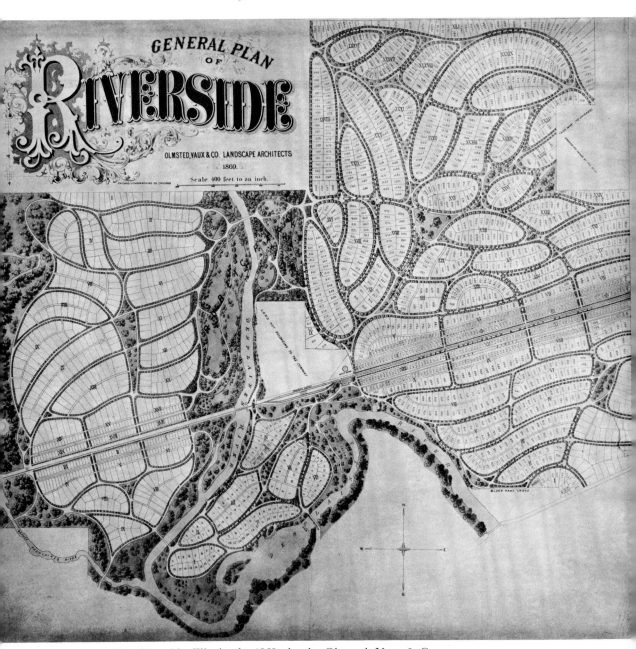

292. Riverside, Illinois: the 1869 plan by Olmsted, Vaux & Co.

by subterranean silt-basins and surface gratings" (272). The report also explains in simple terms the curvilinear character that would prevail in the Riverside street system, so unusual in its day:

> In the highways, celerity will be of less importance than comfort and convenience of movement, and as the ordinary directness of line in

town-streets, with its resultant regularity of plan, would suggest eagerness to press forward, without looking to the right hand or the left, we should recommend the general adoption, in the design of your roads, of grace-fully-curved lines, generous spaces, and the absence of sharp corners, the idea being to suggest and imply leisure, contemplativeness and happy tranquility (268–269).

In evidence is Olmsted's keen appreciation of the way form affects the character of environment. Here too is recognition of the close correspondence between road alignment and velocity, even given the slow speeds of a hundred years ago.

The 1869 General Plan for Riverside (Fig. 292), examined now, shows how well the reasoning of the preliminary report was applied. The curves have a controlled sweep and continuity of their own, unlike any precedent. On the ground the rural effect is heightened by the careful avoidance of curbs, as cautioned in the preliminary report, and by the subtle placement of the roads in slight depressions, flat-sloped so as to become almost invisible except when directly ahead of the traveler. Aside from the two business streets paralleling the railway, all the roads curve; a major line swings from the station generally northeast past the Long Common to a point on the boundary where the "park way to Chicago" was to have started. Noticeable on the plan are two pieces not owned by the company; today these exceptions have street patterns so ludicrously unlike the rest of Riverside that they serve only to accentuate the gentle smoothness of the system as a whole. At key points throughout, as well as in the Long Common and along the river, there are open spaces that contribute an even greater sense of breadth and calm.

But in the plan of Riverside the greatest quality of all cannot be singled out: the totality, the wholeness of form and spirit captured by Olmsted and Vaux so completely that its own continuity was assured through popular acceptance and affectionate pride. For a century Riverside has stood for the most part unchanged in plan and character (Fig. 293), despite financial ups and downs and the relentless pressure of Chicago growing around its borders. It has been staunchly defended by the residents themselves—what could more eloquently testify to the inherent excellence of the original design? To be sure, not every detail of the 1869 plan has been carried out as intended. The Des Plaines River has suffered tragically with the years, like other American rivers, and no longer "abounds with fish and wild fowl"[4] as it did in 1868. The "park way to Chicago" was never finished. A portion of the original tract west of the river has been occupied, partly by the Chicago Zoological Park, partly by areas of the Cook County Forest Preserve system, which act as a welcome buffer strip. But with the exception of these few curtailments, the initial intent has been adhered to faithfully, and Riverside remains an as-

4. *Ibid.*, p. 267.

tounding monument to the enduring power of excellent design. And quite apart from its technical merit, Riverside is historically significant as the first clearly recorded instance in the United States of the application of landscape architectural design to a real-estate land subdivision project.

Roland Park was begun twenty-two years after Riverside. During the intervening period Olmsted and his firm had been engaged in many land subdivisions for private investors, but none received the recognition ultimately accorded Roland Park. In 1891 Edward H. Bouton, of Baltimore, Maryland, organized the Roland Park Company, capitalized at one million dollars, and bought for development about 550 acres of land then four miles north of the Baltimore city line. The company called in the elder Olmsted as landscape architect. What resulted was an unusually intelligent venture that quickly came to be regarded as a leading example of sound real-estate operation, with customers so uniformly satisfied as virtually to guarantee a continuing market. It was an outstanding early model for carefully formulated deed restrictions, worked out by Olmsted and Bouton together with a view to maintaining high quality, stability of values, and a harmonious community. In terms of design Roland Park is not especially distinguished for any overall unity of form (Fig. 294), but it offers valuable lessons in the adapting of plan to topography.

This is particularly true in the northernmost section, where the terrain is hilly and heavily wooded. Here Olmsted was confronted by a succession of high-ridged promontories thrusting forward with steep slopes to form an

293. Riverside, Illinois: typical roadway and walk along the Des Plaines River.

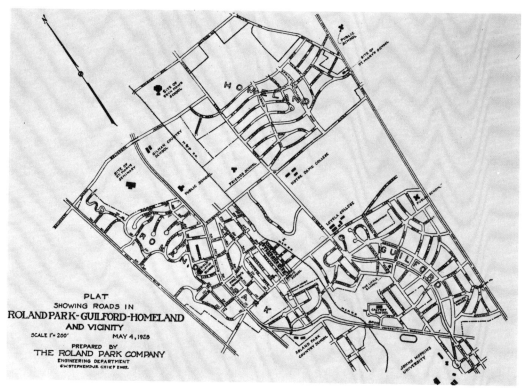

294. Roland Park, Baltimore: the 1891 section is at left, later additions as noted.

irregular bottom edge; from this the land sloped more gently westward toward
Falls Road, one of the property's boundaries. Olmsted placed a cul-de-sac
on each ridge and the winding Edgevale Road along the toe of the slopes.
In two instances, Beechdale and Elmwood Roads, the draw between ridges
was used for an uphill road location. Houses were built on the slopes with
access to the several roads, and in some cases simple stairways from Edgevale
Road still climb the slopes to houses on the culs-de-sac at the top. Throughout
there has been great care in handling exposed slopes and preserving trees
(Fig. 295). Today there are majestic specimens, saved in their youth by flexible
adjustments of grade, with lifted sidewalks, riprapped banks, and similar
indications of early respect for native condition of the site. There has been
remarkably little soil erosion.

The same faithful attention to topographic and other natural features
prevailed in the newer sections that the company found itself called upon
to establish when no more lots were available in the original section. This
was in 1913; to meet the continuing demand, the Roland Park Company
purchased and began developing in 1914 a second contiguous section officially
named Guilford; Olmsted Brothers were the landscape architects. The policy

295. Roland Park: a typical street.

of sensible layout, first-class construction, reasonable profits, and the stability of fully enforced deed restrictions was obviously paying off for the company as predicted. A third section called Homewood was added in 1924; all three were customarily included in the designation Roland Park and eventually came within the corporate limits of Baltimore.

One advantage of the Roland Park situation deserves particular mention: the exceptionally fine boundary protection, a factor of much importance in any community development. The outside property lines of the three sections taken as a whole were shared to a remarkable extent with educational and religious institutions whose considerable open spaces had every likelihood of being maintained. The value of such abutting neighbors, if only as a matter of visual surety, is obvious. This is probably one of the major external factors contributing to the enviable reputation that Roland Park gained in its time, as a real-estate enterprise and as a comfortable environment in which to live.

The continuity of market would no doubt have prevailed unbroken had it not been for the disastrous financial collapse of 1929. Already embarked on further extension, the company added a fourth section, Northwood, in 1934. Its first portion was developed during the 1930s, but the depression took a heavy toll. The company's assets were in large part tied up in vacant land, and the neighboring subdividers began offering cheaper developments of distinctly lower quality that nevertheless proved acceptable on the market of the day. This was a sad commentary on the decline of standards in America. Under pressure, the stockholders and board of directors were increasingly tempted to give up the Roland Park type of first-class operation and liquidate the company. A few other faltering efforts were made to keep things going, and two garden-type apartments were built in 1939 and 1941; but the policy of selling off the company's assets was continued, and in 1959 the directors voted to dissolve the Roland Park Company. Despite the lamentable closing chapter in the history of the company as a business enterprise, the physical Roland Park—especially the hilly northern section started in 1891—will long remain for landscape architects one of the important milestones of community development in America.

Another city-embedded project is the famous Country Club District of Kansas City, Missouri, also a large-scale real-estate operation based, like Roland Park, on confidence in continuity of market. It has been carried on with phenomenal success since its modest beginning in 1907 when Jesse Clyde Nichols, on capital borrowed from friends, bought a ten-acre piece of land on the southern outskirts of Kansas City and started what eventually expanded to an area of several thousand acres. Hare and Hare, of Kansas City, were the landscape architects from 1913 for about the next twenty years, during the formative period when the renowned physical character of the County Club District was being established in the area between 59th and 71st Streets, east of Ward Parkway. Thereafter Hare and Hare served mainly as consultants. When Nichols died in 1950, the company continued under his name; it still actively extends its operations southward and westward.

The Country Club District (Fig. 296) differs in plan from the usual subdivision by having no readily discernible outline form or boundary. This condition arose from the way the district grew, by successively acquiring for new development sizable blocks delimited by major thoroughfares within the gridiron street system of Kansas City. The district comprises today over fifty named subdivisions, each added in its time and integrated to the greatest feasible degree with those already completed. Within most of the large blocks,

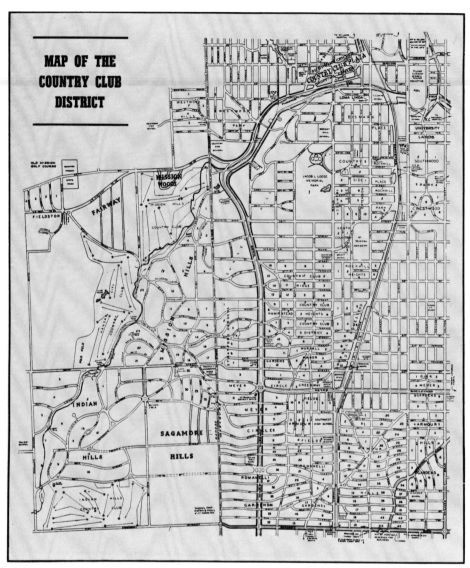

MAP OF THE
COUNTRY CLUB
DISTRICT

296. The Kansas City Country Club District in 1939.

at least during the formative period, the landscape architects were able to modify the stiff gridiron system somewhat so as to recognize existing valleys of the rolling terrain. The district early began reaching across the state line into Kansas, and the total development is now about half in each state. The road systems in the older parts of the Kansas portion, designed by Hare and Hare, follow the topography almost without exception.

Across this general framework of street pattern, two main arteries run roughly north-south, the broad Ward Parkway and the slightly less ample Brookside Boulevard. Toward the northern edge of the district the two swing together and join at the Country Club Plaza, a ten-block commercial area and shopping center early noted for its provision of off-street parking space well in advance of the times. From Country Club Plaza the Mill Creek Parkway runs north into the center of Kansas City.

The Country Club District is made up almost entirely of single-family detached houses, except for some apartment buildings at the plaza and a few more recent additions. Lot sizes vary from a minimum of fifty-foot frontage to large places of five to ten acres in some of the Kansas developments. The income level is relatively high, the population predominantly executive, clerical, and professional. In the district there is abundant carefully planned open space, including over two hundred small parks, several golf courses, and many smaller recreational areas. Numerous shopping centers, local and smaller than the plaza, have been erected after meticulous market analysis. There are many schools and an unusually large number of churches.

Throughout the district there is a spaciousness and charm seldom found in such large residential sections with any consistency. The houses are of highly varied and competent though generally traditional architecture, but the streets and individual properties are handsomely arranged and planted. The distinction that characterizes the district—an appreciable sense of domestic stability—is probably in large part the result of shrewd but enlightened business policy, first on the part of Nichols himself and then within the large organization that he assembled and trained: the aim was never merely to make a sale, it was "to create values in the land and then to maintain them,"[5] as he so often said, recognizing that satisfied customers are the surest source of new business. Both in visual results and financial success, the Nichols operations offer a convincing contrast to the sell-and-get-out approach that has cursed the work of so many real-estate subdividers.

Perhaps the major managerial contribution of the Nichols enterprise was the self-perpetuating restriction worked out after years of trial and error and introduced to American practice by Nichols in the Country Club District. The custom is to file certain basic restrictions on all property in a given subdivision at the time the plat itself is filed. By agreement the restrictions run for a stated period, usually twenty-five years, then automatically extend themselves for another similar period unless the owners of a stipulated proportion of the subdivision's front feet agree, five years before the end of the period, to cancel the restrictions. The result has been, to an unprecedented degree, retention of the restrictions by common consent and thus the perpetuation of a high level of quality in the respective subdivisions. The standard restrictions have usually included control of land use, minimum cost of dwellings, setback lines, building projections, free space, outbuildings, and billboards. For many years there were also racial restrictions, the one serious

5. See "The J. C. Nichols Number," *National Real Estate Journal,* February 1939.

flaw in these provisions. Enforcement of the restrictions in each area, as well as that area's general management, is in the hands of a homes association with elected officers.

Enlightened business policy, however, important as it was and is, could not by itself have accounted for the physical excellence that made the Country Club District by general consensus one of the finest residential sections in the United States. Indeed, a clear indication of the Nichols enlightenment was the retention of Sid J. Hare and his son, S. Herbert Hare (in partnership as Hare and Hare since 1910) as landscape architects for all work from 1913 to the 1930s. During these years Herbert Hare, the designer of the firm, was personally responsible for the subdivision planning, for many of the detailed entrances, parks, and parklets, and for the site-planning of many of the individual properties. It was his hand that brought about in road layouts a degree of departure from the gridiron system and the greater recognition of topography. Hare was a widely respected leader of the profession, especially in the midwest, for half a century until his passing in 1960; he was for years a trustee of the ASLA and served as its president from 1941 to 1945. Under his guidance Nichols, too, became intensely interested in landscape architecture and was an enthusiastic supporter of the profession; in token of his long service to the cause he was elected to corresponding membership by the ASLA in 1939.

In 1911, just before Hare and Hare started helping Jesse Nichols with the Country Club District, the Russell Sage Foundation of New York began developing Forest Hills Gardens on Long Island, within the corporate limits of New York City. Also a suburban subdivision, this was intended in a limited sense as a business enterprise even though it was set up by a philanthropic institution. The Russell Sage Foundation had been established in 1907 under a New York State charter committing it "to the improvement of social and living conditions in the United States of America."[6] In her letter of gift the founder, Mrs. Sage, expressed an interest in "investments for social betterment . . . in distinction from investments in securities intended only to produce income."[7] Accordingly, she authorized the Trustees to so invest two million dollars out of capital funds, provided only that, to avoid dissipation of the fund, a return of 3 percent would in their opinion be produced.

After studying many possibilities, the Trustees decided to attempt a demonstration to prove that careful planning and design of a real-estate subdivision could create for people of moderate means a community of top quality while making a reasonable financial return on the investment. If successful in both respects, it was hoped that the project would encourage commercial developers toward a better type of operation than had been usual. Early in

6. John M. Glenn and others, *Russell Sage Foundation, 1907–1946* (New York, 1947), p. 11.
7. *Ibid.,* p. 668.

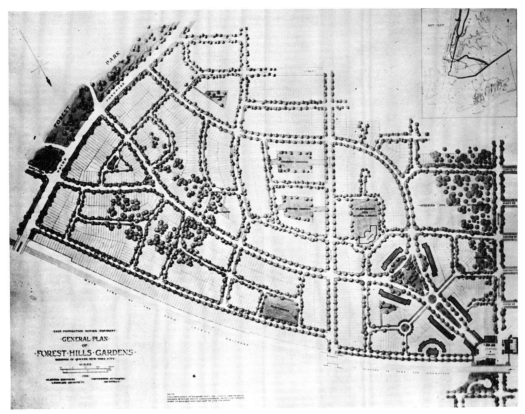

297. Forest Hills Gardens, Long Island: general plan.

1909 a tract of 142 acres of raw farmland was bought on the Long Island Railroad at Forest Hills, Queens. McKim's huge quasi-Roman Pennsylvania Station was being completed; shortly thereafter a railroad tunnel under the East River would bring Forest Hills a mere nine miles, or less than thirty minutes' traveling time, from the station in midtown Manhattan. A residential community at a point like this would be well-nigh perfect for commuters working in New York shops and offices.

In the summer of 1909 the Sage Foundation Homes Company was incorporated, to be financed by the Foundation. Olmsted Brothers were engaged as landscape architects and Grosvenor Atterbury as architect. Studies began at once, field work was under way in 1910, and by autumn 1911 the project was sufficiently established to warrant a public statement of the company's aims, objectives, and proposed sales methods. The plan of Forest Hills Gardens (Fig. 297), developed under the personal supervision of the younger Olmsted, focuses on Station Square—an open space immediately beside and below the station of the Long Island Railroad, whose right-of-way, on a high and slightly curving embankment, forms the northeast boundary of the

·FOREST·HILLS·GARDENS·
·DESIGNED·FOR·THE·SAGE·FOUNDATION·HOMES·CO

STATION·SQUARE·
·RAILROAD·STATION·STORES·AND·APARTMENTS·

298. Sketch of the Forest Hills Station Square, intended to serve as a community center.

project. The square, at ground level, is reached by stairways descending from the station platform. Surrounding it on the remaining three sides and giving it somewhat the appearance of a medieval marketplace (Fig. 298) are the towered Forest Hills Inn and an arcaded shopping center, all charmingly designed by Atterbury in a surprising combination of rough and smooth concrete, brick, and steeply pitched roofs with flat red tiles. From each end of the Inn a covered bridge from an upper floor crosses above a roadway to reach an apartment block at the end of the square, above the shops.

The northernmost bridge arches across Continental Avenue, a straight city thoroughfare passing beneath the railroad and on through the Gardens. The other bridge spans the beginning of two divergent "greenways" curving through the development as major streets. One other city thoroughfare, Ascan Avenue, comes under the railroad and runs straight on through the community in the same manner as Continental Avenue. The narrower local streets, mostly short and curving, have a winsome domestic quality heightened by excellent planting. There is a remarkable visual unity among the dwellings—apartments, row-houses, single-family detached homes—some built by the company, some by individual owners, nearly all of brick, some of stone, and all roofed with the same flat red tile as that used in Station Square (Fig. 299). Between the two Greenways an open panel of grass widens to form a park-like terminal in Flagpole Green; the original intent was also to have six interior parks within blocks of the development, but these did not work out. A site was reserved centrally for a public school, but the space proved inadequate when the school was built and there is still need for play space in the community.

The boundaries of Forest Hills Gardens present an object lesson in several respects. On the northeast, the high embankment of the railroad forms a positive wall, visually and tactually, except for the two penetrations of Continental and Ascan Avenues. On the southern boundary, once well secured by woods of the city's Forest Park with only Union Turnpike intervening, there is now an active barrier of traffic, part of the intricate highway system of the expanding metropolis, and the value of Forest Park has all but vanished. On the north, early sale of some ten acres to the West Side Tennis Club for courts and the world-renowned stadium has created a continuing open-space bulwark against the advancing tide of apartment houses. But the entire western and southwestern boundary, having been formed merely by the irregular property line of the original farm, left the area vulnerable to nondescript development. Fortunately, a measure of harmonious extension was retained through the intelligence of new neighboring owners and the persuasive visual appeal of the existing Forest Hills community.

Forest Hills Gardens is justly regarded as one of the handsomest of American suburban areas, with unusual community solidarity and occupants enthusiastically loyal through the years. There have been numerous community organizations, of which the Gardens Corporation of home owners is probably the most important. In 1923 the Sage Foundation conveyed to the Gardens Corporation the "streets, parks, etc., and rights and powers with

299. Bird's-eye sketch of Forest Hills Gardens.

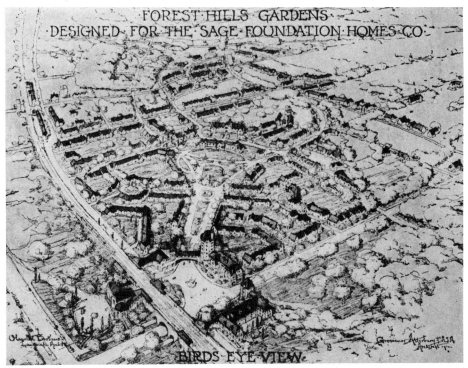

regard to restrictions."[8] This corporation has been, in effect, the local government, enforcing the deed restrictions rigorously and in general managing the community's legal, financial, and social affairs.

The venture has missed its mark in one important respect. Because of rising construction costs and amiable but expensive rivalry among individual home-builders, the income level of the population has been consistently higher than intended. Otherwise, especially considering how little precedent was available, the experiment must on the whole be adjudged a success, at least visually and sociologically, and in these respects a fine chapter in the story of town planning.

The attempt at making Forest Hills an educational demonstration from a commercial point of view has been somewhat less successful. Again the matter of rising construction costs and unpredictable maintenance expenses, together with the interruption of World War I at precisely the wrong time, effectively prevented the investment from realizing the modest 3 percent return conjectured. In order to minimize further risk of its capital fund, the Russell Sage Foundation in 1922 sold to a trustworthy group of residents the Foundation's interest in the Homes Company, absorbing a capital loss of some $360,800. This was looked upon by the Foundation, sensibly enough, as a worthy financial contribution to the elevation of residential standards and the art of community planning.

In the course of years a few weaknesses of plan have been revealed. The difficulty with boundaries has been mentioned, and the shortage of play space. The shopping center at Station Square proved far too limited to serve as a community focus; most of the local trade soon moved along Continental Avenue into what is today the typically gridiron, closely packed, unprepossessing urban development beyond the railroad embankment—an area now reached by the onward-marching New York subway system, with an underground station on Continental Avenue about a block from Forest Hills. This condition renders all the more noticeable the psychological intrusion that was accepted in allowing the two city streets, Continental and Ascan Avenues, to continue straight through the Gardens. This could have been prevented before the streets were dedicated to the city, when title was still held by the Gardens Corporation.

In the eyes of today's visitor, the most glaring fault is a common one, for which the designers can hardly be blamed: a surfeit of automobiles far beyond anything one would have expected in 1910. Station Square is now obviously too small, and too many of the main thoroughfares are lined with parked cars. It is a remarkable testimonial to the intrinsic excellence of Forest Hills Gardens that its quiet charm still shines through the senseless automotive coating.

8. A. C. Comey and M. S. Wehrly, "Planned Communities," in *Supplementary Report of Urbanism Committee of National Resources Committee* (Washington, 1939), p. 108.

XXXIII. Town Planning in the United States: 1915–1929

In the decade that saw Forest Hills Gardens established—in those rollicking, carefree years just before World War I—nothing much more happened in community planning until the war itself burst upon the scene. Certainly there was little evidence of any general preoccupation with the living conditions of the "common people." Such efforts as those described in the preceding chapter were mainly for people in reasonably comfortable circumstances. The concern of British industrialists for housing of factory workers was little echoed in America, though, to be sure, there were a few instances of concern. As early as 1895, the Apollo Iron and Steel Company had engaged the Olmsted office to design a new town around the company's mills in Vandergrift, north of Pittsburgh; but of this plan only a portion was carried out. In 1913 the Kohler Company moved their factory into the country from Sheboygan, Wisconsin, and in time developed Kohler Village around it. In 1915 John Nolen planned industrial Kingsport, Tennessee, but its later growth was haphazard. The Goodyear Company in Akron, Ohio, and the Norton Company in Worcester, Massachusetts, undertook suburban residential development for workers, though not in close connection with their plants. These were isolated cases; it must be conceded that America did not develop a noticeable public conscience about communities for factory workers until the war compelled it. Then the picture changed completely.

In 1917, with America suddenly involved as a belligerent, the country had thrust upon it a swift and urgent dose of workers' emergency housing, as the

United States became for the first time an "arsenal of democracy." There was immediate need for large amounts of shipping, regarded as America's most effective means of contributing to allied war efforts; production of all kinds of armament, ammunition, and other supplies was stepped up drastically. One of the brightest chapters in the annals of American landscape architecture was the profession's quick and extensive mobilization. The younger Olmsted was called to Washington to work with the famous builder Otto Eidlitz on emergency construction for relief of the industrial housing shortage. He was able from this central position to distribute efficiently the services of landscape architects to meet many varied needs.

In the War Department, a Camp Planning Section was set up and teams of architects, landscape architects, and engineers were organized quickly to handle cantonment projects at army stations old and new from coast to coast. An executive governmental agency, the United States Housing Corporation, was charged with providing new housing at industrial sites; within it a Town Planning Division, managed by Olmsted and staffed by landscape architects, worked in close collaboration with architects and engineers on projects throughout the country. Another executive organization, the Emergency Fleet Corporation, set up under the United States Shipping Board, took administrative charge of the vast need for new communities to accommodate the suddenly expanded labor force as shipyards leaped into frenetic action. Here, too, landscape architects did the planning as members of collaborative teams. In 1919, at the end of the war, Olmsted's colleagues in the ASLA presented him a medal "in recognition of his service to his country and to his profession."[1] Regret has often been expressed in recent years that the federal government did not similarly avail itself of professional help during World War II.

With the coming of the 1920s the story of community planning and design changed appreciably. Perhaps it was only a carry-over from the hasty wartime provision of housing for workers, but one would like to believe that America was at last growing up in its realization of the needs of an increasingly industrial and technological society. One of the first postwar manifestations of awakening came with the creation of a new industrial town called Longview, on the Columbia River in Washington. In 1922 the Long-Bell Lumber Company, of Kansas City, bought a huge tract of timber north of the river, and then, seeking a location for mills to produce dressed lumber, chose land northwest of the point where the Cowlitz River empties into the Columbia. It was an almost ideal spot for transportation by water, rail, and highway: on the Columbia, navigable fifty miles either downstream to the Pacific or upstream to Portland via the Columbia and Willamette Rivers; on several railway lines, including the main route from Portland and the south to

1. *Landscape Architecture,* 10 (January 1920), p. 96.

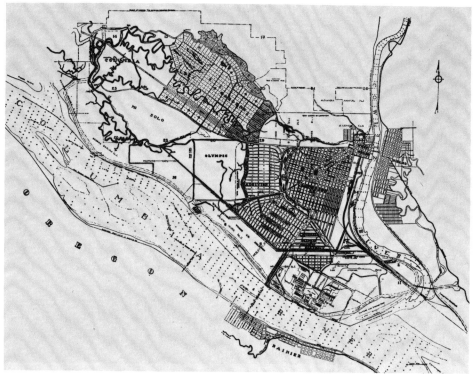

300. Longview, Washington: general plan of 1922 by Hare and Hare.

Seattle; at the junction of main highways through the Columbia and Cowlitz valleys. On the east bank of the Cowlitz was the small town of Kelso; across the Columbia was Rainier, Oregon.

Here on 3,000 acres (already enlarged to 5,200 by 1926) Hare and Hare of Kansas City laid out in 1922 the wholly new town of Longview, planned for an eventual population of 50,000. They had as planning consultant until his death in 1923 George E. Kessler, the landscape architect from St. Louis generally regarded as father of the Kansas City park system. Long-Bell had also retained as realty consultant J. C. Nichols, developer of the Kansas City Country Club District. It was an almost fully Kansas City operation. The plan prepared by Hare and Hare (Fig. 300) provided a central business district, three residential "additions," some tentatively outlined suburban acreage, and a relatively wild public area on Mount Solo, the only high topographic unit, some two or three miles west of the town center. There was a designated "central manufacturing district" for light industry, and a belt of land along each of the two rivers was reserved as a "commercial district." At the mouth of the Cowlitz an area twice the size of the central business district was set apart for the two enormous mills projected by Long-Bell.

Since the land, except for Mount Solo, was relatively flat, with just enough pitch for good surface drainage, gridiron street systems were adopted for the business and residential districts, with longer blocks in the latter and an independent orientation of the grid in each section. Between the central business district and the adjacent residential "additions," a natural drainage channel of the Cowlitz was to be further excavated and formed into a long, narrow, crescent-shaped park containing Lake Sacajawea, with boulevards along both sides.

The plan showed the central business district itself organized about a six-acre civic center later known as Jefferson Park at the high point of the plain. Through this a sight-line running roughly eastward, perpendicular to the main-line railway along the Cowlitz, would focus on the railway station. This line would become Broadway, and the whole grid system of the business district would form on it. From Jefferson Park major diagonals would reach out as thoroughfares: Washington Way southwest to the St. Helen's and Olympic residential "additions" and northeast to the small cross-river settlement called West Kelso; Olympia Way northwest to the Sunset residential "addition," but southeast only a short distance so as to permit better railway service into the industrial district.

Street grading was begun in August 1922, the first lot was sold in February 1923, and a ceremony dedicating the streets and other public land was held in July 1923. The first building to be completed was the seven-story, two hundred-room fireproof Hotel Monticello, set in its own ample grounds facing Jefferson Park. Within ten years Longview grew to a population well over 12,000 with 2,700 permanent homes and many apartment buildings. R. A. Long, of the Long-Bell founding firm, had given a public library; there were four schools, a hospital, nine churches. The city had 160 acres of parks, a golf course, tennis courts, and a stadium. The two vast Long-Bell lumber mills had been joined on adjacent acreage by three mills of the Weyerhaeuser Timber Company. There was a large grain elevator on the extensive docks of the waterfront. A total of thirty-one industries employed over three thousand people; there were eighty-four masonry buildings in the business district. Longview's individual buildings were sturdy and architecturally competent but not exceptional. The general plan, though notably thorough, is hardly one of unusual distinction in design. What is truly remarkable about Longview is its economic and social completeness—and the driving speed with which it was caused to rise almost like a miracle out of raw land.

In 1923, while Longview surged forward, another town was established with an industrial base, though it was not sponsored by industry: Mariemont, Ohio, on the Little Miami River near Cincinnati. Its genesis was philanthropic but practical, much like that of Forest Hills Gardens. Mrs. Thomas J. Emery, of Cincinnati, already for years a dispenser of a wide range of philanthropies, wished to create as a memorial to her husband a complete community that would provide comfortable working and living conditions, primarily for wage-earners, but would nevertheless operate along sound business lines and thus justify itself economically. John Nolen was her land-scape architect, aided by Philip W. Foster and Justin R. Hartzog; Mrs. Emery's local managerial representative was Charles J. Livingood.

Actually, preliminary thinking and study had started in 1914; but the war postponed further action except completion of a topographic survey of the site in 1918, accomplished without disclosure of the purpose. To prevent skyrocketing land prices, the plan to build a town was long kept secret and land was purchased through a real-estate firm in Chicago, not Cincinnati. Even in the Nolen office in Cambridge, Massachusetts, geographical location of the site was not known to the staff until the needed land had been acquired and the general plan was nearly finished. The first Nolen plan of 1921 was labeled with some ambiguity, apparently under instructions from Mrs. Emery: "Mariemont, a new town situated in the Middle West. An Inter-pretation of Modern City Planning Principles applied to a Small Community to produce local Happiness. A National Exemplar."[2]

The tract for which the plan was made contained about 365 acres, though it was later increased. Along the southern edge were high bluffs overlooking a railroad right-of-way and yards, a stretch of bottom land early designated as an industrial section, and the Little Miami River. The Wooster Pike bent its way across the site from west to east. Along most of the north edge of the tract ran the road from Oakley to Plainville, with only a small piece of land called Resthaven lying north of it. Just below the Wooster Pike, on the west edge of the tract and extending north for a slight distance above the pike, was a rough, largely wooded ravine known as Dogwood Park. Otherwise the land north of the bluffs was reasonably level and lent itself well to a community layout.

The plan prepared by Nolen for this tract (Fig. 301) was essentially simple. The route of the Wooster Pike across the property was straightened out and a town center fixed on the new line. Divided roadways and a turfed median strip formed an approach to a village green and church. Strangely contra-dicting this directional quality was the centralized geometry of four diagonal streets through the midpoint of the town center and a strong north-south center-line to an overlook on the lip of the bluffs. The diagonals led northwest and northeast to the Oakley-Plainville road, southwest and southeast to a new street paralleling the pike. On this framework a tree-lined system of streets was laid out, a compromise between rectilinear grid and curved align-ments as required to accommodate the topography. Several culs-de-sac, or "closes" in the manner of Letchworth and Welwyn, were included.

The first public announcement of Mariemont as a new town was made in April 1922. The Mariemont Company, organized to carry out the project, was established in February 1923, and in April 1923 a ground-breaking

2. Conversation, Hartzog and author, 1948.

ceremony was held, Mrs. Emery presiding with a silver spade. Street grading was begun that autumn, and in November building construction was started with the Memorial Church, located next to an existing pioneer cemetery, at the upper edge of the piece of Dogwood Park extending north of the Wooster Pike. This part of the ravine was given the name Dale Park, and the entire northwestern corner of Mariemont was thereafter called the Dale Park section. With the Memorial Church nearing completion, residential construction was begun in April 1924.

The rather unusual procedure was adopted of selecting different firms of architects—twenty-six originally for all of Mariemont—and assigning them respective tasks at specified locations in the Nolen plan. Thus in the Dale Park section a dozen firms designed single-family, semidetached, and group houses, along with a few apartments, the Memorial Church, a fire station, and the Dale Park School—all in 1923 and 1924. In other sections, a few houses were built in Denny Place and Sheldon Close; the Mariemont Inn followed at the town center in 1925. But, with these exceptions, the Dale Park section was the only fully developed part of the new town for many years, until just before World War II.

The unfortunate hiatus in development points up a serious error in community planning illustrated well by Mariemont. Mrs. Emery's dream had been based on the assumption that residents of the town would be largely workers at plants in the bottom-land industrial district, and so it was planned at first. But the decision was early and wisely made to shift industry to a higher area, less vulnerable to flooding, in a gore called Westover, between the railroad right-of-way and the Wooster Pike, west of Mariemont's main residential sections. None of the anticipated industries had actually been secured before development began, however, and when the town was virtually complete none had yet appeared. Then the Cincinnati Milling Company, whose plant had been fully counted on, decided to locate at another site some miles away. As it turned out, no appreciable flow of industry to Mariemont occurred until the late 1930s. In the meantime the Mariemont Company, to protect its investment, felt compelled to raise its sights and aim at an income group higher than intended. Even so, further development just had to wait.

To some degree a similarly optimistic miscalculation affected the treatment of Resthaven, the twenty-five-acre piece of land north of the Oakley-Plainville road. It had been Mrs. Emery's hope to install here a pleasant, small community of cottages and allotment gardens for superannuated pensioners from the Emery enterprises, with a hospital, convalescent home, and workshop. This benevolent plan soon proved impracticable. A nursery had been started in Resthaven in 1922, and in 1924 a demonstration farm group was added. Of the original scheme, the hospital was started hopefully; the central part of a three-wing design was completed and the outer wings indefinitely post-

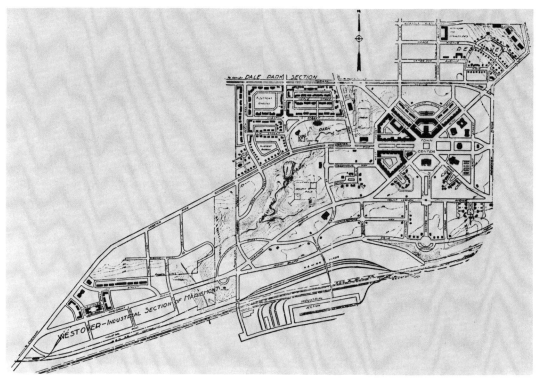

301. Mariemont, near Cincinnati: general plan of development by John Nolen, 1923.

poned. Even then, another miscalculation appeared: it had been intended that a group of doctors would operate this as a private hospital, but such a group had not been assured or organized before construction was begun nor could one be found afterward. The Mariemont Company somehow managed to carry the hospital until 1938, when it was leased for four years to a research institute. In 1942 it was taken over by a religious order and renamed Our Lady of Mercy Hospital; it now serves a highly useful and needed purpose. Meanwhile Resthaven disappeared, both as an idea and as a name; in 1929 the area, except for the hospital and the farm group, was subdivided for lots and single-family houses. It is now known as Lytle Woods.

During Mariemont's most uncertain years, when expected industry failed to materialize, it was feared that the town might remain a permanent bedroom satellite of Cincinnati—and this at a time when transportation facilities were far from optimal. With the passage of years, however, progress has been steady if slow. Industries have at last come to Westover until there is no longer room for more. Meanwhile, Mariemont itself has grown from a population of 1,600 in 1936 to 4,120 in 1960, and the local estimate is that the residential area, now fully built, will not produce a population in excess of the 5,000 originally projected and planned for. The town has had excellent civic spirit throughout; in 1941, when it was rumored that plans were afoot to embrace Mariemont in an expansion of the city of Cincinnati, the townspeople swiftly reacted by incorporating Mariemont as a village.

Thanks to careful control, restrictions, and good interprofessional collaboration in its early years, the town has more visual unity than might have been expected from a multiplicity of architects. The Nolen plan of 1921 has been adhered to remarkably well, and the recreational facilities indicated for the upper level of Dogwood Park and just east of the Dale Park section have been built. Judging by the enthusiastic testimony of people who have lived in Mariemont, it is a happy, harmonious town. Except only for the fact that income levels have always been higher than the original intent, it would appear that Mrs. Emery's dream has finally come true.

Mariemont's landscape architect John Nolen was regarded by many as the dean of American city planners. As noted earlier, he opened his office in 1903; he became a member of the ASLA in 1905, a fellow in 1910. Long an advocate of collaboration, he practiced it successfully on several hundred public projects, including the planning or replanning of dozens of cities. Yet the creation of small, totally new towns was his chief delight, and Mariemont was a favorite. Nolen was a faithful and articulate servant of the profession; he lectured often and wrote several books on the city planning aspects of landscape architecture. After three decades of extremely active practice, he died in 1937.

The industrial town of Chicopee, Georgia, represents a set of circumstances quite different from those in which Longview and Mariemont were born. Unlike Mariemont, Chicopee had a guaranteed industry because industry built it; unlike industry-built Longview, Chicopee was intended solely for the founding industry's own workers. This mill village, about four miles from Gainesville, was established in 1927 by the Chicopee Manufacturing Corporation, a subsidiary of Johnson & Johnson, to supplement the company's plant in Chicopee Falls, Massachusetts—hence the name.

In a sense, the founding of Chicopee was typical of the southward migration that proved so disastrous to the textile-mill towns of New England. The attractions in the present instance could hardly be denied: abundant labor at low wages, cheaper power, inexpensive land, and minimal tax rates—all on a fine site near the main line of the Southern Railway, with clean air and water for the manufacture of a product demanding especially sanitary conditions. Moreover, during the period of industrial resurgence in the South after World War I, many companies availed themselves of the allowable practice of charging against current profits the capital costs of improvement and development in company-owned villages. Because of all these factors, the Chicopee Manufacturing Corporation, after a five-year search, selected and bought some 3,500 acres near Gainesville—much of it to be used to control water supply and for the experimental culture of long-staple cotton —and erected what was advertised as "the world's first modern, single-story cotton mill . . . the technical and aesthetic showplace of the textile industry with its 250-house model mill village for employees."[3]

Chicopee was planned by the landscape architect Earle Sumner Draper, of Charlotte, North Carolina, a pioneer of the profession in the south. After a short period in Massachusetts, he had left in 1915 to represent Nolen as resident city planner in the development of Kingsport, 'Tennessee. In 1917 he set up his own practice in Charlotte—the first professionally trained city planner to locate in the Southeast—where he laid out a score of residential towns, of which Chicopee is generally looked upon as the best, for widely known industrial corporations. Draper was elected to the ASLA in 1920 and to Fellowship in 1927. He was later to have charge of all regional planning studies in the Tennessee Valley Authority and, still later, to serve as deputy commissioner of the Federal Housing Administration until 1945, when he returned to private practice as a consultant in Washington.

Draper's plan for Chicopee was forthright (Fig. 302). The main state highway from Gainesville to Atlanta cut across the property; Draper placed the town on both sides of it. The road traversed the town with two bends, one just before entering from the northeast, the other just beyond what was to become the town center. The plant was kept entirely on the west side of the highway but at some distance from it; the buildings comprised the main mill (an enormous brick and tile structure covering nearly five acres), ware-houses, a powerhouse, and a machine shop with the company's offices. The group was located parallel to the railway, with a pleasant setback from the right-of-way. Between the plant and the highway a large grassy open space was retained. In short, the factory setting was visually peaceful, consisting chiefly of green lawn and trees—a refreshing scene that characterized other Johnson & Johnson installations in later years. The effect of heavy highway traffic crossing the town was minimized by parallel local roads with wide buffer strips and only a few access points.

To the east and south of the highway, the land was devoted to residential development in two broad sections separated by a central band of open space. Only one small residential bit was west of the highway. The gently rolling topography, pitching slightly toward the center, lent itself readily to a com-fortable, tree-lined street system, nicely fitted to the terrain, with good radial flow on the most desirable lines of circulation toward the town center and the mill. The houses were unpretentious, single-family, one-story brick-faced structures in neat and pleasantly kept grounds. All utilities were put under-ground, a measure that contributed greatly to the tranquillity of the area. Today's mature trees make it all the more charming.

3. *Johnson & Johnson Bulletin,* May–June 1966, p. 11.

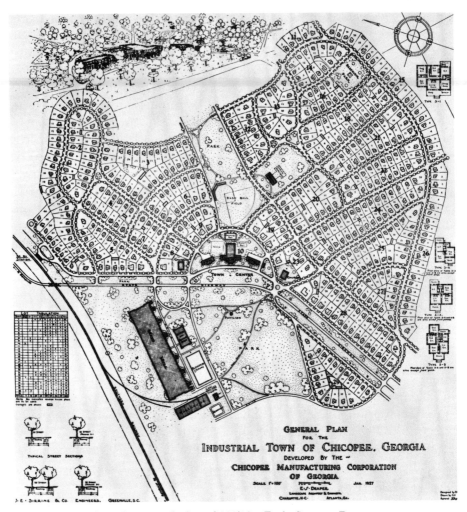

302. Chicopee, Georgia: general plan of 1927 by Earle Sumner Draper.

The town center consisted of a community building, two stores, and two churches. Such a group would be flexible enough to accommodate any changes of function that might develop with the years. The group was set well back from the highway on its own curving access road. Behind it stretched the central open space, with baseball field, park, and school site. Until the school could be built, the corporation maintained a grade school, and a new high school between Chicopee and Gainesville was early used by both towns. There was excellent neighborhood spirit in the new village; even before the community building was erected, several organizations sprang up naturally and received popular support without pressure from the company.

Chicopee was literally a one-industry company town, but not in the derogatory sense often implied by the term. The town was in fact—and still is,

488   *Design on the Land*

though it is now referred to as the Gainesville plant and village—fully owned and operated by the corporation, which manifested from the start a fine sense of social responsibility. A dental and medical clinic was maintained by the company, and child care services were freely available. The company also ran at current regional prices the well-stocked community store and a gasoline filling station.

One of the most heartwarming aspects of Chicopee's early years was the steadily increasing stability of the labor force. Some critics had gloomily predicted that the highly individualistic Georgia hill folk would not take kindly to the new living conditions offered, that there would be a feverishly rapid labor turnover, and that accordingly this would never be a settled community with a stable work force. The history of Chicopee, even within its first few years, clearly showed this prophecy to have been utterly incorrect. Again the power of design had proved itself in the quiet contentment of this tree-shaded industrial town.

While the 1920s were giving rise to varied efforts in the creation of industry-based communities, a deep restudy of the town planning problem was being pursued—a review, as it were, of the tenets of Ebenezer Howard and his garden city idea and, more specifically, of the techniques of Barry Parker and Raymond Unwin at Letchworth. Among the people most intensely involved in the review were two New York architects, Henry Wright and Clarence S. Stein, whose work in the development of lower-cost housing and wiser land use had profound effects. One of the others genuinely interested in these matters and concerned about the housing problem was Alexander M. Bing, an experienced and public-spirited real-estate operator who organized in 1924 a limited dividend company named the City Housing Corporation, the ultimate goal of which was the creation in America of a garden city based on English background.

In order to check out certain assumptions and gain experience in large-scale planning and building, the Corporation first invested in an urban housing development in the Borough of Queens, convenient to Manhattan by rapid transit. Since the land for the project, bought from the Long Island Railroad, had been intended as an addition to the Sunnyside Yards, the new experiment was called Sunnyside Gardens. Although the city compelled them to adhere to the previously platted gridiron street system, Wright and Stein were able to work with entire blocks and to abandon the traditional but deadly subdivision into lots. By using row-housing and concentrating on well-ordered interior spaces, and by profiting progressively from their experience in block after block, they were able in the brief span 1924–1928 to build in clear actuality a revolution in low-cost urban housing (Fig. 303). Working with Wright and Stein was landscape architect Marjorie Sewell Cautley, whose practical but sensitive handling of plant materials brought to completion a surprising atmosphere of almost suburban charm in the city blocks of Sunny-

303. Interior court, Sunnyside Gardens, New York City, about 1926.

side Gardens, much as she did later at Stein's Phipps Garden Apartments and Hillside Homes.

The frankly experimental work in Sunnyside Gardens paved the way for the City Housing Corporation's prime objective, the complete garden city, which they set out to accomplish late in 1927. What resulted was Radburn, New Jersey, a milestone in the history of American town planning. After inspecting many possibilities, the Corporation found and bought about two square miles of raw farmland in the Borough of Fairlawn, near Paterson. The tract lay on a branch line of the Erie Railroad and near the route of a state highway leading to the bridge then being built across the Hudson to New York City; there the Corporation intended to build Radburn, a town of 25,000 people primarily of moderate income.

Applying Ebenezer Howard's requirements for a garden city, Wright and Stein saw early that, although there would be ample land for about three "neighborhoods" of 8,000 to 10,000 people, there would not be enough for surrounding "greenbelt." They soon learned, moreover, that because the location was apparently wrong for it, the chances were slim of drawing the influx of industry upon which a garden city would depend. Despite these two vital deficiencies, it was decided to go ahead. A plan of generous dimensions was drawn up (Fig. 304) and work was begun immediately on the first section near the railway station, where the Erie tracks were crossed by Fairlawn Avenue, an old colonial road (Fig. 305). It had already become evident that the town, in the absence of adequate industrial support, would be a

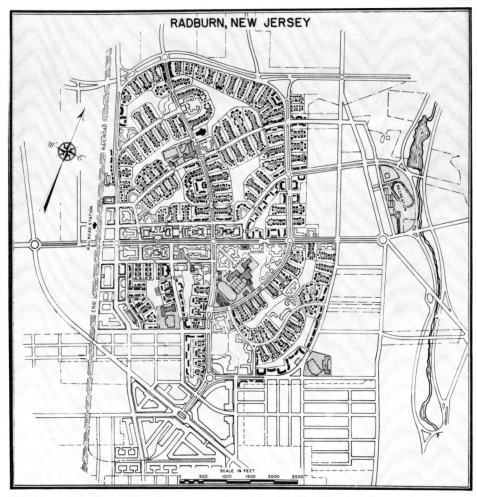

RADBURN, NEW JERSEY

304. Plan of Radburn, New Jersey, as projected by the City Housing Corporation.

bedroom satellite for the metropolitan area of New York City and northern New Jersey.

But the worst was yet to happen. Five months after the first residents moved into their houses, the Wall Street crash of 1929 ended the dream of a completed Radburn. While bemoaning the plight of the City Housing Corporation, forced into bankruptcy through no fault of its own, one can be grateful that at least Radburn's first section, consisting in the main of one entire superblock and part of a second, was in fact finished and occupied (Fig. 306). Its mature charm exists to be enjoyed by residents and visitors, and from it has come Radburn's greatest contribution, surely a classic of community planning, the "Radburn idea." Fundamentally, this meant separating types and speeds of traffic, much as Olmsted had done with grade separations and underpasses in Central Park seventy years earlier. He had kept footpaths,

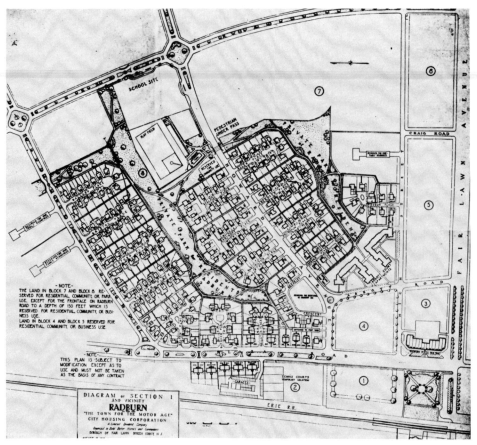

305. Plan of Radburn's Section I, the only portion finished.

carriage roads, transverse streets, and at times even bridle trails distinctly separate. At Radburn the significant separation was between pedestrian and motorcar: the "Radburn idea" meant reserving the interior of a superblock for pedestrians and restricting motors to the surrounding collector roads (if at driving speeds) or cul-de-sac service lanes (if at parking speeds) for direct access to the garages of individual houses. It also meant grouping the houses roughly in U-shaped patterns around these motor or service lanes (Fig. 307). Pedestrian paths then alternated with service lanes to lead in from the collector roads to a core of park space in the middle of the superblock. The combination led to Radburn's wide renown as "a town for the motor age"; and, it was ideally safe for children.

This arrangement, in order to work, required changing the standard type of house plan so as to provide two "front" entrances, one from the service lane, the other from the side toward the park (eliminating the typically unlovely American "back door"). At first the dwellings, aside from the two Abbot Court apartment buildings, were two-story single-family detached

306. Air view of Section I of Radburn in 1930, when nearly completed.

houses, no doubt in deference to a commonly held belief about American preferences. But the resultant spottiness soon led to joining houses, usually by coupling the garages, into doubles and triples. Further experimental plans for group houses were being studied when construction was suspended.

On the side facing the pathway to the park or, in a few instances, facing the park itself, each dwelling unit had its own small yard, treated by the tenant as he wished. The result has been pleasing variety, except in the few cases where hedges have become so high as to make the footway seem cramped and tunnel-like. At their inner ends, the paths joined a circumferential walk around the curving central park-like open space, excellently developed in planting plans by Mrs. Cautley, the landscape architect working with Wright and Stein here as at Sunnyside. At the far eastern end of the central park in the first superblock are the school, an athletic field, a swimming pool, and the underpass beneath Howard Avenue to the second superblock. Across Plaza Road from the railway station, between High Street and Fairlawn Avenue, the Radburn Plaza Building was erected early to house necessary stores on

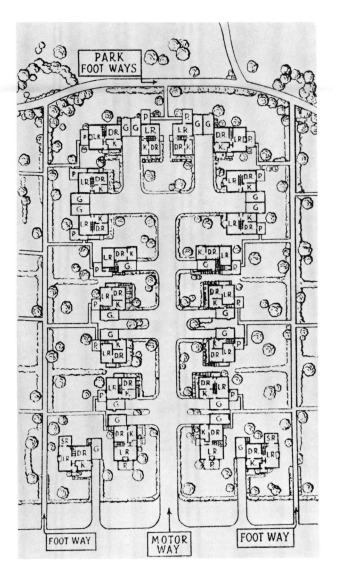

307. Typical unit plan at Radburn, showing full separation of motor and pedestrian traffic.

the ground floor and provide space upstairs for Radburn's various community organizations—numerous and extraordinarily active from the first at Radburn, where the sense of community solidarity has always been unusually strong.

To be sure, some criticisms have been voiced about the Radburn plan. They center mostly on the service lanes, which are of concrete, center-drained for economy, with overhead utilities on poles, and thus tend toward the tawdry appearance of the old-fashioned back alley. To some degree the increased size of automobiles has made the lanes feel cramped for turning—though the cure would more sensibly lie in returning the cars to sane dimensions! The drying of laundry, whether on the service lane or in the space between dwellings, has been a problem, usually solved now by indoor electrical appliances. Most frequent criticism of the service lanes is that their being paved encourages children to use them as play space, thereby exposing themselves to needless danger. A corollary is the claim that the paths on the park side of the houses are too narrow—to invite the play of children and as psychological introductions to the central park space. There is an element of truth in both assertions. It has also been pointed out that Radburn provides insufficient parking space for visitors. This is obviously true, but residents answer that theirs is so tightly knit and self-sufficient a little society as to tend away from outside visitors. The observer must conclude whether this, if true, is a socially desirable solution.

Naturally there have been changes in the total picture as the years have passed. As a community within a larger one, with a fairly constant composition—a relatively young group with social and intellectual interests somewhat above national average—Radburn has felt a degree of tension and political difference with the older and more traditionally burgeoning Borough of Fairlawn, of which Radburn and its fixed population become a continually smaller numerical fraction. To some degree a common meeting ground has been furnished by the regionally oriented supermarket that arose between the Plaza Building and the railway station. The railway itself, even with merger of the Erie and the Lackawanna, provides negligible commuter transportation. Regular bus service, however, plies between Radburn and a splendid new subway station at the New York end of the George Washington Bridge.

In its impact as a visual experience, Radburn has changed only to the extent of looking more mature in its quasi-rural sense of pastoral contentment. Its residents remain loyal—and eager to exhibit its salient features to a visitor with enthusiasm that is unforgettable. Details of the Radburn plan have been improved upon in subsequent community developments; but none can minimize the historic importance and validity of the "Radburn idea." In the story of American town planning, the first decade after World War I has a distinguished final monument.

XXXIV. Town Planning in the United States: 1929–1948

In 1929, just before things began falling apart with the Wall Street crash, Henry Buhl, Jr., of Pittsburgh, left some thirteen million dollars to establish a foundation dedicated to the welfare of the people of that smoky city. Charles F. Lewis, director of the Buhl Foundation, successfully recommended using part of the fund to provide housing for families of limited income while simultaneously testing the financial security of a 100-percent investment in a large-scale housing project completely under Foundation control.

A thorough study was made of the local housing market while possible low-cost sites were sought and examined. Investigation of limited dividend companies, especially the experience of the City Housing Corporation of New York in Sunnyside Gardens and Radburn, led to calling in Wright and Stein as consultants. A forty-five-acre tract of unencumbered land was secured on the heights known as Mount Washington, across the Monongahela River from downtown Pittsburgh, two miles by road from the Golden Triangle and at an elevation four hundred feet above it. The land was well wooded, though rougher than any usually considered appropriate for housing, but about half looked possibly buildable. But preliminary analysis quickly revealed that the single-family detached houses requested by the Buhl Foundation—again on the assumption that "own your own home" was the only tenable American policy—would be far too costly to meet the intended market and its needs; brick row-houses, to be rented rather than sold, would be financially workable.

As a consequence, the project named Chatham Village (for William Pitt, later the Earl of Chatham) became an outstanding object lesson in the town

496

planning story: rental row-housing on rough land, in a plan of such brilliance as to be universally accepted even decades later as one of the country's most charming and successful housing projects. Following the studies of Wright and Stein, landscape architect Ralph E. Griswold and architects Ingham & Boyd, all of Pittsburgh, developed in 1932 the first Chatham Village unit of 129 houses. The result was such a resounding success that in 1936 a second unit of 68 additional houses was built on the wooded point extending southward from the first. The landscape architect of the addition was Theodore M. Kohankie—Griswold yielded in 1934 to the urging of Pittsburgh citizens to accept appointment to public office as superintendent of the city's Bureau of Parks. The two units of Chatham Village are entirely harmonious; the project is without question a single work and is so to be judged.

The built-up part of the project (Fig. 308), bounded on the north by a city street, Virginia Avenue, covers only about 16 acres; the remaining 29, most heavily wooded with mixed hardwoods, with two miles of foot-trails, constitutes a small protective greenbelt on three sides. The built-up area, further bounded on the east by Bigham and Pennridge Roads, on the west by Olympia Road, is in three distinct pedestrian blocks (Fig. 309). Sulgrave Road runs between the northeast and northwest blocks, comprising the first or 1932 unit. The second or 1936 unit is the southern block of the development, separated from the first by a continuation of Bigham Road. Each block has a frame of row-houses along the street, plus occasional others stepping up the steep slope from Olympia Road. Within the blocks are cores of open, sun-dappled park space (Fig. 310)—two in each block except the northeastern, which has only one—with walks leading to a park entrance in each house. Tucked into corners of the park spaces are small sandboxes surrounded by low hedges.

The fall of the land, instead of being a hindrance, is availed of to contribute both visually and operationally to the excellence of Chatham Village. The high point of the built-up area is near the northeast corner; from this point the surface drops about fifty feet across to west and south. By using the row-houses, in effect, as retaining walls and thus designing to two levels, one on the street and the other a story higher on the park face, it has been possible to put basement garages in almost half of the 197 houses. Most of these are along Bigham and Pennridge Roads, along the east side of Sulgrave Road, and at the southernmost tip of Olympia Road.

The fall of the grade has also brought added interest to the project through the skillful use of steps and crisply delimited slopes to form a further architectonic tie between rows of houses, taking the place of retaining walls that could have been used had cost not been a major factor. At one point on Pennridge Road a bull-nosed stone retaining wall was built to save the so-called William Penn oak, a huge tree believed to have been there when the Penns owned the property. The tree succumbed to a hurricane some years ago, and the replacement looks a bit forlorn; but it will grow, and the wall

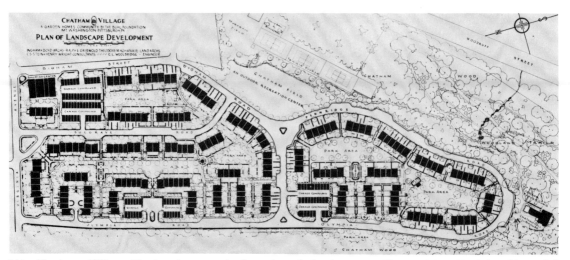

308. Chatham Village, Pittsburgh: general plan of total development. First unit (1932, Griswold) at left, second (1936, Kohankie) at right.

309. Air view of Chatham Village from the south after completion of the second unit (in foreground).

310. Chatham Village: central space of the first unit.

meanwhile serves to remind one how carefully the site's amenities have been safeguarded.

Since the individual garages provide cover for only about half as many cars as there are houses, each block also contains a garage compound, entered directly from the street and connected by walks to houses in the immediate vicinity. On the streets there are numerous parking bays for visitors' cars; the Radburn shortage is not repeated here. There is ample opportunity for recreation in Chatham Field, east of Bigham Road; on the west Olympia Park, a municipal area, offers other facilities. The former manor house at the south end of the built-up area, the only structure erected on the site in its previous history, has been remodeled as Chatham Hall, a clubhouse for community activities. Indeed, for many observers the most noticeable merit of the project is the community spirit, the obvious pride of the residents in their homes, individually and collectively. To the overall excellence of the planting design, which is simple and sturdy with overhead canopy of trees now well matured, the residents have added careful maintenance of the little outdoor spaces attached to all individual dwellings.

Of course Chatham Village cannot pretend to be a complete town in itself; it has no industry, for its occupants are chiefly workers in downtown Pittsburgh offices. It has no schools, churches, or library, but these were already in the vicinity when the site was chosen. At the very northeast corner of the project a small shopping facility was incorporated, along with an office for operation and management of the entire project. Until 1960, management was a responsibility of the Buhl Foundation. In that year, however, a co-operative organization consisting solely of residents, Chatham Village Homes, Inc., set up for the purpose, bought the Foundation's interest and took title to the property. The cooperative is governed by a board of five directors elected from its membership; the board appoints management. With typical good sense, the board has continued in office the managing personnel who have done such a capital job through the years.

The complete success of Chatham Village is perhaps best indicated by the satisfaction it has given in every direction. As an investment, it brought a steady though modest return to the Buhl Foundation through three decades of ownership; the cooperative then had no difficulty in arranging with an insurance company for financing of the 1960 purchase. As a collaborative effort of architects and landscape architects, it has had enthusiastic acclaim from the design professions. As a place to live, it has consistently held the affection of its residents—and even of the permanent maintenance crew. The remarkably low rate of turnover has meant only infrequent vacancies and a long waiting list. What greater evidence of success could one ask for in a housing project?

Whereas Chatham Village was achieved through private investment, Norris, Tennessee, and Greenbelt, Maryland, were public works, creations of President Franklin Roosevelt's New Deal. When the Tennessee Valley Authority was established in May 1933, one of its first projects was Norris Dam, named in honor of the Nebraska Senator known as the father of the TVA. To house construction workers reasonably near the dam the town of Norris was authorized. Design and building of the town in 1933–34 was under the TVA Division of Land Planning and Housing, of which Earle Sumner Draper was director. His team at Norris included landscape architects Tracy B. Augur and Carroll A. Towne and architect Roland A. Wank.

Because a temporary town would have to be built well enough to stand up for several years while TVA construction continued and abandonment thereafter would entail considerable loss, it was early decided to plan for a permanent town, to become eventually a valuable member in a network of communities around Knoxville. A site was found in the sparsely settled, rugged, undeveloped country about four miles from the dam location and twenty-three from Knoxville. Its 2,000 acres, acquired in the name of the people of the United States, were to include a genuine greenbelt surrounding a rise of land on which the town would be placed.

The prevailing note was urgency; while single workers on the dam could be housed in barracks in a construction camp, complete dwelling units were needed at once for families. Small portions of the town were built in final form and fitted into the general plan while the latter was still being designed (Fig. 311), rendering the technical excellence of the planning all the more

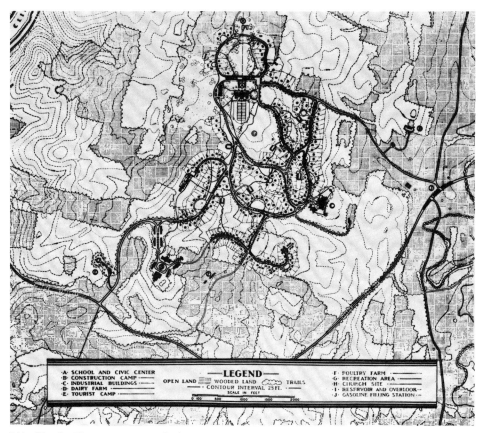

311. Norris, Tennessee: general plan.

astonishing. Perhaps the need for quick decisions contributed somehow to the casual charm that critical visitors have noted at Norris ever since the little town was finished. The atmosphere of sheer naturalness, almost inevitability, probably stems directly from the wholly sympathetic treatment of the undulating, partly wooded land. The street system was fitted in flowing lines closely to the terrain. Only the town center, with administration building, school, stores, and athletic field, was given rectilinear character—although, as the town developed, this was not followed exactly.

House sites, in most cases either on culs-de-sac or loop roads or well set back from the street, were individually related to the topography rather than lined up with the roads in the dull, all-too-familiar pattern of American developers' subdivisions. The houses were tied to each other and to the town center by means of a pedestrian path system, with underpasses and only a few grade-crossings of roads. Along with the ample provision of play spaces, the safe path system—plus elimination of sidewalks on the winding streets—made Norris a joy for children.

According to Draper, the members of the Norris design team were familiar with Radburn and were to a degree influenced by it. The rugged topography precluded adoption of the "Radburn idea" in its complete form; but some dead-end streets were used to serve groups of houses, in most of the large blocks there is a central core of undeveloped open space, and garage compounds within the blocks take the place of individual garages, with cars otherwise restricted to the streets.

Another factor in the visual nicety of Norris is no doubt a reflection of the basic grass-roots policy of the TVA. To a laudable degree the houses follow local or regional norms in both materials and form, giving the place a completely native look. In countless ways the grass-roots policy—a firm belief that TVA administration should depend upon local and regional will rather than imposition from "distant" Washington—acted as a sort of guarantee that what was built by TVA would quickly become an integral part of the land, freely accepted as natural by the region's people. So it came about with Norris.

But that was not all. When the dam was finished, in 1936, the waters of the Clinch River piled up behind it to create Norris Lake. Along the shores, with the aid of the National Park Service and Civilian Conservation Corps camps, TVA built Norris Park and, on another arm of the lake, Big Ridge Park with its abundant provisions for public use. The project's rock quarry, when no longer needed, was allowed to fill from the lake as a boat harbor, provided with a marina and floating docks. The parks are still in active use as facilities of the State of Tennessee, to which they were turned over some years ago. Similarly, Norris Freeway, the first rural freeway in America, has now become a state highway. This limited access road, a forerunner to today's many "thruways," was built in 1933 to connect the dam site with Knoxville and the railhead at Lake City. It bypassed the Norris community, though connected with the town, and served to haul men and materials to both Norris and the dam. It was later turned over to the state as part of the regional road net, although it is by now obsolete in highway standards.

The determination of TVA to be an integral component of the region was further manifested in 1948, when the federal government sold the entire town of Norris at public auction to a private corporation for over two million dollars—actually a little more than building the town had cost the United States. The corporation later resold the property to individual residents, who now own all of it; the town also became a self-governing municipality of Tennessee. Built not as a showcase "model town" but as an intensely practical affair to serve a pressing need for living accommodations—and therefore less publicized than other town planning efforts of the 1930s—Norris has hitherto not had the attention it merits as an outstanding contribution to the American community planning story.

Greenbelt, Maryland, received far wider notice than Norris, not only because it was practically on the doorstep of the national capital, but also because it was an end in itself as a demonstration. It differed markedly from Norris in that it had no industry and became a dormitory satellite of Washington. It was one of three "greenbelt towns" constructed by the Resettlement (later Farm Security) Administration. In April 1935 President Roosevelt combined certain agricultural and land conservation programs in a new agency, the Resettlement Administration. At its head he placed Rexford Guy Tugwell. In addition to organizing cooperative farming projects, Tugwell advocated building, just outside cities, communities of a new type based on his long interest in Ebenezer Howard's Garden City. To further this notion he set up within the new Administration a division called Suburban Resettlement and installed it, with a dash of pure incongruity, in the fantastically elaborate mansion of a former multimillionaire on Massachusetts Avenue in overcrowded Washington.

In that incredible environment, almost as though in protest, some epochal planning was done for the accommodation of low-income families. Under the general guidance of Frederick Bigger an extremely able, dedicated planning staff was assembled—architects, landscape architects, engineers, technicians, and draftsmen. Among the landscape architects were Harold B. Bursley, Jacob L. Crane, Justin R. Hartzog, Elbert Peets, William A. Strong, and Hale J. Walker; they were paired off in teams with their appropriate architectural counterparts to design the three new greenbelt towns: Crane and Peets were to do the plan of Greendale, near Milwaukee; Hartzog and Strong Greenhills, near Cincinnati; Bursley and Walker Greenbelt, near Washington. A fourth projected town, Greenbrook (New Jersey), was never built. The towns were intended not only as badly needed means of employment for some thousands of workers, but also as demonstration projects to establish viable communities "primarily for families of modest income"[1] along lines closely patterned on Howard's Garden City ideal.

Of the three new towns, Greenbelt was soon the best known because of its location and size. Five miles northeast of the District of Columbia line and a dozen miles from downtown Washington, the government acquired about 2,000 acres of land, protected on the north by an additional 5,000 taken for a National Agricultural Research Center. Approximately in the middle of the main acreage, a long crescent-shaped plateau became the heart of the town—a developed area of some 225 acres, around which the remainder of the tract formed a permanent protective belt of fields and forest in the best Garden City tradition (Fig. 312).

The actual construction of Greenbelt took about two years. In October 1935 large crews were set to preparing the site, starting with clearance of the 23 acres of swamp that became Greenbelt Lake a year later. The housing was begun quickly, and in June 1937 the town was incorporated in accordance

1. O. K. Fulmer, *Greenbelt* (Washington, 1941), p. 12.

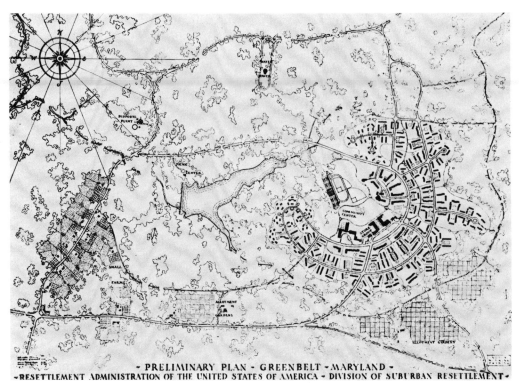

312. Preliminary plan of March 1936 for Greenbelt, Maryland.

with the laws of Maryland. The first families moved in at the end of September 1937, and in short order the Greenbelt Citizens' Association was organized, marking the start of a noteworthy story of spirited community activity that still continues. Late in 1937 the Resettlement Administration was terminated and replaced by the Farm Security Administration, under which Greenbelt lived most of its federal existence.

Working with Walker and Bursley on Greenbelt were architects Douglas D. Ellington and Reginald J. Wadsworth. As carried out, the plan of the town, done chiefly by Walker, is structured basically on two nearly parallel roads outlining the central crescentic plateau; they are continuous at their west end but spread apart at the north as the plateau widens. These are the main streets of the town; the inner is Crescent Road, the outer Ridge Road. The area between them is crossed radially by connecting roads at intervals of about 1,000 feet, so as to form five superblocks of some 14 acres each. At roughly the midpoint of Crescent Road, on the northwest or inner side of the curve and on its own access road, is the Community Center (Fig. 313), containing several shops, a supermarket, post office, branch bank, theater, auto service, municipal office, and police and fire station (Fig. 314). Sizable parking areas flank the group. Down the slope to the northwest, behind the Center,

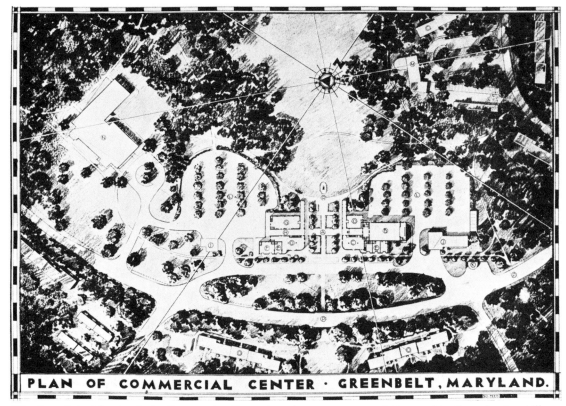

PLAN OF COMMERCIAL CENTER · GREENBELT, MARYLAND.

313. Greenbelt, Maryland: the Community Center is on its own access road; the combination school and library is at left.

314. Greenbelt: along the front of the Community Center, 1958.

are a bath house and the main Greenbelt swimming pool. Along Crescent Road, somewhat to the west of the Center, is the combination library and community school. Walkways connect the components, and an underpass leads from the Center beneath Crescent Road to the opposite superblock of residences.

Except for a few apartment buildings near the Center and about sixty two-family houses, all the dwelling units of Greenbelt are in row-houses of four to eight units per structure. They are disposed within the five pedestrian superblocks in variations of the Radburn system. Here, however, individual dwellings do not have integral garages; as a consequence the service lanes are usually long and narrow, with a back-around at the inner end, but in some instances they become wider service courts with grouped garages. As at Radburn, each dwelling unit has its own small, carefully tended garden on the opposite face of the house, but here the paths on this side lead to no appreciable core of park space. In effect, this means that at Greenbelt the open space is generously distributed among row-houses of the superblocks, but that the unifying force of a central space, so noticeable at Radburn, is lacking.

The plan has a different kind of cohesive sense, furnished by the Community Center both visually and psychologically, though many critics feel that a spatial core would have been more effective. To be sure, the several parts of Greenbelt are strongly connected by pedestrian paths, with underpasses beneath Crescent Road from all the superblocks at appropriate points, and the overall organization of the path system further emphasizes the focal nature of the Community Center and the school, toward which all the paths appear to lead. Children use the paths exuberantly and safely, as they do also the small play spaces interspersed in the interiors of the superblocks. Unfortunately, in 1941, as World War II approached and the national housing shortage became more acute, 1,000 additional dwelling units of "defense housing" were tacked on to what the Resettlement Administration had so carefully planned. Hasty and rather crude, the additions naturally detract from the total sprightly character of Greenbelt.

Without industry support, Greenbelt failed to achieve Howard's garden city ideal. In part this was intentional, in part fortuitous: no serious effort was made to induce industrial organizations to come, though when the program for Greenbelt was being formulated the National Agricultural Research Center north of the town was counted on as an early employment outlet for the residents. But this did not work out well, in part because Greenbelt occupancy was quite properly limited to low-income families, and many workers at the Research Center received salaries too high to qualify. Even today, the majority of Greenbelt's wage-earners commute to and from Washington.

After World War II there were recurrent rumors that Greenbelt was to be sold. The town had been transferred early in 1942 from the Farm Security

Administration to the Federal Public Housing Authority. Then in May 1949 the rumors became actuality, with an Act of Congress authorizing the Public Housing Commissioner to sell all the greenbelt towns by negotiation, giving first preference to veterans' groups organized on a nonprofit basis. The Greenbelt Veteran Housing Corporation (GVHC), forthwith incorporated as required, put in its application. By June 1949 Greenbelt had grown so much that it became a city officially under Maryland law. The Korean conflict then froze all negotiations until 1952. In December of that year all of the original dwelling units except the apartment buildings were sold to the GVHC. Later sales disposed of the rest of the housing. At last, in October 1954, the remainder of the town—the shopping center and a small commercial tract in the north end—was sold, and the federal government, which had built Greenbelt from the ground, was wholly withdrawn from ownership and responsibility.

Opinions in such matters naturally differ, but some observers who knew Greenbelt in the days of federal sponsorship have remarked that maintenance in the town seems to have fallen off since Uncle Sam moved out. This may of course be nothing more serious than the normal wear and tear of active use. It may be a demonstration that private management, even in a council and city manager form of government such as Greenbelt has had from the first, cannot find the powers that the federal structure has at its disposal. At any rate, reports persist that vegetation is inadequately cared for, that random wearing of vagrant footpaths has caused soil erosion, especially on the banks beside the underpasses, and that litter is evident. To the extent that these comments may be justified they should be mentioned, lest new visitors be unaware of the sparkling, trim freshness that characterized the truly re- markable Greenbelt of the late 1930s and early 1940s.

On the other side of the continent from Greenbelt, and struggling through the financial maze as a private project while Greenbelt enjoyed its palmiest public years, was Baldwin Hills Village, on the southern outskirts of Los Angeles (Fig. 315). It was created not as a whole town but as a rental housing project and as such has had few equals. The originators were four Los Angeles architects, Reginald D. Johnson and the associated firm of Wilson, Merrill & Alexander. They early called in Clarence S. Stein from the east coast as a consultant; the landscape architect was Fred Barlow, Jr., of Los Angeles. A local development corporation was persuaded to undertake the project. It required three hectic years, from 1938 to 1941, with help from the Federal Housing Administration and the Reconstruction Finance Corporation, to obtain the needed financing. The delay was not a total loss, however, for it provided time to do scores of studies of a general plan and to work out again and again details of the housing. Few projects can be given so much attention in the study phase.

The site, an almost flat undeveloped rectangle of some 80 acres of grassland then just beyond the city limits, was part of an old ranch in front of the

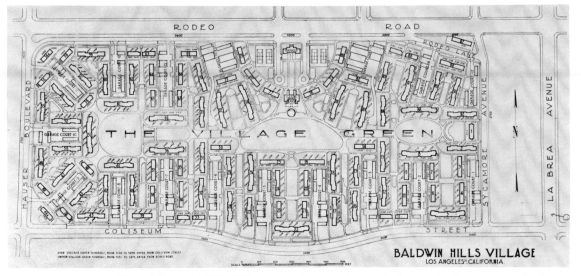

315. Plan of Baldwin Hills Village, Los Angeles: the whole is organized on three major interior spaces.

naked, oil-bearing hills that helped bring riches to "Lucky" Baldwin. As soon as funds were at last available and work could begin, the tract was annexed to the City of Los Angeles so as to bring in the normal city utilities; this also meant, however, a battle with the city's engineers, who insisted that streets already platted to the north be extended southward in traditional gridiron fashion across the new piece.

The city thus threatened the basic plan of making the project a superblock following the Radburn idea. Fortunately, the City Planning Board finally consented to stopping the through streets (except Sycamore Avenue, which lopped off the east end of the tract along La Brea Avenue, to satisfy a silly zoning rule). The ultimate superblock is bounded on the east by Sycamore Avenue; on the north by Rodeo Road; on the west by Hauser Boulevard; and on the south by Coliseum Street, which the designers were allowed to locate as they wished, including the curve that slows down traffic. Rodeo Road is a heavily traveled east-west city thoroughfare; it is accordingly paralleled by a narrower Rodeo Lane, with a buffer of grass and trees between the two. Access from Rodeo Road to Rodeo Lane occurs only at the middle of the long superblock and at one other point, so that Rodeo Lane becomes effectively the northern boundary of the project.

The overall structure of this great superblock is based on three interior spaces known as East Green, Center Green, and West Green, with narrow, tree-shaded malls connecting Center Green to the others; all three collectively are called the Village Green. Between the Greens and the boundary roads the Village as a whole takes form in a striking improvement on the Radburn idea. The 627 dwelling units, all in long, low structures, are arranged in a kind of generally continuous S-shaped sequence; thus spacious garden courts, opening to a Green, alternate with wide garage courts opening to a boundary road. Instead of using Radburn's narrow service lanes, motor access from the boundary road here is to a series of roomy garage courts. Each (Fig. 316) has covered garages or carports (one for each dwelling unit served by the court) and open parking spaces (usually two for each dwelling). Most of the garage courts have group laundries and drying facilities; each is framed by fence or hedge, outside which is a surrounding footwalk with pedestrian access points clearly demarked for the sake of orderliness and safety. The houses embracing a garage court are back far enough from it to provide for each dwelling an enclosed private yard or patio from which a gate opens to the footwalk.

The other side of the long house faces on a garden court, or in some instances directly on a Green. The garden court is a notable improvement on Radburn's narrow, hedge-bordered path leading to a central park space. The counterpart here is an ample grassy bay, at least one hundred feet wide, actually an alcove from a Green (Fig. 317). It is often tree-shaded and always bordered by walks, which are, however, held far enough from the face of the house to insure the rooms their privacy. The belt between walk and house, like other areas that would be difficult to maintain in grass or flowers, is in many cases planted with dark green ground cover, usually Algerian ivy. The garden courts differ considerably from one another, with enough variety of treatment to dispel any feeling of boring sameness.

The houses themselves are long, low, and refreshingly simple, with flattish pitched roofs and wide overhangs above their stucco-faced walls. They are painted in quiet combinations of muted pastel colors. Most of the buildings are of two stories, varying from three to six dwelling units in length. A few have one-story "bungalows" in their ends, and there are nine short one-story buildings of three units each. The long structures contain the bulk of the dwellings, partly in two-story units but mostly in first- or second-floor flats, each with its own ground-floor entrance.

At about midpoint on the north side of the Village, situated comfortably on Rodeo Lane with a motor access from Rodeo Road, is the management office. From it, on the inside of the block, a carefully tended geometric mall connects the office to the club house, which in turn opens on Center Green. The club house, intended at first as a nursery school, then as a center for community recreation, was early remodeled to provide needed apartments. The management office is flanked by two pairs of tennis courts and on plan appears to have its moderate monumentality further emphasized by a line of row-houses arranged in a large semicircle. On the ground, however, all this is not noticeably so centralized. Indeed, the phenomenon leads one to feel the necessity of commenting on a major characteristic—perhaps a true

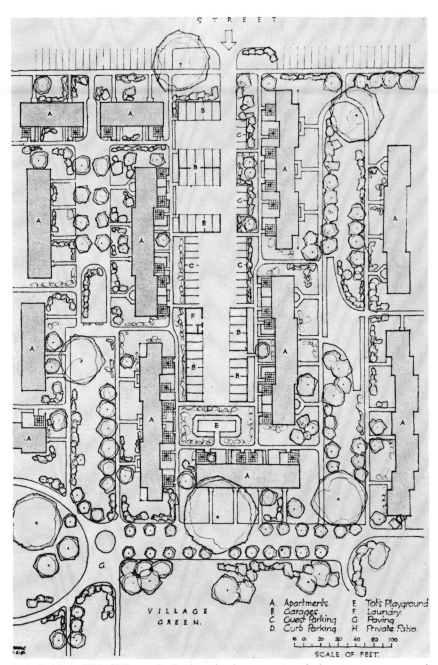

316. Baldwin Hills Village: the basic unit plan, accommodating garage courts and garden courts in a continuous "S" pattern; the service road of the Radburn idea is expanded in size and function.

317. A garden court in Baldwin Hills Village.

paradox—at Baldwin Hills Village. In actuality, of all the relationships in the scheme, only the management office and its tightly rectilinear mall to the club house *look* geometrically structured. Yet, on examining the overall plan, one can see that the whole project is very near full bilateral symmetry and that, in fact, the mirrored reflection on a north-south center-line seems upset only by the loss of the east-end block between Sycamore and La Brea Avenues.

As a consequence of such an arrangement, one might validly expect to find Baldwin Hills Village pompous or dull or both. But, on visiting it what one does feel is a delightful pervading sense of order and serenity. This may well be caused by the strong general structure of the design, but one is quite unaware of any overdone "classical" formalism in the layout—except in the management office and its mall. In explanation, there are two possibilities. First, the color scheme among the buildings, which never echoes the symmetry of the plan: for instance, if a certain row-house is done in a combination of light brown and cream, its balancing counterpart is most likely in, say, smoky blue. Second, it is clear that here is another example of the power of judicious planting to form and modify space and to soften the edges of harshness. Throughout the project, spaces are formed by vegetation as often as by the buildings. The overall spatial organization thus created is well reinforced and supported by the system of footwalks. Many architectural critics have admired the subtlety and skill of Barlow's contribution; some have said the landscape treatment is what makes Baldwin Hills Village so distinctive.

318. Air view of Baldwin Hills Village and the typical real-estate developments that surrounded it almost at once.

That it is in fact so distinctive needs no further proof than an airplane ride over it, embedded as the Village now is in a welter of more traditional developments of the quick-sale real-estate type in appearance (Fig. 318). On the ground, its value is measurable by the satisfaction it has brought to owners as an investment and residents as a home community. Occupancy has been consistently 100 percent, and there has always been a long waiting list. From 1949 until the end of 1961, the Village was owned by the New England Mutual Life Insurance Company, of Boston. It was then sold to Baldwin M. Baldwin, under whom all management policies have remained unchanged. In mid-December 1963 it made national news overnight when the collapse of a reservoir dam in the hills south of the Village cascaded tons of water right across it. But the City of Los Angeles, quite properly, repaired the damage, the Village was restored intact, and the community continued its happy existence almost as though nothing had happened.

What about the period since World War II? It is always risky to attempt an assessment of works too recent to allow for the perspective of time, particularly the effects of aging. Trees mature happily, but buildings are not sure to do so. Nor is maintenance. Much of the effort since the war has been partial or makeshift or both. Such bold essays as Columbia, Maryland, and Reston, Virginia, are still too young and too untested to warrant appraisal. In the last quarter-century a preponderance of massive urban bleakness has too often characterized American town planning developments. But there is an outstanding exception in Fresh Meadows, a 1948 project of the New York Life Insurance Company in New York City. The architects were Voorhees, Walker, Foley, and Smith and the landscape architect Alfred Geiffert, Jr.

The property, about 175 acres of relatively undeveloped land, had been the golf course of the Fresh Meadows Country Club. The company, seeking to make a housing investment productive of not only long-range reasonable financial return but also equally long-range customer contentment and thus good public relations, set forth a heartening program of genuinely humane dimensions. Indeed, the specific aims and requirements outlined in advance by the company are even more impressive than the striking physical development itself. To a degree almost entirely without precedent in such ventures, Fresh Meadows was planned for *people,* not for investment only, not for show, not as a monument to anyone's virtuosity—just for people to live in, belong to, and sense as home and neighborhood over a long period.

First, in recognition of the normal flexibility of space requirements in a given family from a couple's beginning years to their final ones, it was stipulated that not just a single "optimum" size but varied sizes of dwelling units must be made available. This would enable a family, expanding and contracting with the years, always to find an appropriately sized home in Fresh Meadows, instead of having to move elsewhere. The company required, moreover, a diversity of building types and unfailing attention to the creation of realistically sized small groups or subneighborhoods. The project accordingly contains two-story row-houses, three-story and four-story walkups, and two thirteen-story apartment buildings. All are worked into a community of loosely inter-related quadrangles, along with a major shopping center and two minor ones, an ingenious street system, several partly buried parking garages, abundant recreational space, and unstinting provision of lawns and

319. Fresh Meadows, New York: general layout of development.

trees, both existing and newly provided where they will do the most good (Fig. 319).

The street system, though urban in character, is an unusual variant on the gridiron. In pleasant contrast with the intransigence of early years at Sunnyside, the city allowed considerable stoppage of previously platted streets. Of the thirteen north-south streets that might have been forced across the project, only 188th Street was in fact continued through Fresh Meadows, and it has been slowed down with two large oval islands. Of the east-west streets, 64th Avenue is interrupted by one of the ovals and also by retention of a six-acre block of handsome old trees athwart the line of the street; all the other cross-streets have been stopped within the project. With loop-roads and only a few culs-de-sac, good motor roads are taken past all buildings, bringing the car virtually to the door of every dwelling but introducing so many right-angled turns as to render speeding or shortcuts almost impossible. On the basis of one car for every two families (how different from Baldwin Hills!) garages have been provided in several six-level structures sunk into the grade for half their height.

In part the rectilinearity of the street system arose from an earlier decision on organization of the project's residential buildings. The two tall apartments are set by themselves at the corner of a large central open space, with their long elements oriented precisely north-south for desired apartment exposures. All the smaller structures, row-houses and walkups intermingled without any sense of class distinction, are arranged in a loose overall pattern of small rectangular courts related to the street system. Through variety in shape, height, location, and shades of brick every effort has been made to avoid the brittle, mechanical, almost metallic look that so often gives housing projects an institutional cast. Each of the small groupings has its own partly enclosed

320. Fresh Meadows: preservation of existing trees contributed greatly to the suburban character of the community.

central open space with a playground, shaded sitting places, and interior views.

Fresh Meadows has no great schematic design in the sense of long sight-lines organizing the whole, but rather a sort of drifting of casually connected interior spaces through group after group to give the place an almost random but smoothly consistent spatial texture. Its atmosphere of domestic intimacy is all the more surprising when one realizes that the project houses about eleven thousand people. To be sure, the buildings are flat-topped and somewhat severe in their simplicity and the street pattern, though broken up ingeniously, is rectilinear; to this extent the development has an undeniable urban feeling. Yet it is also remarkably suburban in its play of light and shadow (Fig. 320).

It is highly doubtful that the sense of softness could come through as it does if the owners had not taken at the outset a wise position regarding the value of trees. The country club site already had numerous good specimens before work was started; these were carefully saved, notably in the 6-acre block of oaks on the line of 64th Avenue and in the sizable open space at the center of the project. Then, in the small courts and on the streets, the planting of hundreds of new trees under Geiffert's discerning supervision brought a natural quality that contributes enormously to the pervading pleasantness. It has been estimated that the company spent a million dollars on lawns and trees. Nobody is likely to question that the investment was eminently sound.

Fresh Meadows, a big city project in contrast to rural Riverside of eighty years earlier and the intervening cases examined here, would hardly expect to be termed the best; such comparisons really do not make sense. But it has surely faced the most gigantic challenge on grounds of serving the multitude. As such, it illustrates well how helpfully design can operate at a populous extreme of residential requirements.

XXXV. The National Park System: 1872–1929

Americans may seldom stop to realize that in the United States, west of the original thirteen colonies, all the land belonged at first to all the people—it was *public domain,* or at any rate was so declared while its rightful Indian owners were being rudely dispossessed. The story of the National Parks is therefore, for the most part, a tale of creating something for all the people from land already owned by them. But it illustrates too, with often indelible strokes, what a struggle it has been to keep the people from despoiling and squandering their own best possessions: the land and what lives upon it.

Americans did in earliest days give recognition to a certain public value inherent in the land, in spite of their later shameful record in mistreating the natural heritage. In 1641 the Great and General Court of the Massachusetts Bay colony passed the Great Ponds Act, providing that any body of water ten acres or more in extent must be kept open by its owner to public access for purposes of "fishing or fowling." As recently as 1923 an opinion of the Attorney General of Massachusetts held the Great Ponds Act still valid, even with regard to forms of "public rights" that had become customary since passage of the act.

Recognition of such "public rights" eventually gave rise to the national parks as the country grew; their story is in some respects typical of the American west. Of the successive territorial acquisitions that were added to the original colonies as the nation expanded, the Louisiana Purchase of 1803 is the one most closely associated with the national park saga. To explore the far reaches of this enormous tract, the Lewis and Clark expedition made its journey of 1804–1806 up the Missouri River, through the Dakotas and what is now Montana, across the Bitterroot Range into the Oregon country, and so to the Pacific. It was a member of that party, John Colter, who obtained his release on the homeward trip in 1806 and went back west for four more years of trapping and exploration in the mountainous country south of the Missouri's headwaters. On his return to St. Louis in 1810, his wild stories—of great clefts in the rock, thundering waterfalls, underground explosions, and above all gigantic spoutings of boiling water from the bowels of the earth—seemed so utterly unbelievable that he was laughed at and the region he talked about was dubbed "Colter's Hell." His account nevertheless impressed Clark enough to cause "Colter's Route in 1807" to be entered on the official map of the Lewis and Clark expedition, along with reasonably accurate indications of the origin of the Yellowstone River, so named because of the bright color of the rock through which it had carved its way (Fig. 321). Nothing more positive about "Colter's Hell" was known for another sixty years, although fanciful tales kept coming out through individual trappers and mountain men like the famous Jim Bridger. Then in 1862 gold was discovered in Montana and prospectors began flocking in. Numerous parties apparently penetrated the upper Yellowstone, but they kept quiet about it, unwilling to run the risk of being roundly ridiculed for telling of the wonderland that in fact they had seen.

At last a few determined Montana citizens organized in 1870 a large expedition under General Henry D. Washburn and Nathaniel P. Langford, who were sufficiently influential to persuade the War Department to undertake the cost and assign an officer, Lieutenant Gustavus C. Doane, and five cavalrymen as escort. Having traveled up the Yellowstone River, around Yellowstone Lake and through the great geyser basin (Fig. 322), the Washburn-Langford-Doane party was camped along the Firehole River the last night out before leaving Yellowstone country. Around the campfire they fell to discussing what a financial killing would be possible by getting possession of this fantastic natural area. Then one of the number, tradition says Cornelius Hedges, summed up the discussion by suggesting it was in itself clear proof that here was a portion of the public domain too important for any one man or group to own, and that for all time it should continue to belong to *all* the people. Others forthwith agreed, and the notion of a national park was born, or at least became a public issue. The group resolved to spare no pains in getting the true picture before Congress. Doane's brilliant official report of the expedition was published as a Senate Document, and Langford gave lectures on the Yellowstone throughout the east.

The next year, 1871, a scientific party led by geologist F. V. Hayden made an accurate survey of the area and at the end of the summer returned with many charts, photographs, and specimens. Convinced that the region should be made a national park, Hayden joined the campaign to get the needed legislation through Congress. There was the expected opposition from a few

321. In "Colter's Hell": the grand canyon of the Yellowstone River, which John Colter saw in 1807.

322. "Old Faithful" in Yellowstone National Park, established in 1872 as the world's first such park.

benighted legislators, who typified the prevailing era of exploiting the land for enrichment of favored friends. But a park bill of sorts was finally passed, and on March 1, 1872, the signature of President Grant brought into being "in the Territories of Montana and Wyoming" the world's first national park.

The Yellowstone legislation itself was far from adequate for effective administration, as years of experience demonstrated. But in 1872 nobody had any conception of what measures would be needed to protect and manage such a park. No appropriation of funds was requested at the outset; even proponents of the park naively expected the area to be self-sustaining on revenues from ten-year leases, which the bill empowered the Secretary of the Interior to grant. Not even minimal appropriations were voted until 1878, and the annual allowance from Congress remained a mere pittance through the years.

Protection of the park and enforcement of regulations were impossible; the superintendent was given no staff and legally no power beyond ejecting offenders, for no law had been enacted imposing penalties for violations. There was endless poaching and slaughter of the abundant wildlife. Vandalism on the part of curious visitors was a continual problem. The park's boundaries were vague, unmarked, and thus hopeless to control. Not until 1883 was any kind of protection provided when Congress authorized the use of Army troops. These were finally called for in 1886, and for the next thirty years the Army controlled the park under supervision of the Secretary of the Interior. Meanwhile, year after year, the park's friends battled against the scheming of unprincipled legislators who sought to loot the Yellowstone for private gain. In fact, Yellowstone National Park came perilously close to abolition in the 1890s.

By that time, however, much had been done to rectify the earlier mistakes in legislation. Beginning in 1883, Army engineers had built some excellent roads. In 1894 a law explicitly prohibited hunting or killing wildlife and provided stated penalties; a commissioner was appointed to enforce the regulations and funds were appropriated for construction of a jail. The Army continued to furnish protection and in 1896 began marking the park boundaries. As the 1890s saw the Yellowstone safely over the hump as the first national park, so too the decade brought the next members of the slowly growing family: Sequoia, Yosemite, and tiny General Grant National Parks, all in California and all created in 1890. Sequoia and General Grant were set aside purely for preservation of at least some of the great *Sequoia gigantea* of the Sierra Nevada before decimation by greedy lumber interests. The four square miles of the General Grant—actually a single grove of the largest of the giants—were merged many years later into King's Canyon National Park when this was established adjoining the Sequoia.

Yosemite National Park is of course the most famous of the 1890 trio, but in a more confused sense than commonly realized. As observed earlier, the elder Olmsted played a brief but important part in early management of the Yosemite Valley when in 1864 Congress ceded it and Mariposa Grove to California as the first state park in America. As the years passed, California grew less and less enchanted with the heavy responsibility of the park, found the cost of maintenance more and more onerous, and in fact did a barely adequate job of handling it. In 1890, primarily to protect the valley, Congress

323. The upland surrounding the earlier state park in the valley of the Yosemite; the whole became Yosemite National Park.

created Yosemite National Park, but only in the form of some two million acres of high Sierra upland "forest reservation" *surrounding* Yosemite State Park (Fig. 323). This unique doughnut-shaped arrangement lasted until 1906, when California thankfully ceded its holdings back to the United States and Congress made the entire area, including California's part and a much reduced acreage of upland, into Yosemite National Park as it is today. Logically enough, 1890, when the upper ring was set aside, is officially observed as the founding date for the park as a whole.

Yosemite is without question one of the most widely known national parks, not only because of the spectacular grandeur of its glaciated granite peaks, its waterfalls and glaciers and surviving sequoia groves, but also because it is by now so readily accessible (perhaps too readily?) to the thousands who throng to see it. To landscape architects Yosemite is important for another reason. The valley floor, naturally and immutably restricted in extent while tremendously popular, illustrates just about perfectly the problem often referred to as the ultimate calculus: how to find the "right number" between too little and too much. How to open a piece of wild natural environment to the rightful enjoyment of many without ruining it for all? Quite apart

324. Mount Rainier National Park: Wonderland Trail passing Klapatche Lake.

from the question of vandalism, few laymen have even a hazy understanding of how abrasive and erosive to the environment many of the human users' best-intentioned activities can be. The landscape architect *must* understand these factors, and he must use design to counteract them.

At this point in time, passage of the Forest Reserve Act of 1891 should be mentioned. Under it, the president could by proclamation "set apart and reserve" tracts of publicly held forested land "in any State or Territory." Millions of acres of forest were thus made "public reservations" by successive presidents. This meant not only conservation of the country's future lumber supply, but also the saving of many exceptional tracts from chopping up by haphazard homesteading that would otherwise surely have happened in the early days. After 1907 these reservations, in most cases, became national forests.

Before the turn of the century another great park was added, this time in Washington: Mount Rainier National Park, established in 1899 (Fig. 324). Volcanic in origin, 14,410 feet high, snow-capped, with twenty-six active glaciers, the mountain itself covers nearly a hundred square miles, or about one quarter of the park. For many years it was a virtually inaccessible mass

325. Crater Lake National Park.

of bare rock and had no passable roads. Today it is well but modestly developed for tourists and famous for its astonishing range of wild flowers in summer and for winter sports from December to March.

Three years later, Crater Lake National Park, in Oregon, was set apart (Fig. 325). The lake itself, of an incredibly intense blue, lies in the crater of an extinct volcano that geologists believe to have resulted from the titanic explosion of an ancient, still larger volcano, Mount Mazuma. The sapphire hue of the water is presumably caused by the lake's 2,000-foot depth, but nobody truly knows. In Crater Lake, as to a degree also with Mount Rainier, the second of three main reasons for which national parks may be said to have been created emerges: the *scientific* motive. The first, obviously, is *scenic* quality—one might even call it awesomeness, as in the grand canyon of the Yellowstone or the valley floor of the Yosemite. But scientists point out, not without reason, that even the most breath-taking, sublime scenery is invariably also a geological, biological, or ecological phenomenon worthy of dedicated scientific study.

Quick to appear thereafter was a third national park motivation, the *historical*. In 1906, largely through the persistence of Representative John F. Lacey of Iowa, Congress enacted two measures, each important in its distinctive way but both based on the same new awareness of historical values.

326. Devil's Tower National Monument in northeastern Wyoming; the first area so designated by presidential proclamation under the Antiquities Act of 1906.

The first, approved June 8, 1906, was the Antiquities Act, often called the Lacey Act. The second, approved June 29, was the establishment of Mesa Verde National Park. Both actions were aimed primarily at the systematic pilfering and destruction of the remains of Indian civilizations in the southwestern states, a wholesale "pot-hunting" that had been going on far too long. But the Antiquities Act had broader implications. Under it the president was authorized to set aside by proclamation, as a national monument, any area of historic or scientific importance on land already owned or controlled by the United States. Because a presidential proclamation sufficed, instead of the slow processes of Congress required for creating a national park, the Antiquities Act provided a quick method for accomplishing much desirable conservation. In many instances thereafter the initial step toward establishing a national park was a presidential proclamation setting aside a nucleus of the area as a national monument.

Perhaps the most famous instance was the setting aside of the Grand Canyon of the Colorado, in Arizona, as a national monument under jurisdiction of the United States Forest Service, by proclamation of President Theodore Roosevelt in 1908. In 1919 Congress established the area, with some boundary adjustments, as Grand Canyon National Park. More typically, the Antiquities Act facilitated swift and early protection of small areas that would

327. Cliff Palace, Mesa Verde National Park: the most notable and best preserved cliff dwellings and other works of prehistoric man in the United States.

328. St. Mary's Lake, Glacier National Park: planning a sound system of foot trails, horse trails, and motor roads in such an essentially wilderness park is a major task for the landscape architects.

presumably never merit national park status. The first so set aside was Devil's Tower National Monument, a huge column of rock, probably the solidified core of an eroded volcano, in the northeastern corner of Wyoming, declared by public proclamation of President Theodore Roosevelt in September 1906 (Fig. 326).

Meanwhile, just three weeks after approval of the Antiquities Act but quite independent of it, came the establishment of Mesa Verde National Park, an area of about eighty square miles of high green tableland in southwestern Colorado, intersected by deep canyons and containing hundreds of archeological remains mainly in the form of cliff ruins (Fig. 327). Basing their estimates on an ingenious method of counting tree rings and on the carbon test, archeologists believe the mesa was occupied by successive Indian cultures from about the time of Christ until a great drought struck, just before 1300 A.D., and drove southwestward what was left of the depleted population.

Glacier National Park, established in 1910 (Fig. 328), is an exceptionally rugged region of glaciated mountains, with sixty small living glaciers and some two hundred fifty ice-fed lakes. Located against the northern boundary of Montana, its eastern half is continuous with Waterton Lakes National Park in Canada. For many years after its creation, Glacier had the administrative character of a national forest rather than of a national park: rights-of-way were authorized for railways; power and irrigation projects of the Reclamation Service were allowed; twenty-year leases for private summer homes were possible; the Secretary of the Interior was granted authority to sell dead and down timber, and lumber was regarded as a source of revenue. Many of these faults in the act setting up the park were corrected by remedial legislation in later years; Glacier is now regarded as very nearly a wilderness area, with only a few roads, including the brilliantly designed Going-to-the-Sun highway over the Continental Divide, and richly endowed with wild fauna and flora in stupendous primitive scenery.

In 1915 another large park was added directly on the Continental Divide: Rocky Mountain National Park in Colorado, only about fifty miles northwest of Denver and thus within easy reach of a large western and midwestern population (Fig. 329). Its area of some four hundred square miles includes sixty-five named peaks higher than 10,000 feet. Aside from its magnificent scenery, oddly small-scaled in feeling because of its many inward-oriented bowl compositions, it is a veritable outdoor museum of geological processes. Its great range of altitudes, from 7,500 to over 14,000 feet, makes it unusually varied and rich in types of plant and animal life; it is especially noted as the natural habitat of Rocky Mountain bighorn sheep, and beavers abound in its many streams.

As of 1915, with the establishment of Rocky Mountain, there were nine true national parks, plus three areas (Hot Springs in Arkansas, Wind Cave in South Dakota, and Platt in Oklahoma) that were legally national parks

329. Nymph Lake, Rocky Mountain National Park: often referred to as "the first eastern national park" when established in 1915, this is an especially difficult design problem because of the relative proximity of urban concentrations.

but unworthy of the name. But the nine were in no sense a system. Each was administered as a separate entity and each operated under its own specific legislation, in many cases still faulty. The Army had been in charge in most areas, doing a good job of protection and at times road-building; but the military could hardly have been expected to handle with sensitivity such apparent intangibles as scenic values and biotic balance. In some parks the superintendent was an Army officer, in others a civilian; yet the Secretary of the Interior was responsible for all the areas. The division of authority and administration was chaotic.

This was the challenging state of affairs that confronted Chicago industrialist Stephen T. Mather when in January 1915 he accepted appointment under Secretary of the Interior Franklin K. Lane as assistant to the secretary, in charge of national parks. Prior to 1913, when Lane became secretary under President Wilson, there had been practically no provision in Washington for central supervision of these great areas, despite years of agitation by friends of the parks. Lane, when appointed, determined to do something about it and called in a California professor of economics, Adolph C. Miller, to handle the parks along with several other concerns of the Department. Miller brought along another Californian, a young graduate student of economics, Horace M. Albright, who proceeded at once to familiarize himself with the ins and outs of governmental procedures and administration while studying for a law degree. Miller was soon pulled out by the President for another federal assignment, but Albright remained at Interior and so was available to help Mather when the latter assumed the task relinquished by Miller.

Mather's appointment was somewhat extraordinary. A Californian by birth and education, an active member of the Sierra Club, and an outdoor enthusiast since 1905, he had written Secretary Lane in the fall of 1914 complaining about the condition of the national parks as he had experienced them on recent visits. Lane, who recognized the writer as a classmate of Miller's at Berkeley, a self-made millionaire, and a talented organizer of considerable renown, is said to have made this oft-quoted reply: "Dear Steve, If you don't like the way the national parks are being run, come on to Washington and run them yourself."[1] When Mather demurred on grounds of unfamiliarity with "government red tape," Lane promised that the knowledgeable young Albright would be assigned as his assistant. Albright was in fact planning to leave federal service for private law practice in San Francisco, but he and Mather hit it off so perfectly that both agreed to stay. Thus followed the appointment on January 21, 1915, of the man known in later years as "father of the National Park Service": Mather, with Albright at his side.

With characteristic optimism, Mather allowed himself and Albright a year to put the parks on their feet. Mather was widely known as a man with prodigious and seemingly inexhaustible energy, but the task was enormous. Congress needed to be made genuinely interested in the parks and aware of their importance as great national assets, so that reasonable and well-considered appropriations for upkeep would supplant the old specter of

---

1. Robert Shankland, *Steve Mather of the National Parks* (New York, 1951), p. 7.

niggling political bargaining. Public enthusiasm for visiting the parks needed to be aroused, not only through publicity, but through making travel easier and accommodations in the parks less primitive. To this end the railroads would have to be brought to see the investment value of their participation; and, with the growth of motor travel, better roads were required in all the parks. The mixed-up pattern of concessions—for lodging and feeding the public, as well as for transportation within the parks—was in dire need of correction; in this Mather had a back-breaking fight with intrenched political favoritism. Into all these obligations he plunged with reckless vigor, in a ceaseless campaign from coast to coast both in the field and in Washington. He was dead set on creating a system out of the chaos that had prevailed.

Most important of all was the obvious necessity of establishing a separate division or bureau to handle the parks, then staffing it to serve the high ideals that Mather held for it. Authorization of a separate bureau had been proposed annually, though without effect, by successive Secretaries of the Interior and even by President Taft, always in consultation with J. Horace McFarland, of the American Civic Association, and with the younger Olmsted. At last, thanks in no small part to Mather's energy, the bill recommended by Secretary Lane was passed by both houses and approved by President Wilson on August 25, 1916, as the National Parks Act. The Act provided for establishment of the National Park Service in the Department of the Interior and set forth its purpose: "The service thus established shall promote and regulate the use of Federal areas known as national parks, monuments and reservations hereinafter specified by such means and measures as conform to the fundamental purpose . . . to conserve the scenery and the natural and historic objects and the wild life therein, and to provide for the enjoyment of the same in such manner and by such means as will leave them unimpaired for the enjoyment of future generations." The language of the bill introduced by Representative William Kent, of California, was the product of a goodly number of park enthusiasts. The statement of purpose as quoted above was attributed chiefly to Olmsted.

Establishment of the Service did not slow Mather down for a moment. There was still too much to be done, including an unusually trying series of bitter struggles with political patronage about concessions in the Yellowstone. The allotted year that he and Albright had agreed upon was long since past; the second anniversary approached. Mather proceeded to assemble, for January 1917 in Washington, the largest and most ambitious of his many promotional National Park Conferences; then he collapsed, completely exhausted by two years of almost single-handed drive against incredible odds and unrelenting pressures. Mather was kept away from the grind for over a year, resting undisturbed while Albright carried on. Funds for setting up the Service had not been appropriated; they finally came with passage of a deficiency bill in April 1917. Mather was now formally appointed director

330. Hawaii Volcanoes National Park: a night view of the eruption of Kilauea Iki in 1959.

of the National Park Service and Albright assistant director. Meanwhile, the family had grown: Rocky Mountain National Park had been established a few days after Mather's arrival in Washington in January 1915. In 1916 two more parks had been added: Hawaii, with its tremendous display of active volcanoes (Fig. 330), and Lassen Volcanic, in northern California, declared a national monument as a dead volcano in 1907 but suddenly and explosively alive in 1914 before being given national park status. In 1917, just before America's entry into World War I, the huge Mt. McKinley National Park in Alaska was established—almost two million acres in extent, with the nation's highest peak at 20,300 feet of elevation.

Though the war slowed things down to a walk the campaign went on, especially when Mather returned, rested and eager to unleash the old familiar driving energy again. There was much to do in promotion through the press and the railroads, with guided trips into the parks for senators, representatives, writers, and other influential people. Concession problems were still many and vexatious; there were also continuing efforts to get the most worthy new parks established, to prevent unworthy ones, and to remove private holdings from within the parks. To Mather nothing seemed more vitally necessary than staffing the newly created Service with men of ability and integrity, in the completely nonpolitical vein on which he insisted and that became a jealously observed tradition in the Service. He worked strenuously toward a full complement of civilian superintendents for all the parks. To supplant the Army he felt he needed a ranger force of selected and schooled men, and he early saw the importance of trained naturalists as an educational means for interpreting wonders of the parks to visitors, in the outdoors and in museums that he wanted for all the parks.

As though these postwar problems were not enough, Mather discovered that Albright, who had done such fine organizational groundwork in his absence, wanted to leave for private law practice in San Francisco; his resignation was already submitted when Mather countered by offering him the superintendency of Yellowstone and appointment to the new office of Assistant Director in the Field. Albright accepted and for the next ten years filled this double role admirably. For the vacancy as Washington assistant director Mather secured the appointment of Arno B. Cammerer, who knew the governmental ropes from fifteen years of federal service and was eminently suited for the assistant directorship.

Landscape architects will note that it was Cammerer who, in a 1918 conversation with Mather before joining the National Park Service, suggested the need for a division of landscape architecture in the Service and the appointment of Charles P. Punchard, Jr., as its head. Punchard, a member of the ASLA since 1912, had been in Colorado for some years because of his health but had become landscape architect for the District of Columbia in 1917. He welcomed the new appointment, hoping to get back again to the higher and healthier altitudes of the west. A favorite of Mather's from the start, he was deeply respected in the Service and regarded with affection by the field force, but poor health dogged him continually. He died in 1920, and his assistant, Daniel R. Hull, was promoted to head the division.

With the war over, the year 1919 was a rich one, ushering in three new national parks, all of which had first been national monuments. In northern Arizona came Grand Canyon National Park, the stupendous, mile-deep chasm of the Colorado River (Fig. 331), with its hauntingly mysterious distances and the ever-shifting lights and colors of the eroded layers of rock. That same day on the Atlantic coast, Lafayette (later Acadia) National Park was established in Maine, the first park in the east—an exhilarating combination of bare granite mountains, deep green forest, and seas pounding incessantly on the rocky shore (Fig. 332). Later in the year brought Zion National Park, in southern Utah not far from Grand Canyon and, like it, a fantastic spectacle of eroded varicolored rock—but here thrusting majestically above the eyes, against the indigo sky.

The 1920s were no less demanding than earlier years; there were old problems and new. Convinced that a strong state park movement could serve as a buffer against excessive recreational misuse of scenic national parks, and

331. Grand Canyon National Park.

might even help to ward off the rash of proposals for undistinguished additions to the national park system, Mather in 1921 threw his energy behind a large state park conference (discussed later). He continued the usual ceaseless drive in defense of the parks: struggles over boundaries and concessions, against dams and other intrusions. There was a definite bright spot in the turmoil, Bryce Canyon. On Albright's recommendation, Mather had visited this almost inaccessible area in southern Utah, near Zion and of the same in-

332. Otter Cliffs, Acadia National Park.

credibly colorful and even more weirdly eroded rock formations. They succeeded in having it proclaimed a national monument in 1923; its fame spread
rapidly, and in 1924 it became Bryce Canyon National Park.

The 1920s brought a degree of organizational change in the Service. Daniel
R. Hull, appointed chief landscape architect on Punchard's death (and
elected to membership in the ASLA in 1923), continued working out of Los
Angeles on Park Service duties until 1927. In that year Mather decided to

put all the field divisions into one office in San Francisco. Hull preferred not to leave Los Angeles; he resigned, and his first assistant, Thomas C. Vint, was appointed to fill the vacancy. A native of Utah, Vint had lived in California from boyhood and was a graduate of the University at Berkeley, taking his B.S. degree in 1920 after service overseas in World War I. He had worked at all phases of design and construction before, during, and after college when in 1922 he joined the Park Service as a draftsman in the Yosemite. His advancement had been justly rapid.

Not long after his appointment as chief, it fell to Vint to start the building of a strong spirit of professional unity between landscape architects of the National Park Service and those outside it. In a sense this came about by accident. From early days it has been a custom of the successive directors to seek on appropriate occasions advice from the National Commission of Fine Arts, including of course its landscape architect members. The younger Olmsted was a valuable and ever-ready advisor; James L. Greenleaf and Ferruccio Vitale, too, in their turns on the Commission, were called in by Mather for consultation. Late in the 1920s, to help resolve a major disagreement about development at Mammoth Hot Springs in the Yellowstone, Vitale made a visit on behalf of the Commission. After a large conference on the site, he returned to New York singing the praises of "a young fellow named Tom Vint," whom he called "the only person in the group who clearly understood the problem and the site."[2] Later, when Vint was in the east, Vitale arranged for him to see various professional procedures in many offices, meet the established landscape architects, and, especially, get to know his younger colleagues. Friendships were formed that never paled. Sponsored by Olmsted and Vitale, Vint was elected to the ASLA in 1930; when, along with other chiefs of divisions, he was moved from San Francisco to Washington in the early 1930s he was among professional friends from the first.

As chief landscape architect, chief architect, and later in charge of all development by the Park Service, Vint served with distinction for the next forty years, enjoying throughout the respect and affectionate loyalty of all hands. Quiet and unassuming, he was a typical "professionals' professional." He was elected a member of the American Institute of Architects in 1937 and to Fellowship of the ASLA in 1948. Eventually becoming Assistant Director, Design and Construction, Vint retired from the Park Service in 1961. He died in 1967, aged seventy-three.

Among Vint's many professional contributions to the work of the Park Service, perhaps the outstanding one was introduction of the technique of creating and maintaining a master plan for each park area. Fundamentally, the master plan, coordinated by the landscape architects, was a plan of the

2. Conversation at the time, Vitale and author.

ultimate design for the whole area, to assure that work to that end could be done progressively without false motion and waste. Through the use of an ingenious symbol system, devised by Vint, the master plan of an area could be brought up to date annually by simply changing "proposed" components to "existing" as work was completed. Eventually the master plan for an area grew to a sizable stack of bound sheets showing all aspects of the work graphically, including detailed plans of developed areas and statements covering the purpose for establishment of the area, the interpretative aims, and the administrative program for effectuation of the various plans.

To return to the 1920s: one of Mather's pet hopes, more national parks in the east, was gathering momentum. In 1924 a commission of experts appointed at his suggestion studied possibilities in the southern Appalachians for several weeks, then recommended the creation of two parks: one in the magnificently forested region of the Great Smoky Mountains in North Carolina and Tennessee, the other in the Blue Ridge of Virginia. The land problem was considerably different from what was usually the story in the west. It was not here a matter of carving something from the public domain, except for a few pieces of private "inholdings." In these eastern forests virtually all the land for the proposed parks was privately owned and very costly. Moreover, Congress had long held to a policy of not appropriating federal funds to purchase land for the parks. The situation required the utmost in persuasive power from Mather and Cammerer.

After the usual backing and filling, Congress first indicated favorable disposal in 1925 and then, in an act of May 22, 1926, gave advance approval to establishment of these national parks within boundaries determined by the Secretary of the Interior—for administration and protection by the National Park Service, not yet for development—whenever in the future a specified minimum acreage should have been deeded to the United States. This was not enough, by Mather's high standards; nevertheless, the advance approval was an unusual and positive step. It paved the way for further effort, successful a decade later through strenuous work by the states and large private donations, mainly by John D. Rockefeller, Jr. Congress then scaled down the minimum acreage requirements so that the Great Smoky Mountains National Park could be established (at 500,000 acres) in 1934 and Shenandoah National Park (150,000 acres) in 1935.

Attainment of these goals came too late for Mather's enjoyment. Taxed almost beyond endurance by his self-imposed whirlwind activity and the tension of such lengthy battles as that of protecting Grand Canyon against the illegal private claims of Arizona's own Senator, Mather actually began to talk of retiring. In 1927, on an inspection trip to Hawaii, he had a heart attack, but this did not slacken the pace; then in November 1928 he suffered a crippling stroke. Albright, summoned hastily from the west, took temporary charge; in December, Mather resigned and asked that Albright be named

STEPHEN TYNG MATHER
JULY. 4. 1867.   JAN. 22. 1930.

HE LAID THE FOUNDATION OF THE NATIONAL PARK
SERVICE, DEFINING AND ESTABLISHING THE POLICIES
UNDER WHICH ITS AREAS SHALL BE DEVELOPED AND
CONSERVED UNIMPAIRED FOR FUTURE GENERATIONS.
THERE WILL NEVER COME AN END TO THE GOOD THAT
HE HAS DONE.

333. Memorial tablet to Stephen Mather, placed in each national park.

to succeed him. The appointment of Albright as director followed on January 12, 1929, with Cammerer as associate director. Mather struggled on for another year, then died on January 22, 1930, leaving the nation a rich inheritance and the National Park Service a tradition of unselfish integrity that remains an active testimonial to his memory. In a Congressional tribute, the speech of his good friend Representative Louis Cramton included the oft-quoted sentence: "There will never come an end to the good he has done."[3]

3. Shankland, *Steve Mather,* p. 286.

XXXVI. The National Park System: 1929–1964

Albright was director of the National Park Service for only four years after January 1929, but of course he had been an integral part of the Mather regime from its beginning. Under his own administration, three new parks were introduced. Although Jackson Hole was not added until years later, after many involved battles, what came to be known as the "little" Grand Teton National Park, the jagged skyline of peaks south of the Yellowstone, was established in 1929 after Albright's induction. Next came Carlsbad Caverns National Park in southeastern New Mexico—a subterranean wonderland of stalactites, stalagmites, and onyx pendants proclaimed a national monument in 1923 and raised to national park status in 1930. The third unit, Isle Royale National Park, a large island wilderness in Lake Superior, was treated in the same legislative manner as the southern Appalachian parks: in 1931 its future establishment was provided for, to occur whenever the State of Michigan had acquired the lands and given them to the United States. As it turned out, this did not occur until nearly ten years later.

Although the collapse of the American economy came right after Albright's assumption of the directorship, it had no immediate effect on the National Park Service. Albright was able to move forward on several matters of particular interest to him: greater efficiency of organization in the Service; a system of uniform administration for the parks; creation of a Branch of Education and Research, staffed with naturalists and historians; better official recognition of historic sites and buildings, including authorization of the Colonial National Monument to embrace parts of Jamestown, Williamsburg, and Yorktown (Virginia); considerable widening of the Park Service's responsibility to cover national military parks and national battlefield sites already in existence. This last enlargement of duty came after the inauguration of President Franklin Roosevelt on March 4, 1933; it was only one of several reorganizations and massive expansions of opportunity to come in New Deal years.

When Albright saw that the cause of conservation, including the national park system, would be in fully sympathetic hands under President Roosevelt, he felt warranted in yielding at last to the fine offers he had had from private industry. On July 17, 1933, he submitted his resignation, after twenty years of devoted federal service. On August 10 Cammerer was moved up from associate directorship to begin the seven intensive years of his regime as director. What he stepped into was an entirely new era for the National Park Service, as it was for the country. Basic to the President's New Deal policies was use of federal spending to break the coma into which the economy had sunk; this meant engaging thousands of previously unemployed workers on projects of a public nature through a wide variety of agencies old and new. Especially desirable were projects representing a high employment of labor but a relatively small expenditure of raw materials. Obviously, much park work was this kind of endeavor. It is accordingly not surprising that, in Cammerer's years as Director, a vast amount of federal funds became available to the Park Service in many different ways.

Balancing the increase in funds, however, was an equally expanded zone of responsibility. The military-historical areas and national monuments already transferred from the War and Agriculture Departments to the Park Service under Albright in June 1933 were typical of the growing interest in history that brought into the system, under an entirely new classification, the Morristown National Historical Park in New Jersey, where Washington's ragged army wintered in 1779–80 (Fig. 334), and elevated the Colonial National Monument at Yorktown to historical park status. In the same vein, the Park Service initiated with emergency funds the Historic American Buildings Survey, organized and supervised by Vint, to produce a momentous collection of several thousand measured drawings of noteworthy architectural items for the Library of Congress. Further emphasis on eastern problems lay in the intensive campaign still going on, chiefly under Cammerer's personal direction, to assist the states toward acquisition of lands for the Great Smoky Mountains and the Shenandoah, both of which soon achieved establishment. Another eastern problem was the unique ecological area in southern Florida where Everglades National Park, after long years of conflict, was authorized in 1934 for future establishment whenever the lands had been presented by Florida to the federal government.

Assigned to the National Park Service for central guidance and supervision was the tremendous work program, in parks from coast to coast, of the Civilian Conservation Corps, unquestionably the New Deal's most widely acknowl-

334. The Ford Mansion, now restored and furnished with contemporary pieces, Morristown National Historical Park, New Jersey.

edged success. Most CCC work was done in state, county, and metropolitan parks, discussed later; but camps were also located in many national parks. Because the Park Service was ready with master plans prepared by its landscape architects under Vint's regular procedure, much work could be done on buildings, roads, and utilities in all the national parks with funds from the Public Works Administration, which allowed a higher percentage of material cost than that authorized in CCC work. But all of this, too, required central guidance.

The Park Service, in short, was now suddenly faced by a drastic increase in duties. Moreover, the focus of the expansion was in Washington and the east to a degree previously unknown to the Service and its traditionally western orientation. Meeting all these new requirements—with the celerity imposed by the critical situation—obviously meant a geographical shift and a monumental job of staffing. Heads of the technical divisions were called in to Washington by the director, mainly from the field office in San Francisco, and there was an immediate increase of appointments from private life to fill positions not only at headquarters and in the national parks themselves, but also to handle the CCC work and the other emergency programs for which the National Park Service was now responsible. This was the period

335. Readers of Hawthorne's *Scarlet Letter* will recall this Custom House, now part of the restoration comprising the Salem Maritime National Historic Site, the first area developed under the Historic Sites Act of 1935.

that clinched for the Park Service the undisputed title as the largest employer of landscape architects in the history of the profession.

As the months passed, still more tasks confronted Cammerer's forces. In August 1935 came the Historic Sites and Buildings Act that set up another classification, the National Historic Site, to commemorate and illustrate important facets in American socioeconomic history. The first area with this designation was the Salem Maritime National Historic Site, in Massachusetts, dedicated to the maritime history of New England and the American colonies (Fig. 335). Increasingly, the Service had recreational matters assigned to it: in 1936 a five-year study of the park and recreational facilities of all the states; also in 1936, in collaboration with the Bureau of Reclamation, a study of the recreational possibilities of Lake Mead, above Boulder Dam in Nevada; in 1937 development of the Lake Mead National Recreation Area.

Another two entirely new types of land use gained emphasis during the Cammerer regime: national parkways and national seashores. The parkway notion had been initiated by President Hoover, who in 1932 allotted the Park Service some relief money to build Skyline Drive within the area then being acquired by Virginia for Shenandoah National Park. In 1933 an extension of this drive, to be known as the Blue Ridge Parkway, connecting the

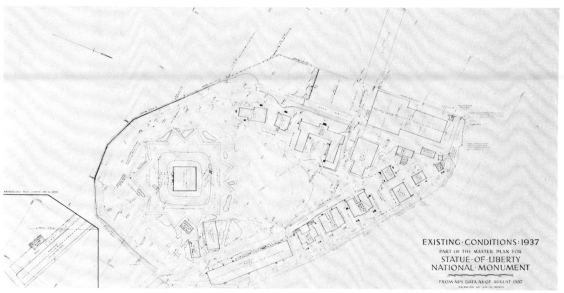

EXISTING·CONDITIONS·1937
PART OF THE MASTER PLAN FOR
STATUE·OF·LIBERTY
NATIONAL·MONUMENT

FROM NPS DATA AS OF AUGUST 1937

336. Another kind of responsibility confronted the National Park Service when the War Department transferred Bedloe's Island, occupied by numerous permanent brick Army buildings and the Statue of Liberty, to the Department of the Interior; this is the base map of existing conditions on the island at the time.

Shenandoah and the Great Smokies, was begun under the National Industrial Recovery Act. Then in 1936 the parkway was established by Congress on terms again prohibiting federal purchase of land, and construction was entrusted to collaboration between the Park Service and the Bureau of Public Roads. In 1938 a second national parkway was established: the Natchez Trace, on the line of an ancient Indian trail from Nashville, Tennessee, to the Mississippi River at Natchez.

Late in 1933 a wide-reaching field reconnaissance—necessarily done under cover to prevent speculative increases in cost of land—was conducted by the National Park Service in a dozen or more seashore locations on all three ocean fronts, wherever there was still a chance that some of the nation's undeveloped beaches might be saved before private "development" could reduce them to the all-too-familiar status of seaside slums. Of the many potential areas only one overcame the lack of comprehension so prevalent in Congress on such issues: in 1937 the Cape Hatteras National Seashore was authorized—to be established, however, only when the specified lands had been given to the federal government by North Carolina or private donors.

Such a recital of extraordinary problems and emergency projects does not mean that the regular functions of the National Park Service, whether on small historical areas (Figs. 336, 337) or vast wilderness tracts, were either slighted or forgotten under Cammerer. There were remarkable contrasts: the

542   *Design on the Land*

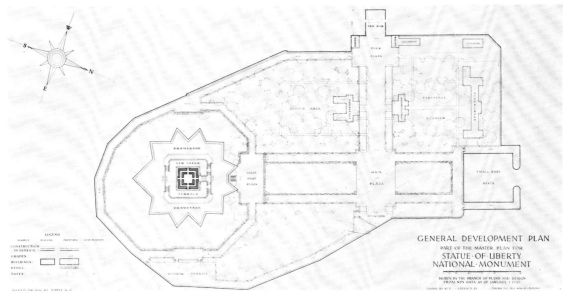

LEGEND

CONSTRUCTION
IN GENERAL
GRADES
BUILDINGS:
HEDGE
TREES

SOURCE   EXISTING   PROPOSED   NOW REMOVED

GENERAL DEVELOPMENT PLAN
PART OF THE MASTER PLAN FOR
STATUE·OF·LIBERTY
NATIONAL·MONUMENT
DRAWN BY THE BRANCH OF PLANS AND DESIGN
FROM NPS DATA AS OF JANUARY 1, 1939

337. General development plan for the Statue of Liberty National Monument, approved by
the Commission of Fine Arts on December 16, 1937: for the National Park Service, Norman
T. Newton, landscape architect. Plan has been carried out except for Small Boat Basin and
two-acre addition to island.

Statue of Liberty stood on about 12 acres. The Great Smoky Mountains
National Park, with the required 500,000 acres at last in federal ownership,
was established in 1934, and the minimal development planned could now
proceed (Fig. 338). Scenically impressive with the permanent blue haze that
gave birth to its name, this great area is also of unusual scientific significance
geologically and botanically. Because of its latitude and range of altitudes
it harbors more native plant species than any comparable area in the world.
Historically, it is noteworthy for its remaining Cherokee Indians and its
retention of the folk culture of its mountain people, including their Elizabethan speech and ballads. It thus combines as clearly as any other member
of the national park family all three of the suggested motivating factors for
the parks.

Shenandoah National Park, the long, narrow area on the Blue Ridge with
picturesque Skyline Drive and the start of the Blue Ridge Parkway, was finally
established in 1935. In 1934 the Everglades National Park in Florida was
authorized, and the same advance approval was given that year to what later
became Big Bend National Park, on the Rio Grande in Texas. In 1938
Olympic National Park and its unique "rain forests," a wilderness of over a
thousand square miles surrounding Mt. Olympus on the great peninsula of
northwestern Washington, was established after some forty years of effort (Fig.
339). In March 1940, nine years after authorization by Congress, Isle Royale

338. Blue haze in the Great Smoky Mountains National Park.

National Park in Lake Superior was established. A month later, the sixty-year battle for King's Canyon National Park in California was successfully ended with its Congressional establishment.

By 1940, Congress had relented somewhat in its determination not to use federal funds to purchase lands for the parks. Even toward the end of Albright's administration some appropriations had been made to buy up private "inholdings," notably in the Yosemite. President Roosevelt allocated emergency relief funds in 1936 for purchase where quick action was needed to protect valuable lands in Isle Royale. Congress in 1938 voted an appropriation to complete acquisition of lands for the Great Smokies, although this was regarded by many as being for the purchase of "inholdings."

To manage the greatly enlarged load of the Park Service in New Deal years, Cammerer adopted a regional structure with offices in Richmond, Omaha, Santa Fe, and San Francisco. These had been set up by Assistant Director Wirth for administration of the huge ECW program in state parks (to be discussed later). Next these offices were given charge of the CCC work in national parks, and finally their effectiveness led to their being given all field responsibilities of the Park Service. Each regional office had a regional director

339. One of sixty glaciers in the Olympic Mountains of Olympic National Park.

and a full complement of branch chiefs, reflecting the makeup of the Washington headquarters. But, even with this degree of decentralization, the burden of the packed emergency years was a staggering one for the director. When heart trouble beset Cammerer, he resigned in August 1940 and, loyal to the core, tried to continue with a reduced load as regional director in the Richmond office. It was still too much, however, and he died April 30, 1941, having literally followed the example of Mather in giving his life for the Service.

To succeed Cammerer, Newton B. Drury of California was appointed on August 20, 1940. For some twenty years he had been executive secretary of the Save-the-Redwoods League and active in the conservation movement. Drury's regime lasted eleven years—four more than Cammerer's—but it hardly seemed that long because of World War II. He took office in a thoroughly defense-minded capital and had been there only about a year when

Pearl Harbor was hit. In the wartime dispersal of nonmilitary offices from Washington, Park Service headquarters moved in 1942 to the Merchandise Mart in Chicago, where it stayed until 1946. The war itself presented many unusual problems in the parks, and the end of hostilities brought an avalanche of others just as intense though of a different kind. Five peacetime years remained for Drury, but they hardly offered unimpeded opportunity, small thanks to war's aftermath.

During the war the parks suffered inroads for emergency cutting of timber and opening of mines. Many areas were temporarily dedicated to troop use; one unfortunate result was a high incidence of vandalism. The Park Service was hit by severe problems of personnel attrition as the CCC program was discontinued and as members of the Service entered the armed forces. Appropriations were of course cut to the bone. With the end of the war, the heavy depreciation of park facilities showed itself all the more in the onrush of peacetime tourists; so did the shortage of trained personnel. Appropriations were a mere fraction of what was needed to restore the parks to levels of reasonable service. A major problem was the plight of the concessioners in the parks; ill-equipped after the meager war years, they were hardly prepared to meet the horde of visitors. In many instances it fell to Drury to persuade concessioners to stay in business; meanwhile—of course—Congress never thought of approving government operation of the concessions!

Despite the discouragement of the war years and the postwar hangover, there were some encouraging additions to the family of parks. In 1940, just after Drury's appointment, President Roosevelt dedicated the Great Smoky Mountains National Park, on which modest development had proceeded since establishment in 1934. Mammoth Cave National Park, in Kentucky, was established in 1941. In 1944 the Chisos Mountains and the cliff-walled canyons of the Rio Grande on the Texas-Mexico border became Big Bend National Park—authorized, though without specific boundaries, in 1935 (Fig. 340). Then in 1947 the long, harrowing process of acquiring land for the uniquely qualified Everglades National Park was brought to completion, at least in a legal sense, and the park was established (Fig. 341); but later events proved that its tribulations were not over. Another protracted battle against dollar-inspired local selfishness was resolved in 1950, when Jackson Hole, recommended by Albright and Mather as early as 1924, was at last added to Grand Teton National Park.

In 1946, recognition came to the Service's chief landscape architect when Vint was promoted to a new office, in charge of all construction work as chief of development. His assistant, William G. Carnes, an ASLA member since 1934, succeeded him as chief landscape architect.

Most of the strictly new units added to the system under Drury were historical in emphasis. In 1945 the Franklin D. Roosevelt home at Hyde Park, New York, became federal property as a National Historic Site, and in 1948

340. Santa Elena Canyon of the Rio Grande, Big Bend National Park, 1944.

the consolidation of an area in the heart of Philadelphia was authorized as the Independence Hall National Historical Park. In 1949 Congress approved creation of the National Trust for Historic Preservation in the United States, a private body modeled somewhat on the similar organization that had existed for years in Britain. And in one way or another during Drury's administration the Park Service became involved in problems connected with water resources. In 1940 the Bureau of Reclamation asked the Service to study the Colorado

341. Circulation for visitors is a peculiarly difficult problem in the Everglades National Park; the water-based ecology is preserved by lifting the walkway.

Basin for scenic, scientific, and recreational potentials. The Service called in Olmsted as a consultant; the resulting report was delayed by the war and not completed until 1946 (Olmsted was seventy-six but a bundle of energy). Next came a series of recreational surveys on various water bodies to be created by new dams; in 1947 no less than twelve separate reservoir areas were being examined by the Park Service. Effort was made to determine whether any archeological resources would suffer from the inundation, and valuable data on early American inhabitants, chiefly pre-Columbian, were uncovered in some of the surveys.

As flood-control dams threatened more and more to invade areas of the national park system, the Service was kept continually on alert to head off intrusions. Most intensely controversial was a proposal by the Bureau of Reclamation to build two dams in Dinosaur National Monument, on the border between Colorado and Utah. The Olmsted report of 1946 had firmly recommended against these dams, and the Park Service opposed their construction. The Reclamation people put on a vigorous propaganda campaign locally, and at last the Secretary of the Interior called hearings, at which Drury staunchly defended the area against the invasion. Eventually flaws were found in the engineering data submitted by the Bureau of Reclamation, the dams were disapproved, and Dinosaur National Monument was saved. But the battle enlisted nationwide interest in defense of the parks.

Director Drury had come to Washington in 1940 under the strong urging of Secretary Ickes, although he had been understandably reluctant to interrupt his conservation work in California. With great distinction he carried the Park Service through the most discouraging period in its history, World War II and the postwar cold-war budget squeezes. For a decade the annual appropriations for the whole NPS system never reached a third of what they had been before the war; but Drury brought the Park Service through this extremely trying period without loss of a single area or aim. When at last his old friend and classmate Governor Earl Warren asked him to come back to California to head the state's system of parks and beaches, the nostalgic pull was too strong to deny and Drury resigned from the Service on April 1, 1951.

To succeed him, Associate Director Arthur E. Demaray was promoted to the directorship for a brief period; he had already expressed a wish to retire at the end of 1951. A faithful member of the family since its beginning, when he was a young draftsman, Demaray had worked his way up through the ranks on sheer ability and was held in deep affection and esteem by the entire Park Service. In December 1951, as long intended, he retired from federal duties. He was succeeded by Conrad L. Wirth, a Fellow of the ASLA, a twenty-year veteran of the Park Service, and through all a mainstay in the headquarters staff. Parks were a part of his natural heritage; his father, Theodore, long an eminent figure in the field of park management, had been for ten years superintendent of parks in Hartford before going in 1906 to head the great park system of Minneapolis. Through the years, Theodore Wirth had many professional contacts with Olmsted; it was the latter's friendly urging that caused the son, Conrad, to go to Washington in 1928. Conrad Wirth's executive skill had been amply demonstrated in the 1930s, when he organized and led for the Park Service the huge program of Emergency Conservation Work performed by hundreds of camps of the Civilian

Conservation Corps in national, state, county, and metropolitan parks throughout the country.

Wirth was Director for thirteen years—years of unbroken effort to keep the parks from being worn out by enthusiastic visitors whose numbers had zoomed at the end of the war and continued soaring while Congressional appropriations lagged and maintenance of the parks became perforce minimal. The problem of overcrowding—of numerical disparity between planned and actual users—is not often understood by the lay population. Nor indeed is it as clearly understood by all landscape architects as it ought to be; the design considerations involved are many and complex. It is not merely a matter of inadequate accommodations on the part of concessioners for lodging, feeding, and transporting people, important as these factors are. It is not simply that visitors may arrive at a park only to find themselves without shelter and meals—or immobilized if they did not come in their own cars. It is not just a question of mechanical shortages, though insufficiency of water supply and sewage disposal can of course be disastrous.

If such inadequacies were the only problem, the deceptively simple answer would be to build larger facilities in more locations, assuming for the moment that concessioners could handle the investment, or that Congress had at last relented about government operation. But the more important question is this: what would these additions do to the natural scenic environment, and how much of it would they affect? Every area of construction or manmade surface arrangement—called a "developed area" in the Park Service—permanently modifies the natural wild condition in a surrounding zone to a depth depending on the total situation. In such a zone many ecological changes occur, the most obvious being disappearance of the normal wildlife. Even a foot trail carries a belt of changed condition to right and left; a horse trail carries a wider one; a motor road so modifies character on both sides as to become virtually a mile-wide strip of land bereft of natural wildness.

With manifest good sense the Park Service has tried zealously to avoid scattering "developed areas" throughout a park, concentrating them instead where needed in carefully selected locations and keeping them as small as possible to serve their respective purposes. The aim, of course, is to avoid general disruption and retain the largest feasible proportion of the park in the superlatively wild condition that was the reason for setting the area aside in the first place and that still is presumably the basic reason for any visitor's coming. Considering these factors, it is clear that the mere addition of more and larger facilities is not as simple an answer as it may seem.

But these are only questions of percentage, of planning and proportion. Equally important in the wild natural environment is outright physical impact of the human individual—multiplied by thousands. It must be obvious that plants tend to die if trampled repeatedly by feet or tires, that tree trunks cannot long withstand being gashed by errant motor cars. What is not so obvious, but is nevertheless true, is the harmful effect of soil compacting. Multiplied footsteps, compressing the soil, form an impervious top layer of earth that interferes with absorption and percolation of needed water and with capillary action in the subsoil, on which trees and shrubs depend for bringing food in solution to their root-hairs. Sooner or later the trees and shrubs die. Moreover, the compacted surface induces rapid runoff of rain and consequent soil erosion.

Under control, these effects can be anticipated and planned for with paths, roads, and other clearly defined areas for human congregation. The trouble is that people, even with the best of intentions, wander unless guided. When there is overpopulation the harmful effects grow explosively worse; there is spillover galore, and the carefully designed use-area swiftly enlarges like a blot, losing all form, integrity, and sense of control. Even so, what happens from trampling feet is as nothing when compared to the damage wrought by the tires of truant motor cars, especially those parked willy-nilly beyond the limits of planned, surfaced, and plainly marked parking spaces. Perhaps the most severe destruction comes from the cumbersome trailer, which seems to arrive in mounting numbers as a major manifestation of overcrowding.

There is at least one other respect in which visitors, the very people for whose enjoyment the parks have been established, turn out to be the chief potential destroyers of what they came for. They are the principal source of forest fires, not only through carelessness with matches but through building fires in places not intended and prepared for the purpose. Control of this hazard is one of the main functions performed by park rangers; but when overcrowding occurs, a given ranger force becomes inadequate in size and the situation can quickly get out of hand. Park rangers are a phenomenally dedicated lot with an admirable ideal of service to the public; it is sheer irony that experience has compelled them, on the whole, to see the visitor principally as a source of danger.

Of course the considerations set forth here form a normal part, albeit only a small one, of the total task confronting landscape architects in the planning of national parks. Theirs is the problem of trying to estimate correctly—in collaboration with engineers, architects, foresters, wildlife technicians, geologists, and sometimes historians—how much development, and in what form, a park can stand without loss of essential character. There is often only the narrowest of margins between too little accommodation and too much development. The problem is tough enough under normal conditions, let alone in the chaos of overcrowding.

For the landscape architects of the Park Service, whether stationed in parks, in regional offices, or at Washington headquarters, these general but controlling considerations govern not only the master plans for the great areas but also the careful, detailed design of concentrated "developed areas" for accommodation and guidance of visitors and ultimately the preparation of construction drawings for installation of the projects. Through a long-standing interagency procedure devised by Vint in 1926, even before he became chief landscape architect, design and construction of park roads and parkways is done collaboratively by the Park Service's landscape architects and engineers of the Bureau of Public Roads.

When by 1955 the national park system was receiving 50,000,000 visitors a year as against the 21,000,000 planned for as recently as 1941, Director Wirth launched a comprehensive ten-year program of reassessment, looking forward to the 80,000,000 visitors expected by 1966, the fiftieth anniversary of the founding of the National Park Service. Appropriately, he called the program "Mission 66." A special booklet, *Our Heritage,* outlined the case for the Service:

> The problem is simply this: the National Parks are neither equipped nor staffed to protect their irreplaceable features, nor to take care of the increasing millions of visitors . . . During World War II, the Korean conflict, and the cold war period, the National Park Service, of necessity, had to curtail all along the line. As a result, the Service and the concessioners were unable to modernize and expand, and the facilities today are insufficient, outmoded, and are wearing out. After fifteen years of patching, and then placing patches on the patches, there is no longer room for makeshift solutions . . . [1]

Eight specific objectives were stated, to provide (1) additional accommodations through greater participation of private enterprise, (2) better government-operated facilities, (3) services leading to better visitor cooperation, (4) operating funds and field staff for a high standard of maintenance, (5) adequate living quarters for field employees, (6) acquisition of needed lands and rights, (7) a coordinated nationwide recreation plan shared by all levels of government, and (8) protection and preservation of wilderness areas. It was estimated that a total of $786,545,600 would be needed for the entire ten-year program.

To head the "Mission 66" staff Carnes, the chief landscape architect, was moved into a new appointment as chief of advanced planning; Merel S. Sager, a Fellow of the ASLA and veteran member of the Park Service family, was promoted to succeed Carnes as chief landscape architect. Another organizational step in 1955 was the establishment of a fifth regional office in Philadelphia. Thanks to the sensible appeal of "Mission 66," Congress stepped up appropriations, and much-needed construction could be undertaken. A major effort was made to reduce congestion in the parks by shifting facilities to new locations, in some cases actually moving them to settlements beyond the park boundaries and in others closing overnight accommodations al-

---

1. National Park Service, *Our Heritage: A Plan for Its Protection and Use* (Washington, D.C., 1955), p. 7.

342. Cape Hatteras National Seashore Recreational Area.

together in recognition of the heavy increase in day use. It was heartening to note that, in much of the new building, full freedom was given to the emancipation of design from its traditional straitjacket, although in fairness one must observe that the National Park Service had never exactly wallowed in architectural eclecticism.

The first new unit added to the system in Wirth's administration was the Cape Hatteras National Seashore Recreational Area in North Carolina, finally established in 1952 (Fig. 342). The original field studies had been done under Wirth's driving guidance eighteen years earlier. In 1954, thanks to private donation of funds, he was able to order resumption of the important study of the nation's few remaining undeveloped seashore areas, picking up the reconnaissance performed by personnel of his branch of the Service in 1933–1934. During the intervening years, as had been feared, many beaches recommended in the earlier study had fallen to private and commercial development. But some success was achieved in 1961, when Congress actually went so far, in reversal of its traditional policy about lands, as to appropriate some sixteen million dollars to purchase sizable acreage for the Cape Cod National Seashore in Massachusetts. Three new national parks, three national monuments, and thirty-one national historic sites were introduced to the system in Wirth's regime. In 1955 the City of Refuge National Historical Park, in Hawaii, was authorized; it was established in 1961. In 1956, thanks to the generosity of the Rockefeller family, the Virgin Islands National Park was established. In 1958 the Petrified Forest National Park, in Arizona, was raised from national monument status, to become effective upon final acquisition of certain inholdings.

Wirth experienced, of course, what had come to be the usual portion of the Service's director: continuous battle against the greed and crass insensitivity of those who will apparently never stop grabbing at the nation's parks; against timber, mining, and power interests; against ill-considered preemption by federal agencies; against the inroads of political chicanery and patronage. Nevertheless, due in large measure to the early success of "Mission 66," Wirth's administration had been marked by steady progress and fine accomplishment when in January 1964 he retired and the directorship passed to George B. Hartzog, Jr., Wirth's associate director. Of the chief landscape architects mentioned, Vint had retired in 1961 as Assistant Director, Design and Construction; Carnes in 1962 as Deputy Assistant Director.

Such in brief is the saga of the national park system from 1807 and "Colter's Hell" to 1872 and the lonesome Yellowstone, to 1916 and Mather's National Park Service and so to the vast system of 1964 with thirty-some national parks and nearly two hundred other units. It is a huge and complex "people's empire," challenging in dimension, inspiring in purpose, difficult to plan and manage. The core of the system, those big tracts of superlative wild grandeur, are being tested as never before by steadily larger throngs of eager visitors. To fence the people out would surely preserve the parks, in an abstract sense. But the parks are for the people to enjoy; their justification is in their human values. Again and again one feels the insistence of that ultimate calculus referred to earlier. In the long run, if the great parks are to survive the onslaught, if they are indeed to remain "unimpaired for the enjoyment of future generations," they will need help—the help that comes from public understanding and respect and the relief supplied by other outdoor recreational areas, high among which are those hundreds of smaller members of the family, the state, county, and metropolitan parks.

XXXVII. The State Park Movement: 1864–1933

The story of American state parks begins with the 1864 cession of the Yosemite Valley and the Mariposa Big Tree Grove, then part of the public domain, to the State of California—unless one prefers to cite anew the remarkable Great Ponds Act of 1641 in the Massachusetts Bay colony. To avoid misunderstanding at the outset: the term *state park* will be used here in its usual generic sense, to include sizable county parks and the larger reservations of metropolitan park systems. All are on occasion referred to as "regional parks," a term that eliminates any question about which level of government has control. Either term is workable; at any rate, the areas, differing considerably in size, ownership, and purpose, are all by custom regarded as products of the "state park movement."

It would perhaps be an exaggeration to say that the *movement* began at Yosemite in 1864, since nothing comparable on a state level happened for another twenty years. But there can be little question that the action on Yosemite was doubly important, not only because it created the first state park in America, but also because of the long-range value of Olmsted's contribution to it (Fig. 343). Whereas Congress withdrew the land from the public domain and granted it to California "for public use, resort and recreation" in June 1864, the state legislature took until 1866 to accept the grant formally. Governor Low meanwhile wisely posted the tract against trespass and appointed an eight-man Yosemite Commission to work out policies for handling the area as a state property. Olmsted was a member of this group, and for it he prepared the preliminary report of 1865, now generally recog-

343. Yosemite Valley: the first state park, 1864.

nized as one of the most significant historic documents of what became the state park movement.[1]

So far as is known today, Olmsted's report, written seven years before establishment of the Yellowstone, presented the first carefully reasoned statement to support the setting aside of great scenic areas for public ownership and enjoyment—a notion that was by no means the outcome of any tumultuous popular demand. In judging the report, one should bear in mind that here, as in the earlier case of Central Park, Olmsted was at heart a social reformer, deeply concerned for the welfare of "the mass of the people." Having spent a month camping with his family in Yosemite during the summer of 1864, he was overwhelmed by its majesty and by the potential

1. Most of the report disappeared for many years; it was brought to light and published with an introductory note by Laura Wood Roper, Olmsted's biographer, in *Landscape Architecture*, 42 (October 1952). The quotations are from that article, pp. 12–25.

of such magnificent scenery for uplifting the health and spirit of those whose need was greatest.

It therefore results that the enjoyment of scenery employs the mind without fatigue and yet exercises it; tranquillizes it and yet enlivens it; and thus, through the influence of the mind over the body, gives the effect of refreshing rest and reinvigoration to the whole system.

Men who are rich enough . . . can and do provide places of this needed recreation for themselves. They have done so from the earliest periods known in the history of the world, for the great men . . . had their rural retreats . . . private parks and notable grounds devoted to luxury and recreation . . . The enjoyment of the choicest natural scenes in the country and the means of recreation connected with them is thus a monopoly, in a very peculiar manner, of a very few, very rich people. The great mass of society, including those to whom it would be of the greatest benefit, is excluded from it . . .

Thus without means are taken by government to withhold them from the grasp of individuals, all places favorable in scenery to the recreation of the mind and body will be closed against the great body of the people. For the same reason that the water of rivers should be guarded against private appropriation and . . . obstruction, portions of natural scenery may therefore properly be guarded and cared for by government. To simply reserve them from monopoly by individuals, however, it will be obvious, is not all that is necessary. It is necessary that they should be laid open to the use of the body of the people.

The establishment by government of great public grounds for the free enjoyment of the people under certain circumstances, is thus justified and enforced as a political duty.

The challenge presented by Central Park, largely a manmade landscape, had been quite different from the one before Olmsted in the existing wild landscape of the Yosemite. He saw clearly the kind of treatment needed here:

Congress enacted that the Yosemite should be held, guarded and managed for the free use of the whole body of the people forever, and that the care of it, and the hospitality of admitting strangers from all parts of the world to visit it and enjoy it freely, should be a duty of dignity and be committed only to a sovereign state.

The duty with which the Commissioners should be charged should be to give every advantage practicable to the mass of the people to benefit by that which is peculiar to this ground and which has caused Congress to treat it differently from other parts of the public domain. This peculiarity consists wholly in its natural scenery.

The first point to be kept in mind then is the preservation and maintenance as exactly as is possible of the natural scenery; the restriction, that is to say, within the narrowest limits consistent with the necessary accommodation of visitors, of all artificial constructions and the prevention of all constructions markedly inharmonious with the scenery or which would unnecessarily obscure, distort or detract from the dignity of the scenery.

In an age when it was common custom on approaching a piece of land to attack it and wrest from it whatever material profit one could—timber, game, ore, crops—Olmsted's admonition regarding preservation and the rights of posterity must have sounded strange indeed:

> It should, then, be made the duty of the Commission to prevent a wanton or careless disregard on the part of anyone entering the Yosemite or the Grove, of the rights of posterity as well as of contemporary visitors, and the Commission should be clothed with proper authority and given the necessary means for this purpose.
>
> This duty of preservation is the first which falls upon the state under the Act of Congress, because the millions who are hereafter to benefit by the Act have the largest interest in it, and the largest interest should be first and most strenuously guarded."

Olmsted, yielding to Vaux's pleas to return east for the Brooklyn work, could not stay on in California long after presenting his Yosemite report; moreover, there is evidence to indicate that the report never reached the floor of the legislature. He certainly had laid the foundations for sound thinking about conservation, and he remained a dominant leader in park matters throughout his life; it is nevertheless clear that California profited less from Olmsted's insight and skill than might have been the case. At any rate, under the circumstances he could not be blamed for California's half-hearted management of the valley in ensuing years. To be sure, the state had the boundaries of the tract surveyed and did its best to remove the few early settlers. But the area was highly inaccessible, and maintaining it was far more costly than the legislature—or anyone else—had realized in those days of inexperience. The logical outcome was return of the state park lands to the United States in 1906.

Meanwhile, after Yosemite's establishment two decades had passed before there was action anywhere about state parks; in fact, development was spotty at best for over a half-century. Thus, although Olmsted, after his return from California (at least as early as 1869) conferred with other conservationists about the preservation of Niagara Falls, no conclusion was reached until 1885. In that year New York created the Niagara Falls Reservation, voting also one million dollars for purchase of land. Also in 1885, the New York legislature established with state-owned lands the huge Adirondack Forest Preserve, essentially a state park in purpose (Fig. 344). A few years later the smaller Catskill Preserve was marked out as a distinct unit. A "park" was later

344. In the Adirondack Forest Preserve of northern New York.

designated within the famous but puzzling "blue line," to include large portions of the Adirondack Preserve but also private holdings under rigorous protective restrictions by the state. Rounding out the three isolated instances of state park addition in 1885, the federally owned Mackinac Island, in the straits between Lake Michigan and Lake Huron, was transferred to the State of Michigan. It had been set aside in 1879, though rather tentatively, as a national military park because of the historically important Fort Michilimackinac of colonial days.

Spasmodic state park progress continued into the 1890s. A step of permanent significance was taken by Minnesota in 1891, when acquisition was begun on lands that became Lake Itasca State Park, containing the headwaters of the Mississippi River (Fig. 345). An earlier chapter contained Charles Eliot's success story in establishing, in 1891, the Trustees of Public Reservations in Massachusetts and then in 1892 the first metropolitan park system in the world. The system's two large forested areas, the Middlesex Fells and the Blue Hills Reservation, are normally classed as state parks in type, although their development for human enjoyment has been relatively slight.

345. Headwaters of the Mississippi River, in Minnesota's Itasca State Park.

The year 1895 was marked by three notable events: the birth of one of the most effective early conservation bodies, the American Scenic and Historic Preservation Society; the start of the first county park organization, in Essex County, New Jersey; the first private acquisition of portions of the Palisades of the Hudson, across from New York City and lower Westchester County, made possible by J. Pierpont Morgan, heading off the mining of this geological marvel for traprock. Five years later, in 1900, the Palisades Interstate

Park was established, to include a strip of land along the west side of the Hudson in New York and New Jersey. Management was ingeniously placed in the hands of two theoretically independent ten-man commissions, one from each state. But by friendly agreement the same ten members, five residents of each state, customarily made up the "two" commissions. This fine example of enlightened cooperation was not covered by legislation until 1937, when an interstate compact was passed by the two legislatures and approved by Congress.

During the first decade of the twentieth century New York State enjoyed the benefits of several separate actions cited here simply to illustrate how state park systems can slowly take shape through private donations accompanied by an appropriately intelligent and receptive public attitude. In 1906, under urging by the American Scenic and Historic Preservation Society, the state acquired Watkins Glen, a fantastic geologic phenomenon of rocky cliffs, cascades, and grottos at the southern end of Seneca Lake. Then in 1907 the legislature approved appointment of the Bronx River Parkway Commission to study and solve the problems presented by that stream on the Westchester approaches to New York City. Again in 1907, William P. Letchworth gave the state his tract of over a thousand acres in the western part of the state,

346. The gorge of the Genesee River in western New York, part of the Letchworth tract.

including Portage Falls and the awe-inspiring gorge of the Genesee River (Fig. 346). Topping even this, in 1910 the Harriman family gave the state over forty thousand acres of rough, forested land reaching to the southwest from Bear Mountain on the Hudson, for addition to the holdings of the Palisades Interstate Park Commission. Almost as though to voice appreciation of its great good luck, the people of the state voted in 1910 to approve a bond issue of $2,500,000, an unprecedented act in both purpose and amount, for purchase of state park lands. Six years later another bond issue, this time for $10,000,000, was approved by the voters. New York was thus well prepared for the momentous upward surge of state park activity right after World War I.

Although the state park movement as such was still sputtering, a modicum of progress was discernible in other states between 1900 and the end of the war. At the turn of the century, Minnesota and Wisconsin created separate interstate parks facing each other across the St. Croix River. At the same time in Massachusetts the Mount Greylock, Wachusett Mountain, and Mount Tom Reservations were set aside. In 1902 Ohio converted into state parks several thousand acres around reservoir lakes left over from an abandoned canal system. As early as 1911, Idaho brought in Payette Lake and Heyburn State Parks, and Illinois established Starved Rock State Park. Wisconsin, having formed a State Park Board in 1907, engaged landscape architect John Nolen to do a study of the state's park potentials, and then saved from destruction Devil's Lake and Nelson-Dewey State Parks; between 1910 and 1914 several thousand acres of forest in the Peninsula State Park were added. During the same years, Pennsylvania assembled the Valley Forge and Fort Washington State Parks, and in 1912 Connecticut set up its State Park Commission, which quickly began acquiring lands for several new parks.

In Illinois, the renowned Cook County Forest Preserve District was created by popular vote in 1914 as an encircling belt of recreational areas about Chicago. New Jersey with Swartswood Lake State Park and North Carolina with Mount Mitchell State Park joined the list in 1915. In 1916 Indiana, under the leadership of Colonel Richard Lieber, established its first units in McCormick's Creek Canyon and Turkey Run State Parks (Fig. 347), preliminary to setting up one of the strongest of the early state park organizations. In 1918, after many years of hard work, the ten thousand-acre California Redwood State Park came into being and the remarkable Save-the-Redwoods League was formed. Also in 1918, Iowa made a start with Backbone State Park and Connecticut added Macedonia Brook State Park.

The foregoing, given in some detail for the sake of fairness to the most progressive states, may seem quite an accomplishment. But in plain fact, at the end of World War I, more than a half-century after establishment of the Yosemite as the first of its kind, there was not a very heartening performance to look back at in terms of a state park movement. Fifty-five years had

347. Turkey Run State Park, Indiana.

produced little more than a handful of state parks, scattered among one-third of the states. Only New York, Indiana, Wisconsin, Connecticut, and possibly California had anything even approaching a firm state park organization, and none of these owned what could reasonably be called a *system* of state parks. Then, within a relatively brief period, things began to happen. At least two specific factors appear to have been catalytic. The impact of the automobile, which had been slowly but surely making the American people more mobile, was highly intensified at the end of the war by the promotion of installment sales of cars. To a degree unknown in earlier years the American family started taking to the road, and the demand for outdoor recreational areas shot upward accordingly. In the two years immediately after the armistice several states, especially those wheelhorses Connecticut, Iowa, Michigan, Minnesota, and Wisconsin, responded with new parks. A number of notable additions were initiated in 1919 and 1920, such as Old Salem State Park in Illinois, Clifty Falls State Park in Indiana, Enfield Glen (later R. H. Treman) State Park in New York, and the huge Custer State Park in South Dakota, that state's first.

A second catalyst was Stephen Mather, who as director of the National Park Service had the sensible notion of looking to an ample, nationwide system of state parks to serve as a buffer to protect the great national parks from a dangerous avalanche of motorized visitors. After all, the most pressing public demand was for intensive recreation—for such day-use facilities as bathing beaches and picnic grounds, for short-term rather than long-term use. State parks could be geared for these purposes just as well as national parks and often better. Moreover, dense urban populations would normally find state parks nearer and more easily accessible than national parks. For intensive recreation, the superlative scenery of the national parks was certainly not a primary requirement; indeed, facilities for swimming would in many cases appear more important. Of a more modest scenic level than national parks, state parks of satisfying quality would be easier to find, justify, and establish. The move toward more state parks, Mather may have surmised, might also curtail the large number of low-grade, unqualified national park proposals then being urged upon the Park Service by ambitious politicians and local groups.

To Mather, having a thought meant acting on it; in this case it meant organizing one of the national conferences for which he was already famous. Beginning in 1920, he enlisted the interest and services of conservationists in many states. He called to a meeting in Chicago a small group of key reliables; they agreed with the proposal for a big conference and settled on Des Moines as a good central place. Mather immediately engaged, at his own expense, a young enthusiast whom he sent to Des Moines two months in advance to pave the way. Secretary of the Interior John Barton Payne, impressed by Mather's reasoning, had given the endeavor his blessing; the hearty cooperation of Iowa's Governor W. L. Harding was readily obtained.

At Mather's request the Governor sent out thousands of formal invitations to a general park conference, especially urging the governors of the other states to send delegations. When the forces gathered at Des Moines for what turned out to be an epochal meeting early in 1921, twenty-five states were represented by over two hundred individuals. This group quickly organized as the National Conference on State Parks, with Secretary Payne as its first chairman. The Des Moines meeting had profound results, not only in the founding of the NCSP, which still holds annual meetings and is a source of strength, but also in such a resurgence of interest and determination that it could at last be fairly said that a state park movement was on the way. The years following the meeting showed the value of a shared concern and concerted efforts. Wholly new parks were added in twenty states, including eight that had

348. Buttermilk Falls State Park, a unit of the Finger Lakes State Park Commission.

349. Jones Beach State Park, Long Island, an outstanding example of state park planning and design: air view from the west.

owned no state parks before 1921. Despite the known slowness of democratic legislative processes, no less than seventeen states created their first state park boards or commissions between 1921 and 1927 or otherwise enacted laws clarifying the responsibility and authority for management of the state's recreational and scenic areas.

An example of such legislative remodeling was that of 1927 in New York. A State Council of Parks, organized in 1924 on studies reaching back to 1922, was placed under a new Division of Parks in the state's Department of Conservation. Replacing a patchwork situation under which various independent boards and societies had administered areas all over the state, the new legislation provided final cement for one of the nation's largest and strongest unified state park systems. This divided the state into regions, each under the charge of an unpaid commission of private citizens appointed by the governor and each with a professional staff, including in most cases at least one landscape architect. The chairmen or presidents of the several regional commissions constituted the State Council, which was responsible for allocation of funds provided by the state's budget. When final adjustment of regional boundaries had been effected, the divisions were Niagara Frontier, Allegany, Genesee, Finger Lakes (Fig. 348), Central New York, Thousand Islands, Adirondack, Taconic, Palisades Interstate, and Long Island. Robert Moses, president of the Long Island State Park Commission, was elected chairman of the State Council when it organized in 1924.

The need for such consolidations was obvious in a state the size of New York, with so many parks of wide diversity in location, topography, vegetative cover, and manner of use. According to a report of the NCSP, New York had by 1928 fifty-six units, with over two million acres of land. These parks included large tracts of near-wilderness, to be sure, but they also illustrated the increasing trend toward intensive recreation that had caused Mather to reach his conclusions about the national role of state parks. Outstanding in the category of areas for intensive use is Jones Beach State Park (Fig. 349), installed on the south shore of Long Island in the summer of 1929. A superb work of landscape design, this great park extends along several miles of wide ocean beach, dispersing with astonishing evenness a use-population of unbelievable thousands. Toward one end is the East Bathhouse (Fig. 350); toward the other, with an enclosed fresh-water pool, is the West Bathhouse. Midway between them is the Central Mall (Fig. 351), with its widely recognized water tower and the main arrival circle of the Wantagh Parkway. There are snack and dining facilities at all three points. The entire length of the

350. The East Bathhouse at Jones Beach State Park.

351. The Central Mall and water tower at Jones Beach State Park.

park is tied together in simple, straightforward geometry, chiefly by means of a wide, raised boardwalk that fronts on the beach from one bathhouse to the other, with carefully delimited game areas along its north side throughout. A long, straight road runs the length of the park on the landward side of the bathhouses, with arrival turns at each of these and at the Central Mall. North of the road there are enormous parking areas for thousands of cars, with pedestrian underpasses leading to bathhouses and beach. Drinking fountains, benches, inconspicuous trash receptacles, and occasional sun-shelters are distributed at logical points in the geometry of the plan.

One of the most remarkable aspects of Jones Beach is the way the site accepts it. All the land outside the clearly bounded use-areas has been allowed to remain in its native ocean-front condition. The dunes, firmly anchored by beach grass, bayberry, beach plum, and jack pine, have flourished un-harmed for forty years. The heartening fact is that these wild areas are simply not invaded by the public. Indeed, the whole place illustrates brilliantly the power of design to affect human behavior and, if need be, control it. One looks in vain for litter; uncouth activity is virtually unknown. The overall landscape design is a masterpiece; it was done in large part by Clarence C. Combs, landscape architect of the Long Island State Park Commission, with help from, among others, Melvin B. Borgeson, a landscape architect on emergency loan from the Westchester County Park Commission.

New York was thus providing by 1929 a type of state park devoted almost wholly to intensive recreational use by large numbers of people. The Empire State was no doubt more advanced in this direction than other states, but the recreational trend was moving along in many of the twenty-five states with state parks by the end of the 1920s. One of the most noteworthy of this kind of park system was the Cook County Forest Preserve District around Chicago, a belt of partially connected holdings totaling over thirty thousand acres. Though not state property, but an autonomous entity within Cook County, these parks have customarily been regarded as of the state park type and are usually so classified. In the words of a Commissioner, the Cook County Forest Preserve District is "a forested sanctuary with recreational facilities for appropriate forms of intensive use on the fringes."[2] This brief statement merits attention, especially in view of the tremendous amount of recreation actually provided by the District through the years.

In 1929 Charles G. Sauers, the landscape architect who had been Colonel Lieber's right-hand man in Indiana, became general superintendent of the Cook County Forest Preserve District. The District's landscape architect was John Barstow Morrill. Under their guidance and that of their professional colleagues at the headquarters in River Forest, the system demonstrated how well a set of parks can accommodate intensive recreation. Surely no sterner test could be imposed than the pressure of such nearby metropolitan masses of eager users. Yet, basic policy of the District required that its areas must remain essentially pieces of near-wild nature. No situation could more in-sistently have demanded continual invention of appropriate new techniques of design and management to keep the parks in service without thereby destroying them through wear and tear. And this is precisely what Sauers and Morrill accomplished. Their job was of incalculable value, not only for

2. Forest Preserve District of Cook County, Illinois, *Annual Report, 1957,* p. 5.

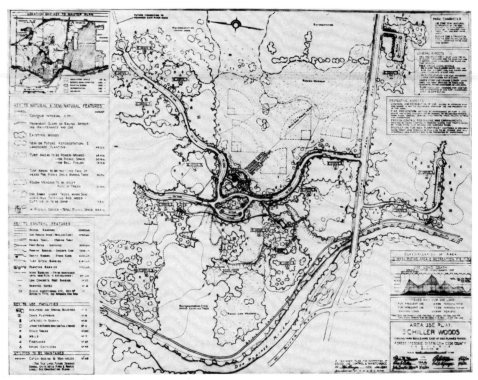

352. Cook County Forest Preserve District of Illinois: the layout of Schiller Woods picnic groves, illustrating the value of careful planning for mass use of wooded areas.

its own practical purposes, but also because it showed how a design problem tends to solve itself if permitted to do so on its own terms of site and function, without the designer's imposing a preconception of form.

Among other departures from standard practice, Sauers and Morrill devised simple new ways of employing durable building materials, particularly straightforward types of concrete structures that did not pretend to be something else, yet looked comfortably at home in the forest about them. The two experimented with—and applied with marked success—a policy of alternate areas for group picnicking, so that a "grove" could be chained off and rested through a season or more, enabling it to restore itself naturally to usable condition while its mate was being used (Figs. 352, 353).

The Forest Preserve District was an all-year operation, with winter sports an integral part of the program, notably in the Palos Hills ski area with its multiple toboggan slides. In summer the major activity was of course at the swimming pools, with thousands of picnic permits running a close second. The parks of the District, in short, were used throughout the year by the people of Cook County in enormous numbers, but the basic "forested sanctuary" character was not lost. The reason for this was primarily a careful adherence

353. Air view of Schiller Woods, looking north (from right in the plan); alternating use of picnic groves aids in maintaining healthy vegetation year after year.

to the fundamental caution already quoted: "facilities for *appropriate forms* of intensive use on the fringes."

The question of what constitutes an "appropriate form" of recreation arises often in discussions of state park policies. There appears to be general agreement against providing a facility that requires too large an area of carefully graded and treated surface, such as baseball diamonds, tennis courts, running tracks, or athletic fields; not only because in form such areas would be incongruous in the normally rough or undulant terrain of a state park, but also because psychologically they would introduce an equally incongruous urban atmosphere. The following language from an annual report of the Cook County District suggests a somewhat differently stated reason for the fine success of its many programs: "The District offers no organized recreation . . . we believe organized recreation belongs in the truly municipal park system."[3]

While in the east and the midwest 1929 brought such intensive recreational developments as Jones Beach and the parks of the Cook County Preserve,

3. *Ibid.*, 1940, p. 174.

other events of great import were taking place on the west coast. In California, Olmsted's famous state park report, one of his most widely cited writings, was published in 1929. Events there had begun in 1927, with the enactment in Sacramento of legislation establishing a state park commission, authorizing a popular referendum on a bond issue of six million dollars for purchase of state parks, and providing for a survey of the state's park potentials. California had at the time five state park areas, but these had been assembled rather fortuitously, without any overall plan, and were administered by different appointive bodies. Perhaps the strongest single organization was the private Save-the-Redwoods League. Pursuant to the 1927 legislation, Governor Young appointed five distinguished Californians to the new centralized commission. They in turn, to implement the provision for a study of the state's potentials, engaged Olmsted. How appropriate it was that this report should be made by the man whose father wrote the first state park report in California! To assist him, Olmsted took on a small staff: Daniel R. Hull of Los Angeles, former chief landscape architect of the National Park Service, Harry W. Shepherd, of the University of California at Berkeley, and Emerson Knight, of San Francisco. All were members of the ASLA. Together with advisers from "the twelve territorial divisions into which the state was divided for the purposes of the survey,"[4] Olmsted and his staff worked during 1927 and 1928. The result, entitled *Report of State Park Survey of California,* was signed by Olmsted on December 29, 1928, and published by the state early the next year. By consensus it is still regarded, both technically and historically, as one of the most valuable of all known documents on state parks.

In his oft-quoted report Olmsted, referring to "the values arising directly and indirectly from the enjoyment of scenery and from related pleasures of non-urban outdoor life," lists in his usual minute manner "the variety and extent of the means by which these values are sought." He continues:

> The kinds of values sought by such means have always been part of the joy of living for many people, but in our time, in America, there has been an enormous increase in the proportion of people who have time left for the pursuit of such values after earning the bare necessities of existence.
>
> These values, together with others which directly make life worth living, as distinguished from things which are valued only because they can be exchanged for something one really wants, are the final things which economic prosperity enables people to buy. In California, today, people are using their economic wealth in the ways above indicated to buy values of this particular kind enormously—incredibly to anyone of a former age or another country. And they will probably seek to buy this kind of values more and more.

4. F. L. Olmsted, *Report of State Park Survey of California* (Sacramento, 1929), p. 9.

How far such values *can* be bought, at any price, by succeeding generations in California will depend largely on the degree to which the physical conditions which make them possible are permanently conserved or are destroyed by the first comers through their wasteful methods of exploiting them.

The enormous development in California of the use of these scenic and recreational values of the out-of-doors has resulted . . . in part from the lavish abundance of naturally favorable conditions of landscape and climate.

But there are signs on every hand that because of this very abundance (and of the increasing rate at which the favorable conditions are being put to use), careless, hasty, shortsightedly selfish methods of exploiting the natural assets of scenic value are rapidly killing the geese that lay the golden eggs.[5]

The California State Park Survey, as the 1929 report is commonly called, contains Olmsted's general specifications for state parks:

The chief criteria for determining which of them should be included in an "ultimate, comprehensive state park system" . . . appear to be these:

1. They should be sufficiently distinctive and notable to interest people from comparatively distant parts of the state to visit and use them . . . Also they should, in general, be situated beyond the limits of urban and suburban communities which have sufficient population and wealth to assume the obligation of providing parks that would be mainly serviceable for the daily use of their own citizens . . .

2. They should be characterized by scenic and recreational resources of kinds which are unlikely to be reasonably well conserved and made available for enjoyment under private ownership . . .

3. They should be as nearly as possible just sufficient in number and extent and character to meet the prospective demands of the people for the kinds of enjoyment which they can provide, and which cannot or will not be supplied by such other means as local parks, national parks and forests, and the use of scenic highways . . .

4. They should be geographically distributed with a view to securing a wide and representative variety of types for the state as a whole, and at the same time making a reasonable assortment of them equitably accessible to the people in each part of the state (pp. 49–51).

Olmsted received recommendations for new state parks from the regional advisers and many other sources. A total of 330 proposals were studied, of which only 125 seemed "projects for favorable discussion in this report" (57).

5. *Ibid.,* pp. 15–17.

354. Richardson Grove State Park, a unit in California's superb system of state parks and beaches.

But, since even these could not possibly be acquired within the limits of the bond issue just popularly approved, Olmsted simmered the list down to a final total of 79, which were then listed and discussed briefly. It is largely on the basis of this list that California's present excellent system of parks and beaches has been built (Fig. 354).

Thus in 1929, sixty-five years after establishment of the first example, the state park movement had at last achieved recognizable momentum. In the course of these years, the role of state parks as vehicles for social service had come to be far more widely understood and accepted. They had become more varied in character as the importance of intensive recreation asserted itself. As they grew more complex, with vastly larger use-populations, the parks confronted landscape architects with ever more demanding problems of design. Also in 1929, of course, came the breakdown of the economy, with its consequent throttling effect on state expenditures. For the next four years the state park movement was, understandably, at almost a standstill as the national catastrophe deepened. Then came the 1932 election of Franklin Roosevelt and, in March 1933, the founding of the Civilian Conservation Corps, credited with having advanced the state park movement by at least a half-century.

XXXVIII. State Parks and the Civilian Conservation Corps

It has been said repeatedly that, of all the measures initiated by President Franklin Roosevelt and his New Deal, the Civilian Conservation Corps was the least controversial. It was certainly an unqualified success in many directions. It provided employment and a healthful outdoor experience for thousands of young men at a critical moment in their lives, and enabled them to acquire useful skills that would otherwise almost surely have evaded them. It sought to conserve not only the face of the land but the nation's human resources as well; in both respects its accomplishments were tremendous. There is general agreement that it was the greatest single step in conservation of natural resources since the first Conference of Governors, called in 1908 by President Theodore Roosevelt to discuss correlation of conservation efforts among the states. As earlier suggested, the CCC program sent the state park movement forward a good fifty years.

Naturally the enterprise gave a badly needed boost to the national economy. Specifically important in the context of this book is the unexpected employment it afforded thousands of professional men—including landscape architects—in supervisory capacities, both in CCC camps and on administrative staffs for the United States Forest Service, the National Park Service, and later the Soil Conservation Service. Not to be overlooked was the experience the program gave the Army, and several thousand reserve officers, in the cooperative management of civilian camps and personnel without dependence on military means.

That President Roosevelt should institute such a program did not come as a complete surprise. He was known to have been long concerned about conservation; as governor of New York he had engaged the services of thousands of unemployed men on reforestation; he had earlier been a member of the Taconic State Park Commission. On March 31, 1933, only twenty-seven days after his inauguration, he signed an Act of Congress conferring extremely broad executive authority for national recovery "in order to provide for the restoration of the country's depleted natural resources and the advancement of an orderly program of useful public works."[1] Several of the New Deal's best-known efforts were based on the executive powers granted under this act. One was Emergency Conservation Work (ECW); on April 5, 1933 (Executive Order No. 6101), the President began implementing the basic act with the appointment, as Director of Emergency Conservation Work, of Robert Fechner, a well-known labor leader. Fechner's presence at the apex of the organization would allay fears of unions that workers employed under ECW might undermine the labor market. The same executive order set up funds for the program and directed that the Secretaries of War, Agriculture, the Interior, and Labor would each appoint a representative to an Advisory Council assisting the director of ECW.

On April 17, the Civilian Conservation Corps was organized as a work force to carry out the ECW program.[2] The entire effort was in legal fact Emergency Conservation Work until July 1, 1937, when another Act of Congress changed the name of the program to Civilian Conservation Corps and the term ECW was dropped. To man the program, physically fit enrollees—mainly unemployed, unmarried men eighteen to twenty-five years of age, from needy families—were selected by representatives of the Department of Labor in each state, in numbers proportionate to the state's population. In addition to these "junior enrollees," the President approved selection of several thousand older, skilled, but unemployed "local experienced men" (eventually called simply LEMs) to serve in ECW camps. These men, in number usually about sixteen to a two hundred-man camp, provided helpful practical guidance and instruction for the younger enrollees and quieted any local fears that enrollees would take jobs from established workers in the territory around a camp. A further addition to the rolls of the CCC was a group of about thirty thousand unemployed veterans, irrespective of age, to be selected by the Veterans' Administration.

Meanwhile, the United States Forest Service, the National Park Service, and several smaller conservation agencies in Agriculture and Interior—all generally referred to in the ECW setup as the Technical Services—had studied applications for allocation of camps, supported in each case by specific pro-

1. *Public No. 5, 73d Congress.*
2. Robert Fechner, *Second Report of the Director of Emergency Conservation Work* (Washington, 1934), p. 1.

grams of needed conservation work, and on this basis had approved the establishment of camps in particular locations. The Army had prepared appropriate housing for two hundred-man companies at the approved sites, mostly in tent camps during the first spring and summer and in barracks-type installations after September 1933. The Army remained responsible for construction and physical maintenance of the camps throughout the ten years of ECW and CCC.

When representatives of the Department of Labor had selected the younger enrollees and the Veterans' Administration had chosen the veterans, the Army was charged with receiving the men, assembling them in centers for physical conditioning, outfitting them with appropriate work clothes and off-duty nonmilitary uniforms, and then assigning them to companies and transporting them to the camps. Once the enrollees were settled in camp, they became the responsibility of a rather unique cooperative effort conducted jointly by the Army and one of the Technical Services. The Army was represented by a camp commander and one or two junior officers; the Technical Service had a civilian camp superintendent with a staff of about a dozen technical supervisors or foremen. Except while the enrollees worked in the field under the Technical Service they were the Army's responsibility. At the beginning of each work day all the enrollees, save only a small housekeeping detail to care for the camp itself, were turned over by the camp commander to the superintendent for execution of the work program; conduct of the program was the camp superintendent's responsibility.

The majority of the CCC camps were in national or state forests, working under the Forest Service; a smaller number, under the National Park Service, were located in national, state, county, or metropolitan parks. Cooperation with state agencies presented no special problem to the Forest Service, which had been authorized for many years to work with state forestry departments and could therefore act according to standard procedures. The National Park Service, on the other hand, had not customarily worked with state park agencies except on an advisory and informal basis. But the basic Act of Congress provided for extending the work into state areas and "to lands owned by counties and municipalities." The ECW program thus confronted the Park Service with the necessity of devising quickly a workable set of procedures, not only for employing the camps in national parks, but also for entering the unfamiliar territory of administering officially, in cooperation with state and local park authorities, State Park ECW and the work of CCC camps in state, county, and metropolitan parks.

This task—not a small one—Director Albright gave to Assistant Director Wirth, who immediately set up and staffed at Park Service headquarters a new Branch of Planning and State Cooperation. To act in effect as Wirth's executive officer for the new work, Herbert Evison, previously executive secretary of the National Conference on State Parks, was appointed supervisor

355. Distribution of park camps (NP and SP) of the Civilian Conservation Corps in the peak year, 1935.

of State Park ECW. Wirth divided the country into regions for Emergency Conservation Work and secured the appointment of a regional officer in each. Later, as the program expanded, the regional organization was modified; but in every case the regional office had to be staffed with newly appointed inspectors to oversee the work of groups of SP camps, the term for those in state, county, and metropolitan parks. Each regional officer was a man experienced in park work; by profession most regional inspectors were landscape architects, though some were civil engineers familiar with park construction. In time, a technical staff comprising several professions was set up for each regional office.

At the end of the first year of operation—March 31, 1934—there were 239 of the SP camps, plus 67 NP camps in the national parks. For each camp it had been necessary to provide a superintendent and supervisory personnel, in cooperation with the park authorities in the case of SP camps. The superintendents were usually landscape architects, foresters, engineers, or experienced practical construction men. The supervisors or foremen were generally of the same professional range, but with emphasis on practical builders. From the first, an effort was made to have at least one landscape architect in the supervisory personnel of every SP camp. Later, the admirable practice was instituted of appointing also, on nomination from university departments, student trainees in architecture or landscape architecture for service at many SP camps during the summer.

In 1935, the peak year of ECW efforts, there were 452 park camps distributed among all the states except one,—Delaware (Fig. 355)—this was a force of over 90,000 men working on the parks of the country! In order to apply to the National Park Service for installation of CCC camps of new areas, no less than 16 states had by 1935 increased their state park holdings by some 600,000 acres. Five states that had previously owned no state parks at all developed entirely new park systems: Mississippi, New Mexico, Oklahoma, Virginia, and South Carolina. Such figures as these indicate how vast a quantity of work was being done by the CCC in the state parks of the nation (Figs. 356–361). But even more significant was its *quality*. Haphazard, unplanned work was not allowed; for every park an approved master plan was required, showing the intended ultimate development of the whole park and the inter-relationship of all projects for which funds and man-hours would be requested. For every project there had to be detailed plans, prepared usually by the park authority or the camp staff and submitted through channels for review, comment, and approval by the professional staff of the regional office and by Washington headquarters. This at times seemed tedious, but it was one of the main reasons for the steadily improving level of quality in the work of the camps. By 1936 project plans were receiving the benefit of professional advice, in either the regional office or Washington or both, from landscape architects, engineers, foresters, architects, naturalists, and geologists. Few park authorities could have had professional service of such completeness in the absence of ECW and the CCC.

Another extremely valuable attribute of State Park ECW arose in part from the sheer quantity of work performed by the camps and in part from the influx of designers prompted by genuine curiosity. The combination fostered experimentation in design, as against mere perpetuation of old but often inadequate standards. If perchance an experiment wound up with a negative result, the single "mistake" represented only a tiny fraction of the total production, yet something positive had usually been learned. This encouragement of a progressive attitude was surely one of the chief contributing reasons behind the remarkable improvement enjoyed by standards of state park design in the CCC decade.

Of like importance in effect on standards in the state parks was the considerable infusion of landscape architects who in earlier practice had been schooled in the most demanding and meticulous types of design, often under eminent practitioners. In countless instances the impact of strong architectonic design prevented what had too often been the accepted formlessness of various kinds of use-area, especially such common ones as group picnic grounds, parking areas, and bathing facilities. In such cases, instead of the usual shapeless blob of amorphous, undifferentiated space with no perceptible order, the park acquired a use-area that was thoughtfully designed, clearly delimited, and orderly (Fig. 362). The changed approach recognized the power of simple

356. Among the many types of work done by CCC camps under guidance of the National Park Service were cabin colonies like this one in Gilbert Lake State Park, New York.

spatial geometry to influence human responses and resulted in easy, relaxed use by the public rather than chaos. Convincingly enough, another consequence was the almost invariable lessening of litter.

In assessing the rise of standards in state parks during CCC days, one must not overlook the contribution of the enrollees themselves as they became more

357. Swimming facilities were developed by CCC in state parks from coast to coast; this lake and beach are in Fairy Stone State Park, Virginia (one of the five state park systems brought into being by the availability of the CCC program).

358. Quite different in character was the pool development at R. H. Treman State Park, New York; in all cases, the natural environment was carefully preserved.

359. Hundreds of miles of horse trails were built by the CCC, like the Lynd Saddle Trail in Itasca State Park, Minnesota.

360. Winter sports facilities were not overlooked; the Old Silver Mine Ski Center in the Harriman Section of Palisades Interstate Park, New York and New Jersey.

361. For the Cook County Forest Preserve District, the CCC reclaimed swampy land in back of Chicago's North Shore and created the Skokie Lagoons.

362. Among the CCC's most successful bathing establishments was the complex of bathhouse, canoe house, beach, and parking area built in Parvin State Park, southern New Jersey.

and more skillful with experience; this was surely one of the most heartening aspects of the entire program. Here were young men deprived by hard times of all the normal opportunities to learn trades through apprenticeship, yet eager to learn and hard working under unusually able supervision, frequently developing to a point where their capacities surpassed even those of the "local experienced men" in the camp roster (Figs. 363–365). Moreover, because they were young, flexible, and curious toward the learning process, the skills they acquired were imaginative and often genuinely creative. This youthful development was especially noticeable in handwork with native materials, such as the stone and timber that every camp used in abundance. It was evident, too, in use of the camp's heavy equipment—trucks, bulldozers, roadgraders— and their maintenance under guidance of the master mechanic that every camp had among its supervisors. Another important aspect of the enrollees' progress, and a clear long-term gain for the cause of conservation in America, was their surprisingly rapid familiarization with the conditions of wild nature—"learning the woods," they sometimes called it. It was remarkable how quickly some of those youngsters, usually city-bred, absorbed a sympathetic understanding of the fields and forests and a rudimentary grasp of ecology.

In addition to the work performed by the camps, with its consequent educational effect on enrollees, supervisors, and public, the CCC period made several other significant contributions to the cause of conservation and of state parks. In part, these endeavors were possible through the authorized use of ECW funds and technical personnel for efforts not immediately connected

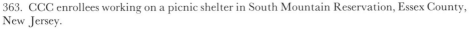

363. CCC enrollees working on a picnic shelter in South Mountain Reservation, Essex County, New Jersey.

364. Building a heavy-duty vehicle bridge under skilled supervision in Parvin State Park, New Jersey.

with specific CCC camps. One was the seashore survey alluded to in an earlier chapter. Beginning in the winter of 1933–34, inspectors from the regional offices of State Park ECW did field reconnaissance of several stretches of ocean beach where there still remained hope of staving off the degradation too long the unhappy lot of the American seaside. By 1936 over a dozen such areas had been examined on all three ocean fronts. Though only the Cape Hatteras National Seashore achieved early realization, the survey was a solid basis for the wider campaign conducted two decades later when Wirth had become director of the Park Service.

A second ancillary project was the 1935 publication, *Park Structures and Facilities,* intended primarily as a guide for newer park authorities and the CCC camps. The book was so hungrily received that work was begun at once on expanding it to a three-volume paperback edition, published in 1938. It consisted of photographs, with plans and sections in some cases, of examples drawn from all over the country of such usual items as entranceways, signs, fences and guardrails, fireplaces, drinking fountains, picnic tables and benches, bridges and culverts, shelters, cabins, comfort stations, bathhouses, and other buildings. The selections were made by a special committee, appointed from Park Service headquarters and from the regional offices, who worked under the inspiring chairmanship of architect Albert H. Good; he also wrote the helpful—and often hilarious—explanatory notes.

Another product of the CCC period was the comprehensive study carried out by the National Park Service pursuant to a Congressional directive: the Park, Parkway and Recreational Area Study Act of 1936. The purpose of

365. Enrollees constructing
the concrete core of a dam
at High Point State Park,
New Jersey, preparatory to
restoring a large lake for
bathing, fishing, and camping.

this effort, undertaken by Wirth's Branch of Planning and State Cooperation, was a complete survey of the park situation in America at all levels of government and an analysis of ways and means for meeting the nation's fantastically growing need for recreational facilities. The work took several years; the resulting report, published in 1941, was entitled *A Study of the Park and Recreation Problem in the United States*. It was in two equal sections: first a text, containing a thorough treatment of the varied facets of recreational planning and "a park and recreational land plan for the United States," and second charts and tables listing for each state all existing and proposed recreational facilities, whether national, state, or local, and giving an outline map of the state with the approximate location of each area. The volume is still one of the few indispensable reference publications in the field of state parks.

But perhaps the most remarkable collateral product of CCC days was the series of Recreational Demonstration Projects in twenty-four states. This endeavor involved government purchase of nearly four hundred thousand acres of submarginal land and the use of CCC camps and funds of the Federal Emergency Relief Administration (FERA) to plan and develop the areas for recreational purposes under supervision of the National Park Service. The RDP program arose in a somewhat roundabout way. It started in 1934 with what was known as the FERA Land Program, an effort by the Roosevelt administration to solve the vicious problem of submarginal land—millions of acres from which the essential plant nutrients, and sometimes even the topsoil itself, had been washed away, leaving relative sterility. Countless American farmers were in a hopeless fix on such land; it was so clearly below the margin of agricultural productivity that the farmer could neither make a living from it nor find someone willing to buy it. As a cure for the blighted land and as a partial solution to the desperate economic plight of the farmer, the government used FERA funds—and later the Resettlement Administration—to purchase the pitifully cheap submarginal acreage, relocate the farmers on better sites, and reforest the leached-out land, which in almost every case was still fertile enough for trees. The tracts were looked upon as "demonstration areas," showing what could be done toward recovering submarginal lands and assigning them to a productive conservation purpose— a step long overdue in America.

Then the thought suggested itself—naturally enough among park-minded people—that if some "demonstration areas" could be obtained for development as recreational facilities of the state park type, the building of such parks could become another valid method for restoring submarginal land to human usefulness. In the process, furthermore, the Park Service would have an independent opportunity to create some sizable recreational areas capable of serving a specific purpose not workable in many existing state parks: the development of large group camps, or "organized camps" as they came to be called, for use by accredited welfare organizations to provide otherwise unlikely outdoor vacations for masses of underprivileged children from the cities. Anyone reasonably familiar with the American camping picture knew of the huge unmet need for such facilities. There were charitable organizations that could provide funds for maintenance and operation, though not capital funds for purchase of land and erecting facilities.

Wirth accordingly directed the regional offices of State Park ECW to have their inspectors comb the states in search of submarginal lands within reasonable distances from metropolitan centers that might serve such a purpose. Often in the company of state soil specialists, inspectors from coast to coast visited and studied outstanding submarginal areas. But they quickly discovered a stumbling block: an area fully submarginal as to agriculture tends often to be equally submarginal for recreational development, and a tract of land clearly suitable for recreation is likely to have considerable portions not at all agriculturally submarginal. The reason is not complex. It is a well-known working rule that a recreational area of the state park type has no hope of complete success without a water body large enough for swimming. This means at least one sizable topographic unit of concave or bowl composition. Though the slopes of such a conformation may indeed be agriculturally submarginal, and even denuded of topsoil, chances are that the topsoil has collected in a rich bottomland of reasonable fertility—unless the bottom holds a swamp that will lend itself to flooding. At any rate, without bottomland where a water body is feasible, the submarginal slopes are in effect useless for recreational development.

The authorities in charge of the land program had of course adopted a basic figure for the maximum percentage of nonsubmarginal land allowable in a tract marked for acquisition with FERA or Resettlement funds. It soon became apparent to the Park Service, especially to personnel seeing conditions in the field, that for recreational demonstration projects the percentage was often prohibitively low. In view, however, of the many social benefits that would accrue from the proposed recreational projects, the authorities were persuaded to allow for RDPs a somewhat higher percentage of nonsubmarginal land. Encouraged by this modest easing of restrictions, Wirth intensified the search for approvable RDP areas, enlisting the counsel of state land-planning agencies and of local advisory committees from urban centers to be served by the organized camps of RDPs. For effectuation, a compact administrative and technical RDP staff was set up in close liaison with each regional office of State Park ECW. Eventually, through use of FERA funds and CCC camps, forty-six RDPs were found, acquired, planned, and developed. Of these, thirty-four were intended primarily as vacation areas, outfitted with organized camps; the other twelve were for series of "Waysides" along the Blue Ridge Parkway and in South Carolina, or for extension of existing national or state parks. As completion of the RDPs approached, their temporary "project" status was dropped and they became known as full-fledged Recreational Demonstration Areas (RDAs), ready to prove their value. It was contemplated from the start that in time the thirty-four vacation and camping RDAs would be turned over to the states, or possibly in some cases to federal agencies or departments.

The RDAs were usually within fifty miles of some urban complex. Of all the states Pennsylvania, with five, had the largest number; they illustrated well the typical distribution—Raccoon Creek RDA near Pittsburgh, Laurel Hill near Johnstown, Blue Knob near Altoona, Hickory Run near Scranton and Wilkes-Barre, French Creek between Philadelphia and Reading (Figs.

366. Horseshoes as social cement at Raccoon Creek RDA, Pennsylvania.

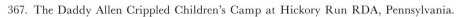

367. The Daddy Allen Crippled Children's Camp at Hickory Run RDA, Pennsylvania.

368. Sixpenny swimming area, French Creek RDA, southeastern Pennsylvania.

366–368). In Tennessee, for another example, were Shelby Forest RDA near Memphis, Montgomery-Bell near Nashville, Fall Creek Falls near Knoxville and Chattanooga. In Missouri, Montserrat near Kansas City, Lake of the Ozark near Jefferson City midway between Kansas City and St. Louis, Cuivre River near St. Louis. Some of the locations were virtually interstate: Versailles RDA in Indiana was about equidistant from Cincinnati, Louisville, and

Indianapolis. On the west coast Portland, Oregon, was served by Silver Creek Falls RDA; on the east coast Portland, Maine, had the Camden Hills RDA.

In some of the RDAs, day-use facilities—mainly picnic grounds and bathing beaches—were installed for the sake of daytime visitors. But, as indicated earlier, the chief aim of the program was provision of organized camps, intended for lease or rental to competent welfare organizations and for management by these agencies. Surveys had shown conclusively that a great number of such organizations were prepared to operate camps and would eagerly do so if some other source could meet the larger cost of land purchase and installation of facilities. Provision of these is precisely what the National Park Service was doing through the RDAs.

The master-planning of entire RDAs and then the design of the various organized camps within them, in collaboration with the architects and engineers, were among the most interesting and rewarding jobs that faced landscape architects of the Park Service, both in Washington headquarters and in the field. Certainly no other problem of landscape architectural design illustrates more clearly the necessary close relationship between physical form and consequent social results. Elsewhere this time-tested precept no doubt appears at times only vaguely theoretical; here it is immediately practical and visible. Here is an instance in which the ultimate psychological effects on the users themselves—the campers as individuals and as social groups— *must* be the major design determinants, along with topographic and climatic conditions. Because the organized camp offered landscape architects a challenge with relatively little precedent, and because it so clearly demonstrates the ability of a problem to "solve itself," it merits somewhat detailed consideration.

Fundamental to the layout of an organized camp, as a reflection of the camp's operational program, was decentralization and a scaling-down of the component parts, with the welcome result of minimizing the heavy-handed institutionalism too often found in mass camping. The camps were organized in a unit system, the smallest element being a tent or cabin for four campers. These were assembled in clusters of four, five, six, or on rare occasions eight cabins; this group, with accessory structures, was termed the "unit." The unit thus comprised, in multiples of four, from sixteen to thirty-two campers (most usually twenty-four in six cabins), plus a unit lodge and kitchen, a unit wash-house and latrine, and one or two counselors' cabins.

In execution of the plans, unaffected simplicity and a sensible economy of construction were keynotes, leading to visual strength and the lowest possible rental rates consistent with excellence. Complementing this wholesome attitude was the first-class craftsmanship developed by the CCC enrollees who in most instances carried out the work. The ultimate size of an entire organized camp depended on the site and on a careful estimate of the needs of the community to be served, worked out in consultation with the

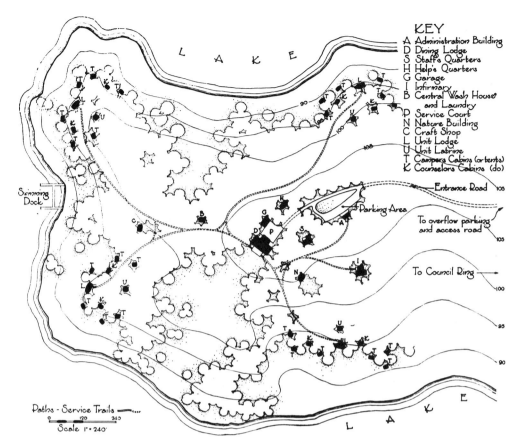

369. Plan of a typical organized camp.

welfare agencies that would eventually use the installation. The most customary size was a camp of ninety-six campers, four units of twenty-four
campers or six cabins in each (Fig. 369). In every case the units were located
out of sight and sound of each other and of an administrative core, which
contained the main recreation and dining hall; a central hot-shower house,
laundry, and latrine; an infirmary; an administration building; quarters for
the director, staff, and helpers. In some of the larger camps there might also
be a craft shop, a nature-study building, and a council ring for camp gather-
ings. The entrance road of the camp was allowed to penetrate only as far
as an arrival space and parking area at the administration building, beyond
which a mere service road for trucks extended to the kitchen wing of the
dining hall. All other connections among parts of the camp and with the
swimming beach were by foot trail only. The whole plan was of course fitted
closely to the topography.

In operation, the completed camp functioned as a clear expression of this
typical layout. The unit, with a high degree of self-sufficiency, was the camp-

er's immediate focus of action. Within it, each member had a personal role, for each was expected to take his turn in preparing the breakfast and midday meals. These were served in the unit lodge; only for the evening meal did the whole camp go to the central dining hall. In its essentials the program was thus sociologically and educationally sound: it inculcated a sense of individual freedom, coupled with equal assumption of personal responsibility. It promoted healthy group loyalties in the child—with a strong aura of belonging, first to the cabin's team of four, next to the unit of twenty-four, then to membership in the wholeness of the camp. In its way it presented a microcosm of life in a viable society. To preserve for each organized camp this atmosphere of self-reliant, self-contained integrity, avoiding the distraction of outside interferences, it was customary to surround the camp with a considerable belt of undeveloped and if possible forested terrain. Whenever an RDA contained two or more organized camps, they were therefore separated as widely as total acreage permitted, with always at least a mile between them.

As described above, the organized camp was for children; but the unit system lent itself well to camping by youngsters in groups of different ages, or indeed in some RDAs by family groups. The camp's remarkable flexibility was one of its most widely applauded merits. If any doubt had existed as to the effective demand for organized camps, it was quickly dispelled in 1937, the first operational summer. For example, two camps in the 15,000-acre Chopawamsic RDA in northern Virginia, one of the first opened for use, were immediately rented for the summer of 1937 by the Family Service Association of Washington, representing some twenty-two accredited welfare agencies of the District of Columbia. During that first summer, twenty organized camps in sixteen RDAs were operated by welfare organizations in twelve states. As in the Washington case, the using agencies were varied in type: councils of Boy Scouts, Girl Scouts, and Campfire Girls; church, sunday school, YMCA and YWCA groups; the board of education of one large city, the park and playground association of another; the incorporated camps association of one state, the 4-H clubs of another, the Crippled Children's League of a third.

By the second summer, 1938, the number of organized camps in RDAs had risen to forty-nine, providing in that year alone a total of about 376,000 camper-days. By 1942, when Congress authorized conveyance of the RDAs to the states or to federal agencies, the thirty-four vacation and camping RDAs had upwards of eighty fully operative organized camps. Distribution went on apace, and by 1948 transfer of all the RDAs had been virtually completed. In the tabulation for 1950 by the National Conference on State Parks, twenty-nine of the former RDAs are listed as state parks—forming another notable increment to the total acreage of state parks in the United States.

The RDAs and their exemplary organized camps were obviously a great contribution to the progress of the state park movement. Indeed, the temptation is to evaluate them as the most outstanding accomplishment of the CCC period. But such a judgment would overlook the magnitude of the total ECW program and the enormous production of the CCC camps. In fact, even so far as organized camps were concerned, it should be noted that many were built in state parks, as well as in the RDAs, within the regular work program of SP camps of the CCC. All of this, however, represented only a part of the total CCC output. One must not forget the miles of roads, trails, telephone lines, and power lines, the systems of water supply and waste disposal, the acres upon acres of erosion control, fire protection work, plant disease and insect pest control, and corrective planting, the scores of dams built and lakes created—all in relatively unseen addition to the thousands of structures of the various types illustrated in the book *Park Structures and Facilities,* referred to earlier.

The CCC program inevitably became a casualty of World War II. As pressure mounted for total concentration of national effort upon winning the war, Congress in July 1942 ordered liquidation of the Corps. By June 30, 1943, all the camps had been closed and all equipment transferred to other agencies, chiefly the Army and the Navy. The greatest decade in the history of state parks had come to an end.

The postwar story for state parks was even more harrowing than that discussed in an earlier chapter for the national parks. With the CCC gone, what had often seemed hauntingly probable turned out to be only too true: that on the whole, the states could not possibly continue expenditures on the same level as the federal government. The pace of development slackened and, with notable exceptions, even the maintenance of CCC-built installations fell off badly. Slowly but surely, however, the momentum was at least in part regained. The state park systems strong before 1933 naturally showed the way, and the roster of states with a serious interest in their park systems had grown prodigiously. In the 1950 NCSP tabulation referred to above, forty-eight states listed a total of 1,346 state parks and 353 state historic monuments, surely a recognizable advance from the handful of parks owned by some fifteen states just thirty years earlier at the end of World War I and prior to the Des Moines conference.

XXXIX. Parkways and Their Offspring

It is doubtful that any single type of park area has been more widely misunderstood and misinterpreted than the parkway. The confusion is hardly to be wondered at when one considers with what free and easy imprecision the term "parkway" has been used. Unfortunately, it has even been employed by real-estate developers in recent years as a sort of status label. Truthfully, it would seem that something of this kind may have been the effect, despite the most innocent of motives, when the landscape architectural pioneers—Olmsted, Vaux, Cleveland, Eliot—used the term for roadways that were simply wider and more richly furnished than ordinary streets: "boulevard," the more usual early title, was of course borrowed from the French. Then Olmsted and Vaux, in about 1870 in Brooklyn, designed a handsome boulevard as "a grand approach from the east"[1] to the Plaza of Prospect Park. They called it the Jamaica Parkway and, though its name was modified almost at once to Eastern Parkway, the designation stuck. Indeed, Eastern Parkway remained a pleasantly impressive combination of carriageways, "parked" pedestrian strips, and overarching elms until years later, when an extension of New York's vast subway system was run under its length and started its downfall from splendor.

A few years later in Boston, when Olmsted began working on the Back Bay Fens, he saw the possibility of establishing a long continuity of park land from the Boston Common and Public Garden along the wide boulevard that was the existing inner end of Commonwealth Avenue, then through his newly

1. Brooklyn Park Commissioners, *Annual Report, 1872,* p. 481.

created Fens and out the Muddy River to Jamaica Pond. This, with an extension to the Arboretum and Franklin Park added later, Olmsted called "the Promenade" in his 1880 report. "The Parkway" was the Boston Park Commissioners' 1887 label for the entire stretch of Muddy River from the tidegate on the Charles out to Jamaica Pond; and they authorized the sectional names that eventually became today's Charlesgate, Fenway, Riverway, Jamaicaway (through Olmsted Park), and Arborway.

Cleveland, in his 1869 pamphlet on "public grounds" for Chicago, recommended a "grand avenue or boulevard" some fourteen miles long to connect the parks. He even went so far, despite his usual vehement antagonism to gridiron systems, as to present a lengthy argument favoring straightness rather than successive curves in the boulevard. He did not use the term "parkway," but he did use it in 1883 when he submitted to Minneapolis authorities a report on "Parks and Parkways" for that city.

In the 1890s, when Eliot was advising the Metropolitan Park Commission in Boston, he repeatedly urged the creation of "parkways or boulevards" as connections between units of the park system. Even though he wrote that "parkways or boulevards . . . are generally merely improved highways,"[2] he seemed to have sensed the importance of a major function that parkways would in later years be called upon to serve, that of providing psychological carryover of the restful influence of one large park area to its echo in another, with little or no interruption on the way.

But on the whole early "parkways" could more accurately be described as boulevards. It was only with completion of New York's Bronx River Parkway after World War I that the modern parkway came into being with its clear set of distinguishing characteristics. The term now denoted a strip of land dedicated to recreation and the movement of pleasure vehicles (passenger, not commercial automobiles). The parkway was *not* itself a road, it *contained* a roadway. The strip of land was not just a highway with uniform grassy borders; it was of significantly varying width, depending on immediate topographic and cultural conditions. The roadway itself differed markedly from that of an ordinary highway in that it was meant for comfortable driving in pleasant surroundings, not merely for getting from one place to another as fast as possible. The alignment was accordingly one of gentle curves, designed for speeds in keeping with the times. Perhaps most important was the distinctive provision that abutting owners had no right of light, air, or access over the parkway strip. It was lack of the *limited access* factor that most clearly kept the early boulevards from functioning as parkways in the modern sense. To appreciate the point, one need only experience the interruptive effect of frequent access roads and private driveways from the side on such older "parkways" as the Fenway and the Riverway in Boston, Eastern Parkway

2. Eliot, *Charles Eliot,* p. 596.

370. Condition of the Bronx River valley prior to creation of the Bronx River Parkway Commission in 1907.

in Brooklyn, Mosholu Parkway in the Bronx, the Mystic Valley Parkway in Arlington, Massachusetts, or Memorial Drive in Cambridge.

The Bronx River Parkway, introducing the new combination of characteristics, was completed at Kensico Dam in New York's Westchester County in 1923, but it represented the culmination of eighteen years of effort that had begun simply as a cleanup job. In 1905, William W. Niles, a public-spirited citizen of New York deeply disturbed over the filthy condition of the little Bronx River as it came down from Westchester County to enter the city's Zoological Park and Botanic Garden in the Borough of the Bronx, enlisted the support of the directors of the two institutions and sought relief in the New York State Legislature for a study of the problem. Not only was the Bronx River valley an unsightly mess; the polluted water of the river was injurious to wild fowl in the Zoological Park.

Unsuccessful in the 1905 session of the legislature, Niles tried again in 1906 and won passage of a bill authorizing "a commission of three to be appointed

371. The same view as in the preceding figure, after cleanup by the Commission.

by the Governor to inquire into the advisability of preserving the waters of the Bronx River from pollution and creating a park reservation of the lands on both sides of the River."[3] The investigating Commission was duly appointed, with Niles as secretary and counsel; it met often, spent the summer inspecting the river and its valley, and prepared a report indicating areas recommended for acquisition as a long park to protect the flowing water. It is to be noted that at this time the thought of including a drive along the river was purely incidental. The report was presented to the Governor and the legislature in 1907. Submitted next, with the concurrence of Mayor George B. McClellan of New York City, was a second bill directed toward implementation of the Commission's report; passed by both houses and signed by Governor Charles Evans Hughes in 1907, it created the Bronx Parkway Commission. By now the thought had emerged that here was also an excellent

3. *Chapter 669, Laws of 1906.*

opportunity to provide a pleasant drive from Bronx Park out to the city's water-supply reservoirs in Westchester County and to give New York the sort of visually acceptable approach from the north that it needed badly.

The newly appointed Commission first had accurate surveys made, then proceeded with acquisition of the necessary lands and with making them more tolerable to the eye. This early essay in removal of negative values from the landscape would alone have more than justified taking the land and creating the parkway strip, even if no roadway had been built. The before and after views of the cleaned-up Bronx River valley, appearing in popular magazines, did much to arouse the interest of lay citizens all over the country (Figs. 370, 371). In at least one known case, it convinced a future landscape architect that this was the profession he wanted to enter.

Meanwhile, design of the proposed roadway had been undertaken, with full attention to the offscape as well as to the road itself. Of course this meant getting rid of billboards and other eyesores, particularly those that for years had assailed commuters' eyes on railway lines entering the city. Curvatures were planned according to prevailing speeds, then in the neighborhood of twenty-five miles an hour. Construction was begun, halted for the duration of World War I, resumed in 1919, and substantially completed in 1923 at the intended terminus, the high Kensico Dam of the New York water-supply system just north of White Plains. The cost of development had been borne three-quarters by the City of New York, one-quarter by Westchester County. This fifteen-mile stretch, the original Bronx River Parkway, is generally regarded as the first "true" parkway in the United States.

The roadway was a four-lane affair; its curvatures began with an almost horse-and-buggy carriageway look in Bronx Park (Fig. 372), then gradually eased out into arcs of longer radii as the alignment crept northward (Fig. 373). Because it was in a valley, local streets could bridge overhead. The roadway had no dividers of any kind (even painted lines were a late development), but in two different places the northbound and southbound lanes were separated to slip at independent levels around hillocks with excellent stands of trees—an early example of the divided roadway technique that later became standard practice. In recent years the New York City end of the paved way has been drastically altered for modern automotive speeds, but it is to be hoped that the remainder of the original Bronx River Parkway, up to the Kensico Dam, will be retained in its early form for the sake of historical values despite the necessity of holding for these few miles to slower but still acceptable speeds.

A memorable technique was the use of generous parkway width to defeat the billboard menace. Of course no such monstrosities were permitted on parkway land; abutting owners, however, though they had no right of access, sometimes in early days weakened before the onslaught of outdoor advertising interests and rented out billboard locations just beyond the boundary of the

372. The new Bronx River Parkway, with its narrow and twisting roadway, near the Wood-lawn section above Bronx Park in 1922.

parkway strip. In such cases, dense plantations on parkway land in front of erected billboards, repeated if necessary as locations were moved, eventually provided a sufficiently convincing discouragement. This is still one of the most persuasive reasons for taking the widest practicable parkway strips from the very beginning of a project.

The Bronx River Parkway had one major unexpected result: for West-chester County the new facility was a resounding success, not only in public acclaim but also in the notable increase in market value, and therefore in assessed valuations and tax returns, of properties nearby. It so strongly im-pressed the county's authorities that as it neared completion the Board of Supervisors obtained from the 1922 session of the New York State Legislature a law setting up an entirely new body, the Westchester County Park Com-mission, with authority to acquire lands for parks and parkways. The Bronx Parkway Commission, on completion of its task, was abolished by agreement, and the portion of the Bronx River Parkway lying in Westchester County was transferred to jurisdiction of the new commission.

The Westchester County Park Commission (WCPC) organized an out-standing technical staff. The chief engineer, Jay Downer, had held that post under the Bronx Parkway Commission. The landscape architect, Gilmore D. Clarke, had been superintendent of construction on the newly completed

373. Air view of the Bronx River Parkway approaching Scarsdale.

parkway. Under their leadership a heartening spirit of interprofessional collaboration was induced within the staff, and the WCPC proceeded to create during the next decade a system of parks and parkways that soon achieved fully merited world renown.

Essentially, the Westchester County park system (Fig. 374) comprised a series of sizable recreational units linked by a network of parkways that were

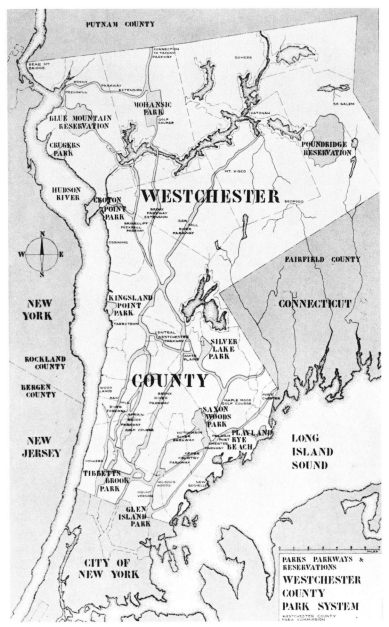

374. The park and parkway system of the Westchester County Park Commission, 1923.

constantly improving in design. First, acting as agent for the State of New York, the WCPC extended the Bronx River Parkway northward some thirty miles from Kensico Dam to Bear Mountain Bridge on the Hudson. The Bronx River Parkway Extension, as it was known, continued the trend toward longer, sweeping curves and more effective superelevation for higher speeds. The taking-lines spread farther apart as the parkway snaked its way through less

375. Easier curves and wider takings of the Bronx River Parkway Extension, done by WCPC as agent for the State of New York.

populated areas, and the abundant use of native plant materials included an occasional seemingly accidental drift of wild flowers (Fig. 375). The overall effect was to eliminate any perceptible borderlines between the parkway and the terrain through which the traveler made his way; visually the parkway was more and more just a natural part of the countryside.

376. Bridge carrying a local road over the Saw Mill River Parkway at Pleasantville, 1930.

During the decade from 1923 to 1933 the WCPC built over a dozen parks, and several new parkways: the Saw Mill River, Hutchinson River, Briarcliff-Peekskill, and Cross County Parkways. All were connectors between units of the park system. The Saw Mill River Parkway (Fig. 376), starting from Van Cortlandt Park in the Bronx, passed along the edge of Tibbetts Brook Park in Yonkers, with its large bathhouse and outdoor swimming pool, then skirted the V. Everit Macy Memorial Park, with a lake and the Woodlands Tavern, on the way north to intersect the Bronx River Extension. The latter ran through Mohansic Park, which held a large golf course; the Briarcliff-Peekskill Parkway had the big Blue Mountain Reservation near its northern end. On the Hutchinson River Parkway were Willson's Woods, Saxon Woods Park, and the Maplemoor Golf Course. The Cross County Parkway, toward its eastern end, led to Playland at Rye Beach on Long Island Sound.

Westchester County is of course best known for its exemplary system of parkways, but Playland is a brilliant accomplishment on so many counts that it deserves more than passing mention as a parkway adjunct. For landscape architecture it is a milestone in a special sense (Fig. 377). For a long time such places as the Luna Parks and Coney Islands of America, with their mediocre, littered bathing beaches and honky-tonk amusement parks, had been notorious for untidiness, boisterous behavior, and a degree of hoodlumism. Indeed, trouble of this sort was widely assumed, at least by laymen, to be inherent in any attempt at combining a bathing beach with the carnival atmosphere of amusement facilities. An insistent argument of some younger landscape architects, with their abiding faith in the power of strong design, was that the two types of activity could safely be combined—without consequent rowdyism—if they could be spatially organized and given the benefit of a clearly perceptible order. This, of course, was purely theoretical. But

377. Playland, Rye Beach: air view just after completion, 1930.

then along came Playland at Rye Beach to prove the confident claim beyond
a doubt; for this is precisely what Playland was and is—a well-designed
combination of bathing beach and amusement park where for over four
decades now abundant joy and merriment but no serious problems of bothersome behavior have prevailed.

Aside from the simple, straightforward geometric structure of the overall
plan, the foremost contribution to Playland's orderly effect was probably the
designers' recognition that the usual amusement devices—rides, wheels,
merry-go-rounds—present a chaotic appearance when grouped in the open.
At Playland they were screened behind a gaily painted colonnade bordering
a central mall. The mall itself was made an impressive space, turf-paneled,
with bright flower beds, rows of red oaks, and the colorful colonnade all
around, leading to a fanciful "music tower" at the far end. Soft music
(amplified records, to be sure, but at a time when such background music
was not common) came from the tower, adding a calming touch to the total
psychology of the place. A spacious plaza at the open end of the mall acted
as a kind of fulcrum, joining the amusement area with the curving beach
by means of an overlook and a continuous boardwalk. Restaurants and a
year-round casino faced on the plaza; at its western edge was the arrival

turnaround and unloading point. Connected with this were an ample bus terminal on one side and a huge parking space on the other. Swinging firmly from the plaza overlook along the excellent white sand beach, the boardwalk led to a twin-towered bathhouse that enclosed a fresh-water swimming pool on an upper level.

Fortunate as the people of Westchester County were to have Playland, this was not their only reason for gratitude. As had been the case with the beginnings of the Bronx River Parkway, so at Playland the first accomplishment was the elimination of offensive negative values. For many years the place had been, to quote a WCPC Annual Report, "a waste expanse of tidal marsh with an adjoining seaside slum area which by gradual accretion had hedged in the County's best salt water beach."[4] With speed that seems little short of miraculous, beginning on Labor Day 1927, the tawdry shacks and hot-dog stands were razed, land was created by dredging and filling, piles were driven, and enough construction and planting was completed to allow the WCPC to open the park for public use just eight months later, in May 1928. A few additions were made in the following two years, even while some five million visitors a year were being accommodated; by 1930 Playland was finished. The maturity of growth that has come to it through the years has made it all the more delightful. It is still an outstanding example of the capacity of strong design to affect human behavior in helpful ways.

Credit for the superb work of the WCPC is rightly to be shared by many individuals because of the prevailing spirit of interprofessional collaboration. Of all the members of the staff, none more truly merit commendation than Downer and Clarke. As chief engineer, Downer was in a unique position to demonstrate his interest and confidence in landscape architecture, which the ASLA recognized in 1932 by electing him to honorary membership. Clarke, as landscape architect of the Commission, heading an unusually competent staff, early showed the ability that made him one of the profession's most distinguished figures. A graduate of Cornell, he worked briefly with Charles N. Lowrie and then with the Bronx River Parkway and the WCPC until 1935. In that year he opened an office in New York and simultaneously accepted a faculty appointment at Cornell, where he was dean of the College of Architecture from 1938 to 1950. His private practice on public works, in partnership with Michael Rapuano, has covered a vast range of projects. He was a member of the national Commission of Fine Arts from 1932 to 1950 and its chairman for the last thirteen years of that period. Elected to the ASLA in 1915, he became a Fellow in 1924 and was president from 1949 to 1951.

North of Westchester County is the rougher territory of the Taconic State Park Commission, one of the regions under the New York State Council of

4. Westchester County Park Commission, *Annual Report, 1930*, p. 30.

Parks. Here the progress achieved in Westchester County carried over into the Taconic State Parkway, from its beginning at the Putnam County line. When in 1933 the WCPC opened a brief connection from the Bronx River Parkway Extension to the start of the Taconic, the parkway route became effectively continuous from Bronx Park northward into the tier of counties east of the Hudson River.

The treatment of side slopes, so well and inconspicuously practiced in Westchester, acquired greater emphasis in the rougher Taconic topography, where cuts and fills were necessarily more frequent and bold cuts in rock were used on many occasions to save good stands of forest growth. As in Westchester so, too, in Putnam County the softening of cuts in earth by means of ogee-curved slopes was an integral part of the effort to blend the parkway into the surrounding scenery. Planting on these easy slopes was with native materials, which naturally took hold quickly and prospered, contributing not only to the desired visual effect but also to the prevention of soil erosion.

Progressive changes of alignment, as already noted in Westchester, became more pronounced as the traveler drove up the Taconic Parkway, with curves continually easing out to accommodate higher speeds (Fig. 378). In Putnam County the roadway was still a simple four-lane ribbon without dividers, but an occasional overlook acknowledged the urge to stop and view the magnificent scenery. At first there was only an outward swelling of the line of the fieldstone retaining wall, and the roadway bulged out into the space thus provided. But in such a mere widening of the roadway one felt not entirely at ease, for the parking space for viewing was not clearly separate from the road and its onrushing cars; so, as work progressed, the next examples had a curbed cushion or belt of turf between the overlook space and the roadway, with entry and exit openings at the ends of the cushion (Fig. 379).

In embryonic form, the need felt intuitively in the case of these overlooks was probably the basic one so often sensed by an observer in outdoor space, especially whenever motor traffic is involved: a need for the use of strips or cushions, acting much as partitions do indoors, to demark spaces clearly and thus ensure full visual integrity. The need is psychological as well as operational; fortunately, experience teaches that one of the surest ways of getting sound mechanical operation from a driver is to provide for his guidance a plan that has visual clarity. The same basic need—plus a dash of common sense—is what led to adoption of the center-strip or divider, which happened simultaneously in many highways. The first cushions were usually only a few feet wide; but it did not take people long to sense that the width of the divider should be at least equal to the length of a car, so that a driver wanting to make a U-turn could pause for a moment at one of the occasional cut-through places, in a space clearly containing his car, without either front or rear protruding into the roadway. Today, with dividers of at least fifteen or twenty feet standard, it seems incredible that anything so obvious could ever have

378. Taconic State Parkway in Putnam County, 1933.

been disputed. Yet arguments on this point occurred again and again in the mid-1930s.

At any rate the Taconic Parkway, as construction proceeded northward through Dutchess and Columbia Counties, continued to follow an enlightened pattern, not only with center-strips but with fully independent alignment and

379. Overlook with cushion, Taconic State Parkway, about 1934.

profile for the freely divided northbound and southbound lanes in generously wide rights-of-way (Fig. 380). This technique allowed the separate roadways to bypass on either side of interesting topographic features such as low glacial mounds, instead of bulldozing them flat. It preserved significant trees and masses of native vegetation in the median strip and created less disfiguring scars on the land in hillside situations. Moreover, it permitted the locating of an occasional service station in the median, readily accessible to both northbound and southbound lanes. In short, it made driving immeasurably safer and more comfortable.

The total effect of all this was to make the upper reaches of the Taconic Parkway a sheer delight—and in its time the pinnacle of achievement in recreational travelways. Eventually it was possible for a driver actually to experience for himself, in one continuum, the steady development of parkway techniques. All he needed to do was start in Bronx Park, before the recent changes at that end of course, and drive north, following first the Bronx River Parkway and then from Kensico Dam the Taconic State Parkway (including the former Bronx River Parkway Extension, renamed by the State of New York as the southern end of the Taconic) up through Putnam, Dutchess, and Columbia Counties to its junction with the Berkshire Section of the New York

380. Taconic State Parkway in Dutchess County, late 1930s: divided ways become normal practice, with wider takings and indistinguishable boundary lines.

State Thruway north of Chatham. As the miles passed he would feel the curves lengthen and see the parkway strip widen; then the roadways at last would separate and pursue their independent sinuous routes with remarkable grace. More and more he would find the parkway merging quietly with the landscape of wooded hills and valleys, imparting to him a welcome sense of profound peacefulness.

During the years when the Westchester parkways were evolving, a notable system of state parks and parkways was being created by the Long Island State Park Commission, another of New York State's regional organizations, under its dynamic chairman Robert Moses; the tremendously successful Jones Beach State Park was described earlier. Moses, one of the great lay figures in park activity, was also chairman of the New York State Council of Parks, commissioner of parks in New York City through the administrations of four mayors beginning with LaGuardia in 1934, and city construction coordinator. With Clarke as one of his consultants, Moses combined various federal, state, and municipal sources of financing to produce an eminently distinguished system of parks, parkways, and expressways within the city, including the Henry Hudson Parkway along the west shore of Manhattan Island. All of these city projects he tied effectively into the scheme of parkways on Long

Island and in Westchester County, forming an unusually fine metropolitan system of motorways in and about New York City.

Between 1929 and 1932 the Bureau of Public Roads, with Clarke in consultation, built the Mount Vernon Memorial Parkway down the Potomac from Washington; between 1934 and 1940 the State of Connecticut installed Merritt Parkway, extending the line of Westchester's Hutchinson River Parkway. Both the Mount Vernon and the Merritt had the controlled-access provision and employed central dividers.

The first of several federal parkways was Skyline Drive along the crest of Virginia's Blue Ridge Mountains, designed in 1931 by the National Park Service and the Bureau of Public Roads. Construction was begun in 1932 and completed in 1940; meanwhile Shenandoah National Park, containing Skyline Drive, was established in 1935. The Drive was precisely that: a roadway snaking along the ridge, with narrow Shenandoah Park on both sides, so that in effect the entire park could be regarded as a parkway. The roadway had no median divider, but there was full control over side access. In 1936, when Shenandoah National Park was dedicated, the first specifically named national parkway was also provided for by Congressional action: the Blue Ridge Parkway, to connect the end of Skyline Drive in the Shenandoah at the north with Great Smoky Mountains National Park as the southern terminus, a run of almost five hundred miles. The right-of-way was to be acquired and deeded to the United States by Virginia and North Carolina except where the parkway would run through national forests in its path. Again, following the normal practice in national parks, the project was to be designed and built collaboratively by the National Park Service and the Bureau of Public Roads. Representing the Park Service in the field as superintendent was landscape architect Stanley W. Abbott, who had worked under Clarke in the Westchester County Park Commission before joining the Service.

The Blue Ridge Parkway was intended for pleasure-driving at reasonable speeds and for moderate traffic. It was in no sense an expressway, but side access was fully controlled. The roadway was a simple ribbon of pavement without a central divider. It was fitted closely to the land and every effort was made, as in the Bronx River Extension and the Taconic, to blend it into the native scene. An underlying point of view recalls Prince Pückler-Muskau's attitude over a century before: the activities of humans are a fully natural part of any total landscape. In the Blue Ridge Parkway this gave rise to effective use of the scenic easement over adjacent farmlands; the owner, instead of having to sell, merely agreed for a modest consideration to keep the land in its normal agricultural use. Thus, along many portions of the route, visual protection of the parkway did not require outright purchase of lands; and use of the scenic easement actually intensified the feeling of being in entirely native surroundings, without affectation or the intrusion of anything exotic (Fig. 381).

381. On the Blue Ridge Parkway in Virginia: the use of scenic easements helps the parkway merge with the existing native countryside.

The atmosphere was further maintained by faithful attention to local ecology, whether in vegetation or in things manmade. Only native materials were used in planting, and these with restraint, so that one never felt enclosed in a tortuous man-planted bowling-alley, as too often happens in highways with "roadside landscaping" applied as a vegetative afterthought. Where fencing of any sort was required along the right-of-way, purely indigenous methods and means were adopted: walls of local stone, post and rail barriers, zigzag snake-fences of split rails. Whenever possible, structures that had been significant in local life were retained or, as in the case of the old Mabry Mill in Virginia, carefully repaired and restored to activity.

The recreational character of the Blue Ridge Parkway was continually emphasized; travel on it was meant to be fun. Camping grounds and picnic areas were built at convenient intervals; there were coffee shops, service stations, and comfort facilities along the way. Occasionally there were clearly indicated halting spots from which foot trails led to nearby vantage points, often for otherwise inaccessible views across to distant mountains. Although the Skyline Drive, as its name implies, stayed mainly along the crests, the Blue Ridge Parkway as a whole, by varying its elevation from hollows to heights and back again, avoided the oppressive monotony that so often comes from too much of a good thing.

The Blue Ridge Parkway, bringing to thousands each year the chance for a leisurely drive in unspoiled Appalachian hill country, is a notable addition to the national park system. Because of its great length and difficult terrain it took years to build but is now near completion. Abbott continued as

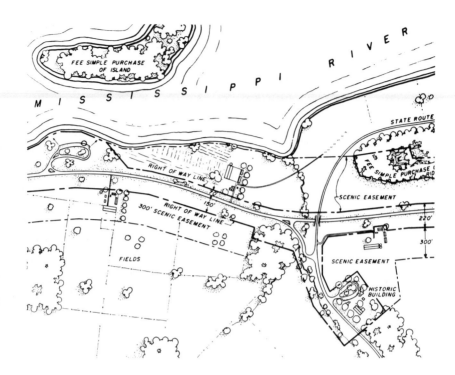

PARKWAY LAND CONTROLS IN RURAL AREAS

HYPOTHETICAL DRAWING TO ILLUSTRATE VARIABILITY
OF PARKWAY LAND TAKINGS SO AS TO PROVIDE:

1- A DEVELOPMENT WIDTH OF 220 FEET WITH SPACE FOR
WIDENING OF PAVEMENT IF NECESSARY IN THE FUTURE.

2- CONTROL OVER THE SIGHTLINESS OF RURAL SCENERY BY
MEANS OF EASEMENTS, SO THAT LANDS COULD CONTINUE
IN PRESENT OWNERSHIP AND REMAIN IN USE AS FARMS.

3- OUTRIGHT PURCHASE OF OCCASIONAL HISTORIC SITES
WOODED ISLANDS, SWAMPS, BLUFF FACES, AND
MARGINAL LANDS.

382. Mississippi River Parkway Survey: diagram of different types of land controls.

superintendent until 1949, when he was called away to head the National Park Service field staff working on the Mississippi River Parkway Survey. This endeavor, undertaken by the Park Service and the Bureau of Public Roads pursuant to an Act of Congress approved August 24, 1949, contemplated the feasibility of a national parkway along the Mississippi from its headwaters in Minnesota's Lake Itasca all the way to the Gulf of Mexico—to be done, with federal aid, by the ten states bordering upon the river. Preliminary studies quickly indicated that such an entirely new parkway, built to national standards with an 850-foot right-of-way, was utterly impracticable in a region with so much development on the river front. Accordingly, it was decided to recommend that wherever possible existing state and county roads be incorporated into the line of a modified parkway. A Parkway Commission of one hundred representatives from the ten "river states" was organized at St. Louis in November 1949. They and the technical staff pursued with enthusiasm the study "to marry the road and the river" and in January 1952 submitted their closing report to Congress. The recommended standards, including the 220-foot right-of-way accepted as a workable compromise but proposing other protective measures, were clearly and helpfully set forth (Fig. 382) in the diagram entitled "parkway land controls in rural areas." Meanwhile, two national parkways in addition to the Blue Ridge had been authorized by Congress in the 1930s: the Colonial Parkway linking Jamestown and Yorktown in Virginia and the Natchez Trace, on the old Indian trail from Nashville to Natchez.

Strangely enough, considering the manifest advantages of the divided roadway technique illustrated in the upper Taconic, that principle was followed slowly elsewhere. The Blue Ridge and Colonial Parkways, and the Mississippi proposals, were thought to have insufficient traffic volume to warrant the divided ways. Two outstanding examples that did adopt the technique were built in New Jersey: the Palisades Interstate Parkway, con-

383. Palisades Parkway, along the west shore of the Hudson. Clarke & Rapuano, landscape architects, for New Jersey Department of Public Works and Palisades Interstate Park Commission.

384. Garden State Parkway near Red Bank, New Jersey, 1955.

necting the lower Palisades of the Hudson with Bear Mountain State Park (Fig. 383), and the Garden State Parkway, running from a junction with the New York State Thruway north of the state line to Cape May at the southern tip of the state.

The Garden State, completed in 1956, is a notable illustration of the progress made in parkway design (Fig. 384). The preliminary plans and estimates, prepared by the firm of Clarke & Rapuano, of New York, determined the width of the right-of-way, the general alignment of the two separate roadways, profiles, and cross-sections, and related details including the location and preliminary design of bridge structures, access drives, and the like. The work was then divided into sections and several different engineering firms were engaged to prepare the final contract documents. The resident landscape architect was Oliver A. Deakin, who served with the state's highway forces from 1930 until his untimely death in 1964.

The Garden State meets parkway standards in excellent fashion, with median strips of variable widths from thirty feet in the urban sections of the north to as much as four hundred through the pine barrens of the south. Valuable experimentation with lengthwise visual barriers in the medians, varying from preservation of heavy existing growth where possible to erection of rough wooden screens or baffles where the median is narrow, has resulted in virtual elimination of the troublesome headlight glare from oncoming cars. The generous right-of-way in the open country has permitted the use of long, flat, softly rounded side slopes. Only indigenous material has been used in new plantings and for erosion control.

In short, the Garden State Parkway is a most welcome addition to the family of recreational travelways; it satisfies all the technical requirements and, except in urban areas, succeeds in maintaining the sensation of effortless passage through wholly native scenes. The most noticeable difference between the Garden State and earlier parkways—the sweep of its long, easy curvatures—is the result of its having been designed for much higher speeds than its predecessors, in response to technological improvements of motorcars and to changing public demand regarding "leisurely travel." However, despite the higher indicated speeds, the Garden State has a remarkably low accident rate—one of the lowest in the nation, in fact.

By having successfully raised the level of safe and pleasurable speeds, the Garden State has rather effectively answered one of the two objections that have done most to keep the parkway, as a type of motorway, from multiplying to the extent that its merits would appear to warrant. The other objection, of course, the Garden State does not attempt to answer: the denial of parkway passage to commercial vehicles. In an age that has come to depend so heavily on truck transport, this limitation often rules out a parkway. The result has been the freeway—or expressway, thruway, or turnpike, as the term varies from state to state (Fig. 385). Even if the parkway as a means of travel should go out of use (an unlikely eventuality) the freeway, or "complete highway," as some engineers like to call it, has profited greatly from experience in parkway development. In fact, it would now seem undebatable that all the parkway's distinctive physical characteristics can and should be incorporated in the design and construction of freeways if these are to be of truly superlative quality, commensurate with the advances of technology.

Most important is the principle of controlled access. It will be recalled that the first utilitarian road to be given the new name was the Norris Freeway, built by the TVA in 1933; the feature that so distinguished it in its day was just this freedom from interruption by access roads from the side. To make controlled access even more effective against the dangers of billboards and "ribbon development" of other unsightly roadside structures, wide rights-of-way are needed. The divided roadway technique is no longer open to serious question in freeways, but the use of medians with variable but ample width, between roadways aligned and profiled to fit ever more snugly into the topography, is not yet as general as it deserves to be.

Certain geometric precepts, evolved in ordinary highway design through the years, should not be overlooked in the rush for innovation. They are valid both visually and operationally: the need for a short tangent with spiral

385. New York State Thruway: section north of Suffern, 1957; the Thruway swings in from the right and curves into the distance up the Ramapo River valley; the complex in the foreground is for toll gate and access to N.Y. Route 17. Clarke & Rapuano, landscape architects.

transitions between horizontal curves in opposite directions, lest the change seem abruptly yanked; the desirability of a flat compounded curve rather than a tangent between horizontal curves in the same direction, to avoid a "broken back" appearance; especially, the substitution of flat curves for long straight stretches because such excessive tangents, contrary to common belief, have proved to be exceedingly dangerous through their hypnotic, tiring effect upon the driver.

But geometric standards, including those inherited by the freeway from its cousin the parkway, are in the long run no more important than a certain quality that does not yet submit itself to mathematical analysis. This is the overall "feel" of the freeway, the result of civilized attention to visual and psychological factors, and primarily what makes the best parkways a delight. It recognizes the humanity of humans, their functional difference from animals, their intuitive capacity to react—to sights and sounds, form and color and texture—in ways and to degrees that animals apparently do not. It rejects the purely mechanical solution as inadequate for humans. It postulates that the travelway of the future shall have the operational perfection of the most advanced freeway, coupled with the pleasantness and visual charm of the parkway. It is what occurs when engineer and landscape architect merge their talents in genuine collaboration.

And when these two collaborate, it should be from inception of the project. Essential to the ultimate excellence of the finished freeway is the skillful and land-sensitive location of the route, in relation not only to immediate terrain but to distant offscapes as well. Collaboration certainly does not mean "roadside landscaping" or "roadside beautification" or any other mere cosmetic treatment along a strip of paving already built. How can an object that is itself fundamentally ugly be "beautified" by adding plants, or anything else? This is not to deny that trees and shrubs and ground cover, judiciously employed, can contribute much to the whole—to erosion control, to baffling out sounds and headlight glare, to composing the views, and to fitting the freeway into the countryside. But the planting must be integral, not an additive. The kinds of excellence sought so eagerly in the freeway are not superficial; they rest in the basic structure of the design. For a landscape architect, the planting design is only a small part of his total professional task in parkway and freeway projects.

All of the above considerations, and any others leading to excellence, become even more compelling today, when the sheer magnitude of federally aided highway programs raises ever more seriously a legitimate question of whether the country may not soon be submerged under pavement. Slaves of an overproduced outer metal integument on wheels, like so many roadrunning beetles, Americans might in the end find greater peace and comfort if they drastically curtailed the number of cars and then found to their great relief that they simply did not need all those duplicate miles of often badly located highways.

XL. Urban Open-Space Systems

Before closing this account of an ancient art that became a new profession in the designing of a city park, the story should return briefly to the urban scene. If Olmsted and Vaux were to look about them in an American city today, what kinds of parks or open spaces would they find their professional descendants creating, as compared to the work they did on Central and Prospect Parks a century ago? They would of course be aghast at the mess people seem determined to make of things, not only in social maladjustments and conflicts, but in the creeping physical decay and disintegration from which ever more widespread slums result. They would be appalled by the unbearable clogging of streets with excessive motor traffic, by heedless pollution of the air and the fouling of water as well wherever it exists in fevered contact with the city. Indeed, Olmsted and Vaux might well find themselves reflecting on the age-old biological precept that no organism can long survive in an atmosphere made up solely of its own by-products.

Recovered from the shock and back with their original query, the two pioneers would find, perhaps to their surprise, that landscape architects today are seldom if ever engaged in the design of new "country parks" of the type first made famous by their partnership and perpetuated in city after city throughout the country during the nineteenth century. The reasons are partly fact, partly conjecture. In fully developed cities that do not have "country parks" it is too late, and in any event would be too costly, to acquire or reserve the necessary large tracts of land. Meanwhile, urgent need has arisen for other open-space facilities that require less extensive acreage.

Then, too, there are those who assert that the "country park," with its pastoral, softly meandering tree-formed space, is no longer needed within the city in view of the relative nearness of countryside in this motor age. This is undoubtedly one reason for diminished popular demand, considering numerical terms at least. Psychologically, however, under the tensions, pressures, and incessant clamor of the hectic urban condition, there is even greater need today for the quick relief of the quiet, contemplative atmosphere of the quasi-rural "country park." And to assume glibly that the countryside is "near at hand for everybody"—a statement frequently heard—is a cruel exaggeration; it will continue to be so until public transportation to the open country is freely or at least reasonably available to the lowest-income urban population.

Nevertheless, whatever the reasons and however justified or false, the fact remains that a new "country park" is a rarity. This is by no means to say that existing parks are a matter of no particular concern to enlightened persons; indeed, one of the major preoccupations of many landscape architects and other citizens is the tendency of public officials to divert park lands to other uses, almost always on the specious grounds that the cost of buying land for those other purposes is thus avoided. The struggle to save the parks, once they have been acquired and appropriately developed, makes a long, sad story beginning a hundred years ago with Olmsted's many battles to fight off the invasion and eventual ruin of Central Park. Almost every city has its troublesome cases.

The problem is rendered no less acute by the poignant fact that often it is not a question of dishonesty or greed or malice on the part of public officials, but only a matter of failure to comprehend the vitally important social value of the parks they would so thoughtlessly destroy. Against the stupidity of such official behavior the best weapon—often the only effectual one—is popular outcry. On occasion this in turn requires organized education of the voting public, if only to offset the cynical observation of some politicians that "nobody lives in parks" and that accordingly "parks don't vote." The greatest danger is public apathy.

Of course the rule of reason must prevail here as in other matters. The city's manifold needs for open space cannot be met entirely by "country parks" alone. In fact, with the changes wrought by the passage of years it is conceivable on balance, in the intricate competition among different, completely valid needs for land, that a portion of an existing park might reasonably be sacrificed in favor of some other crucial and genuinely more valuable purpose. Such a set of circumstances is not likely to occur frequently, but an open mind about the possibility is essential. Landscape architects called upon for expert testimony in such cases must observe the integrity of their professional judgment. But it is quite generally agreed as a necessary corollary that whenever park land is thus given up to a claim of acknowledged higher priority, an equal acreage of acceptable land, appropriately located, should be given to the park authority in exchange.

Among the new uses of urban open space that would surely be most noticeable to Olmsted and Vaux is the greater incidence of areas devoted

386. Charlesbank, Boston. Olmsted plan of 1892 for this earliest playground, established in 1889 by the Boston Park Commissioners.

primarily to active play and exercise. Both men saw movement in this direction before they retired from practice, but public demand for playground space did not reach major proportions until well into the twentieth century. Municipal authorities were slow to recognize the city's responsibility for recreational facilities; the earliest provisions were all arranged by private charitable bodies. Amusingly enough, by modern standards, what is now generally regarded as the first playground in America was the large sandpile placed in the yard of a Boston mission in 1885 by an organization bearing the resounding title Massachusetts Emergency and Hygiene Association. Called a "sand garden," it proved so popular that by 1887 no less than ten such play centers for small children had been installed in Boston. The 1887 Annual Report of the Board of Park Commissioners records that the Boston City Council had asked the Park Board to report on "the cost and advisability of establishing a suitable playground of five or six acres, for boys and athletic clubs." The report goes on to generalize: "Demands for playgrounds for the youth of the city are frequently made."[1]

In 1885, to create a "public promenade" along the Charles River, the Park Commissioners cleared some industrial buildings from a tract of land acquired two years earlier below the West Boston Bridge. In 1889 they established in this area, known as Charlesbank, an "open-air gymnasium for men and boys." Equipped with play apparatus, pools, and a track, the Charlesbank playground (Figs. 386, 387) had considerable influence on later developments in Boston and elsewhere. In their 1890 Annual Report, the Commissioners voiced their pleasure: "Charlesbank has proved to be a great boon to residents in the West End of the city. The open-air gymnasium has, we think, been of great benefit. Over 100,000 entries for use of the apparatus or grounds were made during the year. The open-air gymnasium for women and girls is nearly finished, and will be open for use in the coming season."[2] By 1894, Boston

1. Boston Park Commissioners, *Annual Report, 1887,* pp. 47, 49.
2. *Ibid., 1890,* p. 44.

387. Photograph of Charlesbank from West Boston Bridge in about 1890.

playgrounds of the "sand garden" type were all on school properties; but they were administered with private financing until 1899, when the City Council at last made a small appropriation for upkeep. Meanwhile, under pressure to provide larger space for athletic activities, the city in 1894 purchased Franklin Field, a short distance southeast from Olmsted's Franklin Park and not to be confused with the latter.

Boston was of course not alone in these halting efforts of the late nineteenth century. New York City was authorized in 1887 to use funds to purchase locations for playgrounds in the most congested parts of the city; in the 1890s a thoroughly equipped playground was built by private initiative in the hope that it would serve as a demonstration for the Park Department to follow. In Chicago a "model playground" was established at Hull House in 1892. A dozen cities, thanks usually to private beneficence, had playgrounds of sorts before 1900. Although many cities by this time had parks of considerable size, mostly on the order of Olmsted's Central and Prospect Parks, few were used for active recreational pursuits other than hiking or riding, except in such casual and unplanned forms as the "free play" of young children in the open meadows and baseball or football in whatever open space presented itself without special equipment or preparation.

With the turn of the century, matters took on a new light. In Charles Mulford Robinson's influential book of 1901 referred to earlier, *The Improvement of Towns and Cities,* one chapter was devoted to "Squares and Playgrounds"; this comment was included: "The subject of playgrounds is one that has come up lately with great vigor. It may be called one of modern philanthropy's favorites . . ." Robinson noted that the Massachusetts Legislature had authorized the City of Boston in 1900 "to borrow at once the money for twenty playgrounds, and this after immense results from private efforts."[3]

In Chicago the epochal year was 1903, when the Illinois Legislature acted favorably on recommendations made the preceding year by the Chicago South Park Commissioners by approving, subject to a public vote of concurrence, a bond issue of several millions for extension of the South Parks. Included in the legislation was a section that the Commissioners quickly implemented, according to their 1903 Annual Report:

> An Act authorizing the issuance of one million dollars ($1,000,000) in bonds to provide small parks or pleasure grounds, containing not more than ten acres each . . . The Commissioners, realizing that, for satisfactory results, the plans for the new parks should be drawn by landscape architects whose experience and work are recognized as of the highest order, entered into a contract with the Messrs. Olmsted Brothers, of Brookline, Mass., to make preliminary plans for Grant Park and the other new parks as acquired from time to time.[4]

This was the very authority for which, thirty years earlier, Olmsted, Vaux & Company had made the famous plan containing the areas later named Washington Park, the Midway Plaisance, and Jackson Park. In fact, the Commissioners in their 1903 report referred to the 1871 plan and noted that "the general satisfaction with Washington and Jackson Parks" had influenced award of the 1903 contract to the firm founded by the elder Olmsted.

By 1905, ten "small parks or pleasure grounds" had been opened, supplementing the more extensive effects of Washington and Jackson Parks, which by then had been refurbished for general use after removal of the Columbian Exposition. Baseball had been allowed in Washington Park for some years; by 1900 cricket and football had been added there, and in Jackson Park two golf courses had been laid out. A total of forty-two "tennis courts" were reported in both parks and the Midway by 1900. (The burgeoning interest in "athletic" activities caused batteries of tennis nets to be erected on the undulating turf of these parks—as occurred in about the same period in Brooklyn's Prospect Park and the Ellicottdale section of Franklin Park in Boston. The game played on these "courts" was little more than a kind of pat-ball—there was little conception of the scale of athletic installations that would be required one day, in tennis as in other sports, by public demand and rising standards.)

3. Robinson, *Improvement of Towns*, pp. 178–179.
4. Chicago South Park Commissioners, *Annual Report, 1903*, pp. 7, 10.

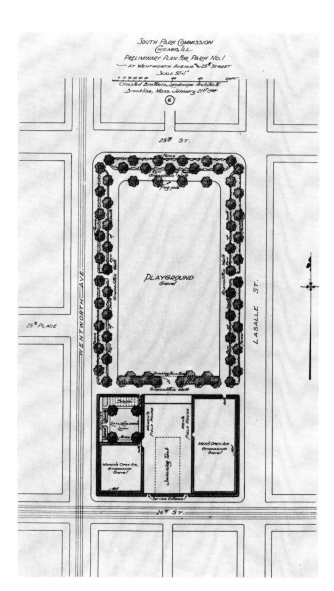

388. Chicago South Parks: preliminary plan (1904) by Olmsted Brothers for Park No. 1 of the newly authorized series of "small parks or pleasure grounds."

The effect of the Chicago South Park playgrounds, designed by Olmsted Brothers for all age groups, was widespread. They were more carefully designed, for varied yet consistent uses, than most playgrounds done before that time (Figs. 388, 389). Age groups were given distinctive areas, appropriately furnished: play spaces for children, open-air exercise areas for men and women, usually divided by sexes, courts for games, wading and swimming pools, and fieldhouses for indoor recreation. In each case the park (its official term) included the bit of greenery thought essential to a visual oasis in the neighborhood. In effect the playgrounds became community centers of great effectiveness and were soon emulated in many cities. The Playground Associ-

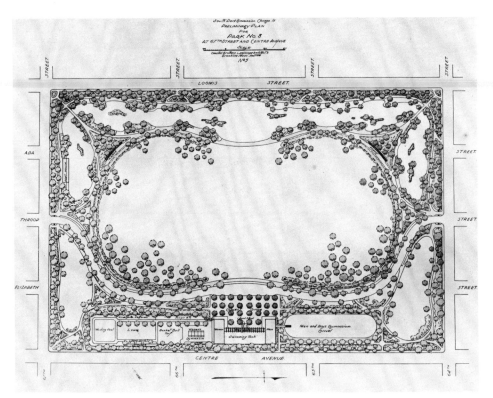

389. Preliminary plan (1904) by Olmsted Brothers for Park No. 8 of the Chicago South Park series.

ation of America, organized in Washington in 1906, had the expectable endorsement of President Theodore Roosevelt, that great outdoorsman, and the recreation movement was well under way.

More and more landscape architects undertook the design of playgrounds all over the country as the movement prospered. By 1914 Henry Vincent Hubbard of Harvard could refer to "a field which is more or less familiar to us all," in a paper entitled "The Size and Distribution of Playgrounds and Similar Recreation Facilities in American Cities" read before the National Conference on City Planning and published in *Landscape Architecture,* the official journal of the ASLA, in July of that year. Hubbard suggested the basis for what became a relatively standard classification for recreational areas:

> (1) The "Reservation," a municipal holding of country land . . . but not yet developed for intensive recreational use . . .
> (2) The large park, or "country park" . . . being the nearest thing to unspoiled country that most of the city dwellers can commonly take time to enjoy . . . fitted to receive large crowds and not to be destroyed by them . . .

(3) The small park, or "intown park," more accessible but less extensive . . .

(4) The playfield, for the active play of adults and young people over
twelve, in games taking considerable space, like baseball, football, tennis,
track athletics, etc., under supervision.

(5) The boys' outdoor gymnasium, or restricted playfield, for very
intensive use by boys over twelve, with apparatus, such as parallel bars,
ladders, etc., and a supervisor.

(6) The girls' outdoor gymnasium, with giant strides, swings, etc., and
a supervisor.

(7) The children's playground, for boys and girls under twelve, with
sand pits, baby hammocks, etc., and a woman teacher in charge.

(8) Special facilities depending upon local opportunities, such as
swimming pools, wading pools, skating ponds, facilities for bathing in
lake, river, or ocean.[5]

Eight years later, when interest in public recreation had zoomed still higher
in the wake of the the War Camp Community Service's wartime efforts,
Hubbard again read a paper before NCCP entitled "Parks and Playgrounds."
In it he remarked: "In a report . . . in 1914 I suggested a general classification
which seemed to me sensible and obvious, and so far as I know no one has
suggested anything especially different since."[6] This paper, published in
Landscape Architecture, also suggested from how large a territory each different
type of area might draw users. The classification offered by Hubbard in 1914
and essentially repeated in 1922 is still rather generally in use—except that
the term "gymnasium" has virtually disappeared among outdoor areas, boys'
and girls' exercise areas are usually called playgrounds, and areas for preschool
children up to five or six years of age are frequently called playlots rather
then playgrounds (some enthusiasts would call them "tot-lots," others find
the term too saccharine).

The Hubbard list indicates the wide range of recreational open-space needs
that had asserted themselves in the city more than forty years ago. It illustrates
particularly the degree to which emphasis had come to be placed on space
for intensive physical activity, even while retaining as desirable the quieter,
more contemplative and even sedentary forms of park space for literally
*re*creating the tired body and spirit. Today's urban needs in recreational space
are surely no less; the populations of cities may have dwindled in many cases,
but the pace of city life seems continually more intense, more in need of relief.
One thing is certain: in most American cities, far more is needed than has
been done.

One of the most remarkable examples of realizing urban potentials in

5. *Landscape Architecture,* 4 (July 1914), pp. 133–135.
6. *Ibid.,* 12 (July 1922), p. 242.

open-space provision was the performance of New York City under Mayor Fiorello LaGuardia's administration in the 1930s. Elected in 1933 by a fusion movement combining the antimachine elements of both political parties, one of LaGuardia's first moves was to ask Robert Moses to serve as director of parks. Moses agreed, subject to certain conditions: first, that the five separated borough park departments, each with a politically appointed commissioner and deputies, be abandoned as such and consolidated under one commissioner for the city; second, that Moses be permitted to retain his unsalaried posts as chairman of the State Council of Parks and of the Long Island State Park Commission, as well as such other offices as would help him coordinate the park and parkway activities of city and state; third, that he have a competent nonpartisan staff of technically trained people. The conditions were gladly accepted, and Moses was duly appointed in January 1934; one of the first consultants he engaged was landscape architect Gilmore D. Clarke. The old Arsenal in Central Park was made over as headquarters of the Park Department (Fig. 390), and an exceptionally able technical staff exempt from relief requirements was recruited to serve in drafting rooms and field. At its peak the planning section totaled 1,800 individuals: landscape architects, engineers, architects, and horticulturists.

390. New York: the Arsenal on Fifth Avenue (at far right), remodeled as Park Department headquarters under Commissioner Robert Moses; behind it, the new Central Park Zoo. Gilmore D. Clarke, consulting landscape architect; Aymar Embury, consulting architect.

To public-spirited New Yorkers the establishment of this new, professionally-oriented Park Department seemed little short of a godsend. For years they had watched with dismay the steady deterioration of the city's parks as the old political machine, treating the parks as stepchildren, sacrificed these assets of the people on the cynical altar of partisan patronage, even at the lowest levels. A broad program of rehabilitation in Central and Prospect Parks, which had been allowed to suffer badly, was undertaken at once. Dead trees dangerous to the public were removed, live ones were repaired by the thousand, the soil was systematically replenished, and planting was added where sorely needed. In Central Park one of the earliest problems attacked was the utterly decrepit old zoo, an effort best described in the retrospective 1940 report of the Park Department entitled *Six Years of Park Progress:*

> The first indication of the efficiency of the new staff was given in February, 1934, when, after sixteen days, plans for the new Central Park Zoo were sufficiently advanced to start work . . . By 1934 the ramshackle sixty-year-old zoo . . . had become a menace to the animals and a smelly nuisance to the public. Ten months after the first plan was started the new menagerie was opened, with nine modern brick buildings forming three sides of a landscaped quadrangle dominated on the fourth by the historic Arsenal Building, completely remodeled to serve as the headquarters office of the Park Department.[7]

In similar vein, the Prospect Park Zoo was rebuilt and by 1936 a new small zoo was installed at Barrett Park on Staten Island.

Many run-down old parks, such as Bryant Park behind the New York Public Library on Fifth Avenue, were redesigned and completely reconstructed (Fig. 391). Filling out the remainder of the double block between 40th and 42nd Streets from the rear of the library to Sixth Avenue, Bryant Park had existed for years in honor of William Cullen Bryant, whose journalistic zeal was so influential in getting land set aside for Central Park in 1853. At the east end, against the high background of the library's rear wall, stood a niche with a bronze seated figure of Bryant; this was a quite respectable memorial, but the rest of the park had become a forlorn, formless mixture of tattered lawns, twisting paths, and rickety benches.

What took the place of this bleakness was soon a bright breathing space in the heart of midtown New York. A green, walk-bordered, central panel of turf had raised terraces on three sides. Those on the north and south, with balustraded parapets, had broad flagstone walks with benches under a canopy of plane trees in beds of English ivy. The terrace on the east, toward the library, served as a setting for the Bryant memorial in the middle and shaded sitting places at the ends toward the entrances from 40th and 42nd Streets.

7. New York Department of Parks, *Six Years of Park Progress* (New York, 1940), pp. 7–9.

391. Bryant Park in the early 1930s; today the elevated railway on Sixth Avenue (Avenue of the Americas) is gone and the plane trees of the park are full-grown.

At the west end, opening on Sixth Avenue opposite 41st Street, the paved and shaded area centered on a handsome raised fountain and basin. Many of the stone details of the new park, incredibly enough, came from warehouses and storage yards of the Park Department, where they had lain on hand but unused. The park has stood up well under thirty-odd years of constant use; it profited greatly some years ago by removal of the elevated railway from Sixth Avenue. With the years the plane trees have grown high, to produce a flickering pattern of sunshine and shadow on the walks and benches, where people from the surrounding department stores and office buildings enjoy the park at all hours of the day in pleasant weather.

One other example of park revision illustrates further the variety of circumstances involved in these wholesale changes. In lower Manhattan there had been from early days a park in some form or other in the triangle between Broadway and Park Row, in front of McComb's graceful City Hall. During the dullest era of American architecture a monstrous Post Office was built at the southern apex of the triangle; what lay between the two buildings was in effect useless. When at last in 1934 the federal government got around to demolishing the bulky Post Office, the Park Department preempted the whole triangle and developed it as a delightful small park, with a bench-lined mall centered on a sight-line from the main door of City Hall to the elegant eighteenth-century portico of St. Paul's Chapel on Broadway (Fig. 392).

Somewhat like the resurrection of Bryant and City Hall Parks but on a much reduced scale was the redevelopment of many awkward remnants of public land, such as those at street intersections, obtained by the Park Department. With unwavering insistence on organizing the city's open spaces around usefulness to the people these plots, though often miniscule in the vastness of New York, were refashioned as comfortable sitting areas where residents were encouraged to gather for neighborly chats. Landscape architects on the Park Department staff treated these little essays in design with amusement and enthusiasm, calling them "conversation pieces" after the play of that name then popular on Broadway.

The great importance of recreation in an urban open-space program, and the extent to which playgrounds had developed in the half-century since those early ones in Boston, are best indicated by further excerpts from the 1940 report (Figs. 393, 394):

> Playgrounds are not impressive as to acreage but are tremendously important in the recreational scheme. Large park areas do not solve the problem of neighborhood recreation, which should be readily accessible to people who can't travel any great distance for fresh air, rest or play.
>
> Few of the 119 playgrounds in 1934 were properly laid out, equipped or maintained. There was little or no indoor activity. Most of these playgrounds have been rehabilitated by installing adequate equipment, paving and landscaping. All of them have been spruced up and one-third have been completely reconstructed.
>
> The playgrounds have been more than trebled in number and range in size from small neighborhood plots to large developments such as Red Hook with its running track, handball courts, football and baseball fields, and stadium. Surfacing of permanent paving material allows year round usage. Chlorinated wading pools, when drained in the fall, winter and spring, are used for basketball and paddle tennis. When weather permits there is ice skating. Trees enhance the appearance and comfort of the areas. Buildings with accommodations for indoor activities in bad weather are provided in one-quarter of the playgrounds.
>
> In Central Park the lawns and landscape areas were being torn to pieces by active children. The problem was largely solved by placing eighteen marginal playgrounds near the entrances to the park, providing children with healthy play which took the place of thoughtless destruction. The same policy is being followed in other large parks. One-half of the east border of Bronx Park has already been so developed.

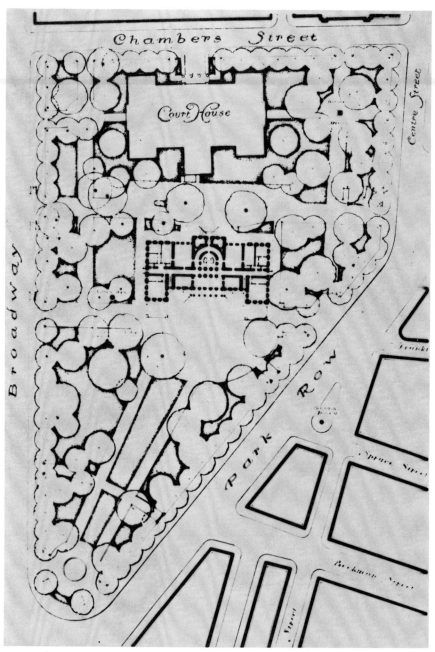

392. City Hall Park, New York: plan after removal of the old Post Office at the apex, 1934.

In rehabilitated parks, wherever necessary, definite areas were set aside for baseball, football, soccer and other open field sports. Hundreds of acres of formerly idle lands were thus made useful.[8]

8. *Ibid.*, pp. 15–16.

393. Typical of opportunities seized upon by Commissioner Moses: Williamsbridge Reservoir in the Bronx, no longer in its original service, taken over intact and redesigned as a playground.

394. Thomas Jefferson Park, redesigned for recreational use in conjunction with New York's East River Drive.

395. Orchard Beach, in the Bronx.

In the course of the six years reported on in 1940, some 6,000 acres had been added to New York's park system: about 800 acres by assignment, 4,000 by condemnation, nearly 400 by gift, purchase, and permit, and about 800 by charter transfer.

> We have attacked the problem in a number of ways. Playgrounds have been constructed on undeveloped land already under the jurisdiction of the Department. By transfer all land suitable for recreation, unused or not required by other City departments or by the State, was turned into parks or playgrounds. Abandoned school houses were torn down, reservoirs drained, construction yards cleared, unnecessary streets ripped up, unused State waterfront properties taken over, all to give way to playgrounds . . .

As new properties were made available through the expansion of the parkway program, playgrounds were developed in connection with them. The most noteworthy examples are the play facilities along the Hudson, constructed as an integral part of the West Side Improvement. The East

396. Henry Hudson Parkway along New York's West Side: regarded by many as Commissioner Moses' greatest administrative achievement, combining five different sources of financing to solve riverfront problems declared insoluble by the Mayor's Committee twenty years earlier.

> River development, to a lesser degree, also provides many new recreational areas, such as East River Park, the new Corlears Hook area, and the small play areas between 92 and 125 Streets . . . In connection with the Belt Parkway there will be twenty-three incidental playgrounds developed in Queens and in Brooklyn.[9]

In addition to open spaces in the built-up sections of the city, there was also the problem of the two public beaches, inadequately planned and developed by previous administrations and inherited by the Park Department under Commissioner Moses. Orchard Beach, in Pelham Bay Park on Long Island Sound, at the far northeastern corner of the Bronx, was completely redesigned and rebuilt (Fig. 395). Tawdry paving-block bathhouses and an unsightly tent and bungalow colony were demolished; an entirely new beach

9. *Ibid.*, pp. 10–12.

397. Fresno, California: Fulton Mall, a highly successful pedestrian shopping facility, the focus of an eighteen-block downtown area enclosed by a loop road. Eckbo Dean Austin & Williams, landscape architects.

was created, bordered by a wide promenade; a modern bathhouse, parking space, and bus terminal were installed. Equally drastic redesign and reconstruction were done at Jacob Riis Park, on the Atlantic Ocean side of the Rockaway peninsula; this was carried out in cooperation with the Marine Parkway Authority, one of the several independent public agencies on which Moses was simultaneously a member.

Reference has been made to the series of parkways and expressways developed by Moses in the city (Fig. 396). He made this great achievement even more significant, in terms of public open spaces, by coordinating his activities as park commissioner with those of his membership on the various Authorities—principally the Triborough Bridge, Henry Hudson Parkway, and Marine Parkway Authorities (the latter two combined in 1938 to form the New York City Parkway Authority). This neat administrative arrangement brought not only the miles of needed parkways, but many other areas as well, for example: in connection with the Triborough Bridge, several large playgrounds, the Randall's Island stadium, and part of the East River Drive; in connection with the New York City Parkway Authority, the parkway and bridge across the islands of Jamaica Bay to Rockaway, followed by the remarkable cleanup and metamorphosis of the mile-and-a-half-long Rockaway Beach Improvement, curing what had been little more than an oceanfront slum.

Though more could be said, especially about projects of historical restoration and land reclamation, what has been recounted here of the New York performance of the 1930s under Commissioner Moses and his landscape architects indicates the kind of open-space program possible in a large city, given a clear understanding of and adherence to the maxim "Parks and politics don't mix"—and a willingness not only to engage professional advice but also to follow it. World War II and the end of munificent federal relief measures naturally put brakes on the whirlwind pace of the 1930s, but the big rebuilding job had been accomplished and the park system was on solid footing by virtue of its own excellence. When activity resumed in postwar years, all that really needed to be done was to hold the great gains already made. This, and more, the Park Department did. Moses remained at the wheel as commissioner until he retired from the office in 1960. In that year, in recognition of the many opportunities he had given the profession of landscape architecture, the ASLA elected him to honorary membership.

A full story of the urban open spaces on which landscape architects are engaged today would have to include types of areas—public, semipublic, and private—not referred to in this book. Examples that come easily to mind are the grounds of schools, museums, and hospitals, the green linkages of space like those in Philadelphia, the all-too-meager open spaces of housing projects everywhere. There are pedestrian shopping malls in cities from coast to coast (Fig. 397), pleasant and often colorful parks atop underground garages and

398. New York: Samuel Paley Park, built on a 42- by 100-foot lot in the East Fifties by a private benefactor for public use. Zion & Breen Associates, landscape architects.

399. Placed by design "where the people are," the vest-pocket Paley Park, with the fascinating "water wall" at the rear its most unusual feature, is gratefully used by workers and shoppers.

multistory ones. And in the last few years some delightful small parks on private properties have been developed by civic-minded individuals for public enjoyment (Figs. 398, 399).

Another recent development certainly deserves mention: a sensible revolution in the design of playlots and playgrounds for younger children, thanks to someone's insight into making use of the greatest asset that such a play area can possibly have—the child's own imaginative powers. The earliest examples appear to have been, incongruously enough, in housing projects, where the usual barrenness was to some degree offset by play areas furnished with the simplest objects—a few lengths of large concrete sewer pipe, a set of railroad ties and rails bedded in the ground, clusters of piles of different heights. Instead of too few fixtures, too readily broken or too limited

400. The Plaza Playground of Riis Houses, New York, seen from above: an arrangement of simple and sturdy sculptural forms that produce a play environment to exercise the imagination of children. M. Paul Friedberg & Associates, landscape architects.

in use, here were abundant unbreakable objects to climb on or over or through—things becoming tunnels or mountains or whatever the children's imagining made them. The simple beginnings have been further developed in many interesting and healthy ways to enrich the lives of children and make the city's open spaces more meaningful (Fig. 400).

All in all, this adds up to a heartening array of kinds of open space for landscape architects to work on in American cities. If Olmsted and Vaux could, indeed, return to inspect the labor of their inheritors on the urban scene today, one can safely guess that they would be happily surprised at their profession's expanded role. In fact, they would find that even the methods and procedures of professional practice had undergone many changes.

XLI. Variations in Professional Practice

The history of landscape architecture as an *art* can justly be compared to variations on a theme in music. Without departing essentially from its basic theme, designing outdoor space upon the land for human use, it has evolved in the course of the centuries a wide variety of forms for an equally wide variety of purposes. Like everything else in the world of actuality, it is never twice exactly the same. In closely parallel fashion, landscape architecture as a *profession* has undergone, in the first century of its existence, considerable variation, not only in type of project and consequently type of client, but also in type of organization for practice. Even without surveying the whole hundred years, remarkable changes can be seen. A landscape architect today is far more likely to be involved in problems of urban renewal than in the design of "country parks." He is far more likely to be an employee of some level of government, from municipal to federal, than would have been the case forty or fifty years ago, when the private office was more the rule and the ASLA had only one or two members in Washington, D.C. Even private practice today is as likely to be engaged on a public project—or on a regional shopping center or the outlying plant of some industrial corporation—as on the type of residential job that was once the main concern of many landscape architects and the only concern of some.

The aim of this chapter is to examine briefly some of the major changes that have occurred in the practice of landscape architecture during the past thirty or forty years. First, a look at the social and political climate surrounding the profession; second, consideration of changes—of kind or, more often, emphasis—in types of client and project; and third, variations in structure of the practicing office. In all these respects, both practice and products in any particular period have generally reflected the fluctuations in American socioeconomic conditions, as would be expected in a human endeavor so consistently expressive of its time and place. Surely the most pronounced, abrupt, and largely irreversible of these changes was that occasioned by the financial crash of 1929 and the economic revolution of 1933, when adoption of new federal tax policies virtually put an end to what is here termed the Country Place Era. To be sure, some landscape architects noticed the change less than their colleagues because they had been engaged primarily in aspects of professional work other than residential—city and town planning, land subdivisions, parks and other public works at city, county, state, and federal levels. But large-scale residential work had in fact been the major output of many offices and constituted a relatively high proportion of the volume of work done by the profession as a whole. Few landscape architects were not affected in some way by the drastic change of direction.

Quite apart from this change for the profession itself, there was also a basic change in the orientation of many of its members. The harrowing experiences of the dark months after the 1929 crash, when disaster spread over the land, closing factories and then banks one after another, gave many Americans a new perspective of what the country's deepest problems actually were. Tragic as the period was, it brought a measure of hope to those younger landscape architects who had grown weary of the plutocratic image inaccurately fastened on the profession as one serving only the wealthy. Now they could see landscape architecture returning at last to its early Olmstedian role of service in the public welfare.

What followed in the 1930s was indeed a decade of public works, a complete reversal of the former proportions. While some residential work naturally continued, as it always would, the majority of landscape architects became involved in some aspect of the efforts of governmental bodies, chiefly the National Park Service. Work of conservation in national, state, and county parks enlisted the energies of more landscape architects than any other single activity had ever done. This phase of the profession's contribution need not be further discussed here, beyond the observation that several excellent state and county technical staffs had been busily engaged on parks in the 1920s; but the collapse of 1929 had shrunk their budgets, so that many members transferred to federal service or to newly reinforced municipal staffs in such outstanding but isolated cases as New York and Cleveland, where operations went forward, supported in large measure by federal relief funds.

The New Deal years brought about yet other changes and preoccupations affecting the profession. It was a busy decade for landscape architects in government service, and even private offices began picking up again, little by little. World War II came along, suspending many aspects of professional practice, though landscape architects collaborated with architects and engineers in the design of some naval and military installations. Those who remembered how effective the teamwork of the World War I period had been, under the leadership of the younger Olmsted, often remarked on the regrettable failure of the government to adopt similar arrangements more often during the later conflict.

But in truth it must be noted that the collaborative climate had already shifted considerably. In the years after the war it could be seen that interprofessional collaboration, especially with architects, had fallen off markedly since the busy 1920s, when it had been an entirely customary practice at least in all the major urban centers. The change is no doubt largely attributable to the shrinkage in residential commissions, an area in which teamwork between architect and landscape architect was of obvious importance, and to the relative increase of large-scale land planning operations in which there is occasion for landscape architects to collaborate with engineers more often than with architects.

There is, however, another possible but little understood cause for at least some of the slump in collaboration with architects. When the world of design finally managed, some twenty-five or thirty years ago, to climb out of the rut of traditional eclecticism and into the clearer light of twentieth-century rationality, many of the leaders in this triumph of good sense were architects whose whole background, training, and professional experience had been European. But up to that time landscape architecture, as a profession of the form and maturity achieved in America, had been virtually unknown in Europe. There were no professional curricula in landscape architecture in European universities or technical schools. To be sure, the technical schools offered some of the old, established courses such as horticulture, forestry, and "garden art," but none in landscape architecture as a design profession on the American model. Thus, in the absence of both practitioners and trainees, it was plainly impossible for the European founding fathers of today's architecture to have worked in collaboration with a landscape architect.

It is therefore not surprising that they should have come to the New World completely unaware of landscape architecture as a profession and blind to the environmental values upon which this profession is based. Such a degree of ignorance or insensitivity could be excused if eventually it had been outgrown—and if it had not been passed on, unmitigated by learning, to disciples and students, conveying a virtual illiteracy about land form and what may best be termed "landscape values." As a consequence the environment suffers and so does the architecture, most often through the unbelievably clumsy placement of buildings on the land. In such instances, early collaboration with a landscape architect, or at least some understanding of how to fit buildings to the surface of the earth, might save the day. But ignorance too often wins out.

The changes that have occurred in specific type of client and project during the past four decades have been primarily shifts of emphasis. Their common characteristic has been a trend from the small to the large, the minute to the comprehensive. What was once a preponderance of residential work for the single individual as client, though long since dwindled to a relatively minor role, has found its expanded echo in residential efforts instead for large numbers of people. One of the methods adopted was land subdivision, a form of development of unfortunate and checkered history. Landscape architects have been doing land subdivisions ever since the work of Olmsted and Vaux at Riverside, Illinois, in 1869. Indeed, all of the American town planning projects discussed earlier, prior to Sunnyside Gardens, were fundamentally essays in land subdivision—a roading-and-lotting procedure, cutting up the land into individual parcels for sale, the whole predicated on the established though questionable American predilection for single-family houses, each with its immediate street access.

So long as these projects were being designed by competent landscape architects, they showed a high order of skill in handling an essentially obstinate problem. But as the growth of population heightened the competition for land, opportunities for swift profits increasingly lured real-estate developers into subdivision projects of ever lower standards of dimension and quality, done wholly without landscape architectural help. Gridiron street systems, argued against so eloquently by Horace Cleveland as far back as 1873, were thoughtlessly plastered on the land, willy-nilly, during the seemingly affluent days of the 1920s. In fact, by 1933 sizable speculative "communities" of gridiron streets, with elementary utilities but devoid of houses and people, had been carved into wooded acreages of undulant land here and there on the peripheries of metropolitan regions throughout the country—ghostly memorials to the unwitting buyers stuck with these graceless lots on butchered land that never received further development.

The ruthless exploitation of land and people was effectively stopped when in 1933 the government set up a professionally oriented Land Planning Division within a Federal Housing Administration. The FHA was established to facilitate credit operations by guaranteeing mortgage loans for carefully scrutinized and approved projects. A bank, before lending money to a real-estate developer, would require FHA approval. The FHA, before granting approval, insisted that the developer present a general plan acceptable to the Land Planning Division. The Division could thus eliminate the fraudulent schemes; it also gave advice freely, showing developers how to improve tentative plans so that FHA approval would be forthcoming. The Division published several timely pamphlets to help developers, beginning with the widely known *Land Planning Bulletin No. 1: Successful Subdivisions* (Fig. 401).

Such efforts did much to improve the overall quality of American subdivisions, raising the common standards to something approaching the level of what landscape architects had been doing for many years. But the new burst of activity meant only a slight increase, if any, in the practice of private landscape offices. The type of commercial developer now encountered usually

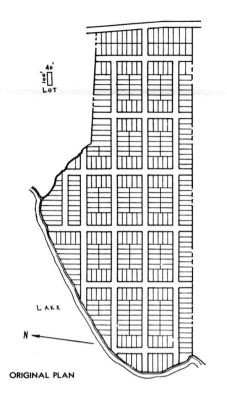

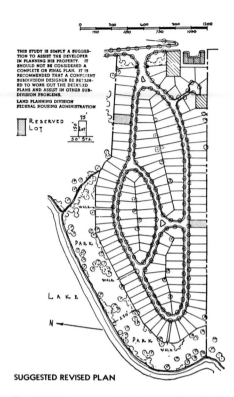

ORIGINAL PLAN

An excessive amount of street construction, the rigid and monotonous layout of streets, the use of "butt" lots, and the subdividing of the wooded lakeshore, as shown in the original scheme, would have made this project costly to develop and difficult to market.

SUGGESTED REVISED PLAN

The revised plan has overcome these objections and every lot has been made a desirable building site. Although this plan provides fewer lots, the changes permit a greater financial return and quicker sales for the developer and a better investment for the buyer.

401. Excerpt from *Land Planning Bulletin No. 1* of the Federal Housing Administration, 1933, showing basic suggestions for "successful subdivisions."

worked on the narrowest of speculative margins, with attention on immediate profits rather than creation of a continuing market. To such operators it seemed senseless to pay the fee of a landscape architect when advice from FHA was free and, if followed, most probably brought approval. Furthermore, to this breed of subdividers quick profits mattered and quality did not.

To be sure, during this period and in later years landscape architects were often called in by responsible individuals or groups for the design and development of high-standard subdivisions backed by FHA guarantees but not so coldly speculative in motivation. These, however, were usually planned for higher income levels; and they were isolated exceptions in a plethora of uninspired, barely approvable FHA projects pushed through without independent professional help by the "fast-sell-quick-escape" type of developer. Then, too, as the years wore on and greedy subdividers multiplied, certain trends appeared that had not been either intended or anticipated by the originators of the Land Planning Division of FHA.

As so often happens with attempts to legislate public standards, what FHA set as minimum requirements became all too soon maximum provisions by the developer: just good enough to get by but no better. Almost inevitably under the circumstances, a sameness of pattern grew so that "typical FHA subdivision" became, perhaps unjustly, the pejorative name for a certain dull stereotype. To top this off, especially in the decades after World War II, there came the virtually runaway expansion of subdivision suburbia, flowing like human lava over the face of the earth in often endlessly monotonous forms—twisting roads bordered by staccato rows of single-family houses of equal size, technically detached but wasteful of the tiny spaces between them. Here was a new curvaceous tedium, ultimately no great improvement over the repetitive banality of urban gridiron schemes and in no sense a solution to low-income housing problems. Possibly the worst examples—and it seems unfair to blame FHA for them even remotely—are the "tract" developments on bulldozed land in southern California, where mistreatment of the topography has reached often vicious proportions, clearly inviting disaster.

But subdivisions, fortunately, were not the only method of attacking the housing shortage in the 1930s; by 1940 the United States Housing Authority was publishing excellent advisory pamphlets on the planning of low-rent housing projects. Landscape architects worked on housing projects, both public and private, with varying degrees of success, depending usually on the size and scope of budgetary allowances for site-development. In visual terms, housing projects have a distinct advantage over subdivisions: since individual lots and street access for each dwelling unit are not requirements in a housing project, road layout does not get top priority, as it must in a subdivision. Primary attention can therefore be given instead to the creation of positive outdoor spaces to serve effectively as the heart of the total development. In short, the whole project becomes perceptibly a spatial composition; the outdoor space is not a leftover or an accident, as all too often it seems in ordinary subdivisions.

Public housing projects, customarily located in cities, have on the whole tended to be bleak and characterless except for some outstanding early instances, where appropriate care was taken in the provision and treatment of interior open spaces. In later years, budgets for site development fell off so lamentably that the landscape architect had little if any chance. Private undertakings in group housing have been a quite different matter; such projects as Chatham Village and Baldwin Hills Village tell their own story. Indeed, one could hardly find a clearer illustration than that provided by the airplane ride over Baldwin Hills Village suggested earlier, to demonstrate the disparity between a successful housing project and the typical real-estate developments that followed and surrounded it.

Many landscape architects in private practice have thus worked on housing projects through the years—and somewhat less on subdivisions. Those in government service have held positions on the administrative and technical staffs of the FHA itself and of other agencies concerned with housing for the multitude. One of the most lively, progressive, and productive of all the agencies was the Farm Security Administration (known as the Resettlement Administration until 1937), the force behind Greenbelt, Maryland. Especially on projects aimed at solving the housing problems of migrant farm workers in California, the FSA moved forward boldly in the late 1930s with an imaginative, nontraditional approach to design in both architecture and landscape architecture. It was in connection with these projects that the landscape architect Garrett Eckbo first became known to the profession.

Reference to new endeavors of the federal government in the 1930s must include mention once again of the internationally famous Tennessee Valley Authority—sometimes called, with more than a little justification, the greatest single landscape architectural project on record, and of course in the finest sense a magnificent interprofessional collaborative effort. From the start, as already noted in discussion of the town of Norris, landscape architect Earle S. Draper was the director of land planning and housing for the TVA; from 1937 to 1940 he was in charge of all TVA regional planning studies.

The trend of projects toward wider implications has been sustained by a growing sense of the profession's social responsibility and by forward-looking ideals, but it must not be supposed that the view has been so limited to the future as to ignore the past. In fact, there has been increasingly active interest in historical restoration, stimulated especially by the notable reconstruction of Williamsburg, Virginia, through the munificence of John D. Rockefeller, Jr. Research was begun in 1928 and construction continued in the 1930s, suspended during the war, and resumed in 1948. The whole was a collaborative between the architects, Perry, Shaw & Hepburn, and the landscape architect, Arthur A. Shurcliff, both of Boston. Shurcliff was one of the elder statesmen of the profession, the first "junior" member elected to the ASLA by the founders in 1899, and active in practice until his death in 1957. The work at Williamsburg is generally regarded as the greatest of his many outstanding accomplishments.

The intellectual honesty of Colonial Williamsburg, the official title of the enterprise, is perhaps its most impressive asset. No claim is made that this is the authentic Williamsburg as it was during its years as the capital of the Virginia colony. In fact, little evidence remained of its original condition, but whatever there was has been faithfully adhered to; as a result, thousands of visitors can see today what may fairly be supposed to have existed in the eighteenth century. Two main features establish the mood: the long Duke of Gloucester Street, lined with restored colonial houses, running from the reconstructed brick capitol at one end to the genuine College of William and Mary at the other; and the magnificent Governor's Palace with its turf-paneled approach and numerous gardens (Fig. 402), all sumptuously done

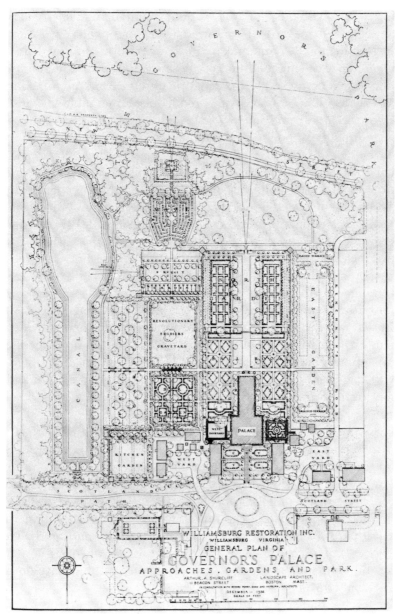

402. Williamsburg, Virginia: conjectural restoration of gardens about the Governor's Palace, based on meticulous research.

as the royal governor and his residence were an ever-present symbol of the distant Crown.

The Williamsburg reconstruction was so admirably carried out that from the beginning its impact was widely felt. Influential also was the complete restoration of General Washington's beloved Mount Vernon, started in 1931 by Morley J. Williams for the Mount Vernon Ladies' Association—fortuitously timed in view of the approaching national celebration of the George Washington Bicentennial in 1932. The work continued until 1938, resulting in the excellent condition of the shrine today. Although in the 1930s economic stringency severely limited private endeavors of this kind, these years saw the National Park Service produce the remarkable Historic American Buildings Survey and undertake several restorations, developing in the process an exemplary policy of the most rigorous accuracy.

With the close of World War II the postponed historical activities of the National Park Service were resumed, principally on the pre-Revolutionary Atlantic seaboard, with emphasis on Philadelphia's Independence Hall complex and on outlying sites around Boston in connection with the Minute Man Historical Park project between Lexington and Concord. Private efforts were again possible at points throughout the country. In the early 1950s Alden Hopkins, then resident landscape architect of Williamsburg, carried out for private sponsors his superb restoration of Gunston Hall, the eighteenth-century home of Washington's friend and counselor George Mason, a few miles down the Potomac from Mount Vernon. Another noteworthy American contribution was the recent landscape restoration of the ancient Greek agora in Athens by Ralph E. Griswold, who continues to be consulted on landscape problems of archeological excavations in Asia Minor. In the United States, largely in the interest of public education, historical restorations and reconstructions have become an active concern for many architects and landscape architects.

Likewise in the field of education itself, activity has risen at a remarkable rate in the design of school grounds and college campuses. Because of the widespread commitment to one-story buildings for elementary, and to some degree even secondary, schools, more attention than in the past has necessarily been centered on site planning. School boards and architects have come to see the crucial importance of careful design in what must be understood as an integral part of the school even though located beyond the shelter of the roof (Fig. 403). This becomes all the more insistent when, as now happens so often, the school as a whole is spread out in rambling fashion on land that is seldom conveniently like a table top.

At the level of higher education, landscape architects have been concerned with the design of college and university campuses ever since the elder Olmsted prepared in 1866 his plan for the "College of California" in Berkeley. But until the last quarter-century campus commissions were at best occasional in most landscape offices. Since World War II there has been a boom in this field, partly the result no doubt of a certain proliferation of upgraded institutions—normal schools being classed as colleges, colleges as universities—and physical expansion at all levels to accommodate the "postwar bulge" as it reached college age. From coast to coast there have been calls for new campus

403. Entrance front of the Country School at Weston, Massachusetts, typical of the trend toward one-story schools closely fitted to interesting sites. Chambers & Moriece, landscape architects; Hugh Stubbins & Associates, architects.

404. Foothill College, Los Altos, California: a new junior college for an eventual enrollment of six thousand. Vehicular traffic is held to the periphery, making the campus a wholly pedestrian domain. Sasaki, Walker and Associates, landscape architects; Ernest J. Kump and Masten & Hurd, associated architects.

plans or amendments to old ones (Fig. 404). The most significant change, regarded as a variation in professional practice, has been the emphasis on statistical analysis and long-range planning of an institution's educational and administrative needs. In projects for colleges and universities, landscape architects now must often spend more time and energy on the institutions' internal program-planning—on speculation and prediction of future probabilities—than on the subsequent physical site planning or design.

Another project area that deserves mention is the "new" discipline called urban design, consisting in the main of shaping city spaces, a type of collaboration with which landscape architects have in fact long been concerned. It is downright amusing to see with what excitement urban design has been "discovered," chiefly by architects who would appear thereby to confess having been unaware of the existence and functioning of outdoor space in the city. The situation presents another curious coincidence. One need only recall the discussion of city planning in an earlier chapter to observe that this "new" urban design is in effect simply a revival of the *sound* part of the City Beautiful movement translated into present-day idiom and cleared of its eclectic overtones. Yet the people most enthusiastic today about the allegedly "new" field are of the same persuasion as those who only a few years ago derided everything in any way associated with the City Beautiful. Truly a phoenix risen from its own ashes!

To landscape architects, the study of urban open space has been a familiar story for years. For instance, as long ago as 1915, when the American Academy in Rome formulated its regulations for work required of the Fellow in Landscape Architecture, one of the first-year assignments was measuring and drawing up a Roman piazza. Among outstanding recent examples of the handling of city spaces by landscape architects are Ghirardelli Square in San Francisco by Lawrence Halprin & Associates; the garage-roof park of Pittsburgh's Mellon Square by Simonds and Simonds; and two works by Sasaki, Dawson, DeMay Associates, Constitution Plaza in Hartford and the winning solution in a national competition for redesign of Boston's Copley Square (Figs. 405–409). Normally less exciting and spectacular than these instances are the frequent landscape architectural involvements in various projects of urban renewal.

Contrasting sharply with problems of urban design and renewal, perhaps the greatest change of all in landscape architectural projects has come from the persistent flow of population and industry away from the cities ever since World War II. This explosive decentralization has multiplied professional opportunities in two areas particularly: regional shopping centers to serve new or expanded suburban communities (Fig. 410), and industrial installations of all sorts ranged along new arterial trucking routes. The shopping center, usually a clear site-planning problem of locating large volumes of interconnecting indoor space and vast parking areas on raw land, is obviously a task

405. San Francisco: Ghirardelli Square, a colorful provision of urban open space descending to a waterfront. Lawrence Halprin & Associates, landscape architects; Wurster, Bernardi and Emmons, architects.

that requires first of all the skills of a landscape architect. In all parts of the country these regional centers have been built, their constituent parts usually branches of major shops and department stores in the nearest city. Combining as they do elements as diverse as massive motor circulation and the intimate

406. Pittsburgh: looking down on the pattern of Mellon Square, a garage facility with a park developed on its roof.

407. Partial shade, bright floral color, and the splash of fountains combine to make Mellon Square a refreshing spot in the heart of Pittsburgh.

408. Constitution Plaza, the pride of Hartford, an urban essay on several levels.

409. Boston: the famous Copley Square redesigned at last. Perspective rendering.

410. The Riveroaks Shopping Center, one of several such regional centers on the outskirts of Chicago. Lawrence Halprin & Associates, landscape architects.

detail of gardenesque sitting areas, such great shopping centers are among the most challenging jobs to a designer.

The treatment of grounds for industrial installations is not, strictly speaking, a completely new field for landscape architects. Forty or fifty years ago commissions were being executed by some of the older landscape offices for industrial firms, but in nearly every case this work was merely to enhance the external appearance of an existing plant. There were of course a few instances of companies moving factories into the country and having whole communities developed around them, as in the textile villages in the southern states done by Earle Draper (his Chicopee, Georgia, was described earlier). But all of this was as nothing when compared with the situation that burst forth after World War II. The flight of industries from the cities, begun before the war in the name of dispersal against aerial bombing, was magnified prodigiously in the postwar period by mounting urban congestion and zooming municipal tax rates (Fig. 411). Real-estate developers took to promoting "industrial parks" on available tracts approachable by railway spurs. Then came the arterial highways; and industries of the light, electric-powered variety, dependent less on railways than on trucking facilities and eager to be out on open land, quickly sought roadside locations. There followed for landscape architects the problem of siting a wide range of building types in a still wider range of relationships, along with the inevitable parking space for plant and office personnel. When, as happens fairly often, the new highway follows a valley, the slope of adjacent land renders the task all the more difficult. Luckily, most industrial installations do not need the wide acreages that regional shopping centers must have.

On the whole, then, and in varied ways, the professional practice of landscape architecture has shown in recent years a definitely expansive trend, whether in the number of people served by a project or in the size of land area encompassed by it. Of basically similar character has been the growing awareness that people and places do not exist in isolation, a resurgence of the deep concern for entire regions that began many years ago in the brilliant work of Charles Eliot. In his method of working with large areas and through agencies of government, Eliot built a solid base for those broad phases of landscape architecture generally known today as regional planning. Since that day Eliot's broadly conceived approach has been continued by many other landscape architects, among them the younger Olmsted, Henry V. Hubbard, Arthur C. Comey, Earle S. Draper, Justin R. Hartzog, Russell V. Black, and Eliot's nephew, Charles W. Eliot II. Through its landscape architects the National Park Service, too, except in the more detailed site planning of developed areas, has necessarily practiced regional planning in its own specific way throughout its existence.

In short, there is nothing essentially new about the regional planning aspect of the profession. The difference recently noticeable is rather one of degree and emphasis as federal and state agencies, reacting almost as though in a hurry at last to do something about natural resources before it is too late, have undertaken various forms of regional planning. The Virgin Islands and Puerto Rico have been commendably active in protecting their futures. Some agencies have employed private firms; others have merely engaged consultants to advise the agency's staff; practically all have offered staff jobs to recent graduates of schools of landscape architecture. As a consequence, more and more time is being apportioned in the schools for study of large regional problems, always basically in physical terms but never without appropriate investigation of the historical, social, economic, and political factors as these affect the lives of the region's people.

A heartening corollary of this growing interest in large areas has been the simultaneous revival of attention to ecology. Some of the more progressive

411. General office building of the Upjohn Company near Kalamazoo, Michigan: an example of executive headquarters moving to suburban areas. Sasaki, Walker and Associates, landscape architects; Skidmore, Owings & Merrill, architects and engineers.

members of the profession have long advocated an ecological approach to practically all landscape architectural problems, but somehow the notion did not seem to take hold until its applicability to regional areas became obvious. This is of course a *total ecology,* not merely one of plants and animals—an ecology that sees humans as living organisms, participating as integral parts in the wholeness of nature rather than as something innately in conflict with the rest of the natural world.

Thus in a number of different ways the recent trend of specific projects has been toward more comprehensive dimensions. These changes have been in a measure paralleled by changes in the organization of some of the private offices practicing landscape architecture. As though to compensate for the decline of interprofessional collaboration between firms or offices, a new phenomenon has arisen in recent years that makes the collaborative process an internal affair, so to speak, rather than the external one of former times.

This has been done in one or more of several ways by individual firms in the three professions. For example, just as the larger landscape offices, in the 1920s and earlier, had normally employed architects and engineers within their own staffs, after World War II some of the larger architectural firms, recognizing their inability to handle site-planning problems adequately with their ordinary procedures, began to hire young landscape architects. The move often proved so successful as to warrant retaining a fully experienced landscape architect and setting up a sizable site-planning section to work within the office under his professional guidance. A few of the larger engineering firms have followed about the same procedure, in the hope of being thus equipped to do site-planning or regional planning projects with something more than mechanical utility, stability, and economy alone. Conversely, landscape architectural firms may still have their own architects and engineers, just as the older offices had them in the past.

Perhaps the most interesting solution of all is the one adopted by a few landscape firms that have evolved what may be called a group or corporate approach to problems. Such a firm consists of professionals from all the design fields, buttressed at times by economists, sociologists, or other specialists as needed. This new type of organization tackles problems of all kinds in outdoor design and land planning, rural or urban, from the largest to the smallest, on a worldwide basis. Here is internal collaboration in its purest form, with all of the professions participating as equal partners in a group endeavor from the very outset: an excellent example of successful collective responsibility. Because many of the problems are of extraordinary complexity, such a firm normally lays great but by no means exclusive emphasis on the analytical, program-planning phases of the total design process.

The evolution of this internal collective approach would seem to be a natural outcome of the trend, perceptible within each of the professions after World War II, to work in a group rather than as separate practitioners. There has also been partial disappearance of the traditional view of the practitioner as an individual who offers a distinctly personal service to clients. Instead, the notion of the group offering its *corporate* service has evolved. Indeed, there has come about an almost complete reversal of the one-time attitude that the strictly personal nature of the service automatically precluded incorporating architectural and landscape architectural offices—or at least that incorporation was generally frowned upon within the professions themselves. Today many firms in both professions are incorporated, although in most states a license to practice can legally be granted only to individual practitioners, not to the corporation.

The same trend toward group action has caused many offices to enlarge the sharing of authority, responsibility, and profits among a much larger number of associates than was once customary. Public declaration of the fact has also appeared in the names adopted by firms. Again and again one learns that a familiarly-named firm is no longer "So-and-So," but "So-and-So and Associates," or even more simply just "So-and-So Associates." What would seem the utmost in depersonalization is the frequency with which offices now operate under entirely impersonal titles such as "North Shore Architects," or "Land Planning Associates," to invent two that are typical but fictional. The above refers, of course, to offices in private practice, which account today for little more than half of the profession, judging as well as possible by membership lists of the ASLA. Though the Society as a whole has grown enormously, with an increase of over 1200 percent in the past half-century, the changes *within* it are more significant.

As the ASLA comes to the end of its seventh decade it approaches a membership of 1500, plus well over 1200 associates (graduates of professional schools but not yet tested as to capacity in actual practice); in 1920 the membership numbered 112. About 92 percent of the members in 1920 were in private offices; only 4 members were in some level of government service; 5 were principally educators, though they may have practiced, also. Comparing 1920 figures with the best available estimates for the present, one finds interesting signs of the profession's ramifications, perhaps into areas where landscape architecture was little known fifty years ago. In terms of distribution, today's approximately 1500 members are:

In private landscape architectural offices	51.9%
In government service, all levels	28.1%
In education (principally)	8.2%
In offices of other professions	6.2%
Employed by nonprofessional corporations	2.4%
Retired	3.2%

In the long run, the various changes recounted in the foregoing pages, to the extent that they indicate a trend toward wider horizons and stronger design, constitute a gratifying augury for the profession. They reveal a steady growth toward deeper awareness of man's intelligent role as a part of nature and a clearer sense of the landscape architect's responsible position as a student, servant, and protector of the total environment. For by aptitude, training, and outlook the landscape architect is ideally prepared to help society attain the ever-beckoning goal of greater predictability in the *wise use of land.*

XLII. Conservation of
Natural Resources

It has long been known that the term *conservation* makes little sense if taken to mean just saving everything indiscriminately. But it can be an extremely helpful guide to constructive action if taken in its currently accepted sense, meaning *wise use.* Wise use of the land and the clear design of spaces upon the land when that wise use calls for human accommodation: how better to describe the central theme of landscape architecture?

To what may seem a surprising extent, questions arising in the field of conservation are remarkably similar to those facing a landscape architect. Consider, for example, the conservation precept of wise use. It obviously implies an evaluational process, a demand for judgment and some system of priorities. It necessarily presents many instances of dilemma, for there seems always to be some form of competition between or among conflicting uses for a given piece of land miniscule or vast. The situation is best illustrated in large tracts, but only because there the dimensions involved make the problem easier to see. In great forested areas, a conservationist is frequently confronted by the question of whether to give primary consideration to preservation and protection of what exists or to development of a new use or procedure to meet a genuine human need. Both are legitimate purposes, yet they conflict. Which, in a given case, most clearly constitutes wise use of the land's resources?

This typical conservation question is almost precisely the same as the ones implied by the landscape architect's ultimate calculus, referred to earlier in regard to national and state parks—the problem of finding the "right number" between too little and too much. This is particularly true if the case under examination is in a national park. There the fundamental statutory purpose is preservation of the great scenic tract "unimpaired for the enjoyment of future generations." Preservation of course; yet it would make no sense to hide the place away in mothballs, even figuratively, and exclude all development. Intelligent visitation by the people is also one of the purposes, and people need accommodation—but in appropriate numbers. How many would be an appropriate number? Great skill, much experience, and a deal of luck are all needed for a workable estimate. Even then, today's mass invasions can upset the best calculations; small wonder that serious attention is being given to housing visitors outside the boundaries of national parks. At any rate, it is obvious that facilities designed for present and future use in the park must be just right in character and just right in capacity, lest they lead to destruction of the very values for which the area was set aside in public trust and is visited by eager citizens. In this case, then, preservation must be the overriding factor and any development held to a minor role.

But what if the example under study is in a state park? Here, it will be remembered, the major purpose is often, and quite validly, one that does not depend primarily on outstanding scenery. It is normally expected that at least some state parks will be reasonably accessible to sizable urban populations, since one of the chief hopes is that of attracting a considerable number of city folk into the out-of-doors. If such an area has all the desirable characteristics of size, location, vegetation, and topography except that it contains no recreational water body, then experience decrees the necessity of creating a lake for swimming and boating, even at some loss in strictly scenic values, if the park is to serve its purposes fully. In this case, development becomes the overriding factor. But here again the development, no matter what elements it involves, must be just right in character and capacity or the result is likely to be a mess for everybody.

In each of these instances, the essential and crucial point is a balance between two broad factors, between preservation of the existing and development of the new. So it is with all the other relevant competing factors: in each case what must be found for a successful outcome is just the right balance for the purposes at hand. This means not necessarily the most or the least of any one factor, but the best in all of them taken as a whole. Not a maximum, nor a minimum, but an *optimum*. The notion of the optimum is fundamental to landscape architecture. It offers a comprehensive means for describing the ultimate goal of the profession: *optimum relations between people and their environments*. The constant aim of landscape architecture is to determine, to create, and then to keep current optimum relations between humans and the rest of the environment of which they too are a living part.

And what is meant by optimum relations? The expression refers to relationships that permit people not only to find sources of abundant satisfaction in the environment and enjoy them according to the varying specific purposes involved, but to find them in optimal numbers and enjoy them in optimal degree with optimal expenditure of human and other natural resources, lest through overuse or misuse the sources of satisfaction themselves be injured or ultimately exhausted and lost entirely. In brief, landscape architecture seeks to enable people to use the sustaining values of the environment, whatever they may be, without using them up.

Landscape architecture thus follows, in its broadest and deepest aspects, the same pattern as conservation; for the notion of the optimum is equally fundamental to the conservation of natural resources. Wise use involves not necessarily the biggest use or the smallest use, or the most or the least, but the *best*, everything considered. Another convenient way of expressing the optimum, with respect to a given piece of land and a given proposed use, is applicable equally to landscape architecture and to conservation. Two questions are involved: Is this piece of land better suited to the proposed use than any other available land? Is this piece of land better suited to the proposed use than to any other possible use for it? To either the landscape architect or the conservationist, an affirmative answer to both questions indicates the desirable optimum relation between the piece of land and the proposed use: in short, wise use of the land.

The more one looks at it, the more clearly one sees that landscape architecture, in its most general sense, is virtually synonymous with conservation: the wise use of the resources, including human resources, to be found on and in the land. And, to repeat what merits frequent repetition, the land, public or private, is the greatest single possession of any people and the basic source of their national wealth (Fig. 412). It is fair to say that no person fully comprehends the central meaning of either conservation or landscape architecture who does not see how fundamental to both is a considerate popular attitude toward the land. For unless the people of the world are profoundly and actively concerned with what poets have called "the smiling face of the land," there are not likely to be smiles on the faces of many humans who live upon that land.

Essentially, this is but the restatement of an ancient historic truth. Through the centuries the story of man's developing capacity to live happily on the face of the earth has been also, to an astonishing degree, the story of his evolving attitude toward the rest of nature and especially toward the land. It is a story that can be encompassed by three words descriptive of a recurring cycle: fear, adjustment, fulfillment.

Judging by the world's few remaining primitive peoples, it would appear that early man must have regarded with consuming fear the mighty forces of wild nature that swirled about him. To grasp the sensation one need only stand today before the Grand Canyon of the Colorado, or Niagara Falls, or the eruptions of Kilauea. Later, bit by bit, man went through adjustment to the great outdoors as he slowly came to see that he was indeed but a part

412. Even at timberline America's greatest national asset, a healthy land, normally maintains its own living vegetative cover.

of the whole scheme of nature. He learned that the tremendous powers of wild nature did not have to be feared as something hostile, so long as he acted with them rather than against them, resiliently and sensibly, using his inborn capacity for understanding.

Then at long last he seems to have achieved the blissful state of fulfillment, in which his attitude toward the rest of nature could honestly be described as *love of the land*. This joyous stage of development has fortunately come—and unfortunately gone—again and again in the long history of civilization. Love of the land: the trait that leads men to regard the land not as the "dirt under their feet" but as "Mother Earth." This is the attitude that has been the hallmark of human progress during many of the world's greatest ages. It is the earnest plea today of landscape architects and conservationists alike that, through dedication and the understanding now available, such an attitude may again one day become a normal characteristic. For in truth the opposite—disappearance of affection for the land—has also made its mark on the pages of history. Civilizations have perished through indifference to the values inherent in a well-husbanded earth, as the following tale illustrates.

What is meant by the common expression "living like a Sybarite?" The term has long signified living in the lap of luxury, because the ancient Greek city of Sybaris was in classical times the embodiment of all that was rich and extravagant. An American soldier thought of this one day during the early months of the Italian campaign in World War II as he stood at the edge of a flea-bitten hamlet on a height of land in the bottom of the Italian boot. All about him were the sinister, denuded hills of an incredibly grim terrain, sullen under the sunless late autumn sky. Below those barren Calabrian slopes, stretched out inert and lifeless along the Gulf of Taranto, lay the bleak expanse of a sodden coastal flood-plain. A far cry, he thought, from the "laughing, sunny Italy" he had known in other days, farther north.

As he stood, it came to him that here was a sample of what happens if men lose sight of what they have known about nature and about the land. Here was the very heart of onetime Magna Graecia, the opulent overseas colony of Greater Greece. Here had been hills covered with fine stands of forest reaching to a sparkling shore; here had been fields and vineyards, a veritable land of milk and honey, of culture and wealth. All too soon, the men of Magna Graecia had lost their touch with nature. They cut down the forests and neglected the land. The rains washed the topsoil down off the hills to form great plains of silt along the shore. Still more rains cut vagrant channels through the plains and then, having clogged the streams, brought floods and swamps and malaria, virtually destroying the land and rendering it unfit for man and beast. Though historians have diverse views of exactly what brought about the final downfall of Magna Graecia, they agree that the ravages of malaria were at least a major cause.

And what has this to do with "living like a Sybarite?" The little village where the soldier stood that day was known as Nuovo Sibari—New Sybaris; and somewhere hidden under that great plain below his eyes lay the remains of Sybaris, so completely vanished that archeologists hardly knew where to begin probing for it.[1] Sybaris, the richest city of Magna Graecia, the city whose name would go down through the centuries as a symbol of luxury—gone perhaps for all time except as a legend and as the memory of a name because men had lost their love of the land.

The sad example of Sybaris offers a lesson well worth remembering: a civilized outlook upon the land is to be acquired and held, not merely for its own sake, but because it has desirable consequences in human terms—and because its neglect can be disastrous. Vitally needed by every citizen is at least an elementary understanding of the processes of nature, including a grasp of how the individual can best fulfill his role as an organic part of the whole in a total ecology. He needs not only to see the forces of nature as helpmate rather than foe, he needs also to resolve not to use his increased knowledge

1. Twenty-five years after this occasion, in December 1968, archeologists reported having struck some underground and underwater walls that they believe may be the remains of the city of Sybaris.

of those forces, as modern technology too often does, to "conquer" and crush the natural environment itself. The achievement of optimum relations between people and environment requires something more than apathy on the part of the people—and certainly not destructiveness.

This highlights the earlier observation that anyone seeking to understand the basic meaning of landscape architecture needs to comprehend the importance of conservation, of the wise use of the land. Virtually every work of landscape architecture, whatever its dimensions, entails the wise use of a portion of the earth's surface. Even the smallest private garden, on close examination, reveals itself as a case of conservation in microcosm. For instance, why does one pave some areas in the garden? Because it is known that grass will not long stand up under the continued trampling of feet or the dragging of furniture. It is known that if the grass wears down to bare earth the moisture-retaining layer of interwoven, soil-binding roots and fibres will also soon be gone. The exposed soil will quickly start drying out, and before long the errant winds will blow that portion of the garden through the air as dust, to drop it where neither the owner nor anybody else wants it. Or the rain will run swiftly off the slick surface, carrying soil with it, and that small portion of the garden will go jauntily down the drain.

Is this not a miniature of what has actually happened to the American people on a national scale? The pioneers, understandably enough, cut down trees to cultivate crops for living. But for generations, with the westward movement of the frontier the hacking and bleeding of the land, beating it to a frazzle, has been continued heedlessly—there was always more fresh land, farther west. Like senseless profligates men mowed down the trees, allowed the forest floor to dry out, and aimlessly watched the rich topsoil wash away into the rivers. As the rivers became more and more silted up, and as the rains came rushing faster and faster off the badly cut-over upland slopes (Figs. 413–415), the nation suffered—and still suffers—disastrous floods. In other sections of the country the pasture lands were overgrazed, killing the natural grassy layer that would have absorbed and held the moisture and warmth of the sun. The great plains were overcultivated, using up and washing away at a prodigal rate the deep topsoil that had taken nature thousands of years to develop. The western winds in time moved in to lift the dry soil into airborne clouds and make deserts of the dust bowls (Fig. 416).

If this kind of catastrophe does not happen in someone's own sample private garden, isn't it simply because he has come to understand something of the processes of nature and to respect the action of its powerful forces, so that the cooling winds and the life-sustaining rains remain friends rather than enemies? He has learned, in that garden microcosm, to treat all of nature and the land with affection, honoring the stewardship that is man's privilege. In like fashion the outlook of the wider national scale does not have to be dark and hopeless. There, too, men have learned and can continue learning,

413. When upland slopes are stripped of trees, rains rush from the cut-over slopes and gullies begin.

414. Wrath among the grapes of California; too rapid mountain runoff did this.

415. Once begun, gully erosion can exact a ghastly toll.

416. Airborne clouds of soil make deserts: dust storm approaching Springfield, Colorado, May 1937.

417. Given a chance, the forest floor continually replenishes itself, even under unusual conditions: a rain forest in Olympic National Park.

especially from ecology. They need not perpetuate former follies, if they will just profit by the wisdom of the wise and by the bitterness of past experience.

Men have learned to take hints from the processes that wild nature herself uses when unimpeded, and to go along with these natural processes, aiding instead of ignoring or fighting them (Fig. 417). Men can see how neatly nature

418. Dying trees fall and turn to humus as a natural part of the life cycle in a forest; if pressed to earth, the "dead-and-down" are not a fire hazard.

provides volunteer growth when fire has cut a gash in the woodland. When they take timber from the forests they now know how to cut selectively, leaving some trees intact to maintain a continuing cycle of growth and planting new trees in sound programs of reforestation, especially on lands

419. East of Boise, Idaho: terraces and contour furrows enable fields to hold water and thus keep their topsoil.

that are submarginal for general agriculture. By leaving the understory in place, to follow the natural processes of decay, they permit the forest floor to replenish itself with essential organic matter (Fig. 418). All of these measures help the land retain its moisture in the soil, where it is needed, instead of letting the rains run off in a gully-gouging rush. They reinforce wild nature's phenomenal capacity to be her healthy self when free from man's heavy-handed stupidities; moreover, by following natural processes, man can restore or at least retain the normal habitat of wild animal life. Indeed, these methods contribute to the maintenance of the remarkable dynamic equilibrium of flora and fauna called *biotic balance.*

To similar effect in croplands, farmers have learned to plow along the contours instead of making channels up and down the slopes. With cover crops, strip farming, terraces, and other common-sense techniques, cultivated fields can hold the water that falls on them—and thus hold the soil (Fig. 419). By means of check-dams and storage basins, some headway can be made toward controlling in streams the runoff from upland heights. In the United States, thanks to efforts of the Soil Conservation Service and to formation of sensible conservancy districts in several states, appreciable steps have been

420. Toward healing the wounds: a severely gullied tract in Georgia was planted with kudzu vine, following nature's own method of recovery.

421. The tract in the preceding figure after three seasons of kudzu growth.

made toward healing the wounds that a once-reckless agriculture inflicted on the land (Figs. 420, 421).

In the wise use of land for agricultural production, then, man's improving ability to behave intelligently as a participant in the natural order has been demonstrated. Yet here is another supreme irony. Even while exhibiting this degree of agricultural enlightenment, Americans somehow permit a cancerous invasion by developers' subdivisions to usurp prime agricultural lands from the Atlantic to the Pacific. The potato and truck-garden farms of Long Island, the dairy farms and citrus groves of California, for example, are sacrificed wholesale to the greed of real-estate operators insensitive to the value of anything but the dollars in their pockets. The ultimate loss to society developers of this breed apparently consider none of their business.

Though men have advanced commendably in saving land through soil conservation, they seem strangely helpless before the depredations committed against the streams on the land and the air above it. They appear unable to discipline themselves into reducing the number of motorcars that foul the atmosphere, unable to combat with much effect the industries that spew their wastes into the air and water of the land, reaping financial gain at the cost of the nation's health (Figs. 422, 423). In this problem, for a change, there is no dilemma; the simple answer is recapture and preservation of the purity of air and water that existed only a few short decades ago. This in turn means prevention—and it may mean prosecution, given the courage to insist on defense of a clean environment. Surely this is one of America's most monumental challenges.

Unhappily, Americans still tend to pursue a psychology of cataclysm in these matters, doing nothing until some crisis arises and then bursting forth with typical energy. What a difference it would make if every citizen were to use his franchise to demand a rational policy of steady progress along lines of proven efficacy. The fault lies not in ignorance about what to do but in inertia about doing it, in time. Nevertheless, strides have been made in the sensible growing of foodstuffs, livestock, and trees. Americans have become alarmed at last, though certainly not enough, over the despoiling of their air and water. But they have lagged behind in general comprehension of some other aspects of conservation that can directly affect one's enjoyment of the land. The active role of the animal world in the biotic balance of nature is well understood by relatively few. Particularly lacking is a grasp of the predator-prey relationship, one of nature's most fascinating systems of checks and balances, and of the way this often ties in with vegetation, especially when man interferes with natural processes of the wild.

The famous tale is told fairly often, almost always with an aura of disbelief, of the Kaibab deer on the north rim of the Grand Canyon: of how ex-President Theodore Roosevelt in 1913, with the best of intentions, encouraged the hunting of cougar in the Kaibab because these "murderers" were preying

422. Air pollution: even mile-high Denver has a smothering smog to combat.

423. In mountain creeks the clear water starts, then man's industry pollutes it in the rivers; Virginia's historic James is already fouled at Lynchburg.

upon the deer; how the cougar were soon slaughtered and the deer, no longer kept in check by their major enemy, multiplied abnormally, eating themselves out of house and home, and then within a few years began to die of starvation. A well-meant interference turned into a major conservation disaster. The predator-prey relationship was simply not understood in 1913.

The less well known and less ravenous tale of a swamp at the end of an upland lake in an eastern state park might also be considered. Residents in nearby towns were proud of the swamp for its remarkable masses of large buttonbush (*Cephalanthus occidentalis*), but they also complained that it was a mosquito-breeding hazard. When the complaints grew too insistent the park authorities drained the swamp, or tried to. The buttonbush, which likes its feet in water, dried out and died. Small fish, which had previously fed on the mosquito larvae, could no longer survive in the puddles of stagnant water left behind. But the larvae could and did—producing more mosquitos than before. Flooding the swamp slightly would have been wiser. As it was, failure to follow nature's processes resulted in loss of the handsome buttonbush and obviously no solution to the mosquito scare.

Aside from the inroads man can make on animal populations by shooting, even risking the extinction of some species, the harm done to wildlife by humans is generally not malicious but rather the consequence of well-intentioned but ill-advised interferences with the normal processes of nature. The key to action here is simple: leave well enough alone. On the whole, biotic balance in the natural world is such a magnificent symphony of inter-woven, mutually supportive activities that what is sound conservation for fields and forests is most often best for wildlife, too (Fig. 424). And perhaps of greatest importance, such a harmony is best for the human values involved: for the education, inspiration, and sheer enjoyment that humans derive from observing, and sharing, the healthy totality of nature.

Full human values—the aspects of conservation that transcend even skill at agricultural production, that are immediately associable with conservation measures in those vast scenic areas, the national parks. Measures that preserve the sights and scents and sounds of the untrammeled wild, and the humbling experience of great solitudes. This points up the truth referred to early in this book: the human requirement of sustenance for the *whole* man, not just food for the stomach. Sooner or later, it was suggested, man would not be content with edibles alone, but would find the joy of using all the senses to nourish his inner self. Add to this his sense of satisfaction from understanding better the ways of nature and from seeing more clearly his integral place within the great scheme of things.

It is in this national park situation that the unity of conservation and landscape architecture can perhaps best be comprehended. The accepted policy of optimum relations between people and environment makes rigorous demands on both fields. But landscape architecture has the additional duty of providing necessary spaces and facilities for human accommodation. To

424. Biotic balance, the natural condition of undisturbed fauna and flora in the wild: Canada geese in the Yellowstone.

solve this phase of man's participation in the natural scene, the landscape architect employs design—the intimate concern for specific form and spatial structure that is an indispensable component of landscape architecture. But it must not be supposed that the manmade forms introduced by design escape the test of wise use; indeed, if the design process is soundly handled, the forms it evolves will themselves induce wise human behavior on the land, for such is the paramount power of design.

In their attitude toward the vast natural order of which man is an organic part, the American people have traveled in only a few generations well up the path of a small cycle: fear, then adjustment, now toward fulfillment. The ultimate historic stage can be reached only with *will*. It is within man's power truly to love the land, if he will but allow this latent affection to come into flower and bear fruit. What is required, of course, is not only to make popular understanding of the natural world more widespread; more crucially needed is a firm belief in the value—in human terms, rather than in mere dollars—of a healthy, vibrant earth, and then the determination to achieve it.

To the attainment of such a goal, the epitome of success in conservation, landscape architecture is fundamentally dedicated. A hope for similar dedication on the part of the reader was a major reason for the conviction, expressed at the outset of this book, that a sympathetic understanding of the development of landscape architecture can bring new richness to the life of an intelligent citizen. If all men join in commitment to this high purpose—seeking complete rapport between people and their environments on the face of the earth—then each nation can indeed have a happy land; and our civilization need not fear the fate of Sybaris.

Select Bibliography
Acknowledgments
Illustration Credits
Index

Select Bibliography

General

Giedion, Sigfried. *Space, Time and Architecture,* 5th ed. Cambridge: Harvard University Press, 1967.

Hamlin, Talbot. *Architecture through the Ages.* New York: G. P. Putnam's Sons, 1940.

Hubbard, Henry Vincent, and Theodora Kimball. *An Introduction to the Study of Landscape Design.* New York: Macmillan, 1917.

Newton, Norman T. *An Approach to Design.* Cambridge: Addison-Wesley Press, 1951.

Peets, Elbert. "The Landscape Priesthood," *The American Mercury,* January 1927, pp. 94–100.

Pond, Bremer Whidden. *Outline History of Landscape Architecture.* Cambridge, Mass.: privately printed, 1936.

Tillinghast, William H., trans. *Ploetz Manual of Universal History.* Boston: Houghton Mifflin, 1925.

Wells, H. G. *The Outline of History.* New York: Macmillan, 1921.

I. Ancient Times

Badawy, Alexander. *A History of Egyptian Architecture: The Empire (The New Kingdom).* Berkeley: University of California Press, 1968.

Blanckenhagen, Peter H. von. "The Imperial Fora," *Journal of the Society of Architectural Historians,* vol. 13, no 4 (1954), 21–26.

Bühlmann, Josef, and Alexander von Wagner. *Das alte Rom mit dem Triumphzuge Kaiser Constantins im Jahre 312 nach Cristi.* Munich: Franz Hanfstaengl, 1903.

Crema, Luigi. *L'Architettura Romana,* Book I, vol. 12, pt. 3: *Enciclopedia Classica.* Milan: Società Editrice Internazionale, 1959.

Gerkan, Arnim von. *Griechische Städteanlagen.* Berlin: W. de Gruyter & Co., 1924.

Giuliano, Antonio. *Urbanistica delle Città Greche.* Milan: Casa Editrice Saggiatore, 1966.

Gothein, Marie Luise. *A History of Garden Art,* trans. Mrs. Archer-Hind. London: J. M. Dent & Sons, 1928. Chapters i–iv.

Hanfmann, George M. A. *Roman Art: A Modern Survey of the Art of Imperial Rome.* New York: New York Graphic Society, 1966.

Harte, Geoffrey Bret. *The Villas of Pliny.* Boston: Houghton Mifflin, 1928.

Lugli, Giuseppe. *Roma Antica: Il Centro Monumentale.* Rome: Bardi, 1946.

Mumford, Lewis. *The City in History.* New York: Harcourt, Brace, & World, 1961.

Naville, Edouard. *The Temple of Deir-el-Bahari.* London: Egypt Exploration Fund, 1908.

Perrot, Georges, and Charles Chipiez. *A History of Art in Ancient Egypt,* trans W. Armstrong. London: Chapman and Hall, 1883.

Price, Thomas D. "Horace's Sabine Villa," *Memoirs of the American Academy in Rome,* 10 (1932), 135–142.

Rosellini, Ippolito. *I Monumenti dell'Egitto e della Nubia.* Pisa: N. Capurro, 1832–1844.

Showerman, Grant. *Monuments and Men of Ancient Rome.* New York: Appleton-Century, 1937.

Smith, W. Stevenson. *The Art and Architecture of Ancient Egypt.* Baltimore: Penguin Books, 1958.

Tanzer, Helen H. *The Villas of Pliny the Younger.* New York: Columbia University Press, 1924.

Thompson, Dorothy Burr, and Ralph E. Griswold. *Garden Lore of Ancient Athens.* Princeton: American School of Classical Studies at Athens, 1963.

Whycherley, R. E. *How the Greeks Built Cities.* London: Macmillan, 1949.

II. Middle Ages

Crisp, Frank. *Medieval Gardens.* London: John Lane, 1924.

Gothein, Marie Luise. *A History of Garden Art,* trans. Mrs. Archer-Hind. London: J. M. Dent & Sons, 1928. Chapter vi.

Mumford, Lewis. *The City in History,* New York: Harcourt, Brace, & World, 1961.

Thompson, James Westfall. *History of the Middle Ages.* New York: W. W. Norton Co., 1931.

Triggs, H. Inigo. *Garden Craft in Europe.* London: B. T. Batsford, 1913. Chapter ii.

Zucker, Paul. *Town and Square.* New York: Columbia University Press, 1959.

III, IV. Islam

Byne, Arthur, and Mildred Stapley Byne. *Spanish Gardens and Patios.* Philadelphia: J. B. Lippincott Co., 1924.

Goodhue, Bertram Grosvenor. *A Book of Architectural and Decorative Drawings.* New York: Architectural Book Publishing Co., 1914.

Gothein, Marie Luise. *A History of Garden Art,* trans. Mrs. Archer-Hind. London: J. M. Dent & Sons, 1928. Chapter v.

Gromort, Georges. *Jardins d'Espagne.* Paris: Vincent, Fréal & Cie., 1926.

Ingalls, George F. "The Generalife," *Landscape Architecture* 14 (October 1923), 1–14.

Pope, Arthur Upham. *An Introduction to Persian Art.* London: Peter Davies, 1930.

Triggs, H. Inigo. *Garden Craft in Europe.* London: B. T. Batsford, 1913. Chapter x.

Wilber, Donald N. *Persian Gardens and Garden Pavilions.* Tokyo: Charles E. Tuttle, 1962.

V–X. Italy

Ackerman, James S. *The Cortile del Belvedere.* Vatican: Biblioteca Apostolica Vaticana, 1954.

────── *Palladio's Villas.* Locust Valley, New York: J. J. Augustin, 1967.

Brinckmann, Albert E. *Platz und Monument.* Berlin: Wasmuth, 1908.

Cantoni, Angelo. *La Villa Lante di Bagnaia.* Milan: Electa Editrice, 1961.

Coffin, David. *The Villa d'Este at Tivoli.* Princeton: Princeton University Press, 1960.

Dami, Luigi. *The Italian Garden,* trans. L. Scopoli. Milan: Bestetti e Tumminelli, 1925.

Davis, E. Gorton. "Villas of the Italian Lakes: Balbianello," *Landscape Architecture,* 12 (April 1922), 136–147.

Ernouf, Alfred Auguste, and Adolphe Alphand. *L'Art des Jardins.* Paris: Rothschild, 1868.

Falda, Giovanni Battista. *Li Giardini di Roma.* Rome: alla Pace, n.d.

Gardner, Edmund G. *The Story of Florence,* 10th ed. London: J. M. Dent's Sons, 1924.

Griswold, Ralph E. "Villa Caprarola, the Upper Garden," *Landscape Architecture,* 13 (January 1923), 106–121.

Gromort, Georges. *Choix de Plans de Grandes Compositions Exécutées.* Paris: Vincent, Fréal & Cie., 1910.

Latham, Charles. *The Gardens of Italy.* London: Country Life, 1905.

Lawson, Edward G. "Villa Gamberaia," *Landscape Architecture,* 8 (January 1918), 76.

———— "The Cascade in Villa Torlonia at Frascati," *Landscape Architecture,* 11 (July 1921), 186–188.

Le Blond, Aubrey. *The Old Gardens of Italy: How to Visit Them.* London: B. T. Batsford, 1912.

Mori, Attilio, and Giuseppe Boffito. *Firenze nelle Vedute e Piante.* Florence: Seeber Libreria Internazionale, 1926.

Newton, Norman T. "Villa Medici at Fiesole," *Landscape Architecture,* 17 (April 1927), 184–198.

———— "In a Roman Villa Garden (Villa Chigi)," *House and Garden,* 52 (October 1927), 116, 206, 216.

Percier, Charles, and Pierre F. L. Fontaine. *Choix des plus Célèbres Maisons de Plaisance de Rome et de ses Environs,* 2nd ed. Paris: Didot, 1824.

Shepherd, J. C., and Geoffrey A. Jellicoe. *Italian Gardens of the Renaissance.* London: Ernest Benn, 1925.

Sitte, Camillo. *L'Art de Bâtir les Villes.* Geneva: Eggiman, 1902.

Triggs, H. Inigo. *The Art of Garden Design in Italy.* London: Longmans Green & Co., 1906.

Wharton, Edith. *Italian Villas and their Gardens.* New York: The Century Co., 1910.

Williams, Edgar I. "Isola Bella," *Landscape Architecture,* 4 (July 1914), 167–170.

Zocchi, Giuseppe. *Vedute delle Ville e d'Altri Luoghi della Toscana.* Florence, 1744.

Zucker, Paul. *Town and Square.* New York: Columbia University Press, 1959.

XI–XII. France

Du Cerceau, Jacques Androuet. *Les plus excellents Bastiments de France.* Paris, 1579. Facsimile ed. by H. Destailleur, Paris: A. Lévy, 1870.

Gothein, Marie Luise. *A History of Garden Art.* trans. Mrs. Archer-Hind London: J. M. Dent & Sons, 1928. Chapters ix, xii.

Gromort, Georges. *Choix de Plans de Grandes Compositions Exécutées.* Paris: Vincent, Fréal & Cie., 1910.

Lansdale, Maria Hornor. *The Châteaux of Touraine.* New York: Century Co., 1906.

Nolhac, Pierre de. *Les Jardins de Versailles.* Paris: Henri Floury, 1924.

———— *La Création de Versailles.* Versailles: L. Bernard, 1901.

Pean, P. *Jardins de France.* Paris: Vincent, Fréal & Cie., 1925.

Pfnor, Rodolphe. *Le Château de Vaux-le-Vicomte.* Paris: Lemercier, 1888.

Triggs, H. Inigo. *Garden Craft in Europe.* London: B. T. Batsford, 1913. Chapters iv, v.

XIII–XV. England

Allen, B. Sprague. *Tides in English Taste.* Cambridge: Harvard University Press, 1937.

Campbell, Colen. *Vitruvius Britannicus: Or, the British Architect.* London, 1731.

Clifford, Derek. *A History of Garden Design.* London: Faber and Faber, 1962.

Gilpin, William S. *Practical Hints on Landscape Gardening.* London: T. Cadell, 1832.

[Kip, Johannes]. *Nouveau Théatre de la Grande Bretagne,* 3 vols. London: D. Mortier, 1713–1716.

Loudon, J. C. *The Suburban Gardener and Villa Companion.* London: Longman, Orme, Brown, Green, and Longmans, 1838.

——— *The Landscape Gardening and Landscape Architecture of the late Humphry Repton, Esq.* London: Longman & Co., 1840.

——— *The Villa Gardener,* 2nd ed. Mrs. Loudon. London: Wm. S. Orr & Co., 1850.

Price, Uvedale. *An Essay on the Picturesque.* London: Robson, 1794–1798.

Repton, Humphry. *The Art of Landscape Gardening,* ed. John Nolen. Boston: Houghton Mifflin, 1907.

Shepherd, J. C., and Geoffrey A. Jellicoe. *Gardens and Design.* London: Ernest Benn, 1927.

Stroud, Dorothy. *Humphry Repton.* London: Country Life, 1925.

——— *Capability Brown.* London: Country Life, 1950.

Tipping, H. Avray. *English Homes,* 8 vols. London: Country Life, 1920–1937.

——— *English Gardens.* London: Country Life, 1925.

Triggs, H. Inigo. *Formal Gardens in England and Scotland.* London: B. T. Batsford, 1902.

Whately, Thomas. *Observations on Modern Gardening.* London, 1771.

XVI. Transition to Public Service

Chadwick, George F. *The Works of Sir Joseph Paxton, 1803–1865.* London: Architectural Press, 1961.

——— *The Park and the Town: Public Landscape in the 19th and 20th Centuries.* London: Architectural Press, 1966.

Church, Richard. *The Royal Parks of London.* London: Her Majesty's Stationery Office, 1965.

Ernouf, Alfred Auguste, and Adolphe Alphand. *L'Art des Jardins.* Paris: Rothschild, 1868.

Fein, Albert. "Victoria Park: Its Origins and History," *East London Papers,* 5 (October 1962), 73–90.

Olmsted, Frederick Law. *Walks and Talks of an American Farmer in England.* London: David Bogue, 1852.

——— *Forty Years of Landscape Architecture,* I: *Early Years,* ed. Frederick Law Olmsted, Jr., and Theodora Kimball Hubbard. New York: G. P. Putnam's Sons, 1922. Cited as *Olmsted Papers: Early Years.*

Reilly, Sir Charles, and N. J. Aslan. *Outline Plan for the County Borough of Birkenhead.* Birkenhead, 1947.

XVII. Pückler-Muskau and Alphand

Alphand, Jean Charles Adolphe. *Les Promenades de Paris.* Paris: J. Rothschild, 1867–1873.

Chapman, J. M., and Brian Chapman. *The Life and Times of Baron Haussmann.* London: Weidenfeld & Nicolson, 1957.

Gross, Felix. *Grand Seigneur: The Life and Loves of Prince Hermann Pückler-Muskau.* New York: Creative Press, 1943.

Haussmann, Georges Eugène. *Memoires du Baron Haussmann.* Paris: Victor-Havard, 1893.

Olmsted, Frederick Law. *Forty Years of Landscape Architecture,* II: *Central Park,* ed. F. L. Olmsted, Jr., and Theodora K. Hubbard. New York: G. P. Putnam's Sons, 1928. Cited as *Olmsted Papers: Central Park.*

Pückler-Muskau, Prince Hermann Ludwig Heinrich von. *Hints on Landscape Gardening,* trans. Bernhardt Sickert, ed. Samuel Parsons. Boston: Houghton Mifflin, 1917.

XVIII. Early American Backgrounds

American Society of Landscape Architects. *Colonial Gardens: The Landscape Architecture of George Washington's Time.* Washington, D.C.: U. S. George Washington Bicentennial Commission, 1932.

Betts, Edwin Morris, ed. *Thomas Jefferson's Garden Book: 1766–1824.* Philadelphia: Memoirs of the American Philosophical Society, vol. 22, 1944.

Downing, Andrew Jackson. *A Treatise on the Theory and Practice of Landscape Gardening Adapted to North America.* New York: Wiley and Putnam, 1841.

Eberlein, Harold Donaldson. *The Manors and Historic Homes of the Hudson Valley.* Philadelphia: J. B. Lippincott Co., 1924.

——— *Manor Houses and Historic Homes of Long Island and Staten Island.* Philadelphia: J. B. Lippincott Co., 1928.

Frary, I. T. *Thomas Jefferson, Architect and Builder.* Richmond: Garrett and Massie, 1931.

Garden Club of Virginia. *Houses and Gardens of Old Virginia.* Richmond: J. W. Fergusson & Sons, 1930.

Kimball, Fiske. *Domestic Architecture of the American Colonies and of the Early Republic.* New York: Charles Scribner's Sons, 1927.

Lambeth, William Alexander, and Warren H. Manning. *Thomas Jefferson as an Architect and a Designer of Landscapes.* Boston: Houghton Mifflin, 1913.

Lockwood, Alice G. B., *Gardens of Colony and State.* New York: Scribner's, 1934.

Morison, Samuel Eliot. *The Oxford History of the American People.* New York: Oxford University Press, 1965.

Root, R. R., and G. R. Forbes. "Notes upon a Colonial Garden, at Salem, Mass.," *Landscape Architecture,* 2 (October 1911), 16–20.

Sale, Edith Tunis, ed. *Historic Gardens of Virginia.* Richmond: James River Garden Club, 1923.

Wilstach, Paul. *Mount Vernon: Washington's Home and the Nation's Shrine.* New York: Doubleday Page & Co., 1916.

XIX. Central and Prospect Parks

Brooklyn, City of. Board of Park Commissioners. *Annual Reports,* 1861–1896.

Central Park, Board of Commissioners of the. *Annual Reports,* 1857–1870.

New York, City of. Department of Public Parks. *Annual Reports of the Board of Commissioners,* 1871–1906.

Olmsted Papers: *Early Years.*

Olmsted Papers: *Central Park.*

Olmsted, Frederick Law. "The Yosemite Valley and the Mariposa Big Tree Grove," *Landscape Architecture,* 43 (October 1952), 12–25.

XX. Olmsted's Work in Boston

Baxter, Sylvester. *Boston Park Guide.* Boston: Small, Maynard & Co., 1898.

Boston, City of. Board of Park Commissioners. *Annual Reports,* 1876–1905.

——— *Notes on the Plan of Franklin Park.* Boston, 1886.

Olmsted Papers: *Early Years.*

Olmsted, John C. "The Boston Park System," *Transactions of the ASLA,* vol. I (1899–1908).

XXI. Weidenmann and Cleveland

Cleveland, Horace William Shaler. *Public Grounds in Chicago: How to Give Them Character and Expression.* Chicago: C. D. Lakey, 1869.

——— *Landscape Architecture: As Applied to the Wants of the West.* Chicago: Jansen, McClurg & Co., 1873.

——— *Suggestions for a System of Parks and Parkways for the City of Minneapolis.* Minneapolis: Johnson, Smith & Harrison, 1883.

—————— *Public Parks, Radial Avenues, and Boulevards: Outline Plan of a Park System for the City of St. Paul.* St. Paul: Globe Office, 1885.

—————— *Park Systems of St. Paul and Minneapolis.* St. Paul: H. M. Smyth, 1887.

Copeland, Robert Morris, and H. W. S. Cleveland. *A Few Words on the Central Park.* Boston, 1856.

Hubbard, Theodora Kimball. "H. W. S. Cleveland, an American Pioneer in Landscape Architecture and City Planning," *Landscape Architecture,* 20 (January 1930), 92–111.

Isaacs, Reginald R. *Goals for 2012: A Retrospective and Prospective View of the Twin Cities.* Minneapolis: University of Minnesota School of Architecture, 1962.

Kimball, Theodora. "American Landscape Gardening in 1857," *Landscape Architecture,* 12 (January 1922), 99–106.

McNamara, Katherine. *Notes on Jacob Weidenmann.* Cambridge, Mass.: mimeograph, n. d.

Minneapolis, City of. Board of Park Commissioners. *Annual Reports,* 1884–1900.

Olmsted Papers: *Early Years.*

XXII. Charles Eliot

Baxter, Sylvester. "Thirty Years of Greater Boston's Metropolitan Park System," *Boston Transcript,* September 29, 1923.

Eliot, Charles William. *Charles Eliot, Landscape Architect.* Boston: Houghton Mifflin, 1902. Cited as Eliot: *Charles Eliot.*

Massachusetts, Commonwealth of. *House No. 150: Report of the Board of Metropolitan Park Commissioners, 1893.*

—————— Board of Metropolitan Park Commissioners. *Annual Reports,* 1893–1898.

XXIII. Single-Track Eclecticism

Biltmore Company. *Biltmore House and Gardens.* Asheville N.C.: The Biltmore Company, 1959.

Early, James. *Romanticism and American Architecture.* New York: A. S. Barnes & Co., 1965.

Lamb, Martha J. *The Homes of America.* New York: D. Appleton, 1879.

Moore, Charles. *The Life and Times of Charles Follen McKim.* Boston: Houghton Mifflin, 1929. Cited as Moore: *McKim.*

Olmsted Papers: *Early Years.*

XXIV. Columbian Exposition 1893

Chicago, City of. South Park Commissioners. *Annual Reports,* 1871–1906.

Chicago Record. *The Chicago Record's History of the World's Fair.* Chicago: Daily News Co., 1893.

Coles, William A., ed. *Architecture and Society: Selected Essays of Henry Van Brunt.* Cambridge: Harvard University Press, 1969.

Johnson, Rossiter, ed. *A History of the World's Columbian Exposition.* New York: D. Appleton & Co., 1897.

Monroe, Harriet. *John Wellborn Root.* Boston: Houghton Mifflin, 1896.

Moore, Charles. *Daniel Hudson Burnham: Architect, Planner of Cities.* Boston: Houghton Mifflin, 1921. Cited as Moore: *Burnham.*

Moore: *McKim.*

Mumford, Lewis. *Roots of Contemporary American Architecture.* New York: Reinhold Publishing Co., 1952.

Olmsted, Frederick Law. "The Landscape Architecture of the World's Columbian Exposition," *Proceedings of the 27th Annual Convention of the A.I.A.* Chicago, 1893.

Olmsted, F. L. & Co., John W. Root, and D. H. Burnham. *Report to Joint Committee on Site.* Chicago, 1890.

Olmsted Papers: *Early Years.*

Sullivan, Louis H. *The Autobiography of an Idea.* New York: Press of the A.I.A., 1924.

XXV. Charles A. Platt

Eliot: *Charles Eliot.* Pages 547–549.

Lay, Charles Downing. "An Interview with Charles A. Platt," *Landscape Architecture,* 2 (January 1912), 127–131.

Platt, Charles A. *Italian Gardens.* New York: Harper & Bros., 1894.

—————— *Monograph of the Work of Charles A. Platt,* intro. Royal Cortissoz. New York: Architectural Book Publishing Co., 1913.

XXVI. Founding of ASLA

American Society of Landscape Architects. *Transactions of the ASLA,* vol. I (1899–1908), vol. II (1909–1921), vol. III (1922–1926).

—————— Official Files. Resolution on the Death of Daniel W. Langton, 1909.

—————— Memorial Minutes, *Landscape Architecture,* 10 (April 1920), 109–113 (Barrett); 12 (April 1922), 129–135 (J. C. Olmsted); 14 (July 1924), 231–234 (Parsons); 16 (July 1926), 280–281 (Vaux); 22 (April 1932), 234–235 (Simonds); 28 (April 1938), 148–149 (Manning); 30 (April 1940), 123–124 (Lowrie); 48 (April 1958), 144–157 (F. L. Olmsted); 49 (Summer 1959), 216–224 (Farrand).

Eliot: *Charles Eliot.* page 703.

Pond, Bremer Whidden. "Fifty Years in Retrospect: Brief Account of the Origin and Development of the ASLA," *Landscape Architecture,* 40 (January 1950), 59–66.

XXVII. American Academy in Rome

American Academy in Rome. *Annual and Quinquennial Reports.* New York and Rome: American Academy in Rome 1914–1969.

La Farge, C. Grant. *History of the American Academy in Rome.* New York: American Academy in Rome, 1915.

La Farge, C. Grant, *et al. The American Academy in Rome: Twenty-fifth Anniversary MCMXX.* New York: American Academy in Rome, 1920.

Moore: *Burnham.*

Moore: *McKim.*

XXVIII. McMillan Commission of 1901

Caemmerer, H. Paul. *Historic Washington: Capital of the Nation.* Washington: The Columbia Historical Society, 1948.

Fine Arts, Commission of. *Thirteenth Report.* 76th Congress, 3rd Session, House Document No. 648.

Moore: *Burnham.*

Moore: *McKim.*

XXIX. City Beautiful Movement

Adams, James W. R. *Modern Town and Country Planning*. London: J. & A. Churchill, 1952.

American Society of Landscape Architects. "Minute on the Life and Services of Charles Mulford Robinson, Associate Member," *Landscape Architecture,* 9 (July 1919), 180–193.

Burnham, Daniel H. *Report of D. H. Burnham on the Improvement and Adornment of San Francisco*. San Francisco: City of San Francisco, 1905.

——— *Report on Proposed Improvements at Manila, June 28, 1905*. Washington: Government Printing Office, 1906.

Burnham, Daniel H., and Edward H. Bennett. *Plan of Chicago*. Chicago: The Commercial Club, 1909.

Moody, Walter D. *Wacker's Manual of the Plan of Chicago*. Chicago: Chicago Plan Commission, 1920.

Moore: *Burnham.*

Nolen, John, ed. *City Planning*. New York: Appleton & Co., 1915.

Robinson, Charles Mulford. *The Improvement of Towns and Cities*. New York: G. P. Putnam's Sons, 1901.

——— *Modern Civic Art*. New York: G. P. Putnam's Sons, 1903.

XXX. Country Place Era

American Society of Landscape Architects. *Illustrations of Work of Members*. New York: House of J. Hayden Twiss, 1931–1934.

——— Memorial Minutes, *Landscape Architecture,* 23 (July 1933), 219–220 (Vitale); 24 (October 1933), 1–4 (Greenleaf); 24 (April 1934), 166–168 (Gallagher); 37 (October 1946), 29–30 (Flanders); 37 (January 1947), 57–59 (Fleming); 47 (April 1957), 431–432 (Coffin); 48 (October 1957), 48–49 (Geiffert). Also *ASLA Bulletin,* no. 105, August 1962 (Whiting).

Caldwell, Alfred. "Jens Jensen: The Prairie Spirit," *Landscape Architecture,* 51 (January 1961), 102–105.

Eaton, Leonard K. *Landscape Artist in America: The Life and Work of Jens Jensen*. Chicago: University of Chicago Press, 1964.

Elwood, Philip H., ed. *American Landscape Architecture*. New York: Architectural Book Publishing Company, 1924.

Fleming, Bryant. "Views in Estates and Gardens at Grosse Pointe, Michigan," *Landscape Architecture,* 19 (January 1929), 84–90.

Jensen, Jens. *Siftings*. Chicago: Ralph Fletcher Seymour, 1939.

Miller, Wilhelm. *The Prairie Spirit in Landscape Gardening*. Urbana: University of Illinois, 1915.

Whiting, Edward Clark. "The Gardens at Ormston." *Landscape Architecture,* 28 (July 1938), 191–199.

XXXI. English Town Planning

Adams, James W. R. *Modern Town and Country Planning*. London: J. & A. Churchill, 1952.

Bournville Village Trust. *The Bournville Village Trust, 1900–1955*. Bournville: The Village Trust, 1955.

Buckingham, James Silk. *National Evils and Practical Remedies: With the Plan of a Model Town*. London: P. Jackson, 1849.

Cadbury Brothers. *Bournville 1924*. Bournville: Cadbury Brothers, 1924.

Creese, Walter L. *The Search for Environment: The Garden City, Before and After*. New Haven: Yale University Press, 1966.

Davison, T. Raffles. *Port Sunlight: A Record of its Artistic and Pictorial Aspect.* London: B. T. Batsford, 1916.

Frankl, Mrs. D., ed. *Welwyn Garden City, Hertfordshire.* London: J. Burrow & Co., 1953–1954.

Howard, Ebenezer. *Tomorrow: A Peaceful Path to Real Reform.* London: Swan Sonnenschein, 1898 (2nd ed. entitled *Garden Cities of Tomorrow*).

Lever, W. H. *The Buildings Erected at Port Sunlight and Thornton Hough.* London: Architectural Association, 1902.

Osborn, F. J. *Green-belt Cities: The British Contribution.* London: Faber & Faber, 1946.

Purdom, C. B. *The Building of Satellite Towns.* London: J. M. Dent's Sons, 1925.

——— *The Letchworth Achievement.* London: J. M. Dent's Sons, 1963.

Turner, Ralph E. *James Silk Buckingham, 1786–1855; A Social Biography.* London: Williams & Norgate, 1934.

XXXII. Town Planning in the United States: 1869 to 1915

Bush, Donald W. Letters for Hare and Hare, Inc., to Norman T. Newton, May 17 and 27, 1968.

Comey, Arthur C., and Max S. Wehrly. *Planned Communities,* pt. 1, vol. II: *Urban Planning and Land Policies,* Supplementary Report of Urbanism Committee of National Resources Committee. Washington: U. S. Government Printing Office, 1939. Cited as *Comey: Planned Communities.* Authoritative for all communities until and including Greenbelt.

Fuller, S. S., *et al. Riverside Then and Now.* Riverside: The Riverside News, 1936.

Glenn, John M., *et al. Russell Sage Foundation: 1907–1946.* New York: Russell Sage Foundation, 1947.

"J. C. Nichols Number" of the *National Real Estate Journal,* February 1939.

Menhinick, Howard K. "Riverside Sixty Years Later," *Landscape Architecture,* 22 (January 1932), 109–117.

Mowbray, John McC. Letter regarding Roland Park Company to Norman T. Newton, May 14, 1968.

Olmsted, Frederick Law. "Riverside, Illinois: A Residential Neighborhood Designed Over Sixty Years Ago," selections from the papers of Olmsted & Vaux, *Landscape Architecture,* 21 (July 1931), 256–291.

Simmons, George B. *A Book of Pictures in Roland Park.* Baltimore: George B. Simmons, 1912.

Tourtelot, George. Photocopies from J. C. Nichols' Scrapbooks, May 1968.

Whitmer, Robert E. Letter for J. C. Nichols Company to Norman T. Newton, May 13, 1968.

XXXIII. Town Planning in the United States: 1915 to 1929

Chamber of Commerce. *Longview, Washington.* Longview: Longview Chamber of Commerce, 1933.

Chicopee Manufacturing Company. *Chicopee, Georgia.* Chicopee: Chicopee Manufacturing Company, 1927.

——— "The Story of Chicopee Companies," reprinted from *Textile Age,* December 1949, n.p.

——— *This Is Chicopee.* New York: Chicopee Manufacturing Company, 1960.

——— "Chicopee Celebrates 50 Years with J & J," *Johnson & Johnson Bulletin,* 24 (May-June 1966), 10–12.

Comey: *Planned Communities.*

Draper, Earle Sumner. "Southern Textile Village Planning," *Landscape Architecture,* 18 (October 1927), 1–28.

——— Letters regarding Chicopee to Norman T. Newton, June 16, 21, July 2, 6, 1968.

Hare, S. Herbert. "The Planning of a New Industrial City," *American City,* 29 (November 1923), 501–503.

Lambuth, B. L. "A Small City Whose Growth is Aided and Controlled by a Plan," *American City,* 35 (August 1926), 186–191.

McClelland, John M., Jr. *Longview.* Portland: Binfords & Mort, 1949.

Mariemont Company. *A Descriptive and Pictured Story of Mariemont.* Cincinnati: The Mariemont Company, 1925.

Nolen, John. *New Towns for Old.* Boston: Marshall Jones Co., 1927.

Parks, Warren Wright. *The Mariemont Story.* Cincinnati: Creative Writers, 1967.

Stein, Clarence S. *Toward New Towns for America.* Liverpool: Liverpool University Press, 1951. (American edition, Reinhold Publishing Corporation, 1957.)

XXXIV. Town Planning in the United States: 1929 to 1948

Augur, Tracy B. "The Planning of the Town of Norris," *American Architect,* 148 (April 1936), 19–26.

Bauer, Catherine. "Description and Appraisal, Baldwin Hills Village," *Pencil Points,* 25 (September 1944), 46–60.

Berry, Richard D. "Baldwin Hills Village, Design or Accident?" *Arts and Architecture,* 81 (October 1964), 18–21, 32–35.

———— "Experiences in a 25-Year-Old Planned Neighborhood," *Journal of Housing,* 4 (April 1966), 214–219.

Comey: *Planned Communities.*

Draper, Earle Sumner. "Landscape Architecture in the Tennessee Valley," *Landscape Architecture,* 28 (July 1938), 185–190.

———— Letter regarding Town of Norris to Norman T. Newton, June 21, 1968.

"Final Sale of Government Property in Greenbelt," *American City,* 69 (September 1954), 207.

"Fresh Meadows, Queens, New York City," *Architectural Record,* 106 (December 1949), 85–97.

Fulmer, O. Kline. *Greenbelt.* Washington: American Council on Public Affairs, 1941.

"Greenbelt Homes Sold to Cooperative Group," *American City,* 67 (December 1952), 125.

"Greenbelt Planning," *Pencil Points,* 7 (August 1936), 401–419.

"Greenbelt Towns," *Architectural Record,* 80 (September 1936), 215–234.

Griswold, Ralph E. Letter regarding Chatham Village to Norman T. Newton, June 25, 1968.

Johnston, Margaret M. Letter for Chatham Village Homes, Inc., to Norman T. Newton, June 21, 1968.

Kyle, John H. *The Building of TVA.* Baton Rouge: Louisiana State University Press, 1958.

Lilienthal, David E. *TVA: Democracy on the March.* London: Penguin Books, 1944.

Mumford, Lewis. "Baldwin Hills Village," *Pencil Points,* 25 (September 1944), 44–45.

Nelson, Otto L. "Fresh Meadows: An Equity Investment by a Life Insurance Company," *Journal of the AIA,* 10 (December 1948), 254–261.

"Norris, Tenn.: To be Sold by TVA," *American City,* 62 (August 1947), 101.

Schlesinger, Arthur M., Jr. *The Age of Roosevelt,* vol II: *The Coming of the New Deal.* Boston: Houghton Mifflin, 1958.

Stein, Clarence S. *Toward New Towns for America.* New York: Reinhold Publishing Corp., 1957

Warner, George A. *Greenbelt: The Cooperative Community.* New York: Exposition Press, 1954.

XXXV–XXXVI. National Parks

Buck, Paul Herman. "The Evolution of the National Park System of the United States," unpub. disc., Ohio State University, 1921. Printed for official use by U.S. Government Printing Office, 1946.

Cahn, Robert. "Will Success Spoil the National Parks?" series in *Christian Science Monitor*, May–August 1968.

Chittenden, Hiram M. *The Yellowstone National Park: Historical and Descriptive.* Cincinnati: Stewart & Kidd, 1917.

Ise, John. *Our National Park Policy: A Critical History.* Baltimore: The Johns Hopkins Press, 1961.

Muir, John. *Our National Parks.* Boston: Houghton Mifflin, 1901.

National Park Service. *Glimpses of Historical Areas East of the Mississippi River.* Washington: U.S. Government Printing Office, 1937.

————— *Glimpses of Our National Parks.* Washington: U.S. Government Printing Office, 1941.

————— *Our Heritage: A Plan for Its Protection and Use ("Mission 66").* Washington: National Park Service, 1955.

Shankland, Robert. *Steve Mather of the National Parks.* New York: Alfred A. Knopf, 1951.

Tilden, Freeman. *The National Parks: What They Mean to You and Me.* New York: Alfred A. Knopf, 1951.

Wirth, Conrad L. Comments and letters to Norman T. Newton, May 5, 11, and 18, 1969.

XXXVII–XXXVIII. State Parks

Evison, Herbert, ed. *A State Park Anthology.* Washington: National Conference on State Parks, 1930.

Fechner, Robert. *First Report of the Director of Emergency Conservation Work* (April 5, 1933–September 30, 1933). Washington: U.S. Government Printing Office, 1934.

————— *Second Report of the Director of Emergency Conservation Work* (April 5, 1933–March 31, 1934). Washington: U.S. Government Printing Office, 1934.

Forest Preserve District of Cook County, Illinois. *Annual Reports,* 1927–1957.

National Conference on State Parks. *1952 Yearbook: Park and Recreation Progress.* Washington: National Conference on State Parks, 1952.

National Park Service. *Park Structures and Facilities.* Washington: U.S. Department of the Interior, National Park Service, 1935.

————— *Park and Recreation Structures,* 3-vol. ed. of preceding work. Washington: U.S. Government Printing Office, 1938.

————— *Recreational Demonstration Projects, as Illustrated by Chopawamsic, Virginia.* Washington: U.S. Department of the Interior, National Park Service [1936].

————— *Proceedings of Conference on Camp Planning.* Washington: National Park Service, Branch of Planning and State Cooperation (mimeograph), 1936.

————— *The CCC and Its Contribution to a Nation-wide State Park Recreational Program.* Washington: U.S. Government Printing Office, 1937.

————— *1937 and 1938 Yearbooks: Park and Recreation Progress.* Washington: U.S. Government Printing Office, 1937–1938.

————— *A Study of the Park and Recreation Problem of the United States.* Washington: U.S. Government Printing Office, 1941.

Nelson, Beatrice Ward. *State Recreation: Parks, Forests and Game Preserves.* Washington: National Conference on State Parks, 1928.

New York, State of. *New York State Parks: Twenty-fifth Anniversary Report.* Albany: State Council of Parks, 1949.

Olmsted, Frederick Law. *Report of State Park Survey of California.* Sacramento: State Printing Office, 1929.

Salomon, Julian Harris. *Camp Site Development.* New York: Girl Scouts of America, 1959.

Shapiro, Sidney M. Letter regarding Jones Beach to Norman T. Newton, January 15, 1969.

Tilden, Freeman. *The State Parks: Their Meaning in American Life.* New York: Alfred A. Knopf, 1962.

Wirth, Conrad L., *Civilian Conservation Corps Program of the United States Department of the Interior* (March 1933–June 30, 1943). Final Report to Secretary Harold L. Ickes, January 1944. Washington: U.S. Government Printing Office, 1945.
———— Comments and letter to Norman T. Newton, May 5, 1969.

XXXIX. Parkways and Their Offspring

Abbott, Stanley W. "The Mississippi River Parkway Survey." Informational bulletins published by the Survey, 1949–1951.
———— "The Mississippi River National Parkway," *Planning and Civic Comment,* March 1951.
Boston, City of. Board of Park Commissioners. *Annual Reports,* 1876–1905.
Brooklyn, City of. Board of Park Commissioners. *Annual Reports,* 1861–1896.
Clarke, Gilmore D. Comments and letters to Norman T. Newton, January 3 and 15, 1969.
Eliot: *Charles Eliot.* Page 596.
Snow, W. Brewster, ed. *The Highway and the Landscape.* New Brunswick, N.J.: Rutgers University Press, 1959.
Westchester County Park Commission. *Annual Reports,* 1927–1933.

XL. Urban Open-Space Systems

Boston, City of. Board of Park Commissioners. *Annual Reports,* 1876–1905.
Butler, George D. *Introduction to Community Recreation.* New York: McGraw-Hill, 1940.
Chicago, City of. South Park Commissioners. *Annual Reports,* 1871–1906.
Hubbard, Henry Vincent. "The Size and Distribution of Playgrounds and Similar Recreation Facilities in American Cities," *Landscape Architecture,* 4 (July 1914), 133–144.
———— "Parks and Playgrounds: Their Requirements and Distribution as Elements in the City Plan," *Landscape Architecture,* 12 (July 1922), 240–264.
New York, City of. Department of Parks. *Six Years of Park Progress.* New York: Department of Parks, 1940.

XLI. Variations in Practice

American Society of Landscape Architects. *Transactions of the ASLA,* vol. II (1909–1921).
———— *Membership Rosters,* 1920–1969.
Federal Housing Administration. *Land Planning Bulletin No. 1: Successful Subdivisions.* Washington: U.S. Government Printing Office, 1933.
———— *Technical Bulletin No. 5: Planning Neighborhoods for Small Houses.* Washington: U.S. Government Printing Office, 1936.
Newton, Norman T. "Annual Report of the President, July 1960 to June 1961," *ASLA Bulletin,* no. 97, August 1961.
———— "100 Years of Landscape Architecture: Centennial of the Profession," *Landscape Architecture,* 54 (July 1964), 260–265.
U.S. Housing Authority. *Design of Low-Rent Housing Projects: Planning the Site.* Washington: U.S. Government Printing Office, 1939.

XLII. Conservation

Coyle, David Cushman. *Conservation: An American Story of Conflict and Accomplishment.* New Brunswick, N.J.: Rutgers University Press, 1957.
Graham, Edward H. *Natural Principles of Land Use.* New York: Oxford University Press, 1944.

Lord, Russell. *To Hold This Soil.* Misc. Pub. No. 321, U.S. Department of Agriculture. Washington: U.S. Government Printing Office, 1938.

President's Council on Recreation and Natural Beauty. *From Sea to Shining Sea.* Washington: U.S, Government Printing Office, 1968.

Sears, Paul B. *Deserts on the March.* Norman: University of Oklahoma Press, 1935.

———— *This is Our World.* Norman: University of Oklahoma Press, 1937.

Wright, George, and Ben H. Thompson. *Fauna of the National Parks of the United States.* Washington: U.S. Government Printing Office, 1935.

Acknowledgments

It must be obvious that without the help of a great many individuals this book could not have been written. The longest outstanding of my debts is one of the spirit, an inheritance from Professor E. Gorton Davis of Cornell, who, through the magic of his own enthusiasm in my undergraduate days, aroused within me an abiding curiosity about the story of landscape architecture. Next I suppose I should thank the students and fellow practitioners who extracted from me, years ago, the promise to do a book of this kind whenever I could find the time for it. They are to blame only for having got me started; for whatever faults they now find lurking in this volume, the blame must be assigned to me. I accept it gladly.

My indebtedness through the years to Dean Gilmore D. Clarke has been again increased by his expert comments on the chapter about parkways and his aid with illustrations in that chapter and in the account of the New York Park Department. Similarly, my gratitude goes to Conrad L. Wirth, former director of the National Park Service, for his critical reading of the chapters on national and state parks, and to Charles W. Eliot II for assistance with the chapter about the life and work of his uncle.

For kindness in reading and criticizing chapters of the manuscript in areas of their special interest, I am happily obligated to Professors James S. Ackerman, Herbert Bloch, George M. A. Hanfmann, Peter L. Hornbeck, Reginald R. Isaacs, David G. Mitten, and Eduard F. Sekler, all of Harvard, and to Professor Elaine P. Loeffler of Brandeis. For detailed factual data about specific projects and areas of concern, I offer cordial thanks to my fellow landscape architects Donald W. Bush, William G. Carnes, Earle S. Draper, Ralph E. Griswold, Charles W. Harris, Sidney N. Shurcliff, and John L. Wacker; also to Professor Leonard K. Eaton of the University of Michigan,

Sidney M. Shapiro of the Long Island State Park Commission, John McC. Mowbray of Baltimore, the J. C. Nichols Company of Kansas City, the Chicopee Manufacturing Company of New Brunswick, New Jersey, Chatham Village Homes, Inc., of Pittsburgh, and the office of Baldwin Hills Village in Los Angeles.

I have depended often and thankfully on that constant source of information about landscape architects and the profession, Mrs. Edwin D. Lundquist, for many years administrative secretary of the ASLA and more recently secretary of the Department of Landscape Architecture in the Harvard Graduate School of Design. I am especially conscious of what I owe Thomas W. Vint for allowing access to the personal files of his late father, my friend Thomas C. Vint, chief of development in the National Park Service.

I am grateful to Miss Caroline Shillaber, librarian of the Harvard Graduate School of Design, not only for her unfailing aid and that of her staff in the many areas both visual and verbal covered by this extraordinary library, but also for sharing with me her extensive knowledge of the history of early American landscape architecture. For the few relevant items not available in the GSD Library, I have enjoyed the usual exemplary service of Harvard's Widener Library, Houghton Library, Map Room, and Fogg Museum of Art.

The Publication Board of the ASLA and Grady Clay, editor of *Landscape Architecture,* the Society's quarterly journal, have kindly allowed me to draw heavily upon its pages; several sections of this book are based on articles of mine that have appeared in the quarterly in past years. I am likewise beholden to the other publishers who have graciously permitted reproduction of text and illustrative material, as indicated in every instance.

For generous response to the search for illustrations I am indebted to many, notably Haines Lundberg & Waehler, architects, and landscape architects Stanley W. Abbott, Walter L. Chambers, Garrett Eckbo, Walter A. J. Ewald, M. Paul Friedberg, Lawrence Halprin, Hideo Sasaki, John O. Simonds, and Robert L. Zion; also to numerous public and private agencies, here and abroad, as noted in each case. Many of the illustrations, historically valuable mainly because of their early dates, were made perforce from negatives resurrected out of an often dim past. For painstaking skill in the task of reproducing them, I wish to pay special tribute to James K. Ufford and his efficient staff in the photographic laboratory of the Fogg Museum.

No statement of gratitude would be complete without an expression of the thanks I owe my wife, Lyyli Lamsa Newton, not only for her patience in putting up with this almost daily stint of mine over the years, but also, and perhaps primarily, for the quick sensitivity with which she has participated in the manuscript's every thought and word.

N. T. N.

Cambridge, Massachusetts
January 1970

Illustration Credits

Abbreviations

ASLA   American Society of Landscape Architects
CCFPD   Cook County Forest Preserve District, Illinois
FAAR   Fellow, American Academy in Rome
HGSD   Harvard Graduate School of Design ("HGSD slide" refers to any slide or negative
          in the collection with origin no longer known)
NPS   National Park Service, U.S. Department of the Interior
SCS   Soil Conservation Service, U.S. Department of Agriculture
WCPC   Westchester County Park Commission

1. Photo Specter, in HGSD Library.
2. Naville, *Deir-el-Bahari*, VI, pl. 169.
3. Rosellini, *Monumenti dell'Egitto*, II, pl. 69.
4. Perrot and Chipiez, *History of Art*, II, 31.
5. Von Gerkan, *Griechische Städteanlagen*, pl. 6.
6. *Ibid.*, pl. 9.
7. Wiegand-Zippelius, HGSD slide.
8. HGSD slide.
9. *Ibid.*
10. *Ibid.*
11. *Ibid.*
12. *Ibid.*
13. *Ibid.*
14. Lugli, *Roma Antica, Il Centro Monumentale*, pl. 5.
15. Bühlmann and von Wagner, *Das alte Rom.*
16. Restoration by George S. Koyl, FAAR, photo in HGSD Library.
17. Restoration by Thomas D. Price, FAAR, photo in HGSD Library.
18. *Ibid.*
19. HGSD slide.
20. *Ibid.*

21. *Ibid.*
22. Crisp, *Medieval Gardens,* II, pl. 224.
23. MS in British Museum, courtesy Trustees British Museum.
24. Photo Sears, in HGSD Library.
25. Drawn by Richard D. Sias, photo in HGSD Library.
26. Photo Newton.
27. *Ibid.*
28. HGSD slide.
29. Photo Newton.
30. Gromort, *Jardins d'Espagne,* pl. 25.
31. HGSD slide.
32. *Ibid.*
33. *Ibid.*
34. *Ibid.*
35. Drawn by George F. Ingalls, photo in HGSD Library.
36. Photo Newton.
37. HGSD slide.
38. *Ibid.*
39. Photo Harris, in HGSD Library.
40. *Ibid.*
41. Zocchi, *Vedute delle Ville,* pl. 31.
42. *Ibid.,* pl. 33.
43. *Ibid.,* pl. 39.
44. Measured and drawn by N. T. Newton, FAAR, photo in HGSD Library.
45. *Ibid.*
46. Photo Bochkor, in HGSD Library.
47. Photo Newton.
48. *Ibid.*
49. Measured and drawn by N. T. Newton, FAAR, photo in HGSD Library.
50. Photo Newton.
51. Gromort, *Choix de Plans,* pl. 18–19.
52. Courtesy Fogg Museum, Harvard.
53. *Ibid.*
54. *Ibid.*
55. HGSD slide.
56. Restoration by R. M. Kennedy, FAAR, photo in HGSD Library.
57. Measured and drawn by Edward G. Lawson, FAAR, photo in HGSD Library.
58. Falda, *Giardini di Roma,* pl. 7.
59. HGSD slide.
60. Measured and drawn by James Chillman, FAAR, photo in HGSD Library.
61. HGSD slide.
62. Percier and Fontaine, *Maisons de Plaisance,* pl. 64.
63. Measured and drawn by Edward G. Lawson, FAAR, photo in HGSD Library.
64. Photo Newton.
65. *Ibid.*
66. Ernouf and Alphand, *L'Art des Jardins,* p. 42.
67. Measured and drawn by Michael Rapuano, FAAR, photo in HGSD Library.
68. Photo Newton.
69. HGSD slide.
70. Photo Newton.
71. *Ibid.*

72. Cantoni, *La Villa Lante,* pl. B.
73. *Ibid.,* pl. A.
74. Photo Moscioni, in HGSD Library.
75. Photo Newton.
76. *Ibid.*
77. HGSD slide.
78. *Ibid.*
79. Measured and drawn by Ralph E. Griswold, FAAR, photo in HGSD Library.
80. Measured and drawn by James E. Lister, FAAR, photo in HGSD Library.
81. Photo Newton.
82. HGSD slide.
83. Model by Ralph E. Griswold, FAAR, photo in HGSD Library.
84. Measured and drawn by Edward G. Lawson, FAAR, photo in HGSD Library.
85. *Ibid.*
86. Courtesy Pierpont Morgan Library and International Exhibitions Foundation.
87. Photo Newton.
88. *Ibid.*
89. *Ibid.*
90. Drawn by Edgar I. Williams, FAAR, photo in HGSD Library.
91. HGSD slide.
92. Measured and drawn by N. T. Newton, FAAR, photo in HGSD Library.
93. Photo Newton.
94. Recorded and drawn by N. T. Newton, FAAR, photo in HGSD Library.
95. Paced and drawn by Ralph E. Griswold, FAAR, photo in HGSD Library.
96. Photo Newton.
97. HGSD slide.
98. Mori and Boffito, *Firenze nelle Vedute e Piante,* p. 144.
99. Gromort, *Choix de Plans,* pl. 12.
100. Courtesy Italian Government Travel Office.
101. *Ibid.*
102. HGSD slide.
103. Gromort, *Choix de Plans,* pl. 14–15.
104. Courtesy Italian Government Travel Office.
105. Photo Newton.
106. *Ibid.*
107. *Ibid.*
108. *Ibid.*
109. Sitte, *L'Art de Bâtir les Villes,* p. 105.
110. HGSD slide.
111. *Ibid.*
112. *Ibid.*
113. Courtesy Italian Government Travel Office.
114. Du Cerceau, *Les plus excellents Bastiments de France,* II, unnumbered pl.
115. *Ibid.,* II, pl. 3.
116. HGSD slide.
117. Redrawn at HGSD from Du Cerceau, *Les plus excellents Bastiments de France,* II, unnumbered pl.
118. Du Cerceau, *Les plus excellents Bastiments de France,* II, unnumbered pl.
119. From Gomboust map of Paris, 1652, in Harvard Map Room.
120. Photo Newton.
121. *Ibid.*

122. HGSD slide.

123. From Gomboust map of Paris, 1652, in Harvard Map Room.

124. Pean, *Jardins de France,* II, frontispiece.

125. Photo Newton.

126. *Ibid.*

127. HGSD slide.

128. Nolhac, *Création de Versailles,* p. 43.

129. HGSD slide.

130. *Ibid.*

131. *Ibid.*

132. *Ibid.*

133. Photo Newton.

134. HGSD slide.

135. *Ibid.*

136. *Ibid.*

137. Drawn by Jesse V. Stensson, photo in HGSD Library.

138. Photo Newton.

139. *Ibid.*

140. Triggs, *Formal Gardens in England and Scotland,* pl. 1.

141. Photo Newton.

142. *Ibid.*

143. Triggs, *Formal Gardens in England and Scotland,* pl. 25.

144. *Ibid.,* pl. 26.

145. *Ibid.,* pl. 52.

146. Photo Newton.

147. Shepherd and Jellicoe, *Gardens and Design,* p. 194.

148. Photo Ingalls, in HGSD Library.

149. *Ibid.*

150. *Ibid.*

151. Kip, *Nouveau Théatre de la Grande Bretagne,* I, pl. 6.

152. HGSD slide.

153. Triggs, *Formal Gardens in England and Scotland,* pl. 32.

154. Photo Hornbeck, in HGSD Library.

155. Campbell, *Vitruvius Britannicus,* III, pl. 72.

156. Tipping, *English Homes, Period IV,* II, 95.

157. Photo Hornbeck, in HGSD Library.

158. *Ibid.*

159. *Ibid.*

160. Photo Newton.

161. *Ibid.*

162. *Ibid.*

163. *Ibid.*

164. Courtesy Public Record Office, Crown copyright.

165. HGSD slide.

166. Courtesy Greater London Records Office.

167. HGSD slide.

168. Ernouf and Alphand, *L'Art des Jardins,* p. 217.

169. HGSD slide.

170. *Ibid.*

171. Pückler-Muskau, *Hints on Landscape Gardening,* pocket of cover.

172. HGSD slide.

173. *Ibid.*
174. *Ibid.*
175. Alphand, *Promenades de Paris,* pl. 3.
176. *Ibid.,* pl. 4.
177. HGSD slide.
178. Prepared by E. Gorton Davis, photo in HGSD Library.
179. HGSD slide.
180. Courtesy Mount Vernon Ladies' Association of the Union.
181. Restoration by Morley J. Williams, photo in HGSD Library.
182. *Ibid.*
183. Downing, *Treatise on the Theory and Practice,* p. 364.
184. *Ibid.,* p. 358; quotation is from p. 359.
185. *Ibid.,* p. 73.
186. *Ibid.,* frontispiece.
187. *Olmsted Papers, Central Park,* p. 214.
188. *Ibid.*
189. HGSD slide.
190. Brooklyn Park Commissioners, *Annual Report, 1867,* p. 117.
191. Courtesy Olmsted Brothers, in HGSD Library.
192. Central Park Commissioners, *Annual Report, 1860,* p. 35.
193. HGSD slide.
194. *Ibid.*
195. *Ibid.*
196. Photo Newton, in HGSD Library.
197. Brooklyn Park Commissioners, *Annual Report, 1868,* p. 246.
198. Photo Newton, in HGSD Library.
199. HGSD slide.
200. Boston Park Commissioners, *Annual Report, 1879,* p. 17.
201. Boston Park Commissioners, *Notes on the Plan of Franklin Park,* 1886.
202. Courtesy Olmsted Brothers, in HGSD Library.
203. *Ibid.*
204. *Ibid.*
205. Boston Park Commissioners, *Annual Report, 1886,* pp. 24–25.
206. HGSD slide.
207. Courtesy Olmsted Brothers, in HGSD Library.
208. *Ibid.*
209. *Ibid.*
210. *Ibid.*
211. *Ibid.*
212. *Ibid.*
213. Cleveland, *Suggestions for a System of Parks,* 1883.
214. Eliot, *Charles Eliot,* frontispiece.
215. *Ibid.,* pp. 670–671.
216. HGSD slide.
217. *Ibid.*
218. *Ibid.*
219. Eliot, *Charles Eliot,* p. 738.
220. HGSD slide.
221. Lamb, *Homes of America,* p. 178.
222. *Ibid.,* p. 175.
223. *Ibid.,* p. 205.

224. HGSD slide.
225. *Ibid.*
226. Courtesy Olmsted Brothers, in HGSD Library.
227. *Ibid.*
228. *Ibid.*
229. *Ibid.*
230. *Ibid.*
231. HGSD slide.
232. *Ibid.*
233. Chicago South Park Commissioners, *Annual Report, 1872.*
234. Johnson, *History of the World's Columbian Exposition,* I, 17.
235. Moore, *Burnham,* I, 36.
236. *Town Planning Review,* 6 (January 1916), pl. 38.
237. Johnson, *History of the World's Columbian Exposition,* I, 1.
238. *Ibid.,* I, 352.
239. *Ibid.,* I, 486.
240. Courtesy Reginald R. Isaacs, in HGSD Library.
241. HGSD slide.
242. Courtesy Olmsted Associates, Inc.
243. Platt, *Monograph,* p. 178.
244. *Ibid.,* p. 179.
245. *Ibid.,* p. 19.
246. HGSD slide.
247. *Ibid.*
248. Platt, *Monograph,* p. 100.
249. HGSD slide.
250. *Ibid.*
251. Platt, *Monograph,* p. 37.
252. Photo Bolton, in HGSD Library.
253. HGSD slide.
254. Courtesy Commission of Fine Arts.
255. HGSD slide.
256. *Ibid.*
257. *Ibid.*
258. *Ibid.*
259. *Ibid.*
260. *Ibid.*
261. *Ibid.*
262. Courtesy Ferruccio Vitale, in HGSD Library.
263. Burnham, *Report on San Francisco,* insert.
264. Burnham, *Report on Manila,* insert.
265. Burnham and Anderson, "Preliminary plan of Baguio" (clipping from "Philippine Commission Report, 1905") in HGSD Library.
266. Burnham and Bennett, *Plan of Chicago,* pl. 129.
267. Courtesy Olmsted Brothers, in HGSD Library.
268. *Ibid.*
269. *Ibid.*
270. HGSD slide.
271. *Ibid.*
272. *Ibid.*
273. Eaton, *Landscape Artist in America,* p. 99.

274. *Ibid.,* p. 101.
275. Drawing by N. T. Newton, photo in HGSD Library.
276. Photo Gottscho-Schleisner.
277. *Ibid.*
278. Courtesy Walter A. J. Ewald.
279. *Ibid.*
280. *Landscape Architecture,* 19 (January 1929), p. 86.
281. HGSD slide.
282. *Ibid.*
283. Buckingham, *National Evils,* frontispiece.
284. HGSD slide.
285. Courtesy Bournville Village Trust, in HGSD Library.
286. *Ibid.*
287. Howard, *Tomorrow,* pl. 2.
288. Courtesy Letchworth Garden City Corporation, in HGSD Library.
289. HGSD slide.
290. *Ibid.*
291. *Ibid.*
292. Courtesy Olmsted Associates, Inc.
293. Photo Walsh, in HGSD Library.
294. Comey, *Planned Communities,* p. 89.
295. HGSD slide.
296. Courtesy J. C. Nichols Company, in HGSD Library.
297. Courtesy Olmsted Brothers, in HGSD Library.
298. *Ibid.*
299. *Ibid.*
300. Comey, *Planned Communities,* p. 42.
301. *Ibid.,* p. 93.
302. *Ibid.,* p. 25.
303. HGSD slide.
304. Comey, *Planned Communities,* p. 97.
305. HGSD slide.
306. *Ibid.*
307. Stein, *Toward New Towns for America,* p. 42, permission Van Nostrand Reinhold Company.
308. Courtesy Chatham Village Homes, Inc.
309. *Ibid.*
310. Photo Newton, in HGSD Library.
311. Comey, *Planned Communities,* p. 71.
312. HGSD slide.
313. *Ibid.*
314. Photo Newton, in HGSD Library.
315. Courtesy Baldwin Hills Village administration office.
316. Stein, *Toward New Towns for America,* p. 197, permission Van Nostrand Reinhold Company.
317. Photo Newton, in HGSD Library.
318. Stein, *Toward New Towns for America* (photo Fairchild Aerial Surveys), p. 191, permission Van Nostrand Reinhold Company.
319. Courtesy Haines Lundberg and Waehler, architects.
320. *Ibid.,* photo Martin.
321. Courtesy NPS, photo Grant.
322. Courtesy NPS, photo Keller.
323. Courtesy NPS.

324. *Ibid.,* photo Kirk.
325. Courtesy NPS, photo Grant.
326. Courtesy NPS, photo Boucher.
327. Courtesy NPS, photo Mang.
328. Courtesy NPS, photo Grant.
329. Courtesy NPS, photo Keller.
330. Courtesy NPS, photo Haugen.
331. Courtesy NPS, photo Williams.
332. Courtesy NPS, photo Boucher.
333. Courtesy NPS.
334. *Ibid.,* photo Grant.
335. Courtesy NPS.
336. *Ibid.,* photo in HGSD Library.
337. Designed and drawn by N. T. Newton for NPS, photo in HGSD Library.
338. Courtesy NPS, photo Grant.
339. Courtesy NPS.
340. *Ibid.*
341. *Ibid.,* photo Williams.
342. Courtesy NPS, photo Anderson.
343. *Ibid.*
344. Courtesy New York Department of Conservation, photo NYSPIX-Commerce.
345. Courtesy Minnesota Department of Conservation, photo Wettschreck.
346. Courtesy Genesee State Park Commission, photo Bassett.
347. HGSD slide.
348. Courtesy Finger Lakes State Parks Commission.
349. Courtesy Long Island State Park Commission.
350. *Ibid.*
351. *Ibid.*
352. Courtesy CCFPD.
353. *Ibid.*
354. HGSD slide.
355. Drawn by N. T. Newton from NPS data.
356. Courtesy Central New York State Park Commission.
357. Courtesy Virginia Conservation Commission.
358. Courtesy Finger Lakes State Parks Commission.
359. Courtesy Minnesota Department of Conservation, photo Wettschreck.
360. Courtesy Palisades Interstate Park Commission.
361. Courtesy CCFPD.
362. Photo Taubert, in HGSD Library.
363. Photo Newton, in HGSD Library.
364. *Ibid.*
365. *Ibid.*
366. Courtesy Pennsylvania Department of Forests and Waters.
367. *Ibid.*
368. *Ibid.*
369. NPS, *Park and Recreation Structures,* III, 117.
370. HGSD slide.
371. *Ibid.*
372. Courtesy WCPC, photo in HGSD Library.
373. *Ibid.*
374. *Ibid.*

375. Courtesy Gilmore D. Clarke.

376. *Ibid.*

377. Courtesy WCPC, photo in HGSD Library.

378. Courtesy Taconic State Park Commission, photo in HGSD Library.

379. *Ibid.*

380. *Ibid.*

381. Courtesy Stanley W. Abbott, photo in HGSD Library.

382. *Ibid.*

383. Courtesy Gilmore D. Clarke, photo Aero Service.

384. *Ibid.*

385. Courtesy Gilmore D. Clarke.

386. Courtesy Olmsted Brothers, photo in HGSD Library.

387. HGSD slide.

388. Courtesy Olmsted Brothers, photo in HGSD Library.

389. *Ibid.*

390. Courtesy Gilmore D. Clarke, photo in HGSD Library.

391. *Ibid.*

392. HGSD slide.

393. *Ibid.*

394. *Ibid.*

395. *Ibid.*

396. *Ibid.*

397. Courtesy Eckbo, Dean, Austin and Williams, photo Tidyman.

398. Courtesy Zion & Breen Associates.

399. *Ibid.*

400. Courtesy M. Paul Friedberg & Associates, photo Hirsch.

401. FHA, *Land Planning Bulletin No. 1,* photo in HGSD Library.

402. Courtesy Shurcliff & Shurcliff, photo in HGSD Library.

403. Photo Newton, in HGSD Library.

404. Courtesy Sasaki, Walker and Associates, photo Morley Baer.

405. Courtesy Lawrence Halprin & Associates, photo Braun.

406. Courtesy Simonds and Simonds, photo Musgrave.

407. Courtesy Simonds and Simonds.

408. Courtesy Sasaki, Dawson, DeMay Associates, photo Hutchins.

409. Courtesy Sasaki, Dawson, DeMay Associates.

410. Courtesy Lawrence Halprin & Associates, photo Bragstad.

411. Courtesy Sasaki, Dawson, DeMay Associates, photo © Ezra Stoller-ESTO.

412. Courtesy NPS, photo Boucher.

413. Courtesy SCS.

414. *Ibid.,* photo Dean.

415. Courtesy SCS, photo Cole.

416. Courtesy SCS, photo Case.

417. Courtesy NPS, photo Haugen.

418. Courtesy U.S. Forest Service, photo in HGSD Library.

419. Courtesy SCS, photo Everts.

420. Courtesy SCS, photo Welch.

421. *Ibid.*

422. Courtesy National Air Pollution Control Administration.

423. Courtesy Federal Water Pollution Control Administration.

424. HGSD slide.

Index

Italic numbers indicate pages bearing illustrations

Abbott, Stanley W., 612–615
Acadia National Park, 532, *534*
Addison, Joseph, 209, 215
Adler & Sullivan, 361, 363, *369, 370*
Agora (Greek), 6, 8, 648
Agrigentum, 6
Akron, O., 479
Alatri, 22
Albany, N.Y., 289, 416
Albright, Horace M., 529–533, 536–539, 544, 546, 578
Alcazar gardens, *see* Seville
Aldobrandini, *see* Villa Aldobrandini
Aldred, J. E., residence of (Ormston), 429–431, *429–431*
Alexander VII, 149
Alexandria, Va., 250
Algiers, 50
Alhambra, *see* Granada
Alphand, J. C. Adolphe, 233, 243–245, 273, 319, 354; *Les Promenades de Paris, L'Art des Jardins* (with Ernouf), 244
Amboise, 154–155, *154,* 160, 164
Amenhotep III, court of, 4, *5*
American Academy in Rome, 367, 393–399, *396,* 436, 650; Fellowship in Landscape Architecture, 396–398, 436, 650
American Academy of Arts and Sciences, 378
American colonists: early Spanish, French, Swedish, Finnish, Dutch, 246–247; early English, 247–255
American Institute of Architects (AIA), 359n, 388, 403, 405, 535
American Institute of Planners (AIP), 425
American Park and Outdoor Association, 386
American Scenic and Historic Preservation Society, 560, 561

American School of Architecture, 394
American School of Classical Studies, 394–396
American Society of Landscape Architects (ASLA), 384, 387–391, 416, 425, 431, 435, 474, 486, 487, 532–552 *passim,* 572, 607, 626, 637, 640, 646, 658; founding, 385–387; small size, 391
Anderson, Peirce, 417
André, Edouard, 319
Anet, 158–159, *158,* 188
Anne, Queen, 197, 207, 219
Antiquities Act of 1906, 524–527
Appalachian Mountain Club, 321
Appleton, Thomas G., "cottage" of, 339, *341*
Arborway, Boston, 300, *300,* 304, 597
Arizona, 525, 532, 536
Armsmear, residence of Samuel Colt, 338–339, *338*
Army, U.S., 521, 528–529, 576, 578
Arnold Arboretum, Boston, 289, 300, *300,* 304, 319, 321, 388, 389, 597
Ashraf, 51–52
Assisi, 55, 56
Atterbury, Grosvenor, 475, *476*
Atwood, Charles B., 361–363
Augsburg, 22
Augur, Tracy B., 500
Aurelia, *see* Villa Aurelia
Aurora, *see* Villa dell'Aurora
Avila, 22

Babylon, Hanging Gardens of, 1, 50, 51, 122
Back Bay Fens, Boston, 291–294, *292,* 299, 300, *300,* 304, 319, 596, 597
Baghdad, 50
Bagnaia, 99, 101, *101,* 103, 107
Baguio, 417, 419–420, *420*
Balbianello, *see* Villa Balbianello

Baldwin Hills Village, Los Angeles, 507–513, *508, 510–512,* 645
Baltimore, Md., 289, 468, 470
Barillet-Deschamps, 244, 354
Barlow, Fred, Jr., 507–513, *508, 511*
Barlow Report, 462
Barrett, Nathan F., 387
Baxter, Sylvester, 325–326, 330, 333; *Greater Boston,* 326
Beaver Brook Reservation, Belmont-Waltham, Mass., 328, 331
Bellagio, 129
Belmont, Mass., 260, 328
Belvedere, Cortile del, 67–72, *68, 70–72,* 117, *151,* 188
Beman, S. S., 361, 363
Bennett, Edward H., 417, 420
Berkeley, "College of California," 275, 648
Bernini, Gian Lorenzo, 149–150, *152,* 179
Big Bend National Park, 543, 546, *547*
Bigger, Frederick, 503
Biltmore, N.C., 346–351, *347–350,* 372, 428
Bing, Alexander M., 489
Biotic balance, 529, 669, 671–673
Birkenhead, 220, 225, 227, 229, 232, 245, 449; park at, 223, 225–232, *229–231,* 267, 268, 270, 273, 344, 447; docks at, 229
Birmingham, Eng., 448, 449, 451
Black, Russell V., 424, 655
Blashfield, Edwin, 362, 394
Blenheim, 210, 212–214, *213, 214,* 259, 345
Blois, 154–156, *155,* 160, 164, 346
Blomfield, Reginald, *The Formal Garden in England,* 377
Blue Hills Reservation, Boston, 328, *329,* 331, 559
Blue Ridge Parkway, 351, 541–543, 589, 612–613, *613,* 615
Boccaccio, 56, 59
Bois de Boulogne, 241–245, *242, 243,* 273, 406
Bordeaux, 242–244
Borgeson, Melvin B., *566,* 569
Borromeo, Carlo, 120
Boston, Mass., 249, 259, 260, 277, 290–306 *passim,* 318–343 *passim,* 385, 386, 389, 394, 406, 414, 596, 597, 622–624, 631; Common, 249, 294, 299, 300, 596; Public Garden, 300, 596; Common-wealth Avenue, 300, 596; Trinity Church, 341, *653;* Public Library, 321, 343, *343;* Copley Square, 650, *653;* Storrow Drive, 294. *See also* Arborway; Arnold Arboretum; Back Bay Fens; Charlesbank; Charlesgate; Charles River; Franklin Park; Jamaica Pond; Jamaicaway; Riverway
Boston & Albany Railroad, 293, 294, 301, 319
Bournville, 449, 451–453, *452,* 460, 463, 465
Bouton, Edward H., 468
Boyceau, Jacques, 160, 162, 164, 172
Bramante, Donato, 67–69, *68, 70,* 117, 146, 154, 188
Bramham Park, 198–202, *200, 201*
Brandon, Va., 251, 253, 405
Branitz, 235, 241
Bridgeman, Charles, 210–212
Bronx River Parkway, N.Y., 597–601, *598, 599, 601, 602,* 603, 607, 610

Brookline, Mass., 289, 294–307 *passim,* 318, 324, 332, 361, 373, 378, 389, 624
Brooklyn, N.Y., 268, 275–279, 310, 596, 598, 624; Eastern Parkway, 596–598
Brosse, Salomon de, 163, 172
Brown, Lancelot ("Capability"), 211–216, *213, 214,* 217, 235
Brunelleschi, 57
Bryant, William Cullen, 266, 268–269, 270, 629
Bryce Canyon National Park, 533–534
Buckingham, James Silk, 448, *449*
Budapest, 405
Buffalo, N.Y., 289, 440
Buhl Foundation, 496, 500
Bureau of Public Roads, 542, 552, 612, 614
Bureau of Reclamation, 541, 547, 549
Burling & Whitehouse, 361
Burnham, Daniel Hudson, 357–362, 368–370, 393, 394, 400–423 *passim, 418–420, 422;* Burnham & Root, 357, 359–361
Bursley, Harold B., 503–506, *504, 505*
Bushnell, Rev. Horace, 308
Bussey Institution, 318, 319, 429
Buttermilk Falls State Park, N.Y., *565*
Byrd, William II, 251

Cadbury, George and Richard, 448–449, 451–453, 456, 464
California, 246, 274–275, 445, 521, 522, 545–563 *passim,* 572–574, 646; state park system, 563, 574; Redwood State Park, 562; Save-the-Redwoods League, 545, 562, 572; Olmsted Report of 1929, 572–574; Richardson Grove State Park, *574. See also* Yosemite State Park
Cambridge, Mass., 249, 268, 294, 318, 320, 389, 424, 483, 598
Cammerer, Arno B., 532, 537, 539–545
Camp Planning Section, War Department, 480
Cantoni, Angelo, 100
Cape Cod National Seashore, 553
Cape Hatteras National Seashore Recreational Area, 542, 553, *553,* 586
Capitol, U.S. national, 289, 401, 403, 405–407
Caprarola, 99, 103, 107, *109;* Villa, 107–113, *108–112*
Carcassonne, Cité, 22–23, *22*
Careggi, *see* Villa Careggi
Carlsbad Caverns National Park, 538
Carnes, William G., 546, 552, 554
Casablanca, 50
Castello, *see* Villa di Castello
Cautley, Marjorie Sewell, 489, *490,* 493, *493*
Caux, Salomon de, 194
Cemeteries, American, 268, 308, 391
Central Park, New York, xxi, 244–245, 266, *272,* 275, 276, *278, 282–284, 288,* 290, 295, 309, 310, 312, 344–345, 348, 390, 465, 491, 556, 557, 620, 621, 623, *628,* 629, 631; Park Act of 1851, 266, 267, 269; amended Park Act of 1853, 269; competition of 1857, 270–271, *272,* 310; development, 269–274; comparison with Prospect Park, 277–286; subsequent interference with, 286–289

Cerceau, Androuet du, *154*, 155, *155*, 156–158, *158*, 159, *159*

Chambers & Moriece, *649*

Chambers, William, 209

Chambord, 156

Chandler, F. W., 394

Chantilly, 166

Charles I, 196

Charles II, 196, 205

Charles V, 36, 37, 41, 43, 75, 183

Charles VIII, 154

Charles IX, 159

Charlesbank, Boston, 622, *622, 623*

Charlesgate, Boston, *292*, 293, 294, 300, 304, 597

Charles River, Boston, 260, 291, 294, 327, 328, *328*, 331, 597, 622

Charleston, S.C., 319

Charleval, 159, *159*

Chatham Village, Pittsburgh, 496–500, *498, 499*, 645

Chatham, Va., 251

Chatsworth, 227, 228

Chenonceaux, 156–157, *157*

Chicago, Ill., 289, 310–312, 314, 330, 353–370 *passim*, 390, 391, 406, 414, 433, 440, 465, 467, 546, 562, 564, 597, 623–625; Burnham plan, 416, 420–422, *422*; City Plan Commission, 421; South Parks, 289, 311–312, *356*, 357, *358, 367*, 624–625, *625, 626*; West Parks, 433, 435; Grant Park, 624; Riveroaks Shopping Center, *654*

Chicopee, Ga., 486–489, *488*, 654

Chigi, *see* Villa Chigi

Chiswick, 211

Church, Frederick E., residence of, 339, *340*

Church, Thomas D., 445

Cincinnati, O., 482, 485, 503

"City Beautiful" movement, 393, 413, 415, 422–424, 426, 650

City Housing Corporation, 489–491, 496

City of Refuge National Historical Park, 554

City planning as a collaborative area, 426

City Point, Boston, 319

Civilian Conservation Corps (CCC), 502, 540–550 *passim*, 575–595, *579, 585–587;* establishment of camps, 577–580; camp operation, 577–578; effect on park standards, 580–585

Clarke, Gilmore D., 411, 426, 601–607, *604–606*, 611, 612, *615*, 616, *616, 618*, 628, *628, 633–635*

Clement VII, 73–75

Clermont, N.Y., 260n

Cleveland, Horace W. S., 271, 308–317, *314*, 385, 414, 464, 465, 596, 597, 643; writings, 309–317

Cleveland, O., 416, 420, 422, 641

Cleveland, Ralph, 317

Climate, xxiii, 3, 4, 26, 28, 31, 50–51, 81, 122, 184, 250

Cloisters, 23–26, *24, 25*, 183

Cobb, Henry Ives, 361, 363

Codman, Henry S., 306, 330, 354, 357–360, 361, 362, 368, 385

Coffin, Marian, 441–443, *444*

Collaboration, interprofessional, 353, 357, 361, 365–367, 391–399 *passim*, 426, 551–552, 642, 646

Colonial National Historical Park, 538, 539

Colonial Parkway, 615

Colter, John ("Colter's Hell"), 518, *519, 520,* 554

Columbia, Md., 513

Columbian Exposition of 1893, *see* World's Columbian Exposition

Columbia University, 394, 431

Columbus, Christopher, 246

Combs, Clarence C., *566,* 569

Comey, Arthur C., 424, 655

Commission of Fine Arts, 389, 411–412, 431, 436, 535, 607

Commons (village greens), 249, 267

Como, Lago di, 114, 129, 131

Conditions, physical and evaluational, importance in judging historic works, xxii–xxiii

Connecticut, 549, 562–564, 612; state park system, 562, 563; Macedonia Brook State Park, 562; Merritt Parkway, 612

Conservation and landscape architecture, as synonymous, 659, 661, 664, 674

Cook County Forest Preserve District (CCFPD), Ill., 435, 467, 562, 569–571, *570, 571, 584*

Cooper, Peter, 270

Copeland, Robert Morris, 271, 309–310

Corcoran Gallery of Art, Washington, D.C., 407, 409

Córdoba, 30–32, 40, 50; Court of Oranges, 32, *33*

Cornell University, 426, 440, 441, 607

Cornish, N.H., *374,* 375, *375,* 377

Country Club District, Kansas City, 471–474, *472,* 481

Country Place Era, 371, 372, 427–446, 641

Country School, Weston, Mass., *649*

Cox, Kenyon, 362

Cramton, Louis, 537

Crane, Jacob L., 503

Crater Lake National Park, 524, *524*

Crete, 4

Crowninshield, Frederick, 394

Crystal Palace, 228, 353

Cushing-Payson place, Belmont, Mass., 260

Damascus, 30, 50

Dante Alighieri, 56

Deakin, Oliver A., 616

Deir-el-Bahari, 1, *2,* 3

Delphi, 6

Demaray, Arthur E., 549

Denver, Colo., 527, *672*

Des Moines, Iowa, 308, 564, 595

D'Este, Cardinal, 90

D'Este, *see* Villa d'Este

Detroit, Mich., 404, 441; Belle Isle Park, 289, 404

Devil's Tower National Monument, *525,* 527

Devonshire, Duke of, 227–228

Diane de Poitiers, 156, 158

Dinosaur National Monument, 549

District of Columbia, 401, *402,* 403, 404, *404,* 405–407, 532, 594

Doane, Gustavus, 518

Dominick, William F., 437, *439*

Downer, Jay, 601–602, 607

Downing, Andrew Jackson, 260–266, 268–269, 309, 337, 344; *Treatise on the Theory and Practice of Landscape Gardening*, 261–265, *262, 264, 265*
Draper, Earle S., 424, 487–489, *488,* 500–502, *501,* 646, 654, 655
Drury, Newton B., 545–549
Dutch, influence of in England, 197, 198, 203, 209, 210

Eckbo, Garrett, 445, 646; Eckbo, Dean, Austin & Williams, *636*
Ecological approach, 391, 655–656, 659–674
Ecological damage by park users, 522–523, 550–552
Edinburgh, 319
Egypt, 1–4, 30
Eidlitz, Otto, 480
Eiffel Tower, 354, *355,* 363
Eliot, Charles, 260n, 295, 306, 318, *325,* 333, 336–337, 373–386 *passim,* 414, 428, 559, 596, 597, 655; study and travel, 318–320; and Trustees of Public Reservations, 320–322; and Metropolitan Park Commission, 322–332
Eliot, Charles William, 318, 319, 335–336; *Charles Eliot, Landscape Architect,* 260n, 336
Eliot, Charles W. II, 655
Elizabeth I, 187
Ellicott, Andrew, 401, *404*
Ellington, Douglas D., 504
Ellsworth, James W., 416
Emergency Conservation Work (ECW), 544, 549, 577–580, 585, 586, 589, 595
Emery, Mrs. Thomas J., 482–486
England, 26, 74, 153, 182–232, 234, 235, 249–268 *passim,* 319, 320, 374, 430, 447–463, *464*
Ernouf, Alfred Auguste, *L'Art des Jardins* (with Alphand), 244
Evaluational conditions, importance in judging historic works, xxii
Evelyn, John, 95
Everett, Mass., 324
Everglades National Park, 539, 543, 546, *548*
Evison, Herbert, 578–579
Exposition of 1851, London, 353
Expositions Universelles of 1855, 1867, 1878, 1889 (Paris), 353–354, *355,* 363, 370

Factory Act, 221
Fairy Stone State Park, Va., *582*
Fall River, Mass., 289
Farm Security Administration (FSA), 504, 506, 646
Farnese, *see* Villino Farnese
Farrand, Beatrix Jones, 387–388, 392
Faulkner Farm, Brookline, Mass., 378, *378, 379*
Fechner, Robert, 577
Federal Housing Administration (FHA), 487, 507, 643–645, *644,* 646
Federal Public Housing Authority, 507
Fenway, Boston, 300, *300,* 304, 597
Fez, 49
Fiesole, 61, 62, 114, 117
Flanders, Annette Hoyt, 443, *445*
Fleming, Bryant, 440–441, *442, 443*

Florence, 29, 57–59, 67, 114, 117, 132–135, *133, 134, 136,* 146, 153, 182, 319
Florida, 539, 543, 546
Fontainebleau, 157, 162, 167, 405
Fontana, Domenico, 87, 147, 149
Foothill College, Los Altos, Calif., *649*
Fora of the Emperors, 15–18, *15–17,* 46, 132
Forest Hills Gardens, N.Y., 474–478, *475–477,* 479, 482
Forest Reserve Act of 1891, 523
Forest Service, U.S., 576–578
Forum Romanum, 13–15, *14, 17,* 132
Foster, Philip W., 483
Fouquet, Nicolas, 167, 172
France, 22, 77, 146, 153–182, 184, 209, 241–246, 259, 260, 319, 320, 374
Francini, Tommaso, 162
Francis I, 75, 155–157, 162, 183, 184, 346
Francis II, 159
Franklin Park, Boston, 277, 295–299, *296–298,* 300, *300,* 304, 319, 389, 623, 624; Franklin Field, 623
Frascati, 81, 83–85, 87, 88
Freeways, 502, 617–619, *618*
French, Daniel Chester, 361, 363, 394
French, influence of in England, 196–202, 205–206, 209, 210
Fresh Meadows, N.Y., 513–516, *514, 515*
Friedberg, M. Paul, & Associates, *639*
Fulton Mall, Fresno, Calif., *636*

Galerie des Machines, 354, *355,* 363
Gallagher, Percival, 429–430, *429–431*
Gambara, Cardinal, 99, 105, 107
Gamberaia, *see* Villa Gamberaia
Garden and Forest, 320–322
"Garden City" movement, 448, 453–462 *passim,* 489, 490, 503
Garden State Parkway, 616–617, *616*
Garibaldi, Giuseppe, 395
Geiffert, Alfred, Jr., 435–440, *438–440,* 513–516, *514, 515*
General Grant National Park, 521
Generalife, *see* Granada
George, Henry, 453
Germany, 233, 235, 319
Giedion, Sigfried, 344
Gilbert Lake State Park, N.Y., *581*
Gilpin, William, *Practical Hints upon Landscape Gardening,* 218
Giotto, 56, 57
Glacier National Park, *526,* 527
Goethe, J. Wolfgang von, 234
Good, Albert H., 586
Goodhue, Bertram G., 430, *430*
Gore, Christopher, 259–260
Gore place, Waltham, Mass., 259–260, 344
Governors, Conference of, 576
Graham, Gillespie, 230
Granada, 31, 32, 40–41, 47, 49; Alhambra, 40–47, *41–45,* 49, 52, 54; Generalife, 47–49, *48*
Grand Canyon National Park, 525, 532, *533,* 536
Grand Teton National Park, 538, 546

Grant, Ulysses S., 520
Gray, Asa, 270, 289
Great Ponds Act, 517, 555
Great Smoky Mountains National Park, 536, 539, 542–544, *544*, 546, 612
Greece, 4–6
Greeley, Horace, 270
Greenbelt, Md., 502–507, *504*, *505*, 646
Greenleaf, James L., 411, 431–433, *432*, *434*, 535
Green Park, London, *222*, 223
"Greensward" plan of Central Park, 271, *272*
Greenwood Cemetery, Brooklyn, 268
Griswold, Ralph E., 496–500, *498*, *499*, 648
Guardian, The, 209, 215
Guerin, Jules, 407, 421
Gunston Hall, Va., 251, 253, 648
Gwinn, in Cleveland, O., 380, *382*, *383*

Haddon Hall, 183, 185, *186*
Hadrian's Villa, 18, *18*, 20, 81, 88, 405
Ha-ha, 211
Halprin, Lawrence, 445, 650; Lawrence Halprin & Associates, *651*, *654*
Hampton Court, 198, 203–206, *203–205*, 212, 259, 405
Hare, S. Herbert, 416, 471–472, *472*, 474, 480–482, *481*
Hare, Sidney J., 416, 471–472, *472*, 474
Harriman family, 562
Hartford, Conn., 270, 289, 308, 332, 338, 549, 650; Constitution Plaza, 650, *653*
Hartzog, George B., Jr., 554
Hartzog, Justin R., 424, 483, 503, 655
Harvard University, 318, 336, 389, 416, 424, 429, 626
Hatfield House, 194–196, *195*, 405
Hatshepsut, Queen, mortuary temple of, 1, *2*, 15
Haussmann, Eugène, 233, 241–244, 353–354
Hawaii Volcanoes National Park, 531, *531*
Hayden, F. V., 518
Hedges, Cornelius, 518
Henri II, 156–159, 162
Henri III, 159, 160
Henri IV, 159–163
Henry VIII, 182–185, 204, 206, 267
Herodotus, 1
Heyland, Clara Jessup, 395
High Point State Park, N.J., *587*
Hippodamos, 6
Historical restoration, 646–648
Historic American Buildings Survey (HABS), 539, 648
Historic Sites and Buildings Act, 541
Holland, 197, 235, 319
Honolulu, 415
Hoover, Herbert C., 541
Hopkins, Alden, 648
Horace, Sabine villa of, 12, *19*, 20
Hot Springs Reservation, 308, 527–528
Housing Authority, U.S., 645
Housing Corporation, U.S., 480
Housing projects, 645–646

Howard, Ebenezer, 453–457, *456*, 460, 463, 464, 489, 490, 503; *Tomorrow: a Peaceful Path to Real Reform* and *Garden Cities of Tomorrow,* 453
Hubbard, Henry Vincent, 219, 416, 424, 626–627, 655
Hudson River places, 260–261, 265, *265*, 339, 344
Hughes, Charles Evans, 599
Hull, Daniel R., 532, 534–535, 572
Hunt, Richard Morris, 339–340, 346, *350*, 360, 361, 363, *365*, 369
Hutton, Edward F., residence of, 443, *444*
Hyde Park, Boston, 328
Hyde Park, London, 223, *223*, *224*, 241, 405
Hyde Park, N.Y., 260, 546

Ickes, Harold L., 549
Idaho, Heyburn and Payette Lake State Parks, 562
Illinois, 311, 387, 562, 564, 624; University of, 384, 416; Starved Rock State Park, 562; Old Salem State Park, 564
Independence Hall National Historical Park, 546–547, 648
India, Mogul, 52, 54, *54*
Indiana, 311, 562–564, 569, 591; Colonel Richard Lieber and, 562, 569; state park system, 562, 563; McCormick's Creek and Turkey Run State Parks, 562, *563*; Clifty Falls State Park, 564; Versailles Recreational Demonstration Area, 591–592
Industrial projects, 650–655, *656*
Ingham & Boyd, 497, *498*
Iowa, 311, 562, 564; Backbone State Park, 562
Ipswich, Mass., 249
Iran, 1, 4, 50–52; "paradises," 1, 4, 50; later gardens, 50–54, *52*, *53*
Iron technology, effects of, 221
Irrigation, ancient networks, 1
Irving, Washington, 270
Isfahan, 51, *52*, *53*
Islam, 30–54; conquest of Spain, 30–31; conquest of Middle East, 50–51; Mogul India, 52, 54
Isle Royale National Park, 538, 543–544
Isola Bella, 114, 119–122, *120*, *121*, 128, 129
Italy, 28–29, 55–152, 154, 157, 160, 182–191 *passim,* 209, 319, 320, 373, 374, 398
Itasca State Park, Minn., 559, *560*, *583*, 614

Jackson, Andrew, 401
Jackson Park, Chicago, 289, 356–359, *356*, *358*, 361, 365, *367*, 624
Jamaica Pond, Boston, 291, 294, 300, *300*, 597
Jamaicaway, Boston, 300, *300*, 304, 597
James I, 194, 196
James II, 197
James River places, 251–253, *251*, *252*, 405
Jamestown, Va., 250, 251, 538, 615
Janin, Jules, 421, *422*
Jefferson, Thomas, 255, 258–259, 401, 403, 405; *Garden Book,* 258; switch from classicism to "landscape gardening," 259; Jefferson Memorial, 408
Jenney & Mundie, 361, 363
Jensen, Jens, 433–435, *436*, *437*

Johnson, Reginald D., and Wilson, Merrill & Alexander, 507–513, *508, 510–512*
Johnson & Johnson, 486, 487
Jones, Inigo, 194, 196, 197
Jones Beach State Park, N.Y., *566,* 567–569, *567, 568,* 571, 611
Jones's Wood, New York, 269
Julius II, 67, 69, 149
Julius III, 69

Kansas, 311
Kansas City, Mo., 471–474, *472,* 480–481
Kensington Gardens, London, 211, 223
Kent, William, 211, 212, 216, 217
Kessler, George E., 481
Kings Canyon National Park, 521, 544
Kingsport, Tenn., 479, 487
Kip's views, *203,* 210
Knight, Emerson, 572
Knight, Richard Paine, 216, 218
Knoxville, Tenn., 500, 502
Kohankie, Theodore M., 496–500, *498*
Kohler Village, Wis., 479

Labor, Department of, 577, 578
Lacey, John F., 524–525
LaFarge, John, 394
LaGuardia, Fiorello H., 611, 628
Lake Mead National Recreational Area, 541
Lamb, Martha J., *The Homes of America,* 337–339, *338, 340, 341*
Land Program, Federal Emergency Relief Administration, 588–589
Landscape architecture: meaning, xxi; profession established, xxi, 273; design an essential ingredient, xxi, 391, 674; as a social art, xxii, 391; value from historical study, xxii–xxiii; skills and interests required, 391–392
"Landscape Gardening School," 207–220; imitated in America, 259
Landscape nurserymen, 445
Landscapes, rural, as manmade product of "landscape gardening school," 220
Lane, Franklin K., 529
Langford, Nathaniel P., 518
Langley, Batty, 216
Langton, Daniel W., 387, 388
Lante, *see* Villa Lante
Lassen Volcanic National Park, 531
Leasowes, 216, 259
LeBrun, Charles, 167, 172
Le Corbusier, 397
L'Enfant, Pierre Charles, 259, 268, 389, 400–414 *passim,* 402
LeNôtre, André, 153, 164–181, *166, 169–171, 174–178, 180,* 182, 206, 217, 246
LeNôtre, Jean, 164, 165
Leo X, 69, 73–75, 99, 146, 183
Letchworth, William P., 561–562
Letchworth Garden City, 456–460, *458, 459,* 461–463
LeVau, Louis, 167, 172–173

Levens Hall, 198, *202,* 203
Lever, W. H. (Lord Leverhulme), 449–451, 453, 456, 464
Lewis, Charles F., 496
Lewis and Clark expedition, 517–518
Lexington, Mass., 249
Lieber, Richard, 562, 569
Ligorio, Pirro, 69, 90
Lincoln, Abraham, 274, 407; Lincoln Memorial, 407
Lippi, Annibale, 77
Liverpool, 223, 227, 232, 319, 447, 449
London, 194, 220–232 *passim,* 259, 319, 353, 405, 406, 447, 453–462 *passim. See also* Royal Parks
London, George, 198, 206, 210
Long-Bell Lumber Company, 480–482
Long Island, N.Y., 260, 395, 430–443 *passim,* 474, 671
Long Island State Park Commission, N.Y., 567, 569, 628; parkways, 611. *See also* Jones Beach State Park
Longleat, *219*
Longview, Wash., 480–482, *481,* 486
Loring, C. M., 317
L'Orme, Philibert de, 158, *158,* 160, 188
Los Angeles, Calif., 508, 513, 534, 572
Loudon, J. C., and "Gardenesque School of Landscape," 218–228 *passim,* 240, 261, 265, 309, 337
Louis XI, 153
Louis XII, 154, 155
Louis XIII, 163–165, 172, 173
Louis XIV, 153, 164–181, 205, 393
Louisiana Purchase, 517
Louisville, Ky., 289, 386, 440
Lowrie, Charles N., 387, 388, 392, 416, 607
Lully, Jean Baptiste, 181
Luther, Martin, 73, 183
Luxembourg, 163–164, *163, 164,* 287, 405
Lyman place, Waltham, Mass., 260
Lynn, Mass., 324

McCann, Charles F., residence of, 443, *445*
McClellan, George B., 599
McFarland, Horace, 530
McKim, Charles Follen, 341, 343, 362, 363, 369, 393–407 *passim,* 420, 475; McKim, Mead & White, 277, 340–343, *342, 343,* 346, 360, 361, 395, *396*
McKinley, William, 403
McLean Hospital, Boston, 290
McMillan, James, 400, 403–407, 410
McMillan Commission (Senate Park Commission of 1901), 367, 389, 393, 400, 403–412, *407–410,* 416, 421
MacMonnies, Frederick, 361, 363
Madama, *see* Villa Madama
Maderna, Carlo, 149, 150
Maggiore, Lago, 114, 120
Maine, 387, 388, 532; Camden Hills Recreational Demonstration Area, 592
Mainz, 22
Mammoth Cave National Park, 546

Manila, 417–420, *419,* 422
Mann, George C., 321
Manning, Warren H., 258n, 385–389, 392, 416, 440
Manors, of N.Y., 249, 261
Marco Polo, 57
Mariemont, O., 482–486, *485*
Mariposa Mining Company, 274
Marrakesh, 49
Marshall, William, *Planting and Rural Ornament,* 216
Maryland, 400, 504, 507
Mason, George, 253, 648
Massachusetts, 290, 321–331 *passim,* 388, 390, 517, 541, 553–562 *passim,* 624; Turnpike, 294
Massachusetts Horticultural Society, 249, 268
Massachusetts Institute of Technology, 321
Mather, Stephen T., 529–538, *537,* 545, 546, 554, 564–565, 567
Mawson, Thomas, 451
Mazarin, Cardinal, 167
Mead, William Rutherford, 341, 360
Medici: Catherine dei, 156, 159, 160; Cosimo dei (Pater Patriae), 57, 59; Ferdinando dei, 77; Giovanni dei (Leo X), 69, 73–75, 99, 146, 183; Giovanni di Cosimo dei, 61; Giulio dei (Clement VII), 73–75; Lorenzo dei, 59, 61; Maria dei, 162, 163
Medici, Villa, *see* Villa Medici
Medieval gardens, 26, *27,* 28
Medina, 50
Melbourne Hall, 198–199, *198, 199*
Melchers, Gari, 362
Mesa Verde National Park, 525, *526,* 527
Mesopotamia, 1, 50
Metropolitan Park Commission, Mass., 323–335, 597
Michelangelo, 69
Michelozzo, *58,* 59, *60,* 61, 62, *61–66*
Michigan, 311, 390, 400, 538, 559, 564; Mackinac Island transferred, 559
Middle Ages, 21–29, 132, 153, 182–183, 204
Middlesex Fells Reservation, Mass., 328, *329,* 331, *335,* 559
Miletus, 6, *7*
Miller, Adolph C., 529
Miller, Philip, 216
Millet, Francis D., 362
Mills, Robert, 403
Milton, John, 207
Milton, Mass., 248, 324
Milwaukee, Wis., 443, 503
Minneapolis, Minn., 314–317, *314,* 549, 597
Minnesota, 559, 562, 564. *See also* Itasca State Park
Minute Man National Historical Park, Mass., 648
Mirafiore, *see* Villa Mirafiore
Mississippi, 542, 580; establishes new state park system to use CCC, 580
Mississippi River Parkway Survey, 614–615, *614*
Missouri: Lake of the Ozarks, Montserrat, and Cuivre River Recreational Demonstration Areas, 591
Molière, 181
Mollet: André, 196–197, 206; *Le Jardin de Plaisir,*

Mollet *(Cont.)*
196; Claude, 160, 162, 165, 196; Gabriel, 196–197, 206
Monasteries, 23–26, *24, 25,* 183–184
Mondragone, *see* Villa Mondragone
Montacute, 187–193, *191–193*
Montaigne, Michel, 94, 99
Montalto, Cardinal, 99
Montana, 518, 520, 527
Montgomery place, N.Y., 260n
Monticello, Va., 255, 258
Montreal, 246; Mount Royal Park, 289
Moody, Walter D., *Wacker's Manual,* 421
Moore, Charles, 360, 405, 406, 411, 421
Morgan, J. Pierpont, 395, 560
Morrill, John Barstow, 569–570
Morristown National Historical Park, 539, *540*
Moses, Robert, 567, 611–612, 628–637
Mount Airy, Va., 251, 253
Mount Auburn Cemetery, Mass., 268
Mount Vernon, Va., 251, 253–255, *254, 256, 257,* 409, 647–648; Memorial Parkway, 612
Mt. McKinley National Park, 531
Mt. Rainier National Park, *523,* 524
Muddy River, Boston, 291, 294, 299–304, *300, 300, 302, 303, 305,* 597
Muskau, Park at, 233–241, *234, 236, 238,* 319
Mystic River, Boston, 327, 331; Mystic River Parkway, 598

Napoleon (Louis) III, 241–244
Nash, John, 224, 225, *226*
Natchez Trace Parkway, 542, 615
National Agricultural Research Center, 503, 506
National Conference on City Planning, 416, 626, 627
National Conference on State Parks, 564–565, 578, 594
National Park Act, 530
National Park Service, 502, 530–554, 576–595, 612–615, 641, 648, 655; master planning, 535–536, 540; regional offices, 544–545, 552, 579, 580, 586, 588–589; "Mission 66," 552–553; State Park ECW (CCC), 577–585; Recreational Demonstration Projects, 588–595
National Trust for Historic Preservation, 547
Nature, limited view of, 208, 239
Neisse, River, 233, 236–237, 239
Neponset River, Boston, 327, 331
Newark, N.J., 289; Essex County Park Commission, 387, 560
New Britain, Conn., 289
Newburgh, N.Y., 260, 344
New England, 464; early landscape architecture, 247–250
New Harmony, Ind., 448, 464
New Jersey, 289, 387, 388, 390, 431, 490–491, 503, 561, 562, 616–617; Swartswood Lake State Park, 562. *See also* Garden State Parkway; Palisades Interstate Park Commission
New Lanark, 447, 448

New Mexico, establishment of state park system to use CCC, 580
New Netherland, 246–247, 249
Newport, R.I., 339
New towns, British, 462–463
New York, N.Y., xxi, 268, 269, 274, 275, 290, 294, 307–310, 315, 354, 373, 386–390, 394, 405, 406, 414, 415, 430–443 *passim*, 474–475, 489–496 *passim*, 513, 535, 560, 596, 598, 611–612, 623, 627–637, 641; Van Cortlandt Park, 249; Battery, 268; Bowling Green, 268; City Hall Park, 268, 630–631, *632*; Riverside Park, 289; Mosholu Parkway, 598; Henry Hudson Parkway, 611, *635*, 636; Bryant Park, 629–630, *630*; Arsenal, 628, *628*, 629; Orchard Beach, *634*, 635; Jacob Riis Park, 636; Rockaway Beach Improvement, 636; parkways, 611–612, 636
New York (state), 247, 249, 269, 270, 276, 387, 388, 391, 394, 558–577 *passim*, 601, 603, 611–612, 628; early landscape architecture, 249, 268; Adirondack Forest Preserve, 289, 558–559, *559*; Niagara Falls Reservation, 289, 558; Watkins Glen, 561; Letchworth gift, 561–562, *561*; Harriman tract, Bear Mountain, 562, *583*; bond issue of 1910, 562; Enfield Glen State Park, 564, *582*; State Council of Parks, 566–567, 611, 628
Nicholas V, 67
Nichols, Jesse C., 471, 473, 474, 481
Nichols garden, Salem, Mass., 248, *248*
Niles, William W., 598–600
Nolen, John, 416, 424, 479, 482–484, *485*, 486, 487, 562
Norris, Tenn., 500–502, *501*, 646; Norris Dam, 500, 502; Norris Park, Big Ridge Park, 502; Norris Freeway, 502, 617
North Carolina, 346, 487, 536, 542, 553, 612; Mt. Mitchell State Park, 562
Norton, Charles Eliot, 290, 368, 370

Offices, professional, changes in, 656–658
Oklahoma, 527; establishment of state park system to use CCC, 580
Olivieri, Orazio, 90
Olmsted, Frederick Law, Sr., xxi, 220, 232, 244–245, 266, 295n, 306–330 *passim*, 337, 344–346, 351, *371*, 372–390 *passim*, 404, 414, 427, 464, 558, 596, 597, 620–648 *passim*; at Birkenhead, 232; books, 232, 270; on Central and Prospect Parks, 270–274, 276–289; in California, 274–275, 604–609; in Boston, 290–306; at Biltmore, 346–351; and Columbian Exposition, 354–362, 368, 370–371; and Riverside, Ill., 465–468
Olmsted, Frederick Law, Jr., 295n, 386–405 *passim*, 411, 416, 420, 429, 431, 475, 535, 549, 642, 655; life summary, 389–390; on McMillan Commission, 405–411; World War I activities, 480; and National Park Act, 530; on Colorado Basin study, 548; and California state park survey, 572–574
Olmsted, John Charles, 294–296, 300, 306, 319, 386, 387, 389, 429
Olmsted, John Hull, 295n

Olmsted, Olmsted & Eliot, 277, 306, 330, 332, 428, 479
Olmsted, Vaux & Company (or Olmsted and Vaux), xxi, 270–289, *278*, *280*, *282–286*, *288*, *356*, 357, 465–468, *466*, *468*
Olmsted Brothers, 389, 424, 429–431, *429–431*, 475, *475–477*, 622, 623, 624–625, *625*, *626*
Olmsted Park, Boston, *301*, 304, 597
Olympic National Park, 543, *545*, *662*, *667*
Omaha, Neb., 544
Optimum relations, people and environment, 660–661, 674
Oregon, 518, 524; Silver Creek Falls Recreational Demonstration Area, 592
Orvieto, 132
Owen, Robert, 221, 447–448, 464

Paestum, 6
Paintings, landscape, influence of and pictorial fallacy, 208–209
Paley Park, New York, *637*, *638*
Palisades Interstate Park Commission, 387, 560–561, 562, *583*; Palisades Parkway, 615–616, *615*
Palmieri, *see* Villa Palmieri
Paris, 158–160, 162–164, 167, 173, 233, 241–245, 287, 319, 353–354, 373, 393, 405
Park and Recreation Problem in the United States, A Study of, 586–588
Parker, Barry, 457, 489
Parks, public, a sequel to "landscape gardening school," 220
Park Structures and Facilities, 586
Parkway, description, 597
Parmentier, André, 260
Parsons, Samuel, Jr., 386–387, 390; Parsons & Pentecost, 387
Parterres developed by Boyceau, 160, 162, 164, 172
Parvin State Park, N.J., *584*, *586*
Pasello da Mercogliano, 154, 155
Patroonships of New Netherland, 249, 260
Paul III, 69, 107, 146
Pavia, Certosa di, 24–25, *24*
Paxton, Joseph, 227–232, *230*, 244, 353
Payne, John Barton, 564
Peabody, Robert S., 318, 360; Peabody & Stearns, 360, 361, 363
Peacock, Thomas L., *Headlong Hall,* 207
Peets, Elbert, 411, 503
Pennethorne, James, 225, *228*
Pennsylvania, 380, 388, 389, 464; University of, 394; Valley Forge and Fort Washington State Parks, 562; Recreational Demonstration Areas (Raccoon Creek, Laurel Hill, Blue Knob, Hickory Run, French Creek), 589, *590*, *591*
Pentecost, George F., Jr., 387, 390, 436
Pérac, Etienne du, 162
Perry, Shaw & Hepburn, 646
Persia, *see* Iran
Peruzzi, Baldassare, 69, 107
Petraia, *see* Villa Petraia
Petrarch, 56
Petrified Forest National Park, 554

Philadelphia, Pa., 400, 403, 547, 552, 637; early landscape architecture, 249, 268, 414; Fairmount Park, 249; Schuylkill Reservoir, 308; Independence Hall National Historical Park, 547, 648
Philippines, 417, 436
Physical conditions, importance of in judging historic works, xxiii
Piazza del Campo, Siena, 29, 135–139, *136, 137*
Piazza della Signoria, Florence, 29, 133–135, *134, 136*
Piazza del Popolo, Rome, 77, 146–148, *148–150*
Piazza di San Pietro, Rome, *68,* 146, 149–152, *151, 152,* 405
Piazza San Marco, Venice, 29, 139–146, *140–144,* 405
Pittsburgh, Pa., 496, 497, 499; Mellon Square, 650, *652*
Plant materials, role in landscape architecture, xxiii
Platt, Charles A., 372–384, 428; principal works, *374,* 375, *375,* 378, *378, 379,* 380, *381–383,* 384; *Italian Gardens,* 372; *Monograph on Works,* 384
Platt, William, 373
Platt National Park, 527–528
Playgrounds, 622–639 *passim, 622, 623, 625, 626, 633, 639;* Playground Association of America, 625–626
Pliny the Younger, villas of, 12, 59
Poggio a Caiano, 59
Polk, Willis, 417, 423
Pollution, air and water, 620, 671, *672*
Pompeii, 6, 8–12, *9–11,* 132
Pope, Alexander, 209, 211, 215
Porta, Giacomo della, 84, 90
Port Sunlight, 449–451, *450,* 453, 460, 463, 465
Post, George B., 360–363, 369
Potomac River, 400, 409
Pratt, George D., residence of (Killenworth), 431–433, *432, 434*
Pray, James Sturgis, 416
Predator-prey relationship, 671–673
Preservation, versus development, 659–660
Price, Uvedale, *Essay on the Picturesque,* 216, 218
Priene, 6, *7, 8*
Prospect Park, Brooklyn, 275, *280, 281, 285, 286,* 287, *287,* 290, 299, 310, 465, 596, 620–629 *passim;* development, 276–277; comparison with Central Park, 277–286
Providence, R.I., 289
Provincetown, Mass., 323
Public Works Administration (PWA), 540
Pückler-Muskau, Prince H. L. H. von, 220, 233–244 *passim, 234, 236, 238,* 263, 283, 319–320, 337, 344, 612
Punchard, Charles P., Jr., 532

Quebec, 246

Rabat, 49
Racine, Jean Baptiste, 181
Racine, Wis., parks, 435
Radburn, N.J., 489–495, *491–494,* 496, 502, 508–509

Raphael, 69, 73–76
Rapuano, Michael, 411, *615,* 616, *616, 618*
Reconstruction Finance Corporation (RFC), 507
Recreational areas, classification of urban, 626–627
Recreational Demonstration Projects and Areas (RDPs, RDAs), 588–595; organized camps in, 588, *590, 591,* 592–594, *593*
Reform Bill of 1832, 223
Reformers, the, 223–225, 268
Regent's Park, London, 223–225, *226,* 227
Regional Planning, 424–426, 655
Reid, Whitelaw, 270
Renaissance, landscape architecture of: prelude to, 55–57; Quattrocento in Florence, 57–66; Cinquecento flowering, 67, 69–73, 89, 99, 146; Italian development, 107, 114; in France, 153–154, 157–160, 164; under LeNôtre, 165, 166; in England, 182–185; revision by Inigo Jones, 194, 196, 197; French influence in England, 196–202, 205–206; Dutch influence, 198, 203, 209; period of confusion, 197–198, 210; breakdown under "landscape gardening" fashion, 210–220
Repton, Humphry, xxi, 216–221, 225, 235, 260, 320, 344
Repton Club, 386
Resettlement Administration, 503–504, 588, 589, 646
Reston, Va., 513
Revere Beach, Boston, 327, *327,* 331
Rhode Island, 289, 339
R. H. Treman State Park, N.Y., 564, *582*
Riario, Cardinal, 99
Ricci, Cardinal, 77
Richardson, Henry H., 293, 301, 340–341
Richardson Grove State Park, Calif., *574*
Richelieu, Cardinal, 163, 166
Richmond, Va., 258, 544, 545
Riis Houses, New York, *639*
Riverside, Ill., 289, 465–468, *466, 468,* 516, 643
Riverway, Boston-Brookline, 294, 299–304, *300–303, 305,* 389, 597
Riviera, 319
Robinson, Charles Mulford, 393, 413–416, 423–424, 623; *Improvement of Towns and Cities,* 414–415, 423, 623–624; *Modern Civic Art,* 415; *Width and Arrangement of Streets,* 416
Robinson, Nelson, 336
Robinson, William, *The English Flower Garden,* 377
Rochester, N.Y., 307, 413
Rockefeller, John D., Jr., 536, 646
Rocky Mountain National Park, 527, *528,* 531
Roland Park, Baltimore, 468–471, *469, 470*
Romano, Giulio, 75
Romanticism, literary, 207
Rome, ancient, 12–18, *14–17,* 132, 267; villas, 12–13, 18, *18, 19,* 20, 59, 81, 89. *See also* Rome, postclassical
Rome, postclassical, 56, 67–83 *passim,* 94, 99, 114, 124, 146, 148, *148–152,* 183, 184, 393–395, *396,* 405. *See also* Rome, ancient
Rome Prize in Landscape Architecture, 396, 398, 436

Roosevelt, Franklin D., 500, 539, 544, 546, 575–577, 646
Roosevelt, Theodore, 395, 406, 411, 576, 626
Root, John Wellborn, 357–361, 368, 369
Rose, John, 206
Rotch Committee, 394
Rousseau, Jean Jacques, 208
Royal Parks, London, *222–224,* 223–225, *226,* 267, 268
Royston, Robert, 445
Rueil, 166
Russell, William E., 322–324, 326
Russell Sage Foundation, 474–475, 477, 478
Russia, 319
Ryerson, E. L., residence of, 435, *436, 437*

Sager, Merel S., 552
St. Catherine's Court, 185–187, *188–190*
St. Francis of Assisi, 55–56
St. Gall, Abbey of, 25, *25*
Saint-Gaudens, Augustus, 361, 365, 394, 400, 405, 406
St. Germain-en-Laye, 162
St. James's Park, London, *222,* 223
St. John Lateran, 23, *24*
St. Louis, Mo., 354, 370, 481, 518, 615
St. Paul, Minn., 314, 316
St. Paul's-without-the-Walls, 23
Salem, Mass., 248, *248,* 309, 541; Salem Maritime National Historic Site, 541, *541*
Salt, Titus, and Saltaire, 448
San Francisco, Calif., 274, 275, 416–422 *passim, 418,* 532, 540, 544, 572, 650; Ghirardelli Square, 650, *651*
Sangallo, Antonio da, 75; the Younger, 69, 107
San Gimignano, 132
Sanitary Commission, U.S., 273, 274, 390
Santa Fe, N.M., 544
Saratoga, N.Y., Congress Spring Park, 308
Sargent, Charles S., 289, 306, 321, 387, 388
Sasaki, Hideo, 411; Sasaki, Dawson, DeMay Associates, 650, *653, 656;* Sasaki, Walker and Associates, *649*
Sauers, Charles G., 569–570
Savannah, Ga., 268, 414
Scandinavia, 319
Schinkel, Friedrich, 344
School grounds, campus plans, 648–650, *649*
Schuylkill Reservoir, Philadelphia, 308
Selinus, 6
Sequoia National Park, 521
Settignano, 114, 115
Seville, 30–40; Casa de Pilatos, 33; Casa de las Dueñas, 33; Alcazar gardens, *34,* 35–39, *36–39*
Shenandoah National Park, 536, 539, 541–543, 612
Shenstone, William, 216
Shepherd, Harry W., 572
Sheridan, Lawrence V., 424
Shipping Board, U.S., 480
Shiraz, 51

Shirley, Va., 251, 253, 405
Shopping centers, regional, 650–654, *654*
Shurcliff, Arthur A., 416, 646, *647*
Sicily, 6, 8
Siena, 29, 99, 124, 135–139, *136, 137,* 146, 149
Sight-lines, xxiv, 3–4, 8–28 *passim,* 46–47, 71–72, 84, 92, 100, 108, 122–159 *passim,* 167, 173–202 *passim,* 220, 237–255 *passim,* 283, 288, 344–345, 359, 389–390, 401, 407, 482, 631
Simonds, Ossian C., 387, 390–391
Simonds and Simonds, 650, *652*
Siracusa, 6
Sixtus IV, 147
Sixtus V, 99, 146–147, 149
Skyline Drive, Va., 541–543, 612
Soil conservation, 664–671, *665–670*
Soil Conservation Service, 576, 669
Soissons, Louis de, 460
South Carolina: establishment of state park system to use CCC, 580; Recreational Demonstration Projects for Waysides, 589
South Dakota, 517, 527, 564; Wind Cave National Park, 527–528; Custer State Park, 564
South Mountain Reservation, N.J., *585*
Spain, 30–49
Spatial structure, xxiii–xxiv; Pompeii, 8–10; ancient Rome, 13, 15–17, 20; medieval town squares, 28–29; Alhambra, 46–47; Belvedere project and later Italian villas, 71–72, 88, 100, 113, 122; evolution in piazze, 132; in France, 157–159, 167, 173–174; confusion in England, 187–188, 196, 203; and "landscape gardening school," 220; and Pückler-Muskau, 220, 237; sequences in Central and Prospect Parks, 283–286; and Central Park, 288, 344–345; and "landscape gardening" in residential work, 337, 345; revival of strong design, 345–346, 351, 370–371; architectonic and pastoral forms merged, 346, 390–391; power demonstrated at Columbian Exposition, 368, 370–371; influence of Platt, 377–378; and Country Place Era, 427–428, 446; strength in state parks, 348–349, 580–581
Spectator, The, 209, 215
State park movement, 274, 521, 532–533, 555–595
Statue of Liberty National Monument, 542–543, *542, 543*
Steele, Richard, 209, 215
Stein, Clarence S., 489–496, *490–494,* 507
Stony Brook, Boston, 291, 293
Stony Brook Reservation, Mass., 328, 331
Stourhead, *215*
Stowe, 211, 212, *212,* 259
Strasbourg, 22
Stresa, 120
Strong, William A., 503
Subdivisions, land, 643–645, *644*
Sullivan, Louis, 361, 363, 369–370, *369*
Sunnyside Gardens, New York, 489–490, *490,* 493, 496, 514, 643
Switzer, Stephen, *Iconographia Rustica,* 215
Switzerland, 25, 308, 389
Sybaris, 663, 674

Taconic State Park Commission, N.Y., 567, 577, 607; Taconic State Parkway, 607–612, *609–611*, 615

Taft, William Howard, 411, 417, 530

Taj Mahal, 54, *54*

Taormina, 6

Taylor, B. E., residence of, 441, *442, 443*

Technical Services in CCC camps, 576–578

Tel-el-Amarna, 3

Tempietto of Bramante, the, 68

Tennessee, 487, 500, 502, 536, 542, 591; Recreational Demonstration Areas (Shelby Forest, Montgomery-Bell, Fall Creek Falls), 591

Tennessee Valley Authority (TVA), 487, 500–502, 617, 646

Thorne, Landon K., residence of, 437–440, *438–440*

Thruway, New York State, 610–611, 616, *618*

Timberline, Pa., 380, *381, 382*

Tivoli, 18, 20, 81, 89, 103

Topiary, 28, 197, 198, *202*, 203, 209

Topography, xxiii, 3, 13, 22, 40, 72, 90–91, 100, 137–138, 160, 184, 197, 237, 279, 313, 348, 419–420, 468–501 *passim*, 589, 608

Torlonia, *see* Villa Torlonia

Toronto, 440

Town squares, 28–29, 132, 152

Towne, Carroll A., 500

Townsend & Fleming, 440

Trier, 22

Trowbridge & Ackerman, 432

Trustee of Public Reservations (now Trustees of Reservations), Mass., 320–326, 559

Tugwell, Rexford G., 503

Tuileries, 160–162, *160, 161*, 165, 166, 405

Udine, Giovanni da, 76

Unwin, Raymond, 459, 489

Upjohn Company, *656*

Urban open space: Middle Ages, 28–29, 132–146; Renaissance times, 146–152; in Paris under Haussmann, 242; New England, 249; in American colonies, 268; lesson of Columbian Exposition, 368, 370–371; monumentality in "City Beautiful" movement, 423; present-day developments, 620–639; "urban design," 650, *651–653*

Utah, 532, 533, 535

Uthwatt Report, 462

Valadier, Giuseppe, 147–148

Vanbrugh, John, 210–214, *213*

VanBrunt & Howe, 360, 361, 363

Vandergrift, Pa., 479

Varé, M., 241–242

Vasari, *Vite degli Artisti*, 62

Vaux, Calvert, xxi, 244, 266, 271–288, 307, 310–312, 344–357 *passim*, 386, 390, 391, 464–468, 596, 620–643 *passim*

Vaux, Downing, 387, 391

Vaux-le-Vicomte, 165, 167–172, *166, 169–171*, 199, 405

Venard, Claude, 95

Venice, 29, 139–146, *140–144*, 405

Versailles, 153, 164–181 *passim, 174–178, 180*, 197, 206, 246, 259, 267, 401, 405; Petit Trianon, 320

Veterans' Administration, 577, 578

"Victoria" model town, 448, *449*

Victoria Park, London, 223, 225, *228*, 267, 268, 447

Vienna, 405

Vignola, 107, 147

Villa, meaning of term, 59, 376

Villa Adriana, 18, *18*, 20, 81, 88, 405

Villa Aldobrandini, 83–84, *83, 85*

Villa Aurelia, 395

Villa dell'Aurora, 394, 395

Villa Balbianello, 114, *128*, 129, 129–131, *129, 130*

Villa Caprarola, *see* Villino Farnese

Villa Careggi, *58*, 59, 135

Villa Chigi, 114, 122–129, *123, 125, 127*

Villa d'Este, 89–98, *90–92, 94, 95, 97*, 103, 107, 113, 117, 405

Villa di Castello, 59

Villa Gamberaia, 114–119, *115, 116, 118, 119*

Villa Lante, 99–107, *100–102, 104–106*, 109, 113, 170

Villa Madama, 73–76, *74, 75*, 81

Villa Medici, Fiesole, *60*, 61–66, *61–66*. *See also* Villa Medici, Rome

Villa Medici, Rome, 76–80, *77–79*, 107, 393. *See also* Villa Medici, Fiesole

Villa Mirafiore, 395

Villa Mondragone, 81–83, *82, 84*

Villa Palmieri, *58*, 59–61

Villa Petraia, *58*, 59

Villard house, New York, *342*, 343

Villa Torlonia, 84–88, *86, 87, 89*, 113, 124

Villino Farnese, 99, 107–113, *108–112*

Vint, Thomas C., 535–536, 539, 540, 546, 552, 554

Viollet-le-Duc, 22

Virginia, 250–258 *passim*, 389–407 *passim*, 536, 538, 541, 580, 594, 612, 615; early landscape architecture, 250; University of, 258; establishment of state park system to use CCC, 580; Fairy Stone State Park, *582;* Chopawamsic Recreational Demonstration Area, 594

Virgin Islands National Park, 554

Visigoths, 22, 30, 50

Vitale, Ferruccio, 396, 411, 435–440, *438–440*, 443, 535

Viterbo, 99, 107, 132

Voorhees, Walker, Foley & Smith, 513–516, *514, 515*

Wacker, Charles H., 421

Wadsworth, Reginald J., 504

Walker, Hale J., 503–506, *504, 505*

Walled towns, 22, *22*

Walpole, Horace, 211

Walters, Henry, 395

Waltham, Mass., 259, 260, 324, 328

Wank, Roland A., 500

Ward, J. Q. A., 394

Warwick Castle, 183, *183*

Washburn, Henry D., 518

Washington, D.C., 259, 268, 273, 289, 354, 400–420

Washington, D.C. (*Cont.*)
  passim, 402, 404, 407–411, 436, 487, 502, 503,
  529–551 *passim,* 594, 612, 626, 640
Washington, George, 253–254, 259, 401, 405, 647;
  Washington Monument, 401, 403, 407, 410; Bi-
  centennial, 648
Washington Park, Chicago, 289, *356,* 357, 624
Waverley Oaks, Waltham, Mass., 320, 328
Weidenmann, Jacob, 307, 308
Weld, Garden of, Brookline, Mass., *379,* 380
Welwyn, 460–463, *461, 462*
Westchester County, N.Y., park system, 601–607,
  603–605; Playland, Rye Beach, 605–607, *606*
Westover, Va., 251–253, *251, 252*
West Roxbury Park, Boston, *see* Franklin Park
West Virginia, 464
Whateley, Thomas, *Observations on Modern Garden-
  ing,* 216, 259
White, Stanford, 341
White House, 259, 401, 403, 407
Whiting, Edward Clark, 429–431, *429–431*
William and Mary, 197, 204–206
Williams, Morley J., *256, 257,* 648
Williamsburg, Va., 250, 405, 538, 646–647, *647*
Wilson, Woodrow, 529
Wind Cave National Park, 527–528

Wirth, Conrad L., 544, 549–554, 578–595
Wirth, Theodore, 549
Wisconsin, 311, 562–564; Nolen state park study,
  562; state park system, 563; Devil's Lake, Nelson-
  Dewey, Peninsula State Parks, 562
Wise, Henry, 198, 206, 210, 212–214, *213*
Wolsey, Cardinal, 183, 203
Worcester, Mass., 479
World's Columbian Exposition, 306, 330, 353–371,
  362, 364–366, 369, 372, 377, 393–416 *passim,* 426,
  624
Wren, Christopher, 196, 197, 203, 205
Wrest Park, 198, 202
Wright, Henry, 489–496, *490–494,* 507
Wyoming, 520

Yellowstone National Park, 518–521, *519, 520,* 530,
  535, 538, 554, 556
Yorktown, Va., 538, 539, 615
Yosemite: State Park (Calif.), 274–275, 555–558,
  556, 562; National Park, 521–522, *524,* 535, 544,
  558

Zion & Breen Associates, *637, 638*
Zion National Park, 532, 533